After the Expulsion

After the Expulsion

West Germany and Eastern Europe
1945–1990

PERTTI AHONEN

OXFORD
UNIVERSITY PRESS

OXFORD

UNIVERSITY PRESS

Great Clarendon Street, Oxford OX2 6DP

Oxford University Press is a department of the University of Oxford.
It furthers the University's objective of excellence in research, scholarship,
and education by publishing worldwide in

Oxford New York

Auckland Cape Town Dar es Salaam Hong Kong Karachi Kuala Lumpur
Madrid Melbourne Mexico City Nairobi New Delhi Shanghai Taipei Toronto

With offices in

Argentina Austria Brazil Chile Czech Republic France Greece
Guatemala Hungary Italy Japan South Korea Poland Portugal
Singapore Switzerland Thailand Turkey Ukraine Vietnam

Oxford is a registered trade mark of Oxford University Press
in the UK and in certain other countries

Published in the United States
by Oxford University Press Inc., New York

© Pertti Ahonen 2003

The moral rights of the author have been asserted

Database right Oxford University Press (maker)

First published 2003

British Library Cataloguing in Publication Data

Data available

Library of Congress Cataloging in Publication Data

Data applied for

ISBN 0-19-925989-5

3 5 7 9 10 8 6 4

Typeset by Cambrian Typesetters,
Frimley, Surrey
Printed in Great Britain
on acid-free paper by
Biddles Ltd., King's Lynn, Norfolk

Matti ja Marjatta Ahoselle ja Sari Dobákille

Acknowledgements

I HAVE INCURRED enormous debts while completing this project, and it is a pleasure to express my gratitude to at least some of the many individuals and institutions whose support has sustained me.

I would like to begin by thanking the History Department of Yale University where this book began as a doctoral dissertation. I am particularly grateful to my *Doktorvater*, Henry A. Turner, Jr., whose guidance and encouragement have been invaluable. Special thanks are also due to the two other members of my dissertation committee, Paul M. Kennedy and Piotr S. Wandycz.

Several friends and colleagues have gone well beyond the call of duty with their help and support for me and this project. Robert G. Moeller, Jeffrey Herf, and William Gray read the entire manuscript and provided excellent suggestions for improvements, as did the anonymous referees for Oxford University Press. Additional highly valuable feedback and encouragement came from Thomas Albrich, Arnulf Baring, Gustavo Corni, Heinz Duchhardt, Jan Gross, Konrad Jarausch, Tony Judt, Ian Kershaw, Andreas Kunz, Marz Mazower, Ralph Melville, Diethelm Prowe, Claus Scharf, Marc Trachtenberg, and Martin Vogt. In addition, I am extremely grateful to all the following, not only for insightful comments on various aspects of this project but also for friendship and human kindness: Tim Baycroft, Frank Biess, Mike Braddick, Maja Brkljacic, Vicki Chirco, Flurin Condrau, David and Ewa Dornisch, Gabriella Etmektsoglou, Gesine Gerhard, Karen Harvey, Charles Lowney, Christof Morrissey, Rainer Ohliger, David Posner, Karine Rance, Greg Rohlf, Bess Rothenberg, Sayres Rudy, Mika Saarela, Barbara Schmucki, Karen Schönwälder, Douglas Selvage, Tim Snyder, Phil Triadafilopoulos, Brian Vick, Anssi Vuorio, Nik Wachsmann, Hugh Wilford, Joachim Wintzer, and Volker Zimmermann. A special thank you also to all my friendly colleagues in the History Department at the University of Sheffield. Having thanked all these good people, I hasten to add that they are of course in no way responsible for the remaining deficiencies of this book. On that score, the fault is all mine.

Numerous institutions have funded my work over the past few years, and I would like to thank them all for their generosity. I am very grateful for the research grants awarded to me by the Academy of Finland; the Department of History, Yale University; the MacArthur Foundation and the International Security Studies Program of Yale University; the Mellon Foundation; the British Academy; and the Department of History, University of Sheffield. I am also deeply indebted to the International Rotary Foundation for providing me with a Graduate Ambassadorial Fellowship at Yale. Special thanks are due to three institutions that granted me residential fellowships during the write-up stage of this project: the Remarque Institute of New York University, the Institut für Europäische Geschichte in Mainz, and the Institut für die Wissenschaften vom Menschen in Vienna. Thank you to all the fellows and staff at each of these fine centres of scholarship, particularly to Tony Judt and Jair Kessler at NYU's Remarque Institute.

I am very grateful as well to all the archivists and other staff members of the various archives and libraries that I visited while researching this book. Their courteousness and professionalism made my work pleasurable. I would like to thank particularly the following people, who helped me gain access to important materials: Gertrud Lenz (Willy-Brandt Archiv); Horst-Peter Schulz (Archiv der sozialen Demokratie); Günter Buchstab and Angela Keller (Archiv für Christlich-Demokratische Politik); Hans-Peter Mensing (Stiftung Bundeskanzler-Adenauer Haus); Roland J. Hoffmann, Edgar Pscheidt, Alois Harasko, and Susanne Habel (Sudetendeutsches Archiv); Markus Leuschner (Bund der Vertriebenen); Andreas Gundrum (Landsmannschaft der Oberschlesier). In addition, the following individuals generously gave me special permission to see restricted collections of personal papers: Marlene Lenz (Nachlass Otto Lenz, Archiv für Christlich-Demokratische Politik); Christa Müller (Nachlass Josef Müller, Archiv für Christlich-Soziale Politik); Sophie von und zu Guttenberg (Nachlass Freiherr von und zu Guttenberg, Bundesarchiv, Koblenz); Michael von Brentano (Nachlass Heinrich von Brentano, Bundesarchiv, Koblenz). Thank you!

Many thanks are due as well to my editors at Oxford University Press, Ruth Parr and Anne Gelling, for all their work on this book and to the editor of *Central European History*, Kenneth Barkin, for permission to reprint a part of my article 'Domestic Constraints on West German Ostpolitik: The Role of the Expellee Organizations in the Adenauer Era', *Central European History*, 31 (1998): 31–64.

Finally, very special thanks to my parents, Marjatta and Matti Ahonen, and my sister, Sari Dobák. As a small sign of my gratitude, I dedicate this book to them.

Contents

List of Abbreviations

AAPD	*Akten zur Auswärtigen Politik der Bundesrepublik Deutschland*
ABdV	Archiv des Bundes der Vertriebenen, Bonn
ACDP	Archiv für Christlich-Demokratische Politik, Bonn/Sankt Augustin
ACSP	Archiv für Christlich-Soziale Politik, Munich
AdG	*Archiv der Gegenwart. Deutschland 1949 bis 1999*, 10 vols. (Sankt Augustin: Siegler, 2000)
AdsD	Archiv der sozialen Demokratie, Bonn
ADL	Archiv des deutschen Liberalismus, Gummersbach
ALdO	Archive of the Landsmannschaft der Oberschlesier, Ratingen
AVBD	*Akten zur Vorgeschichte der Bundesrepublik Deutschland*
BA	Bundesarchiv, Koblenz
BT/PA	Parlamentsarchiv des Deutschen Bundestages, Bonn
Bulletin	*Bulletin des Presse- und Informationsamtes der Bundesregierung*
DoD	*Deutscher Ostdienst*
DuD/DHDF	*Deutschland-Union-Dienst/Der Heimatvertriebene, Der Flüchtling*
DzD	*Dokumente zur Deutschlandpolitik*
FAZ	*Frankfurter Allgemeine Zeitung*
fdk	*freie demokratische korrespondenz*
FDP-Bundesvorstand	FDP-Bundesvorstand. Sitzungsprotokolle (publication series)
FRUS	*Foreign Relations of the United States*
GWU	*Geschichte in Wissenschaft und Unterricht*
IfZ	Archive of the Institut für Zeitgeschichte, Munich
JMH	*Journal of Modern History*
PA/AA	Politisches Archiv des Auswärtigen Amtes, Bonn
SDA	Sudetendeutsches Archiv, Munich
SPD-Fraktion	SPD-Fraktion im Deutschen Bundestag. Sitzungsprotokolle (publication series)
StBkAH	Stiftung Bundeskanzler-Adenauer-Haus, Bonn/Rhöndorf
TzD	*Texte zur Deutschlandpolitik*
Verhandlungen	*Verhandlungen des deutschen Bundestages, Stenographische Berichte*
VfZ	*Vierteljahrshefte für Zeitgeschichte*
WBA	Willy-Brandt-Archiv (in *Archiv der sozialen Demokratie*), Bonn

Introduction

NAZI GERMANY'S SURRENDER in May 1945 brought peace, relief, and liberation to a Europe ravaged by total war. Soldiers inured to daily butchery could finally put down their arms. Surviving concentration camp inmates and other victims of persecution by the Nazis and their allies could take their first hesitant steps towards freedom. Those in hiding could crawl back into daylight, and ordinary civilians could again start to think about a future that stretched beyond the next bombing raid or battle. But millions continued to suffer despite the restoration of peace. Many were dazed and disoriented, struggling to find even the barest necessities of life amidst the destruction. Many also bore mental and physical scars that would burden them for the rest of their lives: tangible traces of injury and torment, memories of injustice, persecution, terror, and death.

In this sea of post-war suffering, some of the hardest-hit were the victims of the so-called 'population transfers' that accompanied the final stages and the aftermath of the war. That euphemism stood for systematic policies of mass expulsion, spurred by planned border changes and ethnic homogenization drives across Eastern and East–Central Europe. Members of many different nationalities were targeted in these 'ethnic cleansing' operations. Although Poles, Ukrainians, Hungarians, Lithuanians, and several other national groups numbered among the victims, the heaviest blows fell against Germans. With its policies of brutal conquest, forced resettlement, and mass murder, Nazi Germany had set the precedent for many of the post-war horrors, and as the decline and fall of the Third Reich was followed by the amputation of many of its eastern territories, a whirlwind of revenge swept Eastern Europe. The number of Germans who either fled or were expelled out of the region was soon enormous. Although precise figures are difficult to establish, the grand total probably reached some fifteen million.[1]

Most of the expelled Germans landed in what was left of the former Reich—the four occupation zones controlled by the victorious Allies. The three western zones that became the Federal Republic bore the brunt of the burden, with some eight million expellees in residence by 1950, while another approximately four million settled, at least initially, in the territory of the German Democratic Republic. These were alarmingly high numbers, and in percentage terms they appeared even more menacing: the expellees constituted over 20 per cent of the total population of the GDR and some 16 per cent of that of the Federal

---

[1] Gerhard Reichling, *Die deutschen Vertriebenen in Zahlen*, i. *Umsiedler, Verschleppte, Vertriebene, Aussiedler 1940–1985* (Bonn: Kulturstiftung der deutschen Vertriebenen, 1986), 28–32.

Republic.[2] As a result, German and occupation authorities alike worried about the possible consequences of this mass influx of the dispossessed into a thoroughly devastated land. How could the expellees be socially and economically integrated into their new surroundings? Would they form a crystallization point for anti-democratic political radicalism? Might they become an irredentist force capable of overturning the post-1945 territorial settlement in East–Central Europe? In short, would they destabilize Germany, and possibly the rest of Europe, right on the heels of the most devastating war in history?

Ultimately such dark fears were not borne out in either German state. In the GDR, the expellee question was subsumed into a broader project of socialist state-building, defined in class terms. Following the implementation of various redistributive social policy measures in the immediate post-war years, the authorities declared the expellee problem solved by the beginning of the 1950s. In the long term, that claim gained validity, as no serious, direct challenge to the system ever arose from the expellees. But this official position also dictated that, during most of the GDR's existence, the expellee issue was discussed only on a very limited scale, largely because of its potentially anti-Soviet implications, and almost exclusively as a socialist success story. The various problems that lingered beneath the surface remained unaddressed. Although cautious steps towards more balanced scholarship and public debate began during the 1980s, a rapidly growing and sophisticated literature on the East German expellee problem has emerged only after reunification.[3]

In West Germany, the focus of this book, the expellee issue has received more attention. Here, too, the potential dangers associated with the newcomers were ultimately averted, albeit with more inclusive and democratic methods than in the GDR. As a result, expellee integration has often been portrayed as one of the Federal Republic's great triumphs. Scholars and publicists alike have sung the praises of the country's enlightened approach to the problem, emphasizing

---

[2] Reichling, *Vertriebene*, i. 59; Gerhard Reichling, *Die deutschen Vertriebenen in Zahlen*, ii. *40 Jahre Eingliederung in der Bundesrepublik Deutschland* (Bonn: Kulturstiftung der deutschen Vertriebenen, 1989), 30–1; Helge Heidemeyer, 'Vertriebene als Sowjetzonenflühtlinge', in Dierk Hoffmann, Marita Krauss, and Michael Schwartz (eds.), *Vertriebene in Deutschland: Interdisziplinäre Ergebnisse und Forschungsperspektiven* (Munich: Oldenbourg, 2000), 237–8.

[3] Key works include Philipp Ther, *Deutsche und polnische Vertriebene: Gesellschaft und Vertriebenenpolitik in der SBZ/DDR und in Polen 1945–1956* (Göttingen: Vandenhoeck & Ruprecht, 1998); id., 'Expellee Policy in the Soviet-Occupied Zone and the GDR', in David Rock and Stefan Wolff (eds.), *Coming Home to Germany? The Integration of Ethnic Germans from Central and Eastern Europe in the Federal Republic* (Oxford: Berghahn, 2002); 56–76; id., 'The Integration of Expellees in Germany and Poland after World War II: A Historical Reassessment', *Slavic Review*, 55 (1996): 779–805; Manfred Wille, Johannes Hoffmann, and Wolfgang Meinicke (eds.), *Sie hatten alles verloren: Flüchtlinge und Vertriebene in der sowjetischen Besatzungszone Deutschlands* (Wiesbaden: Harrassowitz, 1993); Wolfgang Meinicke, 'Probleme der Integration der Vertriebenen in der sowjetischen Besatzungszone', *Jahrbuch für ostdeutsche Volkskunde*, 35 (1992): 1–31; Alexander von Plato and Wolfgang Meinicke (eds.), *Alte Heimat—Neue Zeit: Flüchtlinge, Umgesiedelte, Vertriebene in der sowjetischen Besatzungszone und in der DDR* (Berlin: Verlags-Anstalt Union, 1991); Hoffmann et al., *Vertriebene*; Dierk Hoffmann and Michael Schwartz (eds.), *Geglückte Integration? Spezifika und Vergleichbarkeit der Vertriebenen-Eingliederung in der SBZ/DDR* (Munich: Oldenbourg, 1999).

the supposedly swift success of the integration process.[4] But serious research into expellee issues was slow to develop in West Germany, too. After an early wave of typically partisan and politicized studies, conducted largely by expellee scholars eager to cast their own cause in a positive light, the scholarly tide ebbed by the late 1960s. Mainstream academic interest did not pick up until the 1980s, but it intensified after reunification, with the result that an increasingly nuanced literature on the West German expellee problem has gradually developed.[5]

Several important questions have received sophisticated analysis in this scholarship. The socio-economic integration process, for example, has been re-examined in increasing depth. Without denying the ultimate success of that process, Paul Lüttinger and others have highlighted problems and complications along the way, including tensions between expellees and native West Germans as well as persistent inequalities between the two groups.[6] In a series of case studies Helga Grebing, Johannes-Dieter Steinert, and Franz J. Bauer, among others, have investigated the role of the expellees in West German society on the local and regional levels, particularly during the first post-war decade.[7] The expellees' attempts to

---

[4] See e.g. Horst Möller, 'Die Relativität historischer Epochen: Das Jahr 1945 in der Perspektive des Jahres 1989', *Aus Politik und Zeitgeschichte*, B18–19 (1995), 3–9; Hans-Joachim von Merkatz (ed.), *Aus Trümmern wurden Fundamente: Vertriebene/Flüchtlinge/Aussiedler: Drei Jahrzehnte Integration* (Düsseldorf: Walter Rau, 1979).

[5] On the historiography, see Edgar Wolfrum, 'Zwischen Geschichtsschreibung und Geschichtspolitik: Forschungen zur Flucht und Vertreibung nach dem Zweiten Weltkrieg', *Archiv für Sozialgeschichte*, 36 (1996): 500–22; Thomas Grosser, 'Von der freiwilligen Solidar- zur geordneten Konfliktgemeinschaft: Die Integration der Flüchtlinge und Vertriebenen in der deutschen Nachkriegsgesellschaft im Spiegel neuerer zeitgeschichtlicher Untersuchungen', in Hoffmann *et al.*, *Vertriebene*, 65–85; Ute Gerhardt, 'Bilanz der soziologischen Literatur zur Integration der Vertriebenen und Flüchtlinge nach 1945', in Hoffmann *et al.*, *Vertriebene*, 41–63.

[6] Key works include Paul Lüttinger, *Integration der Vertriebenen: Eine empirische Analyse* (Frankfurt: Campus, 1989); Marion Frantzioch, *Die Vertriebenen: Hemmnisse, Antriebskräfte und Wege ihrer Integration in der Bundesrepublik Deutschland* (Berlin: Dietrich Reimer, 1987); Ther, 'Integration'; Michael L. Hughes, *Shouldering the Burdens of Defeat: West Germany and the Reconstruction of Social Justice* (Chapel Hill, NC: UNC Press, 1999); id., 'Restitution and Democracy in Germany after the Two World Wars', *Contemporary European History*, 4 (1994): 1–18. Hoffmann *et al.*, *Vertriebene*; Hoffmann and Schwartz, *Geglückte*; Sylvia Schraut and Thomas Grosser (eds.), *Die Flüchtlingsfrage in der deutschen Nachkriegsgesellschaft* (Mannheim: Palatium, 1996); Rock and Wolff, *Coming Home to Germany?*; Alexander von Plato, 'Fremde Heimat: Zur Integration von Flüchtlingen und Einheimischen in die neue Zeit', in Plato and Lutz Niethammer (eds.), *'Wir kriegen jetzt andere Zeiten': Auf der Suche nach der Erfahrung des Volkes in nachfaschistischen Ländern. Lebensgeschichte und Sozialkultur im Ruhrgebiet* (Berlin: Dietz, 1985), 172–219; Rainer Schulze, 'Growing Discontent: Relations between Native and Refugee Populations in a Rural District in Western Germany after the Second World War', *German History*, 7 (1989): 332–49; id. (ed.), *Unruhige Zeiten: Erlebnisberichte aus dem Landkreis Celle 1945–1949* (Munich: Oldenbourg, 1990); Michael Schwartz, ' "Zwangsheimat Deutschland": Vertriebene und Kernbevölkerung zwischen Gesellschaftskonflikt und Integrationspolitik', in Klaus Naumann (ed.), *Nachkrieg in Deutschland* (Hamburg: Hamburger Edition, 2001), 114–48; Klaus J. Bade, Hans-Bernd Meier, and Bernhard Parisius (eds.), *Zeitzeugen im Interview: Flüchtlinge und Vertriebene im Raum Osnabrück nach 1945* (Osnabrück: Rasch, 1997).

[7] Major studies include Helga Grebing, *Flüchtlinge und Parteien in Niedersachsen: Eine Untersuchung der politischen Meinungs- und Willensbildungsprozesse während der ersten Nachkriegszeit, 1945–1952/53* (Hanover: Hansche, 1990); Johannes-Dieter Steinert, *Vertriebenenverbände in Nordrhein-Westfalen, 1945–1954* (Düsseldorf: Schwann, 1986); Franz J. Bauer, *Flüchtlinge und Flüchtlingspolitik in*

organize pressure groups and other forms of collective representation have also received attention from a number of scholars.[8] And in some of the most innovative work in the field, Robert G. Moeller and others have explored the expellees' contributions to West German culture and collective memory.[9]

But despite these advances, the literature on the expellees remains insufficiently incorporated into the broader historiography of post-war Germany. The political dimensions of the expellee problem in the Federal Republic form a particular area of neglect.[10] The complicated links between the expellees, their organizations, and the domestic political system remain poorly investigated, especially on the federal level, despite the obvious importance of the newcomers'

Bayern 1945 bis 1950 (Stuttgart: Klett-Cotta, 1982); Rolf Messerschmidt, *Aufnahme und Integration der Vertriebenen und Flüchtlinge in Hessen, 1945–1950: Zur Geschichte der hessischen Flüchtlingsverwaltung* (Wiesbaden: Historische Kommission für Nassau, 1994); Michael Sommer, *Flüchtlinge und Vertriebene in Rheinland-Pfalz: Aufnahme, Unterbringung und Eingliederung* (Mainz: Von Hase & Köhler, 1990); Sylvia Schraut, *Die Flüchtlingsaufnahme in Württemberg-Baden, 1945–1949: Amerikanische Besatzungsziele und demokratischer Wiederaufbau im Konflikt* (Munich: Oldenbourg, 1995); Matthias Beer (ed.), *Zur Integration der Flüchtlinge und Vertriebenen im deutschen Südwesten nach 1945: Bestandsaufnahme und Perspektiven der Forschung* (Sigmaringen: Thorbecke, 1994).

[8] For organizational studies of varying quality, see York R. Winkler, *Flüchtlingsorganisationen in Hessen, 1945–1954* (Wiesbaden: Historische Kommission für Nassau, 1998); Bernd Sonnewald, *Die Entstehung und Entwicklung der ostdeutschen Landsmannschaften von 1947 bis 1952* (Ph.D. diss., Freie Universität Berlin, 1975); Richard Eberle, 'The Sudetendeutsche in West German Politics, 1945–1973' (Ph.D. diss., University of Utah, 1986); Johannes Dieter Steinert, 'Flüchtlingsvereinigungen— Eingliederungsstationen: Zur Rolle organisierter Interessen bei der Flüchtlingsintegration in der frühen Nachkriegszeit', *Jahrbuch für ostdeutsche Volkskunde*, 33 (1990): 55–68; id., *Vertriebenenverbände;* Franz Neumann, *Der Block der Heimatvertriebenen und Entrechteten: Ein Beitrag zur Geschichte und Struktur einer politischen Interessenpartei* (Meisenheim: Anton Hain, 1968); Hans-Josef Brües, *Artikulation und Repräsentation politischer Verbandsinteressen, dargestellt am Beispiel der Vertriebenenorganisationen* (Ph.D. diss., University of Cologne, 1972); Manfred Max Wambach, *Verbändestaat und Parteienoligopol: Macht und Ohnmacht der Vertriebenenverbände* (Stuttgart: Ferdinand Enke, 1971); Hans Schoenberg, *Germans from the East: A Study of their Migration, Resettlement and Subsequent Group History since 1945* (The Hague: Nijhoff, 1970); Ludwig Landsberg, 'Verbände der Vertriebenen und Geschädigten', in *Verbände und Herrschaft: Pluralismus in der Gesellschaft* (Bonn: Eichholz, 1970), 515–62; Michael Imhof, *Die Vertriebenenverbände in der Bundesrepublik Deutschland: Geschichte, Organisation und gesellschaftliche Bedeutung* (Ph.D. diss., Philipps-Universität Marburg, 1975).

[9] See esp. Robert G. Moeller, *War Stories: The Search for a Usable Past in the Federal Republic of Germany* (Berkeley, Calif.: University of California Press, 2001); Moeller's identically named article in *American Historical Review*, 101 (1996): 1008–48; Albrecht Lehmann, *Im Fremden ungewollt zuhaus: Flüchtlinge und Vertriebene in Westdeutschland, 1945–1990* (Munich: Beck, 1991); Michael L. Hughes, ' "Through No Fault of our own": West Germans Remember their War Losses', *German History*, 18 (2000): 193–213; Michael Schwartz, 'Vertreibung und Vergangenheitspolitik: Ein Versuch über geteilte deutsche Nachkriegsidentitäten', *Deutschland-Archiv*, 30 (1997): 177–95; Rainer Münz and Rainer Ohliger, 'Vergessene Deutsche—Erinnerte Deutsche: Flüchtlinge, Vertriebene, Aussiedler', *Transit*, 15 (1998), 141–57; Rainer Schulze, 'The German Refugees and Expellees from the East and the Creation of a Western German Identity after World War II', in Philipp Ther and Ana Siljak (eds.), *Redrawing Nations: Ethnic Cleansing in East–Central Europe, 1944–1948* (Oxford: Rowman & Little, 2001), 307–25.

[10] Grosser, 'Konfliktgemeinschaft', esp. 82–4; Ian Connor, 'Flüchtlinge und die politischen Parteien in Bayern, 1945–1950', *Jahrbuch für deutsche und osteuropäische Ostkunde*, 38 (1995): esp. 133; Frank Bösch, 'Die politische Integration der Flüchtlinge und Vertriebenen und ihre Einbindung in die CDU', in Rainer Schulze (ed.), *Zwischen Heimat und Zuhause: Deutsche Flüchtlinge und Vertriebene in (West) Deutschland 1945–2000* (Osnabrück: Secolo, 2001), esp. 107.

political integration for the Federal Republic's stability.[11] Similar problems are even more obvious in the external realm, where connections between Bonn's foreign policies—above all towards Eastern Europe—and the expellee issue have received very little sustained attention. This is a striking oversight because the expulsions stand out as one of the most problematic legacies of the Second World War, with obvious implications for the subsequent interaction between Germans and their eastern neighbours.[12]

This book aims to demonstrate the centrality of the expellee problem for West Germany's political development. As a means to that end, it provides a long-term case study of a policy field in which the expellee issue's contribution was particularly significant: the Federal Republic's Ostpolitik—or policy toward Eastern Europe. My goal is to untangle a paradox that characterized West German Ostpolitik particularly until the early 1970s and, on a lesser scale, all the way to German reunification in 1990. It derived from the juxtaposition of two seemingly incompatible stances in the statements and actions of the country's leaders.

---

[11] Although comprehensive treatments of the party-political integration of the expellees are lacking, useful studies of specific aspects include Grebing, *Flüchtlinge*; Bauer, *Flüchtlinge*; Connor, 'Flüchtlinge'; Bösch, 'Politische'; Ulrike Haerendel, 'Die Politik der "Eingliederung" in den Westzonen und der Bundesrepublik Deutschland: Das Flüchtlingsproblem zwischen Grundsatzentscheidungen und Verwaltungspraxis', in Hoffmann et al., *Vertriebene*, 109–34; Everhard Holtmann, 'Politische Interessenvertretung von Vertriebenen: Handlungsmuster, Organisationsvarianten und Folgen für das politische System der Bundesrepublik', ibid. 187–202; id., 'Flüchtlinge in den 50er Jahren: Aspekte ihrer gesellschaftlichen und politischen Integration', in Axel Schildt and Arnold Sywottek (eds.), *Modernisierung im Wiederaufbau: Die westdeutsche Gesellschaft in den 50er Jahren* (Bonn: Dietz, 1993), 349–61; Johannes Dieter Steinert, 'Organisierte Flüchtlingsinteressen und parlamentarische Demokratie: Westdeutschland 1945–49', in Klaus J. Bade (ed.), *Neue Heimat im Westen: Vertriebene, Flüchtlinge, Aussiedler* (Münster: Westfälische Heimatbund, 1990), 61–80; Hans-Werner Martin, '. . . nicht spurlos aus der Geschichte verschwinden': Wenzel Jaksch und die Integration der sudetendeutschen Sozialdemokraten nach dem Zweiten Weltkrieg, 1945–1949* (Frankfurt: Peter Lang, 1996).

[12] Relevant contributions include my article 'Domestic Constraints on West German Ostpolitik: The Role of the Expellee Organizations in the Adenauer Era', *Central European History*, 31 (1998): 31–64; and Ph.D. dissertation 'The Expellee Organizations and West German Ostpolitik, 1949–1969' (Yale University, 1999). Samuel Salzborn's two recent books, *Grenzenlose Heimat: Geschichte, Gegenwart und Zukunft der Vertriebenenverbände* (Berlin: Elefanten Press, 2000) and *Heimatrecht und Volkstumskampf: Aussenpolitische Konzepte der Vertriebenenverbände und ihre politische Umsetzung* (Hanover: Offizin, 2001), are marred by polemics and lack nuance. The best older essay is P. von Zur Mühlen, B. Müller, and K. Schmitz, 'Vertriebenenverbände und deutsch-polnische Beziehungen nach 1945', in Carl Christoph Schweitzer and Hubert Feger (eds.), *Deutsch-polnische Konfliktverhältnis* (Boppard am Rhein: Boldt, 1975), 96–161, which concentrates on the years 1955–8 and 1969–71. Hans-Georg Lehmann's contributions, especially his *Der Oder-Neisse Konflikt* (Munich: Beck, 1979), deal with a broader set of problems but provide excellent insights. Also of some relevance are Peter Reichel, 'Die Vertriebenenverbände als aussenpolitische "pressure group"', in Hans-Peter Schwarz (ed.), *Handbuch der deutschen Aussenpolitik* (Munich: Piper, 1975), 233–8; Jörg K. Hoensch, 'Initiativen gesellschaftlicher Gruppierungen in der Bundesrepublik Deutschland bei der Ausgestaltung der deutsch-polnischen Beziehungen', in Wolfgang Jacobmeyer (ed.), *Die Beziehungen zwischen der Bundesrepublik Deutschland und der Volksrepublik Polen bis zur Konferenz über Sicherheit und Zusammenarbeit in Europa* (Brunswick: Georg-Eckert-Institut für internationale Schulbuchforschung, 1987); Hans Hapke, 'Aussenpolitische Einstellung der Vertriebenen als Funktion von Diskriminierung', in Schweitzer and Feger, *Deutsch-polnische Konfliktverhältnis*, 416–53; Ingeborg Zeiträg, *Die Selbstdarstellung der deutschen Vertriebenen als Reflex ihrer gesellschaftlichen Situation* (Ph.D. diss., University of Hamburg, 1970). In addition, other works, particularly those on the expellee organizations, address foreign affairs in passing.

On the one hand, West German politicians persistently proclaimed that their state constituted a new departure in German history, an entity fundamentally different from the preceding regimes, particularly the Third Reich. As a peaceful, westward-looking democracy linked to the humane values of the Western Enlightenment, the Bonn Republic was the perfect antithesis of not only Nazi totalitarianism but also the red variant practised by the rival regime in East Berlin. More concretely, West German leaders also denounced the murderous eastern policies of the Third Reich and pledged to pursue a peaceful reconciliation with the peoples of Eastern Europe.[13]

On the other hand, many of Bonn's statements and actions seemed custom-made to raise doubts about its supposedly peaceful intentions towards Eastern Europe. The West Germans fuelled such suspicions in two ways. First, they were exceedingly slow to normalize their relations with the East European countries. With the exception of the Soviet Union, Bonn failed to establish permanent diplomatic ties to any of the states of the area until the late 1960s, and even then it chose to begin with the regional mavericks Romania and Yugoslavia.[14] The other Eastern bloc governments, including the crucial regimes in Warsaw and Prague, had to wait until the early 1970s.

The second—and more ominous—signal was the steady stream of declarations in which West German political elites appeared to espouse a cause that had wreaked particular havoc in earlier decades: territorial revisionism in Eastern Europe. More specifically, the government and the major parties rejected the current border settlement in the region, above all the so-called Oder-Neisse line that now separated Poland from East Germany. Drawing on the Potsdam Agreement of 1945, they claimed that the Reich—as embodied in the Federal Republic—continued to exist within its 1937 boundaries. And they demanded that any final decisions over territorial questions be postponed, pending a future peace settlement between a free, reunified Germany and the victors of the Second World War, in which the current status quo would presumably be subject to revision.

The seemingly paradoxical behaviour of West German political elites raises a series of intriguing questions. Why did the country's leaders drag their feet about normalizing their relations with the East European countries? Why did they espouse doctrines that bore a disconcerting similarity to the destructive territorial revisionism of an earlier era? In the immediate post-war years, at a time when border readjustments seemed at least theoretically possible, these stances arguably still made some sense. But why did West Germany's leaders stick to their publicly

---

[13] See Jeffrey Herf, *Divided Memory: The Nazi Past in the Two Germanys* (Cambridge, Mass.: Harvard University Press, 1997); German Foreign Ministry's document collection *Die Auswärtige Politik der Bundesrepublik Deutschland* (Cologne: Wissenschaft und Politik, 1995); Hans-Adolf Jacobsen and Mieczyslaw Tomalka (eds.), *Bonn–Warschau 1945–1991: Die deutsch-polnischen Beziehungen* (Cologne: Wissenschaft und Politik, 1992).

[14] Bonn established diplomatic relations with Romania in Jan. 1967 and with Yugoslavia a year later. Diplomatic relations with Yugoslavia had also existed between 1951 and 1957.

proclaimed positions even in the very different context of the 1960s—and in part during the following decades as well—despite the rising actual and potential costs of such practices? With their behaviour, West Germany's political elites provided grist for the mill of anti-German propaganda that Communist leaders used to promote internal cohesion within the Soviet bloc. They also risked growing isolation within the increasingly détente-oriented western alliance and appeared to undermine their presumed primary objective—reunification with the GDR. Given all this, the key question becomes why did West Germany's leaders stubbornly pursue an Eastern policy that appeared increasingly detrimental to their country's broader interests.

The bulk of the relevant historiography has answered these questions with a strong emphasis on calculations rooted in the cold logic of the international system. The prevailing wisdom holds that the key to the Federal Republic's refusal to normalize its relations with most of Eastern Europe was the so-called Hallstein Doctrine: the principle that, in order to keep the GDR internationally isolated, West Germany would eschew diplomatic ties to any country, other than the Soviet Union, that maintained such links with East Germany. Because all the Soviet satellites of Eastern Europe had set up full relations with East Berlin early on, their exclusion from the scope of the Federal Republic's diplomacy was thus a derivative of broader foreign-policy calculations centred on the pursuit of reunification.[15]

The standard explanation for the closely related problem of why Bonn's elites so eagerly proclaimed revisionist territorial demands towards Eastern Europe is similarly heavy on *Staatsräson*. Although most of them did not actually wish to revise the Oder-Neisse line, the argument goes, West German leaders maintained the formal claims because standard diplomatic practice so required. The Potsdam Agreement had, after all, labelled the Oder-Neisse line a temporary demarcation line, pending 'the final delimitation of the . . . frontier' at a future peace conference, and subsequent statements of the Western Allies had seemed to give additional backing to this position.[16] Revisionist territorial demands were therefore valuable bargaining chips that the Federal Republic could not abandon lightly because they might prove crucial for the shaping of a future peace settlement.[17]

---

[15] Werner Killian, *Die Hallstein Doktrin: Der diplomatische Krieg zwischen der BRD und der DDR 1953–1973* (Berlin: Duncker & Humblot, 2001); Rüdiger Marco Booz, '*Hallsteinzeit*': *Deutsche Aussenpolitik 1955–1972* (Bonn: Bouvier, 1995); William G. Gray, *Germany's Cold War: The Global Campaign to Isolate East Germany, 1949–1969* (Chapel Hill, NC: University of North Carolina Press, 2003).

[16] See the text of Article X of the Potsdam Agreement in Ingo von Münch (ed.), *Dokumente des geteilten Deutschlands* (Stuttgart: Kröner, 1968), 42.

[17] See e.g. William E. Griffith, *The Ostpolitik of the Federal Republic of Germany* (Cambridge, Mass.: MIT Press, 1978); Daniel Kosthorst, *Brentano und die deutsche Einheit: Die Deutschland- und Ostpolitik des Aussenministers im Kabinett Adenauer, 1955–1961* (Düsseldorf: Droste, 1993); Klaus Gotto, 'Adenauers Deutschland- und Ostpolitik 1954–1963', in Rudolf Morsey and Konrad Repgen (eds.), *Adenauer-Studien III: Untersuchungen zur Ostpolitik und Bibliographie* (Mainz: Grünewald, 1974), 3–91; and Hans Peter Schwarz's various influential works, including 'Das aussenpolitische Konzept Konrad Adenauers', in Klaus Gotto (ed.), *Konrad Adenauer: Seine Deutschland- und Ostpolitik*

Such diplomatic considerations did play an important role in the formulation of West Germany's policies towards Eastern Europe. But an exclusive focus on them distorts the overall picture by exaggerating the statesmanlike rationality of Bonn's policy-making process. The peculiarities of the Federal Republic's Ostpolitik become fully intelligible only when the foreign-policy problems that hindered improvements in German–East European relations are grounded in West Germany's domestic social and political context. The expellee problem in particular needs to be recognized as a crucial link between the internal and external levels of West German politics.

This book highlights the significance of that link during the cold war. Its primary focus lies on the role of a prominent network of pressure groups—the so-called expellee organizations (*Vertriebenenverbände*)—that claimed to represent the collective interests of ordinary expellees. The groups boasted a self-proclaimed total membership of approximately two million and lobbied the country's political elites to maintain hard-line, revisionist stances towards Eastern Europe, with the ultimate aim of regaining the territories that Germany had lost. Thanks primarily to their presumed electoral leverage on expellees and other nationalistically minded population groups, these organizations quickly became influential political actors whose activities connected the expellee problem to West Germany's relations with Eastern Europe.

This study therefore focuses on the complex interactions among these organizations, the main political parties, and Bonn's federal government. It examines the expellee lobby's efforts to pursue its revisionist agenda, highlighting the various channels through which the expellee activists exerted pressure on Bonn's political elites and the degree to which the latter responded to such pressure. But the book also explores a reverse flow of influence, that is, the extent to which the government and the parties used and manipulated the expellees in pursuit of their own goals. The analysis rests on a large documentary basis, including extensive unpublished material from fifteen German archives, many of which have never before been used for scholarly purposes.

Although primarily a study of West German Ostpolitik in general and its domestic political setting in particular, this book also resonates in broader, related fields. In the context of German history, the story told here forms an integral thread within the wider narrative of the Federal Republic's development. As recent scholarship has shown, West German leaders navigated a tortuous course in building their new state from the ruins of Nazism and total war. The demands of justice had to be balanced against the exigencies of reconstruction, integration, and de-radicalization, which entailed many difficult choices. The political elites had to juggle two often conflicting objectives in their public rhetoric and concrete

(Munich: DTV, 1975), 97–155. Major studies that do combine *Staatsräson* arguments with more extensive attention to other factors include Timothy Garton Ash, *In Europe's Name: Germany and the Divided Continent* (New York: Vintage, 1993); Dieter Bingen, *Die Polenpolitik der Bonner Republik von Adenauer bis Kohl 1949–1991* (Baden-Baden: Nomos, 1998). See also the expellee-related works cited in n. 12.

policies: the promotion of forward-looking, democratic values and structures and the pacification of compromised, discontented elements that posed potential hazards to the new regime.

Ultimately the West German polity proved highly successful, as a stable, democratic system took root and political radicalism remained a fringe phenomenon. But that happy ending does not necessarily justify all the means applied along the way, and much of the relevant historical work of recent years has explored not only the successes but also the costs of the policies pursued by West German elites during the cold war. The many failures of justice in the early Federal Republic have come in for particular criticism in this recent scholarship, which has often, at least implicitly, posed the question of whether alternative policies could have led to equally satisfactory—or even more desirable—ultimate outcomes.[18]

Through its focus on the interaction between Bonn's political elites and the expellee activists, this book throws additional light on the dilemmas of democratic reconstruction in post-war West Germany. The presence of eight million dispossessed and discontented expellees constituted a significant potential threat to the new polity, and the authorities were well aware of the need to placate and integrate this population group. Accordingly, they implemented decisive measures, particularly in social policy. But the Federal Republic's leaders also strove to integrate the expellees on the political level—through party-political manœuvres, rhetorical gambits, and calculated Ostpolitik stances. By highlighting this hitherto neglected aspect of West German state-building, the present study contributes to ongoing debates about the costs and benefits of democratization and identity-formation in the Federal Republic. It asks whether the domestically motivated Ostpolitik positions adopted by the country's leaders were necessary and to what degree they promoted or hampered the long-term stabilization of the new republic. And it raises similar questions about the effects of the activities of the expellees in general and their purported organizational representatives in particular.

Although this study is primarily a work of history, it also relates to broader debates in the social sciences, particularly those concerning the dynamics of foreign-policy formulation. While most studies of West German Ostpolitik have continued to stress the primacy of external factors in policy decisions, political scientists have increasingly moved beyond such overly simplified paradigms. Innovative recent work has tried to connect domestic and international politics in systematic ways through game theory applications and other models.[19] This book

---

[18] Prominent examples include Norbert Frei, *Vergangenheitspolitik: Die Anfänge der Bundesrepublik und die NS-Vergangenheit* (Munich: Beck, 1996); Ulrich Brochhagen, *Nach Nürnberg: Vergangenheitsbewältigung und Westintegration in der Ära Adenauer* (Berlin: Ullstein, 1999). Herf, *Divided Memory*, another key work, is more lenient on West German elites.

[19] Key works include Robert D. Putnam, 'Diplomacy and Domestic Politics: The Logic of Two-Level Games', *International Organization*, 42 (1988): 427–60; Peter B. Evans, Harold K. Jacobson, and Robert D. Putnam (eds.), *Double-Edged Diplomacy: International Bargaining and Domestic Politics* (Berkeley, Calif.: University of California Press, 1993); Ryan K. Beasley, Juliet Kaarbo, Jeffrey S. Lantis,

does not aspire to construct rival models—or to demolish existing ones. But it does provide material for future theory-building through a detailed case study of the long-term interaction between internal and external influences on a particular foreign-policy issue in a major liberal democracy during the cold war.

The key intervening variable between domestic and international affairs highlighted in this study is also of wider, inter-disciplinary significance. Pressure groups and their activities in liberal democracies have received a good deal of attention over the past decades, particularly from social scientists. But as leading experts in the field have lamented, interest in the topic has recently waned, and most relevant studies have focused on the internal dynamics of pressure groups rather than on broader, systemic questions regarding the power and influence of interest groups.[20] By highlighting precisely these broader issues, the present study not only provides empirical material relevant to this wider literature but also offers some conclusions about the extent and limits of pressure group power in liberal democracies.

In addition to this introduction and a conclusion, this book has eight chapters, grouped into three parts. Part I, composed of the first four chapters, opens with the expulsions and the subsequent rise of the expellee organizations in the western occupation zones. The other three chapters then go on to analyse the emergence of an enduring pattern of Ostpolitik interaction among the expellee groups, Konrad Adenauer's government, and the main parties during the period preceding the Federal Republic's attainment of sovereignty in May 1955. In these years, the expellee lobby's revisionist Eastern policy demands—centred on promoting, typically through elaborate legal argumentation, a reannexation of the territories that the Reich had lost to Poland, Czechoslovakia, and the Soviet Union at the end of the Second World War—became instrumentalized by the leading parties and the government. Bonn's political elites knew that the pursuit of these revisionist causes was neither possible nor desirable under post-war conditions. But they cultivated the impression of a far-reaching congruence of interests between themselves and the expellee organizations, primarily because of electoral calculations and the expellee lobby's usefulness for the government's broader domestic and foreign policy agenda.

At the same time, however, governmental and party leaders carefully excluded

and Michael T. Snarr (eds.), *Foreign Policy in Comparative Perspective: Domestic and International Influences on State Behavior* (Washington, DC: CQ Press, 2001); Andrew Moravcsik, 'De Gaulle between Grain and Grandeur: The Political Economy of French EC Policy, 1958–1970', *Journal of Cold War Studies*, 2/2 (2000): 3–43 (part 1); 2/3 (2000): 4–68 (part 2). On Germany specifically, see David F. Patton, *Cold War Politics in Postwar Germany* (London: Macmillan, 1999). For similar attempts by a prominent cold war historian, see Mark Kramer, 'The Early Post-Stalin Succession Struggle and Upheavals in East–Central Europe: Internal–External Linkages in Soviet Policy Making', *Journal of Cold War Studies*, 1/ 1 (1999): 3–55 (part 1); 1/2 (1999): 3–38; 1/3 (1999): 3–66 (part 3).

[20] See e.g. Frank R. Baumgartner and Beth L. Leech, *Basic Interests: The Importance of Groups in Politics and Political Science* (Princeton: Princeton University Press, 1998); William Crotty, Mildred A. Schwartz, and John C. Green (eds.), *Representing Interests and Interest Group Representation* (Lanham, Md: University Press of America, 1994). The classic study that reoriented the field towards internal group dynamics was Mancur Olson's *The Logic of Collective Action: Public Goods and the Theory of Groups* (Cambridge, Mass.: Harvard University Press, 1965).

expellee representatives from key power positions. Final decisions on how far to go with the advocacy of revisionist causes were made in small, closed circles, without direct input from the organized expellee movement. Although disappointed by their exclusion from active policy-making roles, most expellee leaders reconciled themselves to the existing terms of interaction and increasingly focused on monitoring the political elites' continued loyalty to the main tenets of a revisionist Ostpolitik.

As long as West Germany lacked sovereignty and thus the ability to pursue independent policies towards Eastern Europe, the country's political leaders incurred few immediate costs with their manipulative use of the expellee card. But the situation changed with the attainment of sovereignty in May 1955. Possibilities for an active Ostpolitik began to open up, and interest in pursuing such options grew in Bonn. However, the price of earlier promises also became clear, as the political elites found themselves trapped in their publicly proclaimed Eastern policy stances. Although these positions caused growing international image problems for the government and significantly reduced its freedom of action in Eastern Europe, the political leadership refused to budge from them, largely for fear of electoral retribution from the millions of voters whom the expellee lobby claimed to represent. While still lacking active influence—that is, the ability to participate directly in the formulation and implementation of the Federal Republic's foreign policy—the expellee organizations now came to exert an extensive negative influence, as they hindered the government and the main parties from adopting, or even publicly discussing, more flexible Ostpolitik stances.

Part II explores the resulting tensions during their peak, between 1955 and 1965/6. Chapter 5 examines the high summer of the Adenauer era, the years through the end of the 1950s, in which the expellee groups repeatedly flexed their muscles against what they viewed as overly conciliatory Ostpolitik ideas and initiatives. Chapter 6 extends the analysis from the late 1950s to the Bundestag election of 1965 and the last months of Ludwig Erhard's government in 1966, with a special focus on the intensified scramble for expellee votes that took place in these years. The battle's immediate cause was the SPD's concentrated campaign to court this segment of the electorate, which, in turn, was part of the party's larger project of repositioning itself away from the traditional left towards the contemporary political centre. The resulting electoral tussle raised the stakes in expellee politics and seemingly brought the expellee lobby to new heights of political influence in the first half of the 1960s.

But these appearances were deceptive, for in reality the expellee organizations had by then entered a period of decline. Part III traces that process from the 1960s to reunification some three decades later. The gradual erosion of the expellee lobby's position resulted from the confluence of several long-term trends that began to manifest themselves by the early 1960s. On the international plane, the rise of détente generated growing pressure for Bonn to adopt conciliatory policies towards its eastern neighbours. In Berlin, the building of the Wall in August 1961 sounded the death knell for the credibility of Adenauer's 'policy of strength' as a road to reunification and created obvious incentives for the development of new approaches towards the USSR and its East European satellites. Similar incentives also arose on the domestic scene, where a growing chorus of voices—composed primarily of journalists, publicists, and others from beyond the narrow world of Bonn's high-level politics—began to clamour for a more flexible Ostpolitik, inspired in large part by concern about the dead end which hopes for reunification appeared to have hit. In addition, broad generational, social, and attitudinal changes swept West Germany during the 1960s, posing challenges to established patterns and assumptions in many fields of public life, including Eastern policy.

As these changes in the domestic and international context became increasingly obvious during the latter half of the 1960s, politicians reacted by gradually modifying their Ostpolitik positions. Chapter 7 follows the slow adaptation of the Federal Republic's political elites to these shifting conditions, particularly during the three-year period defined by the rule of the so-called Grand Coalition— composed of the CDU/CSU and the SPD—between late 1966 and 1969. Complicated manœuvring during these years culminated in the collapse of the pattern that had characterized the interaction between the expellee activists and the political elites since the founding of the Federal Republic. As the SPD and the FDP switched to a new, more conciliatory line towards Eastern Europe in defiance of the expellee organizations, the public all-party consensus on the expellee lobby's main Ostpolitik demands broke down. For primarily tactical reasons, the CDU/CSU continued to pose as the standard-bearer of expellee causes, but its half-hearted proclamations could not conceal the fact that the formation of the SPD–FDP coalition under Willy Brandt in late 1969 marked the end of an era. Under the banner of the new Ostpolitik, a normalization of the Federal Republic's relations with Eastern Europe could now proceed on the basis of an acceptance of the post-war status quo, regardless of the vociferous protests of the increasingly desperate and marginalized expellee organizations.

Chapter 8 underlines this point. In concise form, it traces key moments in the interaction between the expellee groups and West German political elites from the start of the new Ostpolitik in 1970 to German reunification two decades later. The period was characterized by the continued decline of the expellee lobby's power. The backward-looking organizations found themselves increasingly isolated in West German public life, with ever more tenuous links to most of the political elites, the media establishment, and the general public, including the majority of rank-and-file expellees. At the same time, the expellee activists were still intensively courted by one mainstream party, the CDU/CSU, which acted overwhelmingly out of tactical domestic considerations, as in previous years. However, even the Christian Democrats ultimately had to choose between domestic strategies and political realities. That choice fell in 1990, as Helmut Kohl's government finally dropped its tactical manœuvring and accepted a long-awaited reunification settlement, as a part of which Germany formally abandoned all territorial claims towards Eastern Europe. With that step, the expellee lobby had reached the end of the road in its attempts to shape the Federal Republic's Ostpolitik.

I

Establishing the Pattern
1945–1955

CHAPTER ONE

From the Expulsions to the Rise of the Expellee Organizations

THE EXPULSIONS

Among the many cruelties that darken the history of twentieth-century Europe, mass expulsions of ethnic groups occupy a prominent position. The example set by Turkish deportations of Armenians during the First World War and the forcible Greco-Turkish and Greco-Bulgarian population transfers of the 1920s has been followed on numerous subsequent occasions, most recently in the former Yugoslavia of the 1990s.[1] However, even the 'ethnic cleansings' of recent years are eclipsed, at least numerically, by the largest expulsion of the century, which occurred at the end of the Second World War and targeted members of the self-styled 'master race' of the previous decade—the Germans.

This expulsion, which extended from the last months of the war to the early 1950s, uprooted up to fifteen million Germans from their former homelands in the European east. The bulk of the expellees came from regions which had been part of the Reich since its founding in 1871 but fell under Polish or Russian administration after the Second World War: East Prussia, Pomerania, and Silesia, as well as parts of Brandenburg and Upper Silesia. But extensive forced migrations also originated from three other areas. The first comprised the territories detached from Germany after the First World War, reconquered by the Nazis in the Second, and then incorporated into post-war Poland, such as the city of Danzig, most of West Prussia and Posen, and the eastern-most part of Upper Silesia. Another area hard hit by the expulsion was the Sudetenland, annexed by the Nazis in 1938 and restored to Czechoslovak rule after the war. Further east, considerable numbers of ethnic Germans who had never belonged to the Reich proper were also forcibly uprooted from Hungary, Romania, and Yugoslavia.[2]

---

[1] Norman M. Naimark, *Fires of Hatred: Ethnic Cleansing in Twentieth Century Europe* (Cambridge, Mass.: Harvard University Press, 2001); Michael R. Marrus, *The Unwanted: European Refugees in the Twentieth Century* (New York: Oxford University Press, 1985).

[2] Despite its age and problems, the first work to consult on the expulsions is still Theodor Schieder *et al.* (eds.), *Dokumentation der Vertreibung der Deutschen aus Ost-Mitteleuropa*, 8 vols. (Bonn: Bundesministerium für Vertriebene, Flüchtlinge und Kriegsgeschädigte, 1953–61). On the documentation, see Moeller, *War Stories*, 51–87; Matthias Beer, 'Die Dokumentation der Vertreibung der Deutschen aus Ost-Mitteleuropa: Hintergründe—Entstehung—Wirkung', *Geschichte in Wissenschaft und Unterricht*, 50 (1999): 99–117; id., 'Im Spannungsfeld von Politik und Zeitgeschichte: Das

The process of expulsion began in late 1944, as the Red Army advanced into areas of German settlement. Fear of the Soviets was rife among the Germans, in part as a result of old prejudices and Nazi propaganda but in part also because the behaviour of the Soviets, which was characterized by repeated atrocities as well as forcible transports of civilians to labour service in the USSR, appeared to confirm all the old stereotypes.[3] In fear for their lives, hundreds of thousands of Germans fled westward, first from the south-eastern lands of Hungary, Romania, and Yugoslavia, but by October also from the eastern provinces of the Reich, particularly East Prussia and Pomerania. As the Russians penetrated ever deeper into German-held territory in 1945, the ranks of the German refugees swelled, reaching over seven million from the former Prussian provinces alone by the end of the war. Amidst the chaos and terror of their flight, few of the Germans suspected that they would never return to their former homes. Most regarded the escape as a temporary emergency measure, and many even made vain attempts to return to their old residences in the summer of 1945.[4]

Unbeknownst to the Germans, their systematic expulsion, particularly from Czech and Polish territories, had reached an advanced stage of preparation by the last months of the war. Angered by the brutal Nazi rule in their countries and the perceived 'fifth column' treachery of their interior German minorities, exiled Polish and Czech statesmen had been advocating large-scale expulsions of the Germans throughout the war years. As an additional security measure, the Poles—both the London-based government-in-exile and the rival Communist grouping in the USSR—had also been demanding considerable territorial gains for their country at Germany's expense.[5]

Unsurprisingly, these anti-German ideas found sympathy among the Allies. Stalin, in particular, committed himself by 1943/4 to championing both the expulsion of the Germans from Czechoslovakia and Poland and the shift of Poland's western frontier to the Oder and Neisse rivers, deep within pre-Second World

Grossforschungsprojekt "Dokumentation der Vertreibung der Deutschen aus Ostmitteleuropa" ', *Vierteljahrshefte für Zeitgeschichte*, 49 (1998): 345–89. See also Erik K. Franzen and Hans Lemberg, *Die Vertriebenen: Hitlers letzte Opfer* (Berlin: Propyläen, 2001); Ther and Siljak, *Redrawing*.

[3] On Soviet brutality, see Schieder, *Dokumentation*, i/1. 15E, 7–8; Norman M. Naimark, *The Russians in Germany: A History of the Soviet Zone of Occupation, 1945–1949* (Cambridge, Mass.: Harvard University Press, 1995), esp. 69–140; Atina Grossman, 'A Question of Silence: The Rape of German Women by Occupation Soldiers', *October* (1995): 43–63; Manfred Zeidler, *Kriegsende im Osten. Die Rote Armee und die Besetzung Deutschlands östlich von Oder und Neisse 1944/1945* (Munich: Oldenbourg, 1996). On the forcible labour transports to the USSR, which affected some 400,000 Germans, see Schieder, *Dokumentation*, i/1. 79E–87E; ii. 41E–44E; iii. 75E–80E; iv/1. 31–2; v. 93–7.

[4] Schieder, *Dokumentation*, i/1. 69–78.

[5] Detlef Brandes, *Der Weg zur Vertreibung: Pläne und Entscheidungen zum 'Transfer' der Deutschen aus der Tschechoslowakei und aus Polen* (Munich: Oldenbourg, 2001); Hans Lemberg and Wlodzimierz Borodziej, 'Einleitung', in Lemberg and Borodziej (ed.), '*Unsere Heimat ist uns ein fremdes Land geworden ...*': *Die Deutschen östlich von Oder und Neisse, 1945–1950. Dokumente aus polnischen Archiven*, i (Marburg: Herder-Institut, 2000), esp. 33–55; Viktoria Vierheller, *Polen und die Deutschland-Frage, 1939–1949* (Cologne: Wissenschaft und Politik, 1970); Sarah Meiklejohn Terry, *Poland's Place in Europe: General Sikorski and the Origin of the Oder-Neisse Line, 1939–1943* (Princeton: Princeton University Press, 1983).

War Germany.[6] Stalin was driven by self-interest; the Soviet dictator's plans to annex eastern Poland and uproot its population presupposed compensation of the Communist regime that he planned to install in Warsaw with German territory. However, even the Soviet Union's two Western Allies, who lacked a comparable stake in the region and consequently assigned these matters only secondary importance, expressed their general agreement with the Czech and Polish demands well before war's end. The British showed consistent interest in the expulsions from 1942 on, and even President Roosevelt made his acquiescence clear by the spring of 1943, although his administration's official line on the issue remained rather muted throughout the war. London and Washington also expressed their agreement with the principle of Polish land losses in the east and gains in the west on several occasions, most notably at Teheran in December 1943 and Yalta in February 1945. However, the precise extent of the territorial changes and population transfers remained undetermined, as the Western Allies preferred not to commit themselves prematurely on issues which they hoped to employ as bargaining tools vis-à-vis the Soviets in the post-war settlement.[7]

A formal Allied agreement regarding the expulsions and the associated territorial questions thus did not materialize until the Potsdam Conference of July and August 1945. At the conference, complicated East–West bargaining yielded a compromise: in exchange for Soviet concessions on reparations, the Western Powers accepted the Soviet line on the twin problem of the expulsions and Polish borders.[8] The Potsdam Agreement of 2 August 1945 thus placed the German provinces east of the line formed by the Oder and western Neisse rivers under Polish or—in the case of northern East Prussia—Russian administration, pending the 'final delimitation of the ... frontier' at a future peace conference.[9] Technically, the wording left open the possibility of subsequent boundary changes, as did other declarations in which the Western Allies expressly

[6] Brandes, *Weg*, 200–6, 240–3, 286–90, Edward Taborsky, *President Eduard Beneš: Between East and West 1938–1948* (Stanford, Calif.: Hoover Institution, 1981), esp. 162; Vierheller, *Polen*, 74-6; Vojtech Mastny, 'Soviet War Aims at the Moscow and Teheran Conferences of 1943', *JMH* 47 (1975): 481–50.

[7] Brandes, *Weg*; Detlef Brandes, *Grossbritannien und seine osteuropäischen Alliierten, 1939–1943: Die Regierungen Polens, der Tschechoslowakei und Jugoslawiens im Londoner Exil vom Kriegsausbruch bis zur Konferenz von Teheran* (Munich: Oldenbourg, 1988); Josef Foschepoth, 'Grossbritannien, Sowjetunion und die Westverschiebung Polens', *Militärgeschichtliche Mittteilungen*, 34 (1983): 61–90; Klaus-Dietmar Henke, 'Die Alliierten und die Vertreibung', in Wolfgang Benz (ed.), *Die Vertreibung der Deutschen aus dem Osten: Ursachen, Ereignisse, Folgen* (Frankfurt: Fischer, 1995), 58–85; Carsten Lilge, *Die Entstehung der Oder-Neisse Linie als Nebenprodukt alliierter Grossmachtpolitik während des Zweiten Weltkrieges* (Frankfurt: Lang, 1995); Hans Åke Persson, *Rhetorik und Realpolitik: Grossbritannien, die Oder-Neisse Grenze und die Vertreibung der Deutschen nach dem Zweiten Weltkrieg* (Berlin: Berlin-Verlag, 2001); Wolfgang Wagner, *Die Entstehung der Oder-Neisse-Linie in den diplomatischen Verhandlungen während des Zweiten Weltkrieges* (Marburg: Herde-Gesellschaft, 1968); Michael A. Hartenstein, *Die Oder-Neisse Linie: Geschichte der Aufrichtung und Anerkennung einer problematischen Grenze* (Egelsbach: Hänsel-Hohenhausen, 1997).

[8] Brandes, *Weg*, 401–17; Josef Foschepoth, 'Potsdam und danach: Die Westmächte, Adenauer und die Vertriebenen', in Benz, *Vertreibung*, 58–85; Henke, 'Alliierten', 64–5, 80–1.

[9] Ingo von Münch (ed.), *Dokumente des geteilten Deutschland* (Stuttgart: Kröner, 1976), 42.

confirmed occupied Germany's continued existence within its boundaries of 31 December 1937. In reality, however, all three signatories expected the *de facto* border agreement to become permanent. Accordingly, the Allied Control Council soon defined Germany as the area between 'the Oder-Neisse line and the current western borders', while a memorandum by the British Foreign Minister described a general consensus regarding the fact that 'no change in the Potsdam line will be made in Germany's favour'.[10] Whereas the vagueness of the border paragraph gave ample openings for subsequent cold war manœuvrings, the Potsdam line on the expulsions was much clearer. Article XIII of the agreement expressly sanctioned the 'transfer to Germany of German populations, or elements thereof, remaining in Poland, Czechoslovakia, and Hungary' and prescribed that the 'transfers . . . be effected in an orderly and humane manner'.[11] The expulsions had thus become a matter of consensus among the victorious powers.

With these decisions, the Allies were only reacting to events, however, as mass expulsions of the Germans had started well before Potsdam, particularly in territories under Czech and Polish control.[12] This pre-Potsdam phase of the expulsions, which was characterized by particular brutality and wantonness, began in Czechoslovakia immediately after the German surrender and in the Oder-Neisse territories—where the Soviets had handed administrative control to the provisional Polish government—by early June. During the following weeks, hundreds of thousands of Germans were deported westward, usually under very harsh conditions. Those who stayed behind were deprived of their property and civil rights and often assigned to concentration camps or forced labour, pending later expulsion. Although the first outbreaks of anti-German violence typically erupted spontaneously on the local level, the governments soon took control of the process. During 1945, all five countries which carried out extensive expulsions introduced special legislation to justify and facilitate the collective punishment of the German population.[13] Among the most notorious measures were the so-called Beneš decrees, issued in Czechoslovakia between late May and early August, which provided for the expropriation and denaturalization of the Sudeten Germans and helped to cause the wave of violent retribution that swept the country in the course of the summer.[14]

---

[10] 26 Mar. 1946 decision of the Allied Control Council, in *Dokumente zur Deutschlandpolitik der Sowjetunion*, i (Berlin [East]: Rütten & Loening, 1957), 510; Ernest Bevin's 11 Mar. 1946 memorandum, in Rolf Steininger (ed.), *Die Ruhrfrage 1945/46 und die Entstehung des Landes Nordrhein-Westfalen: Britische, französische und amerikanische Akten* (Düsseldorf: Droste, 1988), 545; Lehmann, *Oder-Neisse*, esp. 55–7.

[11] Münch (ed.), *Dokumente*, 42–3.

[12] On the following, see Schieder, *Dokumentation*, i/1. 135E–143E; iv/1. 105E–115E; v. 97E–102E; Detlef Brandes, Edita Ivaničková, and Jiří Pešek (eds.), *Erzwungene Trennung: Vertreibungen und Aussiedlungen in und aus der Tschechoslowakei 1938–1947 im Vergleich mit Polen, Ungarn und Jugoslawien* (Essen: Klartext, 1999); Emilia Hrabovec, *Vertreibung und Abschub: Deutsche in Mähren 1945–1947* (Frankfurt: Lang, 1995); Ther, *Deutsche*, 50–66.

[13] Schieder, *Dokumentation*, i/1. 125E–135E; ii. 45E–58E; iii. 81E–88E; iv/1. 67E–94E; v. 102E–112E.

[14] Helmut Slapnicka, 'Die rechtlichen Grundlagen für die Behandlung der Deutschen und Magyaren in der Tschechoslowakei 1945–1948', in Richard G. Plaschka *et al.* (eds.), *Nationale Frage*

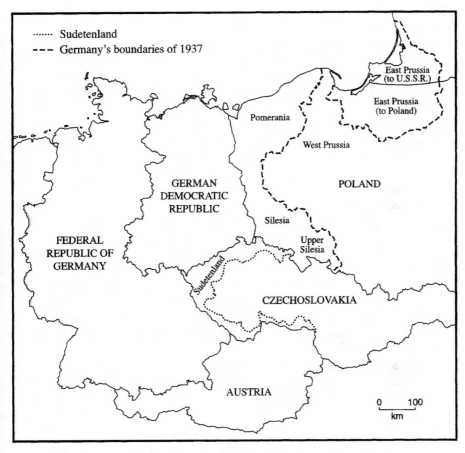

Germany's 1937 and Post-1945 Borders and the Main Areas of Expulsion.

The expulsion article of the Potsdam Agreement was thus in part an attempt by the Western Powers to regulate and humanize a deportation process seen as excessively brutal and chaotic. Regulation seemed necessary not only for altruistic reasons but also because the relentless refugee flood was causing growing organizational problems for the occupying powers, particularly the US and Britain, whose zones drew in the bulk of the newcomers. However, despite an Allied request at Potsdam for a temporary suspension of the expulsions in order to enable the four powers to prepare for further arrivals, brutal and poorly organized deportations continued, primarily from Poland but also from other areas.[15] More orderly transports became the norm only in the first half of 1946, after the Allied Control Council had issued detailed expulsion guidelines in November 1945 and the Western Powers had repeatedly intervened to ensure their enforcement.[16] Admittedly, the material conditions remained very harsh. Deportees from Polish-held territories, for example, still typically had to depart on extremely short notice, march long distances with the meagre but often heavy baggage allowed to them, board crowded freight trains and travel for days, sometimes weeks, without proper nutrition or even elementary medical care. But, in contrast to the earlier phase of the expulsion, the Germans were now much less likely to fall victim to assault, plunder, and rape—or even murder—during their difficult westward journey.[17]

This final, post-Potsdam stage of the deportations extended roughly to the end of the 1940s. After reaching a high of some four million in 1946, the annual expellee total fell to less than a quarter of that the following year.[18] By that time, the bulk of the Germans had already been ousted from Poland and Czechoslovakia, the two main expulsion areas, and during the next few years the refugee flood consequently shrank to a mere trickle. By the end of the decade the process was essentially over, although some three million Germans still remained in the various East European countries.[19] A gradual westward migration of these minorities began soon afterwards and continued throughout the cold war—and beyond.

By 1950, some 12.5 million expelled Germans had found refuge in areas west of their former homelands.[20] The bulk of them—approximately eight million—resided on the territory of the newly founded Federal Republic of Germany. The

und Vertreibung in der Tschechoslowakei und Ungarn 1938–1948 (Vienna: Verlag der österreichischen Akademie der Wissenschaften, 1997), 155–92; Oliver Rathkolb and Barbara Coudenhove (eds.), *Die Beneš-Dekrete* (Vienna: Czernin, 2002).

[15] Schieder, *Dokumentation*, i/1. 143E–147E; Lemberg and Borodziej, 'Einleitung', 55–106; Alfred De Zayas, *Die Anglo-Amerikaner und die Vertreibung der Deutschen: Vorgeschichte, Verlauf, Folgen* (Munich: Beck, 1979), 117–22.

[16] Schieder, *Dokumentation*, iv/1. 118E–122E; i/1. 147E–149E; ii. 59E–63E; Radomir Luza, *The Transfer of the Sudeten Germans: A Study of Czech-German Relations 1933–1962* (New York: NYU Press, 1964), 282–3.

[17] Schieder, *Dokumentation*, i/1. 144E–148E; iv/1. 118E–125E; ii. 62E–64E.

[18] Ibid. i/1. 155; iv/1. 123E–124E; ii. 64E; i/1. 155E; iv/1. 125E–126E; ii. 65E.

[19] Reichling, *Vertriebene*, i, 34.   [20] For the data below, ibid. 26, 30–1.

rival German Democratic Republic housed some four million, while the remaining 500,000 lived in Austria or other foreign countries. Of the eight million West German expellees, five-and-a-half million came from post-war Poland, particularly from the territories that had belonged to Weimar Germany. The Sudeten Germans accounted for another two million of the total, and the ethnic Germans of south-eastern Europe, Russia, and the Baltic region made up the rest. Altogether, the eight million expellees constituted 16.1 per cent of the Federal Republic's population in 1950.

For most of these newcomers, the expulsions had been a deeply traumatic experience that scarred many for life, not least because of the brutalities that typically accompanied the flight and deportation. Downright atrocities took place in many areas. The Red Army set the tone with a systematic campaign of looting, rape, and murder of German civilians during its triumphant offensives of late 1944 and early 1945. Yugoslav partisans followed suit with mass executions and brutal internments of the *Volksdeutsche* soon after their country's liberation from Nazi rule in late 1944.[21] In Czechoslovakia and Poland the Germans faced a variety of harsh punitive measures following the Third Reich's surrender, ranging from confinement in concentration camps to death marches and organized massacres. The slaughter of at least a thousand Germans in the Czech city of Aussig (Usti nad Labem) on 31 July 1945 gained particular notoriety, as did the Polish-run concentration camp of Lamsdorf in Upper Silesia, where at least a thousand German inmates perished from malnutrition, disease, and often sadistic violence in 1945–6.[22] However, even for those who did not have to witness such exceptional cruelties, the expulsions imposed severe affliction: sudden and chaotic dislodgement from a familiar environment; flight or deportation under frightening conditions, sometimes preceded by internment or forced labour; loss of property and civil rights; in many cases separation from family and friends; and frequently beatings, looting, hunger, thirst, and disease. Such hardships posed both a physical challenge to which many, particularly the old and the very young, succumbed, and a psychological burden which the survivors carried with them for years to come. The enormity of the events is reflected in the fact that up to 1.5 million Germans may have died in the course of the flight and deportation.[23]

[21] Schieder, *Dokumentation*, v. 90E–93E, 107E–112E; Hans-Ulrich Wehler, *Nationalitätenpolitik in Jugoslawien: Die deutsche Minderheit 1918–1978* (Göttingen: Vandenhoeck & Ruprecht, 1980).

[22] Schieder, *Dokumentation*, iv/1. 71E–72E; iv/2. 282–6; De Zayas, *Anglo-Amerikaner*, 116, 126; Luza, *Transfer*, 272; Schieder, *Dokumentation*, i/2. 423–32; De Zayas, *Anglo-Amerikaner*, 141; Lemberg and Borodziej, 'Einleitung', 85–99.

[23] The numbers are highly disputed. For seemingly precise figures, see Reichling, *Vertriebene*, i. 34–5. Older German sources give even higher, clearly exaggerated totals, often in excess of 2 million. See e.g. Statistisches Bundesamt (ed.), *Die deutschen Vertreibungsverluste: Bevölkerungsbilanzen für die deutschen Vertreibungsgebiete 1939/50* (Stuttgart: Kohlhammer, 1958), 38–9, 45–7. These figures include not only deaths directly attributable to the excesses of the expulsions but also all civilian war deaths in the East from late 1944 on. Ibid. 32, 42. For much lower estimates, see Rüdiger Overmans, 'Personelle Verluste der deutschen Bevölkerung durch Flucht und Vertreibung', *Dzieje Najnowsze*, 26 (1994): 51–65; id., ' "Amtlich und wissenschaftlich erarbeitet": Zur Diskussion über die Verluste während Flucht und Vertreibung der Deutschen aus der ČSR', in Brandes *et al.*, *Erzwungene*, 149–78.

For all their brutality and inhumanity, the expulsions need to be seen in the broader context of East European ethnic strife on the one hand and Nazi policies on the other. Long-standing tensions between Germans and Slavs, rooted in centuries of often troubled interaction and exacerbated by the rise of modern nationalism, grew particularly acute after the First World War peace settlement broke up the Austro-Hungarian Empire, handed the Sudetenland to Czechoslovakia, and ceded large parts of the German Reich to Poland. As a result, millions of Germans accustomed to a privileged existence within the Habsburg or German Empire suddenly had to settle for a minority status under foreign rule. The grievances of these discontented minorities soon became a prominent source of strife, both within the affected East European countries, particularly Poland and Czechoslovakia, and between these states and Berlin.[24] The tensions grew worse with the rise of National Socialism, whose ideology and programme found a good deal of resonance among the unhappy *Volksdeutsche*. The Nazis exploited these sympathies as an opening for a further development of the financial, cultural, and other links between the Reich and the minorities first established under the Weimar regime. The result was a growing dependence of the *Volksdeutsche* on the Third Reich, which, in turn, enabled Hitler to manipulate the minorities as pawns of his power politics by the late 1930s.[25] The Sudeten Germans received star billing in the Führer's drama. As an active fifth column, they played a key role in the events leading up to the Munich Agreement of 1938 and the subsequent disintegration of Czechoslovakia.[26] In other areas, including Poland, the German minorities were politically less prominent, as dictated by Hitler's initial conciliation of the Polish government.[27] However, by the outbreak of the Second World War, a widespread impression existed, in Eastern Europe and beyond, that the German minorities had constituted a treacherous, destabilizing, and ultimately pro-Nazi force in inter-war politics.

The Second World War not only magnified such sentiments towards the

---

[24] Norbert Krekeler, *Revisionsanspruch und geheime Ostpolitik der Weimarer Republik: Die Subventionierung der deutschen Minderheit in Polen 1919–1933* (Stuttgart: DVA, 1973); Richard Blanke, 'The German Minority in Inter-War Poland and German Foreign Policy: Some Reconsiderations', *Journal of Contemporary History*, 25 (1990): 87–102; id., *The Orphans of Versailles: The Germans in Western Poland, 1918–1939* (Lexington, Ky.: University of Kentucky Press, 1993); Rudolf Jaworski, *Vorposten oder Minderheit? Der sudetendeutsche Volkstumskampf in den Beziehungen zwischen der Weimarer Republik und der ČSR* (Stuttgart: DVA, 1977); Johann Wolfgang Brügel, *Tschechen und Deutsche*, i. *1918–1938* (Munich: Nymphenburger Verlagshandlung, 1967); John Hiden, 'The Weimar Republic and the Problem of the *Auslandsdeutsche*', *Journal of Contemporary History*, 12 (1977): 273–89; Carole Fink, 'Defender of Minorities: Germany in the League of Nations, 1926–1933', *Central European History*, 5 (1972): 330–57.

[25] Valdis O. Lumans, *Himmler's Auxiliaries: The Volksdeutsche Mittelstelle and the German National Minorities of Europe, 1933–1945* (Chapel Hill, NC: University of North Carolina Press, 1993).

[26] Ronald M. Smelser, *The Sudeten Problem 1933–1938: Volkstumspolitik and the Formulation of Nazi Foreign Policy* (Middletown, Conn.: Wesleyan University Press, 1975); Volker Zimmermann, *Die Sudetendeutschen im NS-Staat* (Essen: Klartext, 1999); Ralf Gebel, *Heim ins Reich! Konrad Henlein und der Reichsgau Sudetenland* (Munich: Oldenbourg, 1999); Detlef Brandes and Václav Kural (eds.), *Der Weg in die Katastrophe: Deutsch-tschechoslowakische Beziehungen 1938–1947* (Essen: Klartext, 1994).

[27] Lumans, *Himmler's*, 93–100; Blanke, *Orphans*, 163–237.

Volksdeutsche among the East Europeans but also generated a profound hatred and fear of Germans in general. While the extraordinary viciousness of Nazi rule—in which many members of the inter-war German minority groups became deeply implicated, particularly through service in the *Waffen-SS*—profoundly discredited the Germans, it also provided models and precedents for the expulsions.[28] The parallels between Nazi concentration camps and such post-war counterparts as the Polish concentration camp at Lamsdorf are obvious, and lessons in the feasibility of large-scale forcible population transfers were also provided by the Third Reich. Beginning in late 1939, the Nazis transported some 600,000 *Volksdeutsche* into Germany, primarily from the Baltic states, eastern parts of pre-war Poland, Romania, Bulgaria, Yugoslavia, and the Soviet Union.[29] Many of these Germans were subsequently resettled in the provinces annexed from Poland in 1939, but only after some 750,000 Poles had first been expelled from their homes there.[30] Various other transports ensued: the deportations of the Jews and other victims of the Holocaust brought unspeakable suffering and death for many millions, and a hard fate also befell those shipped for forced labour in the Reich, among them some 1.3 million Poles alone.[31] Even more radical repopulation schemes cluttered the desks of Nazi planners. The infamous *Generalplan Ost* of 1942, for example, envisaged the resettlement of millions of Germans and other so-called Aryans into the Eurasian lands west of the Urals and the consignment of most of the native population to slavery, deportation, or extermination.[32] Although the intended victims did not learn of these plans at the time, the bestiality of everyday Nazi rule in the East made Berlin's basic intentions clear enough to everyone.

Against this background of National Socialist terror, the later deportations of

[28] Schieder, *Dokumentation*, ii. 32E–34E; iii. 51E–58E; v. 64E–75E; Lumans, *Himmler's*, 211–16; George H. Stein, *The Waffen SS: Hitler's Elite Guard at War, 1939–1945* (Ithaca, NY: Cornell University Press, 1966).

[29] Lumans, *Himmler's*, 151–83, 198; Rainer Schulze, 'Forgotten Victims or Beneficiaries of Plunder and Genocide? The Mass Resettlement of Ethnic Germans "Heim ins Reich" ', *Annali dell'Istituto storico italo-germanico in Trento*, 26 (2001): 493–517; Martin Broszat, *Nationalsozialistische Polenpolitik, 1939–1945* (Stuttgart: Fischer, 1961), 84–98; Schieder, *Dokumentation*, ii. 41E–51E; v. 75E–85E; Jürgen von Hehn, *Die Umsiedlung der baltischen Deutschen: Das letzte Kapitel baltisch-deutscher Geschichte* (Marburg: Herder-Institut, 1982); Hellmuth Hecker, *Die Umsiedlungsverträge des Deutschen Reiches während des Zweiten Weltkrieges* (Frankfurt: Metzner, 1971).

[30] Broszat, *Nationalsozialistische*, esp. 198; Robert L. Koehl, *RKFDV. German Resettlement and Population Policy, 1939–1945: A History of the Reich Commission for the Strengthening of Germandom* (Cambridge, Mass.: Harvard University Press, 1957).

[31] Götz Aly, *'Endlösung': Völkerverschiebung und der Mord an den europäischen Juden* (Frankfurt: Fischer, 1995); Christopher Browning, 'Nazi Resettlement Policy and the Search for a Solution to the Jewish Question, 1939–1941', in Browning (ed.), *The Path to Genocide: Essays on the Launching of the Final Solution* (Cambridge: Cambridge University Press, 1992), 3–27; Broszat, *Nationalsozialistische*, 99–105.

[32] Wolfgang Benz, 'Der Generalplan Ost: Zur Germanisierungspolitik des NS-Regimes in den besetzten Ostgebieten 1939–1945', in Benz (ed.), *Vertreibung*, 45–57; Isabel Heinemann, 'Towards an "Ethnic Reconstruction" of Occupied Europe: SS Plans and Racial Policies', *Annali dell'Istituto storico italo-germanico in Trento*, 27 (2001): 493–517; Rolf-Dieter Müller, *Hitlers Ostkrieg und die deutsche Siedlungspolitik* (Frankfurt: Fischer, 1991); Mechtild Rossler and Sabine Schleiermacher (eds.), *Der Generalplan Ost* (Berlin: Akademie, 1993).

the Germans become more understandable. Admittedly, two wrongs do not make a right, and even the enormity of Nazi crimes by no means morally justifies the excesses of the expulsions. But in the end it would be difficult not to agree with Wolfgang Benz's conclusion that 'National Socialist policy was the cause of the misfortune that befell the [German] victims of flight and expulsion at the end of the Second World War.'[33]

THE RISE OF THE EXPELLEE ORGANIZATIONS

For the eight million expellees who reached the western occupation zones by 1950, arrival in the new environment brought only limited relief. While the immediate tribulations of the expulsions had now passed, many other problems remained. The expellees came to an overcrowded, war-ravaged land in which food, housing, and every other useful commodity was in short supply. As a consequence, the vast majority endured long-term unemployment, abject poverty, and substandard accommodation in refugee camps and other makeshift quarters in the immediate post-war period. Most also faced resentment from the local population, which was understandably loath to share scarce resources with strangers easily identified as such by their accents and other idiosyncrasies.[34] Isolated, economically marginalized, and further burdened by memories of the expulsions as well as worries about missing relatives and friends, many expellees took refuge in an idealized vision of the past in the old homelands. The spark that kept many going was a conviction, still strong in the early post-war years, that a return would soon become possible.[35]

With so many important issues at stake, it was logical that the expellees began early on to form special organizations for the representation of their interests. The first groups emerged on the local level for the purpose of establishing contact with other expellees, but organizations with more ambitious objectives also appeared soon. Two became particularly prominent in the immediate post-war months. In Hamburg, Linus Kather, an East Prussian attorney on his way to national fame as a mercurial expellee leader, entered the political limelight by founding the Emergency Association of the East Germans in June 1945. The organization, which sought to defend the interests of all expellees, regardless of their areas of origin, grew rapidly in the following months and renamed itself the Association of German Refugees in early 1946.[36] Meanwhile, a Sudeten German Relief Office, established in Munich in July 1945, launched an array of activities on behalf of the

---

[33] Benz, 'Generalplan', 55.

[34] Schulze, 'Discontent'; id., *Unruhige*; Schwartz, 'Zwangsheimat'.

[35] Pertti Ahonen, 'The Impact of Distorted Memory: Historical Narratives and Expellee Integration in West Germany', in Rainer Ohliger, Karen Schönwälder, and Triadafilos Triadafilopoulos (eds.), *European Encounters: Migrants, Migration and European Societies since 1945* (London: Ashgate, 2003).

[36] The German names were Notgemeinschaft der Ostdeutschen and Arbeitsgemeinschaft deutscher Flüchtlinge. See Linus Kather, *Die Entmachtung der Vertriebenen*, i (Munich: Olzog, 1964), 19–27; Steinert, 'Organisierte', 64.

expellees from Czechoslovakia. These ranged from socio-economic assistance for compatriots to the planning of self-contained Sudeten German settlements in Bavaria.[37]

Both organizations soon encountered hostility from the British and American occupation authorities. The Allies worried about the situation in their zones, which housed nearly all the expellees in western Germany because France—as a non-signatory of the Potsdam Accords—refused to participate in resettlement schemes.[38] The Anglo-Americans realized that the social and political consequences of the expulsions would 'constitute one of the major problems which the authorities in Germany will have to face'.[39] The Americans and the British feared the emergence of a distinct expellee sector within German society. A strong movement of discontented eastern refugees could, they believed, become a base for renewed anti-democratic radicalism. Such a movement would also nurture irredentism because its 'reactionary' leaders would 'certainly [be] planning to go back home' to the East.[40] The Anglo-Americans found the prospect of such territorial revisionism unwelcome in 1945 and early 1946, when the permanence of the Oder-Neisse settlement was 'generally taken for granted', to quote the British Foreign Minister, and when the Western Powers still hoped to achieve at least some co-operation with the Russians over reparations and other key issues.[41]

The Anglo-American recipe for a successful solution of the expellee problem thus stressed integration and assimilation. The expellees were to be treated not as a distinct minority but as citizens with equal rights whose permanent residences now lay in the West. The responsibility for concrete day-to-day policies was delegated to German zonal authorities, while the two occupation powers retained overall control and supervision, including the right to intervene whenever corrective action seemed necessary.[42]

In early 1946 the occupiers made conspicuous use of their prerogatives by cracking down on the organized expellee movement, whose increasing activity

---

[37] Bauer, *Flüchtlinge*; Max Hildebert Boehm, 'Gruppenbildung und Organisationswesen', in Eugen Lemberg and Friedrich Edding (eds.), *Die Vertriebenen in Westdeutschland*, i (Kiel: Ferdinand Hirt, 1959), esp. 531–5, 562–3; Walter Becher, *Zeitzeuge: Ein Lebensbericht* (Munich: Langen-Müller, 1990), 140–4.

[38] The French began accepting organized expellee transports only in 1948. Even as late as 1950, however, the French zone had only some 200,000 expellees whereas the US and British zones accommodated about 3.5 and 4.2 million, respectively. See Schoenberg, *Germans*, 37; Reichling, *Vertriebene*, ii. 32–3.

[39] Ernest Bevin, 'Survey of Present Situation in Germany', May 1946, in Steininger, *Ruhrfrage*, 725.

[40] Lucius D. Clay, *Decision in Germany* (New York: Doubleday, 1950), 312.

[41] Ernest Bevin's 11 Mar. 1946 memorandum, in Steininger, *Ruhrfrage*, 545.

[42] Schraut, *Flüchtlingsaufnahme*; id., 'Die westlichen Besatzungsmächte und die deutschen Flüchtlinge', in Hoffmann and Schwartz (eds.), *Geglückte*, 33–46; Matthias Beer, 'Flüchtlinge—Ausgewiesene—Neubürger—Heimatvertriebene: Flüchtlingspolitik und Flüchtlingsintegration in Deutschland nach 1945, begriffsgeschichtlich betrachtet', in Beer, Martin Kintzinger, and Marita Krauss (eds.), *Migration und Integration: Aufnahme und Eingliederung im historischen Wandel* (Stuttgart: Franz Steiner, 1997), 145–67; Christiane Grosser, Thomas Grosser, Rita Müller, and Sylvia Schraut (eds.), *Flüchtlingsfrage—das Zeitproblem: Amerikanische Besatzungspolitik, deutsche Verwaltung und die Flüchtlinge in Württemberg-Baden, 1945–1949* (Mannheim: Institut für Landeskunde und Regionalforschung, 1993).

they deemed detrimental to integration. First in the British and then in the US zone an extensive ban of expellee organizations came into force, in both cases with the explicit backing of German authorities and party leaders.[43] As a result, the Association of German Refugees, the Sudeten German Relief Office, and a host of other groups disappeared, and a brief time of troubles began for the expellee movement. Even during this period, however, a variety of organizations lived on. Some groups, particularly those whose interests were demonstrably restricted to the social and charitable spheres, remained intact. Many others found ways to circumvent the decrees. In some cases, a banned group simply invented a more inclusive-sounding name to suit the new circumstances. The Sudeten German Relief Office, for example, now became Economic Assistance Ltd. and 'continued [its] activity in full', as a prominent member subsequently admitted.[44] In other cases, organizational work went on under the tutelage of powerful protectors, particularly the Evangelical and Roman Catholic Churches, whose support enabled many expellee activists to carry on with their labours while waiting for the situation to improve.[45]

Better times arrived sooner than many had expected. By late 1946, the two occupation powers began to grow increasingly lax in enforcing the crackdown on the expellee organizations. The reasons lay in the steady intensification of the cold war confrontation over Germany and, more specifically, in the tactical use which the Anglo-Americans now made of the Oder-Neisse issue. The Potsdam package deal, which had coupled Soviet concessions on reparations with the West's *de facto* acceptance of the Oder-Neisse line, collapsed as early as May 1946, when prolonged strife over Soviet non-compliance with the agreement culminated in an American decision to stop reparation shipments to the Russians. The break had major symbolic significance and immediately exacerbated tensions. When V. I. Molotov, the Soviet Foreign Minister, delivered a widely publicized speech in favour of lenient policies towards Germany a few weeks later, the Americans reacted forcefully.[46] Secretary of State James F. Byrnes interpreted Molotov's new line as a challenge to 'battle for the minds of the German people' and responded with his famous Stuttgart speech of 6 September 1946.[47] Byrnes's address signalled a major shift of western occupation policies from a focus on punishment to one on reconstruction and rehabilitation, and it also marked the first time that the United States officially raised the possibility of revising the Oder-Neisse line.[48]

[43] Daniel E. Rogers, *Politics after Hitler: The Western Allies and the German Party System* (London: Macmillan, 1995), 107–11; Bauer, *Flüchtlinge*, 265–7; Steinert, 'Organisierte', 65–7; id., *Vertriebenenverbände*, 19–21; id., 'Flüchtlingsvereinigungen', 57–8; Sonnewald, 'Entstehung', 34–5.

[44] Becher, *Zeitzeuge*, 144.

[45] Boehm, 'Gruppenbildung', 524–30; Wambach, *Verbändestaat*, 28–33; Hartmut Rudolph, *Evangelische Kirche und die Vertriebenen 1945 bis 1972*, i (Göttingen: Vandenhoeck & Ruprecht, 1984).

[46] *FRUS 1946*, ii. 869.

[47] James F. Byrnes, *All in one Lifetime* (New York: Harper, 1958), 366.

[48] Walter LaFeber (ed.), *The Origins of the Cold War, 1941–1947* (New York: Wiley, 1971), 131–4; John Gimbel, 'Byrnes Stuttgarter Rede und die amerikanische Nachkriegspolitik in Deutschland', *Vierteljahrshefte für Zeitgeschichte*, 20 (1972): 39–62; Lehmann, *Oder-Neisse*, 70–1, 82–6.

Admittedly, Byrnes did not state that such a revision in fact *would* take place. In keeping with the wording of the Potsdam Accords, he merely stressed that the territorial question was still formally open and would be regulated only 'when the final [peace] settlement is agreed upon'.[49] But even this careful use of the Oder-Neisse card brought clear benefits. Germans—most of whom chose to read Byrnes's words as an endorsement of their revisionist interests—reacted very positively, whereas the Soviets, flustered by the American offensive, had to commit themselves to the permanence of Poland's Oder-Neisse boundaries and thus increasingly forfeit any hope of winning over all of Germany.[50]

Encouraged by these experiences, George Marshall, Byrnes's successor as Secretary of State, put the Oder-Neisse trump to heavier use in 1947. At the Moscow and London Foreign Ministers' Conferences he advocated the return to Germany of large chunks of territory east of the Oder-Neisse line as well as the establishment of a special four-power border commission to determine the precise extent of these territorial changes. While Britain and—to a lesser degree—France backed many of Marshall's claims, Molotov of course did not, and by the end of the London Conference in December 1947 a complete deadlock prevailed on the issue.[51]

In changing their public position on the Oder-Neisse line, American policy-makers were primarily motivated by two tactical objectives: winning over German loyalties on the one hand and embarrassing the new enemy, the Soviet Union, on the other. Marshall himself admitted in private that the West's 'chances for changing the Polish frontier' remained 'very slender'.[52] But that was not the point. As another leading proponent of the Oder-Neisse propaganda offensive calmly explained, by trumpeting the issue, the Western Powers could score propaganda points in Germany with an issue that promised to prove highly 'embarrassing to [the] Soviet cause'.[53] With an aggressive use of the border theme, the anti-Communist camp could expect to reap a variety of rewards. It could create unrest in Soviet-controlled Eastern Europe while at the same time forcing the Russians to pledge allegiance to the Oder-Neisse cause. The Russian statements, in turn, would put the Western Powers in a position to blame the rise of the Polish–German demarcation line, as well as the expulsions associated with it, on Moscow alone. Such arguments could be expected to win considerable sympathy for the anti-Soviet cause among the Germans. In addition, the advocacy of revising the Oder-Neisse line would allow the Western Allies to pose as resolute champions of German reunification, even as their real priorities increasingly centred on the establishment of a separate West German state.[54]

---

[49] LaFeber, *Origins*, 134.

[50] In an interview some ten days after the Byrnes speech, Molotov for the first time clearly committed the Soviet Union to the irreversibility of the Oder-Neisse line, and Stalin soon said the same. See Lehmann, *Oder-Neisse*, 82–9.

[51] *Europa-Archiv*, 2 (1947): 718–21; *FRUS 1947*, ii. 735, 789; *Europa-Archiv*, 3 (1948): 1071–2; Lehmann, *Oder-Neisse*, 93–102.

[52] Marshall's 9 May 1947 memorandum, *FRUS 1947*, iv. 428.

[53] Walter Bedell Smith, US Ambassador to the USSR, 21 Aug. 1948, *FRUS 1948*, iv. 910.

[54] Lehmann, *Oder-Neisse*, esp. 110–12, 123–4, 140–4.

In this changed context, a continued crackdown on expellee organizations in the western zones began to seem unnecessary and counterproductive. The imperative to suppress revisionist expellee propaganda, an important original justification for the measures, faded quickly at a time when the Western Powers promulgated such material themselves and German publicists and politicians were beginning to do the same, with Allied connivance.[55] Consequently, the two Allies in effect stopped enforcing the organizational bans by late 1946, although formal changes in the regulations ensued only later. The Americans lifted the proscription in their zone in early 1947, and the British, who had not forbidden a single expellee group since autumn 1946, followed suit in the summer of 1948.[56]

Despite this manipulative exploitation of the Oder-Neisse issue, the primary goals of Anglo-American expellee policies remained assimilation and integration. The emergence of a self-conscious refugee minority within Germany was as repugnant an idea to the two powers in 1948 as it had been three years earlier. As a consequence, openly political expellee organizations, particularly political parties, remained forbidden. The occupiers expected the expellees to restrict their organizational activities to the social, cultural, and economic fields and to turn to ideologically oriented, broad-based parties, such as the CDU/CSU or the SPD, for political guidance. Although the strategy was not completely successful—various expellee groups meddled in politics, of course, and some even scored local-level electoral successes during the occupation—it did prevent the development of a politically united expellee movement.[57] By the time the political ban was lifted and the only nationally significant expellee party, the Gesamtdeutscher Bund/ Bund der Heimatvertriebenen und Entrechteten (GB/BHE), founded in early 1950, the Federal Republic's first federal parliament had already been elected and many expellees were safely ensconced in one of the more established parties.[58]

The political restrictions that hindered the emergence of a party like the GB/BHE failed to burden the majority of the expellee groups, which developed in growing freedom during the last phases of the occupation. Of the thousands of different organizations that took shape in these years, many proved ephemeral, but a handful—best divided into three different categories—came to play important political roles in the Federal Republic. The first—and least significant for this study—were groups formed to represent specific professional or vocational interests. An abundance of such organizations emerged in the early post-war years, as expellees sought to capitalize on old connections in their struggle for a new economic footing. Although a handful of these groups, particularly the Representation of Expelled Industry and Commerce and the Association of

[55] Lehmann, *Oder-Neisse*, 112–17.

[56] Bauer, *Flüchtlinge*, 269–70; Steinert, 'Organisierte', 69; id., *Vertriebenenverbände*, 56; id. 'Flüchtlingsvereinigungen', 58–9.

[57] Rogers, *Politics*, 107–11 ; Foschepoth, 'Potsdam', 103–5; Steinert, 'Organisierte', 67–71; id., 'Flüchtlingsvereinigungen', 59–61.

[58] Neumann, *Block*; Richard Stöss, 'Der Gesamtdeutsche Block/BHE', in Richard Stöss (ed.), *Parteien-Handbuch: Die Parteien in der Bundesrepublik Deutschland 1945–1980* (Opladen: Westdeutscher Verlag, 1984), 1424–59.

Expelled Farmers, gained prominence, most remained small and obscure.[59] However, many of the occupational and vocational organizations took on additional weight through their close association with the second main type of West German expellee representation—the Central Association of Expelled Germans (Zentralverband vertriebener Deutschen, ZvD).

The ZvD, a major force in West German politics during the 1950s, was founded in Frankfurt on 9 April 1949, by a small circle of prominent expellee activists. The organization, which changed its name to the League of Expelled Germans (Bund der vertriebenen Deutschen, BvD) in 1954, viewed itself as a non-partisan interest group, whose aim was to unite and represent all expellees on the basis of their current places of residence, irrespective of their pre-1945 origins. It consisted of a hierarchy of member associations (*Verbände*), which rose in a pyramid-like pattern from the local and regional levels to that of the states (*Länder*). The chairmen of the state associations, in turn, were represented in the Federal Executive (*Gesamtvorstand*) in Bonn, which was in principle the organization's main decision-making body. In practice, however, the real decisions often emerged from the presidium, a smaller organ within the Federal Executive, made up of the ZvD/BvD's federal-level president and several of the state associations chairs. In this centralized decision-making machinery, the president's position was strong, particularly because one man, Linus Kather, occupied the post for nine consecutive years, from December 1949 to the organization's dissolution in late 1958. Along with the executive organs, the ZvD/BvD's federal-level structures included a permanent office in Bonn as well as various expert committees and other specialized suborganizations, most of which focused on economic and social policy. In addition, a largely ceremonial federal assembly (*Bundesversammlung*), composed of representatives of the state associations, convened annually to hear activity reports and approve general resolutions. The rank-and-file members, whom the assembly was supposed to represent, allegedly numbered around 1.7 million in the early-to-mid 1950s, although only about one million paid regular membership dues.[60]

The third main organizational force among the West German expellees was that of the homeland societies (*Landsmannschaften*). The movement consisted of individual organizations formed on the basis of their members' pre-1945 origins. The Sudeten-German Homeland Society, for example, sought to unite the former residents of the Sudetenland throughout West Germany; its Silesian counterpart pursued the same aim vis-à-vis the Silesians; and so did the equivalent organizations for the East Prussians, the Pomeranians, and others. The *Landsmannschaften*, which numbered twenty by the early 1950s, were each headed by a speaker (*Sprecher*), who usually presided over a small federal executive committee (*Bundesvorstand*). Both the speaker and the executive committee, the two decisive organs, were typically

---

[59] Boehm, 'Gruppenbildung', 579–86; Wambach, *Verbändestaat*, 44–6.
[60] Boehm, 'Gruppenbildung', 579–80; Wambach, *Verbändestaat*, 53; Kather, *Entmachtung*, i. 45–50. The membership figures should be regarded as estimates, likely to be too high.

elected by a federal assembly (*Bundesversammlung*), composed of representatives of the society's state, regional, and local branches. Many homeland societies also established special suborganizations in key policy fields, particularly in so-called *Heimatpolitik*, which encompassed all aspects of foreign and cultural policy related to the old homelands and an anticipated return to them.[61]

On the national level, several of the *Landsmannschaften* maintained their own lobbying offices in Bonn, and all twenty joined forces in a loose umbrella group intended to coordinate their interests and policies. Baptized the United East German Homeland Societies (Vereinigte Ostdeutsche Landsmannschaften, VOL) upon its founding in August 1949 and renamed the Association of Homeland Societies (Verband der Landsmannschaften, VdL) three years later, the central organization maintained a non-partisan posture, as did its constituent members. The VOL/VdL had two executive organs. The speakers' assembly (*Sprecherversammlung*), composed of each homeland society's top leader, bore formal responsibility for policy decisions. However, the assembly also elected from its midst a small presidium—headed by the VOL/VdL's president—which convened more frequently than its electors, made independent decisions when necessary, and in general exerted significant influence on the larger assembly. From its Bonn headquarters, the VOL/VdL also directed a number of advisory committees in specific fields, such as *Heimatpolitik*, and a range of sub-groups aimed at particular constituencies, including expellee youths and students.[62] In addition, the organization cultivated close ties to several research institutions and cultural centres focused on the German east, such as the Göttingen Circle of East German Scholars and the East-German Cultural Council.[63] The estimated aggregate membership of the twenty *Landsmannschaften* under the VOL/VdL's auspices approximated 1.3 million in the mid-1950s.[64] Although this figure was only a fraction of West Germany's expellee total of eight million, the VOL/VdL—as well as the ZvD/BvD—typically claimed to represent all the expellees.

Given their sweeping representational claims and conflicting organizational principles, it was no surprise that the ZvD/BvD and the *Landsmannschaft* movement often found themselves at loggerheads. An accord reached in November 1949 provided for a division of labour between the two central organizations. The ZvD was to focus on social issues and the VOL on cultural and foreign affairs, but bitter and lasting rivalries nevertheless raged between the two across most policy fields, typically driven less by concrete organizational interests than the personal ambitions and animosities of the leaders.[65] As suggested by the preceding sketches of their organizational structures, both the ZvD/BvD and

---

[61] Wambach, *Verbändestaat*, 55–8; Schoenberg, *Germans*, 77–8.

[62] Wambach, *Verbändestaat*, 46–9, 55–8; Schoenberg, *Germans*, 77–8; Sonnewald, 'Entstehung', esp. chs. 3/3 and 2/41; Boehm, 'Gruppenbildung', 535–9; Imhof, *Vertriebenenverbände*, 201–23.

[63] The German names are *Göttinger Arbeitskreis* and *Ostdeutscher Kulturrat*. See also Schoenberg, *Germans*, 127–9; Imhof, *Vertriebenenverbände*, 275–312; Eberle, 'Sudetendeutsche', ch. 3.

[64] Schoenberg, *Germans*, 318; Imhof, *Vertriebenenverbände*, 132. These figures, too, are probably exaggerated.

[65] On the 20 Nov. 1949 Göttingen Agreement, see Sonnewald, 'Entstehung', 192–4.

the homeland societies-cum-VOL/VdL were directed in a top-heavy fashion by small leadership cadres. Almost without exception, the leaders had occupied elite positions in the old homelands, typically as large-scale landowners, high-level civil servants, or salient members of the free professions. The majority had engaged in right-wing politics during the Weimar era and many had become active NSDAP members in the Third Reich, although only a few of the early Federal Republic's top expellee leaders had been high-ranking Nazis.[66]

Given their shared background as members of an exclusive former elite who had often known each other for decades, many first-tier expellee leaders carried old and deeply rooted grudges against one another. Numerous new antagonisms also arose in the rough and tumble of everyday expellee politics. The interests of the refugee rank and file, which would have been best served by organizational unity, suffered in the process. Clashes within the expellee camp were thus by no means limited to those pitting the ZvD/BvD against the VOL/VdL and its constituent members. Internecine feuds were also rife within the two central organizations and the individual homeland societies.[67]

For the *Landsmannschaften*, heterogeneity presented another problem. Particularly in *Heimatpolitik*, their main area of interest, the individual homeland societies stood on very unequal footing, depending on the kinds of territories they represented. On this basis, the twenty different *Landsmannschaften* fell into four different categories. The strongest group consisted of the five homeland societies whose members stemmed from within Germany's 1937 borders. These organizations could claim to have international backing for their interest in regaining their lost provinces. The Western Allies had, after all, declared as early as June 1945 that Germany continued to exist within its 1937 borders and subsequently reiterated that stance as a part of their Oder-Neisse propaganda offensive. Taken at face value, such statements gave considerable stature to the five organizations in question, whose standing was further enhanced by their numerical strength. Of the eight million expellees in the Federal Republic in 1950, 56.9 per cent belonged to this category.[68]

Of the individual homeland societies within this group, the Landsmannschaft Schlesien was the largest. Established in March 1950 to represent West Germany's 1.55 million Silesians, it had an estimated membership of 300,000 and produced several nationally prominent leaders, among them the CDU Bundestag deputy Walter Rinke, the GB/BHE luminary Erich Schellhaus, and the journalist and SPD politician Herbert Hupka.[69] However, the organization was weakened by particularly intense internal divisions, exacerbated by the founding of a separate Upper

---

[66] By the late 1950s and 1960s, prominent former National Socialists became more visible, particularly within the Sudeten German Homeland Society. See Imhof, *Vertriebenenverbände*, 237–49; Salzborn, *Grenzenlose*, 89–111. [67] Sonnewald, 'Entstehung', ch. 3/3.

[68] Reichling, *Vertriebene*, ii. 30.

[69] Ibid.; and Schoenberg, *Germans*, 94–5. For slightly higher estimates, see Wambach, *Verbändestaat*, 48. See also *Dreizig Jahre Landsmannschaft Schlesien: Eine Dokumentation* (Bonn: Landsmannschaft Schlesien, 1979); Boehm, 'Gruppenbildung', 556–61.

Silesian Homeland Society (Landsmannschaft der Oberschlesier) in late 1950. Some 540,000 Upper Silesian expellees resided in West Germany by then, and among them the new homeland society managed to recruit about 170,000 members.[70] Under the leadership of such forceful speakers as the former Nazi official Otto Ulitz and the CDU parliamentarian Herbert Czaja, the Upper Silesian organization became one of the most centralized and effectively led expellee organizations. But the group also locked horns with the Landsmannschaft Schlesien in a series of prolonged confrontations, which hindered the VOL/VdL's ability to function in the Federal Republic's early years.[71]

Another organization known for its tight leadership structure was the Landsmannschaft Ostpreussen, which claimed as dues-paying members approximately 10 per cent of West Germany's nearly 1.4 million East Prussians.[72] Established in October 1948, the society had its most salient speaker in Alfred Gille, a leading GB/BHE politician and Lübeck lawyer, who headed the group in a sovereign fashion for most of the 1950s.[73]

The two remaining homeland societies representing Germans from within the Reich's 1937 borders were the Pommersche Landsmannschaft and the Landsmannschaft Berlin-Mark Brandenburg. The former, founded in the fall of 1948, distinguished itself with its first speaker, the great-nephew of Germany's legendary founding Chancellor, Herbert von Bismarck. However, even his name could attract to the organization only an estimated 60,000 of the roughly 920,000 Pomeranians resident in the Federal Republic.[74] The Brandenburg Homeland Society, which lacked comparable dignitaries and was also much weaker numerically, remained relatively insignificant. Its total membership reached about 25,000, roughly one-sixth of all Brandenburgers in West Germany. These numbers included not only expellees from East Brandenburg, handed to Polish administration after the war, but also later refugees from the German Democratic Republic, into which western Brandenburg had been incorporated. The resulting diffusion of its members' interests further diluted the *Landsmannschaft*'s strength.[75]

The second group of homeland societies represented territories that had been

---

[70] Reichling, *Vertriebene*, ii. 30; Schoenberg, *Germans*, 95. Wambach, *Verbändestaat*, 48, cites somewhat lower figures. The Upper Silesian Homeland Society also represented, in part, territories that had been ceded to Poland as early as 1921 despite vociferous German opposition. However, because the bulk of Upper Silesia had remained a part of Weimar Germany, the homeland society is best classified under the first category of *Landsmannschaften*.

[71] See *30 Jahre Landsmannschaft Oberschlesien: 15 Jahre Patentschaft des Landes Nordrhein-Westfalen* (Bonn: Landsmannschaft der Oberschlesier, 1979); Boehm, 'Gruppenbildung', 557–60; Schoenberg, *Germans*, 94–5; Sonnewald, 'Entstehung', ch. 3/3.

[72] Reichling, *Vertriebene*, ii. 30; Schoenberg, *Germans*, 316.

[73] Boehm, 'Gruppenbildung', 543–5; Schoenberg, *Germans*, 86–7.

[74] Schoenberg, *Germans*, 316; Reichling, *Vertriebene*, ii. 30. Wambach, *Verbändestaat*, 48, gives slightly higher estimates. See also *20 Jahre Pommersche Landsmannschaft* (Hamburg: Pommersche Landsmannschaft, 1968); Boehm, 'Gruppenbildung', 542–3; Schoenberg, *Germans*, 89.

[75] Schoenberg, *Germans*, 316; Reichling, *Vertriebene*, ii. 30; Boehm, 'Gruppenbildung', 541; Schoenberg, *Germans*, 90.

severed from Germany after the First World War and then reconquered by the Nazis. Although they had no Allied proclamations to bolster their claims, the three *Landsmannschaften* in this category could at least emphasize that their homelands had belonged to the German Reich for nearly half a century. They also could—and did—try to capitalize on the fact that their areas of origin adjoined the 1937 territories, a geographical proximity that offered chances for coalition-building with strategically better placed homeland societies.[76]

Two of the three organizations in question laid claim to lands that had belonged to inter-war Poland. The Landsmannschaft Westpreussen, with some 50,000 members recruited from among West Germany's 500,000 West Prussians, was the larger of the two. However, the organization suffered from serious internal tensions, many of them rooted in competition over potential members with the second representative of inter-war Polish territories, the Landsmannschaft Weichsel-Warthe.[77] Founded in May 1949, the group named itself after two major rivers rather than former provinces in order to broaden its appeal as a general representative of ethnic Germans from the inter-war Polish Corridor, large portions of which had belonged to West Prussia before the First World War. The Landsmannschaft Weichsel-Warthe attracted an estimated 30,000 members and raised to prominence its first speaker, Waldemar Kraft.[78] One of the highest-ranking former Nazis among the early Federal Republic's expellee elites, Kraft quickly established himself in Bonn's political circles as the founder and top leader of the GB/BHE.[79]

The third homeland society in this group represented the former West Prussian capital and inter-war Free City of Danzig. Of the city's slightly over 200,000 former residents in West Germany, nearly one out of four joined the Bund der Danziger, whose launching the British occupation authorities permitted in August 1948. Despite this high participation rate, however, the group remained a relatively minor force in expellee politics, in large part because of its ongoing clashes with the Landsmannschaft Westpreussen over member recruitment and other issues.[80]

Along with their fractiousness, the three homeland societies of the second group shared the problem of having Nazi aggression to thank for their homelands' return under German sovereignty. But the fact that Hitler's actions had produced only a *return* was significant. As representatives of what had earlier been

---

[76] The main avenue for such coalition-building was the North-East German Council (Nordostdeutscher Rat), a consultative suborgan within the VOL/VdL, founded in 1951.

[77] Schoenberg, *Germans*, 316; Reichling, *Vertriebene*, ii. 30; Wambach, *Verbändestaat*, 48; *Westpreussen 1949–1969: 20 Jahre Landsmannschaft Westpreussen* (Münster: Landsmannschaft Westpreussen, 1969); Boehm, 'Gruppenbildung', 545–7; Schoenberg, *Germans*, 87–8.

[78] Boehm, 'Gruppenbildung', 548–9; Schoenberg, *Germans*, 89, 316.

[79] Kraft was *SS-Hauptsturmführer* and *Volkstumsreferent* in the *Reichssicherheitshauptamt*. In addition, he held the post of managing director (*Geschäftsführer*) in the Reichsgesellschaft für Landbewirtschaftung. See Imhof, *Vertriebenenverbände*, 138.

[80] Reichling, *Vertriebene*, ii. 30; Schoenberg, *Germans*, 316. Wambach, *Verbändestaat*, 48, provides a slightly higher estimate. See also Boehm, 'Gruppenbildung', 547–8; Schoenberg, *Germans*, 88–9.

core areas of the *Kaiserreich*, these organizations could also draw upon less troublesome legacies to justify their territorial claims. By contrast, the Sudeten Germans—the third main group among the *Landsmannschaften*—enjoyed no such luxury. The Sudetenland had never belonged to Germany prior to 1938, and its annexation in that year had resulted entirely from the brutal power politics of the Nazi regime. Accordingly, and in striking contrast to the expellees from the 1937 territories, the only diplomatic document which the Sudeten Germans could cite in support of their cause was the notorious Munich Agreement, by which the European powers had imposed the Nazi fiat upon Prague in September 1938.

But the Sudeten Germans also possessed some assets. With 1.9 million compatriots in the Federal Republic, they constituted the largest single expellee group.[81] And unlike the other groups, which were scattered over different parts of the country, the Sudeten Germans were strongly concentrated in one state, Bavaria.[82] This regional convergence offered good lobbying prospects, which the Munich-based Sudetendeutsche Landsmannschaft, founded in early 1950, was well-placed to exploit. The organization, which boasted approximately 350,000 members, possessed a centralized decision-making structure that undergirded the position of the federal executive committee and especially the speaker.[83] The latter's role was further enhanced by the prominence of the individuals who occupied the post. The first speaker, Rudolf Lodgman von Auen, was a veteran right-wing conservative tested in the political battles of pre-First World War Austria-Hungary and inter-war Czechoslovakia.[84] His successor, Hans Christoph Seebohm, counted among West Germany's most durable politicians, with seventeen consecutive years as federal Minister of Transport and eighteen as a Bundestag deputy, first in the Deutsche Partei (DP) and later in the CDU.[85] After Seebohm's death, the speaker's chair passed to Walter Becher, who had distinguished himself as an expellee activist in the Bavarian Landtag before becoming a CSU representative in the federal parliament.[86]

Despite the strength of its top leaders, the Sudetendeutsche Landsmannschaft was no monolith. Admittedly, the speaker and the executive committee generally had the last word on major policy decisions, and subordinates were expected to comply with these decisions. But organizational discipline was never perfect. Internal debates and disagreements flared up from time to time, particularly on *Heimatpolitik*, where four significant and largely autonomous suborganizations routinely made their voices heard. The first, the Sudeten German Council

[81] Reichling, *Vertriebene*, ii. 30.

[82] In 1950, 1,026 of the Federal Republic's 1,918 Sudeten Germans resided in Bavaria. Ibid. 32.

[83] Schoenberg, *Germans*, 317. See also Wambach, *Verbändestaat*, 55–6; Boehm, 'Gruppenbildung', 561–7; Schoenberg, *Germans*, 96–101; Eberle, 'Sudetendeutsche', ch. 4; Sonnewald, 'Entstehung', 185–91.

[84] For contrasting accounts, see Alois Harasko and Heinrich Kuhn (eds.), *Rudolf Lodgman von Auen: Ein Leben für Recht und Freiheit und die Selbstbestimmung der Sudetendeutschen* (Nuremberg: Helmut Preussler, 1984); Imhof, *Vertriebenenverbände*, 136.

[85] Horst W. Schmollinger, 'Die Deutsche Partei', in Stöss (ed.), *Parteien-Handbuch*, i. 1030.

[86] Becher, *Zeitzeuge*; Imhof, *Vertriebenenverbände*, 238.

(Sudetendeutscher Rat), predated the *Landsmannschaft* itself. Established in July 1947 as the Association for the Defence of Sudeten German Interests (Arbeitsgemeinschaft zur Wahrung sudetendeutscher Interessen) and renamed in 1955, this elitist organization originally viewed itself as a kind of government-in-exile, charged with promoting the cause of return to the old homelands. With the rise of the *Landsmannschaft*, the council was gradually relegated to a more advisory role, although some of its members retained a spirit of independence and rivalry vis-à-vis the larger organization. The council was limited by statute to thirty leading Sudeten Germans of all major political persuasions, including the speaker and several top members of the executive committee, and it convened regularly to debate pressing foreign-policy problems.[87]

The other key Sudeten German suborganizations were the three so-called ideological communities (*Gesinnungsgemeinschaften*), elite groupings of politically like-minded activists composed largely on the basis of inter-war Sudeten traditions. The Ackermann-Gemeinde, a Catholic group rooted in the earlier Christian Workers' movement, steered a course close to that of the CSU under its long-time leader and CSU-Bundestag deputy Hans Schütz.[88] The corresponding social democratic organization bore the title Seliger-Gemeinde and developed tight links to the SPD under the direction of such luminaries as Wenzel Jaksch, Richard Reitzner, and Ernst Paul.[89] The third group, the Witiko-Bund, sought to continue the right-wing *völkisch* traditions rooted in the teachings of Othmar Spann and other inter-war neo-conservatives. This organization lacked close ties to any particular party, but it brought to prominence a range of activists, most of them former National Socialists. These included not only the future speaker Walter Becher, whose public activity in the Third Reich had been confined to journalism, but also such Nazi dignitaries as Franz Karmasin, State Secretary for 'German Affairs' (*Deutsche Belange*) in the Slovak puppet regime, and Siegfried Zoglmann, chief of the *Hitler-Jugend* in occupied Bohemia and Moravia.[90]

Despite the Nazi pasts of many of its leaders and the troublesome legacies of the Munich Agreement, the large and internally vital Sudetendeutsche Landsmannschaft was nevertheless in a much stronger position than the fourth group of homeland societies, composed of the ethnic Germans of south-east Europe, Russia, and the Baltics. These eleven organizations, which represented expellees whose native territories had never been part of Germany, were small in

---

[87] Boehm, 'Gruppenbildung', 563, 566; Eberle, 'Sudetendeutsche', 108–10, 247–51; Sonnewald, 'Entstehung', 159–60.

[88] Boehm, 'Gruppenbildung', 526; Eberle, 'Sudetendeutsche', 111–13; Schoenberg, *Germans*, 100; Imhof, *Vertriebenenverbände*, 258–62; Eva Hahn, 'Die Sudetendeutschen in der deutschen Gesellschaft: Ein halbes Jahrhundert politischer Geschichte zwischen "Heimat" und "Zuhause" ', in Hans Lemberg, Jan Křen, and Dusan Kováč (eds.), *Im geteilten Europa: Tschechen, Slowaken und Deutsche und ihre Staaten, 1949–1989* (Essen: Klartext, 1998), 118–19.

[89] Boehm, 'Gruppenbildung', 563–4; Schoenberg, *Germans*, 100–1; Eberle, 'Sudetendeutsche', 115; Imhof, *Vertriebenenverbände*, 263–74; Hahn, 'Sudetendeutsche', 119–20; Martin, *Nicht spurlos*; Martin K. Bachstein, *Wenzel Jaksch und die sudetendeutsche Sozialdemokratie* (Munich: Oldenbourg, 1974).

[90] Boehm, 'Gruppenbildung', 564–5; Schoenberg, *Germans*, 99–100; Eberle, 'Sudetendeutsche', 116–21; Imhof, *Vertriebenenverbände*, 231–57; Hahn, 'Sudetendeutsche', 120–2.

comparison to other expellee groups. Even the largest two, the Homeland Society of Germans from Yugoslavia (Landsmannschaft der Deutschen aus Jugoslawien) and the Homeland Society of Germans from Hungary (Landsmannschaft der Deutschen aus Ungarn), could claim only an estimated 35,000 and 24,000 members, respectively.[91] Regional particularism typically exacerbated the problem of size, especially among the expellees from inter-war Romania, who were splintered into five separate homeland societies.[92] To be sure, these organizations realized their numerical weakness and made attempts to redress it. As a consequence, in 1951 the five Romanian German homeland societies joined those representing expellees from Hungary, Russia, Slovakia, and Yugoslavia in the Southeast German Council (Rat der Südostdeutschen).[93] The council, a VOL/VdL suborganization composed of the delegates of the nine participating homeland societies, strove to coordinate the policies of the member organizations and generate regional unity. In practice, however, it remained only a loose discussion forum that failed to improve the weak standing of the south-east European *Landsmannschaften*.[94]

Ethnic Germans from the Baltic states, most of whom had been resettled to Germany by the Nazis well before the end of the Second World War, were also plagued by factionalism, which manifested itself in the existence of two organizations. The tiny Landsmannschaft der Deutschen aus Litauen claimed to speak for the Federal Republic's 30,000 or so Lithuanian Germans, while the somewhat larger Deutsch-Baltische Landsmannschaft sought to look after the interests of some 40,000 former residents of the other two Baltic states.[95] Both organizations strove to bolster their position by establishing links to the homeland societies representing Prussia's former eastern provinces, both within and beyond the 1937

[91] Schoenberg, *Germans*, 317. For a slightly lower estimate, see Wambach, *Verbändestaat*, 48. See also Boehm, 'Gruppenbildung,' 570–4; Schoenberg, *Germans*, 102–3, 107–8. According to Reichling, *Vertriebene*, ii. 30, in 1950 the expellees from Yugoslavia and Hungary in West Germany totalled 178,000 and 148,000, respectively.

[92] According to Reichling, *Vertriebene*, ii. 30, 149,000 expellees from inter-war Romania resided in the Federal Republic in 1950. They were split into the following organizations (the estimated membership figures in parentheses come from Schoenberg, *Germans*, 317–18, 104): Landsmannschaft der Bessarabiendeutschen (25,000), Landsmannschaft der Siebenbürger Sachsen (20,000), Landsmannschaft der Buchenlanddeutschen (10,000), Landsmannschaft der Banater Schwaben aus Rumänien (6,000), and Landsmannschaft der Dobrudschadeutschen und Bulgariendeutschen (4,000). As the name suggests, the last-mentioned group included some former residents of Bulgaria. See Boehm, 'Gruppenbildung', 574–9; Schoenberg, *Germans*, 103–7.

[93] The two homeland societies not yet discussed claimed to represent Germans from Russia and Slovakia and were named Landsmannschaft der Deutschen aus Russland and Karpatendeutsche Landsmannschaft Slowakei. According to Schoenberg, *Germans*, 317–18, 109, some 2,000 of the Federal Republic's approximately 70,000 Russian Germans were members of the former group, while the latter attracted about 10,000 of the 70,000 expellees from Slovakia. Many of the Russian Germans had been affected by Nazi population transfers during the war and then transported westward by the retreating *Wehrmacht*. See Boehm, 'Gruppenbildung' , 577–8, 555–6; Schoenberg, *Germans*, 101–2, 109.

[94] Boehm, 'Gruppenbildung', 569–70; Schoenberg, *Germans*, 109–10.

[95] Schoenberg, *Germans*, 316. Schoenberg reports the estimated membership of the Lithuanian and German-Baltic Homeland Societies as 5,000 and 20,000, respectively. See also Boehm, 'Gruppenbildung', 549–55; Schoenberg, *Germans*, 91–2.

borders. The main institutional organ for such bridge-building was the Northeast German Council (Nordostdeutscher Rat), a VOL/VdL suborgan akin to its southeastern counterpart, which included the two Baltic *Landsmannschaften* and all but two of the Prussian groups.[96] Although these efforts failed to cure the weakness of the Lithuanian Germans, they did fortify the Deutsch-Baltische Landsmannschaft, the only one of the eleven ethnic German homeland societies to become a relatively salient force in the expellee movement. The group gained prominence through its early leaders, particularly CSU-parliamentarian Georg Baron Manteuffel-Szoege and FDP-activist Axel de Vries, both of whom rose to top positions in the VOL/VdL.

In addition to the main *Vertriebenenverbände* described above, another set of related organizations deserves a brief mention: the various groups that purported to represent the so-called Soviet Zone refugees (*Sowjetzonenflüchtlinge*), that is, the Germans who had fled westward from the territory of the German Democratic Republic. The organizational network of these GDR refugees, who by the early 1960s numbered slightly over three million, resembled that of the expellees but was in some ways even more splintered and complex.[97] The earliest and most ephemeral groups rose and fell on the local level for purposes of self-help, but by the early 1950s three types of broader and more enduring entities had emerged. The first sought to defend the interests of specific vocational and professional groups; the second, labelled *Landsmannschaften*, claimed to represent the former residents of particular provinces; and the third—the so-called *allgemeine Flüchtlingsverbände*—presented themselves as champions of the general interests of all Soviet Zone refugees in West Germany, regardless of their occupational or geographical backgrounds. These organizational principles were clearly very similar to those prevalent among the expellees, and so was the persistence of two competing umbrella organizations: the Vereinigte Landsmannschaften der Sowjetzone—which obviously represented the provincially based organizations—and the Gesamtverband der Sowjetzonenflüchtlinge, which coordinated the activities of the general *Flüchtlingsverbände*.[98]

The refugee representatives were a quarrelsome lot: the two umbrella groups typically engaged in prolonged confrontations, and many of the individual organizations also fought one another frequently. The relations between the various refugee groups and their expellee counterparts tended to be strained as well; disagreements abounded while cooperation remained rare. In addition, the refugee organizations were hampered by low membership levels. The Gesamtverband der Sowjetzonenflüchtlinge, for example, managed to attract as members

---

[96] Boehm, 'Gruppenbildung', 539; Schoenberg, *Germans*, 92–3. The two absentee groups were the Silesian and Upper Silesian Homeland Societies, which formed their own Silesian suborgan within the VOL/VdL.

[97] Helge Heidemeyer, *Flucht und Zuwanderung aus der SBZ/DDR 1945/1949–1961: Die Flüchtlingspolitik der Bundesrepublik Deutschland bis zum Bau der Berliner Mauer* (Düsseldorf: Droste, 1994), 24, 43; Volker Ackermann, *Der 'echte' Flüchtling: Deutsche Vertriebene und Flüchtlinge aus der DDR 1945–1961* (Osnabrück: Rasch, 1995); Heidemeyer, 'Vertriebene'.

[98] For a clear overview, see Heidemeyer, *Flucht*, 315–30.

less than 2 per cent of all the GDR refugees resident in the Federal Republic.[99] For all these reasons, the organizations remained weak and never attained a political status even remotely comparable to that of the main expellee groups. They are therefore not included within the scope of this study. However, occasional reference will be made to the millions of Soviet Zone refugees, primarily because Bonn's leading politicians typically viewed them as an extension of the expellee block, to be courted with similar tactics and arguments for similar political purposes, not least because nearly one-third of these refugees had originally arrived in the GDR as expellees from territories further to the east.

As the preceding pages have shown, an extensive network of expellee representation had developed in West Germany by the beginning of the 1950s. The non-partisan pressure organizations ZvD and VOL—the latter in conjunction with its member groups—dominated the scene, although an expellee political party, the GB/BHE, was soon to appear as well. Meanwhile, the newly founded Federal Republic was increasingly preoccupied with establishing its international position in the context of the intensifying cold war. Crucial issues were at stake: ultimately war and peace, but more immediately Germany's alliance options, internal political order, reunification, and future borders. As these issues were debated by Chancellor Adenauer's government and the main parties, the expellees—nearly one fifth of the voting population—received close attention from all the contestants. Consequently, the Federal Republic's formative years, which culminated in the triumph of Adenauer's Westpolitik in the spring of 1955, as the country acquired both sovereignty and NATO membership, witnessed the emergence of an enduring pattern of interaction among the expellee organizations, the government, and the main parties, particularly in Eastern policy, the expellee lobby's chief area of interest. This pattern was to prove astonishingly resilient in the post-1955 period as well, even after it had clearly outlived its original usefulness, at least for the government and the leading parties.

---

[99] Heidemeyer, *Flucht*, 324. The figures are from 1960/61.

CHAPTER TWO

The Programmes and Strategies of the Expellee Organizations

THE EXPELLEE ORGANIZATIONS began to voice a variety of political demands immediately after their founding. The most urgent calls centred on socio-economic issues, as could be expected, given the poverty and deprivation which afflicted most expellees in the early post-war years. Leaders of the fledgling organizations underscored the 'distress and suffering of the expellee population' and sought to find ways to alleviate the situation.[1] They clamoured for the expellees' 'existence rights', emphasizing the need to overcome persistent discrimination by integrating the newcomers into western German society.[2] Although some leaders recommended a resort to 'self-help' as the high road to equality and integration, the more characteristic stance was to expect the government, in conjunction with the occupation authorities, to provide extensive assistance.[3] Accordingly, the expellee groups soon began to promulgate a number of demands which remained standard features of their social policy agenda for years to come. These included government-funded employment and housing schemes, special credit programmes, and—most significantly—legislation to compensate the expellees for their heavy material losses and thus partially to equalize the disparate burdens which the Second World War had imposed upon different sectors of the German population.[4]

As Walter Rinke—the future speaker of the Silesian Homeland Society—pointed out in early 1949, however, such social demands constituted only a secondary interest, a 'short-term goal', for the expellee activists, whose primary 'long-term objective' remained 'a return to the old homelands'.[5] As a result, Ostpolitik became a central preoccupation of the expellee organizations from early on, and a steady barrage of statements from key leaders underlined the organizations' desire for the reacquisition and resettlement of the lost territories. A

---

[1] Gesamtvertretung der Ostvertriebenen, presidium protocols, 13 Jan. 1949, SDA: NL Lodgman, V/2e.

[2] Rudolf Lodgman von Auen, 'Rundschreiben Nr. 2', 20 Sept. 1949, SDA: NL Lodgman V/2c.

[3] See e.g. Wenzel Jaksch in the Arbeitsgemeinschaft zur Wahrung sudetendeutscher Interessen, 'Verhandlungsschrift über die Zusammenkunft am 15.3.1949 in München', SDA, NL Lodgman, VI/2:2/2, 8.

[4] Presidium of the Gesamtvertretung der Ostvertriebenen, meeting protocols, 13 Jan. 1949, SDA: NL Lodgman, V/2e.

[5] Walter Rinke to Josef Müller, 5 May 1949, ACSP: NL Müller, 344.

typical—albeit maladroit—expression of these sentiments was a 1949 resolution of the Landsmannschaft Schlesien that elevated the return of the eastern provinces into *the* precondition for the 'final solution' *(Endlösung)* of the German expellee problem.[6]

To bolster their revisionist cause, expellee leaders loudly denounced the post-war settlement in Eastern Europe. Predictably, they condemned the expulsions and the accompanying border readjustments, particularly the Oder-Neisse line, in the strongest possible terms. One prominent figure labelled the forcible mass transfer of Germans the 'cause of all evil' in post-war Europe, while another rejected the 'arbitrary' eastern frontiers as a 'mockery of heavenly and earthly justice'.[7] More fundamentally, the expellee elites cursed both Soviet Russia, which they regarded as the main culprit behind the expulsions, and Communism in general. In their words, the post-1945 westward advance of Communist rule had brought 'pan-Slavic imperialism' and 'Asiatic Bolshevism' to 'the borders of Lower Saxony and Bavaria' and thus created a 'colossal' danger to the 'thousand-year-old culture and civilization' which Christian Europe—embodied by the Germans—had traditionally represented in the East–Central regions of the continent.[8]

In their earliest proposals for policies toward the Communist East, the various expellee organizations typically highlighted their own, group-specific territorial interests. Given the official proclamations in which the Western Allies had reaffirmed Germany's continued existence within its 1937 borders, pending a final peace settlement, the organizations that purported to speak for expellees whose former homelands fell under this geographical rubric held the seemingly strongest hand—and produced the loudest noises. Thus the Silesian Homeland Society, for example, publicly demanded in the summer of 1950 that the eastern provinces in question 'absolutely must be removed from Polish administration and returned under German rule'.[9] But other, strategically less well-placed organizations also trumpeted their annexationist intentions in the early post-war years. Homeland societies that laid claim to areas which had belonged to inter-war Poland made no secret of their desire for a *Grossdeutschland* at the Poles'

---

[6] Landsmannschaft Schlesien resolution, 4 Sept. 1949, BA: B 136/6791; Richard Reitzner in the Arbeitsgemeinschaft zur Wahrung sudetendeutscher Interessen, 27 July 1948, SDA: NL Lodgman, VI/2:2/2, 6.

[7] Hans-Christoph Seebohm, 'Die politische Aufgabe der Sudetendeutschen', *Sudetendeutsche Zeitung* (23 May 1953); Walter Rinke, 'Die Grenze des Friedens', a 1948 manuscript, ACSP: NL Müller, 47.

[8] Eichstatt Declaration of Sudeten German leaders, 30 Nov. 1949, in 'Der Landesobmann: Bericht über die Zeit vom Ende November 1949 bis Ende März 1950', SDA: NL Lodgman, I/o/2:3; Seebohm, 'Die politische Aufgabe' (n. 7 above); Linus Kather at the CDU *Parteitag*, Recklinghausen, 28–9 Aug. 1948, in Helmuth Pütz (ed.), *Konrad Adenauer und die CDU der britischen Besatzungszone 1946–1949* (Bonn: Eichholz, 1975), 605; Rudolf Lodgman von Auen's address to the 1949 Sudeten German Whitsun rally, Bayreuth, SDA: NL Lodgman, I/6:1.

[9] Walter Rinke, 'Schlesien meldet sich zum Wort', *hvp*, 24 Aug. 1950, SDA: NL Lodgman, V/4; Silesian Homeland Soviety's resolutions of 12 June 1949, in *40 Jahre Landsmannschaft Schlesien: Eine Dokumentation 1949–1989* (Königswinter: Landsmannschaft Schlesien, 1989), 7–9.

expense, preferably in the frontiers of 1914.[10] Prominent Sudeten Germans, in turn, privately stated their goal to be a new 'Anschluss of the Sudetenland to the Reich' and publicly pressed for a 'return of the *Heimat*' in the 'language bound-aries and settlement frontiers of 1937'.[11] Only the organizations of the *Volksdeutsche* from areas non-contiguous with the former Reich, particularly south-eastern Europe, failed to join the chorus. Aware of their numerical and political weakness, these groups maintained a low profile and by the mid-1950s acknowledged in a seminal closed meeting that a return to their old homelands was neither possible nor desirable, although this conclusion was not to be divulged to the public.[12]

By the early 1950s, the leaders of the expellee organizations had realized that the heterogeneity of their territorial interests presented a serious problem. A cacophony of revisionist demands—a strategy by which 'one constantly cries out his maximum demands for all the world to hear'—was likely to confuse and alien-ate the outside world, as Rudolf Lodgman von Auen, the powerful speaker of the Sudeten-German Homeland Society, pointed out in 1953.[13] A better recipe, again according to the Sudeten Germans, was an arrangement whereby each organiza-tion recognized and supported the 'foreign policy goals of the other . . . groups'.[14] In other words, the expellee activists wanted a united front, a joint Ostpolitik plat-form broad enough to embrace the varied interests of the different organizations and yet moderate-sounding enough to appeal to potential supporters at home and abroad.

As a consequence of these tactics, explicit annexationist demands became increasingly rare in the public rhetoric of expellee leaders by the early 1950s. Admittedly, open calls for 'Silesia undivided in a free Germany', 'Pomerania in its entirety within the German Reich' or the 'reacquisition' of the Sudetenland continued to ring out from time to time.[15] But, as a rule, the expellee organiza-tions' official proclamations on the border question retreated to a stance which the Western Powers had seemed to endorse—at least rhetorically—since Secretary of State Byrnes's famous Stuttgart speech of September 1946. As their minimum territorial programme, expellee leaders now insisted that the post-war border arrangements in the East—particularly the Oder-Neisse line—were

---

[10] See e.g. 'Protokoll der gründenden Mitgliederversammlung der Landsmannschaft der Oberchlesier', Munich, 10 Dec. 1949, SDA: NL Lodgman, V/9.

[11] Friedrich Stolberg to Josef Müller, 23 May 1947, ACSP: NL Müller, 345; Eichstatt Declaration of Sudeten German leaders, 30 Nov. 1949 (see n. 8).

[12] Rat der Südostdeutschen, 'Bericht über die Tagung der Delegierten am 23./24. Juli 1955', SDA: NL Lodgman, XI-93.

[13] Rudolf Lodgman von Auen, 'Grundlagen und Arbeitsziele der sudetendeutschen Aussenpolitik', address to the *Hauptvorstand* of the Sudeten-German Homeland Society, Heiligenhof, 23–5 Oct. 1953, SDA: NL Lodgman, IV/4:13, 3.

[14] 'Thesen' of the Sudeten German *Konklave*, 3–4 Dec. 1949, SDA: NL Lodgman, VI/4.

[15] Walter Rinke at a Silesian rally in Frankfurt, 18 July 1954, *Bulletin* (21 July, 1954); Pommersche Landsmannschaft statement, 6 Jan. 1954, SDA: NL Lodgman, VII/10; Rudolf Lodgman von Auen at the *Sudetendeutscher Tag*, Düsseldorf, 24 May 1953, in A. K. Simon (ed.), *Rudolf Lodgman von Auen: Reden und Aufsätze* (Munich: St. Jörg, 1954), 129.

provisional and illicit. Final decisions about Germany's eastern frontiers could be made only at a future peace conference in which the freely elected government of a reunited Germany would participate on an equal footing and the country's lawful 1937 borders would form the minimum basis for negotiations.[16]

As open territorial demands receded to the background in the rhetoric of the expellee elites, a more abstract—and thus inclusive—programme couched in legal dictates and moral principles rose to the fore by the early 1950s. The first major attempt to publicize the new doctrines was the proclamation of the 'Charter of the German Expellees' at a major rally in Stuttgart on 5 August 1950, the fifth anniversary of the Potsdam Agreement, which had sanctioned the large-scale forcible transfer of Germans from the East.[17] The principles laid down in the Charter and in other key statements issued during West Germany's formative years, prior to the acquisition of sovereignty in May 1955, constituted a general foreign policy programme which leading expellee activists were to promulgate with remarkable consistency throughout the next four decades—and beyond.

The centrepiece of this standard programme was the concept of the 'right to one's homeland' (*Heimatrecht*). This rather vague notion was subsequently defined in an expellee-sponsored study as

the principle . . . that an individual has, or should have, the right to live undisturbed in his homeland (*Heimat*) as long as he wants and that any violation of this right, be it in the form of a forcible transfer of individual people or of an ethnic group from their homeland, or in the form of preventing their return to the homeland, is an injustice.[18]

Expellee leaders regarded the concept as crucial for their interests. As one of them explained in a closed meeting in late 1951, the notion of *Heimatrecht* made it possible to separate the claim to the homeland from the 'biological continuity of the ethnic group' and thus to transform that claim into a question of general justice with an 'all-German, indeed European' appeal.[19] A further advantage of *Heimatrecht* was that—once expellee leaders had declared it to be unaffected by any statutes of limitations—its prerogatives could be passed on to future generations, beyond those immediately affected by the expulsions.[20] In addition, the notion of *Heimat*, with its deep roots in German localist traditions, was likely to

---

[16] Rudolf Lodgman von Auen, 'Die Wiedervereinigung und die heimatpolitischen Anliegen der deutschen Vertriebenen', in Simon (ed.), *Lodgman*, 166–70; Pommersche Landsmannschaft resolution, 29 June 1952, BA: B 136, 27370; ZvD press release, 15 Dec. 1953, SDA: NL Lodgman, VII/10.

[17] Werner Blumenthal and Bardo Fassbender (eds.), *Erklärungen zur Deutschlandpolitik*, i. *1949-1972* (Bonn: Kulturstiftung der deutschen Vertriebenen, 1984), 17–18. For highly critical commentary, see Ralph Giordano, *Die Zweite Schuld oder von der Last Deutscher zu sein* (Cologne: KiWi, 2000), 267–92; Salzborn, *Heimatrecht*, 21–4.

[18] F. H. E. W. Du Buy, *Das Recht auf die Heimat im historisch-politischen Prozess* (Cologne: J. P. Bachem, 1974), 33; Sudeten-German Homeland Society, 'Memorandum des Sudetenproblem betreffend', Dec. 1953, SDA: NL Lodgman, XXIV-02, 5; Salzborn, *Heimatrecht*, 15–30.

[19] Walter Brand in the Arbeitsgemeinschaft zur Wahrung sudetendeutscher Interessen, 8 Oct. 1951, SDA: NL Lodgman, VI/2:2/4, 2.

[20] See e.g. Lodgman von Auen at a VdL meeting in Berlin, 26 Oct. 1952, in Simon, *Lodgman*, esp. 119–20.

evoke positive images and connotations in much of the non-expellee population as well.[21] With these points in its favour, the 'right to the homeland' became the backbone of the expellee lobby's official foreign-policy agenda. One declaration after another praised the concept's international significance and sought to endow it with an exalted moral and ethical stature. Typical statements elevated the *Heimatrecht* into a 'God-given, basic human right' and 'a precondition for the preservation of peace and Christian . . . civilisation in Europe'.[22]

Despite the hyperbole, expellee leaders never considered the *Heimatrecht* alone a sufficient legal basis for their foreign-policy programme. They insisted that the concept was to be coupled with another, more widely recognized notion of international law, namely that of self-determination (*Selbstbestimmung*), and that the expellees had to be granted both in conjunction.[23] The thrust of the leadership's argument was that a return to the old homelands in a minority status under foreign rule would not suffice.[24] The expellees would instead have to receive the right to determine the modalities of their own return, particularly the nature of the political and social system under which they would live.[25]

To pave the way for the realization of their self-proclaimed rights, expellee activists highlighted the need to implement one universal principle—justice. At home, they continued to clamour for fair treatment for the expellees, including 'equal rights as citizens', 'reasonable integration' into the economy, and—most significantly—'just and reasonable distribution of the burdens of the last war among the entire German people'.[26] They also drew direct links between their visions of a just domestic system and a proper international order in at least two ways. First, expellee leaders insisted that satisfactory social legislation at home constituted a precondition for their organizations' approval of the Federal Republic's integration into the cold war West.[27] And second, they maintained that any domestic arrangements to equalize the burdens of the lost war among the population in no way precluded the expellees from later claiming material compensation from the governments that had carried out the forcible population

[21] On *Heimat*, see Celia Applegate, *A Nation of Provincials: The German Idea of Heimat* (Berkeley, Calif.: University of California Press, 1990); Alon Confino, *The Nation as a Local Metaphor: Württemberg, Imperial Germany, and National Memory, 1871–1918* (Chapel Hill, NC: University of North Carolina Press, 1997); Karin Böke, 'Flüchtlinge und Vertriebene zwischen dem Recht auf die alte Heimat und der Eingliederung in die neue Heimat: Leitvokabeln der Flüchtlingspolitik', in Karin Böke, Frank Liedtke, and Martin Wengeler (eds.), *Politische Leitvokabeln in der Ära Adenauer* (Berlin: Walter de Gruyter, 1996), 131–210.

[22] 'Charta der deutschen Vertriebenen' (n. 17); Pommersche Landsmannschaft resolution, 12 May 1951, attached to a letter to Thomas Dehler, 24 May 1951, ADL: N1-1094.

[23] See e.g. 'Die aussenpolitische Linie der Sudetendeutschen Landsmannschaft', *VdL-Informationen* (10 May 1954), 3.

[24] 'Keine Rückkehr unter fremde Souveränität', *Sudetendeutsche Zeitung* (28 Nov. 1953).

[25] In addition to the article in n. 23 see e.g. the VOL's press release 'Kommentar zur Resolution der Sprechertagung über den Sicherheitsbeitrag' (Nov. 1951), SDA: B VIII (VdL/VOL)/4; and the resolution of the Landesgruppe Niedersachsen of the Landsmannschaft Westpreussen, 17 Oct. 1953, BA: B 136, 6790.   [26] 'Charta der deutschen Heimatvertriebenen' (n. 17).

[27] See e.g. the VdL's statement of expectations after the 1953 Bundestag elections, attachment to 'Beschlussprotokoll über die Präsidialsitzung des VdL am 12. Oktober 1953', SDA: B VIII (VdL/VOL)/1.

transfers.[28] As one prominent expellee figure contended in 1952, such transnational compensation would serve the cause of justice in accordance with 'moral and judicial principles before God and mankind'.[29]

Expellee leaders also made a more direct case for a just international system. In their 1950 Charter, they 'renounce[d] all thought of revenge and retaliation' and in other statements declared a ban on 'war' and 'hatred' as well.[30] They called for a new order in which inter-state conflicts would be resolved 'in a peaceful manner' and underscored the urgency of transcending such past evils as traditional nationalism in general and jingoistic 'national egoism' in particular.[31] In the expellee leaders' vision, the high road to a better future ran through European integration. Thus the activists vowed to 'support with all their strength every endeavour directed towards the establishment of a united Europe in which the nations may live in freedom from fear and coercion'.[32] This new Europe, the expellee leaders stressed, would stop 'at neither the Elbe, nor the Oder, nor the Weichsel' but would also include the eastern half of the continent, at least up to the western boundaries of the Soviet Union.[33] Once truly unified, Europe would become a genuine community of peoples, governed by principles of peaceful cooperation. As a consequence, traditional power politics would lose significance, and human rights—including, of course, the German expellees' rights to their homelands and to self-determination—finally receive the respect which they deserved.[34] The end-result of expellee-style unification would thus be a fairytale-like state of peace, happiness, and harmony throughout the continent.

Before real progress toward pan-European unity could commence, however, one major precondition had to be fulfilled—the collapse of Communist rule in Eastern Europe. A key task of the expellee organizations therefore lay in the struggle for the 'liberation' of the East European peoples 'enslaved by Bolshevism', as Rudolf Lodgman von Auen explained in a typical 1953 address.[35] After liberation, Lodgman and other leading expellee figures contended, the captive nations would

---

[28] See e.g. Rudolf Lodgman von Auen in the *Hauptversammlung* of the Landesverband Bayern of the Sudetendeutsche Landsmannschaft, 21 Sept. 1952, SDA: NL Lodgman, I/0/2:5.

[29] Ibid.

[30] Along with the 'Charta der deutschen Heimatvertriebenen' (n. 17), see e.g. the Detmold Declaration of the Sudetendeutsche Landsmannschaft, 25 Jan. 1950, reprinted in Ernst Nittner (ed.), *Dokumente zur sudetendeutschen Frage, 1917–1967* (Munich: Ackermann-Gemeinde, 1967), 352–3.

[31] Walter Rinke at the *Heimattreffen* of the Landsmannschaft Schlesien, Frankfurt, 18 July 1954, *Bulletin* (21 July 1954), 1203; 'Die aussenpolitische Linie der Sudetendeutschen Landsmannschaft', *VdL-Informationen* (10 May 1954), 3; Albert Karl Simon, 'Unsere staatspolitische Aufgabe', *Sudetendeutsche Zeitung* (20 March 1954), 1.

[32] 'Charta der deutschen Heimatvertriebenen' (n. 17).

[33] Walter Rinke's address at the 1953 *Bundestreffen* of the Landsmannschaft Schlesien, 26 July 1953, BA: B 137, 1248; ZvD and VdL joint resolution, attached to 'Beschlussprotokoll über die gemeinsame Tagung des VdL und des ZvD', 22 Jan. 1954, SDA: NL Lodgman, VII/10.

[34] VOL's 2 Apr. 1952 resolution, in *Kurzinformationen der VOL* (4 Apr. 1952), SDA: NL Lodgman, V/2:5; 'Heimatpolitische Entschliessungen des Vorstandes der Vereinigten Ostdeutschen Landsmannschaften', 29 May 1952, SDA: NL Lodgman, XI/9.

[35] Rudolf Lodgman von Auen at the *Sudetendeutscher Tag*, Frankfurt, 24 May 1953, in Simon *Lodgman*, 131.

quickly become converts to the 'European ideas' represented by the West in general and by the expellees, the self-proclaimed 'trailblazers of a real Community of all European peoples', in particular.[36] East Europeans would realize that their true interests—among them, peace, freedom, and anti-Communism—ran 'parallel' to those of Germany's expelled millions and that earlier discord had been the result of Communist machinations.[37] Under these new circumstances, a general agreement between the East Europeans and the German expellees could easily be reached.[38]

At first sight, all this rhetoric about justice and European unity had a rather naive and idealistic ring, its tone supportive of the peacemaker image that expellee leaders sought to project in public. But upon closer examination, discordant and even ominous overtones manifested themselves. One persistent problem was the continual infighting among and within the different expellee organizations. The statesmanlike image to which expellee leaders aspired was hardly bolstered when the umbrella group VOL accused its rival ZvD of trying to marshal the expellee masses into a 'political ... army' organized 'along Marxist principles under the slogan "expellees of all lands, unite" '.[39] Equally unhelpful were squabbles in which competing factions of the Sudetendeutsche Landsmannschaft traded charges of dictatorial ambition and megalomania.[40]

The primary danger to the credibility of the expellee organizations' foreign-policy programme, however, emanated from public statements that conflicted with the officially professed conciliatory principles. Intermittent calls for the reannexation of this or that territory contributed to the problem, as did the tendency of many expellee groups to employ terms and concepts which outsiders, particularly non-Germans, were likely to find offensive. The Sudetendeutsche Landsmannschaft, for example, repeatedly defended the notorious Munich Agreement of September 1938 as 'indisputably valid according to international law' and in general presented the treaty as a significant legal basis for its claims against the Czechoslovak state.[41]

Similarly troubled accents characterized the efforts of several expellee organizations, including the Sudeten-German Homeland Society, to interpret Germany's recent past. The standard portrayal began with a heavy accentuation

---

[36] Ibid. Alfred Gille at the GB/BHE party conference, Bielefeld, 8 May 1954, BA: NL 267/29, pp. 22/7–22/8.

[37] Rudolf Lodgman von Auen at the *Sudetendeutscher Tag*, Stuttgart, 1 June 1952, and at a VOL meeting in Berlin, 26 Oct. 1954, in Simon, *Lodgman*, 113 and 122.

[38] In addition to the sources in the previous three notes, see also Resolution Nr. 2 in 'Auszug aus dem Protokoll der Bundesdelegiertentagung der Landsmannschaft Schlesien', Königswinter, 28–9 Nov. 1953, SDA: NL Lodgman.

[39] Rudolf Lodgman von Auen, 'ZvD—Landsmannschaften: Eine Frage der Organisation?', 14 Oct. 1950, BA: NL 1412/22; Linus Kather to Axel de Vries, 8 Dec. 1950, BA: NL 1412/22.

[40] 'Protokoll über die Plenarsitzung der Arbeitsgemeinschaft zur Wahrung sudetendeutscher Interessen', 2 Apr. 1955, SDA: NL Lodgman, VI/2:2/7.

[41] Rudolf Hilf, 'Das Sudetenproblem in völkerrechtlicher Sicht', *Sudetendeutsche Zeitung* (10 Oct. 1953), 1–2; Rudolf Lodgman von Auen, 'Ein deutsches und ein europäisches Ostprogramm', *Aussenpolitik* (December 1953), reprinted in Simon, *Lodgman*, 147.

of the 'catastrophic mistakes' of the post-First World War settlement, which had humiliated the Reich and left millions of Germans stranded beyond the borders of the Fatherland, unable to exercise their right to self-determination.[42] The narrative then emphasized the injustices suffered by German minorities in inter-war Eastern Europe, while downplaying and relativizing Nazi Germany's crimes. To be sure, the transgressions of the Third Reich were often present in the expellee lobby's public discourse, but only peripherally. The usual rhetorical gambit was first to condemn any 'violent acts' committed by the Nazis, without going into details, and then to relativize that stance with two qualifiers.[43] The organizations typically stressed that the expellees themselves had exerted 'no influence' on the small clique of fanatics who allegedly bore responsibility for the Third Reich's wrongful deeds and that their condemnation extended not only to Nazi crimes but also to those of 'all totalitarian regimes in the world', including, of course, West Germany's cold war nemesis, the Soviet Union.[44]

This brief and cautious distancing from the crimes of the Third Reich contrasted with a thorough and detailed condemnation of the injustices and atrocities inflicted upon the German expellees. The theme of German hardship and suffering highlighted in the standard portrayal of the inter-war years reached its culmination in the expulsions at the end of the Second World War, which expellee leaders never tired of denouncing in the strongest possible terms. In the diction of the *Vertriebenenverbände*, the expulsions constituted not only a 'crime against humanity and a violation of the basic ethical principles of our civilization'.[45] Because of their indiscriminate brutality and sweeping scope, they amounted to something much worse: 'the greatest collective crime in history' which endowed the expellees with a victim status comparable to that of Jewish survivors of the Holocaust.[46]

Such one-sided public comments suggested what behind-the-scenes communications confirmed: that the peace-and-harmony tenets of the expellee organizations' official foreign-policy programme were not to be taken at face value. The absolute rejection of war and violence, for example—a linchpin of the whole programme—came under fire in private exchanges, in which a key Sudeten German figure even advocated all-out war as the only proper policy to be

---

[42] Rudolf Hilf to Lodgman, 25 May 1952, SDA: NL Lodgman, IV/4:9.

[43] See e.g. the Sept. 1952 pamphlet 'Die Tschechoslowakische Frage' by the Sudeten-German Homeland Society, SDA: NL Lodgman; Ahonen, 'Impact'.

[44] Rudolf Lodgman von Auen, quoted in 'Überwältigendes Treuebekenntnis zu Volk und Heimat', *Sudetendeutsche Zeitung* (4 June 1955); the 1952 Sudeten German pamphlet cited in n. 43; Landsmannschaft Schlesien, 'Erwägung zu dem deutsch-polnischen Verhältnis', attached to a 26 Oct. 1957 letter to Konrad Adenauer, BAK: B136/6791.

[45] See the Sudeten German pamphlet in n. 43.

[46] Walter Rinke at the *Heimattreffen* of the Landsmannschaft Schlesien, Frankfurt, 18 July 1954, *Bulletin* (21 July 1954), 1203; Lodgman von Auen at the *Hauptversammlung* of the Sudetendeutsche Landsmannschaft (21 Sept. 1954), SDA: NL Lodgman, I/0/2:5, 18–19. On the broader societal consequences of such rhetoric, see Moeller, *War Stories*; Hughes, 'Through No Fault'; Münz and Ohliger, 'Vergessene Deutsche'; Ahonen, 'Impact'.

pursued.[47] Admittedly, belligerent extremism of this nature remained rare among the expellee elites, whereas another form of dissembling—the pursuit of ulterior motives in the guise of concepts like justice and unity—always loomed large. As Julius Doms, a top figure in the Landsmannschaft Schlesien, pointed out in 1955, the expellee organizations viewed arguments regarding their rights to their homelands and to self-determination primarily as a 'powerful weapon' in the battle over the old *Heimat*. The weapon was to prove its strength by transforming the cause of the expellee organizations from 'a territorial dispute' into a 'question of world views', thus providing cover for the revisionist interests at stake.[48] The combination of the *Heimatrecht* and the right to self-determination into one package formed an essential part of the strategy. Armed with the two rights, a given group of expellees would first return to its former homeland and then self-determine its political fate—including the national affiliation of its territory.[49]

The legal concepts employed by the expellee organizations were thus never far removed from annexationism, and the same could be said of expellee advocacy of European unity as well. From the perspective of Waldemar Kraft, the founder of the expellee party BHE, and Hans Schütz, a leading light of the Sudetendeutsche Landsmannschaft, the main objective of the continent's integration lay in paving the way for 'revision through diplomacy' by ensuring that 'the whole East- and south-east European region, i.e. all the areas where Germans used to live, will again be opened to us'.[50] The hard-nosed rationale behind the abstract argumentation became particularly explicit in an address which Rudolf Lodgman von Auen, the speaker of the Sudeten-German Homeland Society, delivered to a small circle of activists in late 1953. Lodgman proceeded from the premise that an open advocacy of territorial claims to the Sudetenland in the prevailing political and diplomatic conditions would be suicidal folly, akin to 'the case of a military commander who wants to win a battle with his officers and troops and, in order to do so . . . attacks only frontally and in one direction, regardless of how strong the enemy positions are'. Legal arguments and the advocacy of European unification provided tactical flexibility, opportunities to charge from multiple directions. But Lodgman insisted that even the new Europe would be dominated by the hard interests and policies of 'nation states' and suggested that a renewed 'Anschluss' with Germany would provide the best solution to the Sudeten problem.[51] Seen from this angle, argumentation in terms of rights and European unity constituted an attempt by the expellee organizations to build acceptable cover for revisionist

---

[47] Rudolf Hilf to Lodgman, 25 May 1952, SDA: NL Lodgman, IV/4:9, and 4 Jan. 1952, SDA: NL Lodgman, XXIV/10.35.

[48] Julius Doms to Max Jonas, 31 Aug. 1955, BA: B 234, 591.

[49] See e.g. Lodgman von Auen in the *Vorstandssitzung* of the Arbeitsgemeinshcaft zur Wahrung sudetendeutscher Interessen, 31 May 1949, SDA: NL Lodgman, VI/2:2/1, 2.

[50] Schütz in the Arbeitsgemeinschaft zur Wahrung sudetendeutscher Interessen, 8 Oct. 1951, SDA: NL Lodgman, VI/2:2/4, 3; Kraft to Friedrich von Kessel, 31 Aug. 1953, BA: NL 267, 33.

[51] Lodgman, 'Grundlagen und Arbeitsziele der sudetendeutschen Aussenpolitik', address to the *Hauptvorstand* of the Sudetendeutsche Landsmannschaft, Heiligenhof, 23–5 Oct. 1953, SDA: NL Lodgman, IV/4:13.

territorial claims, particularly those that extended beyond the Reich's 1937 boundaries.

To translate their ambitious goals into reality, the expellee organizations needed a practical political strategy, a way to make their voices heard in cold war diplomacy. Finding the proper approach proved a difficult undertaking, however, particularly because many expellee leaders initially had little faith in the political entity through which they could have been expected to assert themselves, the Federal Republic of Germany. Acutely aware of the new state's 'lack of sovereignty' and suspicious of its dependence on foreign powers, expellee leaders—especially Sudeten Germans—wanted to avoid excessive dependence on Bonn by developing alternative, independent policy options.[52] The direction which these efforts should follow became clear in a January 1950 resolution, in which the Sudetendeutsche Landsmannschaft defined 'educational work throughout the world' as its 'best foreign policy' for the time being.[53] By 'educational work' expellee leaders meant systematic propaganda at home and abroad, intended to solicit support for their cause and thus to counter the pernicious anti-German influence exerted by Eastern Europe's Communist governments on the one hand and exiled former leaders on the other.[54]

Such proposals may have sounded glorious, but in the difficult economic and political conditions of the early 1950s they soon proved unrealistic. Most expellee organizations were able to conduct independent propaganda operations only on a very modest scale, if at all. For many a *Landsmannschaft*, the main activity in this field consisted of summer rallies which brought together tens or even hundreds of thousands of supporters for a few days of intense politicking and socializing.[55] Numerous organizations also established their own press organs, but these proved of limited propaganda value because their circulation rarely reached beyond immediate supporter circles.[56]

Only the Sudetendeutsche Landsmannschaft managed to develop a relatively wide array of independent activities, thanks in large part to the generosity of its rank-and-file followers, who donated hundreds of thousands of marks to the organization in a series of fund-raising drives in the early 1950s.[57] With this money, the homeland society put together not only some of the country's largest

---

[52] Lodgman to Josef Schramek, 8 Feb. 1951, SDA: NL Lodgman, XII/3; Waldemar Kraft in a meeting of the VOL's *Geschäftsführer*, Bad Homburg, 24 Aug. 1949, SDA: NL Lodgman, V/2:1/1, 4.

[53] The Detmold Declaration is in the homeland society's newsletter 'Der Landesobmann: Bericht über die Zeit vom Ende November 1949 bis Ende März 1950', SDA: NL Lodgman, I/0/2:3.

[54] See e.g. the presidium protocols of the Arbeitsgemeinschaft zur Wahrung sudetendeutscher Interessen, 16 May 1951, SDA: NL Lodgman, VI/2:2/3.

[55] Schoenberg, *Germans*, 120–3.

[56] Hans-Jürgen Gaida, *Die offiziellen Organe der ostdeutschen Landsmannschaften: Ein Beitrag zur Publizistik der Heimatvertriebenen in Deutschland* (Berlin: Duncker & Humblot, 1973).

[57] According to internal sources, the first of these fund-raisers, entitled *Volksgruppenabgaben*, generated some 200,000 DM (meeting protocols of the Arbeitsgemeinschaft zur Wahrung sudetendeutscher Interessen, 8 Oct. 1951, SDA: NL Lodgman, VI/2:2/4, 7). Two subsequent drives during the first half of the 1950s also raised tens of thousands of marks each, and additional income accrued from publications.

mass rallies but also a number of special publications which it disseminated in several languages.[58] The works included treatises on the history of the Sudetenland, a 'White Book' highlighting the cruelties of the expulsions, and a detailed documentation of Sudeten German property losses.[59] But publications alone did not satisfy the organization's ambitious leaders, who also strove to build alliances with Czechoslovak émigrés in the West. Unsurprisingly, cooperation with groups that purported to represent Slovaks, Magyars, and other discontented minorities of inter-war Czechoslovakia proved relatively easy to arrange, particularly for the purpose of propagating anti-Communist propaganda.[60] Bridge-building to Czech émigrés proceeded less smoothly, although the *Landsmannschaft* did score a seemingly striking success early on. In August 1950, it signed the so-called Wiesbaden Agreement with the Czech National Committee, a London-based émigré group headed by Lev Prchala, a conservative and relatively unknown general. Both signatories pledged to pursue a number of fundamental goals, including democracy, European unity, the liberation of the Czech people from Communism, and a subsequent return of the Sudeten Germans to their old *Heimat*, in which free referenda among the Czechs and the Germans would then determine the 'final state-political make-up' of the region.[61]

In public, Sudeten Germans leaders touted the Wiesbaden Agreement as an event of 'sensational importance', crucial to the cause of 'objective justice' and 'Western culture', but privately they admitted the truth—that Prchala's organization was too small and marginal to carry any real weight even within the narrow Czech émigré community.[62] As a consequence, the *Landsmannschaft* increasingly ignored its presumed partner while struggling to find stronger Czechs as replacements. The efforts led nowhere, not the least because the Sudeten Germans set their preconditions for cooperation impossibly high, rejecting out of hand anyone even remotely linked to the expulsions or to wartime collaboration with the Soviet Union and insisting on a public commitment to the principles of *Heimatrecht* and self-determination from the rest.[63] On these terms, no offers came forward, which forced even the Sudetendeutsche Landsmannschaft to recognize the limited potential of its independent foreign-policy efforts.

[58] According to the Sudetendeutsche Landsmannschaft's own count, the 1953 *Sudetendeutscher Tag* drew 400,000 people. See '400.000 Sudetendeutsche fordern ihre geraubte Heimat', *Sudetendeutsche Zeitung* (30 May 1953). See also Schoenberg, *Germans*, 121.

[59] Walter Becher's report in 'Protokoll über die Sitzung des Plenums der Arbeitsgemeinschaft zur Wahrung sudetendeutscher Interessen', SDA: NL Lodgman, VI/2:2/4.

[60] Correspondence between Lodgman and Ferdinand Durcansky of the Argentina-based Slovak Liberation Committee, SDA: NL Lodgman, XII/10; 'Protokoll über die Sitzung des "Komitees der Vertreter von Organisationen der Völker und Volksgruppen aus dem Raume der ehemaligen Tschechoslowakei" ', Bonn, 10 Oct. 1952, SDA: NL Lodgman, XII/10.

[61] Nittner, *Dokumente*, 357.

[62] Lodgman von Auen at a Munich press conference, 16 Aug. 1950, SDA: NL Lodgman, XII/5:1; Lodgman's comments in 'Besprechung in Grossgmain', 15 Oct. 1950, SDA: NL Lodgman, XII/6:6/1.

[63] 'Bericht des Sprechers der Sudetendeutschen Landsmannschaft vor der Bundesversammlung', 3 June 1954, SDA: Kanzlei des Sprechers, B4/4, esp. 2–4.

By 1951/2, the expellee leaders' willingness to acknowledge the futility of go-it-alone policies was enhanced by another development: the rapidly growing international stature of the Federal Republic. Particularly after the ultimately ill-fated General Treaty of May 1952 had revealed the Allies' intention to end the formal occupation and to endow Bonn with extensive sovereignty, most justifications for the expellee elite's earlier suspicions of the new state were gone. As a result, the expellee organizations shifted the focus of their practical political strategies. At least from 1952 on, they regarded the Federal Republic and its political system as the 'only real basis' for their pursuits.[64] Their main concern therefore became to influence Bonn's policies, either directly, through contacts with government representatives, or indirectly, through the parties and the electoral system. The organizations were to act as political pressure groups and therefore to remain non-partisan, or—in the language of the expellee leadership—'*überparteilich*'.[65] In accordance with the new strategy, the message conveyed through expellee rallies, newspapers, and other publications changed during the early 1950s: an emphasis on exerting influence through the domestic political system increasingly replaced earlier dreams of a direct involvement in international politics.[66]

Admittedly, not all independent initiatives ceased with the ascendancy of this new primary strategy. Sudeten German leaders in particular retained a degree of scepticism vis-à-vis Bonn's willingness to represent the interests of expellees from beyond the Reich's 1937 borders.[67] These doubts were reflected in the continued efforts of the Sudetendeutsche Landsmannschaft to supplement its now-dominant pressure group tactics with some autonomous endeavours. The most significant targets of such policies were American political elites, whom the homeland society sought to convince of the merits of its case with written communications and personal contacts. Representative efforts included memoranda from Speaker Rudolf Lodgman von Auen to Secretary of State Acheson and President Eisenhower, occasional meetings of Lodgman's emissaries with diplomats and lower level State Department officials, and frequent fan mail from key activists to Joseph McCarthy and other right-wing Republicans, fulsomely praising the latter as 'real [*sic*] great Americans' who 'really represent the past traditions of their country and won't be deceived . . . by the present and future

[64] Lodgman von Auen's address 'Grundlagen und Arbeitsziele der sudetendeutschen Aussenpolitik' in the *Hauptvorstand* of the Sudetendeutsche Landsmannschaft, Heiligenhof, 23–5 Oct. 1953, SDA: NL Lodgman, IV/4:13, 5.

[65] See e.g. Rudolf Hilf, 'Landsmannschaften und Parteien', *Sudetendeutsche Zeitung* (15 Nov. 1952), 1.

[66] Compare e.g. the 4 Nov. 1950 resolution of the Sudetendeutsche Landsmannschaft—which maintains that the Federal Republic is 'unable' to represent Sudeten German interests because it 'lacks sovereignty and depends for its existence on foreign powers'—with the article 'Landsmannschaften und Parteien' by Karl Simon, which describes the development of ties to the main parties and the government as the key task for the Sudeten-German Homeland Society: SDA: NL Lodgman, XII/6:1; *Sudetendeutsche Zeitung* (15 Nov. 1952), 1.

[67] 'Tätigkeitsbericht der "Kanzlei des Sprechers" über die sudetendeutsche Aussenpolitik zwischen dem Sudetendeutschen Tag 1952 in Stuttgart und Pfingsten 1953 Frankfurt', SDA: NL Lodgman, IV/4:12a.

sly moves of international communism'.[68] These rather clumsy attempts at ingratiation were unlikely to win many new friends for the expellee cause in North America, particularly once the brief McCarthy era had ended. The same could be said of the organization's main European endeavour between 1952 and 1955, a joint project with Otto von Habsburg to promote a 'Danube Federation', a projected federative reordering of East–Central Europe which suspiciously resembled a restoration of the old Austro-Hungarian Empire under Germanic leadership.[69]

Ultimately, however, these efforts constituted a mere side-show to the central post-1952 preoccupation of the expellee lobby: ensuring that the key tenets of its publicly proclaimed foreign-policy programme were faithfully advocated by the West German government and the major political parties. The expellee leaders' most rudimentary demand was for the political powers-that-be to condemn the expulsions and the territorial changes associated with them and to insist that final decisions about Germany's borders could be made only at a forthcoming peace conference, until which the Reich continued to exist in its 1937 boundaries.[70] Another key claim concerned the expellees' presumed rights to their homelands and to self-determination, which the organizations expected the government and the parties to advocate as a matter of course.[71] On a more practical level, the expellee leaders called for Bonn to pursue a hard-line anti-Communist policy toward Eastern Europe, with no recognition of the regimes currently in place there.[72] To induce compliance with these demands, the expellee groups applied classic carrot-and-stick tactics. They held out a potential reward of millions of expellee votes to parties that backed their cause and predicted dire consequences to those who refused to play along. The projected doomsday scenarios included an *en masse* abandonment of a given party by the expellee voters as well as a possible 'nationalistic radicalization' of the frustrated expellee masses, should their demands go unheeded.[73]

The expellee organizations combined their inflexible rejection of the post-war

---

[68] Walter Becher to Joseph R. McCarthy, 27 Apr. and 29 June 1953, SDA: NL Becher, 440; Lodgman's 26 May 1952 memorandum to Acheson, SDA: NL Lodgman, XII/1; his 16 Jan. 1953 letter to Eisenhower, SDA: NL Lodgman, XXIV-10.00; Karl Simon's report of his US trip in 1953, SDA: NL Lodgman, XXIV-10.32.

[69] On this project and the Salzburg-based Forschungsinstitut für die Fragen des Donauraumes associated with it, see e.g. 'Denkschrift betreffend die heimatpolitische Arbeiten und Planung der Sudetendeutschen Landsmannschaft', 29 Apr. 1952, SDA: NL Lodgman, XXIV-02, 15.

[70] Pommersche Landsmannschaft resolution, 29 June 1952, BA: B 136, 27370; BvD's *Jahresversammlung* resolution, 4–5 June 1955, ABdV: Jahresversammlungen und Jahresberichte 1949–1959.

[71] Lodgman von Auen to Adenauer, 31 Mar. 1953, SDA: NL Lodgman, XXIV–10.33; VdL presidium to members of the Bundestag, 12 Oct. 1953, SDA: B VIII(VdL/VOL)/1.

[72] 'Protokoll über die Sitzung des Präsidiums der "Arbeitsgemeinschaft zur Wahrung sudetendeutscher Interessen" ', 29 Oct. 1954, SDA: NL Lodgman, VI/2:2/5; 'Beschlussprotokoll über die Präsidialsitzung des VdL', 2 Feb. 1955, SDA: NL Lodgman, XI–21.

[73] Hans-Christoph Seebohm to Konrad Adenauer, 14 July 1952, and Lodgman von Auen to Adenauer, 14 July 1952, StBKAH: III/23; Lodgman in the *Hauptversammlung* of the Sudetendeutsche Landsmannschaft, 21 Sept. 1952, SDA: NL Lodgman, I/0/2:5.

realities in Eastern Europe with another, seemingly paradoxical element: a call for an 'active Ostpolitik'.[74] The basic idea was for the government to create a strong Eastern Department (*Ostabteilung*) within the newly established Foreign Office.[75] The department would then serve as the institutional basis for a particular kind of Ostpolitik, whose main focus would lie in the West. Far from making preparations for diplomatic relations or other direct ties to East European governments, the *Ostabteilung* would instead build bridges to 'pro-German émigré groups' and disseminate suitable propaganda throughout the Western world. This way, expellee leaders hoped, their revisionist cause would receive heightened public support and eventually gain ground even on the other side of the Iron Curtain, thereby hastening the demise of Communism.[76]

At its core, active Ostpolitik thus meant a continuation of the expellee organizations' earlier, independent propaganda efforts by other, more government-oriented means. Predictably, expellee leaders therefore considered this work too important to be left to diplomats and politicians alone. As self-proclaimed 'mandate holders' for the lost eastern provinces, they clamoured for an active role in the formulation and implementation of Ostpolitik.[77] The organizations wanted not only regular consultations with top-level policy-makers but also the inclusion of their own representatives into high positions within both the Foreign Ministry in Bonn and key embassies abroad. The objective was to win a formal say in deciding between appropriate and inappropriate Eastern policies.[78] Once the proper measures had been selected, the expellee groups expected a central role in their implementation as well. Highlighting their ability to act 'more elastically and freely' than the presumably stodgy Foreign Office, the expellee leaders showed particular interest in conducting propaganda operations abroad.[79] Their flagship project was the umbrella group VdL's plan for special 'PR offices' in key Western capitals, especially Washington, from which expellee representatives would push their propaganda offensive with the political and financial backing of the West German government.[80]

As the VdL's public relations plans implied, the expellee organizations also expected the government to provide them with a third form of support, along with the advocacy of their general foreign-policy programme and the inclusion of their representatives into the Ostpolitik apparatus. This third demand, a narrower

[74] See, for example, Hansgeorg Loebel, 'Und jetzt aktive Ostpolitik', *Sudetendeutsche Zeitung* (19 Sept. 1953), 2.

[75] See e.g. 'Tätigkeitsbericht der "Kanzlei des Sprechers" über die sudetendeutsche Aussenpolitik zwischen dem Sudetendeutschen Tag 1952 in Stuttgart und Pfingsten 1953 in Frankfurt', SDA: NL Lodgman, IV/4:12a.

[76] 'Vorschläge des Verbandes der Landsmannschaften an die Regierung der Bundesrepublik zur Unterstützung einer aktiven deutschen Ostpolitik', a VdL memorandum to Adenauer, 21 Oct. 1953, BA: B 136, 6515.

[77] Pommersche Landsmannschaft resolution, 29 June 1952, BA: B 136, 27370.

[78] See e.g. VdL, 'Vorschläge des Verbandes der Landsmannschaften an die Regierung der Bundesrepublik zur Unterstützung einer aktiven deutschen Aussenpolitik', attached to a letter to Adenauer, 21 Oct. 1953, BA: B 136, 65615.   [79] Ibid.

[80] Ibid.; VdL presidium protocols, 2 Feb. and 5 May 1955, SDA: NL Lodgman, XI-21.

supplement to the other two, was public funding. Most expellee groups faced financial difficulties from an early hour. The position of the umbrella groups VdL/VOL and BvD/ZvD was particularly precarious, given their high dependence on contributions from various member groups, which often failed to pay their dues. As a consequence, both organizations sought extensive public funding as early as 1950/1, and many individual homeland societies followed suit.[81] By the spring of 1952 even the Sudetendeutsche Landsmannschaft, the financial power-house of the expellee movement, had to acknowledge that its ongoing efforts at internal fund-raising—which by then had generated some 500,000 DM—could no longer keep up with the rising expenses. Like many of their counterparts some-what earlier, Sudeten German leaders saw the solution in 'regular financial support' from the federal government.[82] Well before 1955, all the main expellee groups had thus added financial assistance from state coffers to the litany of demands which they directed at the parties and the government. As Bonn's polit-ical elites reacted to these calls, a complicated pattern of interaction between the expellee lobby, the government, and the main parties gradually took shape during the Federal Republic's formative years. The important role played by the largest political parties in this process requires close examination.

[81] 'Tagung der Sprecher der Ostdeutschen Landsmannschaften', 14 July 1950, SDA: NL Lodgman, V/2:1/1; 'Vorläufige Nachweisung über die Mitnahmen und Ausgaben für die Zeit vom 1. April 1950 bis 31. März 1951 des ZvD', BA: B 137, 2253. The desire of two representative homeland societies—the Landsmannschaft der Oberschlesier and the Landsmannschaft Pommern—for government subsidies is clear in 'Landsmannschaft der Oberschlesier: Vorläufiger Haushaltsplan 1951', ALdO: Bundes-ministerien, sonst. Behörden, AA, Bundesregierung: 17 Nov. 1949–31 Dec. 1956; 'Protokoll der Vorstandssitzung der Pommerschen Landsmannschaft', 28–9 June 1952, SDA: B VIII/13a.

[82] 'Denkschrift betreffend die heimatpolitischen Arbeiten und Planungen der Sudetendeutschen Landsmannschaft', 29 Apr. 1952, SDA: NL Lodgman, XXIV–02, 18–19.

CHAPTER THREE

The Responses and Policies of the Main Parties

THE EXPELLEE PROBLEM became a major issue in the political life of western Germany long before the Federal Republic had even been founded. The three parties that quickly established themselves as the decisive triumvirate of West German politics—the CDU/CSU, the SPD, and the various liberal groupings which merged into the FDP in late 1948—paid extensive attention to the expellee question from an early hour. All three were quick to draw attention to the socio-economic plight of the newcomers and to call for strong measures to alleviate the situation. By 1946, each party had publicly committed itself to the principle of redistributive justice by which those whom the war had left relatively unscathed would have to contribute to the material integration of the hardest-hit segments of the population, particularly the expellees.[1] Disagreements surfaced, however, on how best to carry out such measures, which came to be known as the 'equalization of burdens' (*Lastenausgleich*) in contemporary parlance.[2] A split emerged between the CDU/CSU and SPD on the one hand and the FDP on the other over the 'Immediate Aid Law' (*Soforthilfegesetz*)—the first legislative step in the direction of a comprehensive *Lastenausgleich*—which was passed by the Economic Council, the pre-parliament of the western occupation zones, in November 1948. Whereas the Social and Christian Democrats both championed the measure—which provided standardized monthly support payments, funded by special property taxes, to expellees and select others—the Free Democrats denounced the bill as proto-socialist.[3] However, the FDP also proclaimed that its support for expellee

---

[1] CDU's *Zonenausschuss*, resolution of 1–2 Aug. 1946, in Helmuth Pütz (ed.), *Konrad Adenauer und die CDU der britischen Besatzungszone 1946–1949* (Bonn: Eichholz, 1975), 178–9; CSU's 'Die 30 Punkte der Union', 31 Oct. 1946, in Barbara Fait and Alf Mintzel (eds.), *Die CSU 1945–1948: Protokolle und Materialien zur Frühgeschichte der Christlich-Sozialen Union*, iii (Munich: Oldenbourg, 1993), 1739–40; SPD's 'Politische Leitsätze vom Mai 1946', in Ossip K. Flechtheim (ed.), *Dokumente zur parteipolitischen Entwicklung in Deutschland seit 1945*, iii. *Programmatik der deutschen Parteien* (Berlin: Wendler, 1963), 17–19; the 14 June 1946 programme of Württemberg-Baden's Demokratische Volks-partei, in Peter Juling (ed.), *Programmatische Entwicklung der FDP 1946 bis 1969: Einführung und Dokumente* (Meisenheim am Glan: Anton Hain, 1977), 15, 73–5; Hughes, *Shouldering*; Bösch, 'Politische Integration'; Connor, 'Flüchtlinge'; Grebing, *Flüchtlinge*; Bauer, *Flüchtlinge*.

[2] Reinhold Schillinger, *Der Entscheidungsprozess beim Lastenausgleich, 1945–1952* (St. Katharinen: Scripta Mercaturae, 1985); Hughes, *Shouldering*.

[3] Schillinger, *Entscheidungsprozess*, 119–35; Hughes, *Shouldering*, 73–81.

assistance in general and the equalization of burdens in particular remained unchanged—as long as such policies were carried out on an individual, as opposed to collective, basis; that is, as long as the level of compensation assigned to a given person was determined primarily by the extent of his or her actual property losses and not by group membership as such.[4]

All three parties thus took pains, particularly on the declaratory level, to present themselves as friends of the expellees' social policy interests, and the same tendency was even more pronounced on the second major issue that preoccupied the newcomers—the post-war settlement in the East. In this policy area, in which declarations were in any case the only means available to the Germans of the occupation period, all three parties denounced the post-1945 status quo in strikingly sharp terms early on. The most quotable formulation hailed from the SPD's Kurt Schumacher, a native West Prussian, who underscored the illegitimacy of the eastern border changes and the expulsions by repeatedly proclaiming that he and his party would 'fight with all peaceful means ... over every square kilometre east of the Oder-Neisse'.[5] Speaking for the CDU/CSU, Konrad Adenauer issued numerous similar statements, such as his widely publicized 1946/7 New Year's Appeal, according to which 'no Christian-Democratic politician will ever sign a peace treaty which recognises the Oder-Neisse line and thus definitively robs [the expellees] of their homeland'.[6] In a 1948 speech, Adenauer raised his promises to an even higher plane by describing Germany's claim to the eastern territories as a 'divine right' which the CDU/CSU could 'never abandon'.[7] The FDP displayed somewhat less rhetorical flair in its proclamations, but it, too, made clear that it considered a revision of the post-war settlement in the East a self-evident duty for the party and the nation.[8]

What prompted the leading parties to identify themselves so early and so closely with the two issues nearest to the hearts of the expellee millions? One reason was that many party leaders undoubtedly shared the outrage which most Germans felt about the expulsions and the associated territorial losses in the immediate post-war period. Opinion polls from 1947, for example, suggested that at least 90 per cent of the population regarded the expulsions as completely unjust.[9] Thus the sentiments which Heinrich Krone, a Berlin-based CDU man and a future confidant of Chancellor Adenauer, recorded in his diary shortly after the war's end may well have been representative of those of numerous other contemporary politicians as well, at least in the period preceding the obvious

---

[4] FDP, 'Heppenheimer Proklamation', 12 Dec. 1948, in Juling, *Programmatische*, 86–7.

[5] Schumacher's 1946 declarations at Osnabrück and Hamburg-Bergedorf, in 'Erklärungen und Beschlüsse des SPD-Parteivorstandes, der Parteitage und von Vorstandsmitgliedern der SPD zur Oder-Neisse Frage, zum Selbstbestimmungsrecht und Heimatrecht in den Jahren 1946 bis 1959', BA: B 234, 280.

[6] *Deutscher Pressedienst* (31 Dec. 1946); Kather, *Entmachtung*, i. 295.

[7] Adenauer at the CDU's *Parteitag*, Recklinghausen, 29 Aug. 1948, in Pütz, *Adenauer*, 592–3.

[8] *Deutscher Pressedienst* (7 Jan. 1947); Lehmann, *Oder-Neisse*, 88.

[9] Anna J. Merritt and Richard L. Merritt (eds.), *Public Opinion in Occupied Germany: The OMGUS Surveys, 1945–1949* (Urbana, Ill.: University of Illinois Press, 1970), 146, 186.

hardening of the cold war fronts by about 1947/8. 'And so they expel us from all corners of the world and close us in between the narrow boundaries of the Elbe and the Rhine', Krone wrote in the summer of 1945: 'They do that, and we are powerless. But they will never be able to tear from our hearts the love for the land which we are losing, and the longing for the German Reich will not die.'[10] Krone's attitudes were echoed in various statements in which other prominent politicians of the early post-war years argued that Germany would not be able to support itself without the economic input of the lost eastern territories.[11] The 'love for the land' thus mixed with a fear for the 'existence basis' of the nation in the minds of many political leaders.[12]

However, genuine outrage and existential angst were not the only—nor, by all indications, the primary—motivations for the behaviour of the parties. Two additional considerations loomed even larger in the minds of the leading politicians. The first was the desire to forestall a possible radicalization of the impoverished expellee masses. The early party leaders feared that the expellees would become an embittered and proletarianized 'fifth column' within German society and eventually fall prey to political extremism of either the left-wing or the right-wing variety, thus destabilizing the system in a fashion similar to the fate of the Weimar Republic.[13] The perceived need to lessen such potential was a key reason for the parties' interest in championing social policies aimed at promoting the integration of the expellees.[14] Similar calculations also help to explain, in part, the eagerness of the political elites to advocate territorial revisions in the East. By nurturing hopes of a return to the old homelands, politicians could expect to bolster the expellees' determination to resist the siren calls of despair and radicalization during their difficult transition to a new life in unfamiliar surroundings. The prospect of their mass departure was likely not only to boost the expellees psychologically but also to lessen the hostility and discrimination that they typically faced from more established residents of western Germany.[15]

But the main reason for the parties' willingness to commit themselves to promoting the key interests of the expellees stemmed from yet another source: the cold calculations of electoral politics. With six million of them residing on the territory of the future Federal Republic by October 1946 and another two million

---

[10] Heinrich Krone, *Tagebücher*, i. *1945–1961*, ed. Hans-Otto Kleinmann (Düsseldorf: Droste, 1995), 22; Lehmann, *Oder-Neisse*, 112–20.

[11] CSU's Hans Ehard's comments and D. Dietrich's presentation 'Die deutsche Ernährungsnot', 6–7 June 1947, *AVBD* ii. 513, 519–23; 'Zonentagung der CDU in Lippstadt', 21–3 Oct. 1946, in Pütz, *Adenauer*, 219–20.

[12] Josef Müller in the CSU's *Landesausschuss*, 31 Oct. 1946, in Mintzel, *CSU*, i. 754.

[13] Kurt Schumacher's Zurich speech, 8 June 1947, in Willy Albrecht (ed.), *Kurt Schumacher: Reden, Schriften, Korrespondenzen* (Berlin: Dietz, 1985), 550; Josef Müller in the CSU's *Landesversammlung*, 24–5 Jan. 1948, in Mintzel, *CSU*, ii. 1405–6; Adenauer in the CDU *Zonenausschuss*, Königswinter, 28–9 Oct. 1948, in Pütz, *Adenauer*, 720; Ian Connor, 'The Bavarian Government and the Refugee Problem, 1945–50', *European History Quarterly*, 16 (1986): esp. 133–41.

[14] See n. 13 and Linus Kather at the CDU's *Parteitag*, Recklinghausen, 28–9 Aug. 1948, in Pütz, *Adenauer*, 600–15, esp. 605; Sonnewald, 'Entstehung', esp. 87.

[15] Lehmann, *Oder-Neisse*, 150, 175.

pouring in during the next four years, the expellees constituted a crucial voter bloc in many local and regional elections of the occupation period. This was particularly true in areas with disproportionately high expellee concentrations, such as Bavaria, Lower Saxony, and Schleswig-Holstein.[16] Recognizing that the expellees were likely to cast their votes for the party that best supported their desire to 'overcome' their present 'problems', politicians acted accordingly.[17] They incorporated into their programmes special items which they expected to ring a bell in the expellee camp, such as the whole 'eastern problem' of future borders and related issues.[18] And they closely monitored the activities of their main political rivals, frequently readjusting their own public statements to include themes and slogans with which other parties had made headway among this target audience.[19]

These electoral machinations received additional impetus from the parties' desire to divert attention from the one policy area where open disagreements persisted between them and most leading representatives of the expellee movement throughout the occupation era, even on the declaratory level. The issue at stake was the expellees' freedom to organize politically. From their founding in 1945 to the end of the occupation and even beyond, the three main parties wholeheartedly backed—and indeed encouraged—the Allied policy of not licensing separate expellee parties, for obvious reasons. At least until late 1946, all three also opposed the emergence of other kinds of regional or national expellee organizations, which they feared would isolate the expellees from the rest of society and thus promote radicalization.[20] The SPD followed the strictest line, publicly disputing the need for any but charitable expellee groups even in 1947, at a time when the British and Americans authorities had already begun to tolerate a variety of so-called non-political organizations.[21] The CDU/CSU operated in a tactically cleverer fashion, openly championing extensive organizational freedoms for the expellees from late 1946 on while keeping internal reservations about the matter out of the public eye.[22] The FDP, in turn, projected a less clear profile than its larger rivals on this issue—as on many others—although its firm opposition to expellee parties left no doubt about its general attitude.[23]

The main parties' negative stances on the organizational question were well-known to expellee activists, who generally interpreted them as indications of indifference—or even outright hostility—towards them and their cause.[24] To

---

[16] Reichling, *Vertriebene*, ii. 30–2.

[17] Josef Müller in the CSU's *Landesausschuss*, 28–9 February 1948, in Mintzel (ed.), *CSU*, ii. 1597.

[18] CSU's *Landesausschuss*, 31 Oct. 1946, ibid. 753–4.

[19] Meeting of the CSU's *Erweiterter Landesausschuss*, 6 July 1946, ibid. 448–9; meeting of the CDU's *Zonenausschuss*, Neuenkirchen, 1–2 Aug. 1946, in Pütz, *Adenauer*, 178–9. Unsurprisingly, the political opponent being monitored was the SPD.

[20] Decision of the *Konferenz der Chefs der Länder und Provinzen der britischen Zone*, Oldenburg, 25 Jan. 1946, *AVBD* i. 244; Kather, *Entmachtung*, i. 30, 70; Wambach, *Verbändestaat*, 33–5.

[21] Wambach, *Verbändestaat*, 34–5; Imhof, 'Vertriebenenverbände', 82–3.

[22] Kather, *Entmachtung*, i. 31–8; Wambach, *Verbändestaat*, 33–4; Meeting between General Koenig and the *Regierungschefs* of the French occupation zone, 16 June 1949, *AVBD* v. 612.

[23] FDP, 'Bremer Platform', 12 June 1949, in Juling, *Programmatische*, 99–100.

[24] Kather, *Entmachtung*, i. 30–8, 70; Connor, 'Flüchtlinge'.

convince the activists and, more importantly, the millions of voters whom they presumably represented of the falseness of such suspicions, the parties made use of a whole arsenal of declarations regarding social policy and revisionism in the East, as indicated above. But they also endeavoured to co-opt the expellees in more active ways. All three sought to attract expellees as party members and to put some of the more prominent recruits up as candidates in appropriate local and regional elections.[25] Through this process, the CDU/CSU, SPD, and FDP each raised into prominence a number of expellees figures, both as party leaders and parliamentary politicians. In the early years, these luminaries included the ZvD chief Linus Kather and the Silesian activist Walter Rinke in the Union, the Sudeten German veteran politicians Wenzel Jaksch and Richard Reitzner in the SPD, and the Baltic German publicist Axel de Vries in the FDP.

In the CDU/CSU and the SPD, the co-optation went a step further, as both parties set up a number of special organs aimed at institutionalizing the role of the expellee representatives. The key bodies of the occupation era were the so-called Refugee Committees (*Flüchtlingsausschüsse*), established in the SPD and both constituent parts of the Union in 1946.[26] These small, advisory organs, created first at the central and later also at regional and local levels, provided forums through which expellees could air their concerns and try bring them to the attention of the rest of the party. In the CSU, such efforts could be channelled through another organ as well: the Union of the Expelled (Union der Ausgewiesenen), a broader political and cultural representation of the expellees which emerged in 1947 and gradually subsumed the Refugee Committees.[27]

However, despite all the declaratory and organizational attention devoted to them, the expellees were by no means an all-powerful force within the main parties of the occupation period. In fact, their active influence—the ability to push the parties beyond vague generalities and to shape the concrete agenda on specific issues—was severely limited. In social policy, this showed in the fact that the expellee lobby's pet project—the equalization of burdens—remained secondary to broader concerns of reconstruction and reform in the overall socio-economic plans of the leading parties.[28] Similar reservations manifested themselves in the way in which the parties advocated territorial revisions in the East. Admittedly, party leaders of the early years frequently spoke in deliberately vague and expansive terms of Germany's claims to its 'eastern territories', which

[25] See esp. Josef Müller in the CSU's *Landesausschuss*, 31 Oct. 1946, in Mintzel, *CSU*, i. 689; CDU's *Zonenausschuss* resolution, Neuenkirchen, 1–2 Aug. 1946, in Pütz, *Adenauer*, 178; FDP, 'Bremer Platform', 11–12 June 1946, in Juling, *Programmatische*, 99.

[26] CDU's *Zonenausschuss* meeting, Neuenkirchen, 25–6 Apr. 1946, in Pütz, *Adenauer*, 139, 142; Kather, *Entmachtung*, i. 55; 'Die Christlich-Soziale Union in Bayern und das Flüchtlingsproblem', undated memorandum, ACSP: NL Müller, 47; 'Die Stellung der CSU zum Vertriebenenproblem und zur deutschen Ostfrage', *hvp-Artikeldienst*, 34/53 (27 Aug. 1953), ACDP: VII-004-407/1; Kurt Klotzbach, *Der Weg zur Staatspartei: Programmatik, praktische Politik und Organisation der deutschen Sozialdemokratie 1945 bis 1965* (Berlin: Dietz, 1982), 89; Bauer, *Flüchtlingspolitik*, 271.

[27] The article 'Stellung der CSU' in n. 26; Bauer, *Flüchtlingspolitik*, 275; Connor, 'Flüchtlinge', 135–6; Alf Mintzel, *Die CSU: Anatomie einer konservativen Partei* (Opladen: Westdeutscher Verlag, 1975), 208, 332.   [28] Schillinger, *Entscheidungsprozess*, 7–152.

conceivably could have extended to the frontiers of 1918—or even beyond.[29] But other statements made clear what the vast majority of ranking politicians really meant when making such declarations: the 'lands of the Weimar Republic' within the 1937 boundaries, or only parts thereof.[30] The reannexation of, say, the Sudetenland was thus clearly not on the agenda.

The expellees also proved unable to acquire decisive positions within the party hierarchies. The two highest-ranking figures of the early years were Linus Kather—the second deputy chairman of the CDU in the British Zone—and Wenzel Jaksch—a member of the SPD's top federal-level organ, the *Bundesvorstand*.[31] However, both appointments proved more optical than substantive, as neither man managed to wield power proportional to his formal title. Other party-politically engaged expellees, as well as the special suborgans within the CDU/CSU and SPD, also possessed rather limited influence. As a result, expellee representatives were typically only marginally involved in final decision-making on major issues, including those that affected the expellees directly. This fact was reflected in the composition of the two key appointed bodies that paved the way for the rise of the Federal Republic: the Economic Council—the occupation-era legislature in the western zones—and the Parliamentary Council—the assembly charged with the preparation of what became the Basic Law of the Federal Republic. The former organ had no expellees at all among its original fifty-two members while the latter's seventy-two delegates included only one.[32]

Given these realities, it was no surprise that in the spring of 1949 the Parliamentary Council provided another illustration of the relative weakness of the expellee lobby within the parties. At the time, expellee activists were demanding special 'refugee electoral districts' (*Flüchtlingswahlkreise*) for the first Bundestag elections.[33] The idea was to ensure sufficient representation for the expellees in the first national parliament by creating special districts in which only they would be entitled to vote and run for office. None of the main parties particularly warmed to the proposal, which many politicians regarded as incompatible with the newly minted Basic Law. In a half-hearted but propagandistically clever move the CDU/CSU nevertheless brought the issue up for a vote in the Parliamentary Council, fully cognizant of the fact that the firm opposition of the SPD, the FDP,

---

[29] Adenauer at the CDU's *Parteitag*, Recklinghausen, 28–9 Aug. 1948, in Pütz, *Adenauer*, 592–3.

[30] Schumacher at the SPD's *Parteitag*, Nuremberg, 29 June 1947, in Albrecht, *Schumacher: Reden*, 499; Jakob Kaiser, quoted in the *Neue Zeitung* (20 Sept. 1946); SPD's Paul Löbe, quoted in *Der Sozialdemokrat* (13 Sept. 1946).

[31] Kather, *Entmachtung*, i. 65; Hartmut Soell, 'Deutsche Sozialdemokratie und die Sudetendeutsche Frage', in Wolfgang Göse (ed.), *Die Sudetendeutsche Frage: Entstehung, Entwicklung und Lösungsversuche 1918–1973* (Mainz: Hase & Koehler, 1974), 107.

[32] Wambach, *Verbändestaat*, 106; Kather, *Entmachtung*, i. 65–6; Lehmann, *Oder-Neisse*, 148. Hans-Christoph Seebohm, the future speaker of the Sudetendeutsche Landsmannschaft, was also a member of the Parliamentary Council, but he did not yet claim expellee status. See Kather, *Entmachtung*, i. 67–8.

[33] Kather in the CDU/CSU *Fraktion* in the Parliamentary Council, 2 May 1949, in Rainer Salzmann (ed.), *Die CDU/CSU im Parlamentarischen Rat: Sitzungsprotokolle der Unionsfraktion* (Stuttgart: Klett-Cotta, 1981), 532–3; Kather, *Entmachtung*, i. 71–3.

and the occupation authorities would guarantee the bill's ultimate defeat—which it did.[34]

Expellee leaders were of course aware of their lack of active influence within the parties, and they made their unhappiness known. The loudest voice in the protest choir belonged to the CDU's Linus Kather. On numerous occasions, he castigated his own party for its 'deplorable lack of political vision and real Christian substance' in its dealings with the expellees while condemning rival political forces, particularly the SPD, even more harshly.[35] Expellee spokesmen in other parties echoed Kather's disappointed sentiments, albeit often in less pointed language and with a different evaluation of the relative merits of the largest political groupings.[36] But all this remonstrance was of little avail; it evoked from the main parties only reassuring rhetoric that in effect reconfirmed their unwillingness to move beyond a carefully calibrated, primarily declaratory support of the expellees. The reasons were simple. As national mass parties, the Union, the SPD, and the FDP tried to appeal to the population as a whole and therefore had to avoid commitments that might attract a specific voter group at the cost of alienating other segments of the electorate. The danger of such a voter backlash against a party that allowed itself to be identified too closely with expellee interests was very real in the early post-war years. The expellees were not the only Germans severely hit by the conflict, and their demands for compensation often clashed with those of other 'war-damaged' groups, such as the well-organized war veterans or the so-called *Ausgebombte*—people who had lost their homes and possessions as a result of Allied bombing raids.[37] In addition, general resentment against the newcomers ran deep among native-born West Germans, as indicated by opinion polls which showed, among other things, that even in 1947 nearly half the long-term residents of the US Occupation Zone refused to accept the expellees as German citizens.[38] Similar sentiments also surfaced among party-political elites. In the CSU, for example, prominent native Bavarians argued in 1946 that the expellees had no right to claim 'leading [party] positions or public offices'—or even permanent residences in the state of Bavaria.[39] Against the backdrop of such passions, the parties had every reason to draw a careful balance between their advocacy of expellee interests and of other, broader causes.

---

[34] Salzmann *CDU/CSU*, 559–60; Gerhard Schröder to von Perbandt, 16 Apr. 1949, StBKAH: B 12.02/3 (fiche 12.02, 238–9); Connor, 'Flüchtlinge', 139.

[35] Kather at the CDU's *Parteitag*, Recklinghausen, 28–9 Aug. 1948, in Pütz, *Adenauer*, 613; id., *Entmachtung*, i. 54–69.

[36] Walter Rinke in the CSU's *Landesausschuss*, 3 Jan. 1947, in Mintzel, *CSU*, ii. 1010–11; Bauer, *Flüchtlinge*, 271–3.

[37] James M. Diehl, *The Thanks of the Fatherland: German Veterans after the Second World War* (Chapel Hill, NC: UNC Press, 1993); Michael Krause, *Flucht vor dem Bombenkrieg: 'Umquartierungen' im Zweiten Weltkrieg und die Wiedereingliederung der Evakuierten in Deutschland, 1943–1963* (Düsseldorf: Droste, 1997).   [38] Merritt and Merritt, *Occupied Germany*, 144.

[39] CSU's *Erweiterter Landesausschuss*, 6 July 1946, in Mintzel, *CSU*, 447–8; CSU's Landshut *Kreisverband* to the party's *Landesleitung*, 16 July 1949, ACSP: BTW 1949, 2; Bauer, *Flüchtlinge*, 272–5; Connor, 'Flüchtlinge', 135–42; Bösch, 'Politische', 111–12. Bavarian anti-expellee sentiments also found expression in the short-lived Bavaria Party. See Ilse Unger, *Die Bayernpartei* (Stuttgart: DVA, 1979).

Within these limits, the parties nevertheless paid enhanced attention to the expellees during the 1949 Bundestag election campaign. The fundamental significance of the vote that would determine the composition of West Germany's first federal parliament was obvious to all the contestants, including Konrad Adenauer, who characterized the election as 'the most decisive event . . . that we [Germans] will see for a long time'.[40] The expellees, in turn, constituted a voter bloc potentially large enough to determine the victor in what was expected to be a close race, and as a consequence the Union, the SPD, and the FDP each expended extensive energies on determining how best to court this audience. All three stressed the need to place sufficient numbers of expellee candidates on their electoral lists—a task which Franz-Josef Strauss, the man in charge of organizing the CSU's campaign, labelled 'so crucial that its significance no longer even needs to be particularly emphasized'.[41] The personnel selection was to be conducted with care, however, as the parties expected the proper expellee candidate to show primary loyalty to them instead of one or another of the relevant pressure organizations.[42]

The parties also realized that even the most loyal and appealing candidates would not suffice to pull in the expellee vote unless another, even more important ingredient abounded in the campaign materials—hard-hitting propaganda. Thus Franz-Josef Strauss wanted his party to target the newcomers with posters that highlighted the CDU/CSU's position as the only party to have advocated the creation of the so-called refugee electoral districts for the *Bundestag* election.[43] And Konrad Adenauer insisted that to get the ear of the expellees the Union had to demand the 'revocation of the Oder-Neisse line' in its propaganda materials and provide sufficient attention to 'the German lands in the East' in the party press.[44]

During the campaign, the parties practised what their strategists had preached. They included on their candidate lists significant numbers of expellees—although not significant enough to keep the expellee organizations from demanding many more.[45] They underscored their desire to attend to the socio-economic needs of the expellees through legislation aimed at providing, among other things, housing, work, and, most importantly, a comprehensive *Lastenausgleich*. In their concrete formulas for a proper equalization of burdens the main parties,

[40] Adenauer in the CDU's *Zonenausschuss*, Königswinter, 24–5 Feb. 1949, in Pütz, *Adenauer*, 801–2; Konrad Adenauer, *Erinnerungen, 1945–1953* (Stuttgart: DVA, 1965), 211–12.

[41] Strauss to the CDU/CSU's *Landesverbände*, 24 May 1949, ACSP: BTW 1949, 3; meeting of the CDU/CSU group in the Parliamentary Council, 10 Mar. 1949, in Salzmann, *CDU/CSU*, 428; SPD's 'Grundsätze für die Kandidatenaufstellung zum Bundestag', AdSD: PV-Protokolle 1949, 4; FDP's *Bundeshauptausschuss* protocols, 1–2 July 1949, ADL: A12-1.

[42] Protocols of the FDP's *Bundeshauptausschuss*, 1–2 July 1949 (n. 41), and *Bundesvorstand*, 2–3 Apr. 1949, *FDP-Bundesvorstand*, i/1, 37.

[43] Strauss, 'Rundschreiben an alle Bezirks- und Kreisverbände', 7 July 1949, ACSP: BTW 1949, 2.

[44] 'Kurzbericht über die Sitzung des Presse- und Propagandaausschusses der CDU/CSU am 19.5.1949 in Königswinter'; 'Protokoll der 3. Sitzung des Wahlrecht-Ausschusses und des Presse- und Propaganda-Ausschusses am 19. Mai 1949 in Königswinter', ACSP: BTW 1949, 3.

[45] Kather, *Entmachtung*, i. 73–82.

particularly the SPD and the FDP, still crossed swords. While the former clamoured for a 'radically social *Lastenausgleich*', featuring considerable redistribution of property, the FDP denounced such plans as irresponsible 'socialist experiments' and insisted on legislation organized around an 'individual' principle, according to which the amount of compensation had to be proportional to the original property loss.[46]

Such substantive disagreements were restricted to details of social policy, however; on the problems of the lost eastern territories the parties spoke in unison. All three repeatedly denounced the post-war border settlement in the East and demanded justice for the expellees. The degree of unanimity was reflected in the largely interchangeable phrasing which the three parties employed in their official resolutions. While the SPD demanded a 'redrawing of Germany's eastern boundaries' on the basis of 'international law' to secure the 'future' of the expellees, the Union clamoured for a 'solution of the border problem . . . in keeping with the well-founded claims of the expellees', and the FDP vowed to struggle 'ceaselessly' for the 'return' of the expellees to their 'old homelands'.[47]

The election of 14 August 1949, resulted in a narrow victory of the CDU/CSU over the SPD, with a solid third-place finish for the FDP, well ahead of the several smaller groupings that also gained scattered seats.[48] The expellee contribution to this outcome was by all indications non-decisive. The expellee groups had eschewed partisan stances during the campaign and simply exhorted their followers to vote for parties that promoted expellee candidates and other general interests of the newcomers.[49] Such vague instructions left extensive leeway for individual choice, of which rank-and-file expellees made enthusiastic use. As a result, far from forming a united bloc in favour of one political camp or another, their votes spread out in several directions. Of the minor parties, two in particular received notable support from expellees dissatisfied with the bigger contestants. The German Party (Deutsche Partei, DP), a regional grouping based in Lower Saxony, did well among that *Land*'s numerous expellees, thanks to its anti-Marxist, national-conservative rhetoric and the growing prominence of Hans-Christoph Seebohm, a party leader who, although not a bona-fide expellee in a strict sense, became increasingly involved in the Sudetendeutsche

[46] Schumacher's radio address, 11 Aug. 1949, in Albrecht, *Schumacher*, 679; FDP's 'Bremer Platform', 11–12 June 1949, in Juling, *Programmatische*, 97; Adenauer, *Erinnerungen, 1945–1953*, 212.

[47] SPD, 'Flüchtlingsprogramm für Westdeutschland', 30 May 1949, AdSD: PV-Protokolle 1949, 4; CSU's *Landesversammlung* at Straubing, resolution, 27–9 May 1949, ACSP: LV 27–9 May 1949, 4, pp. 43–4; FDP's 'Bremer Platform', 11–12 June 1949, in Juling, *Programmatische*, 96; Udo Wengst, 'Die CDU/CSU im Bundestagswahlkampf 1949', *VfZ* 34 (1986): 1–52.

[48] The electoral outcome for the eight largest parties was : CDU/CSU: 31.0% of the vote, 139 seats; SPD: 29.2%, 131; the Liberals (FDP, DVP): 11.9%, 52; Bayernpartei: 4.2%, 17; DP: 4.0%, 17; KPD (Communists): 5.7%, 15; WAV: 2.9%, 12; Zentrumpartei: 3.1%, 10. See Gerhard A. Ritter and Merith Niehuss, *Wahlen in Deutschland 1946–1991: Ein Handbuch* (Munich: Beck, 1991), 100.

[49] See e.g. *Mitteilungsblatt des Landesverbandes Bayern der Sudetendeutschen Landsmannschaft* (1949), 1/4, *Ergänzungsblatt* (3 July 1949), SDA: NL Lodgman, I/8; VOL, 'Bericht über die Tagung in Bielefeld vom 5. bis 7. November 1948', SDA: NL Lodgman, V/2b.

Landsmannschaft.[50] In Bavaria, the short-lived Economic Reconstruction Organization (Wirtschaftliche Aufbau-Vereinigung, WAV) had similar success due to its cooperation agreement with an expellee group which American occupation authorities had banned from independent campaigning.[51]

But the bulk of the expellees nevertheless voted for one of the three main parties. Although the available aggregate data are rather scanty, they do suggest that the SPD fared somewhat better than the Union among this segment of the population. The FDP, in turn, obviously received a much lower number of total expellee votes than its two bigger rivals, but in proportion to its size the party occupied an intermediate position: somewhat less successful than the SPD but slightly ahead of the CDU/CSU as a magnet for the ballots of average expellees.[52]

For the expellee movement, the election brought certain benefits, two of which were particularly obvious. First, in contrast to the key appointed bodies of the occupation era, the elected Bundestag came to boast a considerable number of deputies of an expellee background. The precise figure is difficult to determine because of the insufficient biographical information available about many backbenchers, but the best estimates put the grand total at approximately 60, which equals nearly 15 per cent of the 421 total mandates.[53] The number of active expellee deputies, however—those who maintained links to the organized expellee lobby and engaged themselves on a range of relevant parliamentary issues—was considerably lower. Apart from a handful of small-party figures such as Hans-Christoph Seebohm, these activists included close to ten Union deputies, a roughly equal number of SPD mandate-holders, and approximately half a dozen FDP representatives.[54]

Along with these parliamentary connections, the expellees gained another special boon as an immediate result of the 1949 elections: a ministry devoted to their concerns. During the campaign, all the main parties had promised to establish a special ministry to promote expellee interests in general and appropriate social legislation in particular.[55] After the election, the governing coalition

---

[50] Horst W. Schmollinger, 'Die Deutsche Partei', in Stöss, *Parteien-Handbuch*, i. 1025–111; Hermann Meyn, *Die Deutsche Partei* (Düsseldorf: Droste, 1965). Seebohm, born in Upper Silesia in 1903, spent some of his childhood and a few years during the Third Reich in the Sudetenland but resided within Germany's 1937 borders for most of his adult life.

[51] The group was the *Neubürgerbund*, headed by Günter Goetzendorff, who became a WAV Bundestag deputy in 1949. On the WAV, see Hans Woller, *Die Loritz-Partei: Geschichte, Struktur und Politik der Wissenschaftlichen Aufbau-Vereinigung, 1945–1955* (Stuttgart: Klett-Cotta, 1985); Connor, 'Flüchtlinge', 157–9; id. 'Bavarian', 144–7; Goetzendorff's memoir *Das Wort hat der 'Abgeordnete . . .': Erinnerungen eines Parlamentariers der ersten Stunde* (Munich: Herbig, 1990).

[52] Jürgen W. Falter, 'Kontinuität und Neubeginn: Die Bundestagswahl 1949 zwischen Weimar und Bonn', *Politisches Vierteljahrsschrift*, 22 (1981): 236–61. See also Bösch, 'Politische', on confessional issues, particularly the CDU's generally better initial success among Protestant rather than Catholic expellees.   [53] Schoenberg, *Germans*, 135; Wambach, *Verbändestaat*, 106.

[54] For interesting commentary, see Kather, *Entmachtung*, i. 75–82. For a complete list of all deputies, see annex 4 of *Die Bundestagswahl am 14. August 1949* (Wiesbaden: Statistisches Bundesamt, 1952).

[55] Adenauer, Wackerzapp, and Gerstenmaier in the CDU/CSU's *Bundestagsfraktion*, 14 and 16 Sept. 1949, in Udo Wengst (ed.), *Auftakt zur Ära Adenauer: Koalitionsverhandlungen und Regierungsbildung 1949* (Düsseldorf: Droste, 1984), 389, 435.

composed of the CDU/CSU, the FDP, and the DP had no choice but to make good on these promises. With impeccable electoral logic, Chancellor-to-be Konrad Adenauer overrode all objections from party colleagues who doubted the need for the proposed ministry. 'In the campaign almost all of us [in the Union] have called for a Refugee Ministry', Adenauer pointed out to his party's Bundestag deputies in September 1949. 'The Social Democrats have done the same. Therefore we cannot possibly say "no" now.'[56] As usual, Adenauer got his way, and the Ministry for Expellee Affairs became a part of the Federal Republic's first government under the direction of Minister Hans Lukaschek and State Secretary Ottomar Schreiber, two prominent Silesians affiliated with the CDU.[57] In another boost for the expellees, Hans-Christoph Seebohm also gained a cabinet seat as Minister of Transport—a post that he was to occupy for the next seventeen years.

The 1949 election and its immediate aftermath thus witnessed an intensification of the main parties' attention to the expellees and a corresponding enhancement of the organized expellee movement's political position. But these twin trends became even more pronounced from 1950 on, as three developments pushed the parties towards a stronger engagement in the expellee field. First, the expellee organizations increasingly overcame their infantile disorders, chief among them organizational chaos and a tendency towards uncoordinated radicalism, manifest in a cacophony of annexationist oratory. By the early 1950s, most of the expellee groups had become seemingly effective mass movements capable of attracting up to hundreds of thousands of members and uniting around a core programme composed of abstract, appealing-sounding principles. The parties had no choice but to respond to these realities, particularly as public opinion no longer constituted as strong a disincentive to an intensified courting of the expellees. By the early 1950s, most residents of West Germany not only supported territorial revisions in the East—as they had in earlier years—but were also developing a less hostile attitude towards the expellees in their midst.[58]

The parties' interest in the expellee problem was further enhanced by the fact that a steady inflow of refugees continued even after the human flood from Poland, Czechoslovakia, and other primary theatres of expulsion had slowed to a trickle by 1950/1. The point of origin for the vast majority of these post-1950 arrivals was the German Democratic Republic, from which some three million people were to flee west in the period preceding the construction of the Berlin Wall in August 1961. These so-called Soviet Zone Refugees (*Sowjetzonenflüchtlinge*), who had originally

---

[56] Adenauer in the CDU/CSU *Bundestagsfraktion*, 14 Sept. 1949, in Wengst, *Auftakt*, 389.

[57] The German name was Bundesministerium für die Angelegenheiten der Vertriebenen. In 1953, it was changed to Bundesministerium für Vertriebene, Flüchtlinge und Kriegsgeschädigte to reflect the ministry's expanded responsibilities for not only the expellees but also the GDR refugees and other Germans particularly hard-hit by the war.

[58] Anna J. Merritt and Richard L. Merritt (eds), *Public Opinion in Semisovereign Germany: The HICOG Surveys, 1949–1955* (Urbana, Ill.: University of Illinois Press, 1980), 54, 68; Manuela Glaab, *Deutschlandpolitik in der öffentlichen Meinung* (Opladen: Leske+Budrich, 1999), esp. 231–5; Silke Jansen, *Meinungsbilder zur deutschen Frage* (Frankfurt: Lang 1990), esp. 148–52.

been subsumed under the broader rubric of expellees, began to be treated as a separate statistical category in West Germany by the beginning of the 1950s.[59] For the main parties, however, the refugees from the GDR constituted an electoral extension of the expellee bloc, a closely related but numerically and organizationally secondary entity, to be courted with similar nationalistic, anti-Communist slogans. Although this outlook ignored many of the differences separating the two groups—particularly the byzantine quarrels among the various pressure organizations claiming to represent the expellees and the refugees—it did accentuate the significance of the expellee sector for the leading parties. And it had concrete justification in the fact that a disproportionate number of these refugees in fact were expellees, too—people whose flight from the GDR was the latest stage in a westward movement initially set off by expulsion from lands further to the East.[60]

The third, and most significant, development conducive to increasing the main parties' attention to the expellees was the rise of the expellee party, the Bund der Heimatvertriebenen und Entrechteten (BHE). Founded in Schleswig-Holstein in January 1950 under the lead of Waldemar Kraft, the BHE tapped into a groundswell of expellee discontent and scored a series of striking early successes in Landtag elections around the country. In July 1950, it became the second-largest party in Schleswig-Holstein, with 23.4 per cent of the vote, and by the end of 1951 it had raked in double-digit percentages in Württemberg-Baden, Bavaria, and Lower Saxony as well. By early 1952, the party was a coalition partner in all of these four states and thus in a position to exert significant influence not only on the regional level but also in Bonn, where the Bundesrat—the second house of parliament composed of the representatives of the state governments—played a major role in much key legislation.[61] In addition, the BHE even acquired a handful of its own Bundestag deputies, as several expellee legislators originally elected through the WAV or other groupings formally switched their affiliation.[62]

Since the late 1940s, the largest parties had been receiving admonitions that a major expellee party was likely to emerge as soon as the occupation powers stopped enforcing a ban against such entities.[63] These predictions turned out to be very accurate, for the Allied High Commission lifted licensing requirements for new political parties in January 1950, coevally with the founding of the BHE. But despite the forewarnings, the sudden and dramatic rise of the new electoral contender came as a surprise for Bonn's political elites. The first reaction in each of the main parties was to analyse the situation intensively, and the laconic conclusion which the CDU's Linus Kather had reached by the fall of 1950 also

---

[59] Before 1949/50, the term *Flüchtling* generally covered both expellees and Soviet zone refugees.
[60] Heidemeyer, *Flucht*; id., 'Vertriebene'; Ackermann, *Flüchtling*.
[61] Neumann, *Block*, 500–6.   [62] Ibid. 486.
[63] Kather at the CDU's *Parteitag*, Recklinghausen, 28–9 Aug. 1948, in Pütz, *Adenauer*, 609–10, 613–14; Hans Schütz in the CSU's *Landesversammlung*, Straubing, 27–9 May 1949, ACSP: LV 27–9 May 1949, 4, p. 183.

reflected contemporary sentiments within the SPD and FDP: 'The threat from the BHE must not be underestimated.'[64]

Leaders of the largest parties saw the threat as emanating from two sources. Some feared that the BHE would promote isolation and radicalization among the expellees and thus eventually destabilize West Germany's fledgling democratic order. The SPD's Carlo Schmid, for example, fretted that the new party would develop into a backward-looking 'restorative movement' comparable to the 'NSDAP', while a CDU colleague regarded the BHE's rise as an alarming throwback to a Weimar-style splintering of the party system.[65] But the most prevalent worries within the main parties were—predictably—of a more direct electoral nature. In the aftermath of such BHE triumphs as the Schleswig-Holstein Landtag election of July 1950, party leaders had good reason to fear that the BHE would drain away a significant segment of their voter base, at least temporarily. An internal CSU memorandum crystallized these sentiments into the argument that, because 'the expellee and refugee sector' was now going to be 'especially important in the extraordinarily hard electoral campaigns' of the future, the Union would have to intensify its attention to this voter 'reservoir' in order to 'remain victorious'.[66]

To forestall the nightmare scenarios of mass radicalization, ongoing election debacles, and the like among the expellees, the main parties took action in several areas. Certain measures were aimed specifically at the BHE. At the most basic level, the parties kept a close eye on the activities of their expellee rival. The CSU, for example, had its spies monitor various BHE events—including restricted leadership meetings—and prepare detailed reports.[67] Each of the big three parties also sought to develop contacts with the BHE and to cooperate with it, both in order to integrate the group into the political mainstream and to gain more power in the process.[68] Thus the CDU/CSU, the SPD, and the FDP all became *Land*-level coalition partners of the BHE during the tenure of Adenauer's first cabinet between 1949 and 1953.[69] But the efforts of one of the main parties to court the expellee group frequently generated concern among the other two. The

[64] Kather at the CDU's *Parteitag* in Goslar, in *Erster Bundestag der Christlich-Demokratischen Union Deutschlands: Goslar 20.–22. Oktober 1950* (Bonn: CDU, 1950), 119; protocols of the SPD's *Parteivorstand*, 29–30 July 1950, AdsD: SPD-PV, Protokolle 1950, 6; and of the FDP's *Bundesvorstand*, 17 July 1950, in *FDP-Bundesvorstand*, i/1. 102–4, 110–13.

[65] Schmid in the SPD's *Parteivorstand*, 29–30 July 1950, AdsD: SPD-PV, Protokolle 1950, 6; Scharnberg in the CDU's *Bundesvorstand*, 16 Dec. 1952, in Günter Buchstab (ed.), *Adenauer: 'Es musste alles neu gemacht werden'. Protokolle des CDU-Bundesvorstandes 1950–1953* (Düsseldorf: Droste, 1988), 248.

[66] Walter Rinke, 'CSU und Heimatvertriebene', 19 Aug. 1952, ACSP: NL Müller, 334; Otto Lenz, *Im Zentrum der Macht: Das Tagebuch von Staatssekretär Lenz 1951–1953*, ed. Klaus Gotto et al. (Düsseldorf: Droste, 1988), 457; FDP's *Bundesvorstand* protocols, 17 July 1950, in *FDP-Bundesvorstand*, i/1. 102–4, 110–13.

[67] 'Tendenzen der BHE-Gruppe', 10 Sept. 1950; 'Bemerkungen zur Landesversammlung der Deutschen Gemeinschaft-BHE in München am 16/17. September 1950', 18 Sept. 1950, ACSP: NL Müller, 395.

[68] Adenauer in the CDU's *Bundesvorstand*, 5 Sept. 1952, in Buchstab, *Alles neu*, 147–8.

[69] Neumann, *Block*, 500–2.

CDU/CSU, in particular, was plagued by oft-expressed fears that the SPD and the BHE might become steady bedfellows and unite in a federal coalition after the 1953 Bundestag election.[70]

More important than the measures aimed directly at the BHE, however, were the intensified attempts of the major parties to court the expellee audience as a whole. These efforts became particularly evident in three broad areas, the first of which centred on social policy. As in earlier years, all three parties continued to profess their commitment to alleviating the suffering of the expellees and promoting their societal integration—but with a new rhetorical flair that reflected the heightened urgency assigned to this task. Konrad Adenauer, for example, now labelled the adoption of proper social policies towards the expellees 'a political question of the first order', while the FDP elevated expellee integration into a 'moral duty for the entire nation', and Kurt Schumacher labelled the social side of the expellee problem a 'central question' for not only the Germans but the Socialist International as well.[71] Beyond the rhetoric, the whole issue also became a matter of practical politics, as the governing coalition pushed through the Bundestag several pieces of legislation that laid the foundation for the Federal Republic's social integration policies. The first major law, passed in May 1951, gave special benefits to civil servants (*Beamten*) who had lost their positions as a result of the Reich's collapse in 1945. The beneficiaries included a large number of former Nazis—but also many expellees.[72] Next came the Equalization of Burdens Act of August 1952, which provided for a partial material compensation of expellees and several other hard-hit groups through a complicated system of benefits and pensions funded primarily by taxes on properties left unharmed by the war.[73] The final key measure was the Federal Expellee Law (*Bundes-vertriebenengesetz*) of 22 May 1953, whose primary provisions were twofold.[74] On the one hand, it gave a legal definition of the 'expellees'.[75] On the other, it spelt

---

[70] Adenauer in the CDU's *Bundesparteiausschuss*, 14 June 1952, quoted in Kather, *Entmachtung*, i. 229–30; CDU's *Bundesvorstand* debate, 15 July 1953, in Buchstab, *Alles neu*, 632–8. On the CDU–BHE relationship, see also Frank Bösch, *Die Adenauer-CDU: Gründung, Aufstieg und Krise einer Erfolgspartei, 1945–1969* (Stuttgart: DVA, 2001); id., 'Politische', 116–20, 174–80.

[71] Adenauer in the CDU's *Bundesvorstand*, 5 Sept. 1952, in Buchstab, *Alles neu*, 146; the *Deutsche Programm* of the Nordrhein-Westfalen FDP, 25 July 1952, in Juling, *Programmatische*, 123; Schumacher's Frankfurt address, 1 July 1951, in Albrecht, *Schumacher*, 987.

[72] The law was known as the 'Gesetz zu Artikel 131 des Grundgesetzes' because Article 131 of the West German *Grundgesetz* had obligated the new state to produce legislation that would provide employment or public support to former civil servants. See Curt Garner, 'Public Service Personnel in West Germany in the 1950s: Controversial Policy Decisions and their Effects on Social Composition, Gender Structure, and the Role of Former Nazis', *Journal of Social History*, 29 (1995): 25–80.

[73] Schillinger, *Entscheidungsprozess*; Hughes, *Shouldering*. Along with the expellees, those particularly damaged by the war or the currency reform of 1948, Soviet zone refugees, and victims of political persecution were singled out for compensation. In its final form, the law was a mixture of the individual and social organizational principles. [74] Heidemeyer, *Flucht*, 203–20.

[75] The law provided for two different identification documents (*Ausweise*) for expellees. Germans whose permanent residences on 31 Dec. 1937 had been in areas from which expulsions later took place—regardless of whether these areas had been part of Weimar Germany—were entitled to *Ausweis* A and the title *Heimatvertriebene*. Those who had entered the expulsion areas after 31 Dec. 1937 were entitled to *Ausweis* B and the title *Vertriebene*. Expellees in both categories could pass their status on

out the government's concrete responsibilities towards the people covered by that definition, chief among them the active promotion of their social integration and the cultivation of their cultural heritage, which soon began to occur primarily through the granting of governmental subsidies to expellee groups and causes.[76]

As could be expected, the governing parties loudly claimed the credit for these legislative advances. The CDU/CSU, in particular, trumpeted the measures as *its* triumphs in one declaration after another.[77] Equally predictably, the SPD opposition played a very different public tune, lamenting that the government's efforts had fallen sorely short of the mark.[78] The Social Democrats also swore to do much better once they became the ruling party.[79] But the public oratory on all sides obscured the fact that the actual dynamics behind the expellee legislation had been much more complicated. The SPD had given at least tacit—and in some cases active—support to the measures, while the government camp had suffered from internal divisions. In addition, expellee representatives on either side of the government–opposition line had repeatedly crossed swords with all of the main political forces, and the end-result of the complex bargaining had been a legislative compromise tolerable to all sides.[80] However, such technical niceties remained in the background because they did not fit into the politically charged interpretations which the main parties preferred to present to the broad expellee audience.

Social policy thus constituted one field in which the main parties intensified their consideration of the expellees after 1950. The same trend was also evident in the ongoing institutionalization of expellee representation within each of the three leading parties. The refugee committees which the CDU/CSU and the SPD had established for this purpose during the occupation era were now superseded and supplemented by a number of new creations. The Union boasted by far the most elaborate organizational framework, in which a small number of key activists typically occupied multiple posts. The most prominent of the party's various expellee organs was the Working Group of Expellee and Refugee Deputies (Arbeitsgemeinschaft der Vertriebenen- und Flüchtlingsabgeordneten).[81] As its name suggested, the group brought together a small circle of CDU/CSU Bundestag deputies of an expellee—and, in a few cases, Soviet Zone refugee—background for concerted attempts to influence the party's policies. Other organs in pursuit of the same goal included two whose immediate roots reached back to the occupation era. The CDU's Federal Expellee Committee (Bundesvertriebenenausschuss)—a

to their progeny. In addition, the law also granted *Ausweis* C and the title *Flüchtling* to officially recognized refugees from the so-called Soviet Occupation Zone.

[76] Heidemeyer, *Flucht*, esp. 217–19.

[77] Adenauer's radio address, 3 Apr. 1955, *Bulletin* (5 Apr. 1955), 534–5.

[78] *Jahrbuch der SPD 1950/1951* (Bonn: SPD, 1952), 42–6; *Jahrbuch der SPD 1952/1953* (Bonn: SPD, 1954), 49–52.   [79] *Jahrbuch der SPD 1952/1953*, 278.

[80] Schillinger, *Entscheidungsprozess*, 153–282; Hughes, *Shouldering*, 129–50.

[81] Unless otherwise noted, on this and the other CDU/CSU organizations, see Brües, *Artikulation*, 113–24; Wambach, *Verbändestaat*, 94–7.

consultative organ within the central party executive (Bundesvorstand)—was a direct descendant of the earlier refugee committee. In the CSU, the analogous formation bore the name Union of the Expellees (Union der Vertriebenen) and simply carried on the labours of the occupation-era Union der Ausgewiesenen.[82]

Three additional entities further contributed to the complicated organizational substructure within the CDU/CSU. The first consisted of the small and obscure expert groups (*Vertriebenenreferate*) which the party bureaucracy employed in both Bonn and most *Land* capitals, primarily for routine administrative tasks. Somewhat more importance accrued to the other two formations: the Landesverband Oder-Neisse and the Exil-CDU. These organizations were conceived as special supplements to the state-level associations (*Landesverbände*) which the CDU/CSU maintained in each constituent *Land* of the Federal Republic. The Landesverband Oder-Neisse, which by the party's own admission had been created to fulfil 'propaganda needs', represented the lost eastern provinces, and the Exil-CDU, whose primary responsibility was for the GDR territories, also frequently advocated expellee interests.[83]

In the other two main parties, the organizational substructures in the expellee field were much less byzantine. The FDP created only one major organ in this area, the Federal Expellee Committee (Bundesvertriebenenausschuss), which served a function analogous to its namesake in the Union. Revealingly, the group was established in September 1950 expressly for the purpose of 'responding to the work of the BHE'.[84] In the SPD, in turn, a trinity of relevant organizations arose. The Committee for Expellees, Refugees, and War Victims (Ausschuss für Vertriebene, Flüchtlinge und Kriegsgeschädigte)—a direct descendant of the pre-1949 refugee committee—served the central party executive (Parteivorstand) in a primarily advisory capacity. In the party's parliamentary group in the Bundestag, a special Working Group for Expellee Issues (Arbeitskreis für Vertriebenenfragen) provided a loose forum for the coordination of expellee interests. But the key organ in the Social Democrats' organizational scheme was the Referat für Vertriebenen- und Flüchtlingsangelegenheiten, a section of the central party bureaucracy in Bonn that coordinated the SPD's policies towards the expellees in general and the pressure organizations purporting to represent them in particular.[85]

Although the leading parties struggled to catch the attention of the expellees with both social-policy moves and organizational innovations in the post-1950 years, the main battle over expellee loyalties was joined in yet another field: foreign policy, particularly policy towards Eastern Europe. In the crucial years preceding the Federal Republic's attainment of sovereignty as a part of the

[82] Mintzel, *Geschichte*, 182–3.

[83] CDU's *Bundesvorstand* protocols, 11 Mar. 1953, in Buchstab, *Alles neu*, 466; correspondence between Heinrich von Brentano and Bruno Heck, 17 and 25 July 1952, ACDP: VII-001-102/1; Sabine Lee, 'CDU Refugee Policies and the Landesverband Oder/Neisse: Electoral Tool or Instrument of Integration?', *German Politics*, 18 (1999): 131–49.

[84] 'Bericht über die konstituierende Sitzung des Vertriebenenausschusses der Gesamtpartei am 21. und 22.9.1950', ADL: A13-4.

[85] Brües, *Artikulation*, 127–32; Wambach, *Verbändestaat*, 97–8; *Jahrbuch der SPD 1952/1953*, 368–72.

Western bloc in the cold war in May 1955, each of the three leading parties prop-agated a particular vision of the general foreign-policy course which the new country should follow. In the CDU/CSU, the party line was set by Konrad Adenauer, who as Chancellor, Foreign Minister, and party chair possessed an unrivalled foothold on power. As a consequence, party-internal critics of his key ideas had to either leave the Union or learn to live with the standard, publicly promulgated policy line, which proceeded from two premises. First, the USSR pursued an aggressive, expansionist long-term policy aimed at taking over all of Germany as a way-station to dominating Europe as a whole. Second, the division of Germany was a direct result of Soviet expansionism and could never be over-come through independent German efforts. The newly founded Federal Republic was much too weak for such attempts, which would only lead to the country's isolation and eventual subordination to Soviet Communism.

Given these realities, the dreams of reunification through neutrality which numerous publicists and politicians of the early 1950s bandied about had to be rejected as particularly dangerous siren calls. The only correct way forward ran through the West. The Federal Republic needed to achieve a reconciliation with the non-Communist powers—particularly the Reich's old arch-enemy, France, and the new superpower, the United States—and become politically, economi-cally, and militarily integrated into the Western community. Although this policy would require some short-term concessions from Germany, such costs would be easily outweighed by the benefits: security against the Communist colossus, sovereignty for the Federal Republic within the Western camp, and—as the grand prize—reunification on Bonn's terms because the strength and attractiveness of the West would eventually bring the Communist systems of the East to their knees.[86]

As a junior coalition partner of the CDU/CSU, the FDP followed Adenauer's foreign policy lead fairly closely throughout the 1949-55 period.[87] The Liberals shared the CDU/CSU's fear of the Soviet Union; they rejected neutrality as a possible solution to the German problem; and they supported the Federal Republic's integration into the West. But for existential reasons, the FDP also had to assert its own identity, build an independent profile, and thus avoid being completely overshadowed by the CDU/CSU. This need became particularly press-ing in the second Adenauer cabinet, formed in the aftermath of the 1953 election, which had brought contrasting fortunes to the two parties: moderate losses to the

---

[86] For a clear, concise overview, see Wolfgang Benz, Günter Plum, and Werner Röder, *Einheit der Nation: Diskussionen und Konzeptionen zur Deutschlandpolitik der grossen Parteien seit 1945* (Stuttgart: Frommann-Holzboog, 1978), esp. 31–52.

[87] Sebastian Glatzeder, *Die Deutschlandpolitik der FDP in der Ära Adenauer* (Baden-Baden: Nomos, 1980); Christof Brauers, *Liberale Deutschlandpolitik, 1949–1969. Positionen der FDP zwischen nationaler und europäischer Orientierung* (Münster: Lit, 1993); Michael Schmidt, *Die FDP und die deutsche Frage, 1949–1990* (Hamburg: Lit, 1995); Jörg Gutscher, *Die Entwicklung der FDP von ihren Anfängen bis 1961* (Königstein: Anton Hain, 1984, 2nd edn.); Theo Rütten, *Deutschland- und Gesellschaftspolitik der ost- und westdeutschen Liberalen in der Entstehungsphase der beiden deutschen Staaten*, Ph.D. diss. (University of Bonn, 1984).

FDP and large gains to the Union. In response, the Liberals became increasingly assertive. Their preferred field of profile-building was foreign policy. Party leaders beat a nationalistic drum on certain key issues, especially the ongoing conflict between West Germany and France over control of the Saar region, and repeatedly called for more attention to reunification. However, as the FDP also concurrently remained a member of the Bonn coalition and thus continued to defend and represent the government's general foreign-policy line, it often appeared to be speaking with a forked tongue. The image of internal confusion was enhanced by the unauthorized solo acts of prominent party members, most notably the Bundestag deputy Karl Georg Pfleiderer. In several speeches and memoranda, Pfleiderer presented overarching alternatives to Adenauer's policy line, featuring such concepts as a military disengagement of the opposed blocs from Central Europe and German reunification as a part of a comprehensive East–West security system.[88] The FDP disowned these proposals at the time, but after it left the Bonn coalition in March 1956 and began to attack the government's foreign-policy programme in earnest, many of Pfleiderer's ideas made a remarkable comeback.

Despite the apparent confusion, the FDP's foreign-policy concepts were nevertheless more coherent than those of the third leading political contender, the Social Democrats. The SPD shared the anti-Communist and anti-Soviet fervour of the other two parties, but it sought to combine its defiance of the Soviets with a heightened advocacy of German national causes, chief among them unity and sovereignty.[89] In the immediate post-war years, the party—which was dominated by Kurt Schumacher until his death in autumn 1952—had dreamt of a united, socialist Europe that would include a unified Germany and constitute a neutral third force between the two superpowers. As cold war realities ruled out such a possibility, the party shifted its ground and reluctantly accepted the need for a West German state—but only as a temporary expedient. The SPD also agreed, in principle, that the Federal Republic should be linked to the West—but only if certain preconditions were fulfilled. The main prerequisite was that integration with the West must not become an obstacle to the pursuit of Germany's first national objective: reunification. In addition, the party demanded that Germany be treated as an equal of the other West European countries and that the integration process culminate in reformed economic and political structures rather than a simple restoration of old-style capitalism.

From late 1949 on, Schumacher applied these principles to measure the

---

[88] Karl-Heinz Schlarp, 'Alternativen zur deutschen Aussenpolitik 1952–1955: Karl Georg Pfleiderer und die "Deutsche Frage"', in Wolfgang Benz and Hermann Graml (eds.), *Aspekte deutscher Aussenpolitik im 20. Jahrhundert* (Stuttgart: DVA, 1976), 211–48; Hans-Heinrich Jansen, 'Karl Georg Pfleiderer: Gegenentwürfe zur Deutschlandpolitik Adenauers', *Historisch-politische Mitteilungen*, 4 (1997): 35–72.

[89] Benz *et al.*, *Einheit*, 77–109; Klotzbach, *Staatspartei*; Rudolf Hrbek, *Die SPD, Deutschland und Europa: Die Haltung der Sozialdemokratie zum Verhältnis von Deutschlandpolitik und West-Integration* (Bonn: Europa-Union Verlag, 1972); Ulrich Buczylowski, *Kurt Schumacher und die deutsche Frage* (Stuttgart: Seewald, 1973).

acceptability of the Adenauer government's foreign policy. Having found the Chancellor's programme wanting, he then steered the SPD to a course of hard, principled opposition, despite the demurrals of several other party leaders. As a consequence, the Social Democrats objected to every practical step taken towards Western integration taken by the government during the first half of the 1950s. But the relentless nay-saying did the party little good. It only tarnished the SPD's credibility as a serious contender for foreign-policy leadership, particularly because the party proved unable to accompany its criticisms with a consistent alternative to Adenauer's agenda. While stressing the primacy of reunification, SPD leaders failed to explain in clear terms how they expected to reach that goal. In the first years of the Federal Republic, they repeatedly called for four-power negotiations on reunification and bandied about several vague suggestions for the future status of a united Germany, including a limited neutralization and a special system of UN supervision. By 1954, the party had adopted a broader platform, featuring the creation of a collective security system within which reunification was supposed to become possible.[90] However, these ideas, which bore many similarities to the FDP's post-1956 plans and remained central to the SPD's thought until the end of the decade, were still too vague and conceptually unclear to generate much popular appeal.

The general foreign-policy concepts of the three main parties thus differed in several important ways, particularly on the Western integration–reunification nexus. But the divergences did not extend to the issues that affected the expellees most directly: the status of the lost eastern territories and of Germany's claims to them. On these questions, all three parties held remarkably similar public positions. As in previous years, party leaders rejected the post-war settlement in the East, particularly the Oder-Neisse line, in sharp terms. The CDU's Eugen Gerstenmeier, for example, compared the Oder-Neisse line to a 'wound' that threatened to bleed all of Europe dry, while Kurt Schumacher underscored the SPD's 'obligation' to close ranks with the expellees in opposing a perpetuation of that line.[91] Such a perpetuation could not be allowed, all three parties agreed, because the boundary in question was only a temporary, administrative expedient, subject to revision at the upcoming peace conference.[92] What the parties expected this future revision to look like was abundantly clear in their public statements. The obvious goal, to quote a representative declaration of the SPD's Erich Ollenhauer, was 'the return [to Germany] of the areas beyond the Oder and the Neisse'—an objective which the parties vowed to pursue with all peaceful means available to them.[93]

---

[90] The SPD's 'Aktionsprogramm', as amended at the 1954 Berlin *Parteitag, Jahrbuch der SPD 1954/1955* (Bonn: SPD, 1955), esp. 290–2.

[91] Gerstenmaier to Alfred Gille, 13 Feb. 1950, SDA: B VIII/23; Schumacher in *Protokolle der Verhandlungen des Parteitages der SPD vom 21. bis 25. Mai 1950 in Hamburg* (Bonn: SPD, 1950), 158–9.

[92] See e.g. the 5–6 Dec. 1952 Bundestag resolution, quoted in Kather, *Entmachtung*, i. 300.

[93] Erich Ollenhauer at the SPD's *Parteitag*, Dortmund, 24–8 Sept. 1952, in 'Erklärungen und Beschlüsse des SPD-Parteivorstandes, der Parteitage und von Vorstandsmitgliedern der SPD zur Oder-Neisse-Frage', BA: B 234, 280; resolution of the CSU's *Landesversammlung* in Kempten, 17–18 June 1950, ACSP: LV 17–18 June 1950, 4, p. 118; Adenauer's address at a Landsmannschaft Schlesien rally, 28 June 1953, *Bulletin* (30 June 1953), 1020.

The parties' declarations of support for Eastern revisionism took several different forms. As in previous years, relevant proclamations often emanated from the
party press or major partisan gatherings, such as party congresses.[94] But from the
early 1950s on, many promises were also made in front of expellee audiences.
Representatives of all the main parties—and of the government—typically
attended mass rallies organized by the expellee organizations and delivered
supportive addresses in which the fate of the eastern territories figured prominently.[95] At a more formal level, the parties also underscored their revisionist
commitments through Bundestag resolutions, the most notable of which was
adopted by all the parliamentary groups except the Communists on 13 June 1950.
In reaction to an earlier Polish–East German agreement that had recognized the
Oder–Neisse line as a 'border of peace' (*Friedensgrenze*), the resolution denounced
the agreement and reiterated the parties' standard arguments about Germany's
continued claims to the lands east of the Oder–Neisse.[96]

These basic territorial arguments, rooted in the provisions of the Potsdam
Agreement, formed one half of the foreign affairs platform with which the parties
sought to court the expellees. The other half consisted of an open advocacy of the
twin concepts on which the expellee lobby had based its foreign-policy
programme by the early 1950s: the rights to the homeland and to self-determination. The sanctity of the *Heimatrecht* became a matter of far-reaching political
consensus early on, most notably through a Bundestag resolution espoused by all
the parties except the Communist KPD in July 1950. The resolution—whose main
purpose was to refute a treaty between East Berlin and Prague aimed at legitimiz-
ing the expulsions from Czechoslovakia—elevated the *Heimatrecht* into an 'inviolable' human right never to be abandoned.[97] Subsequent declarations from the
three main parties endorsed the concept further. Each party vowed to struggle for
the realization of the *Heimatrecht*, which Konrad Adenauer at one point labelled
'the most elementary right given to man by God'.[98] In addition, the parties also
committed themselves to championing the expellees' right to self-determination.
A December 1952 Bundestag resolution, again adopted by all the parties except the
KPD, waxed particularly eloquent: it declared that a 'lasting peace' could only
emerge with a universal recognition of 'general human rights', including the right
of all individuals to reside in their 'ancestral homelands' and to determine their
own 'state system and citizenship'.[99]

---

[94] See e.g. Schumacher in *Protokolle der Verhandlungen des Parteitages der SPD vom 21. bis 25. Mai 1950*, 62–7, 158–9; Jakob Kaiser in *Erster Parteitag der Christlich-Demokratischen Union Deutschlands, Goslar 20.–22. Oktober 1950* (Bonn: CDU, 1950), 149–54.

[95] See e.g. Adenauer's address to a Landsmannschaft Schlesien rally, 28 June 1953, *Bulletin* (30 June 1953), 1020; Schoenberg, *Germans*, 118–21; Brües, *Artikulation*, 59–60.

[96] *Verhandlungen*, 13 June 1950, 2457–8.   [97] Ibid., 14 July 1950, 2688–9.

[98] Adenauer's official greeting to the 1954 *Bundestreffen* of the Silesian Homeland Society, sent to Walter Rinke, 8 July 1954, BA: B 136, 6791; Schumacher in the Bundestag, 13 June 1950, in Albrecht, *Schumacher: Reden*, 789; Widermann at the FDP's Munich *Parteitag*, 21–3 Sept. 1951, ADL: AI-22, 11–13.

[99] Johannes Maas (ed.), *Dokumentation der deutsch–polnischen Beziehungen nach dem Zweiten Weltkrieg, 1945–1959* (Bonn: Siegler, 1960), 80; Kather, *Entmachtung*, i. 300.

The 1953 Bundestag election campaign highlighted the overarching consensus which the main parties had reached on the expellee organizations' key foreign-policy demands. The standard tenets, including the rejection of the Oder-Neisse line and the endorsement of the *Heimatrecht*, featured prominently in the official programmes of all three parties.[100] But the campaign also underscored the general significance which the leading political forces assigned to the expellee constituency. The parties fielded numerous expellee candidates, targeted the expellees with large amounts of tailor-made propaganda, and sent their representatives to all the major—and many minor—expellee rallies of the pre-election months.[101] A good example of media-effective exploitation of a minor event was Chancellor Adenauer's participation in a special pilgrimage procession of Catholic Silesians in late June, some two months prior to the crucial election.[102]

The election, in which the expellee organizations had again adopted an explicitly neutral stance, culminated in a crushing CDU/CSU victory. The party scored over 45 per cent of the total vote, an increase of 14 percentage points from the 1949 election, while the SPD and the FDP both suffered slight percentage losses and most of the small parties faded into obscurity.[103] By all indications, the expellees contributed significantly to the Union's gains. The aggregate expellee vote shifted noticeably to the benefit of the Union and to the disadvantage of the SPD.[104] Internal estimates within the CDU/CSU even contended that the party had pulled in over 50 per cent of the expellee electorate.[105] But additional parties still remained in the picture. The FDP and the DP both apparently maintained a relatively steady base among the expellees, and the BHE—which had supplemented its name with the prefix All-German Alliance (Gesamtdeutscher Bund, GB) in an ultimately unsuccessful attempt to broaden its support base—scored a total of 27 seats with 5.9 per cent of the vote, almost all of which came from the expellee sector.[106]

The election and its aftermath bolstered the formal representation of expellee interests in Bonn. The number of expellee Bundestag deputies rose to about

---

[100] CDU/CSU's Hamburg Programme, in Peter Hintze (ed.), *Die CDU-Parteiprogramme: Eine Dokumentation der Ziele und Aufgaben* (Bonn: Bouvier, 1991), 33; SPD's *Aktionsprogramm*, in *Jahrbuch der SPD 1952/1953*, 277, and electoral programme, cited in 'Zur Information: Das Wahlprogramm der SPD—ein Armutszeugnis in 12 Punkten', *CDU-Rednerdienst*, 18/1953, ACSP: BTW 1953, 3; FDP's 'Wahlprogramm 1953', in Juling, *Programmatische*, 128–9.

[101] CDU/CSU manifestos 'Die CDU und die Vertriebenen' and 'Die Stellung der CSU zum Vertriebenenproblem und zur deutschen Ostfrage', *hvp-Artikeldienst*, 34/53, ACDP: VII-004-407/1; SPD pamphlet 'Heimat und Heimatrecht der Flüchtlinge und der Vertriebenen: Ein Querschnitt durch die Vertriebenenpolitik der SPD-Fraktion des Bundestages von 1949–1953', AdsD: SPD-Bundestagsfraktion, 2. WP, 286; Wolfgang Hirsch-Weber and Klaus Schütz, *Wähler und Gewählte: Eine Untersuchung der Bundestagswahlen 1953* (Berlin: Franz Vahlen, 1957), 103–7.

[102] Lenz, *Zentrum*, 659; *Bulletin* (30 June 1953), 1020.

[103] The following parties gained parliamentary seats: CDU/CSU: 45.2% of the vote, 243 seats; SPD 28.8%, 151; FDP/DVP 9.5%, 48; GB/BHE 5.9%, 27; DP 3.3%, 15; Zentrum 0.8%, 3.

[104] Falter, 'Kontinuität', esp. 252–3; Hirsch-Weber and Schütz, *Wähler*, esp. 238.

[105] Peter Paul Nahm to Otto Lenz, 17 Sept. 1953, ACDP: I-172-66; Linus Kather 'Vermerk über die Fraktionssitzung vom 16.10.1953', ACDP: VIII-001-1006/4; Kather, *Entmachtung*, ii, 7, 10; Bösch, *Adenauer-CDU*, 148–59.

[106] Hirsch-Weber, *Wähler*, 184–5, 236–9, 268–9; Neumann, *Block*, 91–7.

seventy, thus clearly exceeding the total of the previous electoral period, although true activists still remained relatively few.[107] The entry of a sizeable GB/BHE group into the parliament also tended to increase the expellee lobby's prominence, at least in the short term, and the same could be said of the party's inclusion into the second Adenauer cabinet. Admittedly, the main coalition partners brought the GB/BHE in for reasons other than affinity for expellee interests as such. The main motives were the desire to secure a solid two-thirds majority in the Bundestag—necessary for the passage of many hotly contested foreign-policy measures—and to accelerate the GB/BHE's demise by undermining its ability to maintain an independent, demagogic profile.[108] But the new cabinet nevertheless came to include three expellee representatives, as the DP's Hans-Christoph Seebohm was joined by the GB/BHE's Theodor Oberländer as Minister for Expellee Affairs and Waldemar Kraft as Minister without Portfolio.[109]

As could be expected, the foreign-policy interests of the expellee organizations remained in the limelight after the 1953 election as well. The leading parties continued to pledge allegiance to a revisionist Eastern policy in general and the special rights of the expellees in particular. Such avowals surfaced repeatedly not only in party programmes and other declarations of principles but also in heated partisan exchanges over a concrete policy problem—the fate of the Saarland. The status of this coal-rich region had become a source of renewed Franco-German discord when the post-war governments in Paris began to promote separatism there, hoping to bring the area under permanent French control. The Germans resisted, and after years of friction a compromise was finally reached in October 1954 as a part of the so-called Paris Treaties that eventually endowed West Germany with both sovereignty and NATO membership in May 1955. Adenauer and his French counterpart Mendès France agreed to turn the Saarland into an autonomous entity under international supervision and to subject the arrangement to final approval by a plebiscite of the Saarlanders.[110]

---

[107] For slightly contrasting counts, see Schoenberg, *Germans*, 135; 'Wir fordern Zusammenarbeit', *Sudetendeutsche Zeitung* (19 Sept. 1953), 2. The exact total is less significant than the number of deputies who engaged themselves on expellee issues and maintained close ties to the *Ver-triebenen-verbände*. This figure grew somewhat from the first electoral period, primarily because of the GB/BHE's entry to the Bundestag, although not all GB/BHE deputies were close to the expellee groups. In the other parties, the numbers remained essentially unchanged.

[108] Adenauer in the CDU's *Bundesvorstand*, 10 Sept. 1953, in Günter Buchstab (ed.), *Adenauer: 'Wir haben wirklich etwas geschaffen'. Protokolle des CDU-Bundesvorstandes, 1953–1957* (Düsseldorf: Droste, 1990), 6–8; Eugen Gerstenmaier, cited in Kather, 'Vermerk'; Erich Mende and August Martin Euler in the FDP's *Bundesvorstand*, 11 Sept. and 23 Oct. 1953, in *FDP-Bundesvorstand*, i/2. 1144 and 1187. On the CDU's absorption strategies vis-à-vis the GB/BHE, DP, and other small right-wing parties, see Bösch, *Adenauer-CDU*, 139–94.

[109] On Oberländer, see Philipp-Christian Wachs, *Der Fall Theodor Oberländer: Ein Lehrstück deutscher Geschichte* (Frankfurt: Campus, 2000); John P. Teschke, *Hitler's Legacy: West Germany Confronts the Aftermath of the Third Reich* (New York: Lang, 1999), 105–71.

[110] Robert H. Schmidt, *Saarpolitik 1945–1957*, 3 vols. (Berlin: Duncker & Humblot, 1959–62); Herbert Elzer, 'Adenauer und die Saarfrage nach dem Scheitern der EVG: Die Pariser Gespräche von 19. bis 23. Oktober 1954', *VfZ* 46 (1998): 667–708.

In West Germany, the Saar Agreement caused an immediate political storm. The SPD rejected the compromise loudly, as did the bulk of the FDP and the GB/BHE. A key argument of the treaty's opponents drew upon the favourite concepts of the expellee organizations, many of which also harboured serious doubts about the Saar arrangement.[111] A voluntary abandonment of German territory prior to a peace agreement, the argument ran, would create a dangerous precedent. It would jeopardize Bonn's analogous claims to the lost eastern provinces and thus potentially betray the *Heimatrecht* of the expellees.[112] Adenauer and his supporters disagreed, of course. Their counter-arguments portrayed the Chancellor's Saarland policy as an ideal defence of expellee interests. According to this view, the agreement provided only a temporary solution to a particular problem that in no way prejudiced Germany's claims to the territories beyond the Oder-Neisse line.[113] On the contrary, the plebiscitary formula included in the Saar arrangement constituted a beacon of hope for the expellees, whose right to self-determination might eventually find expression through similar mechanisms.[114] In the end, the Bundestag narrowly approved the Saar Agreement in February 1955. The plebiscite of October 1956, in turn, brought a surprise result that did seem to underscore the power of self-determination: a clear majority of the Saarlanders rejected the treaty and thus paved the way for their region's subsequent return under German rule.

As evidenced by the Saar debate—as well as by numerous other statements, addresses, and resolutions—by May 1955 the leading parties had firmly committed themselves to championing the pet foreign-policy causes of the expellee organizations. The party leaders' motives had been mixed, particularly in the early years. In the immediate post-war era, many prominent figures, sharing the outrage of the expellees, had viewed a revision of the Oder-Neisse settlement as a matter of moral duty and existential necessity. Through the early 1950s, many had also been motivated, at least in part, by a desire to obviate the perceived danger of mass demoralization and radicalization among the expellees by nurturing their hopes of an eventual return to their old homelands.

During the first few years of the new decade both factors waned in importance. A large-scale radicalization of the expellees became a much less serious concern for the parties by 1953. By then, the economic miracle had generated employment opportunities for many of the newcomers; the government's social programmes had begun to alleviate the plight of numerous others; and the second Bundestag election had, once again, highlighted the failure of radical splinter groups to gain

---

[111] Rudolf Lodgman von Auen to Richard Reitzner and Hans Schütz, 19 February 1955, SDA: NL Lodgman, XII/6; BvD's *Aussenpolitischer Ausschuss* protocols, 12 Oct. 1954, SDA: NL Lodgman, VII/10.

[112] Ollenhauer in the SPD's *Bundesvorstand*, 30 July 1953, AdsD: PV-Protokolle 1953, 11; and in the SPD's *Bundestagsfraktion*, 2 Nov. 1954, in *SPD-Fraktion*, i/2. 106–26; Erich Mende, *Die neue Freiheit* (Munich: Herbig, 1981); Rütten, *Gesellschaftspolitik*, 248–50; Erich Kosthorst, *Jakob Kaiser* (Stuttgart: Kohlhammer, 1972), 312–54.

[113] Adenauer, *Erinnerungen 1945–1953*, 372–3, 426–8.

[114] Adenauer in the CDU's *Bundesvorstand*, 5 Feb. 1955, in Buchstab, *Etwas geschaffen*, 351.

a large following among the expellees—or any other segment of the population. The moderation and advancing integration of the expellees had also been underscored by another aspect of the election result: the inability of the GB/BHE to draw more than a small fraction of the expellee vote away from the leading parties.

The conviction that a reacquisition of the lost eastern provinces constituted a national obligation, to be pursued as a matter of principle, also faded from the minds of most leading politicians during the first half of the 1950s. Chancellor Adenauer had never shared these dreams, and the harsh realities of the cold war soon forced others to realize the hopelessness of the situation as well. Thus a leading FDP politician acknowledged in a closed party meeting in July 1950 that 'the expellees raise demands which we will never be able to fulfil, despite our repeated promises'.[115] Some two years later, a close associate of Adenauer waxed even more specific, admitting in private that he saw 'no chance' for a return of the lost eastern territories.[116] By 1954/5, internal deliberations within all three main parties had concluded that the claims to the lands beyond the Oder-Neisse line were highly problematic, potentially dangerous, and in insoluble conflict with the pursuit of reunification with the GDR.[117] But the leaders of each party also felt that all controversial public statements on these issues had to be avoided—largely 'for reasons of domestic politics', to quote an SPD source.[118] Accordingly, the political elite's general lack of faith in the viability of Eastern revisionism remained unpublicized, as did the tendency of several leading politicians, most notably Chancellor Adenauer, to dismiss out of hand the practical value of expellee-style foreign-policy concepts couched in the abstract terms of presumed rights and privileges.[119]

As earlier fears and convictions faded, electoral calculations became an ever more predominant motive for the parties' continued public advocacy of the main foreign-policy tenets of the expellee organizations. Acutely aware of the 'several million votes' at stake, party leaders consistently stressed the need to view the expellee problem 'from the perspective of the coming . . . elections'.[120] In this outlook, central importance accrued to the expellee organizations, which were widely assumed to exert far-reaching influence over the expellee rank and file.

---

[115] Hoffmann in the FDP's *Bundesvorstand*, 17 July 1950, in *FDP Bundesvorstand*, i/1. 112.

[116] 15 June 1952 diary entry in Lenz, *Zentrum*, 364.

[117] Protocols of the CDU/CSU's *Bundesvorstand*, 19 Jan. 1954 and 2 May 1955, in Buchstab, *Etwas geschaffen*, 120–3 and 432–3; Adenauer's comments to James B. Conant in May 1955, *FRUS 1955–1957*, v. 148; SPD's 'Kurzprotokoll der Sitzung des aussenpolitischen Ausschusses', 28 Apr. 1955, AdsD: PV, Neuer Bestand, 2868; FDP's *Bundesvorstand* protocols, 27 Feb. 1954, in *FDP-Bundesvorstand*, i/2. 1394–410.

[118] 'Kurzprotokoll der Sitzung des aussenpolitischen Ausschusses', 28 Apr. 1955, AdsD: PV, Neuer Bestand, 2868.

[119] Adenauer in the CDU's *Bundesvorstand*, 26 Apr. 1954, in Buchstab, *Etwas geschaffen*, 195, 155. See also Heinrich von Brentano, ibid. 192.

[120] 'Zur Information: Das Wahlprogramm der SPD—ein Armutszeugnis in 12 Punkten', *CDU Rednerdienst*, 18/1953, ACSP: BTW 1953, 3; FDP *Bundesvertriebenenausschuss* protocols, 19–20 Nov. 1952, ADL: A13-4.

Accordingly, the parties were always eager to woo the organizations, and by the early 1950s most of the courting took place over Eastern policy, which by then had become the main preoccupation of the expellee leaders. Party activists tailored their public statements to fit what the expellee leadership wanted to hear and correspondingly screened out controversial matters, such as their own privately expressed doubts about the revisionist cause. In retrospect, even Erich Mende, a key FDP figure with good links to the expellee lobby, admitted that much of the foreign-policy rhetoric aimed at expellee audiences had 'of course' been electorally motivated.[121]

Despite all the public proclamations and other commitments, the main parties continued to keep the influence of the expellee lobby within clear bounds, much as they had in the occupation era. In all three parties, the terms of interaction were set by small circles of top leaders with no immediate links to the expellee organizations. Predictably, these elites were particularly keen to limit the direct influence which the organized expellee lobby might exert through its party-politically engaged activists. Accordingly, the parties made clear that they would tolerate 'no divided loyalties' among their expellee representatives, to quote Kurt Schumacher's phrase.[122] Expellee politicians were instead expected to obey the commands of the party leadership over those of all external organizations.

To enforce these rules, the parties took several types of action. They castigated expellee activists who acted too independently or without prior consultation with party leaders, particularly in the foreign-policy sphere.[123] More importantly, they consistently kept their internal expellee organs on a short leash. In each party, the various special bodies received only limited financial and logistical support and lacked access to the inner sanctums of power in which key policy decisions were made.[124] In addition, party leaders did their best to hinder inter-party cooperation among expellee representatives, particularly in the federal parliament, where Linus Kather and others strove to establish a formal coordinative organ of expellee deputies from 1949 on. Largely because of the lack of support from the main parties, these efforts bore little fruit. In both the first and the second Bundestag a loose group of some 15–20 expellee deputies did occasionally cooperate across party lines, particularly on social policy.[125] But the only more formal coordinative body to emerge was an extra-parliamentary creation, a special suborgan which the

---

[121] Mende, *Freiheit*, 278. Although not active in the expellee movement, Mende was born in Upper Silesia.

[122] Schumacher in the SPD's *Parteivorstand*, 16 Sept. 1950, AdsD: PV-Protokolle 1950, 6; discussions in the FDP's *Bundesvorstand*, 2–3 Apr. 1949, in *FDP-Bundesvorstand*, i/1. 37, and *Bundeshauptausschuss*, 1–2 July 1949, ADL: A12-1.

[123] The SPD e.g. moved quickly to discipline Richard Reitzner for his unauthorized participation in the signing of the Wiesbaden Agreement between the Sudeten-German Homeland Society and the Czech National Committee in Aug. 1950. SPD's *Parteivorstand*, 16 Sept. 1950, AdsD: PV-Protokolle, 1950, 6; 'Kurzprotokoll der Sitzung des Aussenpolitischen Ausschusses des Parteivorstandes', 19 Jan. 1951, AdsD: PV, Neuer Bestand, 2868.

[124] Wambach, *Verbändestaat*, 94–8, 160; Alf Mintzel, *Geschichte der CSU: Ein Uberblick* (Opladen: Westdeutscher Verlag, 1977), 182–3; Zur Mühlen *et al.*, 'Vertriebenenverbände', 110.

[125] Kather, *Entmachtung*, i. 81–2; Wambach, *Verbändestaat*, 106–11.

umbrella group VdL established in early 1954 as a forum for periodic consultations with select expellee members of the Bundestag. However, because this Parliamentary Advisory Council (Parlamentarischer Beirat) also encountered strong misgivings and resistance from the largest parties, it remained weak.[126]

The limited influence of the expellee lobby was also manifest in the manner in which the main parties advocated its political desiderata. Although willing to identify themselves with most of the expellee organizations' key demands, the parties retained control of the process and held back from commitments which they considered excessive or dangerous. As in the occupation era, this dynamic was particularly evident on matters of foreign policy. Party leaders had no compunction about calling for a restoration of the Reich's 1937 borders—a cause which the Western Allies had endorsed, at least in theory—or declaring their support for the general principles of *Heimatrecht* and self-determination. But they refused to go beyond this standard repertoire. Any open advocacy of further territorial revisions remained taboo. As a consequence, the parties did some delicate balancing when addressing expellees from beyond Germany's 1937 borders—chief among them the Sudeten Germans, by far the largest and most powerful of the groups involved. While endorsing, in principle, these expellees' right to their homelands, party leaders rejected explicit territorial claims to the areas in question and insisted, with an often confusing logic, that the *Heimatrecht* had nothing to do with revisionist ambitions.[127]

Expellee activists within the main parties were aware of their weak position and made their protests heard, much as they had in the occupation years. The complaints raised by individual representatives and their collective organs were very similar in all three parties. The standard lamentations included inadequate attention from superiors, insufficient financial support, and a general lack of influence on decision-making within the parties.[128] Discontent tended to peak in the immediate aftermath of major elections when the concern of party elites for the expellees typically faltered and many campaign promises went unfulfilled.[129] The protests proved of little consequence, however. Party leaders generally responded with verbal reassurances while resisting changes in internal power relations. As a consequence, the expellee organs within the key parties remained relatively weak and received much less general attention than the non-partisan pressure groups, in part because party chiefs felt that their 'own' activists had already been won

---

[126] 'Beschlussprotokoll über die Präsidialsitzung des VdL vom 10. Januar 1954', SDA: NL Lodgman, XI-20; Wambach, *Verbändestaat*, 111–14.

[127] See e.g. Carlo Schmid in the Bundestag, 29 Sept. 1949, in *DzD* II ii. 64–5; Schumacher in the SPD's *Parteivorstand*, 29–30 July 1950, AdsD: PV-Protokolle, 1950, 6.

[128] CDU's *Landesverband Oder-Neisse* to Adenauer, 8 June 1953, ACDP: I-377-04/3; Weigel to Paul Mikolaschek, 25 Jan. 1955, IfZ: ED 720/48; Paul Mikolaschek to Rudolf Riemer, 25 May 1955, IfZ: ED 720/48; FDP, 'Protokoll über die Sitzung des Vertriebenenausschusses am 8.4.53 in Bonn', ADL: A13-3; FDP, 'Protokoll der Sitzung des Vertriebenenausschusses am 19/20. Juni 1954', ADL: A13-3; SPD, 'Protokoll der Sitzung des Vertriebenen-Ausschusses am 18. Februar 1955', AdsD: PV, Alter Bestand, 04335.

[129] Kather, 'Vermerk'; *Vorstand* of the CDU *Bundesvertriebenenausschuss*, protocols, 31 Oct. 1953, ACDP: I-202-27/7; Bösch, 'Politische'.

over for good and therefore no longer needed to be courted as intensively as potential supporters elsewhere.[130]

The behaviour of the majority of party-affiliated expellees lent credence to these assumptions. Despite their grievances, most ultimately sided with their party in the ongoing conflict between the dictates of practical politics and the demands of the expellee lobby. High-ranking expellee figures, in particular, typically reconciled themselves to the power realities and even sought to proselytize other, more sceptical elements of the expellee movement.[131] The most notable exception to this pattern of adaptation was Linus Kather, the difficult and egocentric head of the umbrella group BvD, who in mid-1954 brought his ongoing confrontations with the CDU leadership to a head by leaving the party for the GB/BHE, in his own words in order to demonstrate that he would not 'allow Adenauer to push [him] into a corner like some waste-paper basket'.[132] However, Kather's move was ultimately one of desperation rather than strength, and it underscored the fact that the expellee policies of the leading parties were determined by people other than the expellee representatives themselves, the periodic protests of the latter notwithstanding.

By May 1955, a clear pattern had emerged in the interaction among the three main parties and the expellee organizations over foreign policy in general and policy towards Eastern Europe in particular. As a part of a concerted, multifaceted effort to court the expellees—an effort whose other components included the promotion of relevant social legislation and the co-optation of a seemingly significant expellee representation into the parties—the CDU/CSU, the SPD, and the FDP had all committed themselves to advocating the main foreign-policy demands of the expellee groups. The key components of the programme which the parties now espoused were a revision of the Oder-Neisse line and the granting of the *Heimatrecht* and the right to self-determination to the German expellees. Aware that these demands were unlikely to be fulfilled, party leaders championed them primarily as an electoral strategy, aimed at soliciting expellee votes. At the same time, however, the leaders were careful to keep expellee representatives out of key positions within the parties. The decisions on how far to go with the advocacy of revisionist interests were made at high levels, in the absence of active influence from representatives of the organized expellee movement. The behaviour of the parties was perfectly rational from an electoral viewpoint and imposed no immediate costs as long as the Federal Republic still lacked sovereignty and was therefore unable to pursue its own foreign policies. With the acquisition of sovereignty in May 1955 these cost–benefit balances would begin to change—but only after Chancellor Adenauer had himself put the expellee card to complicated use at home and abroad.

[130] Wambach, *Verbändestaat*, 94–8, 160; Brües, *Artikulation*, 108–32.

[131] Wambach, *Verbändestaat*, 108–9, 160.

[132] Kather's notes of the Arbeitsgemeinschaft der Heimatvertriebenenabgeordneten der CDU/CSU meeting, 24 Feb. 1954, ACDP: I-377-10/5; Kather to Adenauer, 14 June 1954, ACSP: NL Schütz, 12.

CHAPTER FOUR

Adenauer's Foreign Policy and the Expellees

FEW WESTERN STATESMEN of the post-war era have left as large a personal imprint on their countries' foreign policies as the *Gründungskanzler* of the Federal Republic, Konrad Adenauer. Particularly in the earliest phases of the new West German state—between the formation of his first cabinet in September 1949 and his crowning triumph through Bonn's acquisition of extensive sovereignty and NATO membership in May 1955—Adenauer's dominance was impressive. Acting as his own Foreign Minister and counselled only by a small group of trusted advisers, he put into practice a foreign-policy programme whose main tenets had guided his actions since the immediate aftermath of the war and would continue to do so until the end of his Chancellorship. Because the programme aimed at a radical reorientation of German politics and presupposed a *de facto* abandonment of popular national causes, Adenauer regarded systematic public dishonesty at home as necessary for its implementation. False promises, misleading public rhetoric, and other stratagems thus became a key part of his modus operandi. The bulk of this manipulation was directed at presumably nationalistic, traditionally minded sectors of the population, of which the expellees were by far the largest and most significant. The story of the interaction between Adenauer's government on the one hand and the expellees and their purported organizational representatives on the other therefore highlights an often overlooked major theme in the early history of the Federal Republic: the complex way in which the expellee problem functioned as a link between the country's domestic politics and foreign policies.

ADENAUER'S FOREIGN-POLICY PROGRAMME

The basic objective of Adenauer's foreign policy was West Germany's permanent integration into the Western community, an imperative derived from a coolly realistic reading of the post-war balance of power in Europe. As early as autumn 1945, the future Chancellor had concluded that the continent would be split for the foreseeable future. In a seminal October 1945 letter he pointed out that the Soviets held the bulk of Eastern Europe, including 'the eastern half of Germany', firmly under their control. He also contended that, because the 'economic and political principles' being implemented in the East were 'completely different' from those prevalent in the West, the division of the continent would remain a fact in the years ahead. Under these circumstances, only one avenue remained open for 'the parts of Germany not occupied by Russia'. These territories, which constituted 'an integral part of Western Europe', had to be first organized into 'a suitable political entity' and then linked to the Western democracies through lasting institutional ties.[1]

As Adenauer reiterated throughout his years in office, acceptable alternatives to this Westpolitik did not exist. A united Germany under Soviet influence was obviously out of the question, and neutrality between the two blocs had to be rejected as well. In the Chancellor's opinion, the idea of neutrality was both unrealistic—because Germany was simply too big and too centrally located for such a status—and dangerous—because a neutral Germany would inevitably fall under Soviet influence and thus provide a bridgehead for a Communist take-over of all of Western Europe.[2] The Western integration of the Federal Republic therefore constituted an urgent imperative, whose failure would spell 'a catastrophe for Germany'.[3] Accordingly, the Chancellor pursued his Westpolitik goals with a single-minded dedication until his efforts met with success in May 1955, when the Paris Treaties came into force and made the Federal Republic a member of the West European Union and NATO. Having established these Western ties, Adenauer then spent much of the remainder of his tenure jealously guarding his achievements against various real and imagined threats.

In part, the Western orientation of the Federal Republic was a goal in itself for Adenauer, who considered the 'Christian-humanistic *Weltanschauung*' of Western civilization the best possible antidote to the moral and ethical poisons of Nazism and Communism.[4] But two other, instrumental motives carried even more weight in the Chancellor's calculations. The first was the need for security against the Soviet menace. An intense fear of the USSR lodged deep in Adenauer, apparently induced not only by post-war power realities but also by longer term anti-Russian prejudices prevalent in much of German society.[5] For him, the Soviet Union constituted the only 'aggressor in the world', a sinister, 'Asiatic power' whose 'evil intent' was 'absolutely clear to everyone'.[6] Driven by sweeping

[1] Adenauer to Heinrich Weitz, 31 Oct. 1945, in Hans Peter Mensing (ed.), *Adenauer: Briefe 1945–1947* (Berlin: Siedler, 1983), 130; Garton Ash, *Europe's Name*, esp. 48–53.

[2] Adenauer, *Erinnerungen, 1945–1953*, 96; id., *Erinnerungen, 1953–1955* (Stuttgart: DVA, 1966), 64–5.

[3] Adenauer's comment to Hans Globke, 13 Dec. 1952, reported in Lenz, *Zentrum*, 500.

[4] Adenauer, *Erinnerungen, 1945–1953*, 97.

[5] Hans-Peter Schwarz, 'Adenauer und Russland', in Friedrich J. Kroneck and Thomas Oppermann (eds.), *Im Dienste Deutschlands und des Rechtes* (Baden-Baden: Nomos, 1981), esp. 377–8; Gottfried Niedhart and Normen Altmann, 'Zwischen Beurteilung und Verurteilung: Die Sowjetunion im Urteil Konrad Adenauers', in Josef Foschepoth (ed.), *Adenauer und die deutsche Frage* (Göttingen: Vandenhoeck & Ruprecht, 1990), esp. 102; Eric D. Weitz, 'The Ever-Present Other: Communism in the Making of West Germany', in Hanna Schissler (ed.), *The Miracle Years: A Cultural History of West Germany, 1949–1968* (Princeton: Princeton University Press, 2001), 219–32.

[6] Adenauer's address to the Landesverband der bayerischen Industrie, 26 Nov. 1954, quoted in Peter Siebenmorgen, *Gezeitenwechsel: Aufbruch zur Entspannungspolitik* (Bonn: Bouvier, 1990), 69; his

'plans of global conquest', the Soviets pursued a particularly aggressive strategy in Europe, the most significant theatre of the cold war.[7] Their immediate aim was to gain control of western Germany, the linchpin of continental anti-Communist defences, and thus to undermine the unification of Western Europe, to induce the United States to abandon the region, and ultimately to subject all of Europe to Communist domination.[8] If the Soviets reached these objectives, Adenauer predicted the gravest consequences: the definitive 'downfall of Germany' would then be followed by a general annihilation of 'Christian-based Western culture' and of 'Christianity itself'.[9]

Although Adenauer regarded the Soviet Union as a ruthless, expansionist enemy, he nevertheless believed the top men in the Kremlin to be rational, calculating operatives, who—unlike National Socialist elites—would not 'try to ram their heads through the wall'.[10] In his opinion, the Soviet leaders wanted to avoid war—particularly in Europe, where any armed conflict would have been immensely destructive—and instead sought to extend their power and influence through carefully calibrated, primarily political moves.[11] As a consequence, Soviet expansionism could be contained and eventually even tamed, but only with one means: naked 'power'.[12] A potent 'dam', undergirded by uncompromising military strength, had to be constructed to stem the red tide.[13] Aware that Germany could never perform this role by itself, Adenauer logically sought security elsewhere: in 'tight alliances with Russia's opponents', that is, the West European powers and particularly the United States, the post-war Western hegemon.[14]

Security was not the only instrumental consideration behind Adenauer's Westpolitik, however; a desire to restore German national sovereignty and power also loomed large in his calculations. Unsurprisingly, Adenauer resented the total impotence to which his country had been reduced as a result of the Second World War. The imperious way in which the victorious powers had dictated Germany's fate at the war's end provoked in him a lasting fear of further great power deals at his country's expense, a fear which would continue to torment the mistrustful *Gründungskanzler* for the rest of his life. His sentiments found particularly clear expression in a 1953 interview with a trusted journalist: 'I, too, have my nightmare', the Chancellor proclaimed. 'It is called Potsdam. The danger of a joint policy of the great powers at Germany's expense has existed since 1945—and continues to exist even after the founding of the Federal Republic.'[15]

To escape from the most acute 'danger zone' of potential collusion among the wartime allies, Adenauer wanted to restore Germany—embodied by the Federal

---

21 July 1948 speech, in Hans Peter Schwarz (ed.), *Konrad Adenauer: Reden 1917–1967: Eine Auswahl* (Stuttgart: Klett-Cotta, 1975), 120; his comments in the CDU's *Bundesvorstand*, 13 Jan. 1956, ACDP: VII-001-005.

[7] Adenauer in the CDU's *Bundesvorstand*, 19 Jan. 1954, in Buchstab, *Etwas geschaffen*, 114.

[8] Adenauer, *Erinnerungen, 1945–1953*, 472–3; *Erinnerungen, 1953–1955*, 64–6.

[9] Adenauer, *Erinnerungen, 1945–1953*, 472.   [10] Ibid.

[11] Ibid. 471–2; *Erinnerungen, 1953–1955*, 64.   [12] Adenauer, *Erinnerungen, 1945–1953*, 471.

[13] Adenauer, *Erinnerungen, 1953–1955*, 20.   [14] Schwarz, 'Adenauer und Russland', 379.

[15] Adenauer's interview with Ernst Friedlaender, *Bulletin* (13 June 1953), 926.

Republic—to the status of a 'free, independent actor' at home and abroad.[16] As he subsequently explained to a leading member of his cabinet, Western integration served, in part, as a 'necessary springboard' towards that objective.[17] Bonn's potential contribution to Western defence, which became a particularly urgent issue after the outbreak of the Korean War in June 1950, provided the primary lever with which Adenauer gradually extracted more and more sovereignty for West Germany. With considerable skill, the Chancellor linked the Federal Republic's rearmament—which was strongly desired by the United States and without which an effective defence of Western Europe would have been impossible—to concessions on sovereignty. Through prolonged and complicated bargaining, Adenauer eventually got most of what he wanted: the Paris Treaties of October 1954 made the Federal Republic not only a member of NATO and the West European Union but also a sovereign state, albeit with some restrictions.

To what end, then, did Adenauer pursue a restoration of Germany's independence and power potential? Outdated 'exaggerated nationalism' that had once 'ruled Europe' with disastrous consequences was not his objective, he insisted.[18] Instead, the Chancellor typically sang the praises of an integrated Western Europe, in which Germany would be a member with 'equal rights and equal duties'.[19] In this framework, characteristic of much of Adenauer's public rhetoric, sovereignty constituted something of a precondition for a better, supranational future. But despite his rejection of aggressive nationalism and his accompanying embrace of European integration, Adenauer nevertheless continued to think primarily in traditional power-political categories. Such considerations manifested themselves in what Hans-Peter Schwarz and others have labelled Adenauer's 'European nationalism'.[20] The Chancellor frequently emphasized the need to build Europe into a 'third force', militarily and politically powerful enough to constitute an 'authoritative factor in world politics' alongside the superpowers.[21] To be sure, this Europe would still have been a decisively Western entity, both in terms of its geographical composition and its general cold war loyalties, but occasionally it also could have functioned as an independent actor between the blocs.

Europe was not the only arena where Adenauer's power-political 'nationalism' manifested itself, however. The Chancellor also expressed similar sentiments with reference to West Germany, albeit more guardedly. Behind the scenes, he reminisced nostalgically about the impressive 'rank and fame' that the *Kaiserreich* had once possessed and lamented the 'sad and bitter' decline of German national

---

[16] *Bulletin* (13 June 1953), 926; Adenauer, *Erinnerungen, 1953–1955*, 63.

[17] Adenauer to Erhard, 13 Apr. 1956, cited in Hans-Peter Schwarz, *Adenauer: Der Staatsmann, 1952–1967* (Stuttgart: DVA, 1991), 291.

[18] Adenauer, *Erinnerungen, 1953–1955*, 64.

[19] Adenauer to Helena Wessel, 27 Aug. 1949, in Hans Peter Mensing (ed.), *Adenauer: Briefe 1949–1951* (Berlin: Siedler, 1985), 97.

[20] Schwarz, 'Konzept', 147; Gotto, 'Deutschland- und Ostpolitik', 84.

[21] Adenauer's 9 May 1950 speech, in Schwarz, *Reden*, 177; his *Erinnerungen, 1945–1953*, 330, 563; Hans-Peter Schwarz, 'Adenauer und Europa', *VfZ* 27 (1979): 483–4, 517–19.

power since then.[22] Occasionally he even spoke openly of his desire to restore West Germany to true 'great power' status.[23]

At its core, Adenauer's grand design was thus very Western-oriented; Western integration served as the fountainhead from which new, healthy values and—even more importantly—security and sovereignty would spring for the Federal Republic, a state composed of the westernmost sections of the former Reich. The most obvious Eastern interest of Germany and the Germans, reunification, had much lower priority for the Chancellor.[24] To be sure, Adenauer consistently underscored the significance of reunification in his rhetoric. In an October 1950 address, for example, he labelled 'the restoration of German unity . . . our great goal, which we will never neglect', and in a radio interview some two years later he elevated reunification into 'the foremost political objective of the Federal Republic'.[25] At the same time, he drew a causal link between Western integration and the re-establishment of German unity, describing his Westpolitik as 'the only possible means' of overcoming national division.[26]

Adenauer's reasoning was seemingly straightforward—and closely related to his thoughts on West German security. As a totalitarian state, the USSR, which ultimately held the key to reunification, understood only 'the language of power'.[27] It would therefore agree to negotiations and eventual concessions on the German question only when faced with an opponent of superior strength. Because the Federal Republic could never aspire to such stature alone, its only hope lay in integration with the Western bloc, whose power would in due course convince the Russians of the futility of continuing the cold war confrontation in Europe.[28] Two other factors would also help to divert the Soviet leadership's attention: growing domestic problems, particularly in the economy, and the rising Chinese challenge in the East.[29] The end-result would be a decision by the Kremlin to liberate not only the GDR but also the other East European satellites.[30] Only the timing remained unclear in Adenauer's public blueprint for reunification. In 1952 alone,

[22] Adenauer on 13 Jan. 1963, cited in Horst Osterheld, '*Ich gehe nicht leichten Herzens . . .*': *Adenauers letzte Kanzlerjahre: Ein dokumentarischer Bericht* (Mainz: Grünewald, 1986), 179; Adenauer's Oct. 1950 Goslar address, in Schwarz, *Reden*, 183–4.

[23] Adenauer on 1 June 1951, in *Adenauer: Teegespräche 1950–1954*, ed. H.-J. Küsters (Berlin: Siedler, 1984), 93.

[24] My interpretation of Adenauer's attitude towards German unity differs sharply from that promoted by several prominent German scholars, especially since reunification. For strong examples of the argument that presents the events of 1989/90 as a full vindication of Adenauer's Westpolitik concept, see Rudolf Morsey, 'Die Deutschlandpolitik Konrad Adenauers', *Historisch-politische Mitteilungen*, 1 (1994): 1–14; id., *Die Deutschlandpolitik Adenauers: Alte Thesen und neue Fakten* (Opladen: Westdeutscher Verlag, 1991).

[25] Adenauer at the CDU's Goslar *Parteitag*, 20–2 Oct. 1950, in Benz, *Einheit*, 135; his interview in *Bulletin* (26 Apr. 1952), 487.

[26] Interview with Ernst Friedlaender, *Bulletin* (29 May 1952), 1.

[27] Adenauer at the CDU's Goslar *Parteitag*, 20 Oct. 1950, in Schwarz, *Reden*, 185.

[28] Adenauer's press conference, 23 Oct. 1954, cited in Morsey, *Deutschlandpolitik*, 53.

[29] Adenauer's comments to reporters, 3 June 1952, in *Teegespräche 1950–1954*, ed. Küsters, 301; his *Erinnerungen, 1953–1955*, 63–6, 87–8, 211.

[30] Adenauer in *Bulletin* (25 Apr. 1953), 661.

the Chancellor gave several conflicting predictions of when the great day would come, ranging from three to five years to a metaphorically vague 'today, or tomorrow, or the day after tomorrow'.[31]

Despite its rhetorical prominence, however, reunification constituted something of an 'alien element' in Adenauer's westward-looking policy concept, included more out of necessity than heartfelt conviction.[32] Given the political realities in West Germany, the Chancellor had no choice but to preach the gospel of reunification. Popular interest in German unity ran very high throughout the Adenauer era, as confirmed by various opinion polls.[33] In addition, the Chancellor suffered from personal credibility problems on this issue, caused in large part by the SPD-led opposition, which frequently accused him of subservience to the Allies and lack of interest in German unity, particularly in the Federal Republic's early years.[34] Internal divisions within the cabinet and the CDU/CSU over the proper balance between Westpolitik and reunification also contributed to the Chancellor's image problems.[35] Under these conditions, any public statements suggesting lack of interest in reunification would have entailed political suicide for Adenauer.

In reality, however, reunification remained a secondary concern at best for Adenauer. From the immediate aftermath of the war, he was willing to accept indefinite division as the price for his primary goal, the Western integration of the Federal Republic. Accordingly, Adenauer argued in writing as early as the autumn of 1945 that the parts of Germany controlled by the Russians were gone 'for an indeterminate period of time' and that the creation of a viable Western-oriented state in the other three occupation zones had to proceed regardless of the implications for these 'lost' territories.[36] He also voiced his lack of interest in reunification in several confidential discussions during the occupation years. One conversation partner received the impression that Adenauer aimed at re-establishing Germany in 'the historical boundaries of Charlemagne's Reich', while another concluded that Adenauer 'neither looks nor hopes for the inclusion of parts of East Germany' into what became the Federal Republic.[37]

Once the West German state had been founded, the Chancellor focused on implementing his Westpolitik and at least until May 1955 not only lacked interest

[31] Adenauer's comments, 2 Apr. 1952, in *Teegespräche 1950–1954*, ed. Küsters, 233. Also, ibid. 301; Buchstab, *Alles neu*, 139.

[32] Schwarz, 'Konzept', 145.

[33] Elisabeth Noelle-Neumann, 'Die Verklärung: Adenauer und die öffentliche Meinung 1949 bis 1976', in Blumenwitz *et al.*, *Adenauer*, ii, esp. 524–5, 531, 533; Elisabeth Noelle and Erich Peter Neumann (ed.), *Jahrbuch der öffentlichen Meinung 1947–1955* (Allensbach: Verlag für Demoskopie, 1956), esp. 315, 318; Glaab, *Deutschlandpolitik*.

[34] Klotzbach, *Weg*, esp. 154–72, 188–237.

[35] Hans-Erich Volkmann, 'Adenauer und die deutschlandpolitischen Opponenten in CDU und CSU', in Foschepoth, *Adenauer*, 183–206.

[36] Adenauer, *Erinnerungen, 1945–1953*, 35; his memorandum to von Weiss, 17 Sept. 1945, cited in Henning Köhler, *Adenauer: Eine politische Biographie* (Berlin: Propyläen, 1994), 347.

[37] Ernst Lemmer's impressions, spring 1946, Lemmer, *Manches*, 297; Robert D. Murphy's memorandum, 24 Nov. 1948, *FRUS 1948*, ii. 445.

in reunification but also actively sought to prevent unity, which he regarded as a potential danger to the Federal Republic's internal and external freedoms. Adenauer's behind-the-scenes statements gave evidence of this attitude. In December 1950, he explained to the American High Commissioner, John J. McCloy, that he wished to 'renounce . . . the thought of a reunited Germany', at least 'for a time'.[38] Some eighteen months later he admitted that 'no offer of the Soviet Union' could lure him away from the absolute primacy of Westpolitik, and in the summer of 1953 his personal conviction was reported to be that 'a divided Germany' provided 'the safe solution' to the problem of Central European security.[39]

But the Chancellor's negative attitude towards the issue of unity was even clearer in his practical reunification policies—or, rather, in the lack thereof. His government's standard formula for concrete steps towards reunification in the pre-sovereignty period—free all-German elections to a constituent assembly which would then draft a new constitution—originated not with Adenauer himself but with the Americans, who forced the idea on the reluctant Chancellor in early 1950. Anxious to 'seize . . . [the] propaganda . . . initiative' on reunification and frustrated by Adenauer's apparent 'uninterest' in East Germany, High Commissioner McCloy unveiled the free elections proposal to the press, thus compelling Adenauer to follow suit in a government declaration, despite his privately expressed displeasure.[40] The Chancellor feared that the proposal might generate 'consequences . . . which one cannot anticipate in advance'.[41]

To ensure that these unpredictable consequences would not include a premature reunification in the absence of Western integration, Adenauer used the free elections formula as a tool against, rather than for, national unity in the ensuing years. He loudly insisted on free elections as a first step whenever the Eastern bloc advanced alternative reunification proposals—themselves typically propaganda moves aimed primarily at undermining Bonn's Westpolitik—such as the GDR's November 1950 plan for an appointed all-German Constituent Council.[42] When Moscow and East Berlin signalled potential willingness to concede all-German elections, the Chancellor trotted out additional demands. In response to an East German suggestion of talks on the issue in the autumn of 1951, Adenauer set a new precondition—inspection of both parts of Germany by a special electoral commission of the United Nations—which helped to thwart discussions over

---

[38] McCloy's memorandum, 16 Dec. 1950, *FRUS 1950*, iv. 674.

[39] Adenauer's comments, 3 June 1952, in *Teegespräche 1950–1954*, ed. Küsters, 297; Selwyn Lloyd to Churchill, 22 June 1953, cited in Josef Foschepoth, 'Churchill, Adenauer, und die Neutralisierung Deutschlands', *Deutschland Archiv*, 17 (1984): 1300; Hermann-Josef Rupieper, *Der besetzte Verbündete: Die amerikanische Deutschlandpolitik 1949–1955* (Opladen: Westdeutscher Verlag, 1991), 221, 247–8.

[40] McCloy to the Secretary of State, 24 Feb. 1950, *FRUS 1950*, iv. 604; McCloy in the State Department, 9 Feb. 1950, ibid. 594; Rupieper, *Besetzte*, 213–15.

[41] Adenauer's comment to the Allied High Commissioners, 22 Mar. 1950, in *Akten zur Auswärtigen Politik der Bundesrepublik Deutschland*, i. *Adenauer und die Hohen Kommissare 1949–1951* (Munich: Oldenbourg, 1989), 149.   [42] Schwarz, *Aufstieg*, 832–3.

reunification both in autumn 1951 and spring 1952, amid Stalin's famous note offensive.[43]

During the preparations for the January 1954 Berlin Conference of the wartime allies, whose Germany-centred agenda worried him, the Chancellor again tried to raise the hurdles. He now demanded that the East Germans allow the free election not only of an all-German parliament but also of several other bodies: the national legislature of the GDR and the parliaments of its constituent states (*Länder*), which no longer even existed as administrative units in East Germany.[44] In all this defensive negativism, constructive reunification policies were lacking. Revealingly, the only significant reunification initiative that emanated from Bonn prior to the acquisition of sovereignty—a May 1953 proposal for a four-power conference on German unity—was motivated primarily by Adenauer's desire to 'strengthen his . . . electoral prospects', as Walter Hallstein, a close associate of the Chancellor and a top figure in the Foreign Ministry, told the Americans.[45] Another trusted confidant, the CDU parliamentarian Heinrich Krone, summarized the situation tersely in a diary entry of 5 April 1955: 'Do we have a reunification concept? I do not think so.'[46]

What, then, were the motives that held Adenauer back from an active pursuit of reunification, at least in the pre-1955 period? Some of the Chancellor's considerations have already been mentioned, such as his fear that reunification under false auspices would subject Germany to Communist domination. But these calculations explain little; ultimately they only reiterate Adenauer's perception of reunification as a potential danger rather than a pre-eminent objective, while begging the question of what caused the Chancellor to think this way. Adenauer's actual anti-reunification motives reflected deeply rooted personal beliefs and idiosyncrasies that went beyond the unemotional realpolitik arguments about the primacy of anti-Communist security with which he typically justified his Westpolitik in public—and in which he also sincerely believed. Three personal factors, rarely openly discussed but nevertheless detectable, contributed to Adenauer's lack of interest in German unity.

The first factor was the Chancellor's geographical and cultural background. To quote Herbert Blankenhorn, one of his closest advisers, Adenauer could 'only be understood against the landscape of the Rhine'.[47] Adenauer had spent his entire life in the westward-looking, Catholic milieu of the Rhineland. He had never shown much interest in eastern sections of the country and had long harboured a pronounced aversion to Prussia. As early as the 1920s, when Lord Mayor of Cologne, Adenauer had given graphic expression to his sentiments. Describing

[43] Lenz, *Zentrum*, 182; Josef Foschepoth, 'Westintegration statt Wiedervereinigung: Adenauers Deutschlandpolitik, 1949–1955', in Foschepoth, 44–5; Rupieper, *Besetzte*, 225–7.

[44] *FRUS 1952–1954*, vii. 775–7, 779–80; Köhler, *Adenauer*, 818; Schwarz, *Staatsmann*, 128.

[45] David Bruce's diary, 9 July 1953, *FRUS 1952–1954*, vii. 485; ibid. 460–2, 479, 487; Schwarz, *Staatsmann*, 87–9.   [46] Krone, *Tagebücher*, i. 169.

[47] Herbert Blankenhorn, *Verständnis und Verständigung: Blätter eines politischen Tagebuchs 1949 bis 1979* (Frankfurt: Propyläen, 1980), 43.

eastward train trips through Prussia, he had reportedly claimed that 'for him the Asian steppe begins in Braunschweig; in Magdeburg he always closes the curtains; and after crossing the Elbe, he vomits out of the window every time'.[48] Although Hans-Peter Schwarz is correct in demanding that such statements not be taken too literally and that the significance of the Chancellor's Rhineland-centred provincialism not be exaggerated, Adenauer's anti-eastern, anti-Prussian bias nevertheless needs to be seen in connection with his inactive line on reunification.[49] Because of his background and general orientation, the *Gründungskanzler* had an easier time accepting Germany's division along an east–west divide than most other leading politicians in post-war Bonn.[50]

Adenauer's fearful attitude towards reunification had a second and more immediate origin in party-political calculations. Throughout his tenure as Chancellor, he dreaded the possibility that his political nemesis, the SPD, might rise to power in Bonn. In the occupation years he demonized the Social Democrats as a revolutionary Marxist movement, based on an 'absolutely materialistic' outlook 'diametrically opposed' to the ideals of Christian democracy, led by a dictatorial figure, and driven by an 'absolute striving for power' comparable to that of the National Socialists.[51] In the 1950s, he similarly labelled the SPD a 'totalitarian party' whose rise to power would spell an 'end to the freedom of the German people'.[52] While spouting such rhetoric—which probably included a strong dose of tactical exaggeration along with a core of genuine concern—Adenauer also fretted about reunification's likely implications for the respective vote tallies of the two largest parties. In an internal CDU discussion in late 1948, he noted with regret that 'a large part of the *Länder* of the Eastern Zone and of Berlin always [had been] social democratic'.[53] As a result, he argued on another occasion, in case of reunification 'we must expect that the Social Democrats will gain the electoral majority in this new Germany'.[54] In his public declarations, the Chancellor predictably denied that such party-political considerations played any role in his reunification policy, but comments like these tell a different story.[55] Revealingly, foreign statesmen who maintained close contact with the Chancellor also believed that the SPD factor helped to hold Adenauer back on the reunification front. Christian Herter, the American Secretary of State, for example, was convinced that Adenauer 'does not want a reunified Germany' because of his fear of the 'large socialist vote in East Germany'.[56]

---

[48] Arnulf Baring, *Aussenpolitik in Adenauers Kanzlerdemokratie* (Munich: DTV, 1969), 54.

[49] Schwarz, 'Adenauer und Europa', 508–10; id., 'Adenauer und Russland', 376–7.

[50] Baring, *Aussenpolitik*, 48–55.

[51] Adenauer in the CDU's *Zonenausschuss*, Lippstadt, 18 Dec. 1946, and Herford, 18 Mar. 1947, in Pütz, *Adenauer*, 256, 290.

[52] Adenauer in the CDU's *Bundesvorstand*, 15 Dec. 1952, in Buchstab, *Alles neu*, 227; and on 23 Nov. 1956, cited in Konrad Repgen, 'Finis Germaniae: Untergang Deutschlands durch einen SPD-Wahlsieg 1957?', in Blumenwitz *et al.*, *Adenauer*, ii. 303.

[53] Adenauer in the Parliamentary Council's CDU/CSU *Fraktion*, 25 Nov. 1948, in Salzmann, *CDU/CSU*, 188.

[54] Adenauer in the CDU's *Zonenausschuss*, Lippstadt, 18 Dec. 1946, in Pütz, *Adenauer*, 255.

[55] See e.g. Adenauer's interview in *Bulletin* (26 Apr. 1952), 487.

[56] Herter's discussion with President Eisenhower, 21 Aug. 1959, *FRUS 1958–1960*, ix. 4.

But the Chancellor's apprehension of the Social Democrats was ultimately only one component of a much broader angst which stood at the centre of his reluctance to engage in the pursuit of reunification. This was a fear of the Germans as a people, which Adenauer vented behind the scenes on numerous occasions. As early as 1948, he professed to party colleagues that the Germans were a 'weak' and confused nation, innately prone to 'radicalism of both the left and right-wing varieties'.[57] In communications with the British during the mid-1950s he asserted that the shocks of recent history had created an 'unstable' German population, in which he personally had 'no confidence'.[58] Because of these innate weaknesses and faults, the Germans could not be trusted to reunify and to manage their own affairs free of external ties and influences. Left to their own devices, Adenauer felt, his countrymen would eventually 'decide to go with Russia or to dance between the blocs' and thus precipitate their own downfall.[59] The only way to save the Germans from themselves was to imbue them with a new, stabilizing ideology of 'democracy and Europe' within an institutional framework of Western integration.[60] In the Chancellor's eyes, this process was an existential necessity and therefore 'more important than . . . unification'.[61]

For the success of this national rescue operation, Adenauer considered himself indispensable. By his own admission 'terribly mistrustful' of other people and even 'contemptuous of humankind', he feared that other politicians would betray his cause and lead Germany back to its old disastrous path of exaggerated and ultimately suicidal self-assertion.[62] 'When I am no longer there, I do not know what will become of Germany', he lamented to two foreign statesmen in an angst-filled moment in September 1954. 'My God, I do not know what my successors will do, if they are left to their own devices, if they are not bound to follow clearly laid tracks, if they are not linked to Europe . . .'[63] Although such panicky rhetoric probably contained instrumental elements, aimed at bolstering Adenauer's own standing, its taproot was genuine worry about the condition of the German people, combined with a conviction that only he could guide the nation out of the wilderness.[64]

Accordingly, Adenauer clearly stated at the very beginning of his Chancellorship that he would follow a 'higher calling', determining the key policies himself and expecting support from his party even if its members did not agree with all his actions.[65] Such semi-authoritarian principles became the norm in his

---

[57] Adenauer in the CDU's *Zonenausschuss*, Königswinter, 28–9 Oct. 1948, in Pütz, *Adenauer*, 720.

[58] Memorandum of Adenauer's discussion with Anthony Eden, 12 Sept. 1954, BA: NL Blankenhorn, 33a; Sir Ivone Kirkpatrick's memorandum of a discussion with the German Ambassador to Great Britain, 16 Dec. 1955, in Foschepoth, *Adenauer*, 289.

[59] Adenauer, 13 June 1962, cited in Osterheld, *Herzens*, 127.

[60] Memorandum of Adenauer's discussion with Eden, 12 Sept. 1954, BA: NL Blankenhorn, 33a.

[61] Sir Ivone Kirkpatrick's 16 Dec. 1955 memorandum (n. 58).

[62] Adenauer's 1951 letter to Roswitha Schlüter, cited in Schwarz, *Staatsmann*, 95.

[63] Adenauer's discussion with Henri Spaak and Josef Bech, 28 Sept. 1954, *Der Spiegel* (6 Oct. 1954), 5–6.

[64] For contrasting views, see Schwarz, *Aufstieg*, 555; id., *Staatsmann*, 147; Baring, *Aussenpolitik*, 57–8; Köhler, *Adenauer*, 16, 871, 1190.

[65] Adenauer in the CDU/CSU's *Bundestagsfraktion*, 1 Sept. 1949, in Wengst, *Auftakt*, 191.

Chancellor democracy. Adenauer repeatedly made major decisions alone, without consulting his cabinet or other leading governmental actors, particularly in foreign policy, which he continued to regard as his special domain even after giving up the formal post of Foreign Minister in June 1955.[66] He also buttressed his own authority at home by frequently assuming the role of a lone arbiter who granted representatives of pressure organizations direct access to himself, thus bypassing and sometimes overruling relevant ministries and other organs.[67]

But even Adenauer did not govern in total isolation, of course; several close associates played significant supporting roles in his system. The Chancellor's Office (*Bundeskanzleramt*) had central importance as a coordinating agency, and some of its top officials—particularly long-term State Secretary Hans Globke—belonged to the inner circle of Bonn's power elite.[68] A number of other figures also rose to key positions as Adenauer's personal advisers and confidants. They included several foreign-policy experts who began their careers in the Chancellor's Office and later switched to key posts in the Foreign Ministry, such as Herbert Blankenhorn, Walter Hallstein, and Wilhelm Grewe. Additional major influences were Felix von Eckardt, the head of the government's Press and Information Office during most of the Adenauer era, and Heinrich Krone, the long-term leader of the CDU/CSU parliamentary group in the Bundestag. However, even these members of the inner circle remained decisively subordinate to the Chancellor, who kept his personal distance, jealously guarded his executive powers, and often actively fuelled personal conflicts and rivalries among his closest associates. Most other members of the governmental hierarchy were significantly less connected to the centre of power, and the main institutions of democratic control stood on the margins of the system.[69] The Chancellor viewed the parliament and the press as 'necessary evils', to quote his leading biographer, and sought to keep both minimally informed.[70] After one particularly long and arduous parliamentary debate he even professed nostalgia for a 'moderate dictatorship' which, he added sarcastically, would 'save lots of time'.[71]

Despite his somewhat authoritarian sentiments, Adenauer was keenly attuned to the political realities of Bonn's parliamentary democracy. He had a sharp eye for the complex interconnections between domestic politics and foreign policy.

---

[66] Arnulf Baring, *Sehr verehrter Herr Bundeskanzler! Heinrich von Brentano im Briefwechsel mit Konrad Adenauer, 1949–1964* (Hamburg: Hoffmann & Campe, 1974), 89–115; Schwarz, 'Adenauers Ostpolitik', 230–2; id., *Aufstieg*, 795, 840, 902, 925–56; Köhler, *Adenauer*, 1049–69, 1204–5.

[67] Karl-Dietrich Bracher, 'Die Kanzlerdemokratie', in Richard Löwenthal and Hans Peter Schwarz (eds.), *Die zweite Republik: 25 Jahre Bundesrepublik Deutschland* (Stuttgart: Seewald, 1974), 192; Wambach, *Verbändestaat*, 115–17. On chancellor democracy, see also Ronald Irving, *Adenauer* (London: Longman, 2002), 151–98.

[68] On the *Bundeskanzleramt*, see Baring, *Aussenpolitik*, 16–48. On Globke, including his murky past as a high-ranking civil servant in the Nazi Interior Ministry, see Schwarz, *Aufstieg*, 658–66; Köhler, *Adenauer*, 724–37; Teschke, *Legacy*, 173–220; Klaus Gotto (ed.), *Der Staatssekretär Adenauers: Persönlichkeit und politisches Wirken Hans Globkes* (Stuttgart: Klett-Cotta, 1980).

[69] Baring, *Aussenpolitik*, 6–48, 163–86; Sabine Lee, *An Uncertain Partnership: British–German Relations between 1955 and 1961* (Bochum: Brockmeyer, 1996), 53–64.

[70] Schwarz, *Staatsmann*, 22, 93.   [71] Adenauer, 6 Dec. 1952, cited in Lenz, *Macht*, 490.

As he explained to a journalist in autumn 1949, 'in a country like Germany, every measure of domestic politics also affects foreign relations, and each move in international affairs influences political events at home'.[72] Adenauer also followed public opinion very closely, keeping abreast of the latest polls and weighing the likely impact of various potential decisions on his popularity closely enough to cause cabinet colleagues to grumble about his excessive caution.[73] Predictably, such sensitivity translated into a steady concern about the next elections, particularly of the Bundestag variety. From the first federal parliamentary elections in 1949 to the last of his Chancellorship in 1961 and beyond, Adenauer never tired of stressing the significance of electoral considerations in all policy fields.[74]

In his pursuit of victory and power, Adenauer knew few scruples. He was capable of great personal coldness—even cruelty—towards other individuals, including governmental and party colleagues, several of whom he suddenly dismissed after years of loyal service as soon as they no longer served his needs.[75] He also used systematic dishonesty as a key political tool. By his own admission he recognized 'several types of truth: the simple, the plain and the pure' and observed a specific maxim in his interactions with the media: 'you lie to me, and I do not tell you the truth either'.[76] In practice, these axioms translated into consistent false promises and downright lies aimed at courting specific segments of the electorate. These clever but unscrupulous tactics were particularly evident in Adenauer's handling of the expellees in general and the political demands of their purported organizational representatives in particular. As the following pages will illustrate, the Chancellor played the expellee card to his government's advantage in two different contexts during Bonn's pre-sovereignty period: in the domestic consolidation of his Western integration policy on the one hand and in the international bargaining about the precise content of that policy on the other.

ADENAUER AND THE EXPELLEES IN THE DOMESTIC CONTEXT

In the domestic political context, the expellees served several functions in Adenauer's tactical calculations. From an electoral viewpoint alone, their significance was considerable. As a seemingly coherent and well-organized group of more than eight million, they constituted a force that could potentially make or break the government's parliamentary majority. Acutely aware of these realities,

---

[72] Adenauer in a 16 Sept. 1949 interview, cited in Kosthorst, *Kaiser*, 103.

[73] Daniel Kosthorst, *Brentano und die deutsche Einheit: Die Deutschland- und Ostpolitik des Aussenministers im Kabinett Adenauer 1955–61* (Düsseldorf: Droste, 1993), 404; Franz Josef Strauss, *Die Erinnerungen* (Berlin: Siedler, 1989), 333.

[74] Adenauer in the CDU's *Zonenausschuss*, Königswinter, 24–5 Feb. 1949, in Pütz, *Adenauer*, 800; Adenauer's memorandum of a discussion with Franz-Josef Strauss and Karl Carstens, 3 Aug. 1961, cited in Schwarz, *Staatsmann*, 656.

[75] State Secretary Otto Lenz and Foreign Minister Heinrich von Brentano were among those abruptly dismissed. On their reactions, see, Lenz, *Macht*, 706–16; Baring, *Bundeskanzler*, 339–91.

[76] Baring, *Aussenpolitik*, 184–5, with n. 68.

Adenauer stressed that the expellee bloc's electoral significance 'must not be underestimated'.[77] This error was to be avoided not only because of the number of expellees as such but also because of their role as the core component of a broader segment of the electorate: the German nationalists. This crucial voter category—characterized by its members' devotion to the rebuilding of a strong German nation state through reunification, the reacquisition of the lost eastern territories, and other similar causes—encompassed major sections of several subgroups of the population. Along with expellees, Soviet Zone refugees and war veterans—particularly former Eastern front POWs—were well-represented in this camp, which also included numerous influential politicians from Adenauer's own party and its federal coalition partners. Together, such nationalistically oriented circles formed a powerful electoral force, difficult to define in its precise scope but crucial for the Chancellor's success at the polls, not least because the vast majority of the population sympathized with at least some of this bloc's favourite causes.[78]

The expellees' tactical usefulness for Adenauer and his policies was not restricted to the purely electoral sphere, however. A public identification with the expellees and the national causes associated with them also promised to reward his government in several other ways. With hard-line rhetoric, the Chancellor could present himself as a tough, national-minded advocate of reunification and thus build something of an alibi against the opposition's attempts to portray him as an obstacle to German unity.[79] By similar means, Adenauer could also facilitate anti-Communist mobilization among the population. Accordingly, he and his ministers were quick to portray the brutal expulsions as living proof of the evils of Bolshevik totalitarianism, often in language strikingly similar to anti-Communist and anti-Russian oratory prevalent during earlier epochs of German history, including the Third Reich.[80]

In addition, the government's pro-expellee stance contributed to a broader legitimation and identity-building process, in which other actors—such as opposition politicians, free publicists, and expellee leaders—were also engaged. By highlighting Communist crimes, German suffering, and the Federal Republic's stature as a defender of minority rights and international justice, Germans could try to deflect attention from crimes committed in their nation's name under the Nazi regime and thus promote the creation of a new, positive, and forward-looking identity in West Germany.[81] This reassuring image, in turn, was well-suited to ease the new state's acceptance into the Western Alliance as a powerful, remilitarized anti-Communist bulwark only a few years after the end of a global conflict launched by none other than the Germans.

[77] Adenauer to the Minister Presidents of Rheinland-Pfalz, Nordrhein-Westfalen, Bayern, and Schleswig-Holstein, 31 May 1952, in Hans-Peter Mensing (ed.), *Konrad Adenauer: Briefe, 1951–1953* (Berlin: Siedler, 1987), 224.

[78] Schwarz, *Aufstieg*, 655–6; id., 'Konzept', 144–5; Diehl, *Thanks*; Heidemeyer, *Flüchtlingspolitik*; Glaab, *Deutschlandpolitik*, 231–45, 245–51.

[79] Foschepoth, *Adenauer*, esp. 14, 17, 20, 22, 30–1.

[80] Niedhart and Altmann, 'Beurteilung', esp. 112.

[81] Moeller, *War Stories*; id., 'War Stories'; Hughes, 'No Fault'.

With such goals in mind, Adenauer's government also took the additional step of sponsoring a massive, multi-volume publication series entitled 'Documentation of the Expulsion of Germans from East–Central Europe' (*Dokumentation der Vertreibung der Deutschen aus Ostmitteleuropa*). Initially conceived by expellee activists during the occupation era and then quickly adopted by the government, the series combined hundreds of dramatic eyewitness accounts by German expellees with analysis and commentary by selected academic experts. Although serious and scholarly in tone and content, the project's ultimate purpose for the government was highly politicized: to highlight German suffering and thus to serve as an instrument of 'guilt relativization' for the West German state. Accordingly, the various document volumes were widely distributed in both Germany and abroad, including in English translation, largely in order to promote Bonn's broader political agenda.[82]

Although Adenauer's primary motives for championing expellee causes were thus of a tactical—and particularly electoral—nature, he also harboured genuine concerns about the potential hazards posed by the millions of newcomers. At least through the early 1950s, he dreaded a radicalization of the expellee masses. He worried that West Germany's democratic system might be destabilized by the large-scale 'economic and political unrest' which he expected to ensue if the government failed to heed the demands of the expellees.[83] At the same time, he drew a causal link between a pacification of the expellees and the success of his Westpolitik. Because the Federal Republic's 'outer and inner strength and security [could] not be separated from each other', Adenauer argued, the domestic integration of potentially malcontented elements, chief among them the expellees, constituted a key prerequisite of a successful foreign policy.[84] Isolated and resentful minorities would, after all, be likely to follow the siren calls of Communism or old-style nationalism and thus to undermine the westward orientation which the Chancellor hoped to inculcate in the West German citizenry.

For these various reasons, Adenauer made sure that his government paid extensive attention to the expellees and their purported organizational representatives. One of his key areas of engagement was social policy. Particularly during the first few years of the Federal Republic, he repeatedly pressured his cabinet to expedite the passage and implementation of legislation aimed at facilitating expellee integration.[85] The Chancellor was especially active in promoting the

---

[82] Beer, 'Spannungsfeld', esp. 387; id., 'Dokumentation'; Moeller, *War Stories*, 51–87.

[83] Adenauer to Fritz Schäffer, 4 Dec. 1950, StBKAH: III/21 (1).

[84] McCloy to the Secretary of State, 17 Nov. 1950, *FRUS 1950*, iv. 781; Adenauer to Dannie N. Heinemann, 15 Nov. 1950, in Mensing, *Adenauer: Briefe 1949–1951*, 307; *Konrad Adenauer im Briefwechsel mit Flüchtlingen und Vertriebenen*, ed. Hans Peter Mensing (Bonn: Kulturstiftung der Vertriebenen, 1999), 18–22.

[85] Adenauer in the cabinet, on 8 June and 2 Oct. 1951, in *Die Kabinettsprotokolle der Bundesregierung*, ed. H. Booms et al., iv. *1951* (Boppard am Rhein: Harald Boldt, 1989), 427, 672; and on 31 Mar. 1953, in *Die Kabinettsprotokolle der Bundesregierung*, ed. H. Booms et al., vi. *1953* (Boppard am Rhein: Harald Boldt, 1992), 244.

Equalization of Burdens Act of 1952, whose fundamental significance for the Federal Republic's future development he repeatedly stressed.[86]

Adenauer's eagerness to please the expellees showed even more clearly in his readiness to commit his government to a public embrace of the main Ostpolitik demands of the expellee organizations. Prior to the founding of the Federal Republic, Adenauer, like other leading politicians in western Germany, had repeatedly rejected the Oder-Neisse line as a boundary between Germany and Poland and, on the basis of the Potsdam Agreement, insisted on the continued validity of the Reich's 1937 borders. As Chancellor, he committed the Federal Republic to similar stances. From his first government declaration, presented to the Bundestag on 20 September 1949, to the end of his tenure, Adenauer maintained an inflexible public line on the territorial issue. Officially, he and his government rejected the Oder-Neisse settlement, claimed that the Reich continued to exist within its 1937 boundaries, and demanded that decisions over territorial questions be made only in a future peace treaty among a free, reunified Germany and the victors of the Second World War.[87]

Although this carefully calibrated official position, which reflected the maximum demands acceptable to the Western Powers, did not explicitly state what the final peace treaty *should* decide, occasional public addresses by Adenauer and his ministers, particularly in front of expellee audiences, typically went a step further, highlighting Bonn's determination to ensure that the boundaries of 1937 would in fact be restored in the final peace settlement.[88] The expellees' rights to their homelands and to self-determination likewise received avid rhetorical support from the government. In typical declarations, the Chancellor praised the *Heimatrecht* as the 'most elementary right given to humankind by God' and professed that, with 'patience', the just expellee cause would 'prevail . . . in the end'.[89]

The government's rhetorical support of the expellee organizations' Ostpolitik desiderata remained subject to clear limits, however. On the most elementary level, the Chancellor and his representatives categorically renounced violence as an Eastern policy tool.[90] They also carefully balanced their general advocacy of the *Heimatrecht* and the self-determination right of *all* German expellees with an avoidance of open claims to territories beyond the Reich's 1937 borders. This rhetorical juggling was most obvious vis-à-vis the Sudeten Germans, by far the largest and most influential non-*Reichsdeutsche* expellee group. Adenauer himself

---

[86] Adenauer to Fritz Schäffer, 4 Dec. 1950, StBKAH: III/21 (1); Adenauer in the CDU's *Bundesvorstand*, 5 Sept. 1952, in Buchstab, *Alles neu*, 146; Hughes, *Shouldering*, 172–3; Patton, *Cold*, 52–3.

[87] Government declarations of 20 Sept. 1949, 28 June 1956, and 5 Nov. 1959, in *Verhandlungen*, I WP, pp. 29C–D, III WP, pp. 8541A ff. and 4691B–C.

[88] Adenauer's 6 Oct. 1951 Berlin speech, *Keesings Archiv der Gegenwart*, 21 (1951): 3146–7; Jakob Kaiser's 9 Apr. 1955 radio address, *Bulletin* (14 Apr. 1955), 569–70.

[89] Adenauer's greeting to the *Schlesiertreffen* of July 1954, attached to Adenauer to Walter Rinke, 8 July 1954, BA: B 136, 6791; Adenauer's address to the Exil-CDU, 22 Mar. 1953, *Bulletin* (24 March 1953), 473; Mensing, *Briefwechsel*.

[90] Adenauer's address to a Silesian rally, 28 June 1953, *Bulletin* (30 June 1953), 1020; Jakob Kaiser's 22 Mar. 1953 speech at the Exil-CDU's *Parteitag*, *Bulletin* (24 Mar. 1953), 474.

set down the guidelines, stressing that governmental representatives should avoid 'all political notes' when addressing Sudeten German audiences. The *Heimatrecht* problem was to be covered 'only in general form', as a human right that could be denied neither to the Sudeten Germans nor to anybody else.[91] Accordingly, one government representative after another addressed Sudeten German rallies in flowery but vague language which activists of the Sudetendeutsche Landsmannschaft could interpret as supportive of their revisionist goals but whose real purpose was to avoid such commitments without risking an open clash between the government and the expellee lobby.[92]

The deceptive intent evident in Adenauer's stance on the *Heimatrecht* of the Sudeten Germans reflected a much broader pattern: the Chancellor's lack of genuine interest in any of the Ostpolitik causes which he publicly claimed to support. Even the primary revisionist demand—the reacquisition of the lost eastern provinces—left him cold from the start. As early as 1946, Adenauer reportedly professed to a party colleague his joy at the fact that 'we have got rid of the colonial territory in the East'.[93] A string of similar behind-the-scenes statements followed in the ensuing years, highlighting both Adenauer's conviction that the eastern territories were gone for good—not least because the victorious Western Powers had no desire to return them to Germany—and his explicit refusal to reveal this unpleasant fact to the public.[94] In closed circles, the Chancellor also acknowledged his lack of respect for expellee-style foreign-policy arguments phrased in the loose, unenforceable terms of presumed rights.[95] *Heimatrecht* was thus no tool of practical policy for him, and the definition which he and his associates gave to the concept had in any case very little in common with the views of expellee activists. To Adenauer and his advisers, *Heimatrecht* denoted, at best, the possibility that some of the expellees might eventually return to their former homelands as a minority 'under foreign rule'—a prospect which expellee leaders consistently denounced as unacceptable.[96]

Along with social legislation and revisionist Ostpolitik rhetoric, Adenauer's government employed several other, more immediately tangible means of courting and integrating the expellees. The inclusion of expellee representatives into

[91] Herbert Blankenhorn to the Ministry for All-German Affairs, 26 May 1952, PA/AA: Abt. 3. 753.

[92] Franz Thedieck at the 1952 *Sudetendeutscher Tag* in Stuttgart, *Bulletin* (6 June 1952), 699–700; Jakob Kaiser at the 1953 *Sudetendeutscher Tag*, Frankfurt, *Bulletin* (27 May 1953), 831.

[93] Ernst Lemmer's comments to Robert Murphy, 5 Sept. 1948, cited in Köhler, *Adenauer*, 469.

[94] Adenauer's off-the-record discussion with select journalists, 6 Sept. 1951, in *Teegespräche, 1950–1954*, ed. Küsters, 138; his reported remarks to Erich Ollenhauer, 30 Aug. 1953, cited in Fritz Sänger, 'sgr. 30.VIII.1953', AdsD: NL Fritz Sänger, 280; Giulio Andreotti's reminiscences about Alcide De Gasperi's 1952 visit to Bonn, cited in Hans-Jakob Stehle, 'Adenauer, Polen und die Deutsche Frage', in Foschepoth, *Adenauer*, 81; Hanns-Jürgen Küsters, *Der Integrationsfriede: Viermächte-Verhandlungen über die Friedensregelung mit Deutschland 1945–1990* (Munich: Oldenbourg, 2000), esp. 611–13. See also id., 'Konrad Adenauer und Willy Brandt in der Berlin-Krise 1958–1963', *VfZ* 40 (1992): 507–8, and Axel Frohn, 'Adenauer und die deutschen Ostgebiete in den fünfziger Jahren', *VfZ* 44 (1996): 522, for contrasting evaluations of the second source cited above.

[95] Adenauer in the CDU's *Bundesvorstand*, 26 Apr. 1954, in Buchstab, *Etwas geschaffen*, 195.

[96] Report by the US Ambassador in London about a discussion with Blankenhorn, 17 June 1953, *FRUS 1952–1954*, vii. 475.

the governmental machinery played an important role in these efforts. The most obvious beneficiary of the inclusion strategy was the expellee party GB/BHE, which the Chancellor incorporated into his cabinet after the 1953 Bundestag elections. Adenauer harboured no sympathy for the GB/BHE as such, which he regarded as a potentially dangerous, one-issue splinter group.[97] But by assigning ministerial posts to Waldemar Kraft and Theodor Oberländer, the party's two key leaders, he expected to reap several benefits. Most obviously, he wanted a two-thirds majority in the parliament, necessary for the passage of several highly contested Western integration measures.[98] Additionally, he hoped to accelerate the GB/BHE's demise by luring the party into governmental 'responsibility and co-operation' and thus undermining its demagogic, oppositional profile. In the process, he also intended to pull the GB/BHE's 'good elements' into the CDU/CSU's orbit, thus preventing them from allying with the SPD or merging into a nationalistically oriented right-wing party with similarly minded sections of the FDP.[99]

In addition to the two GB/BHE ministers, other expellees also rose to prominent roles in Adenauer's government. Hans Lukaschek, a CDU-affiliated Silesian activist, headed the Ministry for Expellee Affairs from the autumn of 1949 until his replacement by Theodor Oberländer four years later. The Sudeten German leader and Deutsche Partei luminary Hans-Christoph Seebohm became Minister of Transport in the first Adenauer cabinet and clung to that post for nearly two decades. Below the cabinet level, expellee representatives were likewise present, particularly in the Ministry for Expellee Affairs, many of whose civil servants had a history of at least some activity in the various *Vertriebenenverbände*. Similar, albeit weaker, personal links also existed between the organized expellee movement and the career officialdom of other ministries, such as the Ministry for All-German Affairs or—to a much more limited extent—the Auswärtiges Amt.[100] In addition, the expellee organizations carried out certain auxiliary functions in the government's administrative machinery. This role was particularly pronounced in the implementation of the Equalization of Burdens Act, in which expert bodies composed of expellee activists played a crucial role as examiners of the validity of individual compensation claims.[101]

The personal ties fostered by the presence of expellee representatives within the government were complemented by a broader patchwork of contacts between the expellee organizations and several key ministries. From the beginning of the 1950s, regular meetings took place among expellee activists and middle-level civil servants from the Ministries for All-German, Expellee, and Foreign Affairs. Some of these contacts were institutionalized. The Expellee Ministry, for example, established an official advisory council (*Beirat*), which brought together representatives of the

[97] Adenauer in the CDU's *Bundesvorstand*, 5 Sept. 1952, in Buchstab, *Alles neu*, 147.

[98] Adenauer in the CDU's *Bundesvorstand*, 10 Sept. 1953, in Buchstab, *Etwas geschaffen*, 7.

[99] Adenauer in the CDU's *Bundesvorstand*, 19 Jan. 1954, ibid. 108; Adenauer in the CDU's *Bundesvorstand*, 2 May 1955, ibid. 459–61; Lenz, *Macht*, 695; Bösch, *Adenauer-CDU*, esp. 174–80.

[100] Wambach, *Verbändestaat*, 125–37.   [101] Ibid. 65–9, 131–4.

government, the expellee groups, and other interested parties to analyse problems of expellee integration.[102] The three ministries also jointly organized a special consultative forum (*Dämmerschoppen*) under whose auspices expellee leaders, politicians, and government officials periodically convened for informal discussions of foreign policy, particularly Ostpolitik.[103] Additional meetings between ministry functionaries and expellee representatives occurred on an *ad hoc* basis to address various common concerns, especially in social and foreign policy.[104]

Although rank-and-file civil servants were responsible for the vast majority of these contacts, periodically expellee activists also gained access to the men at the very top. Adenauer himself could be reached in several ways. An indirect link between the Chancellor and the expellee lobby ran through party-politically prominent expellee leaders. In the Bundestag, a handful of expellee deputies from various parties was privy to the confidential—albeit guarded and typically untruthful—policy reports which Adenauer periodically provided to select parliamentary committees, particularly the Committee for Foreign Affairs.[105] Somewhat more significance accrued to the personal meetings which the Chancellor occasionally granted to high-level expellee politicians from within the CDU/CSU. Here the activists typically presented themselves as representatives of the party-internal special organs of the expellees.[106] The most important encounters, however, took place directly between the Chancellor or his representatives and delegations of various expellee pressure groups. These meetings occurred in clusters at politically important junctures and were led by either Adenauer himself or one of his closest associates, most frequently the *eminence grise* of the Chancellor's Office, Hans Globke.

Prior to the passage of the Equalization of Burdens Bill in August 1952, problems of social policy dominated the sessions.[107] Thereafter, the prime focus switched to international affairs. Two waves of meetings—the first between late 1952 and early 1953 and the second two years later, each coinciding with a critical phase in the ratification of the Western Treaties—concentrated on the government's foreign policy.[108] Whatever their precise thematic focus, these direct

---

[102] *Bulletin* (18 Mar. 1954), 424; (31 Mar. 1954), 520. Extensive further documentation exists in BA: B 150, 1954.

[103] Kossmann, 'Aufzeichnung betr: Landsmannschaften', 6 July 1953, PA/AA: Abt. 3. 620; 'Betr: 10 Jahres-Gedanken der Vertreibung der Ostdeutschen. Arbeitsbesprechung im "Dämmerschoppenkreis" am 14.2.1955', PA/AA: Abt. 7. 286.

[104] Detailed reports in Wuschek to Lodgman, 20 Oct. 1952 and 25 Feb. 1953, SDA: NL Lodgman, XXIV-01.

[105] See e.g. Adenauer's reports of 27 Mar. and 3 Sept. 1952, BT/PA: Ausschuss für das Besatzungsstatut und für auswärtige Angelegenheiten, I WP, folders 5 and 6.

[106] Kather to Adenauer, 3 Nov. 1952, ACDP: I-377-004/3; Landesverband Oder-Neisse, 'Kurzbericht über die Zeit vom 27.7 bis 16.8.1953', ACDP: VII-004-406/2.

[107] Kather to Lukaschek, 12 Feb. 1950, BA: B 150, 1150/2; protocol of Adenauer's meeting with expellee representatives, 31 Jan. 1951, BA: N 1412, 20.

[108] For examples, see the reports of the 2 Dec. 1952 meeting of BvD representatives with Globke and others, in Wuschek to Lodgman, 3 Dec. 1952, SDA: NL Lodgman, XI/9; of the 3 Feb. 1955 meeting between a VdL delegation and Adenauer, in Manteuffel-Szoege to Lodgman, 4 Mar. 1955, SDA: NL Lodgman, XXIV-01; and of the 7 Mar. 1955 meeting between VdL and government representatives in 'Die Anwälte der Regierung beim VdL', *Sudetendeutsche Zeitung* (12 Mar. 1955).

encounters between the Chancellor and the expellee organizations typically featured queries and complaints from the expellee side and soothing talk and soft promises from the government. The obvious aim of the whole procedure was to provide the organized expellee lobby with a sense of inclusion and to secure its support for key governmental policies.

Along with personal ties of various kinds, another, more tangible medium played a major role in the government's efforts to court the expellees: public money. With the Chancellor's explicit support, the cabinet decided by early 1950 to begin subsidizing 'not only the umbrella organizations of the expellees but also the individual homeland societies'.[109] Within a few months, the money began to flow, and in 1953 the public funding became solidly institutionalized, as the Federal Expellee Law committed the government to supporting the cultural heritage and development of the expellees, which the expellee organizations claimed to embody. The subsidies issued from several different sources. Along with various *Land*-level authorities, five branches of the federal government opened their purse strings. By far the largest sums emanated from the Ministries for All-German and Expellee Affairs, although the Interior Ministry, the Federal Press and Information Office, and the Auswärtiges Amt also provided smaller contributions.[110] The total figures soon grew relatively large. For the 1952/3 fiscal year, for example, the umbrella organization ZvD received some 187,000 DM in federal subsidies, while a year later its rival group VdL drew in approximately 179,000 DM.[111] In the following years, the amounts increased further. According to its own internal figures, the federal government subsidized the various expellee groups to the tune of some 15.5 million DM during the years 1957–9 alone.[112]

At first sight, the concrete support provided by the government in the form of personal connections and generous subsidies appears very impressive, and in many ways it did bolster the expellee movement. But behind the state's seeming generosity there lurked a strong ulterior motive: a desire for control. The financial subsidies, for example, were envisaged as a control instrument from the start. A 1952 Foreign Office memorandum made this rationale particularly clear, explaining in detail how the apparent largesse in fact aimed at creating a situation of financial dependence which, in turn, would facilitate 'the exertion of influence' on the expellee organizations.[113] The strategy paid off, as the expellee groups soon became heavily dependent on public funding. By the mid-1950s, both umbrella organizations, as well as the vast majority of the individual homeland societies, had reached a point where they could no longer function without governmental

---

[109] Cabinet meeting, 17 Feb. 1950, in *Kabinettsprotokolle 1950*, ed. Booms, 213; Kather to Lukaschek, 12 Feb. 1950, BA: B 150, 1150/2. [110] Wambach, *Verbändestaat*, 138–44.

[111] ZvD, 'Verwendungsnachweis' for 1952/3, 27 Apr. 1953, BA: B 137, 2253; VdL, 'Kassenbericht für das Geschäftsjahr 1953/54', SDA: NL Lodgman, V/25.

[112] 'Betr: Bericht der Bundesregierung über die von ihr in den Rechnungsjahren 1957, 1958 und 1959 getroffenen Massnahmen gemäss 96 BVFG', 30 Aug. 1960, BT/PA: Ausschuss für Heimatvertriebene, 3. WP, Ausschuss-Drucksachen, vol. 115, pp. 50–1.

[113] 'Einflussnahme des Auswärtigen Amtes auf die deutschen Heimatvertriebenen', 29 Sept. 1952, PA/AA: Abt. 3. 214.

subsidies.[114] Of the major expellee groups, only the Sudeten-German Homeland Society managed to maintain relative independence. In the mid-1950s, it apparently received well over half of its income from membership dues, voluntary donations, and other sources beyond the public coffers.[115] But even the Sudeten Germans—like all other expellee groups—were obliged to earmark their governmental subsidies to specific, pre-approved purposes and to submit detailed annual reports of their compliance with these prescriptions, which obviously increased the authorities' sway over the organizations.[116]

The government's interest in control also manifested itself in the various personal connections between state representatives and the expellee groups. The regular meetings between the two sides benefited the government in at least two ways. First, they provided reliable first-hand information about internal developments within the expellee lobby. The Foreign Ministry, for example, often received advance notice of planned actions from leading expellee organizations and could thus anticipate upcoming developments.[117] Second, the encounters provided an excellent avenue for the exertion of influence over the expellee movement. As indicated above, Adenauer and his associates used their meetings with expellee leaders primarily for the purpose of persuading the latter to support the government's policies, often with the aid of rhetorical tricks and false promises. Other sessions focused more directly on reshaping stances which the expellee organizations had already adopted but which the authorities considered potentially detrimental to broader state interests. A key objective of some of the informal *Dämmerschoppen* discussions among Bonn's civil servants and expellee activists, for example, was to induce the expellee groups to change their public portrayal of the background of the expulsions. In complete disregard of the historical record—but with considerable success—the Foreign Office insisted that the organizations present the expulsions as an 'eastern product' which the Western Powers had approved only belatedly and under duress.[118]

The co-optation of expellee representatives into state offices also ultimately proved more beneficial for the government than for the expellee organizations. The expellee leaders in question typically underwent difficult role conflicts, torn between the clashing demands of the government and their base organizations. Loyalty to the former usually prevailed. The vast majority of the expellee activists

---

[114] Federal subsidies constituted 187,000 of the ZvD's total income of 215,454.55 DM in 1952/3, whereas the VdL apparently had no other income than its 179,314.50 DM in subsidies in 1953/4. See n. 111. The Landsmannschaft der Oberschlesier illustrates an average homeland society's dependence on the government. In 1954–5, the organization's total budget of 36,586.42 DM included 27,007.40 in subsidies, 'Jahreshaushaltübersicht für die Zeit vom 1.4.1954–31.3. 1955', ALdO: Bundesministerien, sonstige Behörden, AA, Bundesregierung, 17 Nov. 1949–31 Dec. 1956.

[115] The organization's 1954 budget envisaged a total expenditure of 340,000 DM, some 48,000 DM of which was to be governmental subsidies. 'Der politische Standort der Volksgruppe', *Sudetendeutsche Zeitung* (12 June 1954), 4.   [116] Wambach, *Verbändestaat*, 141–2

[117] Descriptions of meetings between Sudeten German and AA representatives in Wuschek to Lodgman, 19 Sept. 1952; and Karl Simon to Lodgman, 25 Feb. 1955, SDA: NL Lodgman, XXIV-02.

[118] Wuschek's account of the 14 Feb. 1955 meeting, Wuschek to Lodgman, SDA: NL Lodgman, XXIV-01.

who held posts in Bonn soon began to identify with the government and its view-points on most issues, which was hardly surprising, given the prospects of personal prestige and advancement provided by a state position. At the same time, however, most of these individuals maintained at least some affiliation with the expellee movement. They thus became important intermediaries who gener-ally sought to promulgate, or at least to defend, the government's viewpoints and policies among the expellees.

This behaviour pattern was evident on the ministerial level, where cabinet and party discipline magnified the pressure for conformity. Hans Lukaschek, the first federal Minister for Expellee Affairs, for example, became pro-government to a degree that sometimes baffled even his co-activists in the umbrella group ZvD.[119] Waldemar Kraft and Theodor Oberländer, the two GB/BHE representatives in Adenauer's second cabinet, fought a prolonged intra-party battle against radical elements opposed to several aspects of Adenauer's Westpolitik.[120] And even Hans-Christoph Seebohm, who in the course of the early 1950s gained growing notoriety for his occasional, radical-sounding addresses to Sudeten German audi-ences, took care to toe the government line on other issues and to explain away any rhetorical excesses as soon as protest emerged within the cabinet.[121]

The same dynamics of loyalty also manifested themselves at lower, civil servant levels. An excellent example was the case of Wilhelm Turnwald, a Sudeten German activist recruited to the Auswärtiges Amt in keeping with the Ministry's plan of increasing its influence over the expellee movement through direct personal ties.[122] Soon after his entry to the Ministry, Turnwald admitted that he now 'had to be very careful in all matters related to the expellee organizations' so as not to lose his credibility as a civil servant. Accordingly, he exhorted Sudeten German representatives to adopt moderate, pro-government Ostpolitik stances and provided his Ministry with detailed reports of internal developments within the Sudetendeutsche Landsmannschaft.[123]

The government's attitude towards the expellee organizations and the degree of control to be exerted over them was by no means monolithic, however. Two ministries generally outshone the others with their sympathy for the expellees, despite the various personal role conflicts and other restraining influences. Predictably, the Ministry for Expellee Affairs topped the list, followed by the Ministry for All-German Affairs, which became a strong advocate of national causes and constituencies under its long-term head, Jakob Kaiser. But even these relative bastions of sympathy provided only limited benefits for the expellee groups. The two ministries engaged in prolonged rivalries over primacy in the expellee sector,

---

[119] Wambach, *Verbändestaat*, 125–6. [120] Neumann, *Block*, 97–167.
[121] For a typical exchange, see Adenauer to Seebohm, 16 June 1953, BA: NL Seebohm, 1a; Seebohm to Adenauer, 18 June 1953, SDA: NL Lodgman, XXIV-21.00.
[122] 'Einflussnahme des Auswärtigen Amtes auf die deutschen Heimatvertriebenen', 29 Sept. 1952, PA/AA: Abt. 3. 214; 'Vermerk, Betr: Bewerbung Dr. Wilhelm Turnwald', 5 Mar. 1953, PA/AA: Abt. 3. 755.
[123] Karl Simon to Lodgman, 25 Feb. 1955, SDA: NL Lodgman, XXIV-02; Turnwald, 'Aufzeichnung, Betr: Konstituierung des Sudetendeutschen Rats in München', 18 Apr. 1955, PA/AA: Abt. 7. 295.

which reduced their joint impact within the government.[124] More fundamentally, neither ministry possessed a particularly solid position within Bonn's Chancellor democracy, and the Expellee Ministry's footing was especially weak.

Accordingly, key policy decisions relevant to expellee causes were usually made elsewhere. Along with the omnipresent Chancellor's Office, the main power centres were the Finance and Economics Ministries on social policy and the Foreign Ministry on Ostpolitik. In addition, all the branches of the central government—even the two ministries closest to the expellees—agreed on the need to minimize the active influence of the expellee groups on policy formulation and implementation. In foreign affairs, this intra-governmental accord was particularly strong and resulted in a total exclusion of expellee representatives from the inner sanctums of the foreign-policy machinery. A good indication of this trend was the expellee organizations' inability to win governmental support for their plans to conduct 'active Ostpolitik' by means of aggressive PR campaigns in the West. Revealingly, the Foreign Ministry rejected such proposals as a misguided and dangerous 'disturbance' and dismissed leading expellee activists as incompetent dilettantes unsuited for diplomatic tasks.[125]

Despite the deception and the ulterior motives, the Adenauer government's efforts at courting and integrating the expellees proved remarkably successful. A comparison of the general situation in the expellee sector between the beginning of the Adenauer era and the mid-1950s illustrates this point. In the Federal Republic's early stages, the problems had seemed severe. The expellees constituted an uprooted, socially and economically deprived mass that was widely assumed to be susceptible to radical influences. The crisis atmosphere was fuelled further by the leaders of the expellee organizations, who frequently vented their doubts about the value of a state that 'lacks sovereignty and depends for its existence upon the will of foreign powers'.[126] By the mid-1950s, the picture looked very different. Expellee activists accepted West Germany's legitimacy and viewed cooperation with Bonn as 'the only real basis' for their political pursuits.[127] The vast majority of the rank-and-file expellees abided by the ground rules of the democratic system and demonstrated loyalty to the government. The dreaded large-scale radicalization had thus failed to take place, and each passing year made such an outcome appear ever less likely.

---

[124] Wambach, *Verbändestaat*, esp. 142–3.

[125] German Mission in Washington to the Auswärtiges Amt, 18 Nov. 1952, PA/AA: Abt. 3. 754; Walter Hallstein, 'Betr: Einrichtung von Werbestellen der Landsmannschaften in den USA', 31 Dec. 1953, BA: B 136/6515; Krekeler to the Auswärtiges Amt, 15 June 1955, PA/AA: Abt. 7. 292; 'Vermerk: Besprechung Botschafter a.D. v. Dirksen—Staatssekretär Thedieck', 6 Dec. 1952, PA/AA: Abt. 3. 623/1. While refusing to yield to the expellee groups' substantive demands, the Foreign Office made other, cosmetic concessions: e.g. it funded occasional private visits to the USA by expellee representatives.

[126] Sudetendeutsche Landsmannschaft, Wiesbaden resolution, 4 Nov. 1950, SDA: NL Lodgman, XII/6:1.

[127] Rudolf Lodgman von Auen's address 'Grundlagen und Arbeitsziele der sudetendeutschen Aussenpolitik' to the *Hauptvorstand* of the Sudeten-German Homeland Society, Heiligenhof, 23–5 Oct. 1953, SDA: NL Lodgman, IV/4:13, 5.

The reasons for this remarkable success were manifold. In the purely domestic context, the obvious key variable was the socio-economic integration of the expellees, which was well under way by the mid-1950s. Although many problems still remained, by mid-decade the expellees had made significant gains in housing and employment, for example.[128] The so-called economic miracle provided the backdrop for these advances, but specific social policies of the government, particularly the Equalization of Burdens legislation, played a major role as well. Although most expellee activists had initially been less than enthusiastic about the 1952 law, which they considered insufficient, their attitudes soon began to change, particularly as numerous amendments fine-tuned the original measure over the ensuing years.[129] By 1955, the umbrella group VdL, for example, no longer shied back from public declarations of faith in the government's good will in this policy area.[130] At the same time, the government also contributed to the growing pacification of the expellees through other means. The inclusive tactics that tied the GB/BHE to cabinet responsibility, built personal and financial bridges to the expellee organizations, and assigned specific administrative tasks to expellee experts helped to reconcile expellee representatives to the existing political system, thus forestalling radical tendencies.[131]

The government's success in persuading the bulk of the expellee movement to support Adenauer's foreign policy also made a key contribution to the Federal Republic's stability and security. By the early 1950s, most expellee leaders had come to accept the basic policy principles promulgated by the Chancellor. On the most fundamental level, the expellee elites shared the government's fervent anti-Communism.[132] As a consequence, they had little trouble approving of West Germany's integration into the cold war West, at least for the moment. They cheered ongoing advances in 'Franco-German cooperation', advocated further steps towards European unity, and in general stressed the need to build Western Europe into a powerful anti-Soviet bulwark.[133] Logically, the activists also gave their blessing to West German rearmament, which they justified as an essential 'defence against Bolshevism'.[134] Less predictable was their somewhat grudging acceptance of the temporal priorities inherent in Adenauer's overall concept,

[128] Reichling, *Vertriebene*, ii. 74, 108.

[129] Signs of dissatisfaction include Rudolf Lodgman von Auen's address at the 1952 *Sudetendeutscher Tag* in Stuttgart, in Simon, *Lodgman*, esp. 105; and his comments in the *Hauptversammlung* of the Sudetendeutsche Landsmannschaft, 21 Sept. 1952, SDA: NL Lodgman, I/0/2:5.

[130] 'Bundespräsident und Bundeskanzler empfingen VdL-Vertreter', 3 Feb. 1955, SDA: NL Lodgman, XXIV-01.

[131] Hughes, *Shouldering*, esp. 165–98; id., 'Restitution'; Holtmann, 'Politische'; Steinert, 'Flucht-lingsvereinigungen', esp. 63–4; Haerendel, 'Politik', esp. 132–3.

[132] See e.g. Rudolf Lodgman von Auen, 'Ein deutsches und europäisches Ostprogramm', Dec. 1953, in Simon, *Lodgman*, esp. 140–4; Walter Rinke's address to a Silesian rally, 18 July 1954, *Bulletin* (21 July 1954), 1204.

[133] 'Europas Einheit nur in Freiheit', *Sudetendeutsche Zeitung* (21 Apr. 1951), 1.

[134] VOL, 'Kommentar zur Resolution der Sprechertagung über den Sicherheitsbeitrag', Nov. 1951, SDA: B VIII/4.

according to which the build-up of Western strength constituted a precondition for progress on reunification and other German national causes.[135]

Despite this far-ranging agreement on a number of basic principles, the expellee elites disagreed with the Chancellor on several specific issues, the most important of which centred on the problem of German unity. The main points of discord were the urgency of reunification and the territorial definition of the future Reich. On the latter issue, periodic protests erupted from the homeland societies whose members came from beyond Germany's 1937 borders. The Sudetendeutsche Landsmannschaft, in particular, repeatedly expressed its unhappiness with the government's careful avoidance of any concrete claims to the Sudetenland.[136] However, because of the sensitivity of the problem, most activists preferred to press their complaints behind the scenes.[137]

Whereas dissent about the wisdom of extending Germany's territorial demands beyond the internationally sanctioned boundaries of 1937 thus largely remained out of the public eye, another, more fundamental question did not. This was the concern, occasionally aired by expellee functionaries, that the advance of Adenauer's Westpolitik might produce a highly unwelcome side-effect: the triumph of a *kleindeutsch* definition of Germany. Under pressure from the Western Allies, the activists feared, the government—and eventually much of the population—might abandon the claims to the eastern territories altogether and reconcile itself to the thought that reunification denoted only 'the merger of the Soviet Zone with . . . the Federal Republic'.[138]

To ward off such dangers, expellee leaders urged the government to intensify its efforts on behalf of a *grossdeutsch* reunification. Although willing to accept the immediate primacy of a Western military build-up, they wanted to ensure that the German problem remained in the international limelight and that openings towards unity would be pursued at the earliest opportunity. Their wishes diverged from Adenauer's on at least three concrete points. First, many activists would have liked to see a more careful exploration of certain Soviet-sponsored reunification initiatives, particularly of the so-called Stalin Notes of spring 1952, which proposed the creation of a reunited and non-aligned Germany through free elections. Although Stalin's offer included elements which the expellee elites found unacceptable—such as a call for a perpetuation of the Oder-Neisse line—key leaders nevertheless took issue with Adenauer's summary dismissal of the initiative, claiming that the offer

[135] See e.g. Lodgman von Auen, 'Die Wiedervereinigung und die heimatpolitischen Anliegen der deutschen Ostvertriebenen', Oct. 1954, in Simon, *Lodgman*, 166–70; Walter Rinke's 18 July 1954 address to a Silesian rally, *Bulletin* (21 July 1954), 1203–4.

[136] Stephan Weickert to Adenauer, 21 Sept. 1949, SDA: NL Lodgman, XXIV/2:20; Richard Reitzner and Rudolf Lodgman von Auen in the Arbeitsgemeinschaft zur Wahrung sudetendeutscher Interessen, 8 Oct. 1951, SDA: NL Lodgman, VI/2:2/4, pp. 1, 4.

[137] Compare the sources in n. 136 with the very circumspect phrasing in 'Für wen spricht Adenauer?', *Sudetendeutsche Zeitung* (6 Oct. 1951), 1.

[138] 'Kommentar zur Erklärung der VOL über die Pariser Konferenz', 28 Nov. 1951, SDA: NL Lodgman, XI/5.

was probably 'serious' and therefore 'should have been examined more carefully'.[139]

Second, many expellee leaders showed a more general willingness to consider 'alternative solutions' to Adenauer's Westpolitik in case the latter were to lose its momentum. These vaguely defined alternatives typically shared the Chancellor's vision of linking the Federal Republic to the West militarily while seeking to preserve a wide degree of political latitude for the pursuit of reunification.[140] Third, the expellee elites wanted the government to complement its promotion of Western integration with what they called 'active Ostpolitik'. The idea was for the Foreign Ministry to launch extensive propaganda drives on behalf of a German reacquisition of the lost eastern territories, preferably in cooperation with expellee representatives.[141]

Despite these divergent accents, the majority of expellee activists had reconciled themselves to the specifics of Adenauer's foreign policy by 1954/5 at the latest. Only a relatively small, radical minority rejected the Chancellor's programme. The split between the two camps became evident during disputes over the so-called Paris Treaties of October 1954, which ultimately paved the way for West Germany's attainment of both sovereignty and NATO membership in May 1955. One component of the treaties proved particularly divisive among the expellee elites: the Franco-German Saar Agreement, according to which the Saarland was to become a separate, autonomous entity under international supervision, provided that the population approved the arrangement in a plebiscite.

The most obvious chasm opened up between the rival umbrella groups VdL and BvD. The latter had harboured resentments against Adenauer's policies for some time, as exemplified in a semi-official 1953 memorandum that urged the government to return to the inter-war traditions of loose western links and activist eastern policies embodied in the Locarno Pact of 1925.[142] In late 1954, the organization went a step further by declaring the Saar deal unacceptable. According to the BvD's official statement, the agreement had to be 'rejected' because it set a bad precedent. By voluntarily abandoning German territory, it 'endanger[ed]' the expellees' 'right to their homelands' and undermined the cause of reunification.[143]

---

[139] Axel de Vries to Jakob Kaiser, 14 Mar. 1952, BA: B 234, 300; von Dirksen in the ZvD's Praesidium, 16 Sept. 1952, ABdV: 'Protokolle des Präsidiums und des Gesamtvorstandes, 1949–1953', 406.

[140] 'Entschliessung der Pommerschen Landsmannschaft', 8 June 1952, AA: Abt. 3. 623; joint VdL-BvD report 'Bericht über die Beratung des Sachverständigen-Ausschusses am 16./17. Januar 1954', SDA: NL Lodgman, VII/10.

[141] 'Tätigkeitsbericht der "Kanzlei des Sprechers" über die sudetendeutsche Aussenpolitik zwischen dem Sudetendeutschen Tag 1952 in Stuttgart und Pfingsten 1953 Frankfurt', 23 May 1953, SDA: NL Lodgman, IV/4:21a.

[142] 'Die Aussenpolitik bestimmt unser Schicksal: Richtlinien für die aussenpolitische Arbeit des BvD', *BvD-Dienst Niedersachsen* (25 Feb. 1953), PA/AA: Abt. 3. 620; BvD's *Aussenpolitischer Ausschuss*, 8 Sept. 1954 memorandum, in Doetichem to VdL, 12 Oct. 1954, SDA: NL Lodgman, VII/10.

[143] BvD Presidium's 28 Oct. 1954 resolution, attached to 'Protokoll über die Vorstandssitzung am 11/12.1954 in Stuttgart', ABdV: 'ZvD und BvD: Protokolle des Gesamtvorstandes, 8.7.1952 bis 11/12.12.1954'.

The VdL, speaking in the name of the various homeland societies, interpreted the situation differently. While acknowledging that the Saar arrangement was problematic from the German viewpoint, the organization defended the deal. It maintained that the conditions in the Saarland did not parallel those in Eastern Europe and that the pact therefore constituted 'no precedent for a future regulation of the eastern problems'. The VdL also stressed that the Saar Agreement formed an integral part of the Paris Treaties and consequently could not be rejected without jeopardizing the significant gains which the treaties as a whole promised to bring to the Federal Republic and—by extension—to the expellee movement.[144]

This latter point became the heart of the dispute over Adenauer's Westpolitik within the expellee camp: pragmatists inclined to accept short-term concessions for the sake of anticipated long-term benefits confronted purists opposed to any deviation from established principles. The dynamics of the conflict were complicated and by no means reducible only to the public clash between the two umbrella groups. In most cases the battle lines formed within—rather than between—individual organizations. The most glaring example of such internal strife was the expellee party GB/BHE, which split as a result of disagreements about the Paris Treaties.[145] While a moderate faction led by cabinet ministers Kraft and Oberländer pushed for an acceptance of the entire package, a radical group—stressing its principled opposition to 'a voluntary abandonment of German soil'—rejected the Saar Agreement.[146] After months of internal turmoil, the crisis culminated in a disaster from which the GB/BHE never recovered. In mid-1955, Kraft and Oberländer left the party and subsequently joined the CDU/CSU, taking with them not only their ministerial positions but also several other key leaders.[147] The rump GB/BHE, meanwhile, began its descent into obscurity as a small and increasingly irrelevant right-wing force.

Similar, albeit less dramatic, tensions also manifested themselves within many other expellee organizations. The VdL and the BvD, for example, were more internally torn than their respective public stances suggested.[148] And the top echelons of the Sudetendeutsche Landsmannschaft included both 'proponents' and 'sharp critics' of the Western Treaties, according to the group's key leader.[149]

In the end, however, the majority of the organized expellee movement proved willing to back Adenauer's policies. Concentrated opposition to the Saar Agreement—or any other component of the Paris Treaties—formed only within

[144] VdL *Sprecherversammlung* resolution, 29 Nov. 1954, in 'Die Ostvertriebenen zum Saar-abkommen', *Bulletin* (4 Dec. 1954), 2100; 'Beschlussprotokoll über die Sprecherversammlung des VdL am 29. November 1954', SDA: B VIII/6a.   [145] Neumann, *Block*, 138–65.

[146] Gerhard Schuchart to Oswald Pohl, 21 Dec. 1954, ACSP: NL Schuchart, 95; GB/BHE's *Bundesvorstand* meeting, 2 Nov. 1954, ACDP: I-378-010/1.

[147] Neumann, *Block*, 144–65.

[148] The VdL had to conduct a lengthy 'general debate' about its Saar resolution; 'Beschlussprotokoll über die Sprecherversammlung des VdL am 29. November, 1954', SDA: B VIII/6a, 3.

[149] Rudolf Lodgman von Auen to Richard Reitzner and Hans Schütz, 19 Feb.1955, SDA: NL Lodgman, XII/6.

the BvD and the GB/BHE, mobilized in large part by a handful of radicals active in both groups.[150] All other expellee organizations, as well as the bulk of the individual activists, followed a more conciliatory line. In addition, even most of Adenauer's critics took care not to burn their bridges. While opposing the Saar Statute, the majority of them supported—or at least tolerated—the other components of the Chancellor's Westpolitik.

Regardless of such widespread conciliation and caution, however, the dispute over the Paris Treaties constituted an important watershed for the expellee movement. It separated a small, increasingly radical minority from the expellee mainstream. The former followed up its opposition to Adenauer's Westpolitik with a persistent push to the right. From 1955 on, this faction adopted an increasingly nationalistic stance, often resorting to the *völkisch*-racist idiom of earlier times and openly espousing far-reaching re-annexations of former Reich territories beyond those of 1937. With such extremist rhetoric, the radicals—whose main organizational base was the declining GB/BHE, although individual sympathisers were also present in the BvD and other groups—pushed themselves into growing isolation.[151] The government and the major parties obviously did not appreciate this nationalistic zealotry, nor did the vast majority of the expellee movement — or the West German population at large.

With some variations, all the principal organizations other than the rump GB/BHE and—to a much lesser degree—the BvD, steered a course close to the government's from 1955 on. They avoided excessively radical rhetoric and publicly backed the main tenets of Adenauer's foreign policy, even if their real sympathies often lay elsewhere. In return, they expected Bonn to keep its promises about maintaining Germany's claims to the eastern territories and advocating the expellees' rights to their homelands and to self-determination. The mainstream expellee movement had thus entered a kind of limited foreign-policy partnership with Adenauer's government by the time the Federal Republic acquired sovereignty.

What motivated the great majority of the expellee activists to take this stance? Naive faith in the Chancellor's good intentions was clearly not the reason, as even moderate expellee activists privately doubted Adenauer's sincerity. One leading Sudeten German, for example, suspected that the Chancellor aimed 'not at reunification but at West Germany's rearmament and integration into Western Europe', while another feared that Adenauer's policies would culminate in the creation of a western entity comparable to 'Charlemagne's Reich'.[152] Expellee leaders also understood that the government's official line on border revisions,

---

[150] On the extensive overlap in leadership cadre, see Neumann, *Block*, esp. 355–9.

[151] Ibid. 168–238. The Sudeten-German Homeland Society also included numerous radicals, particularly within the Witikobund. See the All-German Ministry's report 'Betr: Jahresversammlung des Witiko-Bundes', 11–12 Oct. 1954, BA: B 137, 2245.

[152] Rudolf Hilf to Rudolf Lodgman von Auen, 4 Jan. 1954, SDA: NL Lodgman, XXIV-10.35; Walter Becher in the Arbeitsgemeinschaft zur Wahrung sudetendeutscher Interessen, 8 Oct. 1951, SDA: NL Lodgman, VI/2:2/4.

according to which final decisions had to be deferred until a future peace settlement, by no means guaranteed that Bonn—or anyone else—would actually raise revisionist demands at the peace conference, if one ever took place at all.[153] This scepticism was reflected in the fact that many activists found Adenauer's reunification programme less convincing than those of some of his critics. Two of the Chancellor's gainsayers in particular received considerable sympathy from the expellee lobby, at least in the early 1950s: Jakob Kaiser, the nationalistically oriented Minister for All-German Affairs, and Karl-Georg Pfleiderer, the FDP's lone early advocate of alternative policy concepts.[154]

The decision to side with Adenauer despite all the doubts was based in large part on instrumental considerations. The underlying rationale found particularly clear expression in a 1954 memorandum by Rudolf Hilf, a key policy adviser in the Sudeten-German Homeland Society. According to Hilf, the expellee organizations would be in a 'hopeless' position without the support of the West German government, which, in turn, was dominated by the 'personal policies of the Federal Chancellor'. To develop the appropriate rapport with Adenauer and his 'winning battalions', the expellee lobby had to generate 'an impression of harmony between [their] policies and those of the federal government, particularly of the Chancellor'.[155] The key word was 'impression' because the ultimate aims of the expellee elites obviously diverged sharply from Adenauer's. Whereas the latter wanted the Federal Republic's Western integration to be a permanent measure culminating in a fundamental reorientation of Germany's political life, his bargaining partners in the expellee movement had very different aspirations. To them, the Western orientation was not a 'permanent solution' but rather a temporary, tactical move, aimed at tiding the fatherland over its post-war difficulties and paving the way for a restoration of an 'independent German policy'.[156] This future policy would draw upon traditional German statecraft and make use of the country's position in the middle of Europe to restore the Reich to its past glory, territorially and otherwise.[157] Ironically, the seemingly pro-governmental expellee elites thus hoped to do with the Chancellor exactly what he planned to do with them: mislead and manipulate for tactical gain.

Along with instrumental calculations, another significant motive propelling the mainstream expellee movement towards Adenauer was a perceived lack of alternatives. Like Rudolf Hilf, the majority of the expellee activists regarded close

---

[153] Axel de Vries, 'Kommentar zur Erklärung der VOL über die Pariser Konferenz', 28 Nov. 1951, SDA: NL Lodgman, XI/5.d.

[154] On Kaiser, see de Vries to Kaiser, 14 Mar. 1952, BA: B 234, 300; de Vries in the VOL's *Vorstand*, 2 Apr. 1952, BA: NL de Vries, 19. Pfleiderer was in frequent contact with expellee activists in the early 1950s. See his presentation to the VOL's *Sprechertagung*, 8–9 Mar. 1951, SDA: B VIII/4; de Vries to Pfleiderer, 10 June 1952, BA: NL Pfleiderer, 52.

[155] Rudolf Hilf to Rudolf Lodgman von Auen, 4 Jan. 1954, SDA: NL Lodgman, XXIV-1035.

[156] Rudolf Lodgman von Auen, 'Ein deutsches und europäisches Ostprogramm', Dec. 1953, in Simon, *Lodgman*, 144; VOL resolution 'Generalvertrag und E.V.G.', 29 May 1952, SDA: NL Lodgman, XI/9.

[157] Along with n. 156, see Walter Becher in the Arbeitsgemeinschaft zur Wahrung sudetendeutscher Interessen, 8 Oct. 1951, SDA: NL Lodgman, VI/2:2/4.

links to the Chancellor as an existential necessity. This belief reflected a basic affinity for the government's conservative, anti-Communist values on the one hand and a deep-seated mistrust of the main opposition forces on the other.[158] Right-wing radicalism struck most expellee activists as a hopeless and undesirable cause, suited only for 'nationally minded good-for-nothings'.[159] The Communist alternative was obviously even further beyond the pale, and many expellee leaders also harboured serious misgivings about the Social Democrats, although the non-partisan status of the expellee groups dictated that public expressions of such sentiments remained limited. In part, the doubts about the SPD were rooted in long-standing prejudices which predisposed expellee activists to question the patriotism and reliability of the Social Democrats.[160] But scepticism about the party's current foreign-policy line was also strong. Although the SPD's fervent principled advocacy of reunification struck a chord among the expellee elites, its concrete policy proposals did not.[161] The party's resistance to the remilitarization and Western integration of the Federal Republic, for example, was so unpopular that even expellee leaders within the SPD denounced these stances.[162] Other activists, in turn, concluded that siding with the Social Democrats and their unrealistic policies would benefit the expellee movement 'nowhere where it counts'.[163]

The impression of a lack of alternatives among the expellee elites did not arise unassisted; the government's skilful handling of the expellee movement made a significant contribution to the process. State subsidies quickly engendered financial and political dependency among the expellee groups.[164] The co-optation of individual leaders into government positions also helped to tame the expellee organizations' oppositional potential. Personal meetings with Adenauer and his immediate advisors typically had the same effect. A special session between the Chancellor's confidants and a select group of GB/BHE functionaries in early 1953, for example, was crucial in turning the latter into the core of the party's subsequent pro-Westpolitik wing.[165] At the same time, the careful exclusion of expellee representatives from key positions in Bonn's foreign-policy machinery ensured that the expellee organizations lacked precise information and were thus poorly positioned to challenge the government head-on.[166] Under these conditions, the bulk of the expellee movement had little choice but to adjust to the Chancellor's foreign policy. Adenauer's manipulation of the expellees and their purported

---

[158] Wambach, *Verbändestaat*, 134–5.

[159] Hilf to Lodgman von Auen, 4 Jan. 1954, SDA: NL Lodgman XXIV-10.35.

[160] See the vitriolic 1950 pamphlet *Wenzel Jaksch ohne Maske* by the Sudeten German activist F. Richter, SDA: NL Lodgman, VIII/1:1.

[161] The party's reaction to the Stalin Note of 1952 constituted an exception. See Axel de Vries in 'Niederschrift über die Vorstandssitzung der VOL', 2 Apr. 1952, SDA: B VIII/5.

[162] Jaksch in the SPD's *Bundestagsfraktion*, 24 Feb. 1954, *SPD-Fraktion*, i/1. 35–6.

[163] Hilf to Lodgman, 4 Jan. 1954, SDA: NL Lodgman XXIV-10.35.

[164] For evidence of the expellee elites' awareness of this problem, see 'Beschlussprotokoll über die Präsidialsitzung des VdL am 2. Februar 1955', SDA: NL Lodgman, XI-21.

[165] 'Besprechung am 19.2.1953, abends', BA: NL 267, 25; 'Protokoll über die Sitzung des Bundesvorstandes des GB/BHE am 20.2.1953', ACDP: I-378/010/1; Neumann, *Block*, 101–2.

[166] Wambach, *Verbändestaat*, 123–4.

organizational representatives in the domestic context had thus yielded hand-some dividends by the time the Federal Republic attained sovereignty in May 1955.

ADENAUER AND THE EXPELLEES IN THE INTERNATIONAL SPHERE

The Chancellor also made manipulative use of the expellees, the *Ver-triebenenverbände*, and the causes associated with them on the international, diplomatic plane. One of his key tools was the Oder-Neisse border problem, which he repeatedly wielded as a weapon against unwanted reunification initia-tives. This behaviour pattern was at its clearest between autumn 1951 and spring 1952, a period in which a series of Eastern bloc initiatives appeared to threaten his Westpolitik objectives. The difficulties began in September 1951 when the GDR responded to looming new advances in West Germany's remilitarization by proposing reunification through free elections and a neutral status for the new state.[167] The initiative evoked widespread interest in the Federal Republic, and soon even prominent CDU/CSU ministers and party functionaries began to advocate exploring the proposal.[168]

As a part of his response, Adenauer played up the Oder-Neisse theme. In a widely publicized Berlin speech in early October 1951, he declared that 'the lands beyond the Oder-Neisse belong to Germany' and that his government could therefore only support reunification encompassing 'Berlin, the Soviet Zone, and all of the German east'.[169] Other contemporary addresses by the Chancellor, including a keynote speech at a major expellee meeting, echoed these argu-ments.[170] Adenauer's stance obviously made the GDR's proposal very difficult to pursue, particularly since the East Germans had already recognized the Oder-Neisse line as a permanent 'border of peace' in the 1950 Görlitz Treaty with Poland. The Chancellor was well aware of these realities, of course. A few months earlier he had relayed to the Allied High Commissioners his cabinet's conviction that any use of the Oder-Neisse theme against East German reunification propos-als would 'probably precipitate the immediate collapse of these efforts'.[171] This belief now proved correct, as the territorial argument, together with a number of other propagandistically clever moves, helped to bring the GDR initiative to naught within a few months. To several perceptive critics all this proved that the Chancellor's motive for hammering on about the question of the eastern territo-ries had been to 'prevent "talks" with the GDR at all costs'.[172]

[167] Hans-Peter Schwarz, *Die Ära Adenauer 1949–1957* (Stuttgart: DVA, 1981), 149–52; id, *Aufstieg*, 880–97.   [168] Lenz, *Zentrum*, 136–8.

[169] *Keesing's Archiv der Gegenwart* (1951), 3146.

[170] Adenauer's address to the BvD, 6 Nov. 1951, in 'Bund der vertriebenen Deutschen', *Sudetendeutsche Zeitung* (24 Nov. 1951).

[171] Adenauer in a meeting with the Allied High Commissioners, 14 Dec. 1950, in *Hohe Kommissare, 1949–1951*, 303.

[172] Ernst Lemmer's comments, 29 Oct. 1951, *FRUS 1951*, iii/2. 1804; Jakob Kaiser's comments, reported in Lenz, *Zentrum*, 225; Frohn, 'Adenauer', 495–501.

During the autumn of 1951, Adenauer also briefly trumpeted the Oder-Neisse problem behind the scenes, in his negotiations with the Western Allies. Here, too, his behaviour revealed a pattern of aggressive tactics in the service of defensive—and ultimately anti-reunification—aims. The starting point for the Chancellor's actions was a development among the Western Powers which he perceived as potentially very dangerous. In November 1951, as the negotiations for the so-called General Treaty between the Federal Republic and the three Allies neared their completion, the latter began calling for a written agreement confirming that their definition of German reunification encompassed only the Federal Republic and the 'Soviet Zone' and explicitly excluded 'any commitment regarding the disposition of territory beyond the Oder-Neisse'.[173] To Adenauer, such an arrangement would have been politically calamitous, given his recent rhetorical use of the Oder-Neisse claims and his other public commitments on the issue. In a meeting with the Allied High Commissioners on 14 November 1951, he therefore went on the offensive. Emphasizing the need to heed German public opinion on this 'question of the greatest importance', he rejected the Allied demands and insisted on a 'joint policy'.[174] As a part of the General Treaty, the Western Powers would have to formally pledge their continued support for Bonn's campaign to uphold the boundaries of 1937.[175]

The Chancellor's stance briefly baffled the Allies. They had considered Adenauer's recent oratory about the Oder-Neisse theme 'opportunist[ic]', to quote the British High Commissioner, and had not expected him to push them for formal commitments on this issue.[176] Within a few days, however, the Allies concluded that the Chancellor's demands were 'not fully sincere' and that their aggressive appearance enshrouded a defensive logic born out of 'local political purposes'.[177] John J. McCloy, the American High Commissioner, provided a perceptive analysis of Adenauer's motives. Stressing the 'politically explosive' nature of the eastern border problem within Germany, he argued that the Chancellor aimed at 'fortify[ing] his political position by appearing as a champion of the thousands [*sic*] of refugees from the East'.[178] McCloy also contended that the Chancellor's most concrete objective was to ensure that 'Germany was not precluded from exerting her aspirations for the return of the eastern territories'.[179] In other words, Adenauer did not really expect the Allies to make additional commitments on the eastern border issue. His true aim was rather to prevent the Western Powers from adopting positions that could either damage him domestically or keep him from continuing to use the Oder-Neisse card as a political tool.

---

[173] McCloy to the Acting Secretary of State, 15 Nov. 1951, *FRUS 1951*, iii. 1580.

[174] Wilhelm Grewe's notes of Adenauer's meeting with the High Commissioners, 14 Nov. 1951, *Hohe Kommissare 1949–1951*, 575–8.

[175] Ibid.; McCloy to the Acting Secretary of State, 15 Nov. 1951, *FRUS 1951*, iii. 1580–1.

[176] Sir Ivone Kirkpatrick in Grewe's notes of the 14 Nov. 1951 session between Adenauer and the High Commissioners, *Hohe Kommissare 1949–1951*, 575.

[177] McCloy to the Acting Secretary of State, 15 Nov. 1951, *FRUS 1951*, iii. 1582.

[178] McCloy to the US, British, and French Foreign Ministers, 17 Nov. 1951, ibid. 1585.

[179] McCloy in the Foreign Ministers' Meeting, Paris, 21 Nov. 1951, ibid. 1598.

This analysis proved correct. As he joined the American, British, and French Foreign Ministers in Paris for the final round of negotiations that led to the initialling of the General Treaty on 22 November 1951, Adenauer immediately retreated from his aggressive demands of the previous week and proposed a very moderate compromise. According to this formula, which was quickly approved by all sides, Bonn demanded no further commitments from the Allies regarding the territories east of the Oder-Neisse, provided that the latter agreed not to enter into agreements about this issue with third parties.[180] The phrasing that found its way to the General Treaty reflected this compromise—and the Potsdam Accords—by simply stating that 'the final termination of the boundaries of Germany' had to await a future 'peace settlement'.[181] Once this status quo solution had been reached, Adenauer happily dropped the matter and made no effort to push the Allies any further, having achieved his objective of preserving his freedom to politicize and manipulate the issue.[182]

Shortly after the November negotiations, Adenauer put this freedom to renewed use. The occasion was the famous Stalin Note of 10 March 1952, which again brought an unwelcome reunification proposal onto the political agenda. The note—addressed to Washington, London, and Paris—urged immediate peace negotiations aimed at creating a reunified, non-allied Germany with its own, independent military.[183] These terms were obviously unacceptable for the Chancellor, whose focus at the time lay on removing all obstacles to the impending final signing of the General Treaty and the accompanying agreement about the creation of the European Defence Community. But many other West Germans—including the political opposition, much of the press, and even several leading figures within the CDU/CSU and the federal cabinet—took the offer seriously and wanted to see it explored.[184] In this atmosphere, Adenauer made his main public statement regarding the Soviet initiative in a widely publicized address on 16 March. As in the previous October, he hammered on about the eastern frontier problem, touting Moscow's determination to perpetuate the Oder-Neisse line—a point reiterated in the 10 March proposal—as his main objection to the note.[185] He also reiterated similar arguments on several other occasions during the following weeks.[186] With this use of the territorial card, Adenauer helped to thwart any possibility of serious

---

[180] 'Verlaufsprotokoll der Besprechung zwischen Adenauer und Acheson vom 21. November 1951', in *Hohe Kommissare 1949–1951*, 527.   [181] *FRUS 1952–1954*, vii. 116.

[182] For different perspectives, see Frohn, 'Adenauer', 501–12; Schwarz, *Aufstieg*, 891–3; Köhler, *Adenauer*, 672–4; Küsters, *Integrationsfriede*, 578–81.

[183] For the note, see Rolf Steininger, *Eine Chance zur Wiedervereinigung? Die Stalin-Note vom 10. März 1952* (Bonn: Neue Gesellschaft, 1986), 114–16. For the latest on the huge historiography, see Jürgen Zarusky (ed.), *Die Stalin-Note vom 10. März 1952: Neue Quellen und Analysen* (Munich: Oldenbourg, 2002).

[184] Lenz, *Zentrum*, 273, 276; McCloy to Acheson, 15 Mar. 1952, in Steininger, *Chance*, 146.

[185] *Keesing's Archiv der Gegenwart* (1952), 3388.

[186] McCloy's report of Adenauer's 25 Mar. press conference, in Steininger, *Chance*, 167; Adenauer's comments to the High Commissioners, 17 Mar. 1952, in *Akten zur Auswärtigen Politik der Bundesrepublik Deutschland*, ii. *Adenauer und die Hohen Kommissare 1952* (Munich: Oldenbourg, 1990), 28.

exploratory talks with the Russians and to justify his hard-line position at home. As the Western Allies shared the Chancellor's desire to pursue the *Westintegration* of the Federal Republic without distractions, nothing ultimately came of the Soviet offer. But in the process the Oder-Neisse theme had again served as a tactical tool of Adenauer's Western-oriented foreign policy.

Along with the territorial claims associated with the expellee organizations, Adenauer also instrumentalized the expellee masses as such in his negotiations with the Western Powers. He frequently reminded the Allies of the potential dangers which the newcomers posed for West Germany. The 'political ramifications' of the expellee problem came up particularly often.[187] Various leading statesmen had to listen to the Chancellor's repeated warnings about the possibility of a large-scale radicalization among the expellees. In a December 1951 meeting with the British Prime Minister, for example, Adenauer reportedly labelled this scenario 'the greatest danger for the Federal Republic'.[188]

Although these statements undoubtedly reflected a good deal of genuine concern, their primary function was instrumental. Adenauer typically raised the spectre of expellee radicalization in connection with demands for changes in specific Allied policies, suggesting that the former would set in if the latter remained unheeded. The Chancellor applied these tactics particularly in two policy areas. First, he underscored the potential for an anti-democratic backlash from discontented expellees and other hard-core nationalists if the Allies failed to provide Bonn with extensive sovereignty as soon as possible. At one point in late 1950 he pushed such scare tactics to an extreme, implying that the Western Powers' reluctance to yield fast enough on sovereignty threatened to destroy West Germany's fragile new democracy. The 'psychological situation' among the population, the Chancellor claimed, was 'extraordinarily similar to that of 1933'.[189]

The second major objective of the radicalization rhetoric was to obtain economic concessions. In his negotiations with the Western Allies, Adenauer repeatedly highlighted the 'special social responsibilities' incumbent upon his government, primarily because of the need to assist and integrate the expellees. Should Bonn fail to fulfil these duties, he predicted, 'the internal security of the Federal Republic would be endangered' and 'the will to resist' the Communist threat 'thereby lowered'.[190] The high social expenditures necessary at home, the argument continued, should entitle the Federal Republic to reduced contributions to Western defence coffers—and to special loans and other financial assistance from the Allies, particularly the United States.[191]

---

[187] Adenauer's meeting with John F. Dulles, 17 Apr. 1953, *FRUS 1952–1954*, vii. 439.

[188] Adenauer, *Erinnerungen, 1945–1953*, 509.

[189] Adenauer in a meeting with the Allied High Commissioners, 1 Dec. 1950, *Hohe Kommissare 1949–1951*, 290.

[190] Adenauer's memorandum, in McCloy to Dulles, 17 Nov. 1950, *FRUS 1950*, iv. 781.

[191] On reduced defence contributions, see n. 190; Adenauer's meetings with the High Commissioners, 16 Nov. 1950 and 9 May 1951, in *Hohe Kommissare 1949–1951*, 269, 363–4; and 22 Feb. 1952, in *Hohe Kommissare 1952*, 21. On financial assistance, see Adenauer, *Erinnerungen, 1945–1953*, 478, 574–5; *FRUS 1952–1954*, vii. esp. 420, 423, 439.

Adenauer's use of the radicalization argument did make some impact. It apparently intensified the Allies' general concern about the German expellee problem. The United States, for example, continued to worry about the situation throughout the first half of the 1950s. A good indication of the enduring concern was the Eisenhower Administration's official statement of policy towards Germany—the NSC 160/1 of August 1953—which labelled the 'millions of refugees from the East who have not been fully assimilated and among whom irredentist claims are cherished' a major source of 'potential instability and risk' for the Federal Republic.[192] Adenauer's tactics also helped to elicit some concrete concessions from the Allies. In response to the Chancellor's pressure campaigns, the Americans began to consider providing loans to promote expellee integration.[193] For similar reasons, the Allies also proved willing to reduce the Federal Republic's defence contributions. For the fiscal year 1952–3, for example, the Western Powers backed down from their original demand of a 13 billion DM contribution from Bonn and eventually settled for 8.8 billion.[194]

However, the diplomatic instrumentalization of both the expellee problem and the related Oder-Neisse question also served a more personal function for the Chancellor. It helped him to bolster his personal power position in the eyes of the Allies. To be sure, Adenauer's manipulative tactics threatened to backfire from time to time. His gloomy portrayals of the burdens imposed by the expellees occasionally struck the Allies as exaggerated.[195] More significantly, his sharp rhetoric about the eastern borders generated periodic fears in Western capitals, especially in Paris, where even Vincent Auriol, the President of the Republic, dreaded that Adenauer's real aim might be to drag NATO into a revanchist war against the Communist East.[196]

But on balance, the use of the expellee card served Adenauer well, particularly as Western leaders gradually developed an increasingly sophisticated understanding of Bonn's domestic need for revisionist oratory. The accentuation of the problems and dangers caused by the expellees helped Adenauer to portray himself as an irreplaceable figure, the only reliable bulwark against the dark, unpredictable forces of unbridled German nationalism. In the course of the early 1950s, the Allies—or at least the British and the Americans—increasingly accepted this image of the Chancellor. By mid-1953, both Churchill and John F. Dulles had come to view Adenauer as the only viable choice in West Germany whose loss of power would spell a 'big disaster'.[197] The perceived dependency went so far that

---

[192] *FRUS 1952–1954*, vii. 511–12.

[193] 'Communique on the United States–German Talks', 9 Apr. 1953, *FRUS 1952–1954*, vii. 454.

[194] McCloy to Dulles, 22 Dec. 1951, *FRUS 1951*, iii. 1695–8; 'Wortprotokoll der Sitzung vom 22. Februar 1952', *Hohe Kommissare 1952*, 20–3; McCloy to the State Department, 23 Feb. 1952, *FRUS 1952–1954*, v. 256–7.   [195] McCloy to Acheson, 22 Dec. 1951, *FRUS 1951*, iii. 1697.

[196] Auriol's comments, 30 Sept. 1953, cited in Schwarz, *Staatsmann*, 97; Adenauer, *Erinnerungen, 1945–1953*, 524; Lenz, *Zentrum*, 260, 284, 297–8, 366; Ferguson to Nitze, 26 Sept. 1952, *FRUS 1952–1954*, vii. 361–8.

[197] For the quotation, by Churchill, see Foschepoth, *Adenauer*, 14. See also *FRUS 1952–1954*, vii. 532–3; Schwarz, *Staatsmann*, 102.

Dulles sought to intervene on the Chancellor's behalf in West German election campaigns—not only during the Bundestag election of 1953 but even in the state-level campaign of Nordrhein-Westfalen the following year.[198] As Adenauer thus established himself as the irreplaceable dream partner of the Western world's leading power, his careful manipulation of expellee causes and constituencies had reached its zenith of success.

By the time the Federal Republic acquired sovereignty in May 1955, the domestic interaction between Adenauer's government and the expellee organizations had formed a pattern which in many ways paralleled that between the organizations and the main parties. The government had invested heavily in courting the expellees in general and the expellee lobby in particular. Although personal and financial connections, along with social programmes, played a significant role in these efforts, foreign-policy arguments soon rose to predominance as the government publicly pledged its support for most of the expellee organizations' Ostpolitik interests. For instrumental reasons—and against his true convictions—Adenauer committed his government to defending both Germany's claims to the so-called Oder-Neisse territories and the expellees' rights to their homelands and to self-determination. At the same time, he carefully excluded expellee representatives from the inner sanctums of power in which the government's real policies were formulated and implemented.

The manipulative use of the expellees and the causes associated with them brought Adenauer and his government many benefits. At home, this strategy helped to pacify the expellees and to consolidate the support base of the Chancellor's Westpolitik. Abroad, it gave Adenauer a diplomatic tool for blocking reunification initiatives, extracting concessions from the Allies, and bolstering his own stature. The costs of these tactics remained low as long as the Federal Republic still lacked sovereignty and thus the ability to pursue independent policies towards Eastern Europe. But after May 1955 the balance began to shift; the government and the main parties were soon to discover that their opportunistically adopted public stances had imposed strict limits on their freedom of movement in Ostpolitik.

[198] On the former intervention, see n. 197. On the latter, see *FRUS 1952–1954*, vii. 574–6.

II

The Pattern in Practice
1955–1966

CHAPTER FIVE

Ostpolitik Options and Expellee Influence, 1955–1959

IN SEPTEMBER 1955 the Federal Republic of Germany responded to an earlier Soviet invitation by sending a sizeable delegation, headed by Chancellor Adenauer, to Moscow to explore the possibility of establishing formal intergovernmental relations between the two countries. After five days of hard bargaining an agreement was reached. The two parties decided to set up full diplomatic ties. The Soviets also granted Bonn two special concessions. They agreed to release the nearly 10,000 German POWs still in their custody and to receive a separate statement in which Bonn reiterated its rejection of the Potsdam border settlement and its continued claim to be the sole legitimate representative of the German nation.[1]

The Moscow connection opened up new vistas for West German foreign policy. Having acquired sovereignty and now established official ties to the East European hegemon, the Federal Republic was—at least in theory—in a position to pursue diplomatic relations with lesser members of the Soviet bloc as well. A qualitatively new Ostpolitik had become possible. Although the potential rewards and dangers of this prospect attracted the attention of numerous observers within and without Germany, few followed the situation with deeper concern than the leaders of the expellee organizations.

Even before the Federal Republic had acquired sovereignty, expellee elites had begun to worry about the 'complications' which such a development might generate, including 'the possibility of official relations with the Eastern states'.[2] When the attainment of sovereignty in May 1955 was soon followed by the Soviet invitation for Adenauer's visit to Moscow, the anxieties intensified. On a general level, the expellee elites dreaded that the establishment of relations with the Eastern bloc

---

[1] For contrasting accounts, see Schwarz, *Staatsmann*, 207–22; Kosthorst, *Brentano*, 63–77; Josef Foschepoth, 'Adenauers Moskaureise 1955', *Aus Politik und Zeitgeschichte*, 22 (1986): 30–46. On the POWs, see also Robert G. Moeller, ' "The Last Soldiers of the Great War" and Tales of Family Reunion in the Federal Republic of Germany', *Signs*, 24 (1998): 129–45; Frank Biess, 'Survivors of Totalitarianism: Returning POWs and the Reconstruction of Masculine Citizenship in West Germany, 1945–1955', in Schissler, *Miracle*, 57–82; id. 'The Protracted War: Returning POWs and the Making of East and West German Citizens, 1945–1955', Ph.D. diss., Brown University, 2000.

[2] Hans Schütz in the presidium of the Arbeitsgemeinschaft zur Wahrung sudetendeutscher Interessen, 29 Oct. 1954, SDA: NL Lodgman, VI/2:2/5.

could 'lead to a recognition of the current territorial situation'.[3] They also harboured more specific fears about the Chancellor's planned visit to the USSR, including concerns that the trip might be construed as a sign of a West German capitulation to Soviet demands and even that Adenauer's 'personal safety' might be jeopardized in the Soviet capital. However, the government ultimately managed to gain the expellee groups' acceptance for the opening towards the Soviet Union. Adenauer and his new Foreign Minister, Heinrich von Brentano, personally assured leading expellee activists that their interests would not be compromised in Moscow, and the Chancellor even agreed to include in his large delegation a VdL-affiliated observer, Professor Hans Koch of the Landsmannschaft Weichsel-Warthe.[4]

This seemingly inclusive tactic proved helpful for the government. Although Professor Koch was not given any policy-making powers, he nevertheless provided several expellee groups with highly positive reports of the trip and its results upon his return. Partly prodded by Koch's pronouncements, the leading expellee organizations promptly gave their approval to the outcome of the Moscow negotiations, stressing in particular their satisfaction with the return of the POWs and with the government's uncompromising stance on the eastern border question.[5] Even the relatively radical BvD grudgingly sanctioned the establishment of relations with the USSR as a 'political necessity'.[6]

The expellee elite's willingness to tolerate eastward diplomatic openings applied only to the Soviet superpower, however. The possibility of formal relations between Bonn and the rest of the Eastern bloc, particularly Poland and Czechoslovakia, had long been anathema to most activists, and in the months following Adenauer's visit to Moscow the unconditional rejection of such prospects hardened into a key expellee dogma that was to remain unchanged for years to come. According to expellee functionaries, the establishment of diplomatic ties to the Soviet satellites would jeopardize German interests in several ways. It would lead to an at least *de facto* recognition of the post-war territorial status quo and to an indirect sanctioning of the unjust expulsions.[7] It would undermine the Federal Republic's claim to be the sole legitimate German state by upgrading Bonn's contacts to the only group of countries that had formally recognized the challenger regime in East Berlin.[8] A further undesirable consequence would be a weakening of the 'inner power of resistance' among the East European

---

[3] VdL, 'Heimatpolitische Richtlinien', in 'Beschlussprotokoll über die Sprecherversammlung des VdL am 29. Juni 1955', SDA: NL Lodgman, XI-31.

[4] Manteuffel-Szoege to Adenauer, 27 July 1955, BA: B 136/6786; Manteuffel-Szoege to VdL member organizations, 7 Sept. 1955, SDA: XXIV-01.

[5] Von Doetinchem to VdL member organizations, 15 Sept. 1955, SDA: NL Lodgman, XXIV-01; 'Beschlussprotokoll über die Präsidialsitzung des VdL am 5./6. Oktober 1955', SDA: NL Lodgman, XI-21.

[6] BvD's 26 Sept. 1955 resolution, in Blumenthal and Fassbender, *Erklärungen*, 50.

[7] Sudetendeutsche Landsmannschaft, 'Memorandum C betreffend die offiziellen Beziehungen der Bundesrepublik Deutschland zur Tschechoslowakei', Sept. 1955, BA: B 234/342; VdL pamphlet 'Zur Bundestagswahl am 15. September 1957: Die deutschen Ostprobleme—Prüfstein gesamtdeutscher Verantwortung und Gesinnung', SDA: NL Lodgman, XIX-00, esp. p. 5.

[8] VdL, 'Aide memoire', 26 July 1956, BA: B 234/301; 'Gegen Beziehungen zu Polen', *Sudetendeutsche Zeitung* (10 Aug. 1957).

peoples.[9] In the opinion of the expellee elites, the oppressed populations of the Soviet satellites despised their own regimes and felt 'admiration and respect' for West Germany's hard, anti-Communist policies. A change in Bonn's stance would therefore disillusion the East Europeans and damage Germany's prestige in the region.[10] Similarly negative psychological consequences could also be expected in the West, where a policy switch would probably be interpreted as an irrational abandonment of significant German national interests.[11]

For all these reasons, the expellee organizations opposed official ties to the East European satellite states. Full diplomatic relations were clearly beyond the pale, and formal economic links also had to be rejected because they would 'contribute to the consolidation of the Communist regimes'.[12] For the time being, only two, informal kinds of connections could be promoted. One was humanitarian assistance to the suffering peoples of Eastern Europe, including the small German minorities still left in the region, to be provided primarily through private channels.[13] The second consisted of cultural links—such as academic exchanges, joint sports events, and youth visits—intended to facilitate 'human understanding' between the Germans and their eastern neighbours.[14] But even these informal contacts were to remain subject to strict preconditions and controls. The expellee elites insisted that all cultural exchanges had to be based on 'reciprocity and equality' and that the German organizers of such activities were to possess a 'thorough knowledge' not only of the countries in question but also of 'the German East'—a joint qualification which expellee leaders typically saw embodied only in themselves.[15] A normalization on the governmental level could proceed only much later, once extremely high preconditions had been fulfilled. The East European governments—particularly Warsaw and Prague—would first have to gain real independence, preferably by abandoning Communism, and then accept the main tenets of the *Vertriebenenverbände*, including the German expellees' 'right to self-determination and to their *Heimat*'.[16]

The immobilism advocated by the expellee organizations bore a relatively close resemblance to the official Ostpolitik line adopted by Adenauer's government after the Moscow visit. Admittedly, Bonn's official stance—a derivative of policies aimed at isolating East Germany—was formulated independently of the expellee organizations and with different underlying motives. But its end effect was to

[9] BdV resolution 'Beziehungen zu Polen', 26 Jan. 1958, in Blumenthal and Fassbender, *Erklärungen*, 62.

[10] VdL pamphlet 'Zur Bundestagswhal am 15. September 1957: Die deutschen Ostprobleme—Prüfstein gesamtdeutscher Verantwortung und Gesinnung', SDA: NL Lodgman, XIX-00.

[11] VdL, 'Aide memoire', 26 July 1956, BA: B 234/301.

[12] VdL pamphlet 'Zur Bundestagswahl' (n. 10), p. 5

[13] Pommersche Landsmannschaft resolution, 8–9 Nov. 1958, attached to the organization's letter to the Expellee Ministry, 14 Nov. 1958, BA: B 136/27370.

[14] BdV memoranda 'Beziehungen zu Polen', 26 Jan. 1958, and 'Kulturelle Beziehungen zu Polen', 17 Jan. 1959, in Blumenthal and Fassbender, *Erklärungen*, 63, 64–5.

[15] See the second memorandum in n. 14.

[16] VdL, 'Aide memoire', 26 July 1957, BA: B 234/301.

make a normalization of relations between the Federal Republic and the East European satellites of the USSR very difficult. The government line arose as a response to a post-Moscow dilemma: how to combine the Federal Republic's self-proclaimed status as the only legitimate German state with the fact that it now maintained full ties to a government that had officially recognized the challenger regime in East Berlin.

After extensive deliberations, Bonn's policy-makers agreed on a doctrine that came to bear the name of Walter Hallstein, then Secretary of State in the Foreign Ministry.[17] The government resolved not to tolerate diplomatic ties between the GDR and any other state than the USSR, which as a Second World War victor and occupation power was deemed to deserve special consideration. As Chancellor Adenauer proclaimed in late September 1955, the Federal Republic would consider the establishment of official relations with the GDR by other countries an 'unfriendly act'.[18]

While the precise manner in which Bonn would respond to such unfriendly moves remained unclear at first, the countries most directly affected by the doctrine were immediately obvious: the Soviet satellites of Eastern Europe, which had already set up full relations with the GDR by the mid-1950s. In public, the Hallstein Doctrine soon came to be mainly identified with the inflexible principle that no country other than the USSR could simultaneously maintain diplomatic relations with both the GDR and the Federal Republic. However, behind the scenes Bonn's policy elites discussed various more flexible options, including the possibility of exempting the Eastern bloc states from this rule because their recognition of East Berlin had presumably occurred under Soviet duress.[19] The hard-line definition received a decisive boost in October 1957 when West Germany responded to Yugoslavia's decision to recognize the GDR by severing relations with Belgrade, first established some six years earlier to encourage Tito's neutralist stances.[20] The expellee activists loudly greeted this step, primarily because it further strengthened the seeming congruence between their Ostpolitik programme and that of the government.[21] Soon after acquiring sovereignty the Federal Republic had thus come to espouse an apparently doctrinaire rejection of official relations with the Eastern bloc satellites.

Such appearances were deceptive, however. As we shall see, the government's actual attitude towards diplomatic openings to Eastern Europe during the latter

---

[17] Killian, *Hallstein*; Booz, *Hallsteinzeit*; Gray, *Germany's Cold War*.

[18] Adenauer's government declaration, 22 Sept. 1955, *Verhandlungen*, I WP, 5647.

[19] Booz, *Hallsteinzeit*, 17–32, 39–46; Killian, *Hallstein*; Wilhelm Grewe, *Rückblenden 1976–1951* (Frankfurt: Propyläen, 1979), 251–62.

[20] Marija Anic de Orsona, *Die erste Anerkennung der DDR: Der Bruch der deutsch-jugoslawischen Beziehungen 1957* (Baden-Baden: Nomos, 1990); Holm Sundhausen, 'Jugoslawisch-deutsche Beziehungen zwischen Normalisierung, Bruch und erneuter Normalisierung', in O. N. Haberl and H. Hecker (eds.), *Unfertige Nachbarschaften: Die Staaten Osteuropas und die Bundesrepublik Deutschland* (Essen: Reimar Hobbing, 1989), 133–45.

[21] VdL, 18 Oct. 1957 press release, BA: B 234/342; 'Die befreiende Tat', *Sudetendeutsche Zeitung* (26 Oct. 1957).

half of 1950s was considerably more flexible than a rigid reading of the Hallstein Doctrine would have suggested. Particularly in the period following the so-called Polish October of 1956, a wide array of governmental actors gave serious consideration to various Ostpolitik initiatives. Encouraged by Wladyslaw Gomulka's rise to power in Warsaw, Bonn's policy-makers detected a potential for growing independence in satellite capitals, a potential that might facilitate not only disintegration in the Soviet bloc but ultimately also reunification. The Federal Republic, in turn, could try to promote both developments by normalizing its relations with Eastern Europe. Although Khrushchev's Berlin ultimatum of November 1958, together with earlier indications of renewed cohesion in the Eastern camp, doused these high hopes, interest in Ostpolitik initiatives nevertheless persisted in Bonn through the first half of 1959. That interest waned only in the aftermath of the Geneva Foreign Ministers' Conference of May–July 1959, whose fruitlessness appeared to highlight the futility of such projects in the prevailing international and domestic atmosphere. However, despite the widespread principled backing which Ostpolitik initiatives enjoyed in the West German capital, particularly from prominent representatives of the government, the political opposition, and the business community, Bonn ultimately shied away from revising its concrete policies throughout the 1955–59 period. The following pages will explore the complex reasons for this caution, attempting, in particular, to assign proper weight to the important but often overlooked role played by the expellees and their purported organizational representatives.

IMMOBILITY IN OSTPOLITIK AND ITS CAUSES

Throughout the latter half of the 1950s, the most vocal and consistent advocates of normalized relations between West Germany and Eastern Europe were to be found amongst the political opposition in Bonn. This fact was hardly surprising, given the government's identification with the hard-line Hallstein Doctrine and the opposition's inherent interest in challenging the government's policies in order to enhance its own political profile. Accordingly, leading SPD figures frequently highlighted the need for diplomatic initiatives towards the East, particularly in internal party deliberations. They denounced Moscow's 'monopoly of representation in the satellite states' as harmful to German interests and clamoured for the establishment of both trade and political relations with the Eastern bloc countries, other than the GDR, with which only lower-level contacts were deemed acceptable.[22]

Similar voices also rang out from the FDP after the party left Adenauer's cabinet in early 1956. The Liberals had already begun to cultivate an oppositional

---

[22] Kalbitzer in the SPD's *Aussenpolitischer Ausschuss*, 30 May 1956, AdsD: PV, Neuer Bestand, 2868; Carlo Schmid's 16 Mar. 1958 interview, in Maas, *Dokumentation*, 168–9; Klotzbach, *Staatspartei*, 326–55, 356–68, 467–94; Wolfgang Schmidt, *Kalter Krieg, Koexistenz und kleine Schritte: Willy Brandt und die Deutschlandpolitik, 1948–63* (Wiesbaden: Westdeutscher Verlag, 2001).

profile on reunification and other issues during their six-and-a-half-year tenure as junior coalition partners of the CDU/CSU. On Ostpolitik, however, the FDP leadership had resisted party maverick Karl-Georg Pfleiderer's attempts to commit it to an avant-garde platform.[23] But after 1956 the tone of the party-internal discourse on Eastern policy changed markedly. In closed deliberations, FDP leaders now described German efforts to 'bring gradual movement to the Eastern front as 'essential'.[24] They also outlined the appropriate West German steps in much the same terms as the SPD: the establishment of trade missions and embassies in the East European capitals, accompanied by cautious efforts to build unofficial contacts to East Germany in order to avoid a further consolidation of national division.[25]

Both parties hoped to reap several benefits; the obvious profile-building at home went hand-in-hand with a number of anticipated foreign-policy gains. These expected blessings of an active Ostpolitik included increased trade opportunities, improved information about the satellite states, and reduced East European fears about Germany, all of which would presumably hasten the decline of Communism and the arrival of reunification.[26]

Business interests, particularly the export industry, formed another base for the advocacy of improved ties to Eastern Europe. Throughout the 1950s, prominent business representatives pressed for a liberalization of the various cold war restrictions that hobbled economic exchanges across the Iron Curtain. A particularly important force in that endeavour was the Eastern Committee of German Industry and Commerce (Ostausschuss der deutschen Wirtschaft), a consultative organ of prominent industrialists and bankers established in 1952, with full governmental backing, to coordinate trade between Eastern Europe and the Federal Republic. At that time West German government still lacked the sovereignty to perform such tasks itself, but even after that situation changed in 1955, the committee continued to function as a key intermediary between Bonn and the East European capitals. The committee consistently strove to improve eastward trading opportunities, and many of its members, as well as other business representatives, also favoured the establishment of formal governmental ties, particularly trade missions, between West Germany and Eastern Europe.[27]

Eastern policy initiatives also had numerous advocates within the government.

---

[23] FDP's *Bundesvorstand* protocols, 15 June 1952, *FDP-Bundesvorstand*, i/1. 336–54, and 22–3 Jan. 1954, *FDP-Bundesvorstand*, i/2. 1355–69.

[24] FDP's *Aussenpolitischer Ausschuss* protocols, 22 June 1956, ADL: Aussenpolitischer Ausschuss, 958.

[25] FDP's *Bundesvorstand* protocols , 31 Aug. 1956, *FDP-Bundesvorstand*, ii. 193–5; 'Entwurf für den ersten Teil der Leitsätze der Freien Demokratischen Partei für die Arbeit im dritten deutschen Bundestag', ADL: Aussenpolitischer Ausschuss, 959.

[26] See n. 25; Glatzeder, *Deutschlandpolitik*, 70–94; Brauers, *Deutschlandpolitik*, 74–119; Schmidt, *FDP*, 28–43.

[27] Robert Mark Spaulding, *Osthandel and Ostpolitik: German Trade Policies in Eastern Europe from Bismarck to Adenauer* (Providence, RI: Berghahn, 1997), 296–501; Angela Stent, *From Embargo to Ostpolitik: The Political Economy of West German–Soviet Relations, 1955–1980* (Cambridge: Cambridge University Press, 1981); Michael Kreile, *Osthandel und Ostpolitik* (Baden-Baden: Nomos, 1978).

The main institutional base of Ostpolitik activism was the Foreign Ministry, whose officialdom was overwhelmingly supportive of West German overtures to the satellite states. The Ministry's experts had opposed a rigid application of the Hallstein Doctrine from the start, arguing that the Federal Republic should not paralyse its own policies by ostracizing the satellite states because of a decision—the recognition of the GDR—that had clearly been dictated by the Soviet hegemon.[28] Similarly flexible attitudes persisted among Foreign Ministry officials throughout the latter half of the 1950s, not only among lower- and middle-level policy planners but also among such top-level figures as the Adenauer confidants Herbert Blankenhorn and Wilhelm Grewe. The favoured Ostpolitik scenario of these men consisted of a gradual normalization of West German relations with the Eastern bloc, beginning with the establishment of formal trade ties and culminating in full diplomatic contacts later on.[29] Only the GDR remained excluded from these blueprints, which in large part aimed at isolating and weakening East Berlin. But the Foreign Ministry advocates of an active Ostpolitik—much like their counterparts in the opposition—also dreamt of unleashing broader transformations that reached well beyond the borders of the two Germanys. Herbert Blankenhorn, for example, maintained in late 1957 that the establishment of official ties with Eastern Europe would enable West Germany to exert 'a magnetic force among the satellites, a force that slowly, step by step, strengthens the forces that promote a closer orientation to the West—and thus freedom'.[30]

Similar hopes and interests also manifested themselves on the cabinet level. The most consistent top-level advocate of a more engaged Ostpolitik was probably Felix von Eckardt, the long-term head of the government's Press and Information Office and a close Adenauer associate.[31] But Foreign Minister Heinrich von Brentano also displayed recurring interest in diplomatic overtures to the Eastern bloc. Motivated, like his leading Auswärtiges Amt subordinates, by a desire for progress on reunification and East European liberation, Brentano seriously considered various Ostpolitik options during the latter half of the 1950s. He described the improvement of West German relations with Eastern Europe in general and Poland in particular as a matter 'particularly close to his heart' and repeatedly expressed willingness to consider side-stepping the provisions of the Hallstein Doctrine when dealing with independent-minded Eastern bloc regimes.[32]

Even the man at the very top, chancellor Adenauer, showed at least principled openness to the establishment of official ties with the Eastern satellites. He, too, perceived a potential for positive 'evolutionary development[s]' in the Eastern

[28] Grewe, *Rückblenden*, 252; Kosthorst, *Brentano*, 90–3.

[29] Blankenhorn's diary, 29 Nov. 1956, BA: NL Blankenhorn, 69, pp. 11–12, and 31 Dec. 1956, BA: NL Blankenhorn, 70, pp. 3–4; Grewe *Rückblenden*, 262–3.

[30] Blankenhorn's diary, 4 Oct. 1957, cited in Schwarz, *Staatsmann*, 372–3.

[31] Eckardt to Adenauer, 17 Aug. 1959, StBKAH: III/24; Schwarz, *Staatsmann*, 373; Eckardt, *Leben*.

[32] Brentano interview, 17 Aug. 1957, in Maas, *Dokumentation*, 149–50; Brentano in the Bundestag's *Auswärtiger Ausschuss*, 9 Nov. 1956, as reported by Hans Furler, BA: NL Furler, 40; Brentano in the cabinet, 17 Oct. 1957, as reported by Hans Merkatz, ACDP: I-148-041/1; Kosthorst, *Brentano*, 167–209.

bloc, particularly in the Poland of the early Gomulka period, and spoke of a need for a rapprochement between the Federal Republic and the satellite states to encourage such trends.[33] The right procedure, according to Adenauer, was to move slowly, starting with a build-up of trade relations and then 'continu[ing] step-by-step'.[34] To be sure, the Chancellor repeatedly stressed the need for 'patience' and 'perseverance' in the pursuit of Ostpolitik, and the caution which he preached reflected his ultimately low personal interest in both Eastern Europe and even reunification.[35] But Adenauer was by no means doctrinally opposed to openings towards the Eastern bloc, as long as they were compatible with his definition of the Federal Republic's broader needs in the context of the cold war.

Despite the widespread interest among Bonn's political and business elites, West German Ostpolitik initiatives remained few and unimpressive during the latter half of the 1950s. To be sure, the Foreign Ministry invested a good deal of time and effort in planning potential policy moves. Between late 1956 and late 1958 the ministry's experts produced several memoranda that weighed the pros and cons of various Ostpolitik options and recommended steps towards a normalization of relations with Eastern Europe, beginning with the establishment of trade missions, particularly in Poland and Czechoslovakia.[36] But the only concrete result achieved in this period was a three-year trade agreement with the Soviet Union, signed in April 1958 after difficult and protracted negotiations.[37] Because Bonn had already established diplomatic ties to the Soviets, the trade deal was hardly a monumental breakthrough, particularly since the Federal Republic failed to follow this achievement with similar practical moves in the rest of Eastern Europe. In its official statements, the government instead stuck to vague generalities, typically referring only to West Germany's desire for peaceful, neighbourly relations with Eastern Europe without specifying what steps should be taken and when.[38]

Even the few top-secret overtures that Bonn ultimately did make towards East European satellite states yielded no tangible results. These clandestine efforts unfolded in two main phases. The first covered the year or so immediately following the so-called Polish October of 1956. During this potentially transformative period, the Federal Republic's policy-makers were eager to explore the political landscape through direct contacts with Eastern bloc representatives, particularly

[33] Adenauer, *Erinnerungen 1955–1959*, 230; 'Die aussenpolitische Konzeption Adenauers', *Neue Zürcher Zeitung* (21 June 1958).

[34] Adenauer's CBS interview, 22 Sept. 1957, *DzD* iii/3/3. 1636; his 3 Oct. 1958 press conference, *DzD* iii/4/3. 1760–1.

[35] Adenauer, *Erinnerungen 1955–1959*, 243.

[36] Welck's 18 Oct. 1956 'Aufzeichnung', BA: NL Blankenhorn, 68, p. 143; Fechter's 14 Nov. 1956 'Aufzeichnung', PA/AA: Abt. 7. 138; the 8 Jan. and 8 Oct. 1957 memoranda discussed in Grewe, *Rückblenden*, 263, 751–2; the Sept. 1958 memorandum described in Brentano to Adenauer, 23 Sept. 1958, Baring, *Sehr verehrter*, 250–2, and in Reinhold Schulze to Thomas Dehler, 10 Oct. 1958, ADL: AK Aussenpolitik, 1852.

[37] Stent, *Embargo*, 55–67; Kreile, *Osthandel*, 51–6; Spaulding, *Osthandel*, 440–58.

[38] Adenauer's government declarations, 8 Nov. 1956, in Maas, *Dokumentation*, 126–7; and 29 Oct. 1957, *Verhandlungen*, III WP, vol. 39, 24.

Poles. In the most spectacular action, a high-ranking West German diplomat, acting upon Foreign Minister Brentano's orders, scouted out the prospects for diplomatic relations with Poland in a series of secret meetings with his Polish counterparts in Washington.[39] Although the contacts confirmed Warsaw's strong interest in the establishment of official ties, Bonn backed off in 1957, influenced first by the pressures of the upcoming Bundestag election and then by the post-election crisis triggered by Yugoslavia's decision to recognize the GDR.[40] After a relatively quiet interlude, the government returned to secret Ostpolitik initiatives in the first half of 1959.[41] As we shall see, it carefully prepared a proposal for non-aggression agreements between West Germany on the one hand and Poland and Czechoslovakia on the other. However, this effort also came to naught, leaving the Federal Republic's Eastern policy at a dead end by the time the decade drew to a close.

The opposition's record in promoting concrete Ostpolitik measures was hardly more impressive than the government's, although at first sight the dif-ferences appeared considerable. In contrast to the government and its main party-political component, the CDU/CSU, both leading opposition parties incor-porated explicit calls for a normalization of relations with Eastern Europe into their official programmes. The SPD blazed the trail. As early as 1952 it had declared the establishment of 'normal relations with all states' as one of its goals.[42] Subsequent statements gave more specificity to this general principle, and by 1956 the party had adopted a position which it continued to espouse through to the end of the decade: an endorsement of 'economic and diplomatic relations' with Eastern Europe, particularly Poland and Czechoslovakia.[43] The FDP trod the same path soon after it left the Bonn coalition in February 1956. Within months it had become a public champion of an 'active and constructive policy' aimed at the establishment of diplomatic relations' with the East European satellites.[44]

However, both parties imposed clear limits on their profile-building with this issue. They kept their statements vague, avoiding specific suggestions of how to begin the normalization process. They also portrayed the establishment of official ties to the East European states as an ultimately secondary problem, hedged with

---

[39] Von Kessel to Brentano, 23 Jan. 1957, BA: NL Brentano, 165, pp. 166–74; Baring, *Verehrter*, 192–4; Kosthorst, *Brentano*, 186–9. In late 1956, Brentano and von Eckardt also sought informal contacts to the Polish Military Mission in East Berlin. See Kosthorst, *Brentano*, 182–3.

[40] Von Kessel, 'Aufzeichnung', 19 June 1957, PA/AA: NL Kessel, 8; Kosthorst, *Brentano*, 186–9, 191–203; Hans-Peter Schwarz, 'Vortasten nach Warschau', *Die Politische Meinung*, 42/326 (Jan. 1997): 92; Dieter Bingen, *Polenpolitik*, esp. 47–57; Markus Krzoska, 'Wladyslaw Gomulka und Deutschland', *Zeitschrift für Ostforschung*, 43 (1994): 184–9; Lee, *Uneasy*, 196–8; Spaulding, *Osthandel*, 423–35.

[41] Some secret contacts with Polish representatives continued into 1958. See Schwarz, *Staatsmann*, 420–1; id., 'Vortasten', 93; Bingen, *Polenpolitik*, 57–61.

[42] SPD's 1952 'Aktionsprogramm', *Jahrbuch der SPD 1952/1953* (Bonn: SPD, 1954), 265.

[43] 'Forderungen der Sozialdemokratischen Partei zur deutschen Wiedervereinigungspolitik', in *Protokolle der Verhandlungen des Parteitages der SPD vom 10. bis 14. Juli 1956 in München* (Bonn: SPD, 1956), 345.

[44] FDP's Berlin Programme, 26 Jan. 1957, in Juling, *Programmatische*, 153–4; 'Leitsätze der FDP für die Arbeit im 3. Deutschen Bundestag und in den Landestagen', 2 Mar. 1958, ADL: AK Aussenpolitik, 1852.

preconditions and subordinate to a broader international détente, which both parties hoped to promote with the creation of a European-wide security system that would ideally culminate in a dissolution of the existing military alliances.[45]

The caution characteristic of the SPD and the FDP was evident even in their most spectacular Ostpolitik action: a joint parliamentary motion in favour of diplomatic relations with Warsaw, presented to the Bundestag in January 1958. Although the initiative sounded bold, both parties proved unwilling to press it in the parliament. As a result, the government's dilatory tactics prevailed, and the motion was quietly shunted to a parliamentary suborgan, the Foreign Affairs Committee, which then proceeded to deliberate it for the next three years.[46] More intensive engagement for an active Ostpolitik was detectable only in a handful of individual opposition leaders, whose efforts often encountered public disavowals from their own parties. The most prominent such figure was the SPD's Carlo Schmid, who repeatedly emphasized the need for a normalization of relations with Eastern Europe in his public statements and even undertook a high-profile reconnaissance trip to Poland in early 1958.[47]

Why, then, were Bonn's elites so reluctant to take concrete steps towards a normalization of relations with Eastern Europe despite their interest in such measures? The standard explanations offered by the leading actors at the time stressed cool *Staatsräson*. Among high governmental representatives, four such lines of reasoning cropped up with particular frequency. The first, and most broadly defined, rationale for avoiding a more active Ostpolitik preoccupied the Chancellor more than anyone else. Adenauer worried that an overly active Eastern policy could weaken the Federal Republic's Western links by disorienting its citizens and arousing Allied suspicions of a German return to the traditions of Rapallo-style *Schaukelpolitik* between the USSR and the West. These trends, the Chancellor dreaded, could then culminate in German isolation between the blocs, making the country the 'football of the conflicting interests of the world'.[48]

The other three justifications for an immobile Ostpolitik in terms of *raison d'état* had wider roots within the government. A prominent place accrued to the anticipated consequences of Eastern policy moves for the international standing of the GDR. Despite the widespread willingness in the Foreign Ministry and else-where to consider exempting the Eastern bloc states from the provisions of the Hallstein Doctrine, key decision-makers ultimately shied away from concrete

---

[45] On the SPD, see 'Forderungen der Sozialdemokratischen Partei zur deutschen Wieder-vereinigungspolitik', in *Protokolle der Verhandlungen des Parteitages der SPD vom 10. bis 14. Juli 1956 in München*, 344–7; 'Deutschlandplan' of 1959, *Jahrbuch der SPD 1958/1959* (Bonn: SPD, 1960), 397–401; Siebenmorgen, *Gezeitenwechsel*, 234–40. On the FDP, see n. 44; 'Deutschlandplan' of 1959, in Juling, *Programmatische*, 158–62.   [46] *Verhandlungen*, III WP, 421.

[47] Schmid, 'Besuch der Universitäten in Warschau und Krakau: Tagebuch einer Polenreise im Jahre 1958', in Werner Plum (ed.), *Ungewöhnliche Normalisierung: Beziehungen der Bundesrepublik Deutschland zu Polen* (Bonn: Neue Gesellschaft, 1984), 191–203; Petra Weber, *Carlo Schmid: Eine poli-tische Biographie* (Munich: Beck, 1996), 598–603.

[48] Adenauer, *Erinnerungen 1953–1955*, 418; Schwarz, 'Adenauer und Russland', 381–2; id., 'Adenauers Ostpolitik', esp. 215.

steps in this direction, in good part precisely for fear of upgrading East Germany's stature in the process. This viewpoint found a strong advocate in Foreign Minister Brentano. According to him, the build-up of official ties to the East European countries would 'inevitably' open up the problem of 'the status of the GDR'.[49] More specifically, Brentano feared, 'the establishment of diplomatic relations with the satellite states [would] give other countries an excuse to recognize' East Germany and thus undermine a central founding myth of the Federal Republic, that is, its claim to be the sole legitimate representative of the German nation.[50] As the Foreign Minister explained in an August 1957 interview, in his view the danger of unleashing a wave of recognition of the pariah regime in East Berlin therefore constituted 'the decisive obstacle to a normalization' of West German relations with the Eastern bloc.[51]

Another oft-cited governmental justification for a slow-moving Ostpolitik was the Oder-Neisse problem, as viewed from a foreign-policy-centred perspective. Although Warsaw and Prague, the two key capitals, repeatedly signalled interest in diplomatic relations with Bonn during the latter half of the 1950s, they also made clear that they regarded the post-war territorial status quo, particularly the Oder-Neisse line, as final. They therefore expected the establishment of relations to be accompanied by an at least implicit West German acceptance of this fact.[52]

Such proposals elicited consistent rebuffs from Bonn's policy-makers, whose public statements had committed them to the opposing viewpoint, according to which the Oder-Neisse line was just a temporary, administrative expedient and the final resolution of the boundary problem had to await a future peace settlement. As Foreign Minister Brentano argued in the fall of 1958, the establishment of formal relations on the Eastern bloc's terms would lead to a 'recognition of the Polish viewpoint on the border question', which, in turn, would significantly harm Bonn's international interests.[53] It would weaken the credibility of the West and 'undermine' Germany's 'future negotiating position' vis-à-vis the Soviet bloc, as a high Foreign Ministry official asserted in late 1957.[54] According to this reasoning, a cool diplomatic logic thus precluded any concrete initiatives towards Eastern Europe as long as such steps presupposed unilateral West German concessions on a territorial issue of presumably considerable legal and political significance.

---

[49] Brentano in the CDU/CSU *Bundestagsfraktion's Arbeitskreis* V, 13 Nov. 1956, ACDP: VIII-006-001/1.   [50] Brentano to Adenauer, 23 Sept. 1958, in Baring, *Verehrter*, 251.

[51] Brentano's 17 Aug. 1957 interview, in Maas, *Dokumentation*, 149.

[52] Polish declarations of 17 Mar. 1955, 12 Oct. 1955, and 14 Jan. 1957 in Maas, *Dokumentation*, 109–10, 116, and 129–30; joint Czechoslovak—GDR declarations of 11 Sept. 1956 and 24 May 1957, DzD iii/2/2. 736–8 and iii/3/2. 1076–7; Czechoslovak Prime Minister Siroky to Adenauer, 15 July 1958, DzD iii/4/2. 1456–9. In 1956–8 the Poles also signalled willingness to exclude the Oder-Neisse problem from negotiations about diplomatic relations with West Germany. See e.g. Carlo Schmid, *Erinnerungen* (Berne: Scherz, 1979), 631; Baring, *Verehrter*, 193. However, any agreement to set up official ties that did not address the Oder-Neisse problem would have come very close to a tacit recognition of the existing situation. See also Bingen, *Polenpolitik*, 54–5.

[53] Brentano to Adenauer, 23 Sept. 1958, in Baring, *Verehrter*, 251.

[54] Von Kessel to the AA, 19 Sept. 1957, PA/AA: NL von Kessel, 8.

The government's final *Staatsräson*-based rationalization of a status quo Eastern policy derived from a hard-nosed reading of power politics within the Soviet bloc. In its milder and more widespread version this doctrine posited that the West in general and the Federal Republic in particular had to exercise great caution vis-à-vis the satellite states in order to avoid provoking Moscow. Citing the bloody suppression of the October 1956 Hungarian Uprising as the basis for their fears, many governmental actors argued that overly forward German initiatives towards the East might unsettle the Soviets and culminate in further brutal crackdowns in Eastern Europe, especially in Gomulka's Poland.[55] Such an outcome, in turn, would not only thwart hopes of further liberalization in the satellite states but also run the risk of an escalation, possibly extending the conflict into East Germany or even engendering a direct clash between the superpowers.[56] To avoid these potential calamities, governmental leaders argued, prudence and circumspection were essential. In the words of Foreign Minister Brentano, the Federal Republic had to 'avoid the impression of attempting to meddle in domestic developments in Eastern Europe'—an impression that in his view might be awakened by overly dramatic Ostpolitik initiatives.[57]

In its more extreme form, this power-political logic went several steps further. Whereas the mainstream version of the doctrine located the pitfalls of Ostpolitik initiatives in their potentially dangerous international implications, the more radical outlook sought to deny the usefulness of such initiatives altogether. This line of reasoning—whose proponents included both Chancellor Adenauer and Foreign Minister Brentano, albeit only periodically and inconsistently, typically at times when the political situation in Eastern Europe appeared particularly bleak—proceeded from the premise that the East Europe governments were ultimately too dependent on their bloc hegemon to be able to influence political developments on their own. 'The key' to the fate of East Europe in general and to West German Ostpolitik in particular therefore lay not in Warsaw or Prague but 'in Moscow', as the Chancellor occasionally argued in both public and private.[58] From this coolly calculating perspective, policy initiatives towards Eastern Europe could thus be seen as nothing but minor side-shows to the real cold war drama whose eastern scenes were being directed with dictatorial severity by the puppet masters in the Kremlin.

Several of these *Staatsräson*-based justifications of a cautious Ostpolitik also found support in the opposition. The insistence on the invalidity of the Oder-Neisse line and on the deferral of an eastern border settlement until a future peace treaty was a particularly oft-cited consideration, especially in the SPD but also

---

[55] Adenauer's comments, 17 July and 6 Aug. 1957, in Küsters, *Teegespräche*, ii. 201, 217; Brentano's 17 Dec. 1956 interview, in Maas, *Dokumentation*, 128; Brentano's 5 Nov. 1956 discussion with the US Ambassador to France, PA/AA: Ministerbüro, 156.

[56] John F. Dulles's report of a conversation with Brentano, 13 Dec. 1956, *FRUS 1955–1957*, xxvi. 188.

[57] Brentano's 16 Dec. 1956 interview, in Maas, *Dokumentation*, 127.

[58] Adenauer to Blankenhorn, 14 Feb. 1958, cited in Schwarz, *Staatsmann*, 382; Adenauer, *Erinnerungen 1955–1959*, 240.

among the Free Democrats.[59] In the opposition, as in the government, public attempts to explain why this inflexible stance had to be maintained typically stressed vague foreign-policy calculations, such as the need to refuse concessions on an issue of principle on which Germany's international position appeared strong and which would presumably loom large in future peace negotiations.[60] The 'dangers of an abandonment of the Hallstein Doctrine', particularly the prospect of a major improvement in the GDR's international standing, also preoccupied many opposition leaders and caused them to harbour reservations about Eastern policy initiatives.[61] In addition, individual politicians in the SPD and the FDP worried that Ostpolitik moves might provoke Western suspicions of Bonn's intentions while failing to bring about any changes in Eastern Europe, given the Soviet Union's ongoing dominance in the region.[62]

The various *Staatsräson*-based arguments against a more active Ostpolitik clearly constituted a very significant brake on the freedom of movement of both the government and the opposition. A good indication of this fact is the failure of the West German business community to push Bonn to a more active Eastern policy engagement, even in trade policy. Time and again during the 1950s, the political elites in general and Adenauer's government in particular pulled overly eager business activists back from East European engagements, thus highlighting the 'primacy of politics' over commercial considerations in West Germany's early Ostpolitik.[63] However, the seemingly statesmanlike logic behind such stances was often far from unequivocal, as party-political, electoral, and other tactical motives routinely mixed with foreign-policy considerations as catalysts for specific statements and actions. In addition, leading politicians frequently changed their specific arguments at short notice and often appeared to espouse mutually contradictory views, thus lending an air of muddled inconsistency to their reasoning. But the underlying foreign-policy concerns nevertheless built real and powerful constraints against more innovative Eastern policies in the Federal Republic of the late 1950s.

Unsurprisingly, subsequent scholarly analyses of the country's Ostpolitik have therefore also focused overwhelmingly on these foreign-policy factors, thus evoking in an only slightly modified form the hallowed German tradition of a *Primat der Aussenpolitik* as the premise for explaining state behaviour in the international arena.[64] In stressing this interpretative model, however, both

---

[59] 'Grenzfragen erst im Friedensvertrag', *Parlamentarisch-Politischer Pressedienst* (2 Sept. 1958), AdsD: Seliger-Archiv, NL Jaksch, J3; FDP's *Deutschlandplan*, 20 Mar. 1959 and *Aktionsprogramm 1957*, in Juling, *Programmatische*, 159, 155.

[60] See e.g. the article 'Grenzfragen' (n. 59).

[61] Wenzel Jaksch, 'Grundsätzliches zur Osteuropa-Politik der SPD', AdsD: Seliger-Archiv, NL Jaksch, J5, p. 4.

[62] Ibid.; Brauers, *Deutschlandpolitik*, 101.

[63] Spaulding, *Osthandel*, 368–73; Stent, *Embargo*; Kreile, *Osthandel*; Hanna Paul-Calm, *Ostpolitik und Wirtschaftsinteressen in der Ära Adenauer* (Frankfurt: Campus, 1981).

[64] Prominent examples include Gotto, 'Deutschland- und Ostpolitik'; Hans-Peter Schwarz's various works, including 'Aussenpolitische Konzept', 'Adenauers Ostpolitik', 'Deutschlandpolitische Vorstellungen', *Aufstieg*, *Staatsmann*; Kosthorst, *Brentano*.

contemporary political leaders and subsequent scholars have distorted and over-simplified the actual dynamics of policy-formulation that prevailed in newly sovereign Bonn. The most glaring omission has been the tendency to downplay the domestic roots of Ostpolitik, especially the political elites' calculations and actions vis-à-vis the largest and most influential domestic constituency with a vested interest in this issue: the expellees in general and their purported organizational representatives in particular.

Throughout the latter half of the 1950s, the expellee lobby, together with its potentially millions-strong popular following, continued to preoccupy Bonn's decision-makers in much the same way as in the preceding years. The institutional framework of interaction between the political elites and the expellee organizations, for example, remained essentially unchanged. All four main parties still maintained special suborgans through which expellee representatives could try to articulate their demands. Each party also continued to promote individual expellee leaders within its ranks, keeping a sizeable number of such activists in the national limelight, as both party leaders and parliamentarians. On the governmental level, the continuities were equally striking. At the very top, Hans Christoph Seebohm as Transport Minister and Theodor Oberländer as Minister for Expellee Affairs provided ongoing personal links between the cabinet and the expellee movement, while numerous civil servants of an expellee background continued to serve similar functions on less elevated planes. In a further carry-over from Bonn's pre-sovereignty days, representatives of the expellee groups still enjoyed frequent access to governmental leaders through personal meetings, many of which were hosted either by the Chancellor himself or his key advisers and ministers.[65] In addition, the flow of federal subsidies to the expellee organisations continued unabated.[66]

The ambitions and intentions behind these institutionalized forms of interaction also remained largely unaltered. The expellee organizations continued to regard their various links to the government and the parties as a potential high road to direct involvement in Bonn's top-level politics. With glowing hopes, expellee activists pressed for an active inclusion of their organizations in the formulation and implementation of the Federal Republic's Eastern policies. Echoing standard arguments first introduced in the pre-sovereignty years, they maintained that no Ostpolitik decisions should be made 'without first hearing

---

[65] The VdL alone had the following meetings with Adenauer, Globke, or Brentano between early 1956 and early 1957: Globke ('Beschlussprotokoll über die Präsidialsitzung des VdL am 9. März 1956', SDA: NL Lodgman, XI-22); Brentano and Globke ('Beschlussprotokoll über die Präsidialsitzung des VdL am 4. Juni 1956', SDA: NL Lodgman, XI-22); Brentano and Adenauer (Manteuffel-Szoege to the VdL Presidium, 17 July 1956, SDA: Kanzlei des Sprechers, B4/13); Globke ('Beschlussprotokoll über die Präsidialsitzung des VdL am 22. Oktober 1956', SDA: NL Lodgman, XI-22); Brentano ('Bechlussprotokoll über die Präsidialsitzung des VdL am 26. November 1956', SDA: BVIII/3); Brentano ('Vermerk über die Besprechung mit Bundesaussenminister von Brentano in Bonn am 21. Januar 1957', BA: B 234/300).

[66] 'Betr: Bericht der Bundesregierung über die von ihr in den Rechnungsjahren 1957, 1958 und 1959 getroffenen Massnahmen gemäss 96 BVFG', 30 Aug. 1960, BT/PA: Ausschuss für Heimatvertriebene, 3. WP, Ausschuss-Drucksachen, vol. 115, pp. 50–1.

those directly interested in and co-responsible for the Eastern territories' and that the pattern of interaction between the political elites and the expellee leaders should be one of 'steady, ongoing co-operation based on an exchange of opinions'.[67]

Such pleas for a far-reaching inclusion of expellee activists in the policy-making process had evoked no support among the country's political elites prior to May 1955, and the second half of the decade brought no change in the situation. Especially the government but also the largest parties continued to regard the various institutionalized ties between themselves and the expellee organizations primarily as a means of tracking and influencing the latter and their followers. The kind of cooperation envisaged by the expellee groups did not fit into this framework, and as a consequence the expellee lobby's representatives remained excluded from the inner sanctums of Bonn's foreign-policy establishment.[68]

Although expellee activists repeatedly expressed dissatisfaction with this state of affairs, they steered clear of all-out confrontations with the powers-that-be over the issue.[69] The existing institutional ties did, after all, accord them a good deal of primarily indirect political influence as well as a number of additional benefits. These included considerable financial advantages—albeit at the cost of a growing dependency on governmental coffers—and chances for personal advancement. Many expellee leaders avidly exploited such career opportunities, rising into comfortable party or governmental positions and typically learning to accommodate themselves to most of their political patrons' viewpoints in the process.

On a less institutionalized level, the political elites' ongoing preoccupation with the expellee lobby was also evident in their essentially unchanged public stances on the main Ostpolitik demands of the expellee organizations. As in the pre-sovereignty years, all the main parties and the government repeatedly pledged their support for the *Heimatrecht* and the self-determination right of the expellees. A formal government declaration of June 1956, for example, described the two concepts as 'indispensable prerequisites' of a solution of the expellee problem, and similarly phrased official statements also repeatedly issued from each of the leading parties.[70] Several of the declarations produced by the government and the parties even went a step further, suggesting that the granting of the two rights to the German expellees constituted a precondition for a normalization of the Federal Republic's relations with Eastern Europe. Most of the time such a linkage was only implied. In representative public statements Foreign Minister Brentano and others first lamented the injustice inherent in the denial of the *Heimatrecht* and the right of self-determination to the German expellees and then asserted that a future

---

[67] Manteuffel-Szoege to Brentano, 4 Oct. 1957 and 13 Dec. 1956, SDA: NL Lodgman, XXIV-01.

[68] Wambach, *Verbändestaat*, 106–25.

[69] Manteuffel-Szoege to Brentano, 13 Dec. 1956, SDA: NL Lodgman, XXIV-01; Sudetendeutsche Landsmannschaft, 'Entschliessung zur Heimatpolitik', 2–3 March 1957, SDA: NL Lodgman, IV-33.

[70] Maas, *Dokumentation*, 118; CSU, 'Grundsatzprogramm' of 1957, in *25 Jahre Christlich-Soziale Union* (Munich: CSU, 1970), 95; Erich Ollenhauer's 1955 address to the Seliger-Gemeinde, in the SPD pamphlet *Heimatrecht im Osten, Lebensrecht im Westen* (Bonn: SPD, 1957), 11; FDP, Berlin Programme, 26 Jan. 1957, ADL: A1-106.

normalization of relations with Eastern Europe could proceed only on the basis of 'justice and fairness'.[71] But in some cases the centrality of the two expellee demands was postulated more explicitly. The FDP, for example, incorporated into its January 1957 Berlin Programme references to 'the right to one's homeland' and to 'self-determination' as two 'basic principles' on which the Federal Republic's foreign policies were to be based.[72] And a few months later Franz-Josef Strauss, speaking for the CSU, hyperbolically assigned to the *Heimatrecht* 'priority over all political considerations' in West German external relations.[73]

Discussions of the Oder-Neisse problem provided additional evidence of the continued importance of the expellees and their organizations for the Ostpolitik deliberations of Bonn's elites. As we have seen, both the government and the opposition typically justified their inflexible public stances on this issue with classical foreign-policy calculations, rooted in the logic of international law and the international state system. Although such statements undoubtedly reflected considerable genuine conviction, in part they also served as a screen for domestically rooted considerations which leading politicians preferred not to air too openly in public, presumably for fear of appearing overly dependent on home-grown influences and thus feeding foreign fears of a domestically driven German revanchism.

Regardless of such precautions, the fact remained that the eastern border orthodoxy in West German public discourse—premised on a rejection of the Oder-Neisse line, a postponement of territorial decisions until a peace settlement, and an insistence on the continued legal validity of the Reich's 1937 boundaries in the meantime—was in large part a by-product of the expellee problem. Leading politicians occasionally highlighted this fact even in public, particularly in statements aimed at courting expellee audiences. In a representative declaration to a large expellee rally in the spring of 1957, the SPD, for example, labelled the struggle for the reacquisition of the territories east of the Oder-Neisse line the 'guiding star' of the party's broader Eastern policy programme, which, in turn, aimed at promoting the *Heimatrecht* of the expellees.[74] Behind the scenes, some party leaders waxed a good deal more explicit about their motives. The FDP's Erich Mende, for instance, acknowledged in early 1959 that his party's stance on the Oder-Neisse issue had been motivated 'in no small part' by concerns about domestic 'public opinion' in general and about 'the reflexive reactions of the expellee organizations' in particular. Similar off-the-record admissions also issued from several other prominent politicians, including the SPD's Helmut Kalbitzer and the CDU's Eugen Gerstenmaier.[75]

---

[71] Government declaration, 28 June 1956, in Maas, *Dokumentation*, 118.

[72] ADL: A1-106.

[73] Strauss at the CSU's *Landesversammlung*, 1 June 1957, ACSP: LV 1.6.1957, 5, p. 29.

[74] 'Erklärung zum SPD-Kongress für Vertriebene, Flüchtlinge und Kriegsgeschädigte', Wiesbaden, 13–14 Apr. 1957, AdsD: PV-Protokolle 1957, 16.

[75] Mende in the FDP's *Bundeshauptausschuss*, 21 Mar. 1959, ADL: A12-31, p. 35; Kalbitzer in the SPD's *Aussenpolitischer Ausschuss*, 30 May 1956, AdsD: PV, Neuer Bestand, 2868; Blankenhorn's diary markings about Gerstenmaier, 12 Oct. 1959, BA: NL Blankenhorn, 98a, p. 151.

Although the Federal Republic's political elites were thus willing to continue their public support of the expellee lobby's main Ostpolitik desiderata, their revisionist engagement remained subject to clear limits, much as in the pre-sovereignty period. The government and the leading parties still unequivocally renounced violence as a tool of Eastern policy.[76] They also refused to endorse any open territorial claims that extended beyond the Reich's 1937 borders. To be sure, the decisiveness with which the political elites rejected such claims in their internal deliberations was often not reflected in their public statements, particularly in those targeted at expellees from beyond the 1937 boundaries.[77] The standard calls for the granting of both the *Heimatrecht* and the self-determination right to the German expellees were in many ways ambiguous and could easily be construed as an indirect endorsement of further-reaching annexationist ambitions.

Many politicians also proved adept at addressing expellee audiences with suggestive phrases that seemed to promise a good deal while actually eschewing any real commitments. Chancellor Adenauer showed particular skill at this kind of manipulation, frequently asserting that virtues such as 'perseverance', 'patience', and 'faith in the *Heimat*' would eventually enable even groups like the Sudeten Germans to 'return home in peace and freedom'.[78] However, such statements by the Chancellor and others consistently avoided concrete proposals or promises, thus illustrating the fact that the political elites continued to define the limits of publicly acceptable revisionist rhetoric. Protest though they might, expellee activists simply could not force the government and the parties to espouse causes which were considered dangerous or otherwise inadvisable.

The motives for the political establishment's close public identification with the expellee lobby's key Ostpolitik demands also remained essentially un-changed during the latter half of the 1950s. Any genuine belief in the merits of the cause had been fading fast during the first half of the decade, and after 1955 the absence of such convictions among the country's top politicians became increasingly clear. Foreign Minister Brentano, for example, privately acknowledged that the former Eastern territories were 'forever lost to Germany'.[79] The Chancellor concurred, and so did numerous other key figures in both the government and the opposition. In one behind-the-scenes statement after another, these leaders dismissed Germany's claims to the lands east of the Oder-Neisse as 'politically utopian' 'daydreams' with no international backing and 'no chance' of

---

[76] Foreign Minister Brentano's 25 Apr. 1957 speech, in Maas (ed.), *Dokumentation*, 137–8; FDP's Berlin Programme, 26 Jan. 1957, ADL A1-106; declaration by the SPD's 'Kongress für Vertriebene, Flüchtlinge und Kriegsgeschädigte', Wiesbaden, 13–14 Apr. 1957, AdsD: PV-Protokolle 1957, 16.

[77] Meyer-Lindenberg to Referat A, 4 Sept. 1958, PA/AA: Abt. 7. 261; deliberations in the SPD's *Bundestagsfraktion*, 28–9 May 1956, in *SPD-Fraktion*, iii. 324–6; and in the CDU/CSU's *Bund-estagsfraktion*, 26 June 1956, ACDP: VIII-001-A/1, 1007/2.

[78] Adenauer's telegram to the 1957 *Sudetendeutscher Tag*, *Sudetendeutsche Zeitung* (22 June 1957); Adenauer's speech at the 1959 *Schlesier-Treffen*, 28 June 1959, StBkAH: Reden, Interviews, Artikeln, 1959/1; Mensing, *Briefwechsel*.

[79] Hans-Jakob Stehle, 'Adenauer, Polen und die deutsche Frage', in Foschepoth, *Adenauer*, 89; Brentano's comments to Couve de Murville , 19 Oct. 1957, *Documents diplomatiques français*, 1957/2 (Paris: Impr. Nationale, 1991), 563.

fulfilment.[80] In similarly frank terms, they also lashed out at the expellees' self-proclaimed rights to their homelands and to self-determination. As in earlier years, governmental and oppositional leaders privately dismissed the political efficacy of these legal constructs and defined their content in terms that diverged sharply from those upheld by the expellee activists. To Chancellor Adenauer, for example, the *Heimatrecht* was a theoretical concept of minor significance that might, at best, enable some interested expellees to return to their former homelands which 'as a result of the Peace Treaty will become Polish'.[81] The Foreign Ministry, in turn, insisted that the government would never support self-determination in its extreme expellee definition, that is, as a tool of effecting the 'reannexation' of, say, the 'Sudetenland'.[82]

None of the expellee organizations' key Ostpolitik demands thus accorded with the actual beliefs of the country's political establishment, although this fact remained hidden from the public, as key leaders insisted on keeping their true convictions secret.[83] To be sure, some differences of opinion still existed among Bonn's elites. Politicians and officials linked to the expellee movement through personal connections, institutional functions, or both were predictably less prone to exercise harsh criticism than their less involved colleagues. More significantly, Chancellor Adenauer also proved more tolerant of the expellee activists and their arguments than many other leading figures. Despite his total lack of interest in actually implementing the expellee groups' revisionist Ostpolitik programme, Adenauer cultivated the image of a special friend of the expellees and never indulged in the kinds of behind-the-scenes outbursts in which Foreign Minister Brentano, for example, cursed the expellee activists as 'unteachable nationalists'.[84]

In the continuing absence of genuine convictions, instrumental considerations remained the primary determinants of the public stances by the government and the parties on the expellee lobby's chief Ostpolitik demands. At times, leading politicians still expressed concern about a potential for a large-scale radicalization among the expellees and viewed professions of loyalty to the revisionist Eastern policy canon as a safeguard against such tendencies.[85] However, these fears had

---

[80] Grewe to Brentano, 19 Mar. 1958, PA/AA: Abt. 7. 33; van Scherpenberg to Brentano, 24 July 1959, cited in Baring, *Verehter*, 274; SPD's presidium protocols, 23 Feb. 1959, AdsD: Präsidium-Protokolle, 23.6.58–26.10.59; Adenauer's 17 July 1959 comments, in *Teegespräche 1955–1958*, ed. Küsters, 201–2.

[81] Adenauer's 16 June 1959 comments, in *Teegespräche 1959–61*, ed. Küsters, 94.

[82] Von Welck, 'Aufzeichnung, Betr: Entschliessung der sudetendeutschen Parlamentarier zur sudetendeutschen Frage', 24 June 1957, PA/AA: Abt. 7. 291b.

[83] SPD presidium protocols, 23 Feb. 1959, AdsD: Präsidium-Protokolle, 23.6.58–26.10.59; Ernst Lemmer to Axel Springer, 16 Aug. 1959, BA: NL Thedieck, 144; Brentano in April 1958, as cited in Stehle, 'Adenauer', 89.

[84] Brentano to G. Pohl, 9 Dec. 1956, BA: NL Brentano, 39; 'Vermerk über Bericht Dr. Gilles über Unterredung mit Bundeskanzler am 30.7.1959', SDA: NL Lodgman, XII-30.01; Adenauer, *Briefwechsel*, ed. Mensing.

[85] Adenauer's comments to Hans Furler, 20 Aug. 1959, BA: NL Furler, 98; Brentano in 'Aufzeichnung über ein Gespräch von CDU-Abgeordneten mit Vertretern des "Comite des Amis de la Pologne" ', 23 May 1963, BA: NL Brentano, 68, p. 8.

been waning in importance since the early 1950s, and they continued to decline in the latter half of the decade. Meanwhile, electoral considerations—prominent throughout the post-war years—rose to ever greater salience. As nearly a fifth of the Federal Republic's population, the expellees remained a weighty voter bloc that was generally assumed to be overwhelmingly supportive of the *Vertriebenenverbände* and their demands.

This widespread image of the expellees as an electorally crucial and ideologically coherent group intensified during the latter half of the 1950s, thanks to two internal developments within the expellee camp. First, after prolonged and tortuous negotiations, the rival umbrella groups VdL and BvD finally agreed to merge, establishing a united federal-level umbrella organization, the League of the Expellees (Bund der Vertriebenen, BdV). Officially constituted in December 1958, the new organization, whose self-proclaimed total membership approximated two million, immediately became West Germany's 'strongest pressure group after the labour unions', as Bonn's politicians were quick to note.[86] Because of this newly found unity, expellee activists acquired new prominence and credibility as spokesmen for the nearly nine million citizens whom they claimed to represent.

In the second major development, the expellee party GB/BHE slowly disintegrated. The throes of disarray began in mid-1955, as the party split over disagreements about Adenauer's Saarland policy, and culminated in late 1960, as the increasingly feeble rump BHE ended its independent existence by merging with another fading splinter group.[87] Throughout this period, the largest parties kept a close eye on the BHE, anxious to capture the hundreds of thousands of votes likely to be freed up as increasing numbers of expellees gradually grew disillusioned with their former political representative.[88] This enhanced focus on the BHE and its supporters, in turn, raised the electoral stakes in the expellee sector as a whole, making the political elites even more eager than before to beat the drum of revisionist Ostpolitik, which was generally assumed to resonate widely among the expellees. Such calculations derived additional potency from the widespread expectation that the same themes would also strike a chord among other nationalistically minded segments of the electorate, such as Soviet Zone refugees and war veterans. Opinion polls did, after all, indicate relatively high levels of popular support for revisionist causes, particularly for anticipated changes in the Oder-Neisse line, throughout the latter half of the 1950s.[89]

---

[86] SPD's Arbeitsausschuss für Vertriebene, Flüchtlinge und Kriegsgeschädigte, protocols, 5 Dec. 1957, AdsD: BTFraktion, 4. WP, 327.

[87] The group was the Deutsche Partei. See Neumann, *Block*, 137–234.

[88] CDU's *Bundesvorstand* protocols, 1 July 1957, in G. Buchstab (ed.), *Protokolle des CDU-Bundesvorstandes*, iii. *Adenauer: '. . . um den Frieden zu gewinnen'*, 1957–1961 (Dusseldorf: Droste, 1994), 1264, 1274–85; SPD's Arbeitsausschuss für Vertriebene, Flüchtlinge, und Kriegsgeschädigte, 5–6 Dec. 1957, AdsD: BT-Fraktion, 4. WP, 327; FDP's *Bundesvorstand*, 1–2 Nov. 1957, *FDP-Bundesvorstand*, ii. 1954–60, 314–16. Another reason for the attention to the GB/BHE was its continued importance in some of West Germany's constituent states.

[89] Elisabeth Noelle and Erich Peter Neumann, *The Germans: Public Opinion Polls 1947–1966* (Allensbach: Verlag für Demoskopie, 1967), 483; Jansen, *Meinungsbilder*, 148–53; Glaab, *Deutschlandpolitik*, 231–42.

In light of all these factors, it was hardly surprising that the leaders of the largest parties continued to view the expellees primarily through electoral lenses. The 'millions' of 'expellee votes' were a recurring theme in the internal deliberations of all the main parties, sometimes as a 'great chance' to be exploited, at other times as a potential hazard that could 'make the difference' between triumph and defeat at the polls.[90] Extending this practical logic to more concrete problems, party leaders specifically stressed the need for circumspection in public discussions of Ostpolitik. Anticipated expellee reactions and their likely electoral implications thus became key measuring sticks for the advisability of any potentially sensitive Eastern policy moves.

These calculations, although amply present in each of the leading parties, were particularly pronounced in the two arch rivals, the CDU/CSU and the SPD.[91] Overriding the periodic scepticism of some prominent colleagues—including Heinrich von Brentano in the CDU, along with Carlo Schmid, Willy Brandt, and Fritz Erler in the SPD—the most electorally attuned strategists in each party successfully enforced continued loyalty to the established canon of revisionist Ostpolitik. Konrad Adenauer and Herbert Wehner in particular distinguished themselves in these roles.[92]

Although electoral considerations—sometimes accompanied by concerns about a possible radicalization—were the main motive for the political elite's disingenuous public stances on Eastern policy, one other instrumental consideration also continued to play a role, at least for Chancellor Adenauer: the continued usefulness of expellee-style revisionism for the politics of reunification. In the Federal Republic's early years, Adenauer's first political priority had been to secure sovereignty and Western integration for the new state. In the absence of these two essentials, he had actively opposed reunification and—as we have seen—repeatedly wielded expellee-related Ostpolitik doctrines as a weapon against premature reunification initiatives.

Even after reaching his primary objectives in May 1955, the Chancellor stuck to an agenda that ruled out any chance of German unity for the foreseeable future. To be sure, during the latter half of his Chancellorship he would have accepted reunification, had it been available on his maximum terms, premised on a Soviet capitulation involving an abandonment of the GDR and an acceptance of reunited Germany's unrestricted membership in the Western Alliance. But in the

---

[90] Von Hassel in the CDU's *Bundesvorstand*, 11 July 1958, in Buchstab, *Frieden*, 215; Wenzel Jaksch in the SPD's presidium, 23 Feb. 1959, AdsD: Präsidium-Protokolle, 23.6.58–26.10.59; Siegfried Zoglmann to Karl-Hermann Flach, 27 Aug. 1959, ADL: Aussenpolitischer Ausschuss, 1957–9, 959; *Landessekretariat* report, CSU's Union der Vertriebenen, 20 Sept. 1955, IfZ: ED 720/48.

[91] On the FDP, see Mende in the party's *Bundeshauptausschuss*, 21 Mar. 1959, ADL: A12-31; Karl-Hermann Flach's memorandum, 27 Aug. 1959, ADL: Aussenpolitischer Ausschuss, 1957–9, 959.

[92] On Adenauer and Wehner, see CDU *Bundesvorstand* protocols, 16 Sept. 1959, in Buchstab, *Frieden*, 393–4; SPD's Arbeitsausschuss für Vertriebene, Flüchtlinge und Kriegsgeschädigte, protocols, 5 Dec. 1957, AdsD: BT-Fraktion, 4. WP, 327; Wehner in the SPD's *Parteivorstand*, 14 Dec. 1957, AdsD: PV-Protokolle 1957, 16. On Schmid and Erler, see Hartmut Soell, *Fritz Erler. Eine politische Biographie* (Berlin: Dietz, 1976), 491–3. On Brandt and Brentano, see Schmidt, *Kalter Krieg, passim*; Baring, *Verehrter*, esp. 271.

absence of this extremely unlikely outcome, Adenauer preferred division to an unpredictable reunification and refused to consider any possible solutions that in his view might jeopardize the Federal Republic's Western orientation and, by extension, its internal and external freedoms. His vision allowed for the possibility of German unity only in the very long term, under the kinds of conditions that came about in 1989 but that no one could have realistically predicted in the cold war conditions of the 1950s.

As in earlier years, the Chancellor occasionally verbalized his true sentiments behind the scenes. In a February 1958 letter to a close confidant, for example, he declared his 'main concern' to be 'the Federal Republic's freedom', which he still considered severely threatened and which he wanted to secure 'absolutely' before even considering the 'liberation' of the East Germans.[93] The same priorities were also evident in his practical policies. To prevent unity under false conditions, he continued to set the hurdles for negotiations extremely high. From mid-1955 on, he increasingly portrayed reunification as temporally and thematically subordinate to a broader, two-stage international process, in which worldwide 'controlled disarmament' would pave the way to a general 'lessening of tensions', as a result of which a solution of the German problem would eventually become possible.[94] Although seemingly reasonable in a post-1989 context, at the height of the cold war this concept made German unity very difficult to pursue by elevating the hotly contested issue of controlled disarmament into a precondition of progress.

But such complications failed to deter Adenauer, who in top-secret deliberations made clear his willingness to remove reunification from the international agenda altogether. The reasons lay in his growing fear of a German settlement imposed by the victors of the Second World War that might contain steps towards unity but only at the unacceptable price of curtailed sovereignty and attenuated Western links for the Federal Republic.[95] Particularly after the renewed Berlin Crisis—precipitated by Khrushchev in late 1958—had exacerbated the Chancellor's fears of a comprehensive great-power deal cut behind his back, unorthodox ideas increasingly preoccupied him. In confidential talks with the Americans, he explained that German unity was neither a 'matter of . . . frontiers' nor a 'national problem' but a 'human' one and that the West's main objective should simply be to enable 'the people in the Soviet Zone [to] lead a freer life'.[96] From 1958 on, the Chancellor also pursued the same agenda in several meetings with Soviet representatives. The various proposals drafted by Adenauer and his advisers in preparation for these talks all shared certain core elements: a *de facto*

[93] Adenauer to Blankenhorn, 14 Feb. 1958, cited in Schwarz, *Staatsmann*, 409.

[94] Adenauer's press conference, 15 Sept. 1961, StBkAH: Reden, Interviews, Artikeln, 1961/III; Adenauer in the CDU's *Bundesvorstand*, 3 July 1955, in Buchstab, *Etwas geschaffen*, 524, 527, and in the cabinet, 11 June 1958, ACDP: I-148-041/2.

[95] A key source of concern for Adenauer was possible superpower collusion in formally excluding Germany from access to nuclear weapons. See Trachtenberg, *Constructed*, esp. 230–8, 339–42.

[96] Adenauer's discussion with Eisenhower, 27 Aug. 1959, *FRUS 1958–1960*, ix. 19.

acceptance of the political status quo, including the existence of two German states, at least for an interim period; human improvements in the GDR in the meantime; and—most significantly—continued unrestricted membership in the Western Alliance for the Federal Republic.[97]

These defensive blueprints, which remained top-secret and yielded no concrete results, highlighted Adenauer's concern about the human consequences of national division, particularly for the long-suffering East German population. But they also underscored the low priority that Adenauer assigned to reunification as a political problem and thus cast light on his motives for continuing a public identification with the expellee lobby's standard Ostpolitik demands. By accentuating West Germany's supposed commitment to a revisionist Eastern policy, Adenauer could remind statesmen in East and West of the complicated and potentially destabilizing problems which any premature attempt to solve the German problem was likely to cause and thereby strengthen his hand in opposing unwelcome reunification initiatives.

At first sight, the entire pattern of Ostpolitik interaction between the expellee organizations and Bonn's party and governmental elites thus appeared very similar to what it had been in the pre-sovereignty years. The institutional and personal connections, the insincere public promises, even the instrumental motives behind those promises, testified to remarkable continuities in the system. But the overall effects of this interaction had nevertheless altered significantly. To be sure, the government and the parties still held the upper hand in many ways. They continued to exclude expellee representatives from an active role in foreign-policy formulation, and they also used their extensive connections to the expellee organizations to steer the latter in what were deemed to be politically constructive directions.

But despite these successes in taming and integrating the expellee lobby, Bonn's political elites also discovered that their dominance was far from complete. The impression of a far-reaching national consensus on a revisionist Ostpolitik agenda which their public stances had in large part created began to impose significant political costs. Once the Federal Republic had become sovereign and thus capable of pursuing its own policies in Eastern Europe, many leading figures in both the government and the opposition developed an interest in exploring these possibilities, only to be confronted with the fact that the domestically determined Ostpolitik dogmas precluded progress in this area. The West German demands were anathema not only to the Eastern bloc but increasingly also to the West, and a clear distancing from at least some of them would have been necessary for breakthroughs in Eastern policy to become possible.[98]

---

[97] On Adenauer's 1958 'Austrian solution' idea, see his *Erinnerungen, 1955–1959*, 365–90; Gotto, 'Deutschland- und Ostpolitik', 34–40; Schwarz, *Staatsmann*, 425–30; Matthias Pape, 'Die Deutschlandinitiative des österreichischen Bundeskanzlers Julius Raab im Frühjahr 1958', *VfZ* 48 (2000): 281–318. On the 1959 Globke Plan, see Morsey and Repgen, *Adenauer-Studien III*, 202–9; Gotto, 'Deutschland- und Ostpolitik', 49–55; Schwarz, *Staatsmann*, 478–86. On Adenauer's initiatives in the early 1960s, including the moratorium proposal of 1962/3, see Gotto, 'Deutschland- und Ostpolitik', 70–83; Schwarz, *Staatsmann*, 486–7, 750, 843–4, 850–1. For critical commentary, see Baring, *Verehrter*, 24–5; Köhler, *Adenauer*, 990–9, 1216–17.   [98] Frohn, 'Adenauer', 512–25; Lee, *Uneasy*, 223–35.

However, the expellee organizations were passionately opposed to such policy switches, which in their view would have amounted to a treacherous abandonment of significant national interests. As a result, they devoted most of their energies to policing the political elites' continued compliance with the prevailing orthodoxies, threatening potential apostates with major electoral sanctions and a potential large-scale radicalization among the expellees. These pressure tactics—which only a handful of journalists and other party-politically non-committed figures managed to defy with relative impunity—brought notable results. They endowed the expellee organizations with extensive negative influence, that is, the ability to prevent the government and the main parties from adjusting their stances on the key issues—or even publicly discussing such adjustments. Along with more traditional *Staatsräson* considerations, calculations focused on the expellees thus became a major obstacle to a more active West German Ostpolitik during the late 1950s, and the expellee organizations began to wield *de facto* veto powers over the acceptability of key Eastern policy options. This restrictive dynamic manifested itself repeatedly during the 1955–9 period, on both the party-political and governmental levels.

THE EXPELLEE LOBBY IN ACTION: NEGATIVE INFLUENCE ON THE PARTIES AND THE GOVERNMENT

On the party level, the typical pattern can be illustrated with two concrete incidents, precipitated, respectively, by the SPD's Carlo Schmid in late 1956 and the CDU's Kurt Sieveking in early 1957. In October 1956, Schmid gave two widely publicized speeches in which he cautiously challenged existing Ostpolitik orthodoxies, suggesting that reunification would have to be preceded by a settlement of the Oder-Neisse problem and that the Germans might have to reconcile themselves to certain unchangeable 'facts'.[99] Some three months later, Sieveking—a weighty political figure by virtue of his dual function as Mayor of Hamburg and President of the Bundesrat at the time—echoed these sentiments in an address to foreign journalists. As a part of a broader plea for improved Polish–German relations, he described the abandonment of 'several German illusions'—including the assumption that the pre-Second World War conditions in the East could somehow be restored—as a precondition for progress in this field.[100] In both cases, the expellee organizations reacted swiftly and aggressively. Underscoring the 'deep concern' and 'indignation' which the comments had purportedly provoked 'among very large numbers of expellees', they vehemently rejected the two politicians' statements and demanded public disclaimers from their parties.[101]

---

[99] Herbert Marzian (ed.), *Zeittafel und Dokumente zur Oder-Neisse-Linie*, iii, June 1956 to June 1959 (Würzburg: Holzner, 1959), 12–13; *Der Spiegel* (17 Oct. 1956), 17.

[100] The text is in SDA: NL Lodgman, XXIV-45.

[101] Manteuffel-Szoege to Schmid, 8 Oct. 1956, SDA: NL Lodgman, XXIV-45; Kraft to Adenauer, 5 Feb. 1957, BA: NL Kraft, 42.

Both the SPD and the CDU quickly complied. In internal deliberations, they criticized the unorthodox remarks, less for their content—which SPD chief Erich Ollenhauer, for example, found perfectly acceptable—than for their public presentation, which most leading figures considered divisive and dangerous, particularly because of their impact on the expellees.[102] Bowing to pressure from their superiors, both Schmid and Sieveking soon issued new, carefully phrased statements that in part sought to explain away their earlier comments, recasting them as positive contributions to the expellees' continuing struggle for justice.[103] Official declarations reaffirming the two parties' allegiance to the standard Ostpolitik doctrines and dismissing Schmid's and Sieveking's remarks as unrepresentative private opinions followed next. The SPD rereleased and updated a series of earlier pronouncements, while the CDU switched into higher gear, utilizing a government declaration of 31 January 1957 to lament premature 'public discussion' of the fate of the eastern territories and to reiterate the government's—and thus also its leading party's—dedication to upholding the established Ostpolitik orthodoxies.[104] These measures succeeded in appeasing the expellee activists, who, despite some privately expressed scepticism, generally greeted them as good-faith reaffirmations of the parties' true commitments.[105] In these two incidents, as in several others that followed a similar dynamic, the leading parties thus managed to maintain the appearance of an Ostpolitik consensus, but only at the price of a quick throttling of any dissenting voices from their own ranks. Expellee protests therefore ultimately determined the very narrow confines within which public political debate of these problems could proceed.

In the cases of both Schmid and Sieveking, electoral calculations were the decisive force propelling the two parties to high responsiveness to expellee pressure. Schmid himself made these realities clear in an unpublished account of the October 1956 controversy. According to him, top-level SPD colleagues shared his 'opinions about the issues' but insisted on silence because careless statements 'could cost the party votes in the next election'.[106]

Although this line of reasoning was central to the expellee policies of the largest parties throughout the latter half of the 1950s, it was particularly pronounced at the time of the Schmid and Sieveking incidents because they occurred during the

---

[102] Protocols of the SPD *Bundestagsfraktion*, 9–10 Oct. 1956, *SPD-Fraktion*, i/2. 370; and of the SPD *Parteivorstand, Parteiausschuss* and *Kontrollkommission*, 18 Oct. 1956, AdsD: PV-Protokolle, 1956, 15; CDU *Bundesvorstand* protocols, 7 Feb. 1957, in Buchstab, *Etwas geschaffen*, 1188–9; von Welck's 'Vermerk', 26 Jan. 1957, PA/AA: Abt. 7. 257.

[103] Sieveking's response to the BvD, 29 Jan. 1957, SDA: NL Lodgman, XXIV-45; 'Ostpolitik—auf unsere Kosten?', *Sudetendeutsche Zeitung* (20 Oct. 1956); Schmid's 9 Oct. 1956 comments, in Marzian, *Zeittafel*, iii. 14.

[104] 'Ostpolitik—auf unsere Kosten?', *Sudetendeutsche Zeitung* (20 Oct. 1956); Maas, *Dokumentation*, 130.

[105] 'Ostpolitik—auf unsere Kosten?', *Sudetendeutsche Zeitung* (20 Oct. 1956); Manteuffel-Szoege in the CDU's *Bundestagsfraktion*, 26 Feb. 1957, ACDP: VIII-001-A/1, 1007/3, p. 172; de Vries to Dr Turnwald, 13 Oct. 1956, BA: NL de Vries, 16.

[106] Unpublished draft of Schmid's memoirs, cited in Siebenmorgen, *Gezeitenwechsel*, 236; Schmid to Helmut Thielicke, 5 Nov. 1956, AdsD: NL Schmid, 661.

run-up to the September 1957 Bundestag election. The expellees assumed major significance in this electoral campaign, much as they had in those of 1949 and 1953, thanks in good part to the pressure tactics of the expellee organizations. Anxious to ensure that expellee causes in general and the 'Eastern problem' in particular remained an 'integral part of the national consciousness of all German voters', the organizations bombarded the parties with an array of demands, ranging from the fielding of sufficient numbers of expellee candidates to the continued public reaffirmation of old Ostpolitik commitments.[107] The VdL even sent a six-point Ostpolitik questionnaire to all the parties, requesting explicit public responses to each point and intimating that the answers would in large part determine the voting behaviour of millions of expellees.[108]

The largest parties paid close attention. They deliberated extensively on the best ways to attract expellee voters, placed numerous expellee representatives on their lists of candidates, and issued a variety of reassuring proclamations on Ostpolitik and other key issues, some as planks in official platforms, others as greetings to expellee rallies or as direct responses to the VdL's queries.[109] The intensity of these efforts varied somewhat among the main political groupings. The FDP proved unable—or possibly unwilling—to match the vehemence displayed by the two arch-rivals, the CDU/CSU and the SPD. While the Free Democrats contented themselves with supportive general statements, the other two parties went further, flooding the expellees with tailor-made pamphlets, periodicals, and propaganda films.[110] In addition, the SPD broke new ground by organizing a large-scale expellee rally of its own as the high point of its effort to court this segment of the population.[111]

Even the best attempts of the Social Democrats failed to make much of a dent in the bumper harvest reaped by the CDU/CSU on election day, however. After a campaign run largely on the theme of continuity and security, as embodied in Adenauer, the Christian Democrats added five percentage points to their already impressive 1953 score, winning 50.2 per cent of the vote and thus a historic absolute majority in the new Bundestag. The party's preponderance was further bolstered by the fact that its only remaining cabinet ally, the steadfastly loyal

---

[107] Sudeten-German Homeland Society's *Bundesvorstand* protocols, 2–3 Mar. 1957, SDA: NL Lodgman, IV-33; VdL presidium, 'Beschlussprotokoll', 18 Mar. 1957, SDA: NL Lodgman, IV-23.

[108] 'Zur Bundestagswahl am 15. September 1957. Die deutschen Ostprobleme—Prüfstein gesamtdeutscher Verantwortung und Gesinnung', SDA: NL Lodgman, XIX-00.

[109] CDU *Bundesvorstand*, 7 Feb. and 1 July 1957, in Buchstab, *Etwas geschaffen*, 1188–215, 1274–85; SPD *Parteivorstand*, 8–9 Feb. 1957, AdsD: PV-Protokolle, 1957, 16; FDP *Bundesvorstand*, 29–30 Apr. and 27 June 1957, *FDP-Bundesvorstand*, ii. 262–3, 274–5; CDU's 1957 Hamburg Programme, in *Politisches Jahrbuch der CDU/CSU*, iii. 1957, esp. 44; FDP's 'Aktionsprogramm 1957', in Juling, *Programmatische*, 155.

[110] A representative pamphlet is 'Warum wählt der Heimatvertriebene CSU—CDU—Adenauer?', SDA: NL Lodgman, XIX-00. Periodicals include the SPD's *Leitfaden für die Vertriebenen-, Flüchtlings- und Kriegsgeschädigtenausschüsse*. On films, see Bruno Heck in the CDU/CSU *Bundesvorstand*, 7 Feb. 1957, in Buchstab, *Etwas geschaffen*, 1197–8.

[111] On the 'SPD Kongress für Vertriebene, Flüchtlinge und Kriegsgeschädigte', Wiesbaden, 13–14 Apr. 1957, see *Heimatrecht im Osten, Lebensrecht im Westen: Referate des SPD Vertriebenen-, Flüchtlings- und Kriegsgeschädigtenkongresses* (Bonn: SPD, 1957).

Deutsche Partei, managed to hold on to nearly twenty parliamentary seats—and thus to a junior partnership in Adenauer's government—while all other smaller parties fell short of Bundestag representation. The CDU's main rivals, in turn, were bitterly disappointed. The FDP suffered major losses compared with its 1953 outcome, while the SPD—despite a slight increase in its overall percentage of the vote—lagged nearly twenty percentage points behind the triumphant Christian Democrats.[112]

By all indications, the expellee voters made a notable contribution to the CDU/CSU's success. According to the available evidence, the party fared significantly better among the expellees than either of its chief rivals, thus continuing and intensifying a trend that had first become noticeable in the previous Bundestag elections. Although clearly second to the CDU/CSU in total expellee votes received, the SPD at least managed to maintain its 1953 support base among this sector of the electorate. The FDP fared less well, suffering clear losses and falling far behind its bigger rivals in the battle for the expellee ballot.[113]

The reasons for the diverging fortunes of the CDU/CSU and the leading opposition parties among the expellees voters were complex, but disapproval of the adventurous Ostpolitik ideas of the SPD and the FDP seems to have played at least a contributing role. Although still officially non-partisan, the leading expellee organizations had consistently criticized the opposition's pleas for diplomatic openings toward the East and in their final pre-election statements betrayed much more sympathy for the CDU/CSU's policy concepts than for those of the FDP and the Social Democrats.[114] Such indirect endorsements undoubtedly helped boost the CDU/CSU among the expellee rank and file, whose general responsiveness to the CDU's 'no experiments' campaign was in any case likely to be high, thanks to the growing security and stability which ongoing integration into West German society was giving them by the late 1950s.

Along with the CDU's rise to predominance, the 1957 Bundestag election also featured another event of lasting importance for the expellee sector: the demise of the GB/BHE as a federal-level parliamentary force. The party's failure to win a single seat in the federal parliament proved significant in at least two ways. First, it symbolized the continuing decline of the radical minority faction within the organized expellee movement. After the 1954/5 disputes about the Saar Agreement had separated the radical minority from the expellee mainstream, the GB/BHE

---

[112] The electoral outcome was: CDU/CSU: 50.2% of the vote, 270 seats; SPD: 31.8%, 169; FDP: 7.7%, 41; DP: 3.4%, 17. While failing to reach the 5% electoral threshold, the DP gained representation through an electoral pact with the CDU/CSU. On the CDU's campaign, see Bösch, *Adenauer-CDU*, 161–74.

[113] Statistisches Bundesamt, *Die Wahl zum dritten Deutschen Bundestag am 15. September 1957*, ii. *Wahlbeteiligung und Stimmabgabe nach Geschlecht und Alter der Wähler. Ergebnisse einer Repräsentativsstatistik* (Stuttgart: Kohlhammer, 1958), esp. 42–5, 50–3; and iii. *Textheft* (Stuttgart: Kohlhammer, 1958), esp. 50–1.

[114] 'Ostpolitik—auf unsere Kosten?', 'Die SPD wird antworten müssen', *Sudetendeutsche Zeitung* (20 Oct., 28 July 1956); VdL, 'Zur Bundestagswahl am 15. September 1957. Die deutschen Ostprobleme—Prüfstein gesamtdeutscher Verantwortung und Gesinnung', SDA: NL Lodgman, XIX-00.

had become the main haven for the former. The party had cultivated an increasingly nationalistic profile and by the time of the 1957 campaign even began to advocate a restoration of Germany's 1945 borders.[115] The party's poor electoral showing testified, in part, to the failure of such appeals to excite the expellee rank and file, and several other concurrent developments also underscored the ongoing decline of the radicals.[116] The umbrella group BvD, for example, which had developed into the second major institutional base for the right-wingers, also faded in significance, as evidenced by the failure of the organization's firebrand top figure, Linus Kather, to gain a leadership post in the Bund der Vertriebenen, the new umbrella organization established as the BvD merged with the stronger and more moderate VdL in December 1958.

Although the decline of the radicals—and particularly of the widely detested Kather—was welcome news to most other expellee activists, the latter nevertheless worried about the implications of the 1957 electoral outcome. Many feared that their demands would now receive reduced attention from the leading parties and that a general 'lessening of interest' in 'the Eastern problems' would therefore ensue, both in Germany and abroad.[117] Although such concerns appeared justified at first glance—the total number of expellee deputies, for example, had declined by some 25 per cent from the previous Bundestag—they soon proved to be largely unfounded.[118]

The reason was the second major consequence of the GB/BHE's departure from the Bundestag: the paradoxical intensifier effect which this outcome had on the leading parties' attentiveness to the expellees. Precisely because the GB/BHE had failed to win any seats and was therefore almost certain to disintegrate further, losing whatever supporters it had still attracted in 1957, each of the leading parties saw a chance for increasing its own future vote count. A key SPD figure observed that the 'decisive phase' in the inter-party battle over 'political leadership in the expellee sector' had thus begun, and several prominent colleagues in both the CDU/CSU and the FDP agreed.[119] As a result, the expellee factor remained a prominent party-political issue through the latter half of the 1950s and arguably rose to even greater salience by the early 1960s, as the next chapter will show.

The high relevance and influence of the expellees was by no means limited to party politics, however; the same dynamics also applied at the highest levels of

[115] Neumann, *Block*, 168–210, 454–75.

[116] The GB/BHE received 4.6% of the vote (about 1,374,000 votes).

[117] 'Beschlussprotokoll der Sprecherversammlung des VdL am 27/28. September 1957', SDA: NL Lodgman, XI-33.

[118] Schoenberg, *Germans*, 135, calculates that the previous Bundestag contained 74 expellee deputies, whereas the new had only 53. Exact figures are somewhat questionable, but the total did decline substantially because of the GB/BHE's disappearance.

[119] Wenzel Jaksch, 'Antrag an den Parteivorstand', December 1957, AdsD: PV, Neuer Bestand, 820; Herbert Wehner in the SPD *Parteivorstand*, 14 Dec. 1957, AdsD: PV-Protokolle, 1957, 16; CDU *Bundesvorstand* protocols, 19 Sept. 1957, in Buchstab, *Frieden*, 13, 25–7; FDP *Bundesvorstand* protocols, 1–2 and 30 Nov. 1957, *FDP-Bundesvorstand*, ii. 314–16 and 318–20.

government. Adenauer himself learned this lesson first-hand before the Federal Republic even became sovereign. On 9 September 1953, immediately following his resounding victory in the election to the second Bundestag, the Chancellor suggested to an American correspondent that in the future Germany and a free Poland might establish either a bilateral 'condominium' or some other international arrangement to govern the disputed territories east of the Oder-Neisse line.[120] This suggestion, probably meant to test the waters for possible future openings towards Poland, back-fired immediately. The expellee activists reacted to the publication of Adenauer's remarks with a storm of protest, in the course of which one radical figure even accused the Chancellor of 'treason'.[121] Under attack from the expellee lobby and pressured by his party to recant in order to avoid alienating the millions of expellees who had just 'given their votes to the CDU', Adenauer quickly distanced himself from the comments attributed to him.[122] He repeatedly denied ever having uttered the word 'condominium' and reverted to full revisionist orthodoxy in his public statements, most notably in an October 1953 government declaration in which he reaffirmed Germany's resolve 'never to recognize the so-called Oder-Neisse line'.[123]

Whereas Adenauer learnt his lesson from this 1953 episode and thereafter consistently avoided controversial public comments on Eastern policy, Heinrich von Brentano became more adventurous during his tenure as Foreign Minister. In the course of the late 1950s, his statements led to several confrontations with the expellee lobby, each of which followed the pattern established in Adenauer's paradigmatic encounter with the expellee organizations in 1953: somewhat daring statements by the Foreign Minister provoked violent protests from the expellee activists, which, in turn caused Brentano to backtrack into the safety of the established Ostpolitik dogmas.[124]

The best-known such case started at a May 1956 press conference in London, at which Brentano characterized Germany's claims to the territories east of the Oder-Neisse as 'somewhat problematic' and suggested that for the sake of reunification with the GDR the Federal Republic might eventually have to consider renouncing those claims.[125] The expellee organizations responded with instant and vociferous protests that sent the Foreign Minister reeling.[126] Within forty-eight hours, he had issued two separate statements that sought to explain away his earlier comments, and a few days later he even tried to assure a leading activist that his remarks should be seen as a mere 'slip of the tongue'.[127] As further penance for the London statement and for a subsequent interview to which some activists also objected, Brentano spent much of the next two months placating the

---

[120] Marzian, *Zeittafel*, ii. 10; Schwarz, 'Vortasten', 90.

[121] *VdL-Informationen*, 37 (1953), 2–5.

[122] Peter Paul Nahm to Otto Lenz, 17 Sept. 1953, ACDP: I-172-66.

[123] Marzian, *Zeittafel*, ii. 10–12.

[124] Along with the case covered here, Brentano caused similar confrontations with two Dec. 1956 interviews that mentioned possible territorial sacrifices and with several Apr. 1957 remarks that appeared to question the *Heimatrecht* of the Sudeten Germans.

[125] Marzian, *Zeittafel*, ii. 42.   [126] Ibid. 43–5.

[127] Ibid. 42–3; Kather, *Entmachtung*, ii. 107.

expellee camp.[128] He courted important expellee leaders with personal meetings and reassuring messages, gave a keynote address at a major expellee rally, and provided renewed assurances of his loyalty to the orthodox Ostpolitik line in a formal government declaration.[129]

Along with the ability to silence key leaders on sensitive topics, the expellee organizations also possessed further-reaching obstructionist powers over the government's Eastern policy. The full extent of these capabilities became manifest during the summer of 1959, as expellee resistance proved the decisive obstacle to the implementation of the most significant Ostpolitik initiative produced by Bonn during the entire 1955–9 period: a proposal for bilateral non-aggression (*Gewaltverzicht*) agreements with Poland and Czechoslovakia. The venue for the planned policy move was the Geneva Foreign Ministers' Conference, which convened between May and July 1959, was attended by the four former allies of the Second World War as well as by the observer delegations of the two German states, and featured prolonged wrangling over reunification and the status of Berlin.[130] The conference yielded no results, other than a growing international acceptance of Germany's division as a basic cold war fact, but on its margins it witnessed a domestic West German struggle over the viability of the non-aggression initiative. An examination of the fate of this abortive venture throws direct light on the Ostpolitik interaction between the West German government and the expellee organizations, accentuating both the expellee lobby's exclusion from active participation in policy-formulation and its extensive negative influence on the domestic acceptability of potential Ostpolitik initiatives.

THE EXPELLEE LOBBY IN ACTION: NON-AGGRESSION AT GENEVA

Preparations for the Geneva Conference began in early 1959, at a time when a confident mood reigned in the expellee camp, thanks to the recent founding of the Bund der Vertriebenen (BdV), and so expellee leaders wanted to play an active role at Geneva. They suspected that Germany's eastern border problem would surface in the negotiations and therefore demanded the inclusion of at least two of their 'official representatives' in the government delegation.[131] In addition, the BdV expected Bonn to cover the costs of an additional observer group which the organization planned to send to Geneva under its own name.[132]

---

[128] On the *Yorkshire Post* interview (23 May 1956), see *Bulletin* 1956, 977 and 1001.

[129] Karl Simon to Rudolf Lodgman von Auen, 9 May 1956, SDA: NL Lodgman, XXVI-2; Brentano to Manteuffel-Szoege, 9 May 1956, SDA: NL Lodgman, XXIV-01. For the address to a rally of the Upper-Silesian Homeland Society, 1 July 1956, see Heinrich von Brentano, *Deutschland, Europa und die Welt: Reden zur deutschen Aussenpolitik* ed. Franz Böhm (Bonn: Siegler, 1962), 197–208. For the government declaration of 28 June, see *Verhandlungen*, II WP, vol. 31. 8422C–8423B. See also Kosthorst, *Brentano*, 170–5.   [130] Küsters, *Integrationsfriede*, 786–95.

[131] Discussion between AA Ministerialdirektor Dittmann and BdV President Krüger, 9 Apr. 1959, PA/AA: Büro Staatssekretär, 299a.

[132] Hans Krüger to Hans Globke, 30 Apr. 1959, BA: B 136/6204.

The government rebuffed the expellee elite's pleas for inclusion in the policy process. Both Adenauer and his Foreign Minister Brentano wanted political preparations for the conference to be carried out 'in a very narrow circle', composed of high-level officials of the Foreign Ministry and the Chancellor's Office.[133] Neither man had any desire to admit pressure-group activists to this select company when even representatives of other ministries were to be consulted only if absolutely necessary. Accordingly, Foreign Minister Brentano informed the BdV in late April that he could not accept the presence of its envoys in the West German delegation.[134] The government's only concession to expellee demands was the granting of a modest subsidy to the small, independent observer group which the BdV decided to send to the conference, although the foreign minister reportedly opposed the organization's presence in Geneva even on this level.[135] As the news magazine *Der Spiegel* sarcastically observed on the eve of the conference, the expellee activists had thus failed to reach their objective of active participation in the shaping of German policy and were instead destined to conduct 'unaccredited hotel diplomacy' with their ragtag 'propaganda squadron'.[136]

Der Spiegel's analysis pointed in the right direction, although the full extent of the expellee leaders' failure to win active influence over Bonn's policy-formulation became apparent only behind the scenes, where the government secretly prepared a new Ostpolitik initiative in the first months of 1959. This initiative, intended for possible public presentation at the upcoming Geneva Conference, consisted of a proposal for bilateral non-aggression agreements between Poland and Czechoslovakia on the one hand and the Federal Republic on the other. The final draft that emerged from the government's deliberations underlined Germany's peaceful intentions and called for non-aggression treaties as a 'first step' towards a 'further normalization of relations' among Bonn, Prague, and Warsaw, while also emphasizing that the agreements would not affect the rights and official positions of the signatories on issues 'not specifically mentioned' in the eventual treaties.[137]

Despite the inclusion of the last-mentioned proviso—clearly intended to avoid any appearance of commitments on issues like the Oder-Neisse line or *Heimatrecht*—the West German government had good reason to assume that the expellee organizations would oppose the new initiative. Expellee activists had informed the Chancellor of their objections to possible non-aggression agreements with Eastern Europe as early as 1957, in response to earlier indications of

[133] Globke to van Scherpenberg, 4 Mar. 1959; van Scherpenberg to Globke, 12 Mar. 1959, BA: B 136/6204.

[134] Brentano to Krüger, 20 Apr. 1959, SDA: NL Lodgman, XXIV-41.02.

[135] Janz, 'Aufzeichnung, Betr: Teilnahme des BdV—Vereinigte Landsmannschaften und Landesverbände an der bevorstehenden Genfer Konferenz', 2 May 1959, BA: B 136/6204; 'Oder-Neisse Grenze: Anständige Staatsgesinnung', *Der Spiegel* (13 May 1959), 14.

[136] 'Oder-Neisse Grenze: Anständige Staatsgesinnung', *Der Spiegel* (13 May 1959), 14.

[137] Auswärtiges Amt (ed.), *Die Auswärtige Politik der Bundesrepublik Deutschland* (Cologne: Wissenschaft und Politik, 1972), 408–10.

Foreign Minister Brentano's interest in such measures.[138] However, larger foreign-policy considerations caused the government to spring into action in early 1959. Since the onset of a renewed Berlin Crisis, provoked by Nikita Khrushchev a few months earlier, the Federal Republic faced intensified pressure from its Western allies for a more elastic Ostpolitik. Behind the scenes, the Americans and the British pushed for flexibility, particularly towards Poland, and in the public arena President Charles de Gaulle of France distinguished himself by advocating a German recognition of the Oder-Neisse line.[139]

Bonn's non-aggression proposal was a direct response to such pressures. The initiative's chief sponsors—Minister Brentano and his Foreign Office staff—justified their brainchild as a way of gaining 'breathing space', of adapting to Allied demands while avoiding the hazards of premature action on the Oder-Neisse issue.[140] They stressed the public relations advantages which the measure would generate by improving Germany's image, tarnished at the time by Soviet bloc propaganda that portrayed the Federal Republic as a safe haven for aggressive revanchism and irredentism towards the East. In its advocates' view, the non-aggression proposal was thus a common-sense measure destined to reap considerable international benefits by formally reiterating a principle to which Bonn had already repeatedly committed itself: the rejection of violence as a tool of foreign policy.[141]

The government prepared its initiative with care—and tight secrecy. After Chancellor Adenauer had given his 'explicit and unconditional approval' to the measure in late January 1959, Foreign Office representatives revealed their non-aggression proposal to the NATO working group responsible for coordinating Western policy for Geneva.[142] The Allies welcomed the initiative, and over the next few months the Germans hammered out the details in a very exclusive circle that included representatives of the Western Powers but not those of several key branches of the government at home. The total exclusion of the Ministries for All-German and Expellee Affairs, both of which harboured considerable sympathies for the expellee organizations, was particularly striking.[143] The preparatory work reached its successful conclusion in late April, as the Foreign Ministers of the four Western Powers formally approved the non-aggression proposal as a part of their negotiation package for Geneva.[144]

[138] Manteuffel-Szoege to Adenauer, 20 July 1957, BA: NL 157/6. Brentano had first expressed guarded interest in non-aggression guarantees between West Germany and Poland in a 30 Nov. 1956 press conference, *DzD* iii/2/2. 937.

[139] Albrecht von Kessel, 'Abschluss eines Nichtangriffspakts mit Polen', 27 May 1959, PA/AA: Ministerbüro, 128; de Gaulle's press conference, 25 Mar. 1959, *DzD* iv/1/2. 1268.

[140] Albecht von Kessel, 'Abschluss eines Nichtangriffspakts mit Polen', 27 May 1959, PA/AA: Ministerbüro, 128; Baring, *Verehrter*, 253.

[141] Brentano to Adenauer, 23 July 1959, in Baring, *Verehrter*, 271; Brentano to Lemmer, 21 Aug. 1959, BA: NL Thedieck, 144.

[142] Brentano to Adenauer, 23 July 1959, in Baring, *Verehrter*, 270.

[143] Ibid.; Brentano to Lemmer, 21 Aug. 1959, BA: NL Thedieck, 144; Thedieck to Brentano, 18 Aug. 1959, ACDP: I-148-173/1.   [144] *FAZ* (1–2 May 1959) 1, 4.

The government's closely guarded plans first leaked to the public shortly after the opening of the conference, apparently through an American indiscretion. After *The New York Times* reported on 21 May that Bonn planned to propose non-aggression agreements to Eastern bloc countries at Geneva, the German delegation's first response was to equivocate: Brentano explained to German journalists in a confidential briefing that the government planned no such action at the present time.[145] But after the country's leading newspaper interpreted the Foreign Minister's comments to mean that a non-aggression initiative did in fact exist, Brentano had to admit as much in a press conference on 22 May. However, he still insisted that the proposal would be used only if an appropriate moment presented itself and that any agreements which might result would not affect Germany's established position on the eastern borders.[146]

Expellee activists reacted with dismay to the unexpected news of the German initiative. The BdV's highest decision-making body, the presidium, concluded in the aftermath of the press leaks that the organization's hopes regarding Bonn's loyalty to the expellee cause had been a mere 'illusion'. The presidium took particular offence at Brentano's failure to even mention the non-aggression plans during the audience he had granted to the BdV's observer delegation on 21 May, the day on which *The New York Times* broke the story on its front page. In the BdV's interpretation, the true purpose of the non-aggression initiative was to pave the way for a German acceptance of the post-war borders in the East. The expellee leaders therefore felt that they had to move towards an increasingly oppositional stance towards the government, but only after the Geneva Conference—and the immediate dangers associated with it—had passed.[147] Partly as a result of the BdV's reluctance to press the issue for the time being, and partly because the deliberations in Geneva continued to be dominated by East–West wrangling over Berlin and German reunification, Bonn's initiative lost its sudden prominence within a few days. For the next few weeks, all remained quiet on the non-aggression front.

Bustle and commotion resumed in early July when Foreign Minister Brentano began to promote the initiative in earnest. His main motivations at this point were twofold. On the one hand, he wanted to provide 'new fuel for the discussion of the German question' during the second half of the conference.[148] Brentano hoped to break the complete deadlock which the Geneva deliberations had reached by their halfway point, jump-start the talks with a new proposal, and perhaps even create openings for reunification in the process. On the other hand, he valued the propaganda effects which he expected the initiative to yield even if it failed to generate

---

[145] 'Bonn Plans No-War Pacts with the Poles and Czechs', *New York Times* (21 May 1959); Herbert Dittmann's telegram, 23 May 1959, BA: NL Blankenhorn, 98b, p. 154.

[146] 'Nichtangriffspakte Bonns bei Konzessionen Moskaus erwogen', *FAZ* (22 May 1959); 'Die Westmächte wollen mit Geheimverhandlungen weiterkommen', *FAZ* (23 May 1959).

[147] Karl Simon to Rudolf Lodgman von Auen, 3 June 1959, 12 June 1959, SDA: NL Lodgman, XII-30.01.

[148] Memorandum 'Taktik des Westens im zweiten Konferenzabschnitt', in Baring, *Verehrter*, 264–8.

noticeable progress on German unity. In his view, the proposal would reduce fears of Bonn's presumed 'revisionism' in East and West and thus considerably improve Germany's image in international public opinion.[149]

The Foreign Minister's first move was to inform Adenauer of his intention to present the non-aggression proposal to the Poles and the Czechs during the second half of the conference. The Chancellor gave his written blessing to the idea in early July, with the proviso that the Minister for Expellee Affairs, Theodor Oberländer, approve the final wording.[150] Brentano accepted this condition 'gladly' and also decided to inform Hans Krüger, the moderate president of the BdV and a CDU parliamentary deputy.[151] In Geneva, the Foreign Minister first ensured that the Western Allies still supported his initiative and then briefed the designated expellee representatives. On 18 July both Krüger and Oberländer endorsed the non-aggression proposal, following the implementation of minor changes in the text that underlined Germany's intention to maintain its existing stances on the eastern borders and the rights of the expellees.[152] The final preparations thus appeared to be running smoothly, and two days later Brentano felt confident enough to assure the American Secretary of State that the Bonn cabinet was certain to give its final approval to the non-aggression initiative in a special meeting on 22 July.[153]

The Foreign Minister would have been less sanguine had he known of the large-scale mobilization against the non-aggression proposal under way among the expellee activists at the time. The protest drive began as soon as members of the BdV's observer group in Geneva learnt of the initiative and their president's conciliatory attitude towards it on 17 July. Dismissing Krüger's position as indefensible, the observers exhorted their colleagues in Bonn to mount 'ruthless opposition' against the 'very great danger' posed by the measure.[154] Activists in the capital heeded the call and conducted a feverish resistance campaign over the next few days. BdV dignitaries sent to Chancellor Adenauer and several cabinet ministers personal letters replete with ominous references to the 'unpredictable' domestic consequences of any non-aggression initiatives.[155] The organization also exerted influence from within the CDU/CSU, where expellee politicians and other sympathizers made their objections known through internal channels.[156] And as its crowning effort, the BdV presidium unanimously adopted and dispatched to the government a resolution confirming the organization's resolve to 'neither

[149] Brentano in the cabinet, 22 July 1959, cited in Hans-Joachim von Merkatz's notes, ACDP: I-148-041/2; Brentano to Lemmer, 21 Aug. 1959, BA: NL Thedieck, 144.

[150] Brentano to Adenauer, 23 July 1959, in Baring, *Verehrter*, 270.

[151] Brentano to Adenauer, 10 July 1959, in ibid. 265.

[152] 'Auszüge aus dem Tagebuch zur Genfer Konferenz', 17 and 18 July 1959, PA/AA: Ministerbüro, 124; Brentano to Krüger, 21 Sept. 1959, PA/AA: Ministerbüro, 124.

[153] Brentano to Adenauer, 23 July 1959, in Baring, *Verehrter*, 270–1.

[154] De Vries to von Doetinchem, 18 July 1959, SDA: NL Lodgman, XII-30.01.

[155] Manteuffel-Szoege to Adenauer, 20 July 1959, ACDP: I-148-173/01; Karl Simon to Lodgman von Auen, 23 July 1959, SDA: NL Lodgman, XII-30.01; Manteuffel-Szoege to W. Rumbaur, 25 Nov. 1959, BA: B 234/282.

[156] Manteuffel-Szoege to Hermann Höcherl, 20 July 1959; Guttenberg to Manteuffel-Szoege, 24 July 1959, BA: NL Guttenberg, 175, pp. 131, 130.

approve nor accept' a non-aggression proposal just as the cabinet convened to make final decisions regarding the matter on 22 July.[157]

Contrary to the Foreign Minister's expectations, the cabinet session did not give the green light to the non-aggression initiative. Adenauer chose instead to shelve the issue indefinitely, which saddled Brentano with the thankless task of returning to Geneva and explaining the government's abrupt volte-face to his Western colleagues.[158] The Foreign Minister resented this turn of events, not least because the sudden reversal was likely to damage Bonn's political credibility in the eyes of the Allies, as he argued in an embittered personal letter to the Chancellor the day after the cabinet meeting.[159] Brentano's claim was hard to refute, and it underlined the question of motivations: why had the cabinet, led by Adenauer, decided to drop the non-aggression project at the last minute, after months of preparation and at the risk of undermining its own international prestige and credibility?

The official government explanation, widely promulgated as soon as the whole episode became public shortly after the crucial cabinet session, emphasized traditional *Staatsräson*. Government spokesmen maintained that Bonn harboured no principled objection to non-aggression agreements as such; the problem was rather that these measures were inopportune at the present time. The reason lay in the Soviet bloc's inflexible attitude on Berlin and German reunification, highlighted anew in several belligerent declarations issued by the USSR and its East European allies since mid-July. In the government's view, one-sided initiatives would be pointless at a time when the opposing camp displayed no 'willingness to compromise'.[160] They could even become downright dangerous by generating an impression of Western weakness, which, in turn, might impel the Communists into new 'provocations'.[161] According to the official interpretation, the government's decision had thus been the result of a careful weighing of the policy options in view of the current international environment, with scarce regard for domestic considerations.

The official line was challenged early on in the German press. *Der Spiegel* led the way by pointing to the 'resistance of the expellee organizations' as the crucial unmentioned factor behind the government's decision. Other major representatives of the fourth estate concurred. The *Frankfurter Allgemeine Zeitung*, for example, lamented the impression that the cabinet had caved in to the 'pressure of the expellees', while the *Süddeutsche Zeitung* described the BdV's vocal opposition as the 'decisive' reason for the negative line adopted by Adenauer's cabinet on 22 July.[162]

[157] 'Beschlussprotokoll der Präsidialsitzung des Bundes der Vertriebenen—Vereinigte Landsmannschaften und Landesverbände am 22. Juli 1959', SDA: NL Lodgman, XII-30.01.

[158] Von Merkatz's notes of the 22 July session, ACDP: I-148-041/02.

[159] Brentano to Adenauer, 23 July 1959, in Baring, *Verehrter*, 271.

[160] 'Nichtangriffspakte?', *Bulletin* (31 July 1959), 1395.

[161] 'Brentano holt sich beim Kanzler neue Instruktionen', *FAZ* (23 July 1959).

[162] 'Genfer Aussichten: Alles selber', *Der Spiegel* (29 July 1959); 'Nichtangriffsverträge mit Warschau und Prag', *FAZ* (31 July 1959); 'CDU-Stimmen für aktive Ostpolitik', *Süddeutsche Zeitung* (9 Oct. 1959).

The domestically focused interpretation advanced by the press was correct. Admittedly, classical foreign-policy calculations also contributed to the decision not to proceed with the non-aggression initiative. During the 22 July deliberations, the Chancellor himself expressed concern regarding the Soviet bloc's inflexibility and the consequent image of weakness which any West German initiative might generate.[163] Several other governmental figures seconded these reservations, both in the crucial cabinet session and thereafter.[164] But it is hard to see how such reasoning could explain the Chancellor's sudden change of heart in the thirteen days between 9 July, when he gave his 'explicit . . . approval' for Brentano to move ahead with the non-aggression proposal, provided that the Expellee Minister gave his consent, and 22 July, when the project suddenly struck him as far too risky.[165] The Soviet bloc's attitude had not grown perceptibly more rigid or threatening during this period. On the contrary, compared with the first half of the Geneva Conference when the USSR had even issued a renewed Berlin ultimatum, the Eastern bloc's attitude was arguably softening up in the course of July.[166] Furthermore, the recent declarations by the Soviet Union and its allies, which the government repeatedly quoted to justify its position, did not contain anything fundamentally new, and one of them had not even been issued by the time the cabinet reached its decision on 22 July.[167] Against this background, the government's rhetoric of *Staatsräson* pales into a secondary motivation that also served as an *ex-post-facto* justification for a decision whose immediate roots lay elsewhere—in Chancellor Adenauer's fear of the electoral consequences of an Ostpolitik measure implemented against the vocal opposition of the expellee organizations.

Adenauer made his stance clear in the cabinet on 22 July. His main argument against the non-aggression proposal was a reference to the 'several hundreds of thousands of votes' which the declining GB/BHE still commanded but which the CDU/CSU could presumably draw in by the next Bundestag elections, due in the autumn of 1961.[168] A month later he explained to a party colleague in a private conversation that Ostpolitik initiatives were out of the question for the time being because of the 'very decisive' influence of the expellees in the political system.[169] And in September he waxed particularly explicit in a closed party circle. The Chancellor pointed out that 'the questions of Poland, Oder-Neisse, and so on' continued to be 'of great importance to the expellee circles at home' and that 'the elections of 1961' therefore had to be kept in mind in the formulation of

[163] Von Merkatz's notes of the meeting, ACDP: I-148-041/02.

[164] Ernst Lemmer in the cabinet, 22 July, cited by Merkatz (n. 163); Lemmer to Axel Springer, 16 Aug. 1959, BA: NL Thedieck, 144; Thedieck to van Scherpenberg, 18 Aug. 1959, ACDP: I-148-173/1.

[165] Brentano to Adenauer, 23 July 1959, in Baring, *Verehrter*, 270.

[166] Kosthorst, *Brentano*, esp. 292.

[167] The Warsaw Declaration of 22 July, in which Poland and the USSR stressed their willingness to back the GDR's claims against West Berlin, featured prominently in Bonn's version of events, although it had not even been released by the time the cabinet met on 22 July.

[168] Von Merkatz's notes of the meeting, ACDP: I-148-041/02.

[169] Hans Furler's notes of a conversation with Adenauer, 20 Aug. 1959, BA: NL Furler, 98.

Ostpolitik.[170] He also indicated that the voters whom the GB/BHE was bound to lose in 1961 would go either to the CDU/CSU or the SPD, Adenauer's political arch-rival, which—as we shall see—had recently launched a special campaign to court the expellees as a part of a broader effort to transform itself into a middle-of-the-road mass party free of excessive Marxist baggage. To Adenauer, who had once again demonized the SPD as the gravedigger of the Federal Republic's freedom and security just a few months earlier, the 1961 elections were thus 'immensely important' as a way to 'consolidate and stabilize' the system which his government had built up since 1949.[171] As a consequence, for him the presumed electoral advantages to be gained by continued good ties to the expellee lobby far outweighed the uncertain foreign-policy benefits that an opening towards Eastern Europe might yield—particularly once the opening in question had generated unexpectedly vehement reactions in the expellee camp.

The Chancellor's electoral reasoning had several opponents within the government, the most outspoken of whom was Foreign Minister Brentano. He privately condemned Adenauer's vote-counting tactics as 'completely erroneous' immediately after the 22 July decision and subsequently continued to lament the fact that 'a small group of [expellee] functionaries' could decide the fate of serious foreign-policy measures.[172] However, all the Foreign Minister's protestations could not change the fact that the proposal he had been advocating was dead. Despite his privately stated interest in relaunching the initiative, Brentano soon came to share the Chancellor's view that Bonn had, for the time being, exhausted its Ostpolitik options. In early November the Foreign Minister officially admitted as much, proclaiming to the Bundestag that the proper 'preconditions' for diplomatic openings toward Eastern Europe simply did not exist at the time.[173]

The ostensible reason for this general impasse was the tense international situation. As long as the Berlin Crisis continued to cast its long shadow over Central Europe, repeatedly demonstrating the Soviet Union's apparent recalcitrance, Bonn's policy-makers could credibly claim that the kinds of conciliatory gestures which Eastern policy advances would have presupposed held out very few rewards for West Germany. But the government's inflexible stance was also in large part a product of the domestic inter-party battle for expellee votes. As that struggle entered a new level of intensity by the early 1960s, thanks to a novel offensive recently unleashed by the Social Democrats, the expellee lobby's negative influence on the Federal Republic's Eastern policy also reached its pinnacle, as the next chapter will illustrate.

---

[170] Adenauer in the CDU's Bundesvorstand, 16 Sept. 1959, in Buchstab, *Frieden*, 393.

[171] Ibid. 394; and in the 'Protokoll der Vorstandssitzung der Bundestagsfraktion der CDU', 16 Mar. 1959, ACDP: VIII-001-A/I, 1503/2.

[172] Brentano to Adenauer, 23 July 1959, in Baring, *Verehrter*, 271; Kosthorst, *Brentano*, 304; von Eckardt to Adenauer, 17 Aug. 1959, StBKAH: III/24.

[173] Brentano's 5 Nov. 1959 government declaration, in Marzian, *Zeittafel*, iv. 13–14.

CHAPTER SIX

Ostpolitik Options and Expellee Influence, 1959–1966

AFTER THE HIGHLY disappointing outcome of the 1957 Bundestag election, the SPD underwent a major political reorientation. Under the determined leadership of such figures as Fritz Erler, Willy Brandt, and particularly Herbert Wehner, the party recast its image and fine-tuned its tactics. The most concrete manifestation of this new course was the November 1959 Bad Godesberg programme that cast aside the Marxist doctrines which the party had formally espoused for nearly a century and officially committed the SPD to a policy of pragmatic reformism within the existing socio-economic system. Other signs of change also abounded. In foreign affairs, Herbert Wehner caused a minor sensation by endorsing the government's key policy principles in a June 1960 Bundestag address. In his widely heralded speech, Wehner skilfully distanced his party from its earlier proposals for alternatives to Adenauer's Westpolitik and pleaded for a non-partisan foreign policy, premised on the assumption that the NATO Alliance and European integration provided the best framework for the Federal Republic's interactions with the rest of the world. On a more practical level, the SPD's reorientation showed in the party's concentrated efforts to widen its appeal among segments of the population that had traditionally shunned the Social Democrats. The Roman Catholic and Evangelical Churches as well as the business community were among the audiences that the party began to court by means of carefully retailored statements, special public events, and private meetings with leaders of relevant interest groups.[1]

These practical efforts also extended to the expellee sector. Despite all their earlier attempts at wooing expellee voters, SPD leaders had to acknowledge in the aftermath of the 1957 election that, at least for the moment, the CDU/CSU had gained the upper hand in the battle for expellee support. Anxious to correct the situation, leading SPD figures deliberated on possible policy adjustments and by December 1957 resolved to intensify their struggle for political primacy in the expellee sector.[2] The party leaders' motives were overwhelmingly electoral. The

---

[1] Klotzbach, *Staatspartei*, esp. 410–94; Beatrix W. Bouvier, *Zwischen Godesberg und Grosser Koalition: Der Weg der SPD in die Regierungsverantwortung. Aussen-, sicherheits- und deutschlandpolitische Umorientierung und gesellschaftliche Öffnung der SPD, 1960–1966* (Bonn: Dietz, 1990).

[2] SPD's Arbeitsausschuss für Vertriebene, Flüchtlinge und Kriegsgeschädigte, 5 Dec. 1957, AdsD: BT-Fraktion, 4. WP, 327; Wehner in the SPD's *Parteivorstand*, 14 Dec. 1957, AdsD: PV-Protokolle 1957, 16; *PPP-Mitteilungen* (18 Dec. 1957).

SPD's highest executive organ underscored these priorities by concluding in early 1959 that closer ties to the expellee organizations could reward the party with up to 'two million additional votes' by the next Bundestag election.[3] The primary field in which the Social Democrats intended to impress the expellee groups was Ostpolitik. As a prominent expert stated in internal deliberations, the SPD would have to utilize and 'master' the 'great emotional appeal' that Eastern policy presumably still exerted over the expellees in general and the activists of the expellee organizations in particular.[4]

The Social Democrats' renewed offensive on the expellee front commenced in early 1958 and continued with rising intensity throughout the run-up to the 1961 Bundestag election, masterminded primarily by the coolly calculating Herbert Wehner.[5] In part, the methods employed bore a close resemblance to those prevalent in previous years. Top party leaders still showered the expellee lobby with supportive statements, vowing to uphold Germany's claims to its 1937 borders and to the *Heimatrecht* and the self-determination right of the expellees, while carefully concealing their true beliefs, aptly summarized in the party presidium's conclusion that Germany stood 'no chance' of ever regaining 'the lost eastern territories'.[6] The party also heeded expellee concerns on the delicate issue of possible official relations between the Federal Republic and the East European satellites. While still favouring at least some governmental ties in principle, by the beginning of the 1960s the SPD had lowered its profile on this issue, adopting an increasingly non-committal official stance, avoiding concrete initiatives, and repeatedly stressing that German claims to the territories east of the Oder-Neisse line could never be abandoned as a price for official relations between Bonn and the Eastern bloc.[7]

More significant than these evasive declaratory stances, however, was a novel item in the SPD's strategy: a clever campaign aimed at creating the impression that the party was now offering the expellee activists precisely what the entire political establishment had previously denied them—meaningful inclusion into the policy-making process. The main constitutive element of the campaign was a series of formal bilateral meetings between the top organs of the party and representatives of major expellee organizations. Sanctioned by a formal decision of the party leadership and billed as an unprecedented venue for comprehensive mutual consultation, the meetings began in March 1958, as the SPD parliamentary group received the BdV presidium, and continued with eight other similar conferences prior to the 1961 election.[8]

---

[3] SPD presidium, 23 Feb. 1959, AdsD: Präsidium-Protokolle, 23.6.58–26.10.9.

[4] Reinhold Rehs in the SPD's Arbeitsausschuss für Vertriebene, Flüchtlinge und Kriegsgeschädigte, 5 Dec. 1957, AdsD: BT-Fraktion, 4. WP, 327.

[5] On Wehner, see August H. Leugers-Scherzberg, *Die Wandlungen des Herbert Wehner* (Berlin: Propyläen, 2002).

[6] SPD presidium, 23 Feb. 1959, AdsD: Präsidium-Protokolle, 23.6.58–26.10.59; Ollenhauer's address to the *Seliger-Gemeinde*, 1 Sept. 1958, AdsD: Seliger-Archiv, 2224.

[7] Fritz Erler's 28 Jan. 1961 radio speech, *DzD* iv/6/1. 245–8; the party's 1961 *Regierungsprogramm*, *Jahrbuch der SPD 1960/61*, 493.

[8] *PPP-Mitteilungen* (18 Dec. 1957). The other meetings were with Landsmannschaft Ostpreussen, 1959 (*Jahrbuch der SPD 1958/59*, 516); Landsmannschaft Ostpreussen, 13–14 Jan. 1960, Landsmannschaft Schlesien, 19–20 May 1960; Deutsche Jugend des Ostens, 25–6 May 1960 ('Verheissungsvoller Anfang:

The sessions typically involved serious, in-depth exchanges about issues of particular interest to the expellee groups, including the continued social integration of the expellees and, more prominently, Eastern policy. The meetings were accompanied by press releases that underscored the harmony of the deliberations and reaffirmed the SPD's dedication to promoting the interests of the expellees, as defined by the organizations involved.[9] Predictably, the meeting campaign intensified with the approach of the 1961 election. Seven of the nine sessions took place in the twenty months preceding the election, during which time the language employed by the SPD in the relevant communiqués also waxed increasingly strong. The most adventurous proclamation resulted from a two-day conference between the SPD presidium and the Sudetendeutsche Landsmannschaft in January 1961. In its press release, the party endorsed the *Heimatrecht* and the self-determination right of the Sudeten Germans and stressed that their prerogative to exercise these rights was not precluded by the fact that the Federal Republic laid claim only to the borders of 1937. Self-determination, the SPD declared, was a 'comprehensive idea' that could produce 'many different national and judicial solutions'.[10]

This deliberately ambiguous phrasing provoked concern within the party, with some fearing 'misinterpretations' and others openly wondering how the SPD could have endorsed a formulation that could be construed as favouring 'the incorporation of the Sudetenland into the Reich'.[11] In response, Wehner revealingly defended the statement on tactical grounds, explaining that the party simply had to 'make concrete statements regarding certain questions', questions that in his view were in any case merely 'hypothetical'.[12]

Along with the meeting campaign, the SPD also used other means to promote the impression of a new, inclusive approach towards the expellee organizations. The party provided its most prominent expellee representative, the Sudeten German veteran politician Wenzel Jaksch, with a spot in the so-called *Mannschaft*, an eleven-member shadow cabinet introduced to the public in August 1960.[13] The Social Democrats also incorporated indirect promises of future consultations with the expellee groups into their so-called 'government programme' of April 1961, vowing 'never to pursue policies behind [the] backs of the expellees'.[14]

---

zu den Gesprächen mit den Landsmannschaften', AdsD: Parteivorstand, Neuer Bestand, 750); Landsmannschaft Pommern, 15 June 1960 ('Mitteilung für die Presse', AdsD: BT-Fraktion, 3. WP, 31); Sudetendeutsche Landsmannschaft, 21–2 Jan. 1961 (SPD-Pressedienst, 'Sudetenfrage und Sozialdemokratie', 23 Jan. 1961, BA: NL Seebohm, 15, pp. 35–7); the BdV, 20 Feb. 1961 (WBA: Berlin 1947–66, 63); Rat der Südostdeutschen, 1961 (*Jahrbuch der SPD 1960/61*, 154).

[9] See n. 8 for examples.

[10] SPD-Pressedienst, 'Sudetenfrage und Sozialdemokratie', 23 Jan. 1961, BA: NL Seebohm, 15, p. 37.

[11] Fritz Erler and Helmut Schmidt in the SPD's *Parteivorstand*, 27 Jan. 1961, AdsD: Parteivorstand-Protokolle, 24/25.10.60–14/15.4.61; 'Vermerk für Herrn Korber' by Müller, 21 Feb. 1961, WBA: Berlin 1947–66, 63.

[12] SPD *Parteivorstand*, 27 Jan. 1961, AdsD: PV-Protokolle, 24/25.10.60–14/15.4.61.

[13] Meeting of the *Parteivorstand, Parteirat* and *Kontrollkommission*, 24 Aug. 1960, AdsD: PV-Protokolle, 15.1.60–10.10.60; Klotzbach, *Staatspartei*, 509–10.

[14] 'Das Regierungsprogramm der SPD', 18 Apr. 1961, *Jahrbuch der SPD, 1960/61*, 491.

However, all these gestures and pledges contained far more show than substance. Despite the consultative meetings with the expellee lobby, the party continued to make its key policy decisions in small circles in which expellee representatives played little or no role. The *Mannschaft* of which Jaksch was a member served only for show in the election campaign, and vague promises of future consultations were obviously of little real value in the harsh world of Bonn's top-level politics.[15]

Most expellee activists nevertheless proved highly appreciative of the Social Democrats' efforts. By the beginning of the 1960s the doubts about the SPD's reliability which some key leaders had entertained only a couple of years earlier in view of the party's advocacy of such unorthodox ideas as diplomatic initiatives towards Eastern Europe had largely dissipated.[16] Apparently unconcerned about the possible limitations of the SPD's campaign, one major organization after another praised the new initiatives, particularly the meetings with prominent party leaders. The Sudetendeutsche Landsmannschaft, for example, was so enthused by its January 1961 conference with the Social Democrats that even a particularly conservative key activist subsequently praised the party's strongly worded press release as 'outstanding'.[17] With results like these, the SPD had reason to rejoice. Accordingly, Wehner did not hide his satisfaction as he reported to a small group of key party figures in July 1961 that the hard work which the SPD had 'invested' in the expellees over the previous few years had begun to pay off and that the 'basis of trust' thus established had already provided a significant boost to the party's stature among the expellee electorate.[18]

To the leaders of the other major parties, the Social Democrats' apparent headway among the expellees was unwelcome news. The CDU/CSU in particular took a grim view of the situation. In internal deliberations at the turn of the decade, leading party figures acknowledged that the SPD's general reorientation—as exemplified by the Bad Godesberg programme—had to be taken 'very seriously', given the fact that several population groups with long-standing ties to the Union parties, including progressive Catholic and Evangelical elements, seemed highly susceptible to the Social Democratic charm offensive.[19] In the expellee sector the CDU/CSU's standing appeared even more threatened, both because the party had never achieved overwhelming predominance there and because the non-aggression initiative of 1959 had provoked the ire of most ranking expellee activists.

Interestingly, Adenauer himself never became a target of the expellee elites' post-Geneva protests, not least because he actively helped to propagate a mendacious version of the non-aggression proposal's origins which most expellee

---

[15] Klotzbach, *Staatspartei*, 570–8, 510.

[16] Seebohm to Becher, 4 May 1959, SDA: NL Seebohm, 1.

[17] Becher, *Zeitzeuge*, 291; *Bundesvorstand* of the Sudetendeutsche Landsmannschaft, 4–5 Feb. 1961, SDA: NL Seebohm, 28.

[18] Wehner in the SPD's *Parteivorstand*, 1–2 July 1961, AdsD: PV-Protokolle, 26.4.–15.12.61.

[19] Krone and Dufhues in the CDU/CSU's *Bundesvorstand*, 29 Jan. 1960, in Buchstab, *Frieden*, 601, 598–9.

activists found highly persuasive. According to this highly revisionist account, the project had been the exclusive brainchild of Foreign Minister Brentano and his staff whereas the Chancellor himself had only stepped in at the last minute to veto the misguided measure.[20] Although Adenauer thus managed to guard his pro-expellee image, his party had nevertheless become vulnerable by the beginning of the 1960s. As lingering expellee disillusionment with Foreign Minister Brentano—and, by extension, with at least some elements of the governing party—coincided with the SPD's seemingly successful push for more expellee backing, the CDU/CSU had no choice but to respond by intensifying its own propaganda drive among this segment of the population.

The party's efforts took several different forms, most of which were not new. Declarations of support for the general aims of the expellee organizations, typically delivered by the Chancellor himself or other key leaders at large expellee rallies, retained a prominent place in the party's propaganda arsenal.[21] Another well-established practice—the careful but concentrated use of governmental resources for the promotion of the CDU/CSU's partisan fortunes—also continued to flourish, arguably even better than in previous years. On a passive level, the link between party-political calculations and governmental action showed in Adenauer's persistent refusal to dismiss or publicly reprimand Transportation Minister and Sudetendeutsche Landsmannschaft activist Hans-Christoph Seebohm despite a series of public statements in which the latter appeared to endorse such unacceptable causes as territorial claims to the Sudetenland. Although the Chancellor privately dismissed Seebohm's comments as dangerous 'nonsense', he held back from an open confrontation for fear that such a step would 'have a negative impact on Sudeten German voters'.[22]

A more active attempt to use governmental powers for partisan gain was evident in the periodic audiences that Adenauer continued to grant representatives of the expellee organizations in his capacity as Chancellor. To the dismay of several ministers and ranking civil servants, the Chancellor significantly expanded the agenda of these meetings in the aftermath of the Geneva Conference of 1959. Along with general reassurances about the government's policies—the traditional highlight of the gatherings—he suddenly began making promises on an issue on which Bonn had successfully stonewalled the expellee organizations for years: their demand for public money to stoke projected large-scale public relations campaigns in Western Europe and North America. Between the summer of 1959 and the elections of September 1961, Adenauer repeatedly dangled the prospect of generous funding of that sort before expellee activists, thus posing as a champion of the kind of inclusionary approach to foreign policy which he had always

---

[20] 'Vermerk über Bericht Dr. Gilles über Unterredung mit Bundeskanzler am 30.7.1959', SDA: NL Lodgman, XII-30.01.
[21] Adenauer's addresses to the Landsmannschaft Ostpreussen, 10 July 1960, and Landsmannschaft Schlesien, 11 June 1961, StBKAH: Reden, Interviews, Artikeln, 1960/II and 1961/I.
[22] Adenauer to Globke, 3 June 1960, ACDP: I-028-007/2.

opposed and, in reality, continued to reject, all tactical appearances notwithstanding.[23]

In concrete terms, the expellee organizations benefited little from the Chancellor's manœuvres. Although they did receive a modest public relations allocation in addition to their regular annual subsidies in 1960–1, after the 1961 elections the government gradually shunted the matter aside again, this time for good.[24] But for Adenauer and his CDU/CSU, the public relations card had by then served its purpose in helping to create the impression that the governing party could match the SPD in its willingness to offer the expellee organizations an increasingly active political role.

That impression could not have endured, however, had the CDU/CSU not taken one additional step in response to the Social Democratic initiatives: a series of formal meetings between party and expellee representatives, in open imitation of the formula originally conceived by the opposition. By the summer of 1960, a growing chorus of voices within the party had begun to argue that 'declarations of sympathy' and other traditional methods no longer sufficed at a time when the 'SPD had for some time made special efforts to build better contacts to the expellee organizations' and the CDU/CSU's influence in the expellee sector had 'significantly declined'. Key leaders specifically pressed for bilateral meetings with the largest expellee groups and ultimately got what they wanted by late 1960.[25] Four sessions with four major organizations took place in rapid succession between November 1960 and January 1961, initially with less than optimal success.[26] The meeting between the CDU and the Sudetendeutsche Landsmannschaft on 2 December 1960, for example, proved 'completely unsatisfactory', to quote a CDU-affiliated observer, particularly in comparison to the highly successful session that the SPD was to conduct with the same organization only a few weeks later. The poorly prepared CDU delegation, which included none of the party's most prominent personalities, reportedly alienated its guests with its nonchalant attitude and unwillingness to engage in substantive discussions.[27]

[23] 'Vermerk über Bericht Dr. Gilles über Unterredung mit Bundeskanzler am 30.7.1959', SDA: NL Lodgman, XII-30.01; 'Aufzeichnung betr: Besprechung einer Delegation des BdV bei dem Herrn Bundeskanzler', 10 May 1960, PA/AA: Abt. 7. 290; Manteuffel-Szoege's 'Aktenvermerk', 11 May 1960, BA: NL Manteuffel, 6. For protest within the government, see Brentano to Adenauer, 13 Nov. 1959, BA: NL Brentano, 157, 298–9; 'Betr: Bund der Vertriebenen', 28 June 1961, BA: B 137, 2213.

[24] The 1960 PR allocation for the BdV was only 200,000 DM instead of the originally promised 2 million. See Manteuffel-Szoege to Brentano, 21 Dec. 1960, BA: NL Manteuffel, 7. The government's desire to drop the matter is clear in 'Vermerk betr: Besuch der Herren MdB Hans Schütz und MdL Walter Becher bei dem Herrn Staatssekretär am 30. November 1961', 29 Nov. 1961, PA/AA: Abt. 7. 299.

[25] Manteuffel-Szoege to von Hassel, 11 July 1960, BA: NL Manteuffel, 4; Kraske to Brentano, 3 Nov. 1960, PA/AA: MB, 124; Krone to Adenauer, 7 June 1960, ACDP: I-028-007/2.

[26] The organizations were: Landsmannschaft Ostpreussen, 11 Nov. 1960 ('Vermerk: Unterredung des Bundesvorstandes der Landsmannschaft Ostpreussen mit dem Herrn Bundeskanzler', 17 Nov. 1960, PA/AA: Abt. 7. 293); Landsmannschaft Schlesien and Landsmannschaft der Oberschlesier, 24 Nov. 1960 (invitation in Kraske to Brentano, 3 Nov. 1960, PA/AA: MB 124); Sudetendeutsche Landsmannschaft, 2 Dec. 1960, BA: B 137, 1257); Landsmannschaft Pommern, 20 Jan. 1961 (Adenauer's speech, StBKAH: Reden, Interviews, Artikeln, 1961/I).

[27] Chyla, 'Aufzeichnung zu den Gesprächen der CDU mit den Landsmannschaften, hier insbesondere mit der Sudetendeutschen Landsmannschaft', 13 Dec. 1960, BA: B 137/1257.

Shaken by the experience, the party abruptly cancelled another scheduled meeting because of fears that 'even worse disappointments' might result.[28] However, the CDU also regrouped quickly, conducting a brief but intense internal debate about its recent failings and returning in good form for a session with the Pomeranian Homeland Society in mid-January 1961.[29] Under Adenauer's leadership, the party now cut a good figure, particularly in the all-important field of Ostpolitik, and when the CSU managed to patch up relations with the Sudetendeutsche Landsmannschaft at a special gathering in Bavaria later in the year, the governing party had reason to feel relatively pleased with its propaganda efforts in the expellee sector by the time the elections drew near.[30]

For the FDP, the battle over the expellee vote during the 1961 campaign was a matter of somewhat lesser urgency than for its two bigger rivals, much as it had been in the previous Bundestag election as well. The party's relative detachment showed, for example, in the fact that it publicly—and much more explicitly than the SPD—continued to call for diplomatic relations between the Federal Republic and the East European countries, particularly Poland, Czechoslovakia, and Yugoslavia.[31] However, this particular stance, dictated largely by the FDP's existential need for political profile-building, by no means signified general lack of interest in expellee voters. On the contrary, the party continued to make extensive efforts to court this segment of the electorate, albeit somewhat less aggressively than its two rivals.

Thus the FDP consistently hedged its calls for diplomatic openings towards the Soviet bloc satellites with the familiar proviso that any such steps must not compromise Germany's claims to the boundaries of 1937, a position that effectively precluded any chance of real progress.[32] The FDP also repeatedly vowed continued loyalty to the *Heimatrecht* and the self-determination right of the German expellees and upgraded its propaganda offensive in response to the novel initiatives launched by the Social Democrats.[33] Aware that the 'five to six million expellee votes could well prove decisive' at the polls and that the SPD's 'outstanding' recent record in 'manipulat[ing]' nationalistic sentiments in the expellee movement could not remain unanswered, the party sprang into action in early 1960.[34] As a first step it appointed three parliamentary deputies to coordinate its 'links to the expellee organizations'.[35] This troika then fulfilled its task

[28] Kraske to Thedieck, 21 Dec. 1960, BA: B 137, 1257.
[29] Along with nn. 27–8 see Thedieck to Kraske, 6 Dec. 1960; von Hassel to Thedieck, 11 Jan. 1961, BA: B 137, 1257.
[30] Adenauer's speech for the Pomeranians, 20 Jan. 1961, StBKAH: Reden, Interviews, Artikeln, 1961/I; report of the CSU meeting, 3 June 1961, SDA: NL Seebohm, 129.
[31] FDP, 'Aufruf zur Bundestagswahl 1961', Mar. 1961, in Juling, *Programmatische*, 163; Mende's comments, 28 Jan. 1961, *DzD* iv/6/1. 242–3.
[32] See n. 31; and the speeches by Leverenz and Achenbach at the FDP's Frankfurt *Parteitag*, 23–5 Mar. 1961, ADL: AI-165 and AI-170.
[33] Foreign-policy communique, FDP *Klausurtagung*, 16 June 1960, *fdk*, 22 June 1960, 7–8.
[34] 'Ergebnisprotokoll zur Arbeitstagung des Bundesvertriebenen- und Flüchtlingausschusses der FDP', 20 Aug. 1960, ADL: A13-1, pp. 45 and 43.
[35] The MPs were Siegfried Zoglmann, Heinz Starke, and Wolfgang Rutschke.

by arranging several top-level meetings with specific organizations and staging a special expellee conference, complete with keynote speeches by high party leaders and supportive declarations on several matters, ranging from social policy to *Heimatpolitik*.[36]

The expellee organizations' reactions to the initiatives of the CDU/CSU and the FDP were generally positive, although not as enthusiastic as to those of the SPD. The CDU/CSU in particular received relatively good marks for its efforts, buoyed in no small part by Adenauer's high personal popularity among the expellee elites.[37] However, some criticisms also surfaced. Activists reportedly suspected that the CDU/CSU had launched its campaign of meetings with the expellee groups only in reaction to the SPD and 'with the 1961 elections in mind'.[38] The expellee leaders' patience with the ruling party was also tested by the government's rhetorical contortions on the question of special public relations subsidies for the expellee organizations, although not severely enough to shake the activists' basic trust in the good intentions of the CDU/CSU leadership.[39]

The FDP's performance received slightly more ambivalent reviews. The expellee organizations appreciated the party's efforts to propagate many of their causes and to strengthen its links to them, although they also continued to harbour misgivings about its willingness to advocate the establishment of diplomatic relations with East European states.[40] But despite such limited concerns, an ebullient mood reigned among the expellee elites. As BdV President Hans Krüger jubilantly explained to a Pomeranian audience in January 1961, the expellee organizations had recently made 'remarkable political advances'. In his view, the expellees' objective of 'reacquiring our homelands' had finally become a truly 'all-German cause', thanks to the fact that 'all the parties and the government [had] formed a common front' on the issue.[41] Boosted by this sense of achievement, the expellee activists faced the 1961 elections in optimistic and largely non-partisan spirits, confident that whichever party emerged victorious would faithfully represent their key interests.[42]

The elections of 17 September 1961 produced notable shifts of strength among the three largest parties, whose collective predominance in the Bundestag was

---

[36] *fdk*, 9 Mar. 1960, 3. On meetings with Landsmannschaft Schlesien (twice) and Deutsche Jugend des Ostens, see 'Ergebnis-Protokoll zur Arbeitstagung des Bundesvertriebenen- und Flüchtlingsausschusses der FDP', 20 Aug. 1960, ADL: A13–1; Rademacher to Rumbaur, 6 Feb. 1961, ADL: A31-36. On the Bundeskongress für Heimatvertriebene in Lübeck, 12–13 Aug. 1961, see ADL: A13-8.

[37] 'Gespräch mit dem Kanzler', *Ostpreussenblatt* (19 Nov. 1960); Manteuffel-Szoege to the Nordostdeutsche Landsmannschaften, 30 May 1960, BA: NL Manteuffel, 7.

[38] Chyla, 'Aufzeichnung zu den Gesprächen der CDU mit den Landsmannschaften, hier insbesondere mit der Sudetendeutschen Landsmannschaft', 13 Dec. 1960, BA: B 137, 1257.

[39] Manteuffel-Szoege to Brentano, 21 Dec. 1960, BA: NL Manteuffel, 7; BdV presidium, 20 Jan. 1961, ABdV: Sitzungen des Präsidiums, 1961–2.

[40] Seebohm to Becher, 4 May 1959, SDA: NL Seebohm, 1; Jaksch in the BdV presidium, 15 Dec. 1961, ABdV: Sitzungen des Präsidiums, 1961–2.

[41] Krüger in the Landsmannschaft Pommern's *Bundesvorstand*, 8 Jan. 1961, BA: B 136, 27370.

[42] Mocker's address to the BdV's 'Arbeitstagung', 11 May 1961, SDA: Kanzlei des Sprechers, 11.

now unchallenged, as even the Deutsche Partei, the most enduring smaller force, had first split in 1960 and now failed to re-enter the parliament under a new name. The CDU/CSU suffered a major setback, slipping nearly five percentage points from the absolute majority it had scored in 1957 while still remaining far ahead of its two rivals. The SPD and the FDP, in turn, registered significant gains, of 4.4 and 5.1 percentage points, respectively.[43]

Although the reasons for these shifting electoral fortunes were, as always, complicated, the most obvious short-term factor hurting the CDU/CSU and boosting the opposition was the erection of the Berlin Wall on 13 August 1961, barely a month before the voting. Symbolically, the Wall seemed to indicate that Adenauer's publicly proclaimed reunification concept, according to which a west-ward-looking policy of strength would eventually pave the road to unity, had hit a dead end. The damage was then compounded by the Chancellor's lackadaisical reaction to the crisis. By initially playing down the severity of the situation and continuing to focus on the electoral campaign, Adenauer severely misread the anxious public mood and contributed to his party's losses. To make matters worse for the CDU/CSU, Berlin Mayor and SPD chancellor candidate Willy Brandt simultaneously distinguished himself with decisive, hands-on leadership in the divided city, thus boosting both his own popularity and that of his party. Although the FDP's involvement in the Berlin Crisis was much less direct, it also benefited from the governing party's troubles. As the FDP had consistently sought to portray itself as a necessary corrective to the CDU/CSU while also explicitly ruling out a coalition with the SPD, it presented an attractive option for disaf-fected CDU/CSU voters desirous of chastizing their former party of choice with-out risking a Social Democratic take-over in Bonn.[44]

Although the precise role played by expellee voters in the 1961 election is diffi-cult to determine, the scant available evidence suggests that the SPD reaped major gains in this sector. According to a series of local studies that constitute the best work on the topic, the party consistently recorded major improvements over its 1957 outcome in expellee-dominated electoral districts.[45] The CDU/CSU, in turn, typically suffered losses of at least several percentage points, which brought the two parties to a virtual dead heat in these districts. The Free Democrats also regis-tered small gains vis-à-vis their generally disappointing 1957 results while still continuing to lag far behind their two rivals in their total share of the expellee vote.

The available sources say very little about the motives of the rank-and-file expellee voters, although the public enthusiasm with which the expellee organiza-tions had greeted the SPD's recent initiatives suggests that active approval of the

43 The results: CDU/CSU 45.3% of the vote, 242 seats; SPD 36.2%, 190; FDP 12.8%, 67.

44 Schwarz, *Staatsmann*, 660–8; Köhler, *Adenauer*, 106–15; Kosthorst, *Brentano*, 379–90; Küsters, 'Adenauer', esp. 527–39; Klaus D. Eberlein, 'Die Wahlentscheidung vom 17. Sept. 1961: Ihre Ursachen und Wirkung', *Zeitschrift für Politik*, 9 (1962): 250–3.

45 Brües, *Artikulation*, 196–206. In this election, the Statistisches Bundesamt no longer provided specific data about expellee voting behaviour.

party's performance was a contributing factor for at least some of the expellees. Events associated with the pre-election crisis in Berlin also probably played a role. The FDP's relatively good showing, in turn, intimates that its pleas for diplomatic openings toward Eastern Europe either did not trouble the rank-and-file expellees very much or were simply drowned out by the party's loud insistence that the key causes espoused by the organized expellee movement would not be sacrificed for the sake of Ostpolitik initiatives.

The election brought fewer immediate political changes than the alterations in the composition of the Bundestag might have suggested. The CDU/CSU carried on as the ruling party, albeit with the FDP as its junior coalition partner and with a switch from Adenauer to Erhard in the Chancellor's office in October 1963. In the Foreign Ministry the torch was passed much earlier, as Gerhard Schröder replaced Heinrich von Brentano immediately after the elections. But from the expellee perspective much remained the same. In the cabinet, Hans-Christoph Seebohm continued to serve as Minister of Transport, as he had done in every previous government, thus providing an ongoing direct link between the cabinet and the expellee lobby, a link whose significance was further enhanced by Seebohm's recent election to the top leadership post of the Sudeten-German Homeland Society.[46]

In the parliament, the expellee presence remained essentially unchanged, thanks to the care with which all three main parties had once again fielded appropriate candidates. The new Bundestag included forty-nine deputies of an expellee background, a decline of only four from the previous electoral period.[47] More importantly, the established pattern of interaction between the party elites and the expellee lobby remained intact, as the major parties not only continued but in some ways even intensified their attempts to court the expellee organizations during the years leading up to the next Bundestag election in September 1965. But the early 1960s also witnessed significant new departures in the expellee sector, particularly the emergence of increasingly open challenges to the expellee lobby and its influence, driven not by the political elites but by the mass media.

THE MEDIA, PARTY POLITICS, AND THE EXPELLEE QUESTION

During the late 1940s and most of the 1950s, West Germany's mainstream media—particularly the press, which still dominated the field at the time—had been generally sympathetic to the expellee organizations and their main publicly stated goals. To be sure, critical commentaries had also appeared from time to time, primarily in response to the rhetorical and other excesses that often marred

---

[46] Expellee Minister Theodor Oberländer had to resign in May 1960 as a result of controversies about his Nazi past. See Wachs, *Oberländer*. After that, Seebohm's key role was unchallenged.

[47] Schoenberg, *Germans*, 135.

major expellee rallies.[48] But the general tone of most of the relevant reporting had been at least respectful and often even openly supportive.[49] This balance started to shift after the onset of the second Berlin Crisis in late 1958. Amidst the heightened tensions caused by the crisis, a number of publications—most notably the news magazine *Der Spiegel*—began increasingly to criticize what they perceived as the expellee organizations' excessive ability to restrict the Federal Republic's freedom of movement in Eastern policy.[50] The abrupt collapse of the West German non-aggression initiative during the Geneva Conference further intensified the criticism, at least temporarily, but the decisive shift in the relations between the major media and the expellee lobby did not occur until the construction of the Berlin Wall in August 1961.[51]

To many West German journalists and publicists, the erection of the Wall signified a decisive break in their country's post-war history. It sounded the death knell for previous reunification concepts and necessitated a painful re-examination of the Federal Republic's policies. The historian Golo Mann, a leading public intellectual, crystallized such sentiments in an article published immediately after the mid-August crisis, in which he drew two lessons from the recent events: that the 'promise to "roll back" ' the Soviet Empire had now been exposed as 'nothing but words' and that the time had therefore come for West Germany to stop repeating its old foreign-policy slogans and 'to think of something' more constructive.[52] Mann and others also had very specific ideas of what this 'something' should be. Motivated primarily by a desire to breathe new life into the cause of reunification, at least over the long term, they called for a systematic re-evaluation of Bonn's policies in a number of relevant fields in which long-established taboos had in their view blocked rational discussion of available options.

The most obvious matter for proposed re-examination was the Federal Republic's official attitude towards the GDR. A chorus of journalists and publicists advocated new approaches in this area during the first half of the 1960s, typically proposing a package deal of sorts: some level of formal acceptance of the GDR by Bonn in return for political and socio-economic changes in East Germany that would improve the condition of the population and increase its contacts with the Federal Republic, thus preserving at least a minimum of cohesion and common identity between the inhabitants of the two states.[53]

[48] 'Es hätte gemütlicher sein können', *Stuttgarter Zeitung* (10 June 1954); 'Radikal', *Deutsche Zeitung* (5 Oct. 1955); 'Das Streiflicht', *Süddeutsche Zeitung* (9 Oct. 1956).

[49] 'Machtvolle Treuebekenntnis zu Ostpreussen', *Hannoversche Allgemeine Zeitung* (5 July 1954); 'Massvoll', *Hannoversche Presse* (29 Oct. 1957); 'Heimat', *Die Welt* (13 Sept. 1958).

[50] See the *Der Spiegel* articles 'Anständige Staatsgesinnung' (13 May 1959) and 'Sudetendeutsche: Das Mysterium' (17 May 1961); 'Vertriebenenpolitik mit Fragezeichen', *Stuttgarter Zeitung* (24 Feb. 1960); 'Gespräche mit den Landsmannschaften', *Sonntagsblatt* (Hamburg, 11 Sept. 1960).

[51] 'Nichtangriffspakte mit Warschau und Prag', *FAZ* (3 July 1959); 'CDU-Stimmen für aktive Ostpolitik', *Süddeutsche Zeitung* (9 Oct. 1959).

[52] Golo Mann, 'Das Ende der Bonner Illusionen', *Die Zeit* (18 Aug. 1961).

[53] Prominent contributions included Werner Richter (ed.), *Die Mauer oder der 13. August* (Reinbek: Rowohlt, 1961); and Rudolf Augstein's and Sebastian Haffner's magazine columns. For examples, see *DzD* iv/11/1. 655 and iv/9/1. 304.

The reform offensive also extended to the closely related field of Eastern policy, and here the expellee activists found themselves in the direct line of fire, as both their organizations and favourite Ostpolitik causes became the targets of increasingly open criticism. The most frequent attacks against the expellee lobby appeared in the daily and weekly press, clustered around a number of themes. Proceeding from the premise that the country's political leaders had deliberately concealed their true Eastern policy convictions in order to pose as 'gladiators' in the battle over the expellee vote, involved journalists felt duty-bound to confront the public with the cold facts. Accordingly, they described the Reich's former eastern territories as lost lands which 'not even a miracle' could bring back; denounced the *Heimatrecht* as a politically useless concept with no foundation in international law; and pleaded for a clear distancing from these illusionary causes as a precondition for a political reconciliation between West Germany and the East European satellite states.[54] They also condemned the leading expellee activists as petty 'functionaries' preoccupied with their own careers and out of touch with the true interests of the multitudes whom they purported to represent.[55]

Very similar arguments also appeared in other, higher profile branches of the media, particularly in the works of a handful of prominent publicists and television and radio reporters. Several of these broadcasts and publications attracted extensive attention from the West German public, far in excess of that drawn by the newspaper and magazine articles described above. The bulk of the contributions focused on the problem of the lost eastern territories. The philosopher Karl Jaspers launched the first major charge against the ramparts of Ostpolitik orthodoxy about a year before the Berlin Wall even went up. In a series of highly controversial interviews and articles in the late summer and early autumn of 1960 he challenged Bonn's received wisdom about reunification and Eastern policy, emphasizing that the eastern territories were lost forever.[56] After the construction of the Wall, similar arguments multiplied. Calls for an abandonment of Germany's claims to the lands beyond the Oder-Neisse line featured prominently in the lectures and writings of Golo Mann, in the radio commentaries of Peter Bender, and—most provocatively and controversially—in the policy recommendations provided by the so-called Tübingen Memorandum.[57] Written by eight leading intellectuals with close ties to the Evangelical Church and intended as a confidential background paper for discussions between the authors and select Bundestag deputies in autumn 1961, the memorandum leaked to the press in February 1962, creating an immediate uproar. This was no surprise, given the

[54] 'Die falsche Richtung', *Stuttgarter Zeitung* (24 Mar. 1964). See also 'Europa und die Vertriebenen', *Handelsblatt* (9 June 1965); 'Recht und Realität', *Lübecker Nachrichten* (22 May 1965).

[55] 'Die Flüchtlinge und ihre Funktionäre', *Frankfurter Rundschau* (5 Apr. 1962); 'Fanfaren vor dem Torso der Nazi-Kongresshalle', *Frankfurter Rundschau* (19 May 1964).

[56] Edgar Wolfrum, *Geschichstpolitik in der Bundesrepublik Deutschland: Der Weg zur bundesrepublikanischen Erinnerung 1948–1990* (Darmstadt: Wissenschaftliche Buchgesellschaft, 1999), 226–31.

[57] On Mann, in addition to n. 52, see his 9 Feb. 1964 lecture in Rome, *DzD* iv/10/1. 239–44. On Bender, see his talk in the WDR series 'Von Woche zu Woche', 28 Mar. 1964, ACDP: I-294-075/2.

statement's iconoclastic stance on Eastern policy. The memorandum condemned what it perceived as the political elite's conscious refusal to admit uncomfortable truths to the public and posited that such risk-avoidance had 'poisoned' the political atmosphere in the Federal Republic. It went on to maintain that Bonn's leaders would have to begin explaining to the population that the country's real priorities lay in defending West Berlin and promoting self-determination in the GDR and that all revisionist causes further east would simply have to be discarded because of their harmfulness to these two core objectives.[58]

Similar recommendations also issued from several prominent television journalists, chief among them Hans-Jakob Stehle and Jürgen Neven DuMont. Stehle, a specialist on East European affairs, became a household name in West Germany as a result of an October 1964 television film in which he sympathetically depicted Poland's efforts to rebuild the so-called Oder-Neisse territories and exhorted the Germans to accept 'the facts, even the painful ones'.[59] Neven duMont, in turn, aired a similar programme about Breslau in May 1963, portraying the city as an increasingly thriving and undeniably Polish entity, thus contradicting standard expellee arguments about the hopeless backwardness of the lost territories in the absence of their former occupants. Neven DuMont also launched repeated and increasingly aggressive broadsides against the expellee organizations in several other television and radio reports during the first half of the 1960s.[60]

Expellee activists perceived the new arguments in the mass media as a shameless affront. In their opinion, the latest Berlin crisis had merely confirmed the correctness of Bonn's hard-line anti-Communist stances of the 1950s by once again spotlighting the relentless, probing aggression characteristic of 'Soviet-Russian imperialism'. Because the Kremlin had not changed, neither should West Germany. According to the BdV, the proper response to the latest challenge consisted instead of vigilance and perseverance, coupled with an avoidance of all concessions that could further encourage the Soviets. Any 'recognition of [the] injustices' created by Moscow was particularly undesirable, regardless of whether the outrages had been committed in Berlin during the recent past or in lands further east in connection with the expulsions and the associated territorial changes of the early post-war period.[61]

Expellee leaders were quick to apply this general precept of no concessions to the task of defending their primary Eastern policy causes against challenges in the media. Underscoring a presumed community of interests between the expellees and all other Germans, they contended that the 'right to self-determination' was

---

[58] *DzD* iv/7/2. 919–23; Martin Greschat, ' "Mehr Wahrheit in der Politik!" Das Tübinger Memorandum von 1961', *VfZ* 48 (2000): 491–513.

[59] 'Deutschlands Osten–Polens Westen', Hessischer Rundfunk, 2 Oct. 1964, ALdO: Presse, Rundfunk, Fernsehen, 1961–30 Nov. 1964. See also Hansjakob Stehle (ed.), *Deutschlands Osten–Polens Westen? Eine Dokumentation* (Frankfurt: Fischer, 1965).

[60] 'Polen in Breslau—Porträt einer Stadt', NDR, 7 May 1963; 'Wem nützt das eigentlich?', DFS, 2 June 1961, AdsD: Seliger-Archiv, NL Jaksch, J1; 'Die Deutschen, die Oder-Neisse Grenze: Sind wir Revanchisten?', DFS, 2 July 1963, PA/AA: Abt. 7. 269.

[61] BdV's declaration regarding the Berlin Wall, 18 Aug. 1961, BA: B 136.

'indivisible' and could not be applied only to the Federal Republic and the GDR. The exclusion of the eastern territories—and thus of the expellees—from the scope of this right would sow 'injustice' (*Unrecht*) and consequently preclude a 'lasting peace', a condition that could prevail only in a just international system.[62] Accordingly, the expellee elites perceived themselves as the voice of reason, or— to quote the Sudeten German luminary Wenzel Jaksch—as the spokesmen of the 'patriotically minded majority of our people', a 'silent' multitude that did not 'write pretentious memoranda or seek cheap publicity overseas'.[63] The journalists and other authors who challenged the views allegedly endorsed by this silent majority received quick and forceful condemnation from the expellee activists. In one statement after another, leading expellee figures condemned the media proponents of Ostpolitik revisions as 'false prophets' whose 'tendentious and . . . untruthful' advocacy of a 'policy of abandonment' (*Verzichtpolitik*) promoted 'dangerous pessimism' and severely 'damage[d] . . . German interests'.[64]

The motives attributed to these apostles of 'abandonment' varied. In their more generous moments, expellee leaders simply charged the media figures in question with naivety and lack of realism, rooted in a general 'ignorance of the power realities' in the Soviet bloc.[65] But at other times they purported to detect more sinister forces at play. Dismissing the argument that the political elites had been consciously lying about Eastern policy for electoral reasons, expellee activists asserted that proponents of such outrageous theses were undermining 'society's political and judicial foundations' and thus 'paving the way for the advance of the atheistic-bolshevistic system'.[66] Occasional statements even charged media personalities with deliberate subversion. The BdV, for example, accused the authors of the Tübingen Memorandum of promoting 'treason' and in late 1963 described segments of the media as 'strongly infiltrated' by Communists.[67]

Although press journalists and independent publicists received their share of expellee censure, the activists saved their hardest shots for the electronic media. By the early 1960s, key expellee leaders had recognized the rapidly 'growing significance of radio and television' for the shaping of public opinion.[68] As this realization was soon accompanied by a strong sense of grievance at the 'negative and dismissive treatment' given to them in this media branch, expellee leaders set out on the war path.[69] They launched extensive protest campaigns against several high-profile television programmes whose content they deemed unacceptable,

---

[62] BdV, untitled press release, 29 Mar. 1962, BA: B 234, 46.

[63] Jaksch's inaugural speech as BdV President. See the BdV's *Bundesversammlung* protocols, 1 Mar. 1964, SDA: NL Seebohm, 34; and the speech manuscript, AdsD: Seliger-Archiv, NL Jaksch, J7.

[64] BdV's untitled press release, 29 Mar. 1962, BA: B 234, 46; report of the BdV's *Klausurtagung*, Oct. 1964, attached to BdV to Erhard and others, 28 Oct. 1964, BA: B 137, 1248; BdV, 'Unterschwellig tendenziöses "Panorama" ', 23 Feb. 1962, SDA: Kanzlei des Sprechers (B4), 11.

[65] Manteuffel-Szoege's declaration, 23 Feb. 1962, SDA: Kanzlei des Sprechers (B4), 11.

[66] BdV's press release, 29 Mar. 1962, BA: B 234, 46; Hans Krüger's declaration, 23 Feb. 1962, SDA: Kanzlei des Sprechers (B4), 11.

[67] Hans Krüger's declaration, as in n. 66; BdV, *Jahresbericht 1963*, ABdV: Jahresberichte, 1960–9, 7.

[68] BdV's *Bundesversammlung* resolution, 28 May 1961, SDA: NL Seebohm, 34.

[69] BdV presidium, 11–12 Nov. 1962, ABdV: Sitzungen der Präsidiums, 1961–2, 11.

particularly Stehle's 1964 show about Poland and Neven DuMont's reports about the city of Breslau and the expellee organizations.[70] These campaigns, in turn, further escalated the conflict between the media and the expellee groups, in good part because of the irresponsible demagoguery in which the latter frequently engaged. The vocabulary employed by expellee activists, particularly such loaded phrases as 'treason' and 'abandonment policy', evoked bad memories of similar rhetorical practices in the Weimar Republic, as critical journalists were quick to point out. These associations were reinforced by particularly outrageous statements, such as the June 1962 suggestions by Erich Schellhaus, a leading Silesian activist, that politicians who joined the media campaign in favour of 'an abandonment of German soil' be punished with 'prison sentences'.[71]

Even more troubling to a large number of observers was a violent incident at the Silesian Homeland Society's annual rally in Cologne in June 1963. At the centre of the events stood Jürgen Neven DuMont, the journalist whose controversial report about Breslau had aired only a few weeks earlier and who attended the rally with his television crew. While filming the proceedings in front of the main stage in broad daylight, Neven DuMont was surrounded by a crowd of angry Silesians who attempted to assault him and forced him to flee the area under police escort. In the ensuing days the print and electronic media provided extensive coverage of the events, typically in a vein sharply critical of the expellee lobby and its recent statements—particularly those about the media—which many regarded as the cause of the attack on Neven DuMont and, by extension, as a growing threat to the freedom of expression.[72]

Amidst this uproar, expellee leaders initially harmed themselves further by trying to blame the incident on Neven DuMont. The underlining reasoning, based on the premise that the journalist's very presence at the rally had constituted an irresponsible provocation, found particularly ill-advised expression in the following analogy, given to the press by a leading Silesian activist: 'If I were a known anti-Semite, I would not show my face in the synagogue; that much is clear'.[73] However, the expellee leaders soon realized that they had gone too far. Both the Silesian Homeland Society and the umbrella group BdV expressed regret about the episode and explicitly distanced themselves from violent pressure tactics and other encroachments on individual freedoms.[74] As a result, the episode soon faded from the headlines, although the concerns which it had aroused continued to burden the relations between the media and the expellee groups.

For the country's political elites, the escalating conflict between the expellee

---

[70] Landsmannschaft Schlesien, resolution, 5 Oct. 1964, in *40 Jahre Landsmannschaft Schlesien*, 31; Krüger and Jaksch to Eberhard Beckamm, 15 June 1961, AdsD: Seliger-Archiv, NL Jaksch, J1.

[71] 'Gefängnis für Verzichtpolitiker', *Süddeutsche Zeitung* (3 July 1962).

[72] 'Tumult in Köln: Der Zorn der Schlesier', *Die Welt* (10 June 1963); 'Ist der Nazismus unausrottbar?', *Hamburger Echo* (10 June 1963); 'Politik mit Fäusten', *Die Zeit* (14 June 1963).

[73] Herbert Hupka, cited in 'Der Kanzler schaute zu und gab Autogramme', *Frankfurter Rundschau* (11 June 1963).   [74] *DoD* (22 June 1963), 6–9.

lobby and much of the media was unwelcome news, as the major parties and their leaders soon found themselves caught between the fronts. The true convictions of most key politicians bore a close resemblance to the critical Eastern policy analyses promulgated in the media. To be sure, members of the political elite differed among themselves on the specific attitude to be adopted towards the GDR, but they over-whelmingly agreed that the focus of Bonn's policies in East–Central Europe had to lie on the rival regime in East Berlin and that revisionist causes east of the Oder-Neisse were both untenable and increasingly detrimental to West Germany's general position in the changing international context of the 1960s. Behind the scenes, top politicians openly acknowledged their lack of interest in territorial re-adjustments beyond the present boundaries of the two Germanys. Chancellor Adenauer, for example, explained in a private discussion in late 1961 that 'every rational human being' understood that the 'existing realities' in the East 'cannot be rolled back'.[75] His successor, Ludwig Erhard, repeatedly expressed similar senti-ments off the record, and comparable dismissals of the official revisionist doctrines also surfaced regularly in the internal deliberations of the SPD and the FDP.[76]

These convictions were not reflected in the major parties' public stances, however. On the contrary, all three leading parties continued throughout the period between the Bundestag elections of 1961 and 1965 to pledge loyalty to the standard revisionist repertoire espoused by the expellee lobby. They repeatedly insisted on the continued validity of Germany's claims to its 1937 borders, pend-ing a future peace settlement, and vowed to uphold the expellees' rights to their homelands and to self-determination.[77] To be sure, by this time all the main parties had begun advocating improved governmental relations with the East European satellites other than the GDR. The FDP remained the strongest propo-nent of such measures, frequently calling for full diplomatic relations, whereas the CDU/CSU and the SPD typically championed a more gradual normalization, beginning with trade and cultural ties. However, even the seemingly decisive FDP set a familiar precondition for the establishment of full diplomatic relations with East European states, one that the other two parties also eagerly endorsed: Germany's territorial claims were not to be compromised in the process.[78]

---

[75] Adenauer's 6 Oct. 1961 discussion with Senator Humphrey, cited in Schwarz, *Staatsmann*, 687.

[76] See e.g. Erhard's comments to Robert Kennedy, 26 June 1964, reported in Horst Osterheld, *Aussenpolitik unter Bundeskanzler Ludwig Erhard 1963–66: Ein dokumentarischer Bericht aus dem Kanzleramt* (Düsseldorf: Droste, 1992), 93; Brandt, cited in Siebenmorgen, *Gezeitenwechsel*, 349–51; Wolfgang Schollwer, *FDP im Wandel: Aufzeichnungen 1961–1966* (Munich: Oldenbourg, 1994), 46–8.

[77] On borders, see Herbert Wehner's 10 June 1965 interview, *DzD* iv/11/2. 634; Johann Baptist Gradl's 22 Mar. 1964 speech, in *Der Weg zu Frieden und Einheit: 1. Kongress der ostdeutschen Landesvertretungen am 22. März 1964 in Bonn* (Bonn: BdV, 1964), 31–5; Erich Mende at the FDP's Bundeskongress für Heimatvertriebene und Flüchtlinge, 4 May 1963, *DzD* iv/9/1. 297–8. On rights, see the SPD Regierungsmannschaft's declaration, 8 Jan. 1965, AdsD: Präsidiums-Protokolle, Jan.–Mar., 1965; Franz-Josef Strauss at the CSU's Landesversammlung, 6–7 July 1963, ACSP: LV 6/7.7.1963, 3; Mende's 4 May 1963 address, *DzD* iv/9/1. 299.

[78] Brandt's address to the Seliger-Gemeinde, 4 July 1964, WBA: Publizistische Tätigkeit, 185; Erhard's 22 Mar. 1964 speech in *Der Weg zu Frieden* (n. 77), 27–9; Mende's 22 Mar. 1965 address, ADL: AI-283, esp. 22.

The principal parties thus continued to pose as dedicated champions of the expellee lobby's main Ostpolitik desiderata, much as they had in previous years, and in fact their propaganda efforts peaked in intensity between 1961 and 1965, even as the top politicians' true convictions diverged ever further from their public pronouncements. One indication of their intensified courtship of the expellees was the sharp language employed in several public declarations, particularly by the SPD. A case in point was the SPD's official declaration to the Silesian Homeland Society's 1963 annual rally in Cologne—the event that also witnessed the attempted assault on Neven DuMont—in which the party equated an 'abandonment' of Germany's claims in the east with 'treason' and swore never to conduct Ostpolitik 'behind the backs of those expelled from their homelands'.[79]

The intensification of the propaganda battle in the expellee sector also showed in the fact that the parties extended their relevant public statements into two new areas. The first was the ongoing strife over Eastern policy between the expellee groups and much of the media, in which the largest parties publicly sided with the former on numerous occasions. The publication of the Tübingen Memorandum in early 1962, for example, evoked loud protests from each of the major parties. Predictably, they all rejected the argument that they had been lying to the people about the political realities in the East and dismissed the authors' policy recommendations in strong terms. The SPD's Herbert Wehner, for instance, left no doubt about his displeasure, denouncing the document's conclusions as 'objectively false and politically dangerous'.[80]

Similarly critical statements followed on the heels of several high-profile TV and radio broadcasts, including Jürgen Neven DuMont's controversial report about Breslau slightly over a year later. The SPD labelled expellee attacks against the show 'justified' on the grounds that it had failed to provide a 'true picture' of the city.[81] The CDU/CSU responded with several declarations, in which Chancellor Adenauer dismissed the show as 'dubious' and select Bundestag deputies accused Neven DuMont of 'deliberate, one-sided distortion'.[82] Even stronger words of censure issued from the FDP, whose representatives claimed that the show had 'exceeded all expectations . . . in an exclusively negative sense' and reflected 'not the voice of the Polish people but that of their rulers'.[83]

When Neven DuMont became the victim of attempted assault a few weeks later, party leaders again mustered extensive sympathy for the expellee side.

[79] *Erkenntnis zu Schlesien. Deutschlandtreffen der Schlesier, Köln, 7.–9. Juni 1963* (Bonn: Landsmannschaft Schlesien, 1963), 25, ACDP: I-094-050/1.

[80] Wehner's TV interview, 4 Mar. 1962, *DzD* ii/8/1. 218. See also Martin (CDU/CSU) and Mende (FDP) ibid. 216–17.

[81] SPD spokesman Barsig, cited in 'Bonn äussert sich zum Fall Neven DuMont', *Stuttgarter Zeitung* (11 June 1963).

[82] Adenauer to the Landsmannschaft Ostpreussen, 14 June 1963, BA: B 136, 6792; CDU's 'Arbeitsgemeinschaft der Heimatvertriebenen und Flüchtlinge', press release, 3 July 1963, ACDP: I094-048/1.

[83] 'Breslau—ein Teil Deutschlands', statement by the FDP's 'Bundesausschuss für Vertriebene und Flüchtlinge', 8 May 1963, AdsD: PV, Alter Bestand, 01573B.

Despite the considerable concern about the incident expressed in their internal deliberations, both the SPD and the CDU/CSU adopted a remarkably cautious public stance.[84] Konrad Adenauer characterized the events as an expression of 'justified anger' provoked by Neven DuMont's wrong-headed Breslau broadcast, while the Social Democrats released statements minimizing the severity of the incident and praising the constructive moderation characteristic of the expellee groups.[85] Occasionally party leaders also followed up their various declarations with actions intended to provide further evidence of their support for the expellee organizations' protest campaigns. These efforts included direct interventions with media representatives on behalf of expellee groups that had requested such steps, as well as special party-sponsored forums at which activists could air their grievances in front of sympathetic, hand-picked audiences.[86]

The second new field in which the major parties had to make a growing declaratory engagement during the 1961–5 period centred on a narrow but particularly contentious problem: the character and relevance of the Munich Agreement of 1938.[87] In earlier years, debates about this issue had raged primarily within the Sudeten-German Homeland Society, pitting a large nationalistic faction against a smaller but vocal group of moderates. The former had consistently presented the agreement as an ideal solution to the Sudeten problem, arguing that the treaty had corrected a key injustice of the post-First World War peace settlement by allowing the Sudeten Germans to join the Reich and that the homeland society should base much of its revisionist argumentation on this happy precedent.[88] The moderate wing had disagreed, not about the inherent merits of the Munich arrangement— even Wenzel Jaksch, the most prominent spokesman of this faction, had labelled the incorporation of the Sudetenland into Germany 'the most reasonable' solution to the problem at hand—but about the tactical wisdom of drawing on the treaty. According to the moderates, the general notoriety of the Munich Agreement, particularly outside of Germany, ensured that any attempt to make use of it would immediately backfire, and as a consequence the organization's best practical strategy was to base its case on such legal principles as self-determination, while avoiding public discussion of the controversial accord.[89]

---

[84] Protocols of the SPD's *Parteivorstand*, 14 June 1963, AdsD: PV-Protokolle, 5.9.62–28.6.63) and presidium, 1 July 1963, AdsD: Präsidiums-Protokolle, 1963; Adenauer to Brentano, 10 June 1963, BA: NL Brentano, 160, pp. 133–4.

[85] Adenauer to the Landsmannschaft Ostpreussen, 14 June 1963, BA: B 136, 6792; 'Bonn äussert sich zum Fall Neven DuMont', *Stuttgarter Zeitung* (11 June 1963); 'Radikalisierung wurde verhindert: Erklärung der SPD zu den Angriffen auf die Vertriebenen', *Sozialdemokratische Presse-Korrespondenz* (12 July 1963), AdsD: BT-Fraktion, 4. WP, 356.

[86] See e.g. Gradl to Klaus von Bismarck, 17 Apr. 1964; 'Arbeitskreis IV: Gesamtdeutsches Bewusstsein und Publizistik', in *Freiheit und Recht in Deutschland und Europa: Vertriebenen-Kongress der CDU/CSU in Nürnberg, 3. und 4. Mai 1965* (Bonn: CDU, 1965), 238–99.

[87] Werner Jakobsmeier, 'Das Münchener Abkommen—unüberbrückbarer Graben zwischen Bonn und Prag?', in Haberl and Hecker, *Unfertige Nachbarschaften*, 177–203.

[88] See e.g. Rudolf Lodgman von Auen, ' "Macht endlich Schluss mit München" ', undated, SDA: NL Lodgman, XXIV-21.

[89] Wenzel Jaksch in the *Bundesversammlung* of the Sudetendeutsche Landsmannschaft, 2 Apr. 1960, AdsD: Seliger-Archiv, NL Jaksch, J6.

Although these internal disputes found seeming resolution in a programmatic statement of early 1961, in which the homeland society combined a spirited endorsement of the *Heimatrecht* and the self-determination right with a cautious defence of certain aspects of the Munich settlement, the calm failed to hold.[90] Amidst the rising controversies about Ostpolitik in the media, aggressive, nationalistically oriented elements gained ground within the Sudetendeutsche Landsmannschaft, as within the expellee movement as a whole. As a consequence, the Munich Agreement rose to unprecedented prominence in the deliberations of the Sudeten German leadership. Although annexationist longings remained the key underlying motivation for the activists, more immediate problems now drew the bulk of their attention, chief among them the question of the agreement's validity, accentuated by growing demands from Czechoslovakia and other Eastern bloc states for Bonn to declare the treaty invalid from its inception (*ab initio*).

In the face of this challenge, the homeland society's ranking leaders rediscovered a strong sense of unity. They sharply rejected all challenges to the validity of the Munich pact, claiming that it had come into being as an indisputably legitimate international agreement and that its retroactive invalidation, particularly *ab initio*, would have disastrous legal consequences for the Sudeten Germans. According to the *Landsmannschaft*, the most severe repercussion would be a forfeiture of the German citizenship that the Sudeten Germans had acquired as a result of the Munich arrangement. That loss, in turn, would expose the Sudeten Germans to prosecution as traitors to the Czechoslovak state, undermine their claims for compensation, territorial and otherwise, from that state, and damage the legal standing of the small German minority still extant in Czechoslovakia.[91]

Once these arguments had matured within the homeland society by 1963/4, nationalistically oriented activists began to expound their views to the general public. Although several provocative articles generated some controversy during the latter half of 1963, a real uproar, both within and outside West Germany, did not arise until May 1964.[92] The commotion was caused by Transport Minister Seebohm's address at the annual rally of the Sudeten-German Homeland Society in which he called for 'the return of the Sudeten German homeland territories to the Sudeten German people' and defended the Munich Agreement as a fully legitimate treaty on which 'the judicial position of all Sudeten Germans' was based.[93] With this high-profile proclamation Seebohm had created something of a fait accompli, and although occasional warnings against a suicidal 'death march' under the 'banner of Munich' continued to ring out in the organization's internal

---

[90] '20 Punkte zur Sudetenfrage', ACSP: NL Schütz, 11.

[91] Sudetendeutscher Rat, 'Exposé: Das Münchner Abkommen und die damit verbundenen staatsbürgerschafts- und vermögensrechtlichen Probleme', 20 June 1964, SDA: Sudetendeutscher Rat, 9.

[92] Albert Karl Simon, 'Unsere Heimkehr ins Reich!', *Pressemitteilungen der Sudetendeutschen Landsmannschaft* (12 Aug. 1963), BA: B 137, 1257; Anton Wuschek, 'St. Germain und München', ibid., 28 Aug. 1963, SDA: Sudetendeutscher Rat, 11.

[93] Seebohm's 17 May 1964 speech is in SDA: NL Seebohm, 46.

deliberations, in practice the Sudeten-German Homeland Society had committed itself to an uncompromising defence of the Munich Agreement's validity by the mid-1960s.[94]

By that time, the *Landsmannschaft* was also gaining an increasingly strong position within the umbrella group BdV, thanks in part to its sheer numerical advantage as the largest homeland society and in part to its relative financial and organizational prowess. As a result, the BdV paid increasing attention to the special interests of the Sudeten German activists, including their claims regarding the Munich Agreement. A good indication of this trend was the fact that in late 1966 the BdV elevated the retroactive annulment of the 1938 pact into one of the four potential developments that it most wanted to prevent in the ensuing years.[95]

The country's political elites resented the growing public prominence of the Munich issue. Prior to mid-1964, leading politicians had preferred to let sleeping dogs lie, avoiding discussion of the notorious agreement, but once Seebohm's widely publicized May 1964 speech had roused the hounds of the past out of their slumber, Bonn's leaders were forced to react. As the main governing party, the CDU/CSU, led by Chancellor Erhard, was under the most pressure to clarify its position, but its two main rivals also had to take a stance. All three clearly distanced themselves from the most radical implications of Seebohm's comments, denouncing both the pressure tactics that had preceded the Munich Agreement and the open aggression that had soon followed.[96] But the parties also took care not to risk alienating the expellee audience with overly critical proclamations. They emphasized that the *Heimatrecht* and the self-determination right of the Sudeten Germans remained unaffected by any disputes regarding the Munich Agreement.[97] They also approached the problem of the treaty's validity, particularly *ab initio*, with caution, typically either eschewing specific statements on the matter or declaring that the issue could not yet be definitively settled.[98]

The parties even engaged in some very delicate balancing on the seemingly

[94] Wenzel Jaksch in the Sudetendeutscher Rat, 20 June 1964, PA/AA: Abt. 7. 299a, p. 11; Sudetendeutscher Rat to Willy Brandt, 24 Nov. 1966, SDA: NL Becher, 467.

[95] 'Was sind lebenswichtige Interessen?', *DoD* (22 Dec. 1966). The others were a recognition of the GDR and of the Oder-Neisse line and the assignment of a neutralized status to Berlin.

[96] See e.g. the 23 May 1964 *Bundeskanzleramt* press release, BA: B 136, 6796; Herbert Wehner's 3 June 1964 radio talk, AdsD: BT-Fraktion, 4. WP, 895; FDP's 'Bundeskongress für Vertriebene und Flüchtlinge', 5–6 Sept. 1964, ADL: A13–13.

[97] See e.g. CDU's 16 Nov. 1964 press release, AdsD: Seliger-Archiv, 2010; SPD's 8 June 1964 press release, AdsD: BT-Fraktion, 4. WP, 47; the declaration of the FDP's 'Bundeskongress für Vertriebene und Flüchtlinge', 5 Sept. 1964, ADL: A13-13, p. 15.

[98] See e.g. Fritz Erler in *Parteitag der SPD vom 23. bis 27. Nov. 1964 in Karlsruhe. Protokolle der Verhandlungen* (Bonn: SPD, 1964), 251. Although the SPD and the CDU/CSU both declared that Hitler had subsequently broken the agreement, such statements did not directly address the legal question of the treaty's validity. See Ludwig Erhard's 11 June 1964 address, *DzD* iv/10/2. 682; and the SPD resolution in *Parteitag der SPD vom 23. bis 27. Nov. 1964 in Karlsruhe*, 974. On one occasion, the FDP argued that the treaty remained in force. See 'Aufzeichnung, Betr: Besprechung Bundesvorstand FDP/Bundesvorstand der Sudetendeutschen Landsmannschaft am 16. Oktober 1964', 27 Oct. 1964, PA/AA: Abt. 7. 299a.

clear-cut matter of the Munich Agreement as a potential base for German territorial claims against Czechoslovakia. Taking their cue from Chancellor Erhard,
who repeatedly proclaimed that the Federal Republic—and, by extension, the
CDU/CSU–'raise[d] no territorial demands against Czechoslovakia', the other
two parties adopted virtually identical formulations, simply replacing the verb
'raise' with other similar ones, such as 'cultivate' or 'present'.[99] Although clear
and convincing at first sight, such declarations in fact contained a considerable
dose of deliberate ambiguity, as Sudeten German leaders were quick to note. The
activists attributed extensive importance to the precise wording, interpreting the
use of a verb like 'raise'—instead of the more explicit 'have'—to mean that,
although Bonn possessed no 'political intention' to push such demands at
present, it nevertheless wanted to guard its prerogative to introduce these claims
in the future.[100]

Such interpretations were completely false with regard to the true motives of
the political leadership, as none of the major parties had the slightest interest
in pursuing border revisions vis-à-vis Czechoslovakia, but they did reflect the
political elites' success in delivering their intended message to the expellee
movement.[101] As some key figures have subsequently admitted, Erhard's government—like the largest parties—chose its phrasing on the Munich issue with
calculated care, balancing credibility abroad with electoral viability at home.[102] In
the midst of an unprecedentedly intense bidding war for the hearts and minds of
the expellee electorate, none of the major players wanted to be the first to begin
demolishing the revisionist illusions which they had all nurtured for years and
thereby risk forfeiting millions of expellee votes.

Along with declaratory methods, the major parties also continued to use more
active and inclusive means to court the expellee movement, much as they had in
the previous electoral period. Regular meetings with the most significant expellee
organizations thus remained standard practice for all three parties. The SPD
retained the lead in this field of operations, staging the most frequent meetings
and consistently adopting very supportive stances at the gatherings.[103] The
CDU/CSU responded with a continued meeting campaign of its own, featuring
both governmental representatives, particularly Chancellors Adenauer and

[99] *Bundeskanzleramt's* press release, 23 May 1964, BA: B 136, 6796; Erhard's 14 June 1964 speech,
DzD iv/10/2. 682; Mende's 5 Dec. 1964 speech, *DzD* iv/10/2. 1201; Erler's address and the declaration in
Parteitag der SPD vom 23. bis 27. Nov. 1964, 251 and 974.

[100] Franz Böhm to Karl Carstens, 6 July 1966, SDA: NL Jaksch, 94.

[101] Meyer-Lindenberg, 'Aufzeichnung Betr: Frage der Rechtswirksamkeit des Münchener Abkommens vom 29. Sept. 1938', 1 June 1964, PA/AA: Abt. 7. 299a.

[102] Rainer A. Blasius, 'Erwin Wickert und die Friedensnote der Bundesregierung vom 25. März
1966', *VfZ* 45 (1995): 548–9.

[103] Meetings included: Landsmannschaft Schlesien, 3 Feb. 1962 (report in AdsD: PV, Neuer Bestand,
789); BdV, 4 Feb. 1963 (AdsD: Präsidiums-Protokolle, 1963); Landsmannschaft Ostpreussen, 22 Oct.
1963 (AdsD: BT-Fraktion, 4. WP, 356); Pommersche Landsmannschaft, 9 Dec. 1963 (AdsD: PV-
Protokolle, 28.8.63–6.6.64 (25)); Rat der Südostdeutschen Landsmannschaften, 3 Mar. 1964;
Landsmannschaft Schlesien, 4 Apr. 1964; Deutsche Jugend des Ostens, 8 June 1964; BdV, 19 June 1965
(*Jahrbuch der SPD 1964/1965*, 107–8).

Erhard, and delegations of other high-ranking party leaders.[104] The FDP also held a number of bilateral sessions with select expellee groups—albeit fewer than its two rivals—and arranged a series of special expellee congresses, replete with panels, study groups, and speeches devoted to the main concerns of the expellee movement.[105]

While these meetings and conferences simply continued practices instituted by the parties during the previous electoral period to promote the impression of a growing inclusion of expellee activists into policy-making roles, an additional initiative, again conceived by the SPD under the guidance of Herbert Wehner, further intensified the inter-party rivalry from 1962 on. Wehner's new inclusion-ary project, entitled the All-German Council (*Gesamtdeutscher Rat*), was conceived at a meeting between the SPD leadership and the Silesian Homeland Society in early 1962 and—following a period of heavy public promotion, primar-ily by Wehner—launched at the end of the year.[106] According to the SPD strate-gist, the council was to be a loosely structured forum in which the 'political parties and organizations such as the homeland societies' could 'regularly deliberate on the German question'.[107] In a widely publicized speech, Wehner contended that 'occasional discussions' between the parties and the 'homeland societies or the BdV' no longer sufficed to prevent potential divisions between the expellees and the rest of the population and that the new organ should therefore serve the primary purpose of guaranteeing that 'nothing happens behind the backs of the expellees', particularly in Eastern and reunification policy.[108]

Expellee activists responded to the idea with predictable enthusiasm, which, in turn, quickly persuaded the other parties to overcome their considerable initial reservations about the project.[109] As a result, the council convened a total of six times between November 1962 and October 1963, bringing together a small circle of delegates from the main parties and the expellee organizations for consulta-tions dominated by polemics against allegedly dangerous trends in the media.[110]

---

[104] Adenauer met with the BdV, 1 Feb. 1963 (BdV presidium protocols, 1–2 Mar. 1963, ABdV: Sitzungen des Präsidiums, 1963) and Erhard and other ministers with the Sudentedeutsche Landsmannschaft, 16 Oct. 1964 (joint declaration in AdsD: Seliger-Archiv, 2010). Other CDU delega-tions met with the Sudetendeutsche Landsmannschaft, 16 Nov. 1964 (CDU declaration, same date, AdsD: Seliger-Archiv, 2010) and with the BdV, 20 Jan. 1965 ('CDU Gespräch mit BdV Präsidium', *DoD* (28 Jan. 1965), 9).

[105] The FDP met with the BdV, 4 Dec. 1962 (*fdk*, 5 Dec. 1962, 'Anhang', 3) and with the Sudetendeutsche Landsmannschaft (FDP press release, 15 Oct. 1964, AdsD: Seliger Archiv, 2010). On the expellee congresses, in Lübeck, 15–16 Sept. 1962; Hameln, 4–5 May 1963; and Brunswick, 5–6 Sept. 1964, see ADL: A13-9, A13-11, A13-13.

[106] Report of the 3 Feb. 1962 meeting, AdsD: PV, Neuer Bestand, 789; Wehner in the party presid-ium, 5 Feb. 1962, AdsD: Präsidiums-Protokolle, 1962.

[107] Wehner in *Parteipolitischer Pressedienst*, 6 Feb. 1962, AdsD: PV, Neuer Bestand, 3745.

[108] Summary of Wehner's 'Tag der Heimat' address, Berlin, 4 Sept. 1962, ALdO: Korrespondenz mit Parteien und Abgeordneten, 1951–31 May 1966.

[109] Alfred Gille at the 'Tag der Heimat', Berlin, 4 Sept. 1962, BA: NL Guttenberg, 180, pp. 253–5; Brentano to Guttenberg, 18 Oct. 1962, BA: NL Brentano, 175.

[110] Protocols of the sessions of 8 Nov., 11 Dec. 1962, 22 Feb., 15 May 1963, 12 June, and 17 Oct. 1963 are in AdsD: PV, Neuer Bestand, 3745.

After October 1963, the organ silently faded away, apparently because party leaders—who in reality remained anxious to keep expellee activists out of Bonn's inner sanctums of power—grew frightened of their own creation, particularly as expellee leaders began to draft increasingly ambitious plans for the new council.[111] For tactical reasons, the SPD nevertheless continued to plead for a reactivation of the organ, and although nothing came of these calls, the overall effect of the entire All-German Council episode was to add intensity to the inter-party battle over the loyalties of the expellees.[112]

Despite the intense rivalry and the concomitant pressure for uniformity, none of the leading parties managed to eliminate internal dissent on expellee-related Eastern policy issues. On the contrary, each party faced growing pressure from within its ranks for the adoption of more realistic public stances. The champions of major policy switches included engaged individual politicians, as well as party-affiliated youth groups and local-level party organizations.[113] These internal pressures were at their weakest among the Christian Democrats, who also enjoyed considerable success in shielding existing discord from the public.[114] The other two major parties found themselves in a more difficult position, both because they faced a higher level of internal disagreement and because the dissenting voices occasionally attracted considerable public attention. Whenever such crises erupted, party leaders typically responded with a strategy honed by years of previous practice: prompt disassociation from the unorthodox opinions, combined with attempts to dismiss the controversial statements as mere misunderstandings.

This behaviour pattern manifested itself in the early autumn of 1964, as the FDP found itself in the eye of an Eastern policy storm. After the illustrated periodical *Quick* published a secret memorandum by a key FDP policy planner, Wolfgang Schollwer, which demanded a reordering of the country's foreign-policy priorities, including a scaling back of the short-term reunification drive and an acceptance of the Oder-Neisse line, party elders reacted to vociferous protests from expellee activists and others by immediately denouncing the study and denying all foreknowledge of it, despite the fact that its conclusions had been discussed—and largely endorsed—by the party's top echelons as early as the spring of 1962.[115]

The same dynamics prevailed in January 1965, as Fritz Erler, the SPD's main foreign-policy expert and a long-term critic of the party's charm offensive towards the expellee movement, declared that Bonn and Warsaw should try to settle the

---

[111] Wenzel Jaksch, 'Abschrift: Der Diskussionsstand über Struktur und Aufgaben des Gesamtdeutschen Rates', AdsD: PV, Neuer Bestand, 3745.

[112] Wehner in a meeting with the Landsmannschaft Schlesien, 4 Apr. 1964, AdsD: PV-Protokolle, 28.8.63–6.6.64 (25).

[113] On pressure from youth groups, see the 20 Apr. 1963 discussion in *FDP-Bundesvorstand*, iii. 503–5. On the SPD's local party organizations, see Elsing, 'Polenpolitik', 58; Schmidt, *Kalter Krieg*.

[114] But see the discussion of Erik Blumenfeld's activities, 9 Nov. 1965, ACDP: VIII-001-1010/2.

[115] Schollwer, *FDP*, 47–8, 217–20; Karl Moersch, *Kursrevision: Deutsche Politik nach Adenauer* (Frankfurt: Societäts, 1978), 44–50.

Oder-Neisse border problem before a future peace conference and intimated that Germany might thereby have to abandon its revisionist claims. In reaction to the immediate public uproar, which featured furious expellee protests as well as attempts by the CDU/CSU to portray the Social Democrats as enemies of the expellee movement, the SPD distanced itself from these heretical remarks. Erler, too, quickly recanted, reiterating his commitment to the orthodox principle that the border settlement must await the peace treaty.[116]

However, even as the SPD and the FDP actively cultivated the impression that stances such as those adopted by Schollwer and Erler were merely isolated minority opinions or even slips of the tongue, the realities behind the scenes belied such pretensions. As the next chapter will demonstrate, significant groups of leaders within both parties not only entertained similar thoughts but also made systematic long-term plans for reorienting the Federal Republic's Eastern and reunification policies away from the prevailing dogmas. Among these groups, which typically took considerable care to guard their sensitive projects from premature public exposure, the most significant was the innermost circle of West Berlin's SPD, composed of ruling Mayor Willy Brandt and several close associates, such as Egon Bahr, Heinrich Albertz, and Klaus Schütz.[117]

Unaware of the seriousness of such behind-the-scenes deliberations, the expellee groups praised the stances and initiatives of the major parties. Amidst their worries about hostile trends in the media, expellee leaders took comfort in the 'completely unanimous', supportive public line that the major parties continued to maintain on key Eastern policy issues.[118] The activists were particularly encouraged by the parties' seeming willingness to grant them a more active role in the policy-formulation process, an impression greatly promoted by the All-German Council project.[119] Of the individual parties, the SPD received the most glowing reviews, marred only by occasional complaints about specific statements, particularly Erler's January 1965 comments as well as a handful of remarks by figures associated with the party's West Berlin wing.[120] The CDU/CSU and the FDP also basked in the expellee lobby's good graces, albeit somewhat less fully than their Social Democratic rivals. The expellee activists' generally high appreciation of the two parties' efforts was somewhat tempered by certain lingering reservations, particularly about the CDU's relative passivity, at least in comparison to the SPD, and about the FDP's excessive

[116] *DzD* iii/11/1. 57–9, 69–72, 61–2.

[117] Schmidt, *Kalter Krieg*; Diethelm Prowe, 'Die Anfänge der Brandtschen Ostpolitik 1961–63: Eine Untersuchung zur Endphase des Kalten Krieges', in Wolfgang Benz and Hermann Graml (eds.), *Aspekte deutscher Aussenpolitik im 20. Jahrhundert* (Stuttgart: DVA, 1976), 249–86; id., 'The Making of "ein Berliner": Kennedy, Brandt and the Origins of Detente Policy in Germany', in David Wetzel (ed.), *From the Berlin Museum to the Berlin Wall: Essays on the Cultural and Political History of Modern Germany* (Westport, Conn.: Praeger, 1996); Andreas Vogtmeier, *Egon Bahr und die deutsche Frage* (Bonn: Dietz, 1996).　　　[118] 'Klares Denken, klare Sprache', *DoD* (28 June 1965).

[119] BdV presidium, 1–2 Mar. 1963, ABdV: Sitzungen des Präsidiums, 1963.

[120] Walter Rinke to Will Rasner, 23 Nov. 1964, ACDP: I-294-076/2; BdV presidium protocols, 14 Dec. 1964, ABdV: Sitzungen des Präsidiums, 1964, 2–3; Jaksch to Kurt Mattick, 8 Oct. 1963, AdsD: Seliger-Archiv, NL Jaksch, J2.

interest in alternative foreign-policy concepts, especially diplomatic openings toward Eastern Europe.[121]

Why, then, did the major parties not only continue but noticeably intensify their campaigns to court the expellee lobby, particularly in the field of Eastern policy, despite their lack of desire to implement any of the revisionist causes that they purported to espouse? Two instrumental motives steered the parties' actions. The first was renewed concern about a possible mass radicalization that party leaders feared might ensue, should large numbers of expellees feel abandoned by the political elites. This fear, which had peaked in the early post-war years and then steadily faded, resurfaced in the 1961–5 period, in large part as a result of the angry and intolerant tones that dominated the protest campaigns of the expellee activists against their media critics.[122] However, such apprehensions still remained relatively muted and, in terms of their overall significance, continued to lag far behind the primary motivation of the party elites: electoral calculations.

Throughout the 1961–5 period, the leading parties never lost sight of the potentially decisive significance of the expellee voter bloc. Behind closed doors, they consistently stressed the need to view the expellee question primarily through electoral lenses and jealously tracked all initiatives launched by their rivals, typically rushing to imitate whatever measures appeared to be bringing gains for the competition.[123] The primacy of electoral considerations also showed in the fact that the party leaders' attention to the expellee lobby peaked in the months preceding the 1965 election. During this period, the major parties issued one particularly supportive declaration after another; put out tailor-made propaganda publications; organized a variety of special meetings and rallies; and fielded numerous candidates chosen specifically because of their expellee background.[124] True to its recent habits, the SPD once again went a step further than its rivals, confidentially assuring BdV representatives that an SPD-led cabinet would include 'not just one but several expellee representatives'.[125]

The outcome of the ballot in September 1965 brought renewed disappointment for the Social Democrats. Although the party's results continued to improve, reaching nearly 40 per cent of the vote, the CDU/CSU also managed to add slightly to its 1961 tally, thus maintaining a lead of more than eight percentage

---

[121] Hans-Christoph Seebohm's speech at the *Sudetendeutscher Tag*, 17 May 1964, SDA: NL Seebohm, 46, esp. 20–1; 'Deutsche Interessen vertreten', *DoD* (29 Mar. 1965); Rinke to Rasner, 23 Nov. 1964, ACDP: I-294-076/2; 'Gefährlicher Einbruch', *DoD* (3 Feb. 1964).

[122] Protocols of the All-German Council, 17 Oct. 1963, AdsD: PV, Neuer Bestand, 3745.

[123] CDU's *Bundesvorstand*, 25 Feb. 1964, ACDP: VII-001-013/2, 87–96; Jaksch to Wehner, 11 Dec. 1964, AdsD: BT-Fraktion, 4. WP, 323; FDP's *Bundestagsfraktion*, 29 Nov. 1961, ADL: A040-737.

[124] See Erhard's, Brandt's, and Mende's addresses to the Silesian Homeland Society, cited in 'Erhard: Vertriebene zahlen heute zu den treuesten in der Bundesrepublik', *Die Welt* (14 June 1965). The CDU/CSU held a 'Vertriebenen-Kongress' in Nuremberg, 3–4 May 1965, while the SPD organized a 'Volkspolitischer Kongress' in Bad Godesberg, 26 June 1965. Special publications included the CDU's *Der Heimatvertriebene und der Flüchtling* and the SPD's *Selbstbestimmung und Eingliederung*. On expellee candidates, see Seebohm to Strauss, 12 Apr. 1965, SDA: NL Seebohm, 20; Jaksch to Wehner, 11 Dec. 1964, AdsD: BT-Fraktion, 4. WP, 323.

[125] Wehner to a BdV delegation, 18 June 1965, AdsD: Präsidiums-Protokolle, Apr.–July 1965.

points over its arch-rival. The FDP, in turn, suffered a notable defeat, its share of the vote falling by a quarter from the record levels of 1961.[126] The available evidence suggests that the expellee voters behaved somewhat differently than the electorate as a whole, particularly in their greater tendency to support the Social Democrats. Among the expellees, the SPD appears to have recorded slight improvements on its already impressive 1961 results, thus remaining roughly even with the CDU/CSU, which bounced back from its disappointing 1961 outcome with moderate gains. The FDP proved less fortunate, suffering losses of several percentage points and thus falling further behind its two rivals.[127]

By all indications, the election was not decided on Ostpolitik or any other foreign-policy issue. Post-election opinion polls showed that the key factors swaying the aggregate result in the CDU/CSU's favour had been domestic in nature, including Chancellor Erhard's personal popularity, which, in turn, was rooted primarily in the past record—and future promise—of economic prosperity associated with him.[128] To be sure, one can safely assume that Eastern policy preoccupied expellees more than most other voters and that the parties' exertions in this policy area contributed to both the SPD's successes and the FDP's continued losses in the expellee sector. But there is no reason to doubt that domestic concerns were also crucial for the expellee voters, particularly because their socioeconomic integration was by now well advanced—giving them a growing stake in maintaining established patterns of prosperity at home—and because the main parties' public consensus on key Ostpolitik issue made big policy shifts in that area appear unlikely regardless of the electoral outcome.

The immediate legacy of the 1965 Bundestag election, much like that of 1961, accentuated political continuity. The basic power relations in Bonn remained unchanged, as a coalition composed of the CDU/CSU and the FDP, with Erhard as Chancellor and Gerhard Schröder as Foreign Minister, stayed in office. From the expellee perspective, continuity was evident in other ways as well. At the very top, Hans-Christoph Seebohm, the sole remaining federal minister with active ties to the expellee lobby, entered yet another cabinet as Minister of Transport. In the slightly less exalted halls of the federal parliament the expellees also held their own; the new Bundestag boasted forty-eight deputies of an expellee background, only one fewer than the previous parliament.[129]

The picture was somewhat more complicated on the question of what policies the political elites sought to promote and implement, particularly on Eastern policy and reunification, the two areas that most concerned the expellee movement. As the next chapter will demonstrate, on the party-political level a gradual move away from the established dogmas began soon after the 1965 election,

---

[126] The results were: CDU/CSU 47.6% of the vote, 245 seats; SPD 39.3%, 202; FDP 9.5%, 49.

[127] Brües, *Artikulation*, 196–206; Statistisches Bundesamt, *Wahl zum 5. Deutschen Bundestag am 19. Sept. 1965* (Stuttgart: Kohlhammer, 1965), ii. *Strukturdaten für die neuen Bundestagswahlkreise*; i. *Allgemeine Wahlergebnisse*.

[128] Divo-Institut, *The Oct. 1965 German Election Study: Post-Election Study, Oct. 2, 1965–Oct. 23, 1965* (Ann Arbor: ICPR, 1975), 54–64, 101–3.   [129] Schoenberg, *Germans*, 135.

particularly in the SPD, which underwent another re-evaluation of its stances and strategies as a result of its latest electoral disappointment. Erhard and his cabinet, by contrast, avoided comparable policy readjustments, and as a consequence the high noon of negative expellee influence on the government's Eastern policy extended well past the 1965 election, ending only with the collapse of the CDU/CSU–FDP coalition in November 1966.

THE GOVERNMENT'S OSTPOLITIK AND EXPELLEE INFLUENCE

At the beginning of the 1960s, the federal government—like the major parties and much of the media—developed an increasingly strong interest in concrete Eastern policy initiatives. The primary cause of the government's intensified attention to Ostpolitik was external pressure, rooted in ongoing international developments. Frustrated by the failure of the 1959 Geneva Conference to yield any progress on the German question and anxious about the hazards imposed by the ongoing Berlin Crisis, the Western Allies increasingly viewed Bonn's doctrinaire public stances on reunification and related problems as obstacles to a broader international détente. Accordingly, the Allies put growing pressure on West Germany to readjust its policies. The recommended changes included a more flexible attitude towards the GDR as well as an acceptance of the Oder-Neisse line and the establishment of official ties to the East European satellite states.[130]

Because of their high dependence on the Western Alliance, Bonn's policy-makers had no choice but to listen to these critical voices, and their propensity to heed the advice was further heightened by two additional factors. First, West German business interests, spearheaded by the Eastern Committee of German Industry and Commerce, continued to push for better trading opportunities, export credits, and generally improved relations vis-à-vis Eastern Europe throughout the 1960s. Although still in no position to dictate its view to the government, the business lobby exerted steady pressure which Bonn's policy elites could not ignore.[131] Second, a growing segment of the country's political leadership had come to harbour growing worries about the apparent erosion of international support for West Germany's most elemental interests, including reunification, over the previous years. In response to these pressures and concerns, the government began to reconsider some of its stances by the early 1960s. Such efforts focused particularly on Eastern policy, in part because optimistically minded policy-makers hoped that a more flexible Ostpolitik posture might create openings for reunification and in part because even the pessimists who disregarded such prospects believed that Eastern policy readjustments would

[130] Trachtenberg, *Constructed*, esp. 326–9; Adrian W. Schertz, *Die Deutschlandpolitik Kennedys und Johnsons* (Cologne: Böhlau, 1992), esp. 135–8, 253–64, 435–43; Lee, *Uneasy*, 223–35; Rainer Marcowitz, *Option für Paris? Unionsparteien, SPD und Charles de Gaulle 1958–1969* (Munich: Oldenbourg, 1996), esp. 151–2, 157, 167–8.

[131] Kreile, *Osthandel*, 56–114; Stent, *Embargo*, 68–153; Paul-Calm, *Ostpolitik*, 78–114.

deflect pressure for changes from another, even more sensitive area—the Federal Republic's hard-line stance towards the GDR.[132]

The first signs of a growing interest in a more mobile Ostpolitik became discernible in the last phases of the era defined by Adenauer's Chancellorship and von Brentano's tenure as Foreign Minister. Adenauer in particular traced the shifting political winds with characteristic astuteness, explaining to a trusted confidant in late 1960 that, because the 'Eastern question' would soon 'come alive, not the least because of the Kennedy Administration', West Germany would also have to start considering new initiatives, particularly towards the largest and arguably most significant East European state, Poland.[133]

Such reasoning received additional impetus in the aftermath of the 1961 Bundestag election. The general sense of crisis provoked by the construction of the Berlin Wall generated immediate pressure for policy readjustments, which, in turn, was reflected in important personnel changes in the cabinet. The re-entry to the government of the FDP, a party with a particularly strong profile as an advocate of new departures in reunification and Eastern policy, could be seen as heralding increased future activity in these areas. But the most significant change occurred in the Foreign Ministry, where the increasingly inflexible von Brentano was replaced by Gerhard Schröder, a CDU politician who quickly established himself as the government's chief champion of an active Eastern policy, a distinction that he was to retain throughout his five-year tenure in the Foreign Office.

Schröder's vision of Ostpolitik was rooted in a broader policy concept, aimed at promoting far-reaching changes in Central Europe's political landscape. Although the Foreign Minister typically described his ultimate goals in the sweeping terms of a 'just ... peaceful European state system', the primary long-term transformation that he had in mind was the reunification of the two Germanys.[134] Acutely aware that the growing superpower détente of the early 1960s was steadily increasing the willingness of most of the world to 'accept Germany's division as an existing fact', Schröder regarded an 'activation of [Bonn's] efforts among the East European satellites' as a key way in which Bonn could advance the cause of reunification through its own efforts.[135]

In his view, a more active Eastern policy, based on the development of governmental and other ties between the Federal Republic and the East European satellites, could promote German unity in two ways. First, it could demonstrate to the East Europeans that a reunified Germany was also in their interest. According to Schröder, the establishment of official relations to the East European countries other than the GDR would polish up Germany's tarnished image in the region.

---

[132] Schertz, *Deutschlandpolitik*; Bender, *Ostpolitik*, 58–61; Bingen, *Polenpolitik*, 71, 76–7, 79.

[133] Kosthorst, *Brentano*, 356.

[134] Schröder's 4 June 1962 speech, in Boris Meissner (ed.), *Die deutsche Ostpolitik 1961–1970: Kontinuität und Wandel* (Cologne: Wissenschaft und Politik, 1970), 34. See also Torsten Oppelland, 'Der "Ostpolitiker" Gerhard Schröder: Ein Vorläufer der sozialliberalen Ost- und Deutschlandpolitik?', *Historisch-politische Mitteilungen*, 8 (2001): 73–94.

[135] Schröder, 'Betr: Bundesregierung und Wiedervereinigung', 6 Jan. 1964 *AAPD* (1964), 15 and 16.

Through their presence, Bonn's representatives could gradually refute the 'horror vision' of 'the militaristic, revanchist Germans' that the Communist elites had played up in order to maintain cohesion within their bloc.[136] At the same time, West Germany would also get the chance to make careful but growing use of its economic prowess, granting trade benefits and financial assistance to the East Europeans and thus providing a foretaste of the much larger rewards that could be expected after reunification.[137]

In Schröder's opinion, the combined effect of these efforts would be to encourage incipient 'polycentric tendencies' within the Eastern bloc. The new policies would help the individual satellite states to develop 'a certain level of independence', which, in turn, would gradually translate into growing openness to Western influences and interests, including German reunification.[138] But the Foreign Minister also maintained that an active Ostpolitik would promote the cause of German unity in another way—by intensifying the isolation of the rival regime in East Berlin. He insisted that the Federal Republic would combine its pursuit of closer ties to the GDR's eastern neighbours with the continuation of an uncompromising non-recognition stance towards the entity that Bonn's leaders still contemptuously labelled the 'Soviet Zone'. In Schröder's vision, this double-barrelled policy would put the East Germans on the defensive in their own back-yard and eventually help to persuade even the Soviet Union of the need to 're-examine its situation' and to allow the emergence of a reunified, 'peacefully satiated' Germany.[139]

Schröder's concept provoked criticism within the government camp, both from conservative CDU/CSU leaders who considered the Foreign Minister's blueprint overly adventurous and from Free Democrats who found the plans insufficiently flexible and innovative.[140] But apart from such limited discord, which partly reflected deeper underlying divisions between the so-called Atlanticist and Gaullist foreign-policy factions within the CDU/CSU, Schröder's proposed new course enjoyed strong backing within the government. Unsurprisingly, the civil servants of the Foreign Ministry proved particularly sympathetic to their minister's plans.[141] More importantly, Schröder also received moderate support from both chancellors under whom he headed the Auswärtiges Amt. To be sure, both Adenauer and Erhard were less enthusiastic and consistent advocates of new Eastern policy initiatives than Schröder. Although Adenauer considered a regulation of the 'Eastern question' a key objective for his last years in office, by the time the new Foreign Minister joined his cabinet in November 1961, he had in effect become a lame duck chancellor,

---

[136] Schröder's 28 June 1963 speech, in Meissner, *Ostpolitik*, 44.

[137] Schröder's comments to Couve de Murville, 24 May 1965, *AAPD* (1965), 873.

[138] Schröder's comments to Japanese Foreign Minister Ohira, 7–8 Nov. 1963, *AAPD* (1963), 1421; his 20 July 1964 notes, AA/PA: B 150, Aktenkopien 1964, 3624.

[139] Schröder's radio interview, 4 Nov. 1963, in Meissner, *Ostpolitik*, 70.

[140] See e.g. Brentano in the CDU's *Bundesvorstand*, 3 Sept. 1963, ACDP: VIII-001-1504/1; FDP *Bundesvorstand* resolutions, 4 June 1965 and 23 Sept. 1965, *FDP-Bundesvorstand*, iii. 630, 648.

[141] The published *AAPD* series provide ample evidence.

scheduled to resign midway through his four-year term, and increasingly inconsistent, even erratic, in his day-to-day policies towards the Eastern bloc.[142] Erhard, by contrast, came to office with a healthier power base, albeit one that soon began to disintegrate, and he shared his Foreign Minister's commitment to the pursuit of reunification to a much greater degree than Adenauer. But Erhard's inexperience in foreign affairs, combined with his chronic indecisiveness, significantly hampered his ability to navigate the uncharted waters of Ostpolitik.[143] Despite these limitations, however, both chancellors gave their general approval not only to Schröder's broad policy blueprint but also to the practical measures with which the Foreign Minister and his associates hoped to implement it.

The concrete policy move most frequently endorsed in the government's internal Ostpolitik deliberations was the establishment of formal trade relations between the Federal Republic and the East European satellites. West Germany had signed a trade agreement with the Soviet Union in 1958, and as trade with the Eastern bloc hegemon increased rapidly in the ensuing years, Bonn's interest in official trade ties to the region's other states also grew, facilitated, in part, by ongoing pressure from the business lobby. Adenauer and Brentano highlighted this step as the most appropriate West German overture towards the East as early as 1960/1, and it remained the centrepiece of the government's practical policy agenda throughout the Schröder era.[144]

But Bonn's plans also extended beyond trade missions. Aware that trade representations alone would not provide West Germany with the kind of influence that his ultimate objectives required, Schröder hoped to 'take further steps, patiently and persistently'.[145] In their internal deliberations, the Foreign Minister and his associates stressed the need for 'political contacts' to the East European regimes and, particularly during the last two years of Erhard's chancellorship, produced various secret blueprints for diplomatic openings.[146] Although Erhard himself was initially sceptical of these plans, he, too, gradually changed his mind and by 1966 began to give the green light for such projects.[147]

Hand in hand with this intensifying consideration of a full normalization of relations with Eastern Europe went the growing willingness of key policy-makers to start distancing the government from certain tenets that had precluded serious

---

[142] Adenauer to Krone, 28 Sept. 1962, ACDP: I-028-008/1; Schwarz, *Staatsmann*, 768–9, 840–6, 850–3.

[143] Volker Hentschel, *Ludwig Erhard: Ein Politikerleben* (Munich: Olzog, 1996).

[144] Kosthorst, *Brentano*, 354–9; Bingen, *Polenpolitik*, 71–6, 79–86; Mechthild Lindemann, 'Anfänge einer neuen Ostpolitik? Handelsverhandlungen und die Errichtung von Handelsvertretungen in den Ostblock-Staaten', in Rainer A. Blasius (ed.), *Von Adenauer zu Erhard: Studien zur auswärtigen Politik der Bundesrepublik Deutschland 1963* (Munich: Oldenbourg, 1994), 54–96.

[145] Schröder, 'Betr: Botschafterkonferenz über Ost-West-Fragen, hier: osteuropäische kommunistische Staaten (Stichworte)', 8 Apr. 1964, PA/AA: B 150, Aktenkopien 1964.

[146] Wickert's 10 Jan. 1966 memorandum, *AAPD* (1966), 5; Krapf's memoranda, 28 Jan. and 2 Feb. 1965, *AAPD* (1965), 203–5, 241–3; Werz's draft telegram, 19 July 1966, *AAPD* (1966), 935–7; von Ruete's memorandum, 15 Sept. 1966, ibid. 1208–13.

[147] Osterheld to Ministerialdirigent Simon, 9 July 1965, PA/AA: B 150, Aktenkopien 1965; Karl Carstens's memorandum, 12 Apr. 1966, *AAPD* (1966), 451.

Ostpolitik openings in the past—and continued to do so even in the mid-1960s. One such tenet was the so-called Hallstein Doctrine, the well-established principle according to which the Federal Republic would eschew diplomatic ties to countries that had established such relations with East Berlin, the only exception to the rule being the Soviet Union. A growing group of key leaders, spearheaded by Adenauer, Schröder, and a range of high-ranking Foreign Ministry officials, challenged this dogma during the 1961–6 period. They typically drew on an old argument, contending that the East European satellite states should be exempted from the doctrine because their recognition of the GDR had occurred under Soviet duress.[148] To be sure, such reasoning surfaced almost exclusively in closed, behind-the-scenes debates and did not constitute a consensus opinion, as the established doctrine still enjoyed significant backing within the government.[149] But the controversy did underscore the political elite's growing willingness to consider moves towards an increasingly flexible position on an issue that formed one of the main obstacles to a more active Ostpolitik.

In all these respects, the internal debates about the Hallstein Doctrine closely mirrored those centred on another key policy tenet: the Federal Republic's refusal to accept the finality of the Oder-Neisse line as Poland's western frontier. On this issue, too, the prevailing *Staatsräson*-based orthodoxy, according to which Germany would have to abide by the letter of the Potsdam Agreement and maintain its claims to its 1937 borders as a trump for future peace negotiations, retained a base of support within the government.[150] But the level of that support declined steadily during the 1961–6 period, as the legalistic Oder-Neisse dogmas faced increasingly vehement challenges behind the scenes. High-ranking Foreign Ministry officials led the way in arguing that no other country had any interest in supporting Bonn's territorial claims and that by stubbornly clinging to these outdated doctrines the Federal Republic was undermining 'the willingness of the non-Communist world . . . to support our efforts on behalf of reunification' with the GDR.[151] Policy-makers also drew practical lessons from these developments. State Secretary Karl Carstens, for example, exhorted Bonn to demonstrate its 'willingness to make sacrifices', stressing that changes in the Federal Republic's public stance on the border question had become highly 'necessary' by the mid-1960s.[152]

Despite the far-reaching interest in movement and flexibility evident in the

[148] Adenauer's discussion with Brandt, 19 June 1962, WBA: Berlin 1947–66, 72; Lindemann, 'Anfänge?', esp. 92–3; van Scherpenberg to Schröder, 25 Jan. 1963, *AAPD* (1963), 181–2; Krapf's 28 Jan. 1965 memorandum, *AAPD* (1965), 203–5.

[149] Foreign Ministry memorandum 'Betr: Nichtanerkennung der Zone', 29 July 1963, *AAPD* (1963), 832.

[150] Von Stackelberg's 5 July 1966 memorandum, *AAPD* (1966), 917; Carstens's 5 Aug. 1964 telegram, *AAPD* (1964), 942–3.

[151] Memorandum attached to Schröder's draft letter to Erhard, 8 Oct. 1965, *AAPD* (1965), 1594; Carstens's Jan. 1966 memorandum, *AAPD* (1966), 83; van Scherpenberg to Schröder, 25 Jan. 1963, *AAPD* (1963), 182.

[152] Carstens's memoranda of 27 Jan. and 17 Oct. 1966, *AAPD* (1966), 84, 1382.

government's internal debates, the practical results of Bonn's Eastern policy in the 1961–6 period remained meagre. To be sure, the Federal Republic did make some headway. Under the primary direction of Foreign Minister Schröder, it established formal trade relations with four East European countries: Poland, Romania, and Hungary in the course of 1963 and Bulgaria in early 1964.[153] But this string of successes ended with the Bulgarian trade treaty, and the last years of the Erhard–Schröder era yielded no further advances. The Federal Republic failed in its attempts to reach a similar trade agreement with Czechoslovakia.[154]

Bonn's policy-makers also proved curiously reluctant to put into practice the plans for the development of further political contacts with the main East European states that they had sketched behind the scenes. The government eschewed serious efforts to move towards diplomatic relations with the key East European states. It publicly distanced itself from such projects under the prevailing conditions, and when it finally did begin secret preparations for the establishment of diplomatic ties to an East European satellite in 1966, it chose Romania, a distant and relatively unimportant maverick state, as its preferred partner.[155] However, even the Romanian connection failed to produce results prior to the collapse of Erhard's coalition in November 1966.

The discrepancy between the government's secret deliberations and concrete actions was also evident in Bonn's refusal to make practical efforts to distance itself from either the Hallstein Doctrine or the claims to the so-called Oder-Neisse territories. Despite the sentiments expressed behind the scenes, policy-makers repeatedly clung to both dogmas in their official statements.[156] As a consequence, even the most conspicuous Eastern policy action of the last Erhard years, the so-called Peace Note of March 1966, proved highly disappointing. Far from clarifying West Germany's stances on the key points of dispute or providing a road map for the restoration of diplomatic ties to the satellite states, the note simply stressed Bonn's general desire to improve its relations with 'the countries and peoples of Eastern Europe'. In addition, it proposed negotiations about vaguely defined non-aggression declarations, while reiterating several hackneyed theses, including Germany's continued claims to its 1937 boundaries.[157]

With such policies, the Federal Republic predictably failed to boost its general influence in Eastern Europe to any notable degree. In the absence of diplomatic ties, trade relations alone could not accomplish much, particularly as the East European governments typically imposed strict limits on the political functions of the German trade missions. In Warsaw, for instance, Bonn's chief representative managed to gain only one high-level audience in the Polish Foreign Ministry during his three years of service between 1963 and 1966.[158]

---

[153] The dates were: Poland—7 Mar. 1963; Romania—17 Oct. 1963; Hungary—9 Nov. 1963; Bulgaria—6 Mar. 1964.   [154] Lindemann, 'Anfänge?', 57–91.

[155] Bingen, *Polenpolitik*, 79–86, 89–94; Bender, *Neue Ostpolitik*, 102–15.

[156] Erhard's government declarations, 18 Oct. 1963 and 10 Nov. 1965; the government's 25 Mar. 1966 Peace Note; Schröder's 7 Mar. 1963 interview, in Meissner, *Ostpolitik*, 63, 116, 120–4, 42.

[157] Meissner, *Ostpolitik*, 120–4.   [158] Bingen, *Polenpolitik*, 83–4; Krzoska, 'Gomulka', 194–5.

This failure to foster a political rapprochement with Eastern Europe also contributed to another, much more profound problem for West Germany: an inability to advance towards the ultimate objectives inherent in Schröder's Ostpolitik concept. The policies pursued between 1961 and 1966 brought the Federal Republic no closer to either reunification or an evolutionary diffusion of the Eastern bloc. On the contrary, by the mid-1960s the Soviet Union and its East European satellites expressed increasingly pronounced support for the German Democratic Republic, stressing in one statement after another that the existence of two sovereign German states was a fact that Bonn would simply have to acknowledge.[159] The satellite states also increasingly joined ranks in demanding that the Federal Republic normalize its relations with them—but only with high preconditions. In the July 1966 Bucharest Declaration, for example, all the member states of the Warsaw Treaty Organization intimated that a normalization was long overdue but could occur only after the Federal Republic had recognized the political and territorial status quo, including the existence of the GDR and the inviolability of the Oder-Neisse line, a position that was to harden into a categorical Soviet bloc demand by the following year.[160]

To be sure, the satellite states' unity on the German question was not quite as complete as the Bucharest Declaration suggested. Even towards the end of the Erhard era, Romania, in particular, cautiously signalled to Bonn its interest in the establishment of bilateral diplomatic relations with very few preconditions.[161] But such limited signs of independence remained marginal in the face of an increasingly uncompromising stance adopted by the two key countries, Poland and Czechoslovakia. Under Soviet pressure, Warsaw and Prague were moving towards a special trilateral relationship with East Berlin by the mid-1960s, a relationship based on the premise that all three governments should present a common front towards the Federal Republic, insisting that in order to normalize its relations with any one of these states, Bonn must accept the primary political demands of all three.[162] Far from isolating the GDR and strengthening centrifugal forces within the Soviet bloc, the Federal Republic's Ostpolitik was thus exerting precisely the opposite effect by the time the Erhard–Schröder stewardship over West German foreign policy approached its end.

The failure of Bonn's Ostpolitik to live up to its key architects' expectations was not the fault of the West Germans alone. The systemic, international context of the mid-1960s significantly narrowed the range of opportunities open to

---

[159] See e.g. the Polish–Soviet Friendship, Cooperation and Mutual Assistance Treaty, 8 Apr. 1965, *DzD* iv/11/1. 399–401; Prague's response to Bonn's Peace Note, *DzD* iv/12/1. 650–1; Hacker, *Ostblock*, 750–68; Hannes Adomeit, *Imperial Overstretch: Germany in Soviet Policy from Stalin to Gorbachev* (Baden-Baden: Nomos, 1998), 109–14; Krzoska, 'Gomułka', 196–8.

[160] *DzD* iv/12/2. 1065.

[161] On Romania, see *AAPD* (1966), 643–6, 935–7, 1144–6, 1208–13, 1223–5, 1332–3. On Hungary, see *AAPD* (1966), 866–8, 916–18, 1275–8.

[162] Krzoska, 'Gomułka', 197–8; Douglas E. Selvage, 'Poland, the German Democratic Republic and the German Question, 1955–1967', Ph.D. dissertation (Yale University, 1998); von Ruete's memorandum, 23 June 1966, *AAPD* (1966), 850.

German policy-makers. The ongoing escalation of the Vietnam War, for example, fuelled East–West tensions and arguably increased the Kremlin's reluctance to condone the kinds of unpredictable, potentially destabilizing changes in its East European sphere of influence that a comprehensive alteration of the region's relations with the Federal Republic could have entailed. The steadily exacerbating Sino-Soviet conflict apparently exerted a similarly restraining effect on Moscow, particularly as the tension between the two Communist giants had by the mid-1960s reached a point at which any internal weakening of the Soviet bloc would have redounded to the benefit of the Chinese, at least in propaganda terms.

But the general constraints imposed by such broad, international developments nevertheless proved less detrimental to Bonn's Ostpolitik than the miscalculations and shortcomings of the West Germans themselves. In part, the Federal Republic's troubles were traceable to major conceptual flaws in Foreign Minister Schröder's Eastern policy plans. The most obvious problem was that Schröder intended to promote precisely the kinds of developments that the Soviet leadership had reason to fear and discourage, such as a growing independence of the East European satellites vis-à-vis Moscow and an eventual isolation of the GDR from the other members of the Soviet camp. Although these sweeping transformations would clearly have necessitated the acquiescence of the Eastern bloc hegemon, Schröder lacked a viable strategy for extracting such a reaction from the Kremlin. Primarily focused on developments within and among the East European satellites, the Foreign Minister neglected to pay sufficient attention to the Soviet Union and thereby severely undermined the feasibility of his general Ostpolitik concept.[163]

Although such conceptual flaws did much to undermine the Federal Republic's Eastern policy, even more harm was caused by a more practical problem: the government's persistent unwillingness to commit adequate resources to the implementation of its unpublicized Ostpolitik plans. Despite the considerable significance which key leaders attributed to Eastern policy, Bonn's practical pursuit of relevant measures remained strikingly half-hearted and confused throughout the 1961–6 period, as we have seen. West German policy-makers hesitated to take practical steps towards the establishment of formal political ties to Eastern Europe, regardless of their growing interest in such moves, even after it became obvious that mere trade relations would not suffice to produce the benefits that key leaders had anticipated. Bonn also refused to adjust its official position on such Ostpolitik-related dogmas as its rejection of the Oder-Neisse line, despite a widespread awareness among the country's top policy-makers that this particular stance was increasingly problematic. It not only blocked further progress in Eastern policy but also weakened West Germany's international standing and provided the Soviet bloc states with an issue that greatly facilitated the building of a united front towards the Federal Republic.

---

[163] Griffith, *Ostpolitik*, 120–1, 130; Bender, *Neue Ostpolitik*, 105–7; Kreile, *Osthandel*, 73–4.

The seemingly irrational behaviour of Bonn's policy-makers had several causes. As in previous years, calculations rooted in the logic of *Staatsräson* remained significant, particularly in the government's public statements but to a somewhat lesser degree also in its behind-the-scenes deliberations. The desire to avoid steps that might ultimately enhance the international status of the GDR continued to restrain the West Germans from diplomatic openings towards Eastern Europe, as evidenced by the support that a strict adherence to the Hallstein Doctrine still enjoyed within the government. Similar *Staatsräson* calculations also partly explained Bonn's consistent refusal to alter its official stance on the Oder-Neisse problem. The thesis that the Federal Republic should not abandon its territorial claims in the East unless it at least received tangible, reunification-related concessions in return retained some resonance among major policy-makers, particularly in the early 1960s.[164] But the relative weight of these *Staatsräson*-based arguments was on the wane. As indicated above, key leaders grew increasingly attuned to the foreign-policy costs of the established doctrines and correspondingly interested in revising them during the 1961–6 period. While classical diplomatic calculations thus gradually lost some of their previous significance as obstacles to new initiatives towards Eastern Europe, another long-standing constraint on Ostpolitik became more striking than ever: the domestically based negative influence of the expellee lobby.

At first sight, this claim appears counter-intuitive because the 1960s opened with a switch by the expellee movement to an unprecedentedly flexible stance on the question of official relations between West Germany and the East European states. Throughout the late 1950s, the expellee activists had opposed all kinds of formal ties between Bonn and the satellite capitals, approving only of loose cultural and humanitarian links. But at the beginning of the 1960s the organizations responded to escalating pressure from both the government and some of their own members for a less extreme position with a significant policy readjustment, which became manifest in a June 1961 parliamentary document known as the Jaksch Report.[165]

The report was the end product of a lengthy process begun in January 1958, as the SPD and the FDP presented to the Bundestag a joint parliamentary motion in favour of diplomatic relations with Poland. The Bundestag quickly shunted the matter to its Foreign Affairs Committee, which, in turn, established a special working group to study the matter. Headed by Wenzel Jaksch, the SPD deputy and key Sudeten German activist, the group deliberated the issue at length, granting extensive attention to the expellee organizations and their specific concerns, and then produced a formal report which received not only unanimous approval

---

[164] Schröder's comments to Dean Rusk and Lord Home, 27 Sept. 1963, *AAPD* (1963), 1245–6; Erhard's comments to Rusk, 4 June 1965, *AAPD* (1965), 957.

[165] On internal pressure, see the BdV's 'Ausschuss für gesamtdeutsche Fragen', 5–6 Oct. 1959, SDA: Kanzlei des Sprechers (B 4), 14. On governmental pressure, see Karl Carstens's report about a meeting with expellee leaders, 18 Jan. 1961, PA/AA: Abt. 7. 589b.

from the Bundestag in mid-June 1961 but also subsequent endorsement from the main expellee groups.[166]

The report exhorted the Federal Republic to conduct an increasingly active Eastern policy, aimed at the 'creation of a free, reunited Germany' and the promotion of good, peaceful ties to 'the Soviet Union and all East European states'. To further these ends, the document recommended concrete steps towards a normalization of relations between West Germany and the East European countries 'in the economic, humanitarian, spiritual, and cultural fields'. But the report also imposed several restrictions and preconditions on the projected normalization. It said nothing about relations reaching beyond the level of trade ties, which suggested that the authors wanted to discourage any exploration of such options for the foreseeable future. It also made clear that the build-up of improved ties to the East European states could proceed only as long as 'vital German interests' were not abandoned in the process. Although the report did not provide an explicit definition of these indispensable interests, it did allude to one in general terms, asserting that Bonn was not to give up its legally valid claims against countries that either exercised 'temporary administrative control over German territories' or had earlier expelled Germans.[167]

Another, comparable allusion was included in a supplementary document released in conjunction with the actual report. Entitled 'The Destinies of German Populations in Eastern Europe and the Soviet Union since 1939', this addendum described the past and present suffering of German minorities in the East and urged Bonn to devote 'special attention and care' to the enduring plight of these minorities as it sought to improve its 'relations with the East European countries and the Soviet Union'.[168]

The Jaksch Report has usually been described as a major political breakthrough by both contemporaries and subsequent commentators. The standard interpretation has credited the report with creating 'favourable . . . domestic conditions' for new initiatives and thus serving as 'the beginning of the new German Ostpolitik', a policy that after many twists and turns culminated in a comprehensive normalization of the Federal Republic's relations with the Eastern bloc states under the Social–Liberal Coalition of the early 1970s.[169] Such arguments contain a modicum of truth, as the report did constitute a significant milestone in two ways. First, it marked a switch by the expellee organizations from an uncompromising rejection of all governmental relations between the Federal Republic and the East European satellites to an acceptance of at least some modest contacts, as indicated above. And second, it gave resounding advance approval

---

[166] *Verhandlungen*, 3. WP, 14 June 1961, 9364A–9367C; Becher, *Zeitzeuge*, 293; Czaja, *Unterwegs*, 231–2; Baron Manteuffel's 23 Feb. 1962, declaration, BA: B 234, 46. The records of the working group's meetings are in the Kommission für die Geschichte des Parlamentarismus und der politischen Parteien in Bonn (KGParl).

[167] *Deutscher Bundestag*, 3. *Wahlperiode, Drucksache 2740*, 12.

[168] *Deutscher Bundestag*, 3. *Wahlperiode, Drucksache 2807*, 8.

[169] Kosthorst, *Brentano*, 359; Griffith, *Ostpolitik*, 115. See also Garton Ash, *Europe's Name*, 53; Lindemann, 'Anfänge?', 54; Klotzbach, *Staatspartei*, 564.

from the entire Bundestag for the pursuit of the specific types of initiatives spelted out in the document.

But beyond these two points, the Jaksch Report delivered much less than surface appearances might suggest. Most significantly, it did not provide a domestic base of legitimacy for the kind of Eastern policy envisaged by Foreign Minister Schröder and his associates. On the contrary, the report was specifically designed to restrict the government's freedom of movement in Eastern Europe, and as it fulfilled that function with striking effectiveness throughout the 1961–6 period, it became the chief instrument with which the expellee lobby exerted an unprecedentedly high negative influence on the Federal Republic's Eastern policy.

The report's main author, Wenzel Jaksch, designed his brainchild in a cleverly calculating fashion, with the interests of the expellee lobby foremost in his mind. Although eager to demonstrate some openness to the development of governmental ties to Eastern Europe, partly to accommodate the wishes of Bonn's political elites and partly to forestall the looming danger of the expellee lobby's isolation from the political mainstream, his main objective was to impose limits on the government's future policies. Jaksch's strategy was to endorse the kinds of low-level economic and cultural ties which the expellee lobby probably could not have prevented for long in any case and to draw the line at political relations, albeit in a subtle and seemingly non-confrontational manner. As he confided to fellow expellee activists, many of whom were initially suspicious of his intentions, Jaksch wanted the report to appear to signal principled openness to a far-reaching normalization of West Germany's relations with Eastern Europe, even on the diplomatic level, while at the same time precluding any such normalization in practice by making it contingent on 'preconditions and qualifications' that he knew 'would not be accepted' by the East Europeans.[170]

Even more significantly for the expellee movement, Jaksch also intended to use the report to ensure that the definition of these preconditions, that is, of the 'vital German interests' that were not to be abandoned as a price for Ostpolitik advances, would be a 'matter of domestic politics'.[171] This way, he hoped, he could 'make the expellee organizations a more integral part of the political scene' and thus bolster their position as judges of the acceptability of the government's Eastern policy initiatives.[172]

Far from planning to create favourable conditions for an extensive normalization of the Federal Republic's relations with the Eastern bloc countries, Jaksch thus intended to build a base for domestic obstructionism against such measures, and the expellee organizations were quick to seize the opportunities thereby presented. As soon as the scepticism which some activists had initially expressed about the project had dissipated, the expellee lobby began to cooperate with Jaksch in several ways. In response to an invitation from him, the various homeland societies testified about

[170] Axel de Vries to Manteuffel-Szoege, 14 Sept. 1960, BA: NL 1412/17.
[171] Jaksch in the Sudetendeutscher Rat, 20 June 1964, PA/AA: Abt. 7. 299a.
[172] De Vries to Manteuffel-Szoege, 14 Sept. 1960, BA: NL 1412/17.

their demands and interests to a special session of the parliamentary working group, thus ensuring that their opinions received a formal hearing and could, in part, be incorporated into the Jaksch Report.[173] The published report, in turn, was immediately seized upon by leading activists, who portrayed it as the bedrock of West German Ostpolitik, rejecting any attempts to steer the government away from its principles.[174] At the same time, the expellee organizations also enthusiastically promulgated their definition of the vital national interests whose inviolability the document had elevated into a general precondition of any Eastern policy initiatives. In accordance with the special supplement to the report, activists repeatedly highlighted the Federal Republic's obligation to do everything in its power to improve the living conditions of the German minorities in Eastern Europe.[175] But these humanitarian concerns remained secondary, as the expellee elites laid their primary emphasis on the sanctity of the legal points mentioned in the report itself, emphasizing the government's duty to uphold the revisionist doctrines which the expellee lobby had nurtured for years, particularly the claims to the lost territories east of the Oder-Neisse and to the *Heimatrecht* and self-determination right of the German expellees.[176]

The government reacted to the Jaksch Report in a way that was bound to enhance the expellee lobby's influence: by assigning fundamental significance to the document. Throughout the 1961–6 period, in one statement after another, the government portrayed the report as the guiding light of its Eastern policy. According to one representative declaration, given by Foreign Minister Schröder to the Bundestag in early 1965, the report had been a 'pioneering' achievement with which the government 'fully agree[d]' and in whose 'spirit' the Federal Republic 'shape[d] its policy toward the East European countries'.[177] To be sure, Bonn's policy-makers did not adopt this stance out of love for the expellee activists and their favourite causes. The reasons for the government's interest in accentuating the Jaksch Report as the basis of its Ostpolitik lay rather in the report's favourable parliamentary reception on the one hand and its general short-term political usefulness on the other. The unanimous approval which the document had received in the Bundestag helped to confer an aura of non-partisan legitimacy on the government's Eastern policy. The report itself, although not supportive of a far-reaching normalization of relations with Eastern Europe, at least gave the green light for movement towards the establishment of trade ties, which was where the government's most immediate interest was focused during the early 1960s.[178]

[173] Record of the working group's ninth meeting, 9 Feb. 1961, KGParl.

[174] BdV resolution 'Entspannung und Recht', 6 Oct. 1963, in Blumenthal and Fassbender, *Erklärungen*, 100–1; Sudetendeutscher Rat resolution in 'Protokoll über die Plenarsitzung des Sudetendeutschen Rates am 16/17. Nov. 1963', SDA: B IX/31, 11–13.

[175] See the Sudetendeutscher Rat resolution in n. 174; the declaration of the BdV's Arbeitskreis Oder-Neisse, 8 Oct. 1962, SDA: Kanzlei des Sprechers (B4), 15; Jaksch to Erhard, 18 Oct. 1965, BA: B 234, 361.

[176] See e.g. the Kongress der Ostdeutschen Landesvertretungen declaration, 22 Mar. 1964; BdV resolution 'Aussenpolitische Fragen', 6 Oct. 1964, both in Blumenthal and Fassbender, *Erklärungen*, 105–6, 108–10.   [177] *DzD* iv/11/1. 272.

[178] Lindemann, 'Anfänge?', 54.

However, by repeatedly using the report as a tool of policy legitimation and justification, the government also identified itself with the preconditions that the expellee lobby had sought to attach to the document. Admittedly, the official statements in which Bonn's policy-makers highlighted the Jaksch Report's general significance did not contain assurances of their willingness to honour the expellee lobby's revisionist Eastern policy demands as 'vital national interests'. But given the broader political context in the Federal Republic, the impression that the government intended to do precisely that was bound to arise even in the absence of such specific statements.

Top governmental leaders did, after all, regularly pledge their unwavering support for the expellee lobby's Ostpolitik agenda in other settings. In their capacity as party politicians, they made key contributions to the partisan bidding war in which the country's main political forces sought to capture the votes of expellees, wielding generous Eastern policy promises as one of their chief weapons. Even when speaking in the name of the government, they frequently made similarly strong statements, particularly to expellee audiences, defending not only Germany's claims to the territories east of the Oder-Neisse but also the expellees' rights to both their homelands and self-determination.[179] As such rhetoric then became combined with the government's wholehearted endorsement of the Jaksch Report, Bonn found itself chained more closely than ever to the Eastern policy agenda of the expellee lobby. No matter how vehemently leading policy-makers privately questioned the wisdom of upholding unrealistic territorial doctrines in the East or defending such 'distorted' and 'dubious' concepts as the *Heimatrecht*, they could not distance themselves from these standard stances without breaking their earlier promises and thereby risking punishment at the polls.[180]

With the Jaksch Report, the expellee lobby's negative influence on West German Eastern policy thus became institutionalized to an unprecedented degree, which, in turn, significantly modified the pattern of interaction between expellee leaders and governmental elites. In earlier years, institutionalized forms of contact between the two groups—ranging from regular meetings at different levels to the inclusion of expellee representatives in the state bureaucracy and the granting of sizeable public subsidies to the expellee organizations—had worked overwhelmingly in the government's favour, typically inducing dependency and malleability in the expellee elites. Much of this dynamic persisted even in the 1960s, as the established framework of financial and personal interaction continued to serve the government's interests more than those of the expellee lobby, but the Jaksch Report added a countervailing force to the equation, at least in Eastern policy.

---

[179] See e.g. Erhard's address to the Kongress der ostdeutschen Landesvertretungen, 22 Mar. 1964, Meissner, *Ostpolitik*, 76–8; statement about Erhard's meeting with Sudeten German representatives, 16 Oct. 1964, AdSD: Seliger-Archiv, 2010.
[180] 'Ergänzende Stellungnahme zu den "Erwartungen" des Sudetendeutschen Rates unter aussen-politischen Gesichtspunkten', 28 Sept. 1964, PA/AA: B 150, Aktenkopien 1964; Erwin Wickert's memo-randum, 10 Jan. 1966, *AAPD* (1966), 4.

To be sure, expellee leaders still remained excluded from the kinds of active roles in Bonn's foreign-policy establishment that they had coveted for years. Neither top offices nor major consultative roles in the policy-formulation process were available to them, and leading activists even bitterly complained about being so poorly informed as to have to rely on 'the press' for the latest news about the government's Ostpolitik plans.[181] Key expellee leaders also frequently worried about the government's—and particularly Foreign Minister Schröder's—real intentions and quarrelled among themselves about how confrontational or conciliatory an attitude to adopt towards Bonn's power elites.[182] But despite such limitations and problems, the expellee organizations reached the peak of their negative influence over West German Ostpolitik in the 1961–6 period, since the Jaksch Report strengthened their hand precisely at a time when the government's interest in new policy initiatives was growing stronger than ever before.

On a general level, the expellee lobby's considerable sway was apparent in the behind-the-scenes deliberations of West German policy-makers. As Foreign Minister Schröder explained to his French counterpart Couve de Murville in the spring of 1965, Bonn's established Eastern policy stances were 'extremely sensitive' matters from a domestic viewpoint, given the presence of 'millions of expellees' in the Federal Republic.[183] Accordingly, Schröder and his colleagues repeatedly dwelt on the likely 'domestic consequences' of possible policy readjustments, typically accentuating the high 'risk' which such moves would presumably present.[184] Going a step further, they also stressed the need to 'give careful advance consideration' to these anticipated repercussions and to try to determine how to 'bring them under . . . control' before proceeding with any potentially controversial measures.[185] In effect, Bonn's policy-makers thus routinely acknowledged the power of domestic, expellee-related considerations to prevent them from exploring a whole range of Eastern policy options, and most of the time the expellee lobby's negative influence manifested itself precisely in this quiet but steady form: as self-censorship through which policy-makers held themselves back from steps that could have offended expellee activists.

But occasionally that influence also showed more explicitly in concrete initiatives that either failed altogether or fell far short of their original goals largely because of the government's reluctance to risk alienating the expellee lobby. This dynamic can be best illustrated with two specific examples: the Czech–German trade negotiations conducted between 1963 and 1965 and the West German Peace Note of March 1966.

In the Czech–German negotiations, issues related to the Sudeten Germans,

[181] BdV's Arbeitskreis Oder-Neisse, declaration, 8 Oct. 1962, SDA: Kanzlei des Sprechers (B4), 15.

[182] Protocols of the BdV presidium, 24 Apr. 1964 and of the Sudetendeutscher Rat, 26 June 1964, in ABdV: Sitzungen des Präsidiums, 1964 and PA/AA: Abt 7. 299a; of the BdV presidium, 15 Oct. 1962, ABdV: Sitzungen des Präsidiums, 1961–2, 3–4; and of the BdV *Bundesversammlung*, 30 June 1963, SDA: NL Seebohm/33.

[183] Schröder's comments to Couve de Murville, 24 May 1965, *AAPD* (1965), 868 and 871.

[184] State Secretary Carstens's memoranda, 17 Oct. 1966, *AAPD* (1966), 1383; and 4 Oct. 1964, *AAPD* (1964), 1107.   [185] Carstens's memorandum, 17 Oct. 1966, *AAPD* (1966), 1383.

particularly the status of the Munich Agreement, constituted a major stumbling block. As indicated earlier, the character and relevance of the Munich Pact had become a prominent political issue within the Federal Republic by 1963/4, thanks to provocative statements in which Hans-Christoph Seebohm and other Sudeten German leaders aggressively defended the agreement, rejecting with particular vehemence rising Eastern bloc demands that Bonn declare the treaty invalid *ab initio*. The government, like all the major parties, had adopted a cautious public stance on the issue. While distancing itself from the most odious aspects of the agreement, such as Hitler's violent tactics, it had avoided clear statements on the validity question and even deliberately cultivated false hopes among the Sudeten Germans by phrasing official denials of territorial claims against Czechoslovakia in a calculatingly ambiguous fashion, stating merely that West Germany 'raised' no such demands rather than that it did not 'have' any.

Such public discussion of the Munich Accord predictably elicited expressions of concern from Czech leaders and helped to catapult the notorious accord into a central point of dispute in the Czech–German trade negotiations that began at the end of 1963. In the talks, the Munich problem quickly became linked to another key issue. While the West Germans insisted that West Berlin be specifically included in the anticipated trade agreement, the Czechs in return expected Bonn to distance itself unambiguously from all challenges to Czechoslovakia's territorial integrity, particularly by declaring the Munich Agreement invalid *ab initio*. After prolonged wrangling, the trade negotiations hit a dead end over these twin issues by March 1965, and although both sides had contributed to that outcome with their inflexibility and posturing, Bonn bore the brunt of the blame.[186] Not only had the Federal Republic refused to clarify its stance on the Munich Treaty's validity; it had also rejected a Prague's offer to yield on the Berlin issue in return for West Germany's agreeing to receive a 'unilateral declaration' explaining 'the Czech viewpoint on the Munich Agreement'.[187]

Although the formal negotiations thus ended in deadlock in March 1965, contacts between the two sides continued well into 1966, with the Czechs repeatedly signalling both interest in a trade agreement and willingness to accommodate West German demands regarding West Berlin.[188] However, nothing came out of these overtures, in large part because Bonn refused to adjust its relevant stances, delaying on the Munich issue by conducting a prolonged internal study of the matter and explicitly refusing to make its renunciation of territorial ambitions vis-à-vis Czechoslovakia more unequivocal.[189] According to an internal memorandum, the verb 'raise' remained 'the limit' for the government in this context; more explicit formulations could be used only by private citizens, at their own risk.[190]

---

[186] *AAPD* (1964), 1019–20, 1353–5; *AAPD* (1965), 125–6, 159–63, 463–5, 847–55.
[187] Von Mirbach's report of the 15–26 Feb. 1965 negotiating session and of 11 Mar. 1965, PA/AA: B 150, Aktenkopien 1965.   [188] *AAPD* (1965), 1960–2; *AAPD* (1966), 198–203.
[189] *AAPD* (1964), 1354–5; and *AAPD* (1966), 137–8 n. 17.
[190] Luedde-Neurath's memorandum, 19 Feb. 1966, *AAPD* (1966), 202.

By the end of the Erhard–Schröder era, Czechoslovakia thus remained the only East European satellite state to which the Federal Republic had no formal governmental ties, even on the trade level. This situation was anomalous and paradoxical for several reasons. Relations with Prague were of major significance for West Germany's broader interests, as Bonn's policy-makers well understood. Particularly by the mid-1960s, as Warsaw and Prague were inching towards a special trilateral relationship with East Berlin and starting to present a united front towards the Federal Republic, West German leaders realized that Czechoslovakia constituted the weakest side of this triangle and that improvements in Czech–West German ties would probably help to undermine the whole formation.[191]

At the same time, Bonn's policy-makers harboured deep-seated reservations about the positions that they stubbornly maintained in their talks with the Czechs. Most regarded the Munich Agreement as a general source of embarrassment whose prominence in the negotiations was regrettable. The territorial ambitions that Sudeten German activists sought to promote with their defence of the treaty enjoyed no sympathy within the government. The legal argumentation with which the activists opposed a West German acceptance of the pact's invalidity *ab initio*—the assertion that such a step would deprive the Sudeten Germans of their wartime German citizenship and thus jeopardize their legal standing vis-à-vis Czechoslovakia—also drew explicit rejection from several government experts.[192] In addition, many leading figures argued behind the scenes that the appearance of a close association with the Sudeten German lobby that the government's stances helped to generate was a major liability for the Federal Republic, feeding suspicions of a 'deliberate two-facedness' in West German policies and thus undermining the county's stature and credibility.[193] And yet, despite all these problems and reservations, the government refused to budge from its established positions, primarily because of the Munich Agreement's 'fundamental significance' in view of the 'domestic policy aspects' associated with it, as the leader of the West German delegation to the talks with Prague observed in early 1965.[194]

The government's fear of the expellee lobby was even more evident during the preparation of the government's Peace Note of March 1966. As planning for the note got under-way in early 1966, the involved Foreign Ministry officials, led by Erwin Wickert, the document's main author, intended to improve West Germany's international image with appropriate 'political initiatives' targeted primarily at Eastern Europe in general and Czechoslovakia, the regional problem

---

[191] Von Ruete's memorandum, 23 June 1966, *AAPD* (1966), 850.

[192] AA memorandum 'Aufzeichnung, Betr: Frage der Rechtswirksamkeit des Münchener Abkommens vom 29. Sept. 1938', sent to all West German representations abroad, 15 June 1964, ACSP: NL Schütz, 31. But see also Finke-Osiander's 21 Jan. 1965 memorandum, *AAPD* (1965), 159–63; and the 16 May 1966 AA study, cited in *AAPD* (1966), 137–8 n. 17.

[193] Krapf's 4 Feb. 1966 memorandum, *AAPD*, 138; Carstens's 6 Oct. 1964 memorandum, *AAPD* (1964), 1124–5; 'Ergänzende Stellungnahme zu den "Erwartungen" des Sudetendeutschen Rates unter aussenpolitischen Gesichtspunkten', 28 Sept. 1964, PA/AA: B 150, Aktenkopien 1964.

[194] Von Mirrbach's 4 Mar. 1965 memorandum, PA/AA: B 150, Aktenkopien 1965; von Ruete's 23 June 1966 memorandum, *AAPD* (1966), 852; Blasius, 'Wickert', 548.

child, in particular.[195] Accordingly, Wickert and his associates drafted several foreign-policy proposals, particularly on international security issues, including calls for arms control measures and for the exchange of non-aggression declarations between the Federal Republic and the East European satellite states. But the note's authors also wanted to tackle the domestic side of Ostpolitik. To Wickert, the note presented an opportunity to weaken the sway of the 'expellee organizations', which he considered 'the greatest domestic obstacle to Schröder's Eastern policy'. In his view, the best strategy was to 'crack the expellee groups one by one', starting with the Sudetendeutsche Landsmannschaft.[196]

Accordingly, Wickert incorporated into the original draft of the note several challenges to the Eastern policy doctrines espoused by the expellee lobby. In keeping with his plan to pursue a divide-and-conquer strategy vis-à-vis the expellee movement, he adopted a relatively cautious stance on the Oder-Neisse problem. His original phrasing repeated the standard legal dogma about the continued validity of the Reich's 1937 borders while adding in the next sentence that 'the German people' would be prepared to 'accept sacrifices for the sake of reunification'.[197] On problems directly related to the Sudeten Germans, Wickert hit considerably harder. According to his proposed draft, the Federal Republic regarded the Munich Agreement as 'no longer valid'; 'ha[d] and . . . raise[d] no territorial demands against Czechoslovakia'; and 'distance[d] itself from all statements that could cast doubt on this position'.[198]

The draft note drew prompt and vehement criticism from the cabinet, not because of the foreign-policy concepts themselves—all of which were ultimately endorsed with only minor revisions—but because of the unorthodox statements aimed at the expellee lobby. Several ministers objected to the juxtaposition of West Germany's standard Oder-Neisse doctrine with an allusion to possible sacrifices in the interest of reunification. Expellee Minister Johann Baptist Gradl of the CDU, for example, maintained that the sacrifice reference had to be removed from this context because 'otherwise the expellees will receive the impression that the government is ready for a total abandonment (*Verzicht*) of the Eastern territories'.[199]

Wickert's formulations on the Munich Agreement and related problems provoked even stronger censure. Not only Heinrich Krone, a veteran CDU powerbroker and a junior cabinet member, but also Chancellor Erhard himself baulked at this passage, reportedly for fear of the 'possible objections of the Sudeten-German Homeland Society'. The Chancellor, in particular, had reason to dread such a reaction. Only days before receiving Wickert's draft note, he had personally assured the BdV that his government remained steadfast in its key Ostpolitik stances and 'open to the justified wishes of the expellees'.[200]

---

[195] Blasius, 'Wickert', 544–7; von Ruete's 23 June 1966 memorandum, *AAPD* (1966), 849.

[196] Blasius, 'Wickert', 548.   [197] *AAPD* (1966), 264; Blasius, 'Wickert', 547.

[198] *AAPD* (1966), 265; Blasius, 'Wickert', 548–9.

[199] Gradl's notes, 9 Mar. 1966, ACDP: I-294-070/4.

[200] Blasius, 'Wickert', 548–50; Wickert's 17 Mar. 1966 memorandum, *AAPD* (1966), 318; 'Aus der Reserve treten', *DoD* (18 Mar. 1966), 4–5.

True to their political instincts, Erhard and his ministers implemented major changes in the expellee-related sections of the draft note. The sacrifice reference was moved to a safe distance from the discussion of the Oder-Neisse problem, and after intensive lobbying by several leading figures, including a last-minute intervention by the Chancellor, the Munich passage was stripped of most of its content.[201] The final version of the note thus included neither the admission that the Munich Agreement was no longer valid nor the statements that Bonn 'ha[d]' no territorial claims vis-à-vis Czechoslovakia and that it distanced itself from all suggestions to the contrary. Instead, the Peace Note simply reiterated the standard phrase according to which West Germany 'raise[d]' no territorial claims against Czechoslovakia. As its only concession to Wickert's original intentions, the document repeated a formulation first used by Chancellor Erhard in a 1964 speech, acknowledging that the Munich Agreement had been subsequently 'torn up' by Hitler and that the treaty 'no longer ha[d] territorial significance', which hardly counted as an unequivocal renunciation of all potential territorial ambitions against Czechoslovakia.[202]

In its strongly diluted final form, the Peace Note proved a disappointment, undeserving of the label 'masterpiece of German diplomacy' that some of its architects subsequently sought to bestow upon it.[203] It failed to break any of the domestic taboos that had shackled West Germany's Ostpolitik and as a consequence did little to improve the country's international image. This was particularly true in Eastern Europe, where the note elicited consistently negative governmental reactions that typically lambasted Bonn for its seemingly unflagging allegiance to revisionist causes.[204] Wickert's original hope of dividing and weakening the expellee lobby was also frustrated, as the leading expellee groups joined forces in criticizing even the very cautious formulations contained in the final version of the document. The Sudeten Germans, in particular, expressed strong displeasure about the note, focusing on the 'one-sided representation' of the Munich Agreement and the absence of explicit assurances about the government's continued support for the *Heimatrecht* and the self-determination right of all expellees.[205] The other major organizations endorsed these objections and even adopted a formal 'solidarity declaration' in support of the 'disappointed Sudeten Germans'.[206]

In response to this pressure from the expellee lobby, Erhard soon caved in and further weakened the note's domestic impact. In a written exchange with expellee activists he stated that the government 'did not intend to deviate from its established [Ostpolitik] principles' and that the continued validity of the Sudeten

---

[201] Blasius, 'Wickert', 548–50; Wickert's 17 Mar. 1966 memorandum, *AAPD* (1966), 318.

[202] Meissner, *Ostpolitik*, 121, 82.

[203] Karl Carstens, *Erinnerungen und Erfahrungen* (Boppard am Rhein: Boldt, 1993), 759.

[204] *DzD* iv/12/1. 592–8, 648–55, and 725–30.

[205] Bundesverband protocols of the Sudeten–German Homeland Society, 26 Mar. 1966, SDA: NL Becher, 229; press release by Walter Becher and Herbert Prochazka, 25 Mar. 1966, SDA: NL Becher, 357.

[206] BdV presidium protocols, 3 May 1966, ABdV: Sitzungen des Präsidiums, 1966.

Germans' and other expellees' rights to their homelands and to self-determination remained unaffected by the recent diplomatic initiative.[207] The Chancellor thus did exactly what Wickert had feared. Far from following up the Peace Note with 'firmness', Erhard began 'again to talk about *Heimatrecht* to the Sudeten Germans', thus further 'blur[ring]' the issues and postponing the necessary task of 'tackling . . . the Sudetendeutsche Landsmannschaft'.[208]

This evasive and dilatory approach prevailed throughout the remainder of Erhard's chancellorship as well. Foreign Ministry officials wanted to develop further initiatives towards Eastern Europe and accordingly drafted a specific proposal aimed at Prague that envisaged negotiations about non-aggression declarations, accompanied by a clear 'political and moral condemnation' of the Munich Accord by Bonn and the establishment of a special Czech–West German body of legal experts to examine the legal questions surrounding the treaty.[209] But nothing came out of these plans, largely because of the Chancellor's reluctance to pursue the matter. According to Wickert, the reasons were clear: beset by growing economic problems and declining popularity in the twilight of his chancellorship, Erhard was restrained by the fear that innovative Eastern policy moves might exacerbate his troubles by evoking 'the ire of the expellee functionaries'.[210]

By the time Erhard's government collapsed under the pressures of economic recession and political infighting in November 1966, the Federal Republic's Ostpolitik had reached a dead end and become an increasingly obvious obstacle to the pursuit of other, higher priority goals, including reunification. State Secretary Karl Carstens admitted as much in a secret memorandum discussed at one of Erhard's last cabinet sessions, in which he recommended extensive readjustments in several of Bonn's standard stances, ranging from the Hallstein Doctrine to the Oder-Neisse dogmas. However, Carstens also indicated that these steps would spell domestic difficulties for the government and described an 'open discussion' of the relevant matters with the 'expellee organizations' as 'absolutely necessary'.[211]

Although largely ignored during Erhard's last weeks in office, Carstens's recommendations were to enjoy growing resonance as the Federal Republic entered a new, transitional period under the political leadership of the Grand Coalition, composed of the CDU/CSU and the SPD, in late 1966. During this three-year era, the long-standing pattern of negative expellee influence on the Federal Republic's Eastern policy gradually crumbled, paving the way for the turning point that came when Willy Brandt's Social Liberal Coalition launched its so-called new Ostpolitik in defiance of expellee protests from late 1969 on. As the

[207] Josef Stingl to the BdV's Landesverband Oder-Neisse, 4 May 1966, ACDP: I-094-021/2.

[208] Blasius, 'Wickert', 552.

[209] Von Ruete's memoranda, 12 Aug. 1966 and 23 June 1966, *AAPD* (1966), 1064, 847–55; Blasius, 'Wickert', 552–3.

[210] Blasius, 'Wickert', 553; Franz Böhm to Erhard, 6 July 1966, SDA: NL Jaksch, B1/94.

[211] Carstens's memorandum, 17 Oct. 1966, *AAPD* (1966), 1374–83; 'Schweigen Ehrensache', *Der Spiegel* (24 Oct. 1966).

next chapter will demonstrate, the changes of the 1966–9 period were driven primarily by forces other than the government, which still remained cautious in its official stances. Leadership in challenging the established policy taboos came rather from journalists, intellectuals, and church leaders and, to a lesser degree, from select politicians in the SPD and the FDP, who, in turn, were swept along on a broader wave of long-term changes in West German society. As this offensive began to gather major strength about a year before Erhard's government finally collapsed, a glance back to the autumn of 1965 becomes necessary.

III

The Collapse of the Pattern
1966–1990

CHAPTER SEVEN

The Grand Coalition as the Turning Point, 1966–1969

SHORTLY AFTER THE Bundestag elections of 1965, the West German public discussion about the expellee question in general and its Ostpolitik implications in particular reached a new level of urgency. This development was traceable to novel contributions by two key institutions that had previously kept a low profile in relevant public debates: the Evangelical and Catholic Churches. To be sure, both Churches had played a major role in the early integration of the expellees, providing not only spiritual but also social and organizational support, and remained engaged in later years as well, typically through special suborgans that maintained close ties to the expellee sector. But the Churches had shied away from direct participation in the public debates about the expellees and Ostpolitik that had begun to permeate West German society by the early 1960s. Even the seeming key exception to this rule—the Tübingen Memorandum of 1961, which had exhorted Bonn to abandon its revisionist Eastern policy doctrines in the interest of facilitating reunification with the GDR—had been written by prominent individuals associated with the Evangelical Church without authorization from that institution, which had distanced itself from the document soon after its publication.[1]

This situation changed dramatically in October 1965, as the Evangelical Church released a lengthy memorandum entitled *The Situation of the Expellees and the Relations of the German People to their Eastern Neighbours*.[2] Although it addressed a number of expellee-related issues, the document derived instant notoriety from its arguments regarding Ostpolitik in general and German–Polish relations in particular. Critical of the 'irrational emotionalism' characteristic of much of the country's public discourse about Eastern policy problems, the memorandum aimed 'to bring new movement to the political imagination of the German people and also to offer a new level of dialogue to [Germany's] Eastern neighbours'.[3] It

---

[1] Hartmut Rudolph, 'Fragen der Ostpolitik im Raum der Evangelischen Kirche in Deutschland', in Wolfgang Huber and Johannes Schwerdtfeger (eds.), *Kirche zwischen Krieg und Frieden* (Stuttgart: Klett, 1976), 460–540; id., *Evangelische Kirche und Vertriebene 1945 bis 1972*, ii (Göttingen: Vandenhoeck & Ruprecht, 1985); Hansjakob Stehle, 'Seit 1960: der mühsame katholische Dialog über die Grenze', in Werner Plum (ed.), *Ungewöhnliche Normalisierung: Beziehungen der Bundesrepublik Deutschland zu Polen* (Bonn: Neue Gesellschaft, 1984), 155–78.   [2] *DzD* iv/11/2. 869–97.

[3] Ibid. 895.

explicitly repudiated the 'self-righteousness' inherent in attempts to perpetuate 'rigid and one-sided' revisionist claims rooted in presumed German 'rights', stressing instead the need to move beyond such ethical and judicial categories and to think in realistic political terms.[4]

Without denying the injustice of the expulsions, the memorandum placed that collective tragedy in the broader context of the Third Reich's crimes and underscored two basic facts about contemporary Poland: its existential need for secure western borders and the rise of a new Polish generation that had grown up in the former German territories and thus acquired a *Heimatrecht* there.[5] Combining these realities with a close reading of the prevailing trends of international relations, the memorandum concluded that West Germany had no choice but to adjust to the advance of détente by committing itself to a policy of 'reconciliation with [its] eastern neighbours'. While acknowledging that decisions about the precise direction of that policy had to be left to the country's political elites, the authors intimated that in their opinion the most appropriate German contribution to the process of reconciliation would be an eventual abandonment of the revisionist claims upheld by the expellee lobby.[6]

The Roman Catholic Church's contribution to the contemporary public debate was considerably more guarded. The Church made its move in response to an external stimulus, the November 1965 open letter with which Poland's Catholic bishops invited their German counterparts to a celebration of the thousandth anniversary of the Christianization of Poland. The invitation addressed a number of current political problems. As could be expected, it underscored the immutability of the Oder-Neisse line in view of Poland's tragic past, but it also broke new ground by acknowledging the 'suffering' of the German expellees and pleading for a 'serious dialogue' between the two peoples in a spirit of reconciliation and mutual 'forgiveness'.[7] In their published response, the German bishops accepted the Polish invitation, endorsed the call for dialogue and forgiveness—but equivocated on key points of dispute. To be sure, they expressed sympathy for Poland's desire to retain its new western territories and for the right of a new generation of Poles to live in these lands. But they also defended the *Heimatrecht* of the German expellees as a concept allegedly free of 'aggressive intent' and expressive of a natural human longing to 'remain connected with the old homeland'.[8] Although clearly sympathetic to many Polish arguments, this key Catholic document thus posed a much less direct challenge to the standard expellee doctrines than its Evangelical counterpart.

The joint impact of the statements by the two Churches was to inject new intensity into ongoing public debates about the guiding principles of West German Ostpolitik. Much of the ensuing controversy unfolded along predictable lines. Many leading publicists and mainstream journalists greeted the church commentaries, especially the Evangelical memorandum, as welcome contributions to a

---

[4] *DzD* iv/11/2. 896. [5] Ibid. esp., 877–87. [6] Ibid. 896.
[7] Ibid. 945–7. [8] Ibid. 975.

larger process of questioning past taboos and expanding the political options available to West Germany.[9] The expellee lobby, in turn, reacted with vociferous protest, the bulk of which was directed specifically at the Evangelical memorandum. In one statement after another, activists denounced the document as a 'pseudo-scholarly, pseudo-theological' polemic, authored by a group of 'naive' dilettantes who had unwittingly become pawns in a broader Communist offensive aimed at 'undermining Western defences against Soviet expansionism . . . by means of subversive propaganda'.[10] Expellee leaders also worried about the precedent set as two of the most prestigious institutions in West German society publicly espoused views that, to varying degrees, collided with those of the expellee lobby. A key figure in the Silesian Homeland Society, for example, privately observed in late 1965 that the release of the Evangelical memorandum had 'opened the flood gates to a self-destructive public discussion' through which, he feared, the mass media would attempt 'to crush the expellees'.[11]

In addition to evoking these predictable reactions by the media elites and the expellee activists, the Evangelical and Catholic statements also served as catalysts for two new political trends that were to assume crucial significance during the remainder of the 1960s. The first new development was the failure of the country's political elites to rush to the defence of expellee organizations in the manner that had become customary in the early 1960s. Whereas the parties had quickly sided with the expellee lobby during several of its previous clashes with the media, their initial reaction now was to keep their distance and to issue cautious, carefully balanced statements. Although party spokesmen typically reiterated that their stance on the eastern border question was unchanged, they did so rather mechanically and often in a deliberately ambiguous manner suggestive of a willingness to abandon such territorial claims for the sake of reunification.

In a prime example of such equivocation, Foreign Minister Gerhard Schröder of the CDU declared that his party would not give up 'its position with regard to Germany's eastern territories in isolation from the reunification complex'.[12] The SPD, in turn, proclaimed that it intended to 'save as much of Germany as possible for the Germans' but then identified only one cause that it would 'never abandon'—'the seventeen million compatriots in the GDR'.[13] Elaborate, old-style defences of concepts such as the *Heimatrecht* of the German expellees were absent from the parties' early statements, as were outright attacks against either the

[9] Reinhard Henkys (ed.), *Deutschland und die östlichen Nachbarn: Beiträge zu einer evangelischen Denkschrift* (Berlin: Kreuz, 1966); Wolfgang Huber, 'Die Vertriebenendenkschrift von 1965 und das Verhältnis von Kirche und Öffentlichkeit', in id. (ed.), *Kirche und Öffentlichkeit* (Stuttgart: Klett, 1973), 380–420; Rudolph, 'Fragen', 519–39; id. *Evangelische*, ii.

[10] 'Verzicht in Raten', *DoD* (22 Nov. 1965); 'Vertriebene protestieren', *Pommersche Zeitung* (30 Oct. 1965).

[11] Clemens Riedel to R. Süssmuth, 29 Nov. 1965 and 3 Dec. 1965, ACDP: I-094-048/1.

[12] Schröder's 14 Nov. 1965 interview, cited in 'Zurückhaltung und Kritik: Stellungnahmen der Bundesregierung und der Parteien', *DoD* (22 Nov. 1965).

[13] 'EKD-Denkschrift und Briefe der Bischöfe', *SPD Pressemitteilungen und Informationen*, 11 Dec. 1965, AdsD: BT-Fraktion, 5. WP, 904.

Evangelical or the Catholic Churches. Indeed, party spokesmen typically saluted the church leaders' good intentions and their positive contributions to serious public debate, while taking care not to endorse specific controversial points raised in the two documents.[14] In addition, several key political figures lamented the 'harshness and bitterness' characteristic of much of the ongoing discussion regarding, in particular, the Evangelical memorandum, thus indirectly criticizing the expellee activists, whose vitriolic commentaries had repeatedly overstepped the bounds of customary public decorum.[15]

In part, the party leaders' behaviour was traceable to a general reluctance to be drawn too deeply into a dispute that involved the powerful Churches. But considerations focused directly on the expellee lobby were also important, particularly given the timing of the most recent controversies. In the immediate aftermath of the 1965 Bundestag election, with the end of the Second World War more than two decades in the past, it was only logical that many politicians found the moment auspicious for placing some additional distance between themselves and the expellee movement.

The party leaders' general willingness to begin loosening their ties to the expellee groups was by no means uniform, however. Despite their similar initial reactions to the Evangelical and Catholic documents, Bonn's political elites soon began to give evidence of what amounted to the second major development unleashed by the public controversies of late 1965: a growing differentiation of attitudes towards the expellee lobby's favourite Ostpolitik causes. Disagreements predictably flared up within the main parties, with expellee politicians and other traditionalists crossing swords with reform-minded forces eager to explore some of the options recommended by the Evangelical memorandum.[16] But far more significance accrued to the differences that began to emerge *between* the parties in the months following the appearance of the Evangelical and Catholic statements.

The SPD led the way in this process, thanks to its growing willingness to pose public challenges to established Eastern policy doctrines—albeit still in a cautious and often contradictory manner, with each step forward typically followed by a half-step back. This dynamic, apparently propelled in large part by the party's interest in a gradual disengagement from an overly close association with the expellee lobby after the disappointing 1965 Bundestag election, became evident during the spring of 1966. The SPD's party congress in Dortmund in early June illustrated the trend. Key addresses by Willy Brandt and Helmut Schmidt underlined the responsibility of Bonn's political leaders 'to tell the truth, even when it is inconvenient' and 'not to promise more than [they] can deliver', especially in

---

[14] Johann Baptist Gradl's 17 Jan. 1966 *Der Spiegel* interview, in *DzD* iv/12/1, esp. 102; Herbert Wehner, 'Denkschrift der EKD', *Sozialdemokratische Presse-Korrespondenz*, 29 Oct. 1965, AdsD: BT-Fraktion, 5. WP, 904; FDP's Klaus Scholder's comments, 6 Nov. 1965, in Henkys, *Deutschland*, 55.

[15] Wehner, 'Denkschrift' (n. 14); von Hase's 26 Nov. 1965 press conference, *DzD* iv/11/2. 952–3.

[16] Joint session of the SPD's Arbeitskreis I and Bundestagsfraktion, 17 Mar. 1966, AdsD: NL Schmid, 1415; CDU's Wilhelm Simpfendörfer's interview, *Der Spiegel* (15 Dec. 1965); Henkys, *Deutschland*, 51–2.

view of the fact that West Germany did not technically 'possess' even the lands 'between us and the Oder-Neisse line', let alone the territories further east.[17] At the same time, however, the official reunification and Eastern policy resolutions adopted by the party congress studiously avoided clarity on these disputed issues, and conciliatory post-congress communications by key leaders sought to alleviate the expellee lobby's concerns about the party's unorthodox pronouncements.[18] The SPD's incipient movement towards a new, more critical public posture on the revisionist Ostpolitik doctrines associated with the expellee lobby was thus slow and hesitant but none the less clearly perceptible by the mid-1960s.

The other two major parties, locked in an increasingly strained partnership in Ludwig Erhard's cabinet, showed less interest in readjusting their public stances. To be sure, the FDP demonstrated somewhat greater flexibility than its senior coalition partner. The FDP had, after all, traditionally cultivated the image of an engaged champion of an active Eastern policy and, after some initial hesitation, expressions of approval for some of the unorthodox ideas contained in the two church documents began to emanate from its ranks. One prominent party leader, for example, declared in late 1965 that the Evangelical memorandum had done the country a great service by focusing public attention on the German–Polish relationship, a field in which most West German politicians had 'not uttered a single politically responsible word for years', confining themselves instead to 'the stereotypical repetition of hackneyed formulas'.[19] A more official comment to the same effect appeared in June 1966, when the party executive approved a resolution that praised the memorandum for 'directly addressing earlier taboos'.[20] But on these and other occasions, the FDP hedged its approval of new ideas and initiatives with careful expressions of sympathy for old Ostpolitik doctrines, and it consistently stopped short of the suggestive rhetoric of sacrifice that the Social Democrats were beginning to employ.

The FDP's pronouncements nevertheless exhibited greater potential flexibility than those of its senior coalition partner. To be sure, the CDU/CSU's relevant statements were typically just as befuddled and contradictory as those of its two main rivals.[21] But the Christian Democrats differed from the other two main parties in their greater tendency to accentuate the risks of abrupt Eastern policy readjustments and to highlight the presumed advantages of the traditional positions upheld by the expellee lobby. Behind the scenes, top CDU/CSU leaders thus assured expellee activists that the party continued to place a high premium on 'solidarity and unanimity' with the expellee lobby, in both 'expellee politics' and

[17] *DzD* iv/12/2. 807–16, 827–32, esp. 810–11.

[18] Ibid. 846–52; BdV presidium protocols, 14 June 1966, ABdV: Sitzungen des Präsidiums, 1966; 'Entscheidende Veränderung', *DoD* (13 June 1966); Brandt to Jaksch, 8 July 1966, WBA: SPD/Parteivorstand, Verbindungen mit Mitglieder des Präsidiums usw., 5; Herbert Wehner's address to the Upper Silesian Homeland Society, 25–6 June 1966 ALdO: Bundestreffen der LdO, 1951–68, 385–7.   [19] Klaus Scholder, cited in Henkys, *Deutschland*, 55.

[20] 'Denkschrift der Ev. Kirche—Beziehungen zu Polen', 5 June 1966, in *FDP-Bundesvorstand*, iii, 687–8.

[21] Johann Baptist Gradl's interview with *Berlingske Tidende* (16 Dec. 1966), ACDP: I-294/070-2.

matters related to 'the eastern boundaries of our Fatherland'.[22] Leading party figures also repeatedly sang a similar tune in public. While eschewing direct criticism of the church representatives who had authored the documents that stood at the centre of recent controversies, several CDU/CSU luminaries indicated that their sympathies for the old Ostpolitik doctrines championed by the expellee organizations remained strong. In a representative statement in late 1965, for example, Rainer Barzel, the powerful head of the CDU's Bundestag group, reiterated his party's conviction that Germany had to hold on to its legal positions on issues like the Eastern borders and expellee rights, asking rhetorically whether 'anyone' really believed that Germany and the Germans would 'come one step further by violating these rules and norms'.[23]

By the time Ludwig Erhard's coalition teetered into its final months in office in 1966, the Federal Republic's main political parties were thus moving in different directions on Eastern policy in general and the revisionist causes associated with the expellee organizations in particular. In a significant departure from their previous propensity for consensus politics—first in competing for the favour of the expellee lobby and then in cautiously backing away from some of their most extravagant pro-expellee commitments amidst the public debates provoked by the two church statements—the parties began to display increasing signs of public dissension in late 1965 and early 1966. The SPD trod warily into uncharted territory, issuing carefully choreographed challenges to some of the core revisionist claims that had long dominated West German political discourse. The CDU/CSU chose a less adventurous path, clinging to a closer identification with both the expellee lobby and the traditional Ostpolitik line, a stance that was not altogether surprising, given the party's position as the main pillar of government and its generally conservative orientation. Predictably, the FDP, in turn, found itself squeezed in the middle, demonstrating more of a pioneering spirit than its coalition partner but lacking the sporadic flair of the Social Democratic opposition.

These incipient divisions took on heightened importance at the end of 1966, as Erhard's cabinet collapsed and the formation of the Grand Coalition inaugurated a political partnership of the two parties whose recent Ostpolitik stances had diverged the most. The resulting party-political tensions within the government were to assume major significance during the Grand Coalition's tumultuous three-year term in office.

THE OSTPOLITIK OF THE GRAND COALITION AND THE EXPELLEES

The coalition formed by the Christian and Social Democrats in early December 1966 was in many ways an anomalous entity, seemingly riddled by differences and contradictions. Along with the diverging public profiles of the two parties in

---

[22] Dufhues to Riedel, 29 Nov. 1965, ACDP: I-094-048/1.
[23] *DzD* iv/11/2. 964.

recent public debates about the expellee lobby and Eastern policy, several other, more immediately obvious disagreements appeared to handicap the new government. The two parties had long stood at opposite ends of the ideological continuum of mainstream West German politics, and their interaction had often been characterized by a harsh, intolerant rivalry, particularly prior to the SPD's political reorientation at the end of the 1950s. Given the bitterness of many earlier exchanges, substantive political differences between the two parties were thus likely to be exacerbated by personal animosities, which indeed turned out to be the case.

These personal tensions were particularly evident at the top rung of the new government, where the long shadows of the Nazi past further complicated the picture. The strained relationship between Chancellor Kurt-Georg Kiesinger, an ex-Nazi, and Foreign Minister Willy Brandt, a former political exile and resistance fighter, epitomized this problem. But despite all these divisions—or arguably precisely because of them—the Grand Coalition was also seen, at least initially, by key figures in both parties as a major chance to be seized, a temporary arrangement through which a government backed by an overwhelming parliamentary majority could address long-standing problems and implement badly needed reforms. Accordingly, the new coalition set out to reorient West Germany in several key ways, in both domestic and foreign policy.[24]

In the external sphere, the thrust of the government's efforts was directed eastward—towards reunification on the one hand and the closely related field of Eastern policy on the other. Despite all their apparent differences, the CDU/CSU and the SPD agreed relatively quickly on the main objectives to be pursued in these policy areas, albeit in a somewhat superficial fashion that masked lingering disagreements.[25] The key underlining goal of the government's policies remained what it had been under Erhard and Schröder: a peaceful reunification of the two German states. But the chief decision-makers sensed that this goal now seemed more remote and jeopardized than ever. The continuing advance of superpower détente threatened to push the cumbersome issue of German unity entirely off the international agenda, leaving the Federal Republic increasingly isolated and vulnerable.[26] Danger also lurked in the very nature of the status quo: the continued existence of the two German states as integral members of opposing political

---

[24] Reinhard Schmoeckel and Bruno Kaiser, *Die vergessene Regierung: Die grosse Koalition 1966 bis 1969 und ihre langfristigen Wirkungen* (Bonn: Bouvier, 1991); Klaus Hildebrand, *Von Erhard zur Grossen Koalition 1963–1969* (Stuttgart: DVA, 1984), esp. 241–416; Ulrich Wirz, *Karl Theodor von und zu Guttenberg und das Zustandekommen der Grossen Koalition* (Grub am Forst: Menzner, 1997); Klaus Schönhoven, 'Aufbruch in die sozial-liberale Ära: Zur Bedeutung der 60er Jahre in der Geschichte der Bundesrepublik', *Geschichte und Gesellschaft*, 25 (1999): 123–45; Andrea H. Schneider, *Die Kunst des Kompromisses: Helmut Schmidt und die Grosse Koalition* (Faderborn: Schöningh, 1999); Daniela Taschler, *Vor neuen Herausforderungen: Die aussen- und deutschlandpolitische Debatte in der CDU/CSU Bundestagsfraktion während der Grossen Koalition, 1966–1969* (Düsseldorf: Droste, 2001).

[25] Kiesinger's reports in the CDU/CSU's *Bundestagsfraktion*, 28 Nov. 1966, ACDP: VIII-001-1011/1, 392–3; and *Bundesvorstand*, 29 Nov. 1966, ACDP: VII-001-015/8, 5–11.

[26] Kiesinger at the CDU/CSU's *Wirtschaftstag*, 27 Jan. 1967, in Meissner, *Ostpolitik*, 178; Willy Brandt, *Begegnungen und Einsichten* (Hamburg: Hoffmann & Campe, 1976), 189, 220.

and military alliances, with few day-to-day contacts between them, meant that the two populations were likely, as the Chancellor put it, to 'grow further and further apart', thus gradually precluding any meaningful pursuit of unity.[27] The new government therefore perceived a strong need to readjust some of Bonn's established stances.

Closest to home, change was evident in the key leaders' attitudes towards what was euphemistically called 'the other part of Germany'.[28] While still eager to avoid a recognition of the GDR as a fully legitimate state, key leaders of both parties wanted to move away from the efforts at a strict isolation of East Berlin that had characterized Foreign Minister Schröder's policies. Accordingly, top figures agreed that a more flexible approach, featuring increased contacts between the two countries, would be necessary in order to 'preserve the substance of the nation' and to provide possible 'new openings for overcoming the national division', to quote Herbert Wehner's formulation.[29]

On a more general level, the government also wanted to readjust its general stance vis-à-vis the prevailing trends in the international system. In large part in response to pressure from the United States and other Western Allies, the Grand Coalition intended to embrace détente and its manifestations with less ambiguity than had previous cabinets.[30] Because of their increasing willingness to acknowledge that a general relaxation of international tensions constituted a precondition of any future progress towards reunification, Bonn's new leaders stressed the imperative to construct a 'European peace order', a vaguely defined concept evocative of a peaceful process of pan-European integration as a panacea to all the continent's problems.[31] Ostpolitik, in turn, assumed central significance as the primary West German contribution to this broader development. According to Chancellor Kiesinger and his key ministers, Bonn needed to pursue not only improved relations with the East European states but also 'reconciliation' with 'the peoples' of the region, while avoiding steps that might create the impression that its actions were aimed at dividing the Eastern bloc.[32] The end-result of these efforts, the architects of the Grand Coalition's policies hoped, would be a gradual evolution through which the Soviet Union and its East European satellites would come to realize that peaceful change in the region, most notably on the German question, would serve their long-term interests.[33]

The practical steps through which the Grand Coalition hoped to pursue these overall objectives were spelt out in Kiesinger's government declaration of 13

[27] Kiesinger's 5 Dec. 1966 interview, *DzD* v/1/1. 20.

[28] See e.g. Wehner on West German radio, 24 Jan. 1967, *DzD* v/1/1. 366.

[29] Wehner's 10 Dec. 1966 speech, *DzD* v/1/1. 41.

[30] Schertz, *Deutschlandpolitik*; Andreas Wenger, 'Der lange Weg zur Stabilität: Kennedy, Chruschtschow und das gemeinsame Interesse der Supermächte am Status quo in Europa', *VfZ* 46 (1998): 69–99.

[31] See e.g. Willy Brandt, *Friedenspolitik in Europa* (Frankfurt: Fischer, 1968).

[32] Wehner's 10 Dec. 1966 address, *DzD* v/1/1. 38; Kiesinger and Brandt in *Bulletin* (1967), 33, 60.

[33] See e.g. Kiesinger's 5 Mar. 1967 interview, *DzD* v/1/1. 688–9.

December 1966, as well as in a number of subsequent proclamations.[34] On reunification policy, the government's proposals broke significant new ground. To be sure, Bonn still ruled out any formal recognition of 'a second German state' and portrayed itself as 'the only German government' that was 'freely and democratically elected and therefore entitled to speak for the entire German people'. But the Grand Coalition also stressed its desire to help to 'bridge . . . the gulf' within the nation by promoting 'human, economic, and cultural relations' across the inter-German divide, even by means of limited 'contacts between authorities in the Federal Republic and the other part of Germany'.

Looking further east, the government professed a desire to pursue better relations with the Soviet Union, proposing negotiations about non-aggression declarations as an initial step in that direction. It also extended to the other East European states a call for improved 'economic, cultural, and political' ties, including 'diplomatic relations' in so far as 'current circumstances' allowed. As an additional indication of its serious intentions, the government added to its proclamations new elements aimed specifically at Poland and Czechoslovakia, the two Soviet satellite states whose relationship to the Federal Republic remained especially burdened by the recent past. Apparently in large part as a result of pressure from the SPD, it expressed sympathy for Poland's desire to 'live with secure boundaries', particularly in view of the country's 'hardship-laden history', and declared the Munich Agreement 'no longer valid'. But the government qualified these stances, both of which surpassed the standard formulas employed by all previous cabinets, with some very traditional poses. It reiterated that Germany's eastern borders could not be determined until a final peace settlement and that the government remained committed to protecting the interests of all the German expellees, including the Sudeten Germans, whose citizenship claims and other key problems had to be settled before the Munich Agreement could be definitively removed from the international agenda. For all their innovation, the Grand Coalition's policy proposals thus contained many traces of the received wisdom inherited from its predecessors.

The ideas and initiatives outlined in the government's declarations yielded very few concrete results. Attempts to improve day-to-day contacts between the two Germanys failed, as East Berlin ignored such West German proposals and insisted on talks about a normalization of political relations, which Bonn, in turn, rejected. On the ground, this dialogue of the deaf—which culminated in an unprecedented but unproductive exchange of letters between Kurt Georg Kiesinger and his East German counterpart, Willy Stoph, in 1967—produced the exact opposite of what West German policy-makers had intended: a deterioration of inter-German contacts, as the East Germans imposed a number of new restrictions on travel and communications between the two states from 1967 on.[35] The

---

[34] The following quotations are from *DzD* v/1/1. 56–61. See also Taschler, *Herausforderungen*, 73–8. Other key proclamations include the Chancellor's 'Tag der deutschen Einheit' speech, 17 June 1967, *DzD* v/1/2. 1321–4; and the 13 Oct. 1967 government declaration, *DzD* v/1/2. 1802–5.

[35] Bender, *Neue Ostpolitik*, 144–8; Taschler, *Herausforderungen*, 164–89, 189–204, 261–9.

proposed non-aggression agreement with the USSR also proved to be a losing cause. The relevant exchange of notes initiated by the West Germans failed to gain proper momentum and ground to an abrupt halt in July 1968, as the Soviets unilaterally published some of the confidential communications.[36]

In the rest of Eastern Europe, the practical record of the Grand Coalition's policies also remained highly unimpressive. To be sure, the government scored a seemingly striking early victory in January 1967, as it established diplomatic relations with Eastern bloc maverick Romania, thus successfully completing negotiations begun by its predecessor. But the developments of the following months quickly reduced this apparent triumph into a Pyrrhic victory. Pressured not only by the Soviet Union but also by Poland and the GDR, the other Eastern bloc states—except Romania's fellow mavericks Albania and Yugoslavia—reacted to the breakthrough between Bonn and Bucharest by coordinating their stances towards the Federal Republic. After some arm-twisting at two special conferences, they agreed in April 1967 to elevate a group of demands first introduced in a Warsaw Pact declaration of the previous summer into strict preconditions for any normalization of relations with the Federal Republic. Before negotiations about the establishment of diplomatic relations with West Germany could even begin, Bonn was now expected, among other things, to accept the 'inviolability' of Europe's post-war borders, particularly of the Oder-Neisse line; recognize 'the existence of two sovereign and equal German states'; and declare the Munich Agreement invalid *ab initio*.[37] As the promulgation of these demands was accompanied by additional demonstrations of internal cohesion within the Eastern bloc, including the signing of bilateral friendship and cooperation treaties between the GDR and some of its Warsaw Pact allies—most notably Poland and Czechoslovakia—Bonn soon found its Eastern policy efforts stymied.[38]

Despite concerted West German attempts to persuade several Soviet satellite states, particularly Czechoslovakia, Bulgaria, and Hungary, to begin negotiations about the establishment of diplomatic relations on the basis of the Grand Coalition's policy programme, none of these governments proved willing to break ranks with their socialist brethren.[39] As a consequence, Bonn could boast only two tangible Eastern policy achievements after its initial success with Romania: the agreements to set up long overdue trade ties with Czechoslovakia in

---

[36] Griffith, *Ostpolitik*, 141–7; Günter Buchstab, 'Geheimdiplomatie zwischen zwei bequemen Lösungen: Zur Ost- und Deutschlandpolitik Kiesingers', in Karl-Dietrich Bracher *et al.* (eds.), *Staat und Parteien* (Berlin: Duncker & Humblot, 1992), 883–901.

[37] Declaration of the conference of European Communist parties, Karlový Vary, 26 Apr. 1967, *DzD* v/1/1. 1050. Bonn was also expected to renounce access to nuclear weapons and to recognize West Berlin as a separate political entity. Bender, *Neue Ostpolitik*, 139–41; Griffith, *Ostpolitik*, 142–4; Hacker, *Ostblock*, 750–68; Krzoska, 'Gomulka', 198–200; Hans Georg Lehmann, *Öffnung nach Osten: Die Ostreisen Helmut Schmidts und die Entstehung der Ost- und Entspannungspolitik* (Bonn: Neue Gesellschaft, 1984), 140–3.

[38] For the GDR's treaties with Poland, 15 Mar.; Czechoslovakia, 17 Mar.; Hungary, 18 May; and Bulgaria, 7 Sept. 1967, see *DzD* v/1/1. 740–3, 767–70, 1154–6, v/1/2. 1593–6.

[39] On Czechoslovakia, see *AAPD* (1967), 47–50, 60–4, 756–9, 769–70, 898–901, 1020–5, 1112–14, 1127–32, 1142–5, 1149–51, 1152–5. On Hungary and Bulgaria, ibid. 153–70, 356–8, 521–3, 721–2, 921–2.

August 1967 and to re-establish diplomatic relations with the archetypal East European outsider, Yugoslavia, in January 1968.[40] Additional advances never materialized, as even the potentially promising liberalization process that swept Czechoslovakia in 1968 ended in a violent Soviet crackdown before the Federal Republic could reap any concrete benefits.[41]

Only in the spring and summer of 1969 did the situation become somewhat more favourable, with the Soviet Union and its mainstream allies signalling growing interest in serious negotiations with Bonn. A new Warsaw Pact declaration of March 1969, for example, dropped the *ab initio* annulment of the Munich Agreement from the list of demands directed at the Federal Republic and no longer portrayed the other items on that list as absolute preconditions for the pursuit of diplomatic ties between West Germany and Eastern bloc states.[42] However, by this time the Grand Coalition had become too distracted by internal problems, most of them related to the approaching Bundestag election of September 1969, to be able to respond effectively to such overtures. Measured against its original goals, the government's Eastern policy record thus remained highly unsatisfactory.

As in previous years, West Germany's Ostpolitik problems were partly caused by broad international developments that lay beyond the control of Bonn's policy-makers. During most of its time in office, the Grand Coalition faced an unfavourable international constellation in which neither superpower was inclined to invest in supporting West Germany's endeavours in Eastern Europe. The United States was largely preoccupied with the Vietnam War and its implications, whereas the Soviets worried about their ability to control their sphere of influence in Eastern Europe amidst the tensions caused by the Vietnam conflict on the one hand and the escalating Sino-Soviet rivalry on the other. As a result, the Soviets in particular were reluctant to allow potentially risky diplomatic experiments to proceed in their backyard. To be sure, the Soviets adjusted their attitude by 1969, as we have seen, again primarily in response to changes in the international context. Newly confident about their hegemonic position in Eastern Europe after the intervention in Czechoslovakia and alarmed by the growing likelihood of a Sino-American rapprochement, the Soviets grew increasingly willing to pursue compromise solutions on their western flank. Unfortunately for Chancellor Kiesinger and his government, however, the West German electoral cycle had by then reached a stage at which his government proved unable to seize

---

[40] On the Czechoslovak trade agreement, 3 Aug. 1967, see *DzD* v/1/2. 1498–9. On the negotiations, see *AAPD* (1967), 756–9, 769–70, 898–901, 1020–5, 1112–14, 1127–32, 1142–5, 1149–51, 1152–5. On the re-establishment of relations with Yugoslavia, 31 Jan. 1968, consult *DzD* v/2/1. 138–9; Sundhausen, 'Beziehungen'. On the decision-making process, see *AAPD* (1967), 259–61, 282–3, 412–15, 586–8, 700–3, 1448–54, 1594–7, 1670–2.

[41] Hans Peter Schwarz, 'Die Regierung Kiesinger und die Krise in der CSSR 1968', *VfZ* 47 (1999): 159–86.

[42] On this Budapest Declaration, 17 Mar. 1969, see Griffith, *Ostpolitik*, 167–9; Bingen, *Polenpolitik*, 108–11; Arnulf Baring, *Machtwechsel: Die Ära Brandt-Scheel* (Stuttgart: DVA, 1982), 236–44; Krzoska, 'Gomulka', 200–2.

the resulting opportunities, which ultimately accrued to the benefit of its successor, the Social–Liberal cabinet formed under Willy Brandt's leadership in October 1969.[43]

Bad luck and global politics do not suffice to explain the failures of the Grand Coalition's Eastern policy, however. The main cause of Bonn's problems lay in its own past and present actions. Despite their stated determination to avoid repeating the previous government's mistakes, the country's new rulers opened their Ostpolitik with a move that was bound to be perceived by Moscow and its key allies as an unwelcome continuation of the peripheral, divisive strategies associated with ex-Foreign Minister Schröder. As the West German Ambassador to Moscow reported in March 1967, the establishment of diplomatic ties between the Federal Republic and Romania, a country that took pride in its nonconformist bad-boy image, had struck the Soviets as a 'particular perfidy', and confirmed their suspicion that Bonn intended to keep operating 'behind the Soviet Union's back' with the objective of 'sowing divisions within the Warsaw Pact'.[44]

Predictably, the Kremlin and its key allies responded to this perceived challenge by trying to impede the West Germans, most notably by making further progress in the normalization of relations with the Federal Republic dependent on the strict political preconditions promulgated in April 1967. Here again the West Germans ultimately had their past practices to blame. By persistently refusing to address a number of practical Eastern policy and reunification problems in previous years, they had allowed the emergence of several political taboos and thereby provided the Eastern bloc states with the opportunity to forge a powerful tool of preventive diplomacy out of these troublesome issues. Although the most sensitive taboo of all—the fiction that a second German state did not really exist—was at least understandable, given the painful division of the nation, the others made much less sense in the context of the 1960s, not least because they increasingly militated against attempts to overcome that division. The continued wrangling about Germany's eastern borders may have had a strong base in international law and diplomatic precedent, as Bonn's leaders repeatedly emphasized, and legal considerations may also have played some role in controversies surrounding the Munich Agreement of 1938. But, as the previous chapters have shown, Bonn's overly cautious stances on these issues also owed a good deal to less statesmanlike calculations focused on the expellees as a potential source of short-term electoral gain for the governing parties. In many ways, the West Germans were thus paying the long-term price for such tactical practices as the Soviet Union and its key allies switched to a hard-line position on West German Ostpolitik in the spring of 1967.

The new package of preconditions presented by the major Eastern bloc states put Bonn's policy-makers in a difficult but by no means hopeless position. To be sure, the government's room for manœuvre was rather limited. For reasons of

---

[43] For good, concise accounts, see Baring, *Machtwechsel*, 229–36; Griffith, *Ostpolitik*, 141–9, 162–7.
[44] Ambassador von Walther to Brandt, 14 Mar. 1967, *AAPD* (1967), 470.

prestige and political survival, it could hardly afford a full-scale capitulation in the face of Eastern bloc ultimatums. The demand for a formal recognition of the GDR in particular constituted a hurdle which the Grand Coalition as a whole was in no position to clear, despite growing indications of leading SPD members' willingness to consider making that leap.[45] However, as senior Foreign Ministry officials argued behind the scenes, a continuation, even intensification, of Bonn's Eastern policy efforts was essential in the new circumstances, in which flexibility and innovation had potentially become the key diplomatic tools of the hour.[46]

In the months following the promulgation of the Eastern bloc's new preconditions for a normalization of relations with Bonn, the West Germans did, after all, receive repeated signals suggesting that the publicly presented package of demands did not necessarily have to be taken at face value.[47] Astute manœuvring on Bonn's part might therefore have exposed cracks in the unified façade projected by the major Eastern bloc allies and extracted concessions from individual satellite states or, more importantly, from the Soviet Union itself. By contrast, a continuation of the government's traditional practice of repeating old slogans with seemingly scant regard for their contemporary relevance was likely to damage the Federal Republic's interests. This approach could be expected to provide ample ammunition for the Eastern bloc's anti-Bonn propaganda and thus to delay any hope of the kind of gradual, peaceful evolution through which the architects of the Grand Coalition's policies had hoped to make reunification a practical possibility.

Despite these considerable drawbacks, the government's general course of action continued to conform rather closely to the traditional, conservative paradigm. Admittedly, the Grand Coalition was no monolith on Ostpolitik issues. Particularly towards the end of the cabinet's term in office, SPD ministers posed repeated challenges to Bonn's traditional stances, as the following pages will illustrate. But the general tone of the government's Eastern policy was set primarily by Chancellor Kiesinger and his political associates in the CDU/CSU, who continued to project an image of caution, even stagnation. Although affirmations of the Federal Republic's desire to 'proceed step by step towards normal relations with our Eastern neighbours' remained prominent in the government's proclamations, so did qualifiers that in effect precluded practical gains in the pursuit of that objective.[48]

In a typical formulation of October 1967, the Chancellor explained that West Germany had to 'insist on holding its ground' on key points of dispute vis-à-vis the Eastern bloc.[49] This precept found practical application in the government's

---

[45] Wehner's *Washington Post* interview, 31 Jan. 1967, *DzD* v/1/1. 432–5; Kiesinger's rebuff, ibid. 462; Kroegel, *Anfang*, 115–68.

[46] Foreign Ministry memoranda by Bahr, 22 Feb. 1967, and von Ruete, 26 May 1967, *AAPD* (1967), 314–15, 789–93.

[47] Heinz Timmermann, 'Im Vorfeld der neuen Ostpolitik: Der Dialog zwischen italienischen Kommunisten und deutschen Sozialdemokraten 1967/8', *Osteuropa*, 21 (1971): 393–5; Kroegel, *Anfang*, 214–15; Bahr's 20 July 1967 report, *AAPD* (1967), 1113.

[48] Kiesinger's 23 June 1967 lecture, *DzD* v/1/2. 1367.

[49] Kiesinger's comments to French Ambassador Seydoux, 12 Oct. 1967, *AAPD* (1967), 1369.

official stance towards Poland, for example. To be sure, the Grand Coalition repeatedly highlighted the modest innovations introduced in its inaugural government declaration of December 1966—general expressions of sympathy for Poland in general and its desire for secure national boundaries in particular—and added hints about its willingness to discuss all bilateral problems in a conciliatory spirit. But at the same time it stubbornly continued to insist that a binding demarcation of the Polish–German border could be reached only in a future peace treaty.[50]

In addition, the Grand Coalition kept issuing high-profile declarations about a matter whose public perusal could hardly benefit West Germany: the Munich Agreement of 1938. Filled with seemingly abstruse speculations about the point at which the agreement might have lost its validity and about the legal implications of such technicalities, particularly for the Sudeten Germans, the government's statements played into the hands of the Eastern bloc leaders who accentuated this issue and hoped to keep it in the public limelight for propaganda reasons.[51] In many ways, the Grand Coalition thus remained caught in an outdated Ostpolitik rhetoric that was particularly inappropriate as a response to the political roadblock erected by the major Eastern bloc allies in the spring of 1967.

As in earlier years, the government's behaviour was, in part, motivated by traditional *Staatsräson*. On the most general level, Bonn's leaders stressed, particularly in public, their refusal to cave in to Eastern bloc ultimatums and thereby to create an impression of weakness. 'We cannot submit to these demands', Chancellor Kiesinger declared in June 1967, for example.[52] But such pointed public proclamations belied the fact that, in their internal deliberations, many of the government's policy-makers sought ways not only to avert diplomatic loss of face but also to remain engaged in Eastern Europe with a 'long-term policy' that might necessitate West German concessions, even in the absence of immediate political gains.[53] Bonn's reading of the logic of diplomatic give and take thus did not necessarily preclude a greater degree of Ostpolitik innovation, and neither did the two other *Staatsräson*-based factors that had long exerted a restraining influence on West German policy-makers: the Hallstein Doctrine and the territorial claims in the East, as viewed through the legal lenses provided by the Potsdam Agreement.

The Hallstein Doctrine remained relevant, to the degree that the Federal Republic still stood by its claim to be the sole legitimate German state, which, in turn, implied that it would continue its efforts to curb the GDR's international prestige by forcing third countries to choose either Bonn or East Berlin as the only German capital with which normal relations could be maintained. However, by setting up diplomatic ties with Romania and Yugoslavia, two states that had

[50] Government declaration, 13 Oct. 1967, *DzD* v/1/2. 1805; Kiesinger's Bundestag declaration, 27 Mar. 1968, *DzD* v/2/1. 514–15.

[51] Kiesinger's *Spiegel* interview, 20 Mar. 1967; his 23 June 1967 address, *DzD* v/1/2. 1367–8.

[52] *DzD* v/1/2. 1368.

[53] State Secretary Lahr's memorandum, 26 Apr. 1967, *AAPD* (1967), 677.

normalized their relations with the GDR long before doing so with the Federal Republic, Bonn signalled a significant policy switch, which the Foreign Ministry had been planning and preparing for years. In practice, East European states were now to be exempted from the one-Germany-only rule, primarily because their initial recognition of the GDR had presumably occurred under Soviet duress. As a result, the Hallstein Doctrine lost much of its earlier relevance as an immediate obstacle to an active Ostpolitik, and the main focus of Bonn's anti-GDR efforts shifted to ensuring that adjustments in the relations between the Federal Republic and the Eastern bloc countries would not generate a flood of GDR recognition by other states, particularly in the Third World.[54]

Similarly, the policy-makers' faith in the traditional thesis that the territorial claims rooted in the Potsdam Agreement should be preserved as bargaining chips for a future peace settlement continued to erode steadily during the Grand Coalition's reign. Although the border dogmas retained their place in many of the government's public proclamations, behind the scenes Bonn's leaders acknowledged that 'no major German politician' was interested in pressing these claims and that the whole matter would ultimately have to be settled 'with cool realism'.[55] Increasingly, relevant planning memoranda therefore focused on defining the modalities under which West Germany could best move towards a recognition of the existing territorial realities in the East.[56] In view of these developments, classical diplomatic calculations alone could explain neither the Grand Coalition's fumbling and often contradictory general approach to Ostpolitik nor its public preoccupation with such seemingly suicidal causes as the validity of Munich Agreement.

As in previous years, the missing piece in this Eastern policy puzzle was the domestically based negative influence of the expellee lobby, which continued to make itself felt both directly, through unmediated interaction between the government and the expellee movement, and indirectly, through the main political parties. In the former arena, much of the expellee influence was still exerted in a steady, inconspicuous fashion, manifest in behind-the-scenes deliberations in which policy-makers routinely worried about possible expellee reactions to potentially controversial decisions and shied away from steps deemed to be overly risky. Echoing planning memoranda that anticipated 'very vociferous' opposition from 'the expellees' against major readjustments in key Ostpolitik doctrines, the highest guardians of Bonn's foreign policy vented these concerns in the autumn of 1967.[57] While Chancellor Kiesinger underscored the need to avoid provoking 'resentments' among the expellees who, after all, constituted a 'large percentage of the population', Foreign Minister Brandt stressed the relevance of the 'realities of

[54] Gray, *Germany's*; Booz, *Hallsteinzeit*, 97–134.

[55] State Secretary Lahr's comments to Hungarian Foreign Minister Péter, 25 Jan. 1967, *AAPD* (1967), 158 n. 29; 'Vermerk betr. Koalitionsgespräch am 26. März 1968', ACDP: I-226-010.

[56] Foreign Ministry memoranda by Diehl, 10 Mar. 1967, and by State Secretary Lahr, 26 Apr. 1967, *AAPD* (1967), 460–6, 676–8.

[57] Von Ruete's memorandum, 23 Dec. 1966, *AAPD* (1966), 1698.

domestic politics' for the formulation of the country's Ostpolitik.[58] However, although this kind of partial self-censorship shielded the government from open clashes with the expellee lobby most of the time, occasional confrontations in which the expellee organizations managed to impose more specific restraints on the government, at least temporarily, still continued to take place. The most notable such incident occurred in early 1967, immediately following the formation of the new cabinet.

During the preceding years, expellee activists had gradually grown increasingly wary of the government's Eastern policy, and the controversies following the release of the West German Peace Note of March 1966 had magnified their suspicion that many of the country's policy-makers could not be trusted. When the formation of the Grand Coalition inaugurated a new, politically untested partnership in Bonn, the immediate reaction of the expellee elites was mixed: anxiety intermingled with optimism. The president of the BdV, for example, lamented the ongoing 'leadership crisis' that in his view had caused the country's political elites to weaken their advocacy of 'Germany's rights and claims'. But he also expressed hope that the new cabinet would prove to be a 'government of resistance' against a continuation of such trends.[59] In the same spirit, the BdV provided the country's new leaders with a list of the themes and principles that it wanted to see included in the government's Ostpolitik programme. Along with highlighting the expellee lobby's routine demands—such as a rejection of the Oder-Neisse line and an accentuation of the *Heimatrecht* and the self-determination right of the German expellees—this memorandum also enjoined the government to continue to base its policies on the Jaksch Report and to avoid any unilateral concessions regarding the validity of the Munich Agreement.[60]

When the government declaration of 13 December 1966 failed to heed this advice, most flagrantly on the Munich issue but also more generally in its tendency to strike conciliatory notes towards Eastern Europe while muting traditional expellee themes, expellee leaders felt betrayed. Buoyed by an internal consensus that the declaration had been the worst ever delivered by a West German government, the activists proceeded to mobilize a protest campaign.[61] In a series of declarations and interviews, prominent leaders vented their disappointment and demanded 'clarification' from the government on a variety of issues, ranging from the eastern border problem to the *Heimatrecht* and the new accents on the Munich Accord.[62] The activists also pressed their cause through private channels, bombarding the government's top officials with letters underscoring the 'considerable disquiet' that

[58] Kiesinger's comments to French Ambassador Seydoux, 12 Oct. 1967, *AAPD* (1967), 1369; Brandt's speech, 6 Oct. 1967, *DzD* v/1/2. 1768.

[59] Wenzel Jaksch, 'Bundesrepublik braucht Widerstandsregierung', *DoD* (31 Nov. 1966).

[60] BdV, 'Niederschrift über die Sitzung des geschäftsführenden Präsidiums', 7 Dec. 1966, ABdV: Sitzungen des Präsidiums, 1966.

[61] BdV, *Jahresbericht 1966*, ABdV: Jahresberichte, 1960–9, 5; BdV presidium protocols, 17 Jan. 1967, ABdV: Sitzungen des Präsidiums 1967.

[62] Sudetendeutsche Landsmannschaft resolution, 22 Jan. 1967, *DzD* v/1/1. 352; Reinhold Rehs's radio interview, 31 Dec. 1966, ibid. 228–31; 'Was sind lebenswichtige Interessen?', *DoD* (22 Dec. 1966).

allegedly prevailed among the expellees and requesting reaffirmation of the government's loyalty to expellee causes as well as special consultations with the chancellor and his key ministers.[63]

After some initial hesitation, the government moved to accommodate the expellee lobby. In late February 1967, it arranged two highly publicized meetings with leading expellee organizations, including the Sudeten-German Homeland Society, which had voiced particularly strong criticism of the government's recent stances. Represented not only by Chancellor Kiesinger but also by his ministers for Foreign and All-German Affairs—the SPD's Willy Brandt and Herbert Wehner—the government sought to reassure its guests, vowing, among other things, not to act 'behind the backs of the expellees'.[64] The three ministers also pursued a similar agenda in several public and private statements over the ensuing weeks.

However, while Brandt and Wehner addressed expellee-related Ostpolitik problems only in broad and somewhat ambivalent terms, the Chancellor himself waxed considerably more specific.[65] In a letter to a prominent Upper Silesian activist, he categorically rejected the possibility that the loss of the 'eastern territories' could become 'the price that Germany would have to pay for the war that had been launched and lost by Hitler'.[66] He also struck similar chords in several public statements, arguing, among other things, that the Munich Pact had come into being as an indisputably valid international agreement no different from many other treaties 'signed under comparable conditions of coercion or threat of violence'.[67] These rhetorical exploits culminated in late April 1967, as the Chancellor delivered the keynote address at a major expellee rally. Rejecting what he described as the 'naive romanticism' characteristic of the advocates of a unilateral abandonment of Germany's legal claims, Kiesinger reaffirmed his government's commitment to a reconciliation with Eastern Europe, but only on terms that preserved such key national interests as the expellees' rights to their homelands and to self-determination as well as Germany's prerogative to postpone the final determination of its borders until a future peace conference.[68]

The government's pronouncements soon placated most expellee leaders. Activists interpreted their February 1967 meetings with the key ministers to have signified a 'caving in' by the latter, and some of the Chancellor's subsequent proclamations generated outright enthusiasm among the expellees.[69] His strongly

---

[63] H. Gossing to Kiesinger, 5 Jan. 1967, ABdV: Sitzungen des Präsidiums, 1967; Stingl to Kiesinger, 16 Jan. 1967, SDA: NL Becher, 144.

[64] On the 21 Feb. 1967 meetings with the Sudetendeutsche Landsmannschaft and the Kongress der ostdeutschen Landesvertretungen, see 'Vertrauensvolle Zusammenarbeit unverlässlich', *DoD* (1 Mar. 1967).

[65] Brandt's 20 Apr. 1967 interview, *DzD* v/1/1. 985–9; Wehner, 'Deutsche und europäische Entspannung', *Rheinischer Merkur* (21 Apr. 1967).

[66] Kiesinger to Herbert Czaja, 29 Mar. 1967, BA: NL Guttenberg, 53, pp. 112–13.

[67] Kiesinger's 27 Feb. 1967 address, *DzD* v/1/1. 642; his 20 Mar. 1967 *Spiegel* interview, *DzD* v/1/1. 783–7.

[68] Kiesinger at the Kongress der ostdeutschen Landesvertretungen, 29 Apr. 1967, *DzD* v/1/1. 1074–7.

[69] BdV's Bundesvertretung protocols, 11 Mar. 1967, SDA: BIX/33.

worded April address, in particular, impressed many, including a prominent Silesian activist in whose opinion 'no previous chancellor' had ever addressed the relevant issues with equal 'clarity'.[70]

But this modest victory on the domestic front also entailed high costs for the government, particularly in the international realm. Because the episode occurred at the very beginning of the Grand Coalition's term in office, it set a fateful precedent in the interaction between the cabinet and its critics and contributed to a general image of vacillation and excessive risk-avoidance that soon began to plague the government, especially in foreign policy. To make matters worse, the Grand Coalition's rhetorical contortions followed on the heels of its first diplomatic moves towards Eastern Europe, and the bad publicity engendered by some of the fresh oratory facilitated the formation of a united front towards the Federal Republic by most of the Eastern bloc states later in the spring of 1967. In addition, the relatively rigid positions espoused by the Chancellor and his ministers narrowed the government's short-term policy options and thus made an effective response to the challenge posed by the Eastern bloc ultimatums all the more difficult.

Ironically, even the expellee lobby's newly found contentment with Kiesinger and his cabinet failed to last. Having taken stock of the broader political situation, several of the government's key figures, including the Chancellor himself, began by the summer of 1967 to inch away from some of the positions which they had publicly endorsed a few months earlier. As the cabinet's top echelons cautiously wiggled themselves back towards a slightly more critical reading of the Munich Agreement, for instance, expellee activists watched with a jaundiced eye.[71] Sensing a growing divergence between their own underlying goals and those of the government, they condemned a number of ongoing trends, particularly in their internal deliberations.

At the most fundamental level, the expellee leaders worried about a general diminution of the government's support for their interests, as the Jaksch Report, for example, increasingly faded as a point of reference and ministers spoke 'with a forked tongue', repeatedly promising one thing to the expellees and something very different to everyone else.[72] Complaints also continued to ring out about a long-standing source of expellee discontent: the exclusion of their representatives from active policy-making roles, which became more apparent than ever once the Sudeten German luminary Hans-Christoph Seebohm, a steady presence in every previous cabinet, had been denied a post in the Grand Coalition.[73]

Some specific Ostpolitik steps also provoked grumbling among the expellee leaders. Although willing to endorse the normalization of relations with Romania and the establishment of trade ties with Czechoslovakia—albeit with some dissent, particularly in the latter case—the activists criticized Bonn's decision to

[70] Erich Schellhaus in the Schlesische Landesversammlung, 29 Apr. 1967, BA: B 234, 600, p. 27.
[71] Brandt's 10 June 1967 speech, *DzD* v/1/2. 1268; Kiesinger's 23 June 1967 speech, ibid. 1367–8.
[72] Schellhaus in the Schlesische Landesversammlung, 25–6 Nov. 1967, BA: B 234, 601, p. 17.
[73] 'Den neuen Männern zunächst vertrauen', *DoD* (8 Dec. 1966).

re-establish diplomatic links to Yugoslavia as a step likely to be interpreted as a 'triumph . . . for the Communists'.[74] Because of a steady accumulation of such complaints, the expellee lobby grew increasingly disillusioned with the government, and by the time the Grand Coalition entered its last months in office, radical leaders had begun advocating 'shock therapy' tactics vis-à-vis the cabinet.[75] However, despite the increase in this emphasis in their internal deliberations, in public the expellee organizations avoided polemical attacks against the government and couched their criticism in relatively moderate terms, primarily because key leaders understood that their only chance of influencing the Federal Republic's policies was through cooperation with Bonn, not isolation from it.

The expellee elites also had another reason to avoid blanket condemnation of the government: as close observers of the Bonn scene they were well aware that the Grand Coalition was anything but a political monolith, particularly in Eastern policy. The two governing parties had, after all, entered their joint venture with significant underlying differences on Ostpolitik, and although they had managed to create an initial impression of extensive unity, the disagreements soon re-emerged, especially on expellee-related policy issues. The two parties' top representatives began to strike slightly different notes during the cabinet's charm offensive vis-à-vis the expellee lobby in the early spring of 1967, and in the ensuing months this rhetorical divergence grew steadily more pronounced.

In August 1967, for example, Foreign Minister Brandt declared during a state visit to Romania that attempts to build the vaunted 'European peace order' had to 'proceed on the basis of the existing realities', a position which Chancellor Kiesinger promptly contradicted.[76] Nevertheless, the Foreign Minister continued to promote the same basic argument on other occasions, whereas several of his Christian Democratic cabinet colleagues, most notably Expellee Minister Kai Uwe von Hassel, repeatedly stressed Bonn's obligation to defend its legitimate claims and to 'rescue as much of Germany as possible'.[77] Although both parties publicly sought to belittle the gravity of such differences, tensions kept growing until they exploded into something resembling an open rupture in the spring of 1969. In the shadow of the approaching Bundestag election, the two parties clashed bitterly over specific policy issues—such as the proper application of the Hallstein Doctrine in reaction to Cambodia's recognition of the GDR in early May—and more personal matters, including a perception in each political camp that its leaders and stances were being subjected to unfair, defamatory attacks by the other

---

[74] BdV's presidium protocols, 27 Feb. 1967, ABdV: Sitzungen des Präsidiums, 1967; Reinhold Rehs's statement to Omnipress, 10 Aug. 1967, BA: B 234, 187; Intern-Information der Sudetendeutschen Landsmannschaft, 18 Aug. 1967, SDA: SD Rat, 11; 'Diplomatische Beziehungen zu Jugoslawien noch im Januar?', *DoD* (15 Jan. 1968).

[75] BdV, 'Niederschrift über die Klausurtagung', 30 Nov.–1 Dec. 1968, SDA: NL Becher, 194.

[76] Brandt's 4 Aug. 1967 comments, *DzD* v/1/2. 1507; Kiesinger's press conference, 21 Aug. 1967, ibid. 1545; Kiesinger to Brandt, 22 Aug. 1967, WBA: Aussenminister 1966–9, 13.

[77] See e.g. Brandt's 18 Aug. 1967 speech, *DzD* v/1/2. 1538; von Hassel's *Der Spiegel* interview, 1 Apr. 1968.

side.[78] As a consequence, the Grand Coalition became paralysed several months before its final, election-induced demise, with no chance of effective action on either the reunification or Eastern policy fronts.

The inter-party divisions that ultimately incapacitated the Grand Coalition by the spring of 1969 were obviously complex phenomena with multiple causes. Genuine philosophical and political differences between—and also within—the CDU/CSU and the SPD contributed to these conflicts, as did convoluted personal rivalries and animosities among the top politicians. Ongoing clashes between the Gaullist and Atlanticist factions within the CDU/CSU, for example, contributed to the problems.[79] But the tensions within the cabinet were also in good part caused by an often overlooked process: continued party-political manœuvring focused on the expellees in general and the chief Ostpolitik causes promoted by their purported organizational representatives in particular.

The differences in the main parties' stances on the relevant issues, first evident in the final year of the previous cabinet, increased steadily during the Grand Coalition's term in office, engendering a complicated domestic dynamic of action and reaction among the largest parties and the expellee organizations. As the resulting tensions were then reflected back on the government, most obviously through the growing discord between the coalition partners, the expellee lobby's ability to make an indirect impact on the Federal Republic's Eastern policy remained considerable. The country's domestic politics and foreign policies thus continued to be closely intertwined, with the party system functioning as a crucial transmission belt in the process.

DOMESTIC POLITICS AND THE EXPELLEE QUESTION

While the Grand Coalition's Eastern policy stalled, the West German public discussion about the proper role of the expellees in that policy continued unabated. Sharp criticism still rang out in the print and electronic media, including many television and radio broadcasts as well as commentaries in leading left-liberal periodicals and newspapers, such as *Der Spiegel, Stern,* and *Die Zeit*.[80] But, as in previous years, contributions from beyond the formal media establishment continued to make the strongest impact. One document, in particular, received very extensive attention during this period: the so-called Bensberg Memorandum of March 1968. Written by a group of prominent Catholic intellectuals without formal authorization from the Church, the

---

[78] Kroegel, *Anfang*, 310–30; Booz, *Hallsteinzeit*, 128–31; 'Vermerk betr. Koalitionsgespräch 2.6.1969–3.6.1969', ACDP: I-226-010; Brandt to Kiesinger, 27 June 1969, ACDP: I-226-A001.

[79] On CDU/CSU divisions and their background, see Taschler, *Herausforderungen*; Marcowitz, *Option*; Granieri, *Ambivalent*.

[80] Reimund Klinkhammer's radio commentary 'Stimmungsmache am falschen Platz', 2 Sept. 1968, ABdV: Sitzungen des Präsidiums 1968; 'TV-Vertriebenenjagd', *Der Spiegel* (23 Dec. 1968); 'Zensoren der Ostpolitik', *Die Zeit* (5 Apr. 1968); *Stern* commentary, 10 Mar. 1968, in *DzD* v/2/1. 348–57.

memorandum focused on the Polish–German relationship, promoting in a more pointed form several key arguments highlighted in its Evangelical counterpart of October 1965. Stressing their Christian duty to exercise 'political responsibility', the authors exhorted the Federal Republic's leaders to explain certain inconvenient facts in 'unambiguous' terms, not only to the domestic audience but also to the Poles.[81] The most prominent item on the list was the impossibility of changing Germany's eastern boundaries. According to the memorandum, the Germans would have to atone for the world war which their 'political leadership had launched and lost' in several ways, including by accepting the fact that the former Reich territories east of the Oder-Neisse line had become definitively 'integrated into Poland' and that Germany could 'no longer demand . . . their return'. The expellees, in turn, were to cease regarding this necessary step as an 'abandonment' of something presumed to be rightfully theirs and learn to view it as an important 'contribution' to the building of 'an international peace order'.[82]

By the late 1960s, such calls for new departures in Ostpolitik seemed increasingly consistent with the broader ethos of West German society, which was also dominated by intensifying change. In social and economic terms, the feverish reconstruction of the 1950s had given way to a more tranquil existence for much of the citizenry, which could enjoy the benefits of an established welfare society and channel a growing share of its energies to free-time pursuits. At the same time, a new post-war generation that had played no immediate part in the Third Reich began to rise to the fore. These broad socio-economic and generational changes were, in turn, reflected in several other, more immediately visible phenomena that swept the country during the 1960s. Inspired by a number of high-profile trials of Nazi war criminals within and beyond the Federal Republic's borders, many West Germans—particularly those of the young generation—began to ask new, probing questions about their nation's past in general and the Nazi period in particular.[83] These critical discussions spilt over into the various overlapping protest movements of students, peace activists, and others which reached their culmination in the so-called Extra-Parliamentary Opposition, a large and loosely organized agglomeration of radical activists determined to curb on the streets what they regarded as the Grand Coalition's excessive preponderance within the halls of parliament.[84] As demonstrations and other forms of unrest swept the land, particularly in 1967 and 1968, few could fail to sense that new winds were blowing and that many old beliefs and doctrines could no longer

---

[81] *DzD* v/2/1. 302–14, esp. 304, 309. [82] Ibid. 308, 310, 311.

[83] On the context, see Axel Schildt, Detlef Siegfried, and Karl Christian Lammers (eds.), *Dynamische Zeiten: Die 6oer Jahre in den beiden deutschen Gesellschaften* (Hamburg: Christians, 2000).

[84] Ingo Juchler, *Die Studentenbewegungen in den Vereinigten Staaten und der Bundesrepublik Deutschland der sechziger Jahre* (Berlin: Duncker & Humblot, 1996); Karl A. Otto, *Vom Ostermarsch zur APO: Geschichte der ausserparlamentarischen Opposition in der Bundesrepublik, 1960–70* (Frankfurt.: Campus, 1982); Maren Krohn, *Die gesellschaftlichen Auseinandersetzungen um die Notstandsgesetze* (Cologne: Pahl-Rugenstein, 1981); Gerd Koenen, *Das rote Jahrzehnt: Unsere kleine deutsche Kulturrevolution 1967–1977* (Cologne: Kiepenheuer & Witsch, 2001).

marshal the nearly unquestioning allegiance that they had enjoyed during most of the previous decade.[85]

These ongoing attitudinal shifts were clearly evident on key matters of reunification and Eastern policy. To be sure, public opinion polls indicated that the population's desire for reunification remained high and that only a small minority was willing to accept East Germany as a normal, legitimate state.[86] As late as September 1968, for example, a mere 27 per cent of West Germans wanted their government to recognize the GDR as a fully sovereign, foreign country.[87] But the polls also revealed a growing level of scepticism and resignation regarding the practical chances of reunification in the foreseeable future, as evidenced by the fact that at the end of the Grand Coalition's term in office, 62 per cent of West Germans no longer believed that they would live to see the arrival of unity.[88] Widespread popular resignation to the status quo was even more evident on Ostpolitik issues, particularly on the revisionist doctrines associated with the expellee lobby. The percentage of West Germans who viewed the former Reich provinces east of the Oder-Neisse line as irretrievably lost rose steadily throughout the 1960s, hitting 60 per cent by late 1967 and nearly 70 per cent two years later.[89]

This trend correlated closely with growing popular support for an increasingly active and flexible Eastern policy. In September 1967, for example, 59 per cent of the population maintained that Bonn should pursue improved relations with the East European states in a 'patient and accommodating' spirit, even if the other side continued to 'cause difficulties' with preconditions and other tough demands.[90] But the most revealing indicator of change could arguably be found in the shifting attitudes of average expellees. Whereas most expellees had claimed throughout the first two post-war decades to be at least potentially willing to return to their former homelands, the balance shifted decisively during the latter half of the 1960s. By late 1967, the majority rejected such a prospect, and during the ensuing years the proportion of those uninterested in reclaiming their former homelands continued to grow steadily, reaching approximately 60 per cent by the time the Grand Coalition left office and climbing further under its Social–Liberal successor.[91]

---

[85] Ingrid Gilcher-Holtey (ed.), *1968: Vom Ereignis zum Gegenstand der Geschichtswissenschaft* (Göttingen: Vandenhoeck & Ruprecht, 1998); Wolfgang Kraushaar, *1968 als Mythos, Chiffre und Zäsur* (Hamburg: Hamburger Edition, 2000); Wolfrum, *Geschichtspolitik*, 211–95.

[86] Elisabeth Noelle and Erich Peter Neumann (eds.), *The Germans: Public Opinion Polls 1947–1966* (Allensbach: Verlag für Demoskopie, 1967), 215.

[87] Elisabeth Noelle and Erich Peter Neumann (eds.), *Jahrbuch der öffentlichen Meinung 1968–1973* (Allensbach: Verlag für Demoskopie, 1974), 510.

[88] Ibid. 506; *Emnid-Informationen* (31 Jan. 1967), 4; Glaab, *Deutschlandpolitik*, 245–51; Jansen, *Meinungsbilder*, 93–105.

[89] Gebhard Schweigler, *Nationalbewusstsein in der BRD und der DDR* (Düsseldorf: Bertelsmann, 1973), 116; Glaab, *Deutschlandpolitik*, 235–45; Jansen, *Meinungsbilder*, 148–55.

[90] Noelle and Neumann, *Jahrbuch, 1968–1973*, 567.

[91] Schweigler, *Nationalbewusstsein*, 115; Noelle and Neumann, *Germans*, 483; Grosser, 'Integration', 84–5; Jansen, *Meinugsbilder*, 152.

This growing unwillingness to contemplate a return to the old *Heimat* reflected broader ongoing trends among average expellees in at least two ways. First and foremost, it highlighted their increasingly successful integration into West German society by the mid to late 1960s. The reluctance of most expellees to consider leaving their current environment implied increasing contentment with the status quo, a development confirmed by other evidence, including indications of economic advances among the expellees and of rising rates of intermarriage between them and longer term residents of western Germany.[92] However, social change did not treat all expelled Germans with equal kindness. By the 1960s generational dividing lines had become particularly noticeable, although other factors, such as social class and education, obviously complicated the picture. The 'old generation', which had grown up in the old *Heimat* and experienced the full horrors of the expulsions, typically found successful readjustment to the Federal Republic much more difficult than the 'middle generation', whose members could remember the expulsions and the preceding years only from the perspective of a child, if at all. The young 'post-war generation', which lacked any first-hand exposure to these past traumas and had known only the Federal Republic as its home, was predictably in the best position to take full advantage of the many opportunities available in that environment.[93]

These generational differences, in turn, helped to shape the second significant trend under way among the expellees during the latter half of the 1960s: a steady attenuation of the expellee lobby's support base. Although expellee activists still portrayed their organizations as important political movements attuned to the interests of the vast majority of the people they claimed to represent, the reality belied these claims. The degree to which average expellees identified with the firebrand rhetoric of their purported spokesmen had always been questionable, and during the 1960s the growing gulf between the elite and the base grew increasingly obvious. Surveys and other observations suggest that, by the mid-1960s, a majority of the rank-and-file members regarded the expellee organizations' political activities as secondary to other, social and cultural objectives, such as the maintenance of personal friendship networks.[94]

As a result, a growing minority of ordinary expellees began to issue open challenges to the popular legitimacy of their self-proclaimed representatives, publicly accusing the activists of 'fanaticism' and 'dangerous illusions'.[95] Many others backed away from the expellee lobby with less fanfare, as affirmed by falling membership rates and other statistical indicators. By 1962, internal BdV records indicated that the total membership of the expellee organizations had slipped to

---

[92] Grosser, 'Integration', esp. 73–5; Reichling, *Vertriebene*, ii. 44–9, 72–87.

[93] For good insights, see Lutz Niethammer, 'Traditionen und Perspektiven der Nationalstaatlichkeit für die BRD', in *Aussenpolitische Perspektiven des westdeutschen Staates*, ii. *Das Vordringen neuer Kräfte* (Munich: Oldenbourg, 1972), 76–81.

[94] Zur Mühlen *et al.*, 'Vertriebenenverbände', 132; 'Fast nur eine Familienfeier', *Stuttgarter Nachrichten* (16 May 1967); Imhof, *Vertriebenenverbände*, 342–57.

[95] 'Sprechen nicht für uns', *Die Zeit* (29 May 1964).

1.25 million at most—a far cry from the officially proclaimed figure of two million, and a steady decline continued in subsequent years as well. By mid-decade, the official newspaper of the Silesian Homeland Society, for example, attracted only 25,800 subscriptions from among the more than 1.5 million people that the group claimed to represent.[96]

Even more ominously, the declining organizational engagement of ordinary expellees was accompanied by a troubling corollary: the disproportionate tendency of younger age cohorts to cut their ties to the expellee lobby altogether. A survey of various local branches of the Sudeten-German Homeland Society conducted in the mid-1960s, for example, showed that only 1 per cent of the members were under 25 years of age, while a similar local-level analysis of the Silesian Homeland Society, done a few years earlier, revealed a total absence of anyone under 30.[97] The expellee organizations were thus shrivelling into narrow and increasingly unrepresentative groups of professional functionaries and ageing followers, with many of the latter poorly integrated and economically disadvantaged in West German society.

The leaders of the expellee lobby observed the ongoing changes around them with profound suspicion. They realized that their membership figures were falling; that the youth was increasingly turning its back on the entire movement; and that the 'middle generation', too, had to be somehow 'pulled' back into the fold.[98] In their deliberations, top activists also lamented the sagging enthusiasm of average expellees who seemed to live by the selfish motto 'the evenings belong to me; I will not attend any political events then'.[99] But the leadership cadres failed to agree on practical steps to address such problems. Despite internal calls for the activists to 'represent our cause in the language of today', the organizations stuck to very traditional vocabulary in their public statements.[100] Instead of engaging in self-criticism or proposing bold new initiatives, they directed their rhetorical fire at perceived external enemies, much as they had in previous years.

The various protest movements quickly became a favourite target for these verbal salvoes. According to the expellee elites, such movements were led by 'well-trained professional agitators of the radical left' who aimed at the ultimate overthrow of the Federal Republic's democratic system.[101] But the trouble did not stop with these hard-core leadership cadres. In the activists' view, most of the rank-and-file protesters and much of the younger generation in general had been infected with a similar bacillus. In the words of a senior Silesian figure, the Federal Republic of the late 1960s suffered from a disease called 'the clash of generations',

---

[96] BdV, 'Vermerk, Betr.: Mitgliederzahlen der Landsmannschaften', 18 July 1962, BA: B 234/361; Kempe in the Schlesische Landesversammlung, 9 Oct. 1965, BA: B 234/596.

[97] Sudetendeutsche Landsmannschaft, 'Altersgliederung der Mitglieder—Stand 31.12.1965', SDA: NL Becher, 227; Zur Mühlen *et al.*, 'Vertriebenenverbände', 131.

[98] Max and Segner in the BdV's Klausurtagung, 30 Nov.–1 Dec. 1968, SDA: NL Becher, 194, pp. 10, 4; BdV's Bundesvertretung protocols, 11 Mar. 1967, SDA: BIX/33, 3.

[99] Hupka in the Schlesische Landesversammlung, 29 Apr. 1967, BA: B 234/600, p. 48.

[100] Hupka in the Schlesische Landeseversammlung, 30 Aug. 1969, BA: B 234/603, p. 11.

[101] 'Die Studenten, die Schüler—und?', *DoD* (24 June 1967).

whose most frightful symptom bore a reverse correlation to the age of its victims: 'the younger the people, the greater their readiness to agree to a complete sell-out of German interests'.[102]

This catastrophic situation, in turn, had its roots in the long-term tendency of media elites, publicists, and, most recently, church-affiliated intellectuals to subject the expellees and their organizational representatives to a steady barrage of unfair and mean-spirited criticism. Portraying themselves as 'the centre of resistance' against the evil influences radiating outward from the mass media, expellee leaders firmly condemned the Bensberg Memorandum, for example, and repeatedly lamented what they perceived as 'constant provocations on radio and television'.[103] Some even claimed to detect in recent West German debates a tendency towards a 'second expulsion', a conscious drive to exclude the 'victims of expulsions from the dialogue with the East European peoples'.[104]

Bonn's party elites tracked these controversies as well as the underlying shifts in popular opinions and attitudes with observant eyes. But they chose their official positions carefully, eschewing both an open defence of the expellee lobby against its media critics and a vanguard stance as challengers of the status quo. In general, the party leaders thus continued to behave in a manner that had characterized their Eastern policy stances throughout the Federal Republic's existence, particularly on the revisionist causes associated with the expellee movement. The pattern was one of reacting to pressures from below rather than leading with a consistent larger vision and following public opinion instead of taking major risks to reshape it.

To be sure, each of the main parties could boast some pioneering past contributions on sensitive Eastern policy issues. As previous chapters have shown, individual politicians—such as Carlo Schmid and Fritz Erler in the SPD, Wolfgang Schollwer in the FDP, and Kurt Sieveking in the CDU—had occasionally questioned the prevailing doctrines. More importantly, unorthodox Ostpolitik ideas had also found more institutional bases, particularly in the SPD and the FDP, in which special youth organs and certain regional suborganizations had promoted new departures since the early 1960s.[105]

The most important institutional base of Eastern policy innovation had been the SPD's West Berlin wing. Under the leadership of Willy Brandt and his nimble-minded key adviser, Egon Bahr, a small circle of top leaders had subjected the received political wisdom to a critical re-examination since the 1950s, and particularly since the erection of the Berlin Wall. Based on the assumption that only reduced tensions and improved contacts between East and West—including the

---

[102] Herbert Hupka in the BdV presidium, 21 Apr. 1969, SDA: NL Becher, 193.

[103] Walter Brand in the BdV Presidium, 10 Feb. 1969, SDA: NL Becher, 193; Reinhold Rehs in the BdV Bundesversammlung, 31 Mar. 1968, SDA: NL Becher, 194.

[104] Wenzel Jaksch, 'Sein Vermächtnis: Patriotische Mitte', *Volksbote* (3 Dec. 1966).

[105] Mathias Siekmeier, *Restauration oder Reform: Die FDP in den sechziger Jahren: Deutschland- und Ostpolitik zwischen Wiedervereinigung und Entspannung* (Cologne: Janus, 1998); Brauers, *Deutschlandpolitik*, 162–71; Ludwig Elsing, 'Polenpolitik der SPD 1960 bis 1970', in Plum, *Ungewöhnliche Normalisierung*, esp. 57–9.

two German states—could sustain the possibility of reunification, Brandt and his associates had produced a general policy concept that envisaged a progression of concrete moves toward a normalization of relations with the Eastern bloc states— without side-stepping the GDR or otherwise openly challenging the existing political realities in the region.[106]

Substantively, this concept thus left just as little room for the types of revisionist doctrines espoused by the expellee lobby as did the critical public commentaries of key journalists and other publicists. But the ruminations of Berlin's SPD leaders and other party-based champions of Ostpolitik readjustments had nevertheless made only secondary contributions to broader public debates in the pre-Grand Coalition years. Individual dissenters had typically been silenced by their own superiors before they managed to provoke too many headlines, and most of the SPD and FDP suborgans interested in expanding the country's Ostpolitik options had been simply too marginal to make a lasting impact. The Berlin group of the SPD, in turn, had chosen to toe a cautious public line, despite its inherent weight and innovative ideas. Admittedly, some of its key figures had occasionally made provocative public statements, as exemplified by Egon Bahr's famous, iconoclastic call for a more engaged policy towards the GDR, issued in Tutzing in July 1963.[107] But such moves had remained the exception to the rule of public reticence, primarily because Brandt and his associates had repeatedly stressed the need for restraint on sensitive Eastern policy problems, in large part to avoid creating the impression that the party 'is not sufficiently concerned about the expellees' and their interests.[108]

During the Grand Coalition, the leaders of the main parties continued to shape their Eastern policy stances in accordance with the same basic principles as before. Paradoxically, however, this continuity in approach now began to produce increasing differences in outcome. All the main parties kept up their past practice of closely tracking public opinion and defining their policy options largely in response to it. Each party also continued to face steady resistance from the expellee lobby to any substantive changes in its Eastern policy stances, resistance that was channelled both externally, through interventions by the expellee organizations, and internally, through pressure exerted by expellee politicians active within each party. But in a significant departure from earlier times, the general situation grew increasingly fluid and ambiguous in the late 1960s, with public opinion and organized expellee pressure pulling in opposite directions. Accordingly, the party elites had to make difficult decisions about how to read

---

[106] Schmidt, *Kalter Krieg*; Prowe, 'Anfänge'; id., 'Making'; Abraham Ashkenasi, *Reformpartei und Aussenpolitik: Die Aussenpolitik der SPD Berlin–Bonn* (Cologne: Westdeutscher Verlag, 1968); Siebenmorgen, *Gezeitenwechsel*, 351–71, 381–4; Jeffrey Herf, *War by Other Means: Soviet Power, German Resistance and the Battle of the Euromissiles* (New York: Free Press, 1991), 27–44; Peter Bender, 'Wandel durch Annäherung: Karriere eines Begriffs', *Deutschland-Archiv*, 33 (2000): 971–8.

[107] Vogtmeier, *Bahr*, 59–66; Stephan Fuchs, *'Dreiecksverhältnisse sind immer komplizert': Kissinger, Bahr und die Ostpolitik* (Hamburg: Eva, 1999).

[108] Brandt in the SPD's Bundestagsfraktion, 8 Dec. 1964, *SPD-Fraktion*, iii/2. 538; Albertz to Brandt, 1 Aug. 1963, WBA: Berlin 1947–66, 38.

these conflicting demands and where to place their priorities. As they did so in increasingly disparate ways, the result was a sharpening of the inter-party divisions on the expellee-related Eastern policy doctrines that had begun to manifest themselves in the months preceding the formation of the Grand Coalition and were ultimately to culminate in a pronounced party-political polarization by the 1969 Bundestag election.

As the only opposition party, the FDP had a logical incentive to build a political profile distinct from that of the governing coalition, an endeavour for which Ostpolitik, particularly in connection with reunification policy, provided ample openings. However, the party underwent a prolonged internal struggle on how best to proceed in this area, fought by two opposing factions, each of which was deeply concerned about public opinion and the likely electoral repercussions of any policy readjustments. On one side stood a conservative group that in the course of the 1960s became increasingly identified with Erich Mende, the party chairman from early 1960 to January 1968. According to Mende and his associates, several of whom faced particularly strong pressure from the organized expellee movement, the risks of major policy readjustments outweighed the potential gains because the population in general and most of the party's supporters in particular were not ready for such moves.[109]

The party chairman explained his reasoning in autumn 1967, claiming to detect a 'great difference' between West German 'public opinion' on the one hand and 'a large part of so-called published opinion' on the other.[110] Choosing to read contemporary opinion polls in a way that accentuated the hesitation of much of the public in the face of new Ostpolitik ideas and assigning relatively strong weight to the protests and complaints of the expellee lobby, Mende and his associates advocated a cautious—and profoundly contradictory—Eastern policy stance. While pressing the government to 'establish diplomatic relations with all East and South-East European states' as soon as possible, they also insisted that Bonn must not abandon its claims to the territories east of the Oder-Neisse line or otherwise compromise its legal position. This combination could only be described as completely unrealistic, particularly after the main Eastern bloc states had confronted Bonn with their joint set of preconditions for a normalization of relations in the spring of 1967.[111]

The other FDP faction proceeded from a very different reading of contemporary realities in West German society. Members of this group—best labelled the reformers—believed that the country had undergone a thorough sea change by the late 1960s and that the party should readjust its Eastern policy stances accordingly. One adherent of this general viewpoint, for example, claimed in early 1969, with specific reference to recent opinion polls, that 'no one' in the country 'honestly believes that we could still someday reclaim the [areas east of the] Oder-Neisse'.

[109] Siekmeier, *Restauration, passim.*
[110] Mende in the Bundestag, 13 Oct. 1967, *DzD* v/1/2. 1826.
[111] Mende in the Bundestag, 16 Dec. 1966, *DzD* v/1/1. 156.

Another argued a year earlier that the unrest among West German 'youth' should be viewed as an opportunity for the FDP to show more 'imagination' in 'defining and presenting its policies for tomorrow and the day after'.[112]

The strongest calls for change came from a small but vocal cohort of devoted left-liberals intent on turning their party into a 'crystallization point for all "radical-democratic", liberal forces' and thus presenting a 'true political alternative' to the existing government.[113] The Eastern and reunification policy programme of these radical reformers was presented most cogently in two documents published in the periodical *Stern* in March 1967: a memorandum by policy planner Wolfgang Schollwer, originally meant for internal FDP use only, and a subsequent short article by party treasurer Hans Wolfgang Rubin, written explicitly to defend his colleague's unorthodox ideas. In blunt language, both men exhorted their party—and the federal government—to abandon all revisionist Ostpolitik claims, pursue a full normalization of relations with Eastern Europe, and seek a realistic modus vivendi with the GDR, jettisoning such wasting assets as the Hallstein Doctrine and other measures aimed at perpetuating East Berlin's international isolation.[114] These bold proposals found strong resonance among various other prominent figures on the party's left wing, including such celebrities as Ralf Dahrendorf, the pre-eminent young sociologist, and Rudolf Augstein, the founder and chief editor of *Der Spiegel*.[115]

Following a prolonged internal struggle, the reformist wing prevailed. Particularly after the moderate reformer Walter Scheel had replaced Erich Mende as party chairman in January 1968, the FDP's change of course became increasingly evident. Signals of movement on key Ostpolitik issues had already begun to emerge in the previous year, when—at a party congress marked by bitter disputes between reformers and conservatives—the FDP had included in its new Action Programme a compromise plank stating that 'a possible reunification . . . must not founder on territorial problems'.[116] Similar signals intensified from early 1968 on, as Scheel and the rest of the party's top leadership gradually embraced several of the radical faction's favourite causes. In the hope of broadening the party's appeal among progressive members of the younger generation and others who 'actively participate in ongoing political debates', Scheel and his associates proclaimed their desire to 'clean up' the 'ritualistic language' routinely employed by West German politicians bent on 'skirting the truth on particularly delicate issues'.[117]

---

[112] Schweinfurth in the FDP's Bundesvorstand, 10 Mar. 1969, ADL: BV-Protokolle, 132, p. 142; Scheel's 24 Mar. 1968 address, *DzD* v/2/1. 503.

[113] Wolfgang Schollwer, 'Deutschland- und Aussenpolitik', 23 Dec. 1966, *DzD* v/1/1. 193–210, esp. 199.

[114] Ibid. Rubin, 'Die Stunde der Wahrheit', *DzD* v/1/1. 660–3.

[115] Siekmeier, *Restauration*; Daniel Koerfer, *Die FDP in der Identitätskrise: Die Jahre 1966–1969 im Spiegel der Zeitschrift 'liberal'* (Stuttgart: Klett-Cotta, 1981); Brauers, *Deutschlandpolitik*, 162–71; Schmidt, *FDP*, 55–8; Clemens Heitmann, *FDP und neue Ostpolitik* (Sankt Augustin: COMDOK, 1989), esp. 44–9, 86–95.

[116] Juling, *Programmatische*, 198. On disputes, see ADL: A1-328, esp. 49–143.

[117] Scheel in the FDP's Bundesvorstand, 16 Dec. 1968, ADL: BV-Protokolle, 130, p. 61; his 24 Mar. 1968 address, *DzD* v/2/1. 501.

This drive at linguistic purification was particularly evident in the party's stances towards the GDR. While holding on to the end goal of reunification and rejecting a full recognition of East Germany as a foreign country, the party pressed for a formal renunciation of both the Hallstein Doctrine and the Federal Republic's broader claim to be the only legitimate representative of all Germans. The FDP also called for extensive governmental and other contacts between the two Germanys, and in early 1969 it even published a proposed 'General Treaty with the GDR', which outlined the party's vision of normalized inter-German relations.[118]

On Eastern policy, the FDP moved in a similarly reformist direction, albeit somewhat more cautiously. It advocated full diplomatic relations between the Federal Republic and all of Eastern Europe; declared the Munich Agreement invalid; and made numerous general references to its intention to respect the existing borders on the continent.[119] But the party stopped short of absolute clarity on the territorial problems in the East. With a strong whiff of sophistry, Scheel, in particular, repeatedly argued that the establishment of governmental ties between Bonn and East Berlin would remove the entire Oder-Neisse problem from the West German political agenda because 'the Federal Republic does not border Poland; the GDR does' and Bonn accordingly 'lacks the authority to decide about another state's boundaries'.[120] More explicit renunciations of revisionist ambitions surfaced only in internal deliberations and occasional public statements by radical-liberal leaders, not in official party proclamations, primarily because the pragmatist Scheel wanted to eschew formulations which expellees and other like-minded elements, including conservatives within the FDP, might find 'unnecessarily insulting'.[121] Even amidst their unmistakable disengagement from the standard doctrines that had guided the Federal Republic's earlier Eastern policy, the FDP's top leaders thus proved unwilling to make a complete break with the ritualistic public rhetoric whose use by others they so lamented.

The SPD's relevant stances evolved in a direction parallel to that of the FDP, but with a reversed emphasis on the key points: greater clarity on Ostpolitik and higher caution on policies toward the GDR. To be sure, even on the latter issue, the SPD's top leaders agreed with the key arguments of the Free Democrats. The need to drop the Hallstein Doctrine and to accept the GDR as a second German state was widely acknowledged in the SPD, particularly by the latter stages of the Grand Coalition.[122] But apart from isolated statements by youth and regional

---

[118] Scheel's 14 Dec. 1968 interview, *DzD* v/2/2. esp. 1607–8; FDP's 1969 electoral programme, in Juling, *Entwicklung*, 207; Heitmann, *Ostpolitik*, 199–200.

[119] Scheel's 14 Dec. 1968 interview, and FDP's 1969 electoral programme (n. 118); SPD's Bundesfachausschuss für Deutschland-, Aussen-, und Sicherheitspolitik resolution, 24 Jan. 1969, ADL: Aussen-, Deutschland-, und Sicherheitspolitischer Ausschuss, 1968–71, 964.

[120] Scheel's 14 Dec. 1968 interview, *DzD* v/2/2. 1608; Scheel to Hupka, 26 Feb. 1969, ABdV: Sitzungen des Präsidiums, 1969.

[121] Scheel in the FDP's Bundesvorstand, 27 Apr. 1969, ADL: BV-Protokolle, 152, p. 127; Siekmeier, *Restauration*, 380–420; Schmidt, *FDP*, 82–97.

[122] Baring, *Machtwechsel*; Kroegel, *Anfang*, 115–68; Schneider, *Kunst*.

party groups and some controversial remarks by Herbert Wehner, the party avoided public elucidation of its specific intentions.[123] Far from matching the level of detail in the FDP's draft treaty with the GDR, the Social Democrats typically contented themselves with generalities that underscored the need to come to terms with 'the existence of a state in the other party of Germany' and to achieve a 'regulated coexistence' with East Berlin, while continuing to rule out a full recognition of the GDR as a fully sovereign state.[124]

On Eastern policy, the SPD waxed a good deal more specific. The party never left any doubt about its desire for a normalization of relations between Bonn and the East European capitals, and by 1967 it increasingly began to question key taboos that still hindered this process. As we have seen, Foreign Minister Brandt made several public statements suggestive of a willingness to abandon the Federal Republic's revisionist claims in the East during the latter half of 1967, and so did several other ranking SPD leaders.[125] More explicit public rhetoric surfaced the following year. Helmut Schmidt, who had established a reputation as a tough polemicist, became the party's messenger of choice. In several public appearances, he exhorted his fellow politicians to show 'the courage to be truthful' by distancing themselves from the Eastern policy 'illusions of the 1950s'. According to Schmidt, a particularly dangerous illusion was the dream that 'the borders of 1937 [could] be re-established one day', a cause for which no one outside of Germany felt the slightest sympathy.[126] Similar themes also featured prominently in some of Willy Brandt's addresses, but their most notable application came in a pioneering resolution, adopted by the SPD's 1968 party congress in Nuremberg, in which the Social Democrats pledged to 'respect and recognize the existing European borders, especially Poland's current western boundary', pending a final peace settlement.[127] A further resolution, adopted the following year, pronounced the Munich Agreement not only invalid but also 'unjust from inception', the most explicit distancing from the notorious accord ever issued by a mainstream West German party.[128]

However, all this seemingly clear rhetoric—which the party followed up with intensive behind-the-scenes explorations of practical Ostpolitik prospects through secret meetings with representatives of the Polish government and the Italian Communist Party—remained subject to persistent provisos and qualifications.[129]

---

[123] SPD's Landesausschuss in Berlin, resolution, 23 Sept. 1967, *DzD* v/1/2. 1712–16; Jungsozialisten resolution, 10 Dec. 1967, ibid., 2190–1; Günter Gaus (ed.), *Staatserhaltende Opposition oder hat die SPD kapituliert? Gespräche mit Herbert Wehner* (Reinbek: Rowohlt, 1966); Kroegel, *Anfang*, 130–3.

[124] SPD's party congress resolutions, Bad Godesberg, 16–18 Apr. 1969, *Jahrbuch der SPD 1968/1969*, 437 and 428.

[125] Examples include Wehner's address to the Silesian Homeland Society, 25 June 1967, *DzD* v/1/2. 1378–82, and Bahr's television interview, 4 Sept. 1967, ibid. 1579.

[126] Schmidt's 8 Feb. 1968 interview, *DzD* v/2/1. 191; Schmidt in the Bundestag, 14 Mar. 1968, ibid. 399; Schneider, *Kunst*, 213–19.   [127] *DzD* v/2/1. 464; *Jahrbuch der SPD 1968/1969*, 338.

[128] SPD's party congress resolution, Bad Godesberg, 16–18 Apr. 1969, in *Jahrbuch der SPD 1968/1969*, 436.

[129] Timmermann, 'Vorfeld'; Kroegel, *Anfang*, 212–24; Hansjakob Stehle, 'Zufälle auf dem Weg zur neuen Ostpolitik: Aufzeichnungen über ein geheimes Treffen Egon Bahrs mit einem polnischen Diplomaten 1968', *VfZ* 43 (1995): 159–71.

The party's 1968 resolution pledging to recognize the Oder-Neisse boundary provided a case in point—by leaving that stance subject to change at a future peace conference, at least in theory. Similar obfuscation characterized Helmut Schmidt's public pronouncements, which combined seemingly uncompromising calls for honesty and realism with contradictory asides, including assurances that his intention was not to undermine Germany's 'legal positions' but simply to analyse their chances of implementation.[130] Even the SPD's 1969 declaration about the Munich Agreement contained ambiguous phrasing, including a reaffirmation of the party's obligation to protect the interests of the Sudeten Germans and to ensure that any decisions about the fate of the 1938 accord would not burden this group with 'new disadvantages'.[131]

The SPD's revamped Ostpolitik image thus appeared somewhat schizophrenic, as a strong dose of pioneering boldness clashed with whiffs of defensive hesitation. The reason for this incongruity lay in the party's attempts to reconcile mutually incompatible imperatives. On the one hand, party leaders struggled to accommodate what they viewed as growing domestic pressures for new approaches towards Eastern Europe and the GDR. Willy Brandt, for example, was acutely aware that 'the youth' in particular kept asking 'probing questions' that could not be answered with hackneyed old formulas.[132] Accordingly, his party made a conscious effort to portray itself as '*the* political force that responds to the impulses of the young generation and therefore prepares for the coming new decade from a position of strength'.[133]

At the same time, however, the Social Democrats also faced countervailing pressures from two quarters. The first was the expellee lobby, which tried to restrain the party with vocal protests against its new accents on Eastern and reunification policy.[134] Such interventions no longer swayed the SPD leadership as they once had, in large part because the party's top echelons now believed that the bulk of the rank-and-file expellees 'agreed in principle' with the Social Democratic stances, regardless of what the activists claimed.[135] But the party was nevertheless eager to avoid too dramatic a rupture with the expellee lobby, particularly in view of its past practice of assiduously courting these groups. The Social Democrats therefore continued to hold occasional consultations with leading expellee organizations, albeit without the profuse promises of earlier years, and the contradictions in the party's Ostpolitik proclamations were in large part the result of key leaders' desire to avoid 'formulations' that could provoke unnecessary 'mistrust towards the party and its policies', especially

---

[130] Schmidt's 8 Feb. 1968 interview, *DzD* v/2/1. 191–2.

[131] *Jahrbuch der SPD 1968/1969*, 436.

[132] Brandt, as reported in Karl Carstens's memorandum, 28 June 1966, *AAPD* 1966, 895; Patton, *Cold*, 70–3.

[133] Nuremberg party congress resolution 'Sozialdemokratische Perspektiven im Übergang zu den siebziger Jahren', 21 Mar. 1968, *DzD* v/2/1. 481.

[134] SPD's Bundestagsfraktion protocols, 2 Apr. 1968, AdsD: BT-Fraktion, 5. WP, 91.

[135] SPD's Vertriebenen- und Flüchtlingsausschuss resolution, 2 Dec. 1968, AdsD: BT-Fraktion, 5. WP, 902.

among the expellees[136] But the SPD also had another reason to mince its words somewhat. As a governing party, it was forced to exercise caution, particularly as its coalition partner had chosen to adopt a very different posture on Eastern and reunification policy, a posture that placed it in growing conflict with the steadily converging stances of the SPD and the FDP.

This contrast was clear in the CDU/CSU's official attitude towards the GDR. Although willing to condone 'negotiations and agreements with [East Berlin's] rulers' aimed at improving the living conditions of average East Germans and maintaining a sense of unity across the inter-German divide, the party rejected any kind of recognition of what it still called 'the totalitarian system' in the East.[137] It insisted on the continued validity of the Hallstein Doctrine, at least outside of Eastern Europe, and maintained that the Federal Republic remained the only legitimate representative of the entire German people.[138] Revealingly, the party even refused to use the term GDR, typically preferring the euphemism 'the other part of Germany' and occasionally resorting to the antiquated and inaccurate formulation the 'Soviet-occupied part of Germany'.[139]

On Eastern policy, the CDU/CSU pursued a similarly conservative course. To be sure, the party's top leaders frequently stressed their 'genuine desire' for improved relations with the East European countries, describing 'reconciliation' and 'cooperation' as their overall objectives in the region.[140] They also emphasized the forward-looking nature of their Ostpolitik objectives, denying any restorative intent and underscoring the need for new solutions that would contribute to the building of a broader European peace order.[141] At the same time, however, party leaders highlighted the necessity of basing their Eastern policy on what the CSU labelled 'the vital interests of our people'.[142] As defined by the CDU/CSU's proclamations, these interests bore a close resemblance to the traditional revisionist doctrines advocated by the expellee lobby. The presumed key goal was to safeguard Germany's 'legal positions'. The Federal Republic had to insist that the regulation of the Polish–German border be deferred until a future peace settlement.[143] The government was also obliged to ensure that 'the rights [of the German expellees], particularly the *Heimatrecht*, continue to be represented' with appropriate firmness.[144]

---

[136] AdsD: BT-Fraktion, 5. WP, 902; SPD press releases about a meeting with the BdV, 9 Oct. 1967, AdsD: BT-Fraktion, 5. WP, 878, and with select expellee activists, 28 June 1969, AdsD: BT-Fraktion, 5. WP, 902.

[137] CDU's Berlin Programme, 7 Nov. 1968, in *16. Bundesparteitag der Christlich Demokratischen Union Deutschlands*, 74.

[138] See e.g. Freiherr Guttenberg's memorandum 'Zur Deutschlandpolitik der CDU/CSU (Entwurf)', Apr. 1967, BA: NL 397, 170, pp. 73–8.

[139] See the Berlin Programme (n. 137).

[140] Barzel in the Bundestag, 14 Mar. 1968, *DzD* V/1/1. 387; Barzel's 19 June 1969 speech, cited in *DuD/DHDF* (24 June 1969), 1; CSU's 'Grundsatzprogramm', 14 Dec. 1968, in *25 Jahre Christlich-Soziale Union. Parteitag 15.–17. Oktober 1971, München*, 101.

[141] See e.g. Windelen's 19 June 1969 speech, *DuD/DHDF* (24 June 1969), p. 1; Gradl in the Bundestag, 14 Mar. 1968, *DzD* v/1/1. 428.   [142] CSU's 'Grundsatzprogramm', Dec. 1968 (n. 140), 101.

[143] CDU's Nov. 1968 Berlin Programme, in *16. Bundesparteitag*, 75; Johann Baptist Gradl, 'Wir dürfen nicht nachgeben', *Deutsches Monatsblatt* (10 Oct. 1967).

[144] CDU/CSU's 'Vertriebenen- und Flüchtlingskongress' resolution, Wiesbaden, 22 Nov. 1968, *DzD* v/2/2. 1519–20.

On both counts, CDU/CSU leaders castigated the Social and particularly the Free Democrats for their allegedly lax and irresponsible stances. Franz-Josef Strauss, for example, dismissed the FDP's hopes of trying to facilitate reunification by moving towards an acceptance of the existing Polish–German border as 'illusionary schemes rooted in wishful thinking'.[145] The CDU/CSU also criticized its two main rivals on more marginal Ostpolitik issues which hardly qualified as vital German interests. A case in point was the Munich Agreement, on which the party quickly dissociated itself from the SPD's 'unhelpful' April 1969 resolution that had labelled the treaty 'unfair from inception'.[146]

To be sure, the CDU/CSU was careful and often deliberately ambiguous in its public identification with revisionist Eastern policy causes. While insisting that Germany's Eastern borders could be determined only in a future peace treaty, the party also maintained that 'negotiations with Poland' could commence prior to a peace conference and that the final settlement would have to form the basis for 'a lasting peace' between the two nations.[147] The CDU/CSU also asserted that the *Heimatrecht* was not an exclusive 'entitlement of the German expellees' but a basic 'right for all Europeans everywhere' and combined its cautious defence of the Munich Agreement with a specific rejection of any attempts to use the treaty as a basis for territorial or other claims against Czechoslovakia.[148] However, despite such carefully phrased qualifiers, the Union's stances towards Eastern Europe and the GDR clearly remained much more conservative and traditional than those of the other two main parties.

The CDU/CSU's reluctance to readjust its positions, particularly on Eastern policy, was in large measure a derivative of the Federal Republic's domestic expellee problem. In part, the party's behaviour was traceable to direct pressure from the expellee lobby, transmitted through two different channels. The less important of these was unmediated institutional contact between leading expellee organizations and the party. As in previous years, the typical pattern of interaction consisted of protest against CDU/CSU actions by specific expellee groups, followed by party leaders' attempts to reassure the activists.[149] On several occasions, the party also arranged special bilateral meetings with key organizations, at which it issued proclamations that often struck somewhat more revisionist Ostpolitik chords than its other pronouncements, thus linking the party to these specific promises and thereby limiting its freedom of movement.[150]

---

[145] Strauss, 'Deutsche Rechtspositionen nicht ins Zwielicht', *Bayern-Kurier* (15 Apr. 1967).

[146] 'CSU erklärt sich mit Vertriebenen solidarisch', *DuD/DHDF* (29 Apr. 1969); 'Verständnis für die Wünsche der Vertriebenen', *DuD/DHDF* (12 May 1969).

[147] Communiqué of a CDU–BdV meeting, 27 Mar. 1968, ALdO: Parteien und Abgeordnete, 1.1.68–31.8.69; CDU's Nov. 1968 Berlin Programme, in *16. Bundesparteitag*, 75.

[148] Von Hassel at the CDU/CSU's 'Vertriebenen- und Flüchtlingskongress', Wiesbaden, 21 Nov. 1968, *DzD* v/2/2. 1517–18.

[149] See e.g. Kiesinger's comments, reported in Becher to Gebert, SDA: NL Becher, 2.

[150] Press communiqué about a CDU–BdV meeting, 27 Mar. 1968, ALdO: Parteien und Abgeordnete, 1.11.68–31.8.69; 'CSU erklärt sich mit Vertriebenen solidarisch', *DuD/DHDF* (29 Apr. 1969); 'Verständnis für die Wünsche der Vertriebenen', *Dud/DHDF* (12 May 1969).

Although this form of interaction had its significance, more weight accrued to the second channel through which the expellee organizations exerted direct pressure on the CDU/CSU: the interventions of activists working from within the party. Endowed with a more elaborate organizational infrastructure and more independent-minded leadership than their counterparts in the other major parties, the CDU/CSU's expellee politicians cut a strong figure during the Grand Coalition. To be sure, expellee activists remained excluded from top-level party posts, and they still lacked the power to shape the CDU/CSU's positive agenda, as witnessed by the failure of their campaign to add extensive revisionist content to the Ostpolitik section of the Berlin Programme, the new policy guidelines adopted by the CDU in November 1968.[151] But the expellee leaders wielded considerable negative influence at lower levels of the party organization. Using the various existing expellee suborgans as bases for planning and coordination, the activists made their mark primarily in two arenas: the CDU/CSU's parliamentary group in the Bundestag (*Bundestagsfraktion*) and the CSU's Arbeitskreis fur Deutschland- und Ostpolitik, a special advisory body established in the summer of 1967.[152]

Their major weapon in both organs was protest, predictably directed against any attempt to change the CDU/CSU's traditional doctrines, particularly on Ostpolitik.[153] Such campaigns exerted considerable restraining influence on those associated with the party's mainstream or liberal factions—most notably Chancellor Kiesinger himself—who were not philosophically opposed to gradual readjustments in the party's Eastern policy stances.[154] The restraints were enhanced by the fact that the expellee activists received frequent encouragement from several heavyweights within the party. The CSU, which had built particularly close ties to the expellee lobby, primarily through the Sudeten Germans, produced the most vocal backers of the expellee activists, chief among them Franz-Josef Strauss and Freiherr Theodor von und zu Guttenberg. However, although Guttenberg appears to have been motivated by genuine political and ethical convictions in his support of the expellee leaders, most others, including Strauss, were not.[155] For them, the nationalist Ostpolitik card was a tactical one, to be played for personal and factional gain in internal party battles as well as for the broader benefit of the CDU/CSU, in accordance with a particular reading of the broader situation in West German society.

This broader reading of societal realities provides the ultimate explanation of the CDU/CSU's susceptibility to expellee pressure—an explanation that underscores the continued *indirect* influence of the expellee problem and its foreign-policy

---

[151] BdV presidium protocols, 9 Sept. 1968, p. 9; 11 Nov. 1968, p. 7, SDA: NL Becher, 194; 'Neue Konturen', *DoD* (11 Nov. 1968).

[152] Taschler, *Herausforderungen*.

[153] CDU/CSU Bundestagsfraktion protocols, 12 May 1967, ACDP: VIII-001-1014/1; 12 Dec. 1967, 5 Feb. 1968, ACDP: VIII-001-1015/2; Detlef Bischoff, *Franz Josef Strauss, die CSU und die Aussenpolitik* (Meisenheim am Glan: Anton Hain, 1973), esp. 245–7.

[154] Kiesinger in the CDU/CSU Bundestagsfraktion, 12 Dec. 1967, ACDP: VIII-001-1015/2, esp. 23; his 19 Sept. 1967 speech, *DzD* v/1/2. esp. 1673.   [155] Bischoff, *Strauss*; Wirz, *Guttenberg*.

implications on the party's actions. The CDU/CSU was, after all, not the only party subject to Ostpolitik pressure from the organized expellee movement. The SPD and the FDP also confronted similar problems. Yet these two parties increasingly chose to defy the expellee lobby and to readjust their relevant stances, whereas the CDU/CSU did so only to a very limited degree. The higher relative intensity of the internal pressure faced by the Union contributed to these differences, but only in a secondary way. The main cause of the divergence was rather the fact that CDU/CSU leaders interpreted West Germany's main societal trends and the electoral and other advantages to be gained from them very differently than did their primary political rivals.

Not only the Union's right-wingers but also the bulk of its centrist and more liberal politicians, including the Chancellor himself, doubted that public opinion on Ostpolitik issues had really changed as much as various polls seemed to indicate. In internal deliberations, party leaders argued that the polls reflected 'passing mood[s]', likely to swing 'one way today and the other tomorrow', rather than any 'carefully considered ideas'.[156] They also believed that the bulk of the expellees, as well as a sizeable chunk of the rest of the population, continued to subscribe to many of the old Eastern policy doctrines, irrespective of what the latest polls suggested. Kiesinger himself maintained as late as the summer of 1969 that 'the majority of the population' supported the CDU/CSU's conservative stances on issues such as 'the recognition of the GDR or of the Oder-Neisse line'.[157] Unlike their counterparts in the SPD and the FDP, the leaders of the CDU/CSU thus concluded that continued public loyalty to the revisionist Ostpolitik doctrines associated with the expellee lobby remained electorally profitable, and this calculation, in turn, was the underlying cause of the party's growing divergence from the positions adopted by its two main rivals.

The CDU/CSU's interest in maintaining a relatively close public identification with the traditional Eastern policy doctrines was further bolstered by an additional, closely related factor: the rise of a new and threatening political force, the National-Democratic Party (NPD). Founded in late 1964 as the latest attempt to rally the country's right-wing-radical fringe, the NPD adopted an extreme nationalist posture, mixing apologetic accounts of the Nazi past with thinly veiled calls for a glorious, authoritarian future. An aggressive Eastern policy programme—centred on reacquiring 'all of Germany', including the 'Sudetenland', for the 'German people'—featured prominently in the NPD's proclamations, and the party's leadership cadre came to include several prominent expellee figures, such as the veteran firebrand Linus Kather.[158]

---

[156] Kiesinger in the Bundestagsfraktion, 6 June 1967, ACDP: VIII-001-1014/1, p. 7; Windelen in the Bundestagsfraktion, 12 Dec. 1967, ACDP: VIII-001-1015/2, p. 20.

[157] Kiesinger in the Bundestagsfraktion, 1 July 1969, ACDP: I-226-A010, p. 5; Bösch, *Adenauer-CDU*, 402–8.

[158] Horst W. Schmollinger, 'Die Nationaldemokratische Partei Deutschlands', in Richard Stöss (ed.), *Parteien-Handbuch* (Opladen: Westdeutscher Verlag, 1984), ii. *1922–1994*, esp. 1933; Reinhard Kühnl, *Die NPD* (Frankfurt: Suhrkamp, 1969).

Predictably, the party therefore invested heavily in courting the expellees, particularly those who showed at least some affinity for the organized expellee movement. As a consequence, the spectacle of NPD agitators distributing aggressive propaganda materials at expellee rallies became commonplace during the late 1960s.[159] The possibility of a large-scale radicalization among expellees and other like-minded elements, in turn, again began to worry the country's political establishment, particularly after the NPD had scored a series of spectacular successes in regional elections during the first two years of the Grand Coalition, culminating in a 9.8 per cent share of the vote in the April 1968 Landtag election in Baden-Württemberg.

The CDU/CSU tracked the situation particularly closely, not only out of concern but also because its leaders realized that as the most conservative mainstream party in the West Germany, the Union was in the best position to benefit from the situation. While fearful that overly rapid Ostpolitik readjustments would 'arouse a wave of right-wing radicalism' and thus fuel the NPD's growth, the party's leaders hoped that with continued allegiance to more traditional doctrines the CDU/CSU could kill two birds with one stone.[160] It could serve the common good by providing a moderate, responsible alternative to the genuine revisionism espoused by the NPD. At the same time, it could hope to boost its own partisan fortunes at the expense of both the National Democrats on the right and the FDP and the SPD on the left, in the latter case by siphoning off nationalistically inclined voters unhappy with their parties' new Ostpolitik stances but wary of the extremist NPD.[161] The dangers and opportunities inherent in the rise of the NPD thus strengthened the CDU/CSU's general tendency to see in ongoing societal developments incentives for maintaining a conservative Eastern policy posture, a process that underscored the continued indirect influence of the expellee problem and its implications on the party's decision-makers.

The expellee organizations kept a very close eye on the evolution of the major parties' Eastern policy positions. The new chords struck by the SPD and the FDP found quick condemnation in the expellee lobby's internal deliberations, and during 1967 and 1968 the activists also waxed increasingly vocal in their public censure of the two parties.[162] The FDP, whose links to the expellee movement had traditionally been weaker than those of its two larger rivals, received the harshest censure. As early as the spring of 1967, the BdV denounced the party's 'radical-liberal' faction as a dangerous group of extremists, bent on 'recklessly discarding Germany's rightful claims' in the East.[163] As these left-liberal forces then rose to increasing dominance within the FDP during the following year, expellee activists

---

[159] 'Pfiffe für den Vertreter der Bundesregierung', *Frankfurter Rundschau* (27 May 1969).

[160] Kiesinger's comments, reported in *Stern* (10 Mar. 1968), *DzD* v/2/1. 349; Krone to Kiesinger, 6 Feb. 1968, ACDP: I-226-A005.

[161] Bösch, *Adenauer-CDU*, 397–402; Kühnl, *NPD*, 298–302.

[162] BdV's Bundesvertretung protocols, 11 Mar. 1967, SDA: B IX/33; Hans Stephan's report about the BdV, 31 Oct. 1967, WBA: SPD/Parteivorstand—Verbindungen mit Referaten, 19.

[163] 'Kopfstand der Logik: Die Stunde der Wahrheit—über die FDP', *DoD* (10 Apr. 1967).

responded with continued criticism, while also gradually resigning themselves to the fact that the party was likely to go its own way regardless of their protests and could therefore no longer be trusted.[164]

A similar view of the SPD gained increasing credence among the expellee elites from the spring of 1968 on. The resolution by which the party pledged to 'respect and recognize' the Oder-Neisse line in March of that year was a particularly bitter blow for the expellee leaders. In the immediate aftermath of that proclamation, the BdV accused the party of 'breaking its promises', and subsequent commentaries placed the blame for the perceived 'souring of the formerly good relations between the SPD and the expellees' solidly at the party's doorstep.[165] The relations took a further turn for the worse in early 1969, as the Social Democrats declared the Munich Agreement 'unjust from inception', thereby evoking the wrath of the well-organized Sudeten-German Homeland Society.[166] The rift between the expellee lobby on the one hand and the FDP and the SPD on the other had thus become highly noticeable by the time the Bundestag election of 1969 began to draw near.

Even as their frustration with the Social and Free Democrats increased, expellee leaders found themselves in far-reaching agreement about Eastern policy issues with another party—the NPD. Top activists greeted the NPD's 'honest, national-minded ethos' and concluded that no other party advocated their revisionist core causes with equal decisiveness.[167] However, because of the NPD's extremist reputation—which some activists considered justified in view of the party's aggressive agitational style and its openly apologetic stances towards certain aspects of the Third Reich—the expellee elites expected any open association with the party to be a liability rather than an asset.[168] A special BdV commission set up to study the relationship between the expellee lobby and the NPD resolved that collaboration with the National Democrats would saddle the expellee cause with a 'shady or even offensive image abroad and at home'.[169] Accordingly, despite some dissent within their ranks, the main expellee organizations decided to steer clear of institutional cooperation with the party, although the presence of individual NPD members in the organizations was not seen as a problem.[170]

---

[164] 'Fortschritt in welche Richtung', 'Was heisst "Generalvertrag" ', *DoD* (7 Feb. 1968, 17 Jan. 1969); President Rehs in the BdV's Bundesvertretung and Bundesversammlung, 26–7 Apr. 1969, ABdV: Protokolle—Bundesversammlung, Bundesvertretung, Präsidium, 17.1.67–31.12.69.

[165] BdV's 30 Mar. 1968 declaration, AdsD: BT-Fraktion, 5. WP, 876; 'Woran sich viele stossen', *DoD* (11 June 1968).

[166] Sudentendeutsche Landsmannschaft, Bundesverband protocols, 19 Apr. 1969, SDA: NL Becher, 201.

[167] Jaksch at a BdV Klausurtagung, 12–13 Nov. 1966, ABdV: Bundesvertretungsprotokolle, 1958–67, p. 2; Hilf to Schwarzer, 1 Feb. 1968, BA: B234/167.

[168] BdV memoranda 'BdV—Folgerungen zur NPD' and 'Betr: NPD-Parteiprogramm', attached to Hilf to Schwarzer, 1 Feb. 1968, BA: B234/167.

[169] Neuhoff, 'Betr: NPD-Programm und BdV', 18 June 1969, BA: B 234/167.

[170] BdV presidium protocols, 2 July 1969, SDA: AG zur Wahrung sudetendeutscher Interessen, 4, pp. 3–4.

As a consequence, by the latter stages of the Grand Coalition the expellee lobby was left with only one potentially viable political ally—the CDU/CSU. To be sure, the activists were not fully satisfied with the Union's stances, which many regarded as unnecessarily guarded. The prominent presence within the party of left-leaning Catholic intellectuals, several of whom had contributed to the Bensberg Memorandum, provided a further source of concern.[171] But, compared to the alternatives, most expellee leaders nevertheless regarded the Union as the most 'solid' option for them.[172] The CSU, in particular, drew repeated praise for its receptiveness to the expellee groups and their interests, and the Chancellor himself managed to evoke periodic applause from the key organizations.[173] As the SPD and the FDP increasingly faded from the picture and the NPD remained beyond the political pale, a special relationship between the expellee lobby and the CDU/CSU thus began to take shape by 1969.

The Bundestag election campaign of 1969 turned these long-evolving trends into a full-blown political polarization in the expellee sector. The division of the parties into two camps, composed of the FDP and the SPD on the one hand and the CDU/CSU on the other, with the NPD lurking in the shadows several steps to the right of the Union, was evident in two ways. First, the effort invested by the two camps in courting the expellee lobby with Eastern policy arguments differed sharply. The SPD and the FDP kept a relatively low profile in this area. To be sure, neither party sought to burn its bridges to the expellee activists. Both avoided unnecessarily provocative accents during the campaign, toning down their rhetoric somewhat on the most heated issues, such as the future status of the Oder-Neisse line.[174] But neither party backed down from its core positions, and, when attacked or questioned, key leaders of both parties repeatedly defended the stances they had adopted during the previous few years.[175]

The CDU/CSU, on the other hand, pursued a much more aggressive course. In numerous proclamations the party not only reiterated its continued commitment to protecting the rights of the German expellees and steering Bonn's Eastern policy clear of 'the low road of abandonment and sell-out'.[176] It also reverted to the suggestive rhetorical practices of an earlier era, vowing to 'save as much of Germany . . . as ever possible' and wishing, in language redolent of Adenauer, that

---

[171] 'Wahlkampf 69: Um die Stimmen der Vertriebenen', *Süddeutsche Zeitung* (12 Sept. 1969); BdV presidium protocols, 11 Nov. 1968, SDA: NL Becher, 194, esp. p. 7.

[172] BdV presidium protocols, 30 Mar. 1968, SDA: NL Becher, 200, esp. p. 2.

[173] 'Konservativ und fortschrittlich', *DoD* (23 Dec. 1968); Böhm in the BdV's Klausurtagung, 30 Nov.–1 Dec. 1968, SDA: NL Becher, 194, p. 2; Rehs in the BdV presidium, 30 Mar. 1968, SDA: NL Becher, 200, p. 2.

[174] FDP's election programme, 25 June 1969, in Juling, *Programmatische*, esp. 207–8; SPD's official responses to a BdV questionnaire, 16 June 1969, AdsD: BT-Fraktion, 5. WP, 930.

[175] Wehner's meeting with expellee politicians, 28 June 1969, AdsD: BT-Fraktion, 5. WP, 902; Wehner at the Kongress der Ostdeutschen Landesvertretungen, Bad Godesberg, 31 Aug. 1969, ALdO: Parteien und Abgeordnete, 1.12.69–28.2.70; Walter Scheel on the latter event, 1 Sept. 1969, ADL: BV-Protokolle, 153, esp. 6–8.

[176] 'CDU bekundet Verbundenheit mit Vertriebenen und Flüchtlingen', *DuD/DHDF* (24 June 1969).

'one day . . . a just peace settlement' will provide 'justice to the German people'.[177] With such rhetorical practices, the CDU/CSU found itself approaching the territory of the NPD, which beat the revisionist Ostpolitik drum with a heavy hand throughout the election campaign.[178]

The political polarization on the expellee issue during the 1969 campaign also manifested itself in a second domain: the responses of the expellee organizations to the main parties. Both in public and behind the scenes, the expellee lobby still purported to be strictly non-partisan, with some seeming credibility.[179] The leadership organs of the main expellee groups included individuals affiliated with all the major and several minor parties, including the NPD, and the organizations never specifically instructed their followers to support or shun any of the major parties. But the expellee groups nevertheless engaged in extensive partisan polemics by issuing detailed guidelines, phrased in broad, philosophical terms, about how the expellees should view the upcoming election. These manifestos portrayed the balloting in stark, binary terms. According to the BdV, the election was the most important since 1949 because it found the Federal Republic 'at a crossroads', forced to decide between a future of 'national self-assertion or feckless capitulation'.[180] The champions of the latter course, to be fought by all legal and non-violent means, could be recognized by their advocacy of causes such as a recognition of the Oder-Neisse line, an acceptance of 'the Ulbricht regime', 'an abandonment of Germany's Eastern territories', or declarations that the Munich Agreement was 'void and unjust'.[181] Not coincidentally, all were stances associated with the SPD and the FDP.

Immediately preceding the election, the expellee activists made their partisan message even more explicit. As a part of its last-minute appeal to its followers, the BdV compared the leading parties' recent stances on the key Ostpolitik problems, praising the CDU/CSU for its 'clarity and consistency' while portraying the SPD and particularly the FDP in a much more unflattering light.[182] As these public pronouncements were accompanied by significant rightward shifts in the composition of the expellee lobby's leadership cadres, demonstrated most dramatically by BdV President Reinhold Rehs's highly publicized defection from the SPD to the CDU in May 1969, the expellee groups had in practice forfeited their earlier non-partisan stature in favour of a limited political partnership with the CDU/CSU.[183] The flip side of this development had been a clear rupture between

---

[177] 'Verständnis für die Wünsche der Vertriebenen', *DuD/DHDF* (12 May 1969); 'CDU-Programm für die Jahre 1969–1973 verabschiedet', *DuD/DHDF* (9 July 1969).

[178] 'Vertriebene auf Rechtskurs', *Die Zeit* (30 May 1969); 'Mit nationalen Phrasen gegen "Anerkennungspartei" ', *Süddeutsche Zeitung* (12 Sept. 1969).

[179] 'Aufruf des Bundesvorstandes der Sudetendeutschen Landsmannschaft und der Sudetendeutschen Bundesversammlung zu den Bundestagswahlen', Sept. 1969, SDA: NL Becher, 398; BdV, 'Rundschreiben, Betr: Bundestagswahl 1969', SDA: NL Becher, 193.

[180] 'Die wichtigste Wahl', *DoD* (5 Sept. 1969).

[181] BdV, 'Rundschreiben, Betr: Bundestagswahl 1969', SDA: NL Becher, 193.

[182] 'DoD-Bundestagswahldienst', *DoD* (25 Sept. 1969), 13.

[183] 'Vertriebene auf Rechtskurs', *Die Zeit* (30 May 1969).

the relevant Ostpolitik positions of the Union on the one hand and the SPD and the FDP on the other. The traditional pattern of interaction among the expellee lobby, the largest parties, and the government, based on non-partisan pressure group tactics by the expellee organizations and consensus politics by the political elites, had thus collapsed in the course of the 1969 election campaign.

The election itself served to reconfirm this development and to highlight its fateful consequences for the expellee lobby. The electoral outcome dismayed the expellee activists. Although the CDU/CSU remained the largest party—slipping slightly vis-à-vis its 1965 outcome—and the FDP suffered heavy losses, the biggest winner turned out to be the SPD, which continued its steady advance by adding over three percentage points to its previous record, achieved four years earlier. The NPD, in turn, fell somewhat short of the 5 per cent threshold required for entry to the parliament.[184] The expellee contribution to this outcome remains poorly investigated, but by all indications the rank-and-file expellees had not followed the recommendations of their purported spokesmen very closely at all. According to the available data, the expellees did show a somewhat greater tendency to vote for the CDU/CSU and also the NPD than did the rest of the population. They also largely shunned the FDP, like most other West Germans, but their support for the SPD remained high, declining only slightly from the 1965 levels.[185]

For the expellee lobby, the election of 1969 marked the end of an era. For the first time since the founding of the Federal Republic, the expellee groups had failed to secure the backing of all the main political parties for their primary Eastern policy doctrines, even on a rhetorical level. To make matter worse, the only major political force that still identified itself with the bulk of the expellee lobby's demands soon found itself manœuvred out of power as the two parties whose Ostpolitik proposals the expellee activists had been busy denouncing throughout the election campaign promptly cobbled together a new governing coalition.[186] With the transition to the Social–Liberal era, the main epoch of expellee influence on West German Ostpolitik had come to an end, although the final decline of that influence was to be a prolonged process, stretching from the launching of the New Ostpolitik in the beginning of the 1970s to the reunification settlement of 1990/1 and even beyond. The following chapter will outline and analyse key moments in this process.

---

[184] The results: CDU/CSU 46.1%, 242 seats; SPD 42.7%, 227; FDP 5.8%, 30; NPD: 4.3%.

[185] Brües, *Artikulation*, 183–98; Zur Mühlen *et al.*, 'Vertriebenenverbände', 143–5.

[186] Daniel Hofmann, ' "Verdächtige Eile": Der Weg zur Koalition aus SPD und FDP nach der Bundestagswahl vom 28. Sept. 1969', *VfZ* 48 (2000): 515–64; Baring, *Machtwechsel*, 166–94.

CHAPTER EIGHT

From the New Ostpolitik to Reunification, 1969–1990

THE SOCIAL–LIBERAL COALITION that came to power in the late autumn of 1969 under the leadership of Chancellor Willy Brandt of the SPD and Foreign Minister Walter Scheel of the FDP quickly demonstrated its intention to pursue new policies towards the Eastern bloc. Brandt's government declaration of 28 October 1969 helped to set the tone. Although its most radical innovations had to do with East Germany—Brandt acknowledged the existence of 'two states in Germany' and offered East Berlin 'negotiations on the governmental level, without discrimination' while still rejecting a full legal recognition of the GDR as a foreign country—the declaration also signalled the government's willingness to break new ground in its approach towards Eastern Europe as a whole. Brandt proposed renunciation of force (*Gewaltverzicht*) negotiations with all Eastern bloc states with which Bonn had not yet formalized its relations, explicitly including the GDR, thus underscoring his intention to avoid a repeat of past attempts to isolate East Berlin. Even more menacingly from the expellee lobby's viewpoint, the Chancellor also proclaimed his willingness to seek agreements that would respect the 'territorial integrity' of each East European state and 'move beyond the issues of the past'.[1]

Although these challenges to established revisionist dogmas were still relatively vague, considerably more explicit rhetoric soon began to emanate from the government. Chancellor Brandt, for example, declared in the spring of 1970 that 'the Federal Republic has no territorial demands whatsoever'.[2] Moving beyond mere rhetoric, the Social–Liberal Coalition also quickly took a series of concrete policy steps that demonstrated its changed attitude towards the expellee question and Ostpolitik. In a symbolically significant move, it abolished the Expellee Ministry and transferred the relevant tasks to the Ministry of the Interior, thus signalling that it viewed the expellee problem as a matter of domestic policy alone. It also significantly scaled back the personal and institutional ties that previous governments had maintained to the expellee lobby.

To be sure, the bridges were by no means completely burnt. The Social–Liberal

---

[1] Brandt's government declaration, *AdG* v. 4881, 4889.
[2] Brandt in *Parteitag der Sozialdemokratischen Partei Deutschlands vom 11. bis 14. Mai 1970 in Saarbrücken* (Bonn: SPD, 1970), 470.

Coalition continued to allow sizeable subsidies to flow to the various expellee organizations, but the total amounts were cut back.[3] It also kept up the tradition of consultative meetings between key ministers and government officials and expellee representatives. However, from the early 1970s on such meetings occurred less frequently than in previous years, and their tone and content also altered. Government representatives were now much less willing to engage in elaborate dialogues about the expellee lobby's favourite legal concepts, and they typically no longer hesitated to describe the government's true political objectives in clear terms. Foreign Minister Scheel, for example, told a BdV delegation in the early summer of 1970 that 'a regulation of the border question [could] not be avoided' any longer and that the Federal Republic therefore intended to give formal expression to its 'acceptance of the existing situation'.[4]

The government's new priorities became even clearer once its concrete policies towards Eastern Europe began to take shape. The search for a comprehensive modus vivendi started swiftly, as Bonn dispatched special envoys to the Soviet Union and Poland in the first weeks of 1970. Intensive and complicated negotiations then ensued, paralleled by first feelers between the Federal Republic and the GDR about the possibility of bilateral political relations and by initial talks among the victorious Second World War Allies about a new regulation for Berlin. By the autumn of 1970, the West German efforts had paid off, as the bargaining with the Soviets and the Poles yielded the two agreements that became the cornerstone of Bonn's new Ostpolitik: the Moscow and Warsaw Treaties. In the Moscow Treaty with the Soviet Union, signed in mid-August, both the West Germans and the Soviets pledged to pursue peace in Europe, not to raise territorial demands against anyone now or in the future, and to regard the existing borders of all European states, including those of Poland and the GDR, as 'inviolable'. The Warsaw Treaty of December 1970 repeated similar commitments on the bilateral Polish–West German level, stressing in particular Bonn's recognition of the Oder-Neisse line as Poland's western border.[5] Taken together, the two agreements marked a radical shift in the Federal Republic's Eastern policy, as the country now officially recognized the territorial status quo of post-1945 Europe, which it had consistently questioned, at least rhetorically, throughout previous decades.

Admittedly, the West Germans still held on to some key reservations. A separate note handed to the Soviets stressed that the Moscow Treaty did not contradict the ultimate goal of German unity, and in its official interpretation of the Warsaw Treaty the Bonn government insisted that it could speak only for the

---

[3] BdV financial records, BA: B 234/527. The subsidies were rooted in the 1953 Federal Expellee Law.

[4] Schwarzer, 'Kurzprotokoll über das Gespräch mit dem Bundesaussenminister anlässlich des Arbeitsessens am 3. Juni 1970', BA: NL 397/55.

[5] AdG vi. 5219–523, 5310–19. See also Benno Zündorf, *Die Ostverträge: Die Verträge von Moskau, Prag, das Berlin-Abkommen und die Verträge mit der DDR* (Munich: Beck, 1979); Günter Schmid, *Entscheidung in Bonn: Die Entstehung der Ost- und Deutschlandpolitik 1969/70* (Cologne: Wissenschaft und Politik, 1979); M. E. Sarotte, *Dealing with the Devil: East Germany, Detente and Ostpolitik, 1969–1973* (Chapel Hill, NC: University of North Carolina Press, 2001).

Federal Republic, not for a reunified Germany.[6] But such provisos could not belie the fact that the new agreements made future challenges to the territorial status quo extremely unlikely and thus delivered a direct slap to those who had set their sights on such moves, chief among them the leadership cadres of the expellee organizations.

The expellee activists were acutely aware of the troubles they now faced. The outcome of the 1969 election had already provoked sharp concern among the expellee elites, and the fears intensified when the party-political make-up of the new cabinet confirmed the activists' worst fears. As a result, a growing sense of crisis soon pervaded the main expellee groups. Key leaders sensed not only that the new government's attitude towards them was unprecedentedly cool and detached, but also that 'a large part of the German population' seemed to favour new Eastern policy initiatives and that the expellee lobby's position was therefore growing increasingly 'difficult'.[7] However, although a vocal minority of activists called for innovative concepts that would enable the expellee groups to move beyond 'reactive' stances, in reality the organizations again failed to adjust to the new circumstances and instead largely carried on with their old slogans, much as they had in the 1960s.[8]

At first, most key activists stressed the need to remain non-partisan and to build 'loyal relations' to the new government, seemingly oblivious to the fact that their openly biased stances during the 1969 election campaign had severely undermined the viability of that strategy.[9] Nevertheless, the expellee lobby toed a cautious line for the first few months of the new regime, avoiding radical rhetoric and seeking close personal contacts to the government, while at the same time expressing strong displeasure about such developments as the abolition of the Expellee Ministry, the loosening of personal ties between the government and the expellee lobby, and especially Bonn's new political accents towards Eastern Europe and the GDR.[10]

In the first months of 1970, this relatively moderate pose faded away, as key activists realized that the government intended to proceed with its Ostpolitik regardless of their interventions. As a result, the expellee groups switched to an increasingly confrontational and polemical stance. By April, the umbrella group BdV condemned the government's initiatives towards Poland as nothing short of a 'betrayal' of the Germans' 'rights to self-determination and to the homeland'.[11] Angry rhetoric and fiery protest rallies followed over the spring and the summer,

---

[6] *AdG* vi. 5234, 5317–18.

[7] President Rehs in the BdV presidium, 27 Nov. 1969, SDA: NL Becher, 193.

[8] See e.g. Guillaume and Homeier in 'Niederschrift über die Präsidialsitzung des BdV', 27 Nov. 1969, SDA: NL Becher, 193, p. 4.

[9] Walter Becher in the Bundesvorstand of the Sudetendeutsche Landsmannschaft, 'Niederschrift über die 12. Sitzung des IV Bundesvorstandes', 22 Nov. 1969, SDA: NL Becher, 205.

[10] 'Unklar und unzulänglich: President Rehs zur Regierungserklärung', *DoD* (29 Oct. 1969); Walter Becher's speech for the Sudetendeutsche Landsmannschaft's Bundesversammlung, 29 Nov. 1969, SDA: Arbeitsgemeinschaft zur Wahrung sudetendeutscher Interessen, Box 4.

[11] BdV *Bundesvorstand* resolution, 26 Apr. 1970, *DoD* (30 April 1970).

and in the autumn the main expellee organizations rushed to reject both the Moscow and Warsaw Treaties. According to the BdV's published pronouncements, the agreement with Poland was a dangerous *diktat* whose glorification of so-called 'existing facts' undermined the cause of peace and justice and thereby reflected a crude power-political attitude characteristic of 'Hitler and Stalin'.[12]

Despite their moral fervour in rejecting the government's policies, the expellee groups failed to produce credible alternatives. In a bull-headed fashion, they instead kept repeating their old maxims about the power of justice to overcome all problems in post-war Europe, provided that the *Heimatrecht* and the right to self-determination received the attention they deserved.[13] The underlying agenda remained as revisionist and navel-gazing as ever, however, as the activists stubbornly refused to bow to the realities even on the most untenable planks of their traditional platforms. Particularly absurd was the zeal with which the Sudeten Germans kept producing planning memoranda that described the Munich Agreement as 'valid' and insisted that 'the national affiliation of the Sudeten territory' remained an 'open question'.[14] Such arguments were worthless in the détente-oriented international context of the early 1970s, and even the minor additions that the expellee groups did make to their publicly proclaimed programmes ultimately served to underscore their inability to adapt to the altered circumstances in a meaningful way.

These minor additions comprised three specific items that began to appear in expellee pronouncements with increasing frequency, each of them ultimately aimed at hindering the progress of the Social–Liberal Coalition's Ostpolitik. The least important was an occasional suggestion that Bonn should press claims for material compensation against Poland and Czechoslovakia for the damages caused by the expulsions.[15] While this item remained marginal, in large part because of many activists' fears that a more extensive discussion of 'material claims' could be misconstrued to denote the expellee lobby's 'passive resignation to the Oder-Neisse border', another point rose to greater prominence: the current position of German minorities in Eastern Europe, particularly Poland.[16] Although they had paid some attention to this issue for years, particularly since it had been highlighted by the Jaksch Report of 1961, the expellee groups truly warmed to it once the Polish–West German negotiations got under way. The activists dismissed as insufficient any advances made in the talks, including the unilateral assurances about better emigration possibilities and other improvements ultimately issued by the Poles.[17]

The most important new item in the expellee rhetoric of the early 1970s was a

---

[12] 'Das Warschauer Diktat', *DoD* (27 Nov. 1969).

[13] See the resolutions in Blumenthal and Fassbender, *Erklärungen*, i. 173–221.

[14] 'Stellungnahme zur Prolematik der Sudetendeutschen (Unterlagen für ein Gespräch mit der Bundesregierung)', SDA: Arbeitsgemeinschaft zur Wahrung sudetendeutscher Interessen, Box 4.

[15] BdV resolution in *DoD* (17 Mar. 1972), p. 10.

[16] Gossing in the BdV's geschäftsführendes Präsidium, 20 Nov. 1969, SDA: NL Becher, 193.

[17] Zündorf, *Ostverträge*, 72–3; Blumenthal and Fassbender, *Erklärungen*, i. 201, 213, 219–20.

vague legal construct, developed by expellee scholars during the previous decade and labelled 'ethnic group rights' (*Volksgruppenrecht*). This highly elastic term, which was to become a staple of expellee discourse in subsequent years, described the rights which national minorities and other ethnic groups ideally should enjoy in an enlightened pan-European order. They included an updated version of the *Heimatrecht*—which could have enabled large numbers of expellees to return to their old homelands—as well as extensive self-determination, through which the expellees could ultimately have assumed control of the areas and perhaps even reannexed them to Germany.[18] Underneath the seemingly high-minded rhetorical packaging, even this apparent innovation was thus directly rooted in the expellee lobby's long-standing revisionist dreams.

The inability to adjust to new political realities was only one major problem plaguing the' expellee groups. A closely related obstacle was their growing isolation, manifest in a severe shortage of potential political allies. During the new coalition's first months in office, expellee leaders increasingly began to label the two governing parties as outright enemies, and subsequent internal BdV documents identified the start of the Social–Liberal period as the 'breaking point' in the expellee lobby's relations with the SPD and the FDP.[19] Some of the hostility was soon reciprocated by key Social and Free Democrats, as Willy Brandt, among others, stressed the need to prevent 'restorative elements' from pushing 'the government . . . and the party' into an Ostpolitik 'defensive'.[20] At the same time, however, the main expellee groups continued to exclude the option of an alliance with the right-wing radical end of the party-political spectrum, including the NPD. Although individual functionaries were still involved both in this party and in other right-wing circles, the main expellee organizations carefully distanced themselves from political extremism, in part because of tactical calculations based on the general weakness of right-wing forces but in large part also because of genuine democratic convictions.[21]

With the left-liberal and right-wing radical segments of the political spectrum thus excluded, the expellee lobby increasingly placed its hopes in the only remaining potential ally of significance: the CDU/CSU. Unfortunately for the expellees, the party found itself in a deep crisis at the start of the 1970s. After two decades as *the* key governing force in the Federal Republic, the Christian Democrats had suddenly been relegated to the unfamiliar role of the parliamentary opposition. Reeling from this unexpected shock, the party struggled to find its bearings and to settle on a political strategy for the immediate future, a task that was complicated by abstruse factional divisions and byzantine leadership rivalries within its

---

[18] Sudetendeutscher Rat (ed.), *Referate zum Volksgruppenrecht* (Munich: Sudetendeutscher Rat, 1970); Salzborn, *Heimatrecht*, 30–57; id., *Grenzenlose*, 68–71.

[19] Herbert Schwarzer, 'Der BdV im vorparlamentarischen Raum', 17 May 1972, BA: B 234, 404.

[20] Brandt in the SPD's Bundestagsfraktion, 25 May 1970, AdsD: BT-Fraktion, 6. WP, 31.

[21] BdV, 'Abschlussbericht über die Kundgebung des Bundes der Vertriebenen am 7. Mai 1972 auf dem Marktplatz in Bonn', BA: B 234, 404; 'Klare Abgrenzung: BdV lehnt Unterstützung durch radikale Kräfte ab', *DoD* (16 May 1972).

ranks. Although such conflicts were partly rooted in enduring tensions between the Atlanticist and Gaullist factions of the 1960s, they also reflected the wide-spread sense within the CDU/CSU that the new government, with its razor-thin majority of a mere twelve Bundestag seats, would not survive long and that renewed ministerial opportunities would soon open up for those who prevailed in the party's internal scuffles.[22]

To make these dreams come true, the Christian Democrats needed to challenge the ruling coalition's policies, and in that endeavour Ostpolitik seemed to offer excellent prospects. Many of the party's key figures were genuinely sceptical of the government's new stances towards the Eastern bloc—particularly its willingness to pursue a *de facto* recognition of the GDR—and were therefore eager to take the offensive on this front. But, as in previous decades, instrumental domestic policy considerations also played a crucial motivating role. The CDU/CSU's leadership cadres regarded 'confrontation' on Ostpolitik issues as desirable for 'reasons of domestic policy'.[23] With this approach, the party could hope to strengthen its public profile, appeal to conservatively minded voters, including many expellees, and draw away residual support from the declining NPD—considerations that ex-Chancellor Kiesinger portrayed as 'a great chance for us' in his party's internal deliberations.[24]

Accordingly, the CDU/CSU responded to the opening moves of Social–Liberal Ostpolitik in the first half of 1970 with repeated public criticism, accusing the government of an excessive willingness to concede to Eastern bloc demands.[25] At the same time, the Christian Democrats also made extensive attempts to court the expellee lobby, both rhetorically—with statements supportive of such standard demands as the deferral of an eastern border settlement until a peace treaty—and more concretely, with consultative meetings and special public events aimed at demonstrating the party's continued loyalty to the expellee organizations.[26]

Most expellee leaders reacted to the CDU/CSU's overtures with enthusiasm. They praised the Christian Democrats' 'decisive' opposition to the new Ostpolitik. A particularly passionate attack by the CSU's Baron zu Guttenberg against the government's policies even inspired a leading BdV functionary to

---

[22] Christian Hacke, *Die Ost- und Deutschlandpolitik der CDU/CSU: Wege und Irrwege der Opposition seit 1969* (Cologne: Wissenschaft und Politik, 1975); Clay Clemens, *Reluctant Realists: The Christian Democrats and West German Ostpolitik* (Durham, NC: Duke University Press); Anselm Tiggemann, *Die CDU/CSU und die Ost- und Deutschlandpolitik 1969–72: Zur 'Innenpolitik der Aussenpolitik' der ersten Regierung Brandt/Scheel* (Frankfurt: Peter Lang, 1998); Michael Lemke, *CDU/CSU und Vertragspolitik der Bundesrepublik Deutschland in den Jahren 1969–1975* (Saarbrücken: Dadder, 1992); Oppelland, ' "Ostpolitiker" ', 86–94.

[23] Alfred Dregger in the CDU/CSU's *Bundesvorstand*, 23 Jan. 1970, ACDP: VII-001-331/7 (alte Signatur), 18.

[24] Kiesinger in the CDU/CSU *Bundesvorstand*, 23 Apr. 1970, ACDP: VII-001-331/9 (alte Signatur), 85.

[25] CDU/CSU, 'Grosse Anfrage betreffend Deutschland-, Ost- und Europapolitik', 27 Apr. 1970; 'Resolution der CDU/CSU Bundestagsfraktion zur Ost- und Deutschlandpolitik', 26–7 May 1970, *DzD* vi. 232–7, 292–3.

[26] 'BdV beim CDU Präsidium', AdsD: BT-Fraktion, 6. WP, Altsignatur 690 (A); 'Ver-triebenenkongress der CSU', *DuD/DHDF* (8 Sept. 1970).

compare the speech in question to that of 'Emil Zola in defence of Dreyfus'.[27] But the expellee activists were not fully contented. They complained about the continued exclusion of expellee politicians from the party's key decision-making centres and questioned the true loyalty of a range of CDU/CSU politicians.[28] Most importantly, they left no doubt about what they ultimately expected from the Christian Democrats: the use of 'all constitutional means' to stop the government's Eastern policy.[29] More specifically, expellee activists demanded a 'clear and united' rejection of the Moscow and Warsaw treaties by the CDU/CSU in the federal parliament.[30] From the expellee elites' perspective, the ratification of these two agreements, due to begin in the Bundestag in early 1972, thus became not only the decisive battle in their rearguard fight against the new Ostpolitik but also the litmus test of the loyalty of their lone remaining parliamentary ally.

With their blinkered view of the situation, the expellee activists failed to realize how complicated the broader political context surrounding Ostpolitik had grown by 1972. Several further agreements had by then become linked to the Moscow and Warsaw Treaties, chief among them the Quadripartite Agreement on Berlin, signed by the four victorious Second World War Allies in September 1971, as well as a handful of smaller agreements on practical communication issues reached between the two German states. In addition, a series of long-term trade treaties between the Federal Republic and the East European countries, including the Soviet Union, had been concluded since late 1969, and formal discussions about a far-reaching normalization pact between West and East Germany were well under way.[31] As a result, the outcome of the ratification process in the Bundestag had far-reaching international and domestic implications. A parliamentary rejection of the two agreements that formed the cornerstone of the new Ostpolitik would have jeopardized all these recent advances vis-à-vis the Eastern bloc. In particular, it would have risked an unpredictable crisis with the Soviet Union and endangered the implementation of the new Berlin regulation, thereby crushing all hope of a modus vivendi with the East Germans. Even more ominously, it could also have done unforeseeable damage to the Federal Republic's international standing, particularly as the new Eastern policy had begun to enjoy widespread recognition as a crucial part of détente, not least among Bonn's own allies in the West.[32]

From a domestic perspective, an attempt to reject the Moscow and Warsaw Treaties appeared equally dubious. Opinion polls showed solid, and growing, support for the Social–Liberal Eastern policy throughout the early 1970s. By the

---

[27] Herbert Czaja's 3 April 1970 radio address; ALdO: Parteien und Abgeordnete, 1.9.69–28.2.70; Domes to Guttenberg, 27 May 1970, BA: NL 397/131, p. 227.

[28] Czaja to Heck, 29 July 1970, BA: NL 397/55, pp. 218–25; Döring to Barzel, 23 May 1970, ACDP: I-094-037/2.

[29] Czaja's 3 Apr. 1970 radio address (n. 27).

[30] 'Vertriebene setzen auf Barzel—Sie erwarten von der CDU/CSU geschlossene Ablehnung der Ostverträge', *Osmipress*, 10 Oct. 1971, BA: B 234, 401.

[31] Kreile, *Osthandel*, 115–42; Stent, *Embargo*, 154–91; Zündorf, *Ostverträge*, 117–75, 176–210.

[32] Baring, *Machtwechsel*; Bingen, *Polenpolitik*; Fuchs, *Dreiecksverhältnisse*; Sarotte, *Dealing*.

spring of 1972 less than 20 per cent of the population opposed the two treaties, which would have made a negative vote on them a risky enterprise for any democratic party.[33] In addition, the opposition's chances of finding a Bundestag majority against the agreements were unclear. True, from late 1970 on, the governing coalition had been steadily losing its parliamentary majority, as a string of SPD and FDP deputies, several of them expellees upset about the government's Eastern policy record, defected to the CDU/CSU. In April 1972 the departure of one more FDP politician made the stalemate complete: the CDU/CSU opposition now held exactly the same number of Bundestag seats as the governing coalition. In addition, several more deputies of the governing parties—particularly of the FDP— were known to harbour serious reservations about the new Ostpolitik.[34]

Despite all this, however, the Christian Democrats ultimately stood on shaky ground in the parliament. The political balances were fluid, and the ultimate voting behaviour of several deputies, even those of the CDU/CSU, remained unpredictable. The party learnt a bitter lesson in this regard in late April 1972 as it sought to overthrow the Social–Liberal Coalition through a parliamentary vote of no confidence, only to lose by two votes.[35] An attempt to reject the Eastern treaties could well have culminated in a similar humiliation, which made an already hazardous policy option seem all the more unappealing. The CDU/CSU's leaders were well aware of these potential pitfalls. Behind the scenes, the key figures— particularly the moderates clustered around the CDU's top man, party chair Rainer Barzel—therefore stressed the 'extraordinary importance' of the ratification process, exhorting their party colleagues to avoid a rush to judgement and to consider the broad domestic and international context.[36]

But along with external realities at home and abroad, the Christian Democrats also had to juggle with conflicting pressures inside the party. On the one hand, the CDU, and especially the CSU, contained a sizeable group of devoted opponents of the new Ostpolitik in general and the Moscow and Warsaw Treaties in particular. These hard-liners, many of whom were at least loosely affiliated with the expellee organizations, still had their main power base in the CDU/CSU's parliamentary group in the Bundestag. Their position was further strengthened by the arrival of several similarly minded defectors from the SPD and the FDP in the months preceding the ratification debates. To be sure, the direct influence of these uncompromising Ostpolitik opponents on top-level decision-making within the CDU/CSU still remained limited, as expellee politicians' persistent complaints about a perceived political exclusion testify.[37] But the hard-liners did manage to propagate their views to the party and to the

---

[33] Noelle and Neumann, *Jahrbuch der öffentlichen Meinung 1968–1973*, 573; Glaab, *Deutschlandpolitik*, 241–5; Jansen, *Meinungsbilder*, 148–55.

[34] Baring, *Machtwechsel*, 297–302, 405–10.

[35] Ibid. 396–424.

[36] Gradl to Barzel, 22 Nov. 1971, ACDP: I-294/054-1; Gerhard Schröder, 'Die CDU/CSU und der Moskauer Vertrag', 21 Aug. 1970, ACDP: I-483-176/3.

[37] Protocols of the CDU/CSU parliamentary group's Arbeitskreis V, 24 Feb. 1970, ACDP: VIII-006-002/1.

general public through the parliamentary group and its suborgans, and their influence manifested itself indirectly, as the moderates in charge of the Christian Democrats had to placate this faction in order to avoid open splits within the party.[38] In many ways Barzel and the other top leaders of the early 1970s were thus footing the bill for their predecessors' zeal in integrating expellee representatives into the CDU/CSU.

At the same time, the CDU/CSU also faced strong countervailing pressures from pro-Ostpolitik elements inside the party. Christian groups, youth organizations, and even numerous expellees disgruntled with their political lobby urged the party to back the Eastern policy treaties, typically with arguments that stressed Germany's moral duties towards victims of Nazi aggression.[39] Similar calls also emanated from a vocal group of top-level Christian Democratic politicians, including the future federal president Richard von Weizsäcker.[40] As these internal impulses merged with the powerful external pressures in favour of the new Ostpolitik, the CDU/CSU's central leadership around party chair Rainer Barzel ultimately had little choice but to allow the Moscow and Warsaw Treaties to be approved. The pursuit of this path required a good deal of juggling and tactical finesse, however, and as a result the CDU/CSU's switch to an acceptance of the treaties occurred gradually over the span of some eighteen months.

The first signs of change appeared as soon as the Moscow and Warsaw Treaties took shape in the autumn of 1970. Whereas the CDU/CSU's stances towards the new government's Eastern policy had been very critical until then, a somewhat more nuanced—and thoroughly contradictory—position now emerged. The Christian Democrats continued their general attacks against Social–Liberal Ostpolitik, typically denouncing it as naively soft towards the Soviet Union, while keeping their future options open by avoiding clarity about what concrete changes were needed. At the same time, the CDU/CSU had to react to the specific agreements, which it did in contradictory double talk. In response to the Warsaw Treaty, for example, the party affirmed its desire for reconciliation, stressing 'the right of the Poles to secure borders', while at the same time casting doubt on these sentiments by loudly repeating the cliché that 'the final regulation of Germany's borders' had to await a future 'peace treaty', which hardly rang assuringly to Polish ears.[41] With this approach, the Christian Democrats locked themselves into a highly ambivalent posture of delay, no longer fully opposed to the new Ostpolitik but wary of concrete commitments about their future course.

The next shift in the party's position became noticeable with the beginning of the Bundestag debates about the ratification of the Moscow and Warsaw Treaties in February 1972. Under the pressure of the unfolding parliamentary proceedings,

[38] Clemens, *Reluctant*, 62–4, 315; Hacke, *Deutschlandpolitik*, 75–6.

[39] See the letters by Societas Populorum Progressio (30 Apr. 1972, SDA: NL Becher, 365) and Hans Habenich (22 Oct. 1970, ACDP: VIII-006-010/1) to the CDU/CSU's parliamentary group.

[40] Weizsäcker in the CDU/CSU's Bundesvorstand, 23 Jan. 1970, ACDP: VII-001-331/7 (alte Signatur), esp. 25–6; report by Dichgans and Petersen of a trip to Poland, 28 May 1970; ACDP: I-483-175/1.

[41] CDU/CSU Bundestagsfraktion resolution, 25 Nov. 1970, DzD vi. 547.

CDU/CSU chairman Rainer Barzel made his party's Eastern policy line more explicit: although they disliked the treaties in their current form, the Christian Democrats might approve them with specific adjustments, aimed primarily at reassuring the Federal Republic's links to the West and its continued right to pursue reunification with the GDR.[42] With this new stance, the CDU/CSU had taken a major step towards a conditional acceptance of the Moscow and Warsaw agreements, and in the ensuing months key figures kept nudging the party further down the same road. By early May 1972 the switch was complete: Barzel and his associates now pressed for a positive CDU/CSU vote in the Bundestag, particularly after the opposition and the coalition had jointly hammered out a ten-point joint resolution, intended to be passed in conjunction with the two treaties. The resolution accommodated most key demands recently raised by the CDU/CSU, including the proviso that the treaties in no way prejudiced the final regulation of reunified Germany's borders in a future peace settlement.[43]

Armed with this document, Barzel managed to secure his party's consent to the government's Ostpolitik, although not in the form that he desired. While the party chair still pressed for a 'yes' vote by the entire CDU/CSU, a group of hardliners spearheaded by expellee activists refused to obey him, and as a result the Christian Democrats ultimately fell back on an inelegant face-saving formula intended to mask their internal divisions: abstention. Accordingly, the vast majority of CDU/CSU deputies abstained in the final vote on the Moscow and Warsaw Treaties in mid-May, with the result that both documents passed with a comfortable margin, as did the accompanying joint resolution, which received nearly unanimous support from all parties. A few days later, the CDU/CSU also failed to block the agreements in the Bundesrat, the upper house of parliament, although it held a majority there at the time.[44]

As a result, the Moscow and Warsaw Treaties came into force by early June 1972, watered down somewhat by the joint resolution adopted by the Bundestag, but still clear in their recognition of the territorial status quo of post-Second World War Europe. The passive backing of the Christian Democrats had been crucial for their ratification, and once the treaties had come into force, the opposition's acceptance of them became increasingly explicit. In one representative statement, issued a few months after the ratification vote, the CSU's Franz Josef Strauss clarified the opposition's viewpoint by declaring: 'The treaties with Moscow and Warsaw are indisputably valid. There is no alternative to them anymore.'[45]

For the expellee lobby, the outcome of the ratification process was a 'heavy blow', to quote the BdV president.[46] The Christian Democrats, too, had now failed the organizations, and in the aftermath of the ratification vote the expellee

---

[42] Barzel in the Bundestag, 23 Feb. 1972, *DzD* vii. 454–69.

[43] Baring, *Machtwechsel*, 438–40.

[44] Ibid. 427–47; Tiggemann, *CDU/CSU*, 91–137.

[45] Strauss in the Bundestag, 24 Jan. 1973, quoted in Tiggemann, *CDU/CSU*, 134.

[46] Herbert Czaja, quoted in 'Schwerer Rückschlag', *DoD* (31 May 1972).

elites repeatedly vented their 'disappointment and bitterness' with the CDU/CSU in general and Barzel and other party moderates in particular.[47] The activists' anger reflected the fact that the events of May 1972 marked the definitive end of an era. After some two decades as a major background force in the formulation of West German Ostpolitik, the expellee organizations had now lost their grip not only on the government but on the opposition as well. They could no longer count on any of the Federal Republic's major political forces to back their fully anachronistic revisionist agenda, although the full confirmation of that fact would be slow in coming. The long twilight of the activists' dream of reacquiring the old *Heimat* would endure nearly two more decades, to be ended only by the final reunification settlement of 1990/1.

In the aftermath of the ratification debacle of 1972, the expellee elites still stubbornly refused to face this reality, however. While acknowledging in private that they faced major problems, including growing 'resignation' among rank-and-file followers, the activists insisted on pressing forward without major changes of direction.[48] According to the standard argument, repeated time and again by leading figures, 'everything' was constantly 'in flux' in politics, which meant that 'the last word' about Germany's future had 'not yet been spoken'.[49] The task of the expellees therefore remained 'to keep our courage up and to continue to fight for the *Heimatrecht* and the right to self-determination', with the hope that the Eastern policy treaties could be revised in the future.[50]

For the pursuit of these aims, the expellee lobby still needed political allies, but its options were now more limited than ever. Concerted cooperation with right-wing extremists remained unacceptable for the mainstream expellee groups, and close links to the governing parties could not be rebuilt either, particularly as the coalition pressed on with its established policies towards the East. Fortified by its resounding victory in the Bundestag elections of November 1972, which gave it a majority of thirty-six seats over the CDU/CSU opposition, the government proceeded to sign and ratify two more major agreements: the Basic Treaty with the GDR in December 1972 and the Prague Treaty with Czechoslovakia a year later. Both were anathema to the expellee lobby: the Basic Treaty because it gave East Germany *de facto* recognition as a sovereign state and the Prague Treaty because it declared the Munich Agreement of 1938 'invalid', renounced all territorial claims against Czechoslovakia, and failed to address the expulsions.[51]

Under these circumstances, the CDU/CSU was still the only political option

---

[47] Von Braun to Stücklen, 28 June 1972, SDA: NL Becher, 63; Rudolf Wollner, 'Spricht die CDU mit zwei Zungen?', *DoD* (31 May 1972); Becher to Strauss, 25 May 1972, ADL: N47-83.

[48] Protocols of the Sudetendeutsche Landsmannschaft's *Bundesvorstand*, 10 June 1972, SDA: NL Becher, 212; Schwarzer, 'Der BdV im vorparlamentarischen Raum', 17 May 1972, BA: B 234, 404, p. 3.

[49] Schwarzer's 17 May 1972 memorandum (n. 48); Herbert Hupka, 'Der Auftrag bleibt!', *DoD* (30 June 1972).

[50] 'Die Ostverträge müssen revidiert werden!', *Osmipress* (1 May 1972), BA: B 234, 404.

[51] 'Schwere Bedrohung der Nation!', *DoD* (10 Nov. 1972); 'Der Bund der Vertriebenen lehnt den Prager Vertrag ab', *DoD* (13 Dec. 1973); Zündorf, *Ostverträge*, 211–319, 96–111; Jakobsmeier, 'Münchener'.

left for the expellee groups. Despite their disappointment with the party's recent actions, the expellee activists nevertheless found reason to have faith in the Christian Democrats. Many observed that the CSU, as well as certain conservative circles in the CDU, had been supportive of most expellee demands even during the lobby's recent tribulations.[52] The organizations also valued the joint declaration that the Bundestag had passed in conjunction with its approval of the Moscow and Warsaw Treaties in May 1972. Activists described the document as 'a good starting point for a future policy' and credited the Christian Democrats for incorporating into it the proviso that the final determination of Germany's eastern borders could only occur in a future peace settlement.[53]

The CDU/CSU also scored further points through its subsequent behaviour towards the expellee groups. Unlike the SPD and the FDP, the Christian Democrats kept stressing their intention to continue to 'stand by' the expellee organizations.[54] They invited key activists to consultations in which top party leaders explained away their Ostpolitik switches as responses to external necessities while claiming full credit for the important improvements allegedly contained in the joint declaration of the Bundestag.[55] More importantly, the public rhetoric of the Christian Democrats remained much more supportive of the expellee lobby's Eastern policy agenda than did that of the governing parties. To be sure, the CDU/CSU, too, sounded much more circumspect than in previous decades, cautioned by the fundamentally different political situation and by powerful forces within its ranks that pushed for a switch from 'outdated positions to a more realistic view of the situation'.[56] But the party continued to target the expellee lobby with several carefully measured stock phrases that, with slightly altering emphases, would remain central to its Ostpolitik diction for nearly two decades, all the way to reunification in 1989/90.

On the one hand, the CDU/CSU underscored its political maturity and responsibility by calling for a reconciliation with the Eastern bloc countries and reiterating its commitment to the Ostpolitik treaties. But on the other hand it relativized these statements by praising the joint Bundestag declaration of 1972 as a document of fundamental importance. More specifically, the party highlighted the principle of 'open options' (*Offenhalten*), declaring time and again that the 'German question', including the determination of the nation's ultimate frontiers, had to be kept open until a future peace settlement.[57] With this vague general stance, the Christian Democrats hoped to give something to everyone: reassurances to those concerned about the CDU/CSU's earlier hard-line

---

[52] Rudolf Wollner, 'Spricht die CDU mit zwei Zungen?', *DoD* (31 May 1972).

[53] Herbert Hupka, 'Der Auftrag bleibt!', *DoD* (30 June 1972).

[54] Barzel to Becher, 12 June 1972, SDA: NL Becher, 242.

[55] Riedel's protocol of the CDU–BdV meeting, 26 June 1972, ACDP: I-094-047/1; 'Erneute Beratungen zwischen CDU/CSU und BdV', *DoD* (29 Sept. 1972).

[56] Gradl to Kraske, 4 July 1972, ACDP: I-294-081/1.

[57] 'Regierungsprogramm der CDU/CSU für Vertriebene und Flüchtlinge', 17 Sept. 1972, ALdO: Parteien, Abegeordnete, 1.3.71–31.8.72; 'Erneute Beratungen zwischen CDU/CSU und BdV', *DoD* (29 Sept. 1972).

pronouncements, guarded hope to those eager to view the party as a continued guardian of revisionist interests, and ample room for interpretation for anyone willing to give the party the benefit of the doubt from any angle at all.

While the CDU generally contented itself with these verbal acrobatics, its Bavarian sibling CSU—whose ties to the expellee groups in general and the Sudeten Germans in particular were especially close—took the continued courting of the expellee lobby several steps further. Acting through the Bavarian state government, which it held in a secure one-party grip, it intervened repeatedly with Bonn's authorities on behalf of the Sudeten-German Homeland Society during the Czech–West German talks that culminated in the Prague Treaty of 1973. Although the efforts made very little practical difference, they did evoke a good deal of gratitude among the Sudeten German activists, as did the CDU/CSU's solid opposition to the Prague Treaty during its parliamentary ratification in 1974.[58] Even more successful was the Bavarian government's attempt to challenge the constitutionality of the Basic Treaty with the GDR in the Federal Constitutional Court. After expellee leaders had failed to persuade the CDU/CSU to present such a challenge to the Moscow and Warsaw Treaties, the Bavarians stepped into the breach in the spring of 1973, motivated in part by instrumental calculations about expellees and other nationalists but even more by genuine concerns about the Basic Treaty's implications for the goal of German unity.[59] Although the court's 31 July 1973 decision upheld the treaty's constitutionality, it also provided new ammunition for expellee revisionists by suggesting—in very complex and confusing language—that, from a legal standpoint at least, the German Reich still continued to exist within its 1937 borders.[60]

With all this activity, the CDU/CSU managed to charm the expellee elites. Although their trust in leading politicians had been shaken, for lack of better alternatives the main expellee groups nevertheless linked themselves to the CDU/CSU.[61] While still officially non-partisan, the organizations grew increasingly distant from the governing parties after 1972, with ever more tenuous personal and political links, although governmental subsidies continued to flow into their coffers. For all practical purposes, the expellee groups had by this time become non-partisan in name only. In functional terms, they increasingly resembled right-wing extra-parliamentary auxiliaries of the CDU/CSU, with an extensive overlap in leadership personnel and superficial political rhetoric, albeit with vast differences in ultimate political objectives, particularly in Eastern policy. In

---

[58] Correspondence among Becher, Bavarian Minister President Goppel, and Bonn's Foreign Ministry, SDA: NL Becher, 370.

[59] Johann Baptist Gradl's diary markings, ACDP: I-294-055/1.

[60] Zündorf, *Ostverträge*, 310–19; Karlheinz Niclauss, *Kontroverse Deutschlandpolitik* (Frankfurt: Metzner, 1977), 103–14; Garton Ash, *Europe's Name*, 223–4. A subsequent appeal by individual expellees against the Moscow and Warsaw Treaties produced another decision by the court on 7 July 1975. Expellee activists cheered the decision because it maintained that the two agreements in no way reduced individual citizenship, property, and other rights. See *DzD* x. 404.

[61] Schlesier Verein München to Strauss, 15 June 1973, ACSP: NL Schuchart, 93; 'Die Ausgangslage vor der Wahl', *DoD* (29 Sept. 1972).

this general political situation, the expellee activists had only one remaining source of hope for a realization of their Ostpolitik goals: a change of government that would catapult the CDU/CSU back into power and lead to a drastic shift in the Federal Republic's attitudes towards Eastern Europe. With this dream at the backs of their minds, the expellee elites endured the rest of 1970s and early 1980s, awaiting the end of the Social–Liberal era.

THE KOHL ERA

The hour of change ultimately struck in October 1982, as the CDU/CSU enticed the Free Democrats to swap their partnership with the SPD for a new conservative–liberal coalition spearheaded by the CDU's Helmut Kohl as Chancellor and the FDP's Hans-Dietrich Genscher as Foreign Minister. The expellee organizations cheered the power switch in Bonn, their joy tempered only by the inclusion of the detested FDP in the new cabinet. The activists had high expectations for the future; they hoped for a new, tougher approach towards Eastern Europe that would keep Germany's options open and help to pave the way for at least a partial revision of the territorial status quo.[62] In the event, however, the organizations were headed for a 'big . . . disappointment', to quote the subsequent judgement of a key Sudeten German leader.[63] The Kohl era would culminate not in a return to the old eastern *Heimat* but in a formal renunciation of Bonn's claims to these lands as the price for German reunification.

In its early phases the conservative–liberal period still looked promising for the expellees, as the government's public pronouncements appeared to set new political emphases towards Eastern Europe and the GDR. The coalition stressed certain issues more than its predecessor, chief among them human freedoms—particularly those of the GDR population, but also those of German minorities further east—and the pursuit of German reunification.[64] Even more interestingly for the expellee lobby, the government also appeared to define the area to be reunified more expansively than its predecessor. Leading members of the CSU in particular distinguished themselves with statements suggestive of a revived West German interest in territorial revisionism. In the most notorious example, federal Interior Minister Friedrich Zimmermann assured a Bavarian expellee audience in early 1983 that 'tendencies to reduce the German question to the Federal Republic and the GDR alone, with the exclusion of the areas beyond the Oder and the Neisse, will not exist under this new government'.[65] Similarly suggestive, albeit much less explicit, rhetoric also issued from key figures in the CDU. Chancellor Kohl himself told another expellee audience in the autumn of 1984 that, although

---

[62] Czaja, *Unterwegs*, 603–10.　　　　　　　　　　　　　[63] Becher, *Zeitzeuge*, 365.
[64] Karl-Rudolf Korte, *Deutschlandpolitik in Helmut Kohls Kanzlerschaft* (Stuttgart: DVA, 1998); Matthias Zimmer, *Nationales Interesse und Staatsräson: Zur Deutschlandpolitik der Regierung Kohl 1982–1989* (Paderborn: Schöningh, 1992); Garton Ash, *Europe's Name*, 230–43.
[65] Zimmermann at a Bavarian BdV meeting, 29 Jan. 1983, *DoD* (3/1983).

the Warsaw Treaty's recognition of Poland's current borders was binding for the Federal Republic, it did not apply to 'a future united Germany'.[66] With such statements, the Christian Democrats set themselves apart not only from the SPD and the other emerging left-wing opposition force of the 1980s—the Greens—but also from their Free Democratic coalition partners, who showed no desire to follow the seemingly neo-revisionist path being blazed by Kohl and his associates.[67]

The appearances created by the CDU/CSU's rhetoric were deceptive, however. Most ranking figures measured their public statements carefully, typically restricting themselves to speculations about Germany's legal options and commitments while steering clear of endorsing any specific revisionist objectives or policies. This deliberately ambiguous language, in turn, fitted into a broader, instrumentalized political strategy. Kohl and the other responsible top-level leaders of the CDU/CSU knew perfectly well that territorial changes in Germany's favour in Eastern Europe were neither possible nor desirable, and at times they carefully hinted at this fact even in public statements, particularly in front of foreign audiences. But in the domestic context the party had other, contradictory needs. The CDU/CSU wanted to retain the nationalistically oriented voters, expellees and others, that it had managed to draw into its orbit during the Social–Liberal years. It also hoped to attract additional similarly minded supporters, many of them potential backers of the Republicans and other threatening far-right entities that appeared to be advancing during the 1980s. In addition, the party needed to maintain unity within its own ranks. Some 15 per cent of its members were expellees, and a sizeable proportion had ended up in the CDU/CSU rather than the other mainstream parties precisely because of its recent Ostpolitik stances.[68] For all these reasons, the Christian Democrats had to create the impression that they intended to deliver on promises made while in opposition. Far from being true revisionists, the CDU/CSU's top leaders were thus captives of their tactical choices, forced to continue their domestically driven political posturing because of the success of their earlier domestically driven political posturing.

This Christian Democratic juggling act was a very delicate enterprise, however. If the party's luminaries were too cautious with the rhetorical Oder-Neisse card, they risked alienating real and potential supporters at home. But if they played their revisionist trump card too boldly, even more serious perils loomed. At home, the Social Democratic opposition was certain to try to cash in on the CDU/CSU's alleged extremism; the bulk of the media would probably react with outrage; and even the FDP could be expected to raise objections from within the cabinet. Abroad, the political, economic and cultural bridges between West Germany and Eastern Europe laboriously constructed through détente might be undermined and stereotypes about aggressive, unreliable Germans reinforced, with unpredictable consequences on both sides of the Iron Curtain.

---

[66] Kohl at a BdV rally, 2 Sept. 1984, in Jacobsen and Tomalka, *Bonn–Warschau*, 368.

[67] On the FDP, see Hans-Dietrich Genscher, *Erinnerungen* (Berlin: Siedler, 1995).

[68] Korte, *Deutschlandpolitik*, 243–64, esp. 250; Bingen, *Polenpolitik*, 221–60; Garton Ash, *Europe's Name*, 216–31.

To counteract these lurking dangers, the Christian Democrats under Kohl stuck to a consistent pattern: while normally avoiding any unnecessary provocations in their Qstpolitik rhetoric, on special occasions, particularly in front of expellee audiences, they resorted to bolder moves. If unusually vehement protests resulted, especially abroad, party leaders retreated with contradictory, vaguely reassuring statements This kind of balancing characterized the entire 1982–9 period, and the danger of matters slipping out of control was always present. However, the situation grew particularly critical on two occasions, and both times Kohl's government adjusted by shifting towards a formal renunciation of all territorial claims. The first key episode unfolded in 1985 around the Chancellor's planned presence at an unexpectedly controversial expellee rally. The second encompassed the prolonged wrangling about the terms of reunification in 1989/90 that culminated in Bonn's official acceptance of reunified Germany's existing borders.

The storm that broke in 1985 actually began to rise in the previous year, when Chancellor Kohl agreed to address a mass rally of the Silesian Homeland Society, scheduled for June 1985. The Chancellor's decision was nothing extraordinary as such—he had already spoken at two major expellee meetings during the autumn of 1984—although it did stand out in comparative terms, as the last chancellor to address any large-scale expellee event had been Ludwig Erhard, nearly two decades previously. What ultimately turned this seemingly routine plan into an embarrassing incident was the confluence of two additional factors. First, the fortieth anniversary of the end of the Second World War was rapidly approaching, which meant that observers from around the world were likely to dwell on Germany's dark past, while Kohl's government was eager to avoid any scandals that could serve as reminders of it. Second, the Silesian Homeland Society proceeded to create precisely such a scandal. After announcing Chancellor Kohl as the star guest of its upcoming rally and without consulting the government, the organization picked a slogan for its event that could hardly have been more provocative: '40 Years of Expulsion—Silesia Remains Ours'.[69]

The news of the Chancellor's planned participation at this event set off a lively media debate in West Germany, in which both the Silesians and Kohl received nearly unanimous condemnation. By early 1985 related controversies spread to other countries as well, and political trouble began to brew.[70] The SPD set out on the war path, demanding the government 'make unmistakably clear that the German question . . . does not include the lost eastern territories'.[71] The FDP pressed for similar clarification from within the cabinet. Buffeted by the rising pressure, Kohl hesitated at first but then resorted to damage control by early 1985. In private and public exchanges with Herbert Hupka, a CDU Bundestag deputy and head of the Silesian Homeland Society, the Chancellor exhorted the Silesians

[69] Korte, *Deutschlandpolitik*, 250–64.

[70] Karl-Klaus Rabe (ed.), *Von Oggersheim bis Oberschlesien: Union und Vertriebenenverbände im politischen Einklang* (Bornheim: Lamuv, 1985), 68–79.

[71] SPD deputy Schmude in the Bundestag, 6 Feb. 1985, cited in Korte, *Deutschlandpolitik*, 253.

to avoid 'statements that stir up emotions and cause misunderstandings' and insisted on a new, less provocative slogan for the rally.[72]

The homeland society obeyed the second command, although in a fashion that violated the first. The new slogan was the hardly more reassuring '40 Years of Expulsion—Silesia Remains Our Future in a Europe of Free Peoples'. As a result, the debates within and beyond the Federal Republic raged on throughout the spring, exacerbated by additional Silesian provocations, including an article in one of the homeland society's newspapers, in which a 20-year-old student fantasized about a West German military offensive as a means of liberating the East European satellites from the Communist yoke.[73] Although the enduring controversies created strong pressure to the contrary, Kohl ultimately did attend the mid-June rally, at which he delivered a bland and confusing speech, comparable to many of his earlier and subsequent statements on related topics.[74] Along with defending the German expellees against all charges of revanchism, the Chancellor described the bases of his Eastern policy by simply listing a number of documents ranging from the Moscow and Warsaw Treaties to the Joint Resolution of the Bundestag and the Federal Constitutional Court's 1973 decision regarding the Basic Treaty with the GDR. Studiously avoiding comment on any of the real and potential contradictions among these various texts, he then claimed to have made his position literally 'unmisunderstandable', which clarified nothing and left listeners to draw their own conclusions.[75] The only bolder item in the speech was a passing reference to the fact that 'Silesia today is inhabited almost entirely by Polish families, for whom this land has by now become home' (*Heimat*), which amounted to a gentle snub to the Silesian functionaries, most of whom still refused to extend a *Heimatrecht* to the Polish residents of this area.[76]

More notable than Kohl's words at the Silesian rally itself were other statements issued by the government earlier in the year, under the pressure of the unfolding events. Kohl himself had underlined the need to 'respect' the right of current-day Poles to reside in former German lands in a widely publicized Bundestag speech in late February.[77] More significantly, the Chancellor had also quietly authorized a key emissary, the CDU's foreign-policy spokesman Volker Rühe, to give a much more hard-hitting description of the political realities in another parliamentary debate a few weeks earlier. Rising to the occasion, Rühe had declared not only that the Warsaw Treaty expressed the Federal Republic's desire to respect the Poles' wish to 'live in secure borders' but also that the treaty had a 'politically binding effect' that 'could not be ignored even by a reunified Germany'.[78] Although Rühe's words, too, left some room for interpretation and

---

[72] Kohl to Hupka, 23 Jan. 1985, in Jacobsen and Tomalka, *Bonn–Warschau*, 373–5; Hupka, *Unruhiges*, 339–40; Korte, *Deutschlandpolitik*, 251.

[73] Thomas Finke, 'Nachdenken über Deutschland', *Der Schlesier* (25 Jan. 1985); Hupka, *Unruhiges*, 341–4.   [74] *TzD* iii/3. 310–26.

[75] This literal translation of *unmissverständlich* is from Garton Ash, *Europe's Name*, 228.

[76] *TzD* iii/3. 316–17; Garton Ash, *Europe's Name*, 228–9; Hupka, *Unruhiges*, 353–9.

[77] Kohl's 'Bericht zur Lage im geteilten Deutschland', 27 Feb. 1985, *TzD* iii/3. esp. 63.

[78] Rühe on 6 Feb. 1985, in Jacobsen and Tomalka, *Bonn–Warschau*, 376.

although their effect was undermined by subsequent waffling by Kohl and others, they had great significance as signals. They gave a clear indication of what the government would ultimately do if forced to choose between its legalistic, pseudo-revisionist, domestically driven rhetoric and the actual political realities. The verity of these signals was to be confirmed in the forging of the reunification settlement of 1990.

REUNIFICATION

After several years of relative quiet, the Oder-Neisse border issue reappeared as a topic of heated debate in the summer of 1989, just as unpredictable changes were sweeping several East European countries, including Poland. Pressured by the prospect of political transformations in the Eastern bloc and by the rising popularity of the right-wing Republican party, particularly in Bavaria, the CSU once again sprang into opportunistic action. In early July federal Finance Minister Theo Waigel told yet another large-scale Silesian rally that in his opinion the German question still encompassed the lost provinces east of the Oder-Neisse line.[79] The immediate result was a predictable political controversy, intensified by the fact that it coincided with ongoing preparations for Chancellor Kohl's autumn visit to Warsaw, where the first non-Communist government in four decades had just risen to power.

Waigel's claims were promptly disavowed not only by the political opposition and the media establishment but also by the FDP, whose leading light, Foreign Minister Genscher, proceeded to assure the United Nations that the right of the Polish people 'to live in secure borders will not be questioned by us Germans through territorial demands now or in the future'.[80] The contradictions within the ruling coalition remained unresolved throughout the summer and early autumn—particularly as Chancellor Kohl studiously avoided clear statements on the matter—and found official expression in a resolution adopted by the Bundestag on 8 November 1989, just one day before the start of the Chancellor's visit to Poland. In a typically contradictory fashion, the document juxtaposed a substantial quotation from Genscher's recent comments with a reiteration of the older 'fundaments' of Bonn's Ostpolitik, including the Warsaw Treaty of 1970 and the principle that final border decisions had to await a peace settlement.[81]

On the very next day, just as Chancellor Kohl arrived in Warsaw, the entire context of Bonn's policies towards the Eastern bloc was transformed. As the crumbling regime in East Berlin allowed the opening of the Berlin Wall, all previous calculations suddenly lost their relevance. Whereas talk of German reunification and a final peace settlement had been purely theoretical before, both now

---

[79] Garton Ash, *Europe's Name*, 229; Bingen, *Polenpolitik*, 245.
[80] Jacobsen and Tomalka, *Bonn–Warschau*, 482.
[81] *Europa-Archiv*, 23 (1989): D672.

became real possibilities for the foreseeable future, particularly as the disintegration of the GDR and the other Communist satellite states of Eastern Europe continued apace over the ensuing months, accompanied by ever-stronger indications of Moscow's unwillingness to intervene in the region. With the long-coveted prize of reunification now looming in the distance, the unresolved Eastern border problem became a burning issue for the Federal Republic in general and Chancellor Kohl, Bonn's chief foreign-policy mastermind, in particular.

As in previous years, Kohl's government still faced conflicting pressures on the border question. On the one hand, the forces pushing for a prompt recognition of the existing Polish–German frontier waxed ever stronger as the steady erosion of the East German state became increasingly obvious. At home the bulk of the media and of public opinion, the political opposition, as well as the FDP and even growing elements of the CDU, clamoured for an unambiguous renunciation of all claims to territories beyond the eastern boundaries of the GDR. Abroad, the same viewpoint was adopted by every country whose word counted on the reunification issue, including the Soviet Union, France, Britain, the United States, and—most vehemently of all—Poland. Even the GDR itself unequivocally espoused this position.[82]

On the other hand, however, countervailing domestic forces sought to hold the government back from formal border commitments. While the Republicans and other right-wing political groups exerted such pressure, its primary source was still the expellee lobby, although at first sight the latter appeared to be shifting towards more realistic stances. The Sudeten-German Homeland Society, for example, declared in early 1990 that it saw no border problem between Germany and Czechoslovakia, and numerous other expellee statements focused not on the border claims but on such concrete issues as the position of the German minorities in Eastern Europe or the prospect of material compensation for the property losses caused by the expulsions.[83]

On closer inspection, however, the chimera of territorial revisionism still dominated the expellee lobby's political vision. The main organizations agitated aggressively against a recognition of the Oder-Neisse line in one proclamation after another, and ulterior motives also lurked behind many pronouncements that ostensibly addressed other issues. The attention given to German minorities in Eastern Europe, for example, was far from merely humanitarian. Demands about their treatment could be expected to delay border agreements, and the

---

[82] On reunification, see Philip Zelikow and Condoleezza Rice, *Germany Unified and Europe Transformed* (Cambridge, Mass.: Harvard University Press, 1997); Konrad H. Jarausch, *The Rush to German Unity* (Oxford: Oxford University Press, 1994); Stephen F. Szabo, *The Diplomacy of German Reunification* (New York: St Martin's, 1992); David Schoenbaum and Elizabeth Pond, *The German Question and Other German Questions* (Basingstoke: Macmillan, 1996); Elizabeth Pond, *Beyond the Wall: Germany's Road to Unification* (Washington, DC: Brookings Institution, 1993); Charles S. Maier, *Dissolution* (Princeton: Princeton University Press, 1997); Werner Weidenfeld, *Aussenpolitik für die deutsche Einheit* (Stuttgart: DVA, 1998); Korte, *Deutschlandpolitik*; Küsters, *Integrationsfriede*, 801–80.

[83] Sudetendeutscher Rat declaration, 26 Jan. 1990, *Sudetendeutsche Zeitung* (5 Feb. 1990); Krzysztof Miszczak, *Deklarationen und Realitäten* (Munich: tuduv, 1993), 387–90, 424–6.

umbrella group BdV also pressed the idea of a 'free referendum' in which the German minority in Poland, as well as the 'German expellees and their descendants', would play a key role in determining 'the future of the areas east of the Oder-Neisse'.[84] Even the seemingly clear stance adopted by the Sudeten Germans vis-à-vis the territorial integrity of Czechoslovakia was not wholly unambiguous; the concept of 'ethnic group rights' that continued to be heavily advocated by the Sudeten Germans and other expellee groups left open the possibility of territorial adjustments at some point in the future. But the Sudeten problem had nevertheless become peripheral by 1989/90, at least for the time being. The expellee lobby's main objective was to keep alive the possibility of incorporating into a reunified Germany at least some of the lands that the Reich had lost to Poland after the Second World War.

Caught in this crossfire of conflicting demands, Chancellor Kohl chose the path of delay and evasion. For months he consistently refused to take a clear stance on the Oder-Neisse border question. The joint declaration adopted at the end of Kohl's Polish visit on 14 November 1989, for example, left the border issue open, and the Chancellor's ten-point reunification plan, presented to the Bundestag two weeks later, failed to mention the problem at all.[85] A series of ambiguous statements followed over the following months, typically combining assurances of Bonn's peaceful intentions towards Poland with legal reservations about the impossibility of a border regulation prior to a peace treaty.[86] Even in early March 1990, at a time when formal negotiations about a reunification settlement were already in progress and the pressures for an acceptance of the Oder-Neisse line appeared overwhelming, Kohl hit the brakes. In a high-profile speech he suggested that commitments by Bonn and East Berlin to guarantee the German–Polish border should be conditional on two prior concessions by Warsaw: provision of greater rights for the German minority in Poland and renunciation of war reparation claims against Germany.[87]

Only after this particular intervention had provoked widespread concern about his government's true intentions, particularly abroad, did the Chancellor switch course. During the spring of 1990 Kohl began to set a new tone in his public statements, stressing the need for the two German states to confirm 'the inviolability of the border with Poland' even before reunification.[88] Concrete action followed in the summer. On 21 June, in conjunction with their ratification of the Treaty on Monetary, Social, and Economic Union between the Federal Republic and the GDR, the parliaments of the two German states passed identical resolutions on the Polish border whose key provision the Chancellor summa-

[84] Miszczak, *Deklarationen*, 387–8; Salzborn, *Heimatrecht*, 57–72.

[85] Jacobsen and Tomalka, *Bonn–Warschau*, 501–10; Auswärtiges Amt (ed.), *Die Auswärtige Politik der Bundesrepublik Deutschland* (Cologne: Wissenschaft und Politik, 1995), 632–8.

[86] A prominent example is Kohl's 17 Jan. 1990 Paris speech, in Michael Ludwig, *Polen und die deutsche Frage* (Bonn: Deutsche Gesellschaft für auswärtige Politik, 1990), 197–8.

[87] Kohl in the Bundestag, 8 Mar. 1990, ibid. 215–18; Weidenfeld, *Aussenpolitik*, 479–87.

[88] Kohl's Cambridge speech, 29 Mar. 1990, *Bulletin* (3 Apr. 1990), 333–6.

rized as follows: 'The current border between Germany and Poland is final.'[89] In the debate that preceded the vote in the Bundestag, Kohl elaborated on the significance of this border resolution. He explained that Germans now stood before 'a clear decision. Either we confirm the existing border or we fritter away our chance to national unity.' He also placed that momentous choice in an international context, explaining that 'all [of Germany's] neighbours and partners in Europe and especially the four powers, i.e. the United States, France, Great Britain, and the Soviet Union', insisted on an 'unambiguous answer' to the Polish border question.[90] With such observations, the Chancellor suggested that on this territorial issue his government was primarily reacting to external pressure and possibly even acting against the Chancellor's personal preferences.

After the parliamentary resolution of 21 June, further steps towards the final recognition of the Oder-Neisse border followed quickly. The so-called 2+4 negotiations on German unity—featuring the two Germanys, the four Second World War Allies, and, on this particular question, Poland—settled this issue by mid-July, with the result that the final 2+4 treaty, signed in Moscow in mid-September, declared the Oder-Neisse line to be unified Germany's eastern boundary.[91] The agreement also obliged Bonn and Warsaw to reconfirm the matter in a further bilateral pact, which was achieved through the German–Polish frontier treaty, signed in Warsaw in November 1990. As a further step towards a normalization of relations, the two governments also negotiated a comprehensive, bilateral friendship pact that was seen by both sides as a crucial new beginning. With the ratification of the border and friendship agreements with Poland by unified Germany's Bundestag in October 1991, the decades-long strife about the country's eastern frontier had formally ended. Although the expellee organizations screamed in protest and a handful of conservative CDU/CSU deputies, most of them expellees, voted against the two pacts, Germany's acceptance of the territorial status quo had become final and official.[92]

The West German Chancellor's behaviour on the border problem during 1989/90 bewildered observers, particularly abroad. Kohl's prolonged evasiveness on the seemingly very secondary Oder-Neisse issue to a point where it could have jeopardized the great prize of reunification seemed to defy the rules of rational statesmanship—unless the Chancellor really wanted to pursue territorial revisions. That was never the case, however. In the summer of 1989, amidst the revived West German public discussion of the Oder-Neisse problem, Kohl had privately vowed that he would 'never cave in' to the 'pressure' from revisionist circles, and behind the scenes he consistently expressed similar viewpoints

---

[89] Auswärtiges Amt, *Auswärtige Politik*, 533–4.

[90] Ibid. 535; Weidenfeld, *Aussenpolitik*, 487–500; Küsters, *Integrationsfriede*, 849–61.

[91] Zelikow and Rice, *Germany*, 149–363; Jarausch, *Rush*, 163–76; Maier, *Dissolution*, 244–84; Weidenfeld, *Aussenpolitik*, 500–9, 568–71; Hanns-Jürgen Küsters, 'The Kohl–Gorbachev Meetings in Moscow and in the Caucasus, 1990', *Cold War History* 2 (2002): 195–235.

[92] Bingen, *Polenpolitik*, 261–84; Miszczak, *Deklarationen*, 369–461.

throughout the reunification process.[93] His public vacillation was therefore tactical and rooted 'exclusively in domestic and party political considerations', as his chief foreign-policy adviser subsequently admitted.[94] In the broadest sense, Kohl's strategy was to use suggestive statements and the resulting roars of protest to demonstrate to the nationalist fringe, including the expellee lobby, that they were wrong and that the recognition of the Oder-Neisse was the price to be paid for the unification of the two real existing German states. More specifically, Kohl hoped to neutralize the Oder-Neisse issue as an extremist political theme; court the votes of the 'right-wing section of the electorate'; 'secure a broad majority for his policies towards Poland'; and maintain unity within the CDU/CSU by helping expellee leaders and other extreme conservatives to adjust to the political realities.[95]

The Chancellor's tactics ultimately triumphed. Germany was reunified and the Oder-Neisse line officially recognized. Radicalism among the expellees and other nationalists remained a fringe phenomenon, and the government began the 1990s with a broad popular support base and a large parliamentary majority, secured through the ruling coalition's sweeping victory in the all-German elections of 2 December 1990.[96] Kohl's public manœuvring on the eastern border issue has therefore received frequent praise. One recent observer, for example, labelled 'the manner in which he pushed the expellee politicians to a moderate position' in 1989/90 a 'tactical . . . masterpiece'.[97] But this retrospective conclusion begs the question of whether the Chancellor's rhetorical delaying strategy was really necessary for the positive outcome ultimately achieved. Kohl himself privately admitted in the summer of 1989 that nearly 90 per cent of Germans had accepted the Oder-Neisse line as a permanent boundary for years, and the prospect of an imminent reunification would have raised this percentage further even in the absence of the Chancellor's tactical posturing, particularly as the rejection of any border revisions by all external powers was clear from the start.[98]

Kohl's claims that his ambiguous statements pacified the atmosphere at home by preventing a premature 'reopening' of the 'gaping wound' associated with the 'Oder-Neisse question' also seem questionable.[99] In many ways, the Chancellor's rhetorical distortions had precisely the opposite effect. They fuelled unfounded expectations among expellee activists and other revisionists and thus lent political

---

[93] Kohl's comments to Solidarity leader Geremek, 7 July 1989, in *Dokumente zur Deutschlandpolitik: Deutsche Einheit: Sonderedition aus den Akten des Bundeskanzleramtes 1989/1990*, ed. H.-J. Küsters and D. Hofmann (Munich: Oldenbourg, 1998), 343. See also pp. 481, 639, 802.

[94] Horst Teltschik, *329 Tage: Innenansichten der Einigung* (Berlin: Siedler, 1991), 14.

[95] Ibid., esp. 166, 14; Garton Ash, *Europe's Name*, 227–31; Bingen, *Polenpolitik*, 265; Korte, *Deutschlandpolitik*, 470–1; Weidenfeld, *Aussenpolitik*, 486–8, 505–7.

[96] Hans Georg Lehmann, *Deutschland Chronik 1945–2000* (Bonn: Bouvier, 2000), 443–4; Patton, *Cold*, 137–40.

[97] Bingen, *Polenpolitik*, 276. See also Korte, *Deutschlandpolitik*; Weidenfeld, *Aussenpolitik*.

[98] Kohl's comments to Geremek, 7 July 1989, *DzD Deutsche Einheit*, 343; Glaab, *Deutschlandpolitik*, 244–5.

[99] Kohl's comments to Mitterrand, 15 Feb. 1990, *DzD Deutsche Einheit*, 847.

prominence to an unconstructive issue that could have been removed from the contemporary agenda with much less fanfare. Kohl's domestically driven tactical moves also had serious negative consequences abroad: they rekindled latent fears of Germany, particularly in Eastern Europe, and gave hard-line Communists in Poland and elsewhere a tool for last-stand attempts at popular mobilization against ongoing political changes.[100] On balance, it therefore seems that much of Kohl's 'Machiavellism', to borrow Timothy Garton Ash's phrase, was exaggerated and counter-productive and that firmer, less opportunistic leadership would have yielded the same benefits with less cost.[101]

[100] Miszczak, *Deklarationen.*   [101] Garton Ash, *Europe's Name*, 230.

Conclusion

LIKE ALL HISTORICAL events, German reunification had its winners and losers. The former included most Germans, at least in the initial euphoria, and even most other Europeans, given the liberation of the Eastern bloc and the general relaxation of tensions that accompanied the end of the cold war. Among the losers, the expellee activists formed one prominent cohort. For their organizations, reunification marked the terminus on a long road of political decline. Once potent in their ability to hinder changes in Bonn's policies towards Eastern Europe, these groups had witnessed a steady waning of their powers since the 1960s. The first harbingers of change had been various public intellectuals who began to pose systematic challenges to the expellee groups and the Ostpolitik dogmas associated with them from the early 1960s on. In the course of that decade, these challenges gained growing public backing, thanks in large part to broader generational, social, and attitudinal changes in West German society.

Once public opinion polls had started to provide increasingly firm evidence of such trends, the country's political elites also began to react. The SPD and the FDP moved towards new policy positions, gradually distancing themselves from the expellee lobby, while the CDU/CSU remained much more supportive of expellee-associated Ostpolitik doctrines. As a result of these divergent stances, which largely reflected each party's perceptions of opportunities for partisan gains, the old pattern of consensus politics with regard to Ostpolitik broke down, and the expellee organizations increasingly lost their credibility as purportedly non-partisan interest groups.

The formation of the Social–Liberal Coalition in late 1969 brought these long-term trends to a culmination. The government proceeded to implement its new Eastern policy in spite of vehement protests by the expellee groups, and the concrete results of its efforts—particularly the Moscow and Warsaw Treaties of 1970—constituted major defeats for the expellee lobby. The only remaining hope for the organizations was now the CDU/CSU, which continued to profess loyalty to their cause. However, even this backing was merely rhetorical and highly instrumentalized, as the expellee activists discovered when the Christian Democrats failed to block the parliamentary ratification of the Ostpolitik treaties in the spring of 1972.

After this setback, the expellee lobby's political options grew extremely narrow. Estranged from the governing parties, yet unwilling to ally with far-right forces, the organizations linked themselves ever more closely to the Christian Democrats in general and to the CSU in particular, despite enduring doubts about the party's true intentions. The CDU/CSU, in turn, continued to make manipulative use of expellee concerns about Ostpolitik, both in opposition, and—from late 1982 on—as the senior partner in Helmut Kohl's new ruling coalition with the FDP. With carefully calibrated, deliberately ambiguous language, the new Chancellor and his associates engaged in delicate rhetorical manœuvres, balancing vague suggestions of an interest in future territorial revisions in the East—intended for domestic consumption by expellees and other nationalists—with statements aimed at reassuring everyone else that West Germany did not actually intend to pursue such goals. This strategy succeeded in placating both target audiences for years, but in the end the Christian Democrats had to choose between their incompatible poses once German reunification came up for negotiation. Although complicated—and largely unnecessary—rhetorical acrobatics characterized this process, too, the ultimate decision was never really in doubt. The formal acceptance of unified Germany's existing boundaries by a CDU/CSU-led government in 1990 closed the era of instrumentalized revisionist rhetoric in the Federal Republic and put an end to the irredentist hopes of the expellee organizations.

In the post-unification decade, most expellee leaders have cut an embittered figure. One activist after another has vented frustration with the political settlement of 1990 and complained about a lack of interest in expellee concerns among ordinary Germans and political elites alike.[1] Although most such complaints have been exaggeratedly aggressive in tone, they do contain a core of truth, as the expellee groups and their political demands undoubtedly have grown increasingly marginal in German public life, not only in the most recent decade but in the entire period since the 1960s. In part, the expellee lobby's political downfall was the inevitable result of structural forces beyond the activists' control. On the international plane, the gradual transition from East–West confrontation to détente and growing cooperation between the cold war blocs left increasingly little room for the harsh, revisionist anti-Communism of the expellee organizations. Within the Federal Republic, rising affluence and generational change brought about social and attitudinal transformations that lessened the cohesiveness of the expellee milieu and promoted indifference, even hostility, to the political expellee movement among a growing segment of the population.

But in large measure the expellee activists had themselves to blame for the sorry state in which they found themselves by the end of the 1960s—and from which they never recovered. Their most fundamental failing was an inability to adjust to changing external conditions, particularly on Eastern policy. They stubbornly refused to follow the route increasingly proposed by various politicians and other observers from the late 1960s on: a shift from foreign-policy preoccupations to a focus on the preservation of the cultural heritage of the former Eastern provinces. Instead, the expellee elites stuck to their traditional cold-warrior stances. To be sure, they frequently expressed support for such abstract principles as international cooperation and reconciliation within a peaceful, pan-European framework. But on the Ostpolitik issues that directly affected them they

---

[1] Examples include Czaja, *Unterwegs*; Hupka, *Unruhiges*; Becher, *Zeitzeuge*.

adhered to a more confrontational axiom, which the head of the Sudeten-German Homeland Society once reduced to the imperative not to 'budge a millimetre from the demands that we have raised from day one'.[2] A good example of the resulting absurdities was the reaction of leading activists to the suggestions that the *Heimatrecht* be extended not only to the German expellees but also to the Poles and others who had become established residents of the former German territories. Most key figures refused to issue clear affirmations of the Polish *Heimatrecht* even in the 1980s, and occasional statements continued to dismiss the Polish presence in the area as an 'illegal foreign settlement of eastern Germany'.[3]

The expellee leaders' inability to adjust to changing circumstances was also manifest in their attitudes towards ongoing developments among their own presumed followers. The most obvious problem was the activists' refusal to face the inherent contradiction between the two primary goals that they had pursued throughout the Federal Republic's existence: integration into West German society on the one hand and an eventual return to the old homelands on the other. Even in the late 1960s, the expellee elites typically maintained that their purported followers remained rootless, poorly integrated, and ready to return to the East, thus ignoring rapidly accumulating evidence to the contrary and skirting a difficult issue.[4] Another key problem, growing generational tension within the expellee movement, received somewhat more attention, but only on an abstract, deliberative level. In their closed meetings, activists acknowledged both the growing estrangement of the younger expellee generation from the organizations and the need 'to do more about the youth and its problems'.[5] But in public the activists typically denied the existence of these tensions and failed to adopt new initiatives aimed at the younger generation.[6] As a result, the archetypal message that expellee youths received from their purported organizational representatives was a tirade against Communism and political disaffection rather than a constructive proposal for engagement and inclusion.

This refusal to face reality cost the expellee lobby dearly. It was the main reason for the movement's increasing isolation from the mainstream of West German society. Even more self-defeatingly, it also increasingly alienated most rank-and-file expellees from the organizations. Although the BdV asserted as late as September 1969 that even 'welfare recipients' among the expellees cared more about foreign policy than about such trivialities as the price of 'eggs' or 'butter',

---

[2] Hans-Christoph Seebohm in the *Bundesvorstand* of the Sudetendeutsche Landsmannschaft, 21 Jan. 1967, SDA: BIX/30, p. 5.

[3] *Der Schlesier* (25 May 1984), cited in Rabe, *Oggersheim*, 63.

[4] BdV memorandum 'Betr.: Wahlrechtsreform und Vertriebene', 12 Oct. 1967, BA: B 234/187; Hans-Christoph Seebohm's *Bayern-Kurier* interview, 20 May 1967, DzD v/1/2. 1178; Böke, 'Flüchtlinge', 203–8.

[5] Herbert Hupka in the *Bundesdelegiertenversammlung* of the Schlesische Landsmannschaft, 22–3 Mar. 1967, ACDP: I-401-023/3; *Bundesvorstand* protocols of the Sudeten-German Homeland Society, 22 Jan. 1973, SDA: NL Becher, 216.

[6] Hans-Christoph Seebohm at the *Sudetendeutscher Tag*, Nuremberg, 17 May 1964, SDA: BIX/46, esp. 10; BdV president Helmut Czaja in *DoD* (25 Aug. 1973).

the realities within the organizations belied these claims.[7] The political engagement of expellees declined steadily during the 1960s and continued to drop further in the following decades. The falling membership figures of the various expellee groups testified to this trend, which was made all the more ominous by the fact that members of the younger generation, particularly those under 30, were almost entirely absent from the organizations by the mid to late 1960s. The result was an increasingly skewed age structure, reflective of the growing dominance of ageing and often socially discontented veterans. In the words of one concerned top activist, the organizations were thus ossifying into irrelevant 'old-timers' clubs'.[8] This trend was especially striking at the top leadership levels, where activists of the first hour, most well past the retirement age, held on to the bulk of the key positions even into the 1980s.

Despite their growing isolation, the activists proved unwilling to overstep the boundaries within which their organizations had traditionally operated. Occasional strident public protests notwithstanding, subversive political radicalism remained beyond the pale for the mainstream expellee movement. One important reason for this relative moderation was the lobby's continued heavy dependence on state subsidies. By the 1960s, the smaller homeland societies could not have existed at all without such support, and even the umbrella group BdV received roughly 80 per cent of its annual income from the West German state.[9] Only a handful of organizations enjoyed a significant degree of financial independence, chief among them the Sudeten-German Homeland Society, whose ability to generate revenue from its own members remained considerable. But even the Sudetendeutsche Landsmannschaft received hundreds of thousands of dollars in annual governmental subsidies, rendering it, too, susceptible to the subtle political control exercised through governmental purse strings.[10] The effects of such financial dependence became clear in the Social–Liberal era, as the expellee organizations continued to request, and receive, large amounts of state subvention, which exerted a moderating influence at a time when the political chasm between the expellee lobby and the governing coalition was rapidly widening.[11]

More than money is required to explain the expellee movement's relative moderation, however. The mainstream expellee leaders' unwillingness to seek truly radical solutions by collaborating with the NPD of the 1960s, the Republicans of the 1980s, or other potentially anti-democratic forces had deeper roots. By all indications, the key activists were fundamentally opposed to attempts to undermine the Federal Republic's democratic system. They accepted the basic

---

[7] 'Kriterien der Entscheidung', *DoD* (6 Aug. 1969).

[8] Rinke to Rasner, 23 Nov. 1964, ACDP: I-294-076/2.

[9] BdV *Bundesvertretung* protocols, 11 Mar. 1967, SDA: BIX/33, esp. 3; BdV presidium protocols, 11 Mar. 1968, SDA: NL Becher, 195, esp. 3–4; BdV *Bundesversammlung* protocols, 31 Mar. 1968, SDA: NL Becher, 194, esp. 12.

[10] Sudetendeutsche Landsmannschaft, 'Jahresrechnung 1964' and 'Jahresrechnung 1965', SDA: B IX/30; the organization's draft subsidy request, attached to Becher to Jaksch, 10 Dec. 1963, SDA: NL Jaksch, B1/139.

[11] BdV's finance committee (*Finanzausschuss*) records from the early 1970s, BA: B 234, 527.

rules of the new polity and engaged in the rough and tumble of interest-group politics, ultimately accepting less than optimal solutions and even downright defeats on significant issues. To be sure, expellee elites reacted to such setbacks with cries of disappointment and anger, but they never went so far as to channel their discontent against the political system as a whole. Their grudging acceptance of Adenauer's westward-looking foreign-policy programme illustrates this pattern, as does their reluctant toleration of both the new Ostpolitik and the eventual reunification settlement, all vocal public protest notwithstanding.

The expellee lobby's political prudence was facilitated not only by the constraints of financial dependence but also by the rewards that individual activists drew from their political engagement. Participation in the system brought experience, insight, and often career opportunities in the parties, the government, or the administrative machinery, all of which helped to draw activists ever deeper into the new polity and give them a stake in maintaining its stability. In addition, authoritarian systems of both the left- and right-wing variety were sufficiently discredited in the Federal Republic to ensure that even initially reluctant democrats preferred the existing institutions to the possible alternatives.[12] As a result, the mainstream expellee movement remained within democratic bounds, even as its stubborn inflexibility on Ostpolitik increasingly relegated it to the political margins from the 1960s onwards.

Even more importantly, the expellee lobby's relative moderation was part of a broader pattern in the Federal Republic. The habits of give and take within a democratic framework that took root within the expellee groups also characterized other organizations of disadvantaged and potentially dangerous minorities. As recent work by Michael L. Hughes, James Diehl, and others has shown, pressure groups representing war veterans as well as various types of West German civilians victimized by the war accepted the need for compromise solutions within the existing system while rejecting the siren calls of anti-democratic extremism.[13] Such eminently reasonable behaviour stood in striking contrast to Germany's previous democratic experiment, the Weimar Republic, in which narrow groups had all too often pressed their own interests with ruthless zeal, regardless of the broader repercussions.[14] Thanks to this creeping democratization, Bonn's political path increasingly diverged from that of Weimar, a momentous development that was significantly facilitated by the behaviour of the mainstream expellee leaders.

But the expellee lobby's contributions to the construction and consolidation of the West German polity reached well beyond attitude adjustments among pressure group elites. Particularly notable was the multifaceted role that the organizations played in the long-term integration of millions of rank-and-file expellees whose potential for radicalization had preoccupied decision-makers in the early post-war

---

[12] Diehl, *Thanks*; Frei, *Vergangenheitspolitik*; Jerry Z. Muller, *The Other God that Failed: Hans Freyer and Deradicalization of German Conservatism* (Princeton: Princeton University Press, 1987).

[13] Diehl, *Thanks*; Hughes, *Shouldering*; id., 'No Fault'; Krause, *Flucht*.

[14] See esp. Hughes, 'Restitution'; Holtmann, 'Politische'.

years. At the most fundamental level, the expellee groups made a difference simply by giving a collective voice to a large mass of discontented people. Although the degree to which their political proclamations reflected the views of their purported followers became increasingly dubious, the very existence of the organizations undoubtedly facilitated the integration of the newcomers, particularly in the early post-war period. With their lobbying, the organizations helped to secure important social benefits for ordinary expellees, and their various mass rallies and other events provided opportunities for participation and social interaction, which, in turn, fostered a sense of belonging among their uprooted and disoriented followers.[15]

The expellee leaders' Ostpolitik activities also played a significant, albeit complicated, role in the integration process. The loud demands for territorial revisions and a return to the old homelands assumed particular importance in the immediate aftermath of the Second World War. At a time when millions of impoverished, demoralized, and homesick expellees eked out a very precarious existence, often facing prejudice and discrimination from the native population at every turn, such calls performed integrative functions on several levels. From the expellee perspective, the prospect of an eventual return provided hope of a better future and diverted attention from the harshness of everyday social realities. But the revisionist public discussions also resonated among many long-term residents of western Germany, who welcomed the possibility of the expellees ultimately heading back to the East and thereby ceasing to demand their share of scarce available resources. Thus the illusionary hopes fuelled by the expellee lobby helped to defuse tensions between expellees and native western Germans and to diminish the appeal of political radicalism, particularly during the difficult early post-war years.[16]

The expellee lobby's public rhetoric contributed as well to more comprehensive integrative and identity-building processes in the early Federal Republic. A case in point is the wide appeal that one particular staple of expellee discourse, the concept of *Heimat*, enjoyed in West German society. With its emotionally laden connotations of tradition and close-knit community, the idea of *Heimat* gave comfort to many at a time of great uncertainty and upheaval. To the expellees, it held out hope of a return to the lost homelands while also suggesting that stability could be rediscovered in their new surroundings. To many other West Germans, it accorded similar promise of belonging to a larger whole. Through the popular media—particularly the cinema, where idyllic *Heimat* films became the country's top box office hits of the 1950s—it provided idealized images of harmonious community at a time when most people's everyday reality was likely to be characterized by toil and conflict.[17]

[15] For similar points, see Steinert, 'Flüchtlingsvereinigungen'; Haerendel, 'Politik'; Holtmann, 'Politische'; Hughes, *Shouldering*, esp. 165–98; Schwartz, 'Vertreibung', esp. 186–9.

[16] Ahonen, 'Impact'; Niethammer, 'Traditionen', esp. 80–1.

[17] On the concept of *Heimat* and its appeal, see Böke, 'Flüchtlinge', 131–210; Applegate, *Nation*; Confino, *Nation*; Heide Fehrenbach, *Cinema in Democratizing Germany: Reconstructing National Identity after Hitler* (Chapel Hill, NC: University of North Carolina Press, 1995), 148–68; Moeller, *War Stories*, 123–70.

The expulsions themselves soon became another significant identity-building tool in West Germany. The expellee lobby was quick to promulgate its version of these events, emphasizing the injustices and atrocities suffered by the German victims while providing a severely truncated version of the broader historical context. Such accounts typically sought to relativize the preceding crimes of the Nazi era by comparing them to exaggerated portrayals of the atrocities inflicted upon Germans during the expulsions. This distorted narrative, in turn, found extensive circulation in West Germany early on as politicians, publicists, scholars, and others publicly espoused most of its key elements. As a result, the horrors of the expulsions became a central component of what Robert G. Moeller has labelled West German 'rhetorics of victimization'. Focused on German suffering and its comparability to that of the victims of German crimes, this type of rhetoric enabled West Germans to address the Nazi past while evading questions of collective responsibility and to suggest that the German people, too, had ultimately been victims of Hitler and his psychopathic henchmen. Such public discourse helped to construct an integrative myth of suffering and hardship that served as a source of collective legitimacy and identity for the new state. But it also advanced social cohesion on another, closely related level. By placing the onus for the transgressions against Germany on East European Communists in general and the Soviet Union in particular, the expellee proclamations facilitated anti-Communist mobilization, which, in turn, functioned as a vital social adhesive within West Germany and eased the country's integration into the cold war West.[18]

The expellee organizations thus made various contributions to the stabilization and consolidation of West German state and society, particularly in the early years, roughly through the mid-1950s. To be sure, their contributions had their costs at this stage too, and from the 1960s onwards many of the expellee lobby's increasingly strident activities are difficult to view as constructive. But even in this later period the organizations ultimately made a positive contribution to expellee integration, albeit in a paradoxical fashion. Through their inability to adjust to the social, political, and attitudinal changes of the 1960s, particularly on the contested terrain of Ostpolitik, they increasingly alienated the majority of the people whom they purported to represent. After having claimed for years that Bonn's recognition of the territorial status quo in Eastern Europe would provoke massive expellee protests, spell electoral disaster to the parties involved, and risk large-scale political radicalization, expellee leaders were now forced to recognize that the bulk of their supposed followers refused to conform to such stereotypes. Far from rushing to the barricades to demand continued hard-line stances, the vast majority of West German expellees proved perfectly willing to live with the government's new policies towards Eastern Europe, thus demonstrating that revisionist rhetoric no longer won their allegiance.[19]

The multifaceted West German attempts to integrate the expellees had thus

---

[18] Moeller, *War Stories*; Ahonen, 'Impact'.   [19] Ahonen, 'Impact'.

proved largely successful by the early 1970s. A mass radicalization, much dreaded in the early post-war years, had been averted. Social and economic integration had begun to make headway early on, bolstered by the economic miracle and relevant governmental policies, and by the 1960s and 1970s most expellees had achieved a reasonably secure material existence. The expellee parties that had emerged in the early post-war years had been successfully absorbed by their larger mainstream rivals without a fragmentation of the political landscape or an enduring ghettoization of the expellee voters. The potential irredentist threat posed by the expellees had also faded, as ever-growing numbers had accepted the Federal Republic as their new *Heimat* and rejected the siren calls of backward-looking revisionism.

A variety of factors contributed to this outcome. The expellee organizations facilitated the process in several ways, as we have seen. Even more vital were the contributions of the people the organizations claimed to represent, the millions of average expellees, who endured many hardships while gradually growing into a stabilizing force in the Federal Republic. But ultimately these successes were possible only within a broader framework defined by two more powerful sets of actors. The first comprised the Western victors of the Second World War. Having quickly grasped the urgency of the expellee problem, the Western occupation forces prodded German authorities to address the matter. They prevented the build-up of independent expellee groups long enough to allow the mainstream parties a head start in recruiting followers. Subsequently they stood in the wings as a background force ready to crack down on anti-democratic excesses, thereby exercising a strong moderating influence on all potential extremists. Without their presence and actions, developments might well have taken a different turn.[20]

West Germany's mainstream political elites were the other crucial actors. Like pressure group activists, they had learnt from the fatal divisiveness of the Weimar era and were eager to pursue inclusionary tactics in their renewed attempts to build a German democracy. Accordingly, the federal government and the leading parties strove to accommodate discontented and potentially anti-democratic minorities.[21] As the largest group of this kind, the expellees received extensive attention in several ways. Social legislation and assistance programmes alleviated existential problems and anxieties among the rank and file. Tailor-made posts and organs within parties, ministries, and the administrative machinery served as bridges between expellee leaders and mainstream political elites. Financial strings brought dependence and control into the political elite's relations with the expellee lobby while public rhetoric cultivated the impression of a general accord between top politicians and the expellees. With such steps, Bonn's leaders helped to anchor the newcomers into the political system, gradually drawing the venom out of potential radicalism and territorial revisionism. As a result, the oft-stated claim that expellee integration ranks immediately behind the closely related

---

[20] Schraut, *Flüchtlingsaufnahme*; id., 'Besatzungsmächte'; Rogers, *Politics*, 104–18.
[21] Hughes, 'Restitution'; Holtmann, 'Politische'; Haerendel, 'Politik'.

phenomenon of the economic miracle in West Germany's list of triumphs rings substantially true. The Federal Republic has reason to be proud of its record in this area, especially in view of the many potential hazards that had loomed along the way.

These achievements seem even more impressive in a comparative perspective. The most obvious point of comparison is Bonn's arch-rival, East Germany, which took a very different approach to integrating the approximately four million expellees within its borders. After some initial hesitation and the adoption of various measures aimed at a radical redistribution of wealth and resources, the Communist authorities proclaimed what they euphemistically labelled the 'resettler' problem to be solved by the beginning of the 1950s. As a result, the GDR adopted a policy of no special concessions towards its expellees: no autonomous organizations; no major assistance programmes; and no public discussion of specific expellee demands, least of all territorial ones, which would have constituted open defiance of the Soviet Union.[22] The newcomers were instead expected to assimilate without further ado, an approach that by all indications functioned much less smoothly than its more inclusive counterpart west of the Elbe. Although most East German expellees ultimately did adjust to the socialist system, the intensity of the underlying discontent was reflected in the fact that they constituted a disproportionately high percentage—nearly one third—of the more than three million East Germans who fled to the Federal Republic between 1949 and 1961.[23]

West Germany's record also compares favourably with that of the GDR's immediate neighbour to the east, Poland. Major problems with expellees existed there too, both in repopulating the new western territories from which Germans had recently been removed and in integrating the so-called 'repatriates', ethnic Poles who had been forced out of the formerly Polish eastern territories annexed by the Soviet Union after 1945. Like their counterparts in East Berlin, the Polish authorities resorted to heavy-handed administrative fiats to address these issues. Poles expelled from the East were denied an autonomous voice, and the special problems of the newly gained western territories remained largely unaddressed. As a result, uncertainty and instability plagued the former German lands long into the post-war decades, and Polish society suffered from festering discontent and tension traceable to the expulsions and their consequences.[24]

West Germany's inclusive, consultative approach to expellee integration thus seems to have functioned better than the top-heavy methods of socialist Eastern Europe, which is perhaps not very surprising. But some of the country's achievements also compare favourably with those of other key Western democracies. A

---

[22] Some specific social measures to assist the expellees were adopted in the Soviet Occupation Zone in the first few post-war years, but they were scaled back drastically by the late 1940s, before the GDR was even founded, and discontinued by 1952/3.

[23] Ther, *Deutsche*; id., 'Integration'; id. 'Expellee'; Wille *et al.*, *Alles*; Meinicke, 'Probleme'; Plato and Meinicke, *Alte*; Schwartz, 'Vertreibung'; Hoffmann *et al.* *Vertriebene*; Hoffmann *et al.*, *Geglückte*; Heidemeyer, 'Vertriebene'.   [24] Ther, *Deutsche*; id., 'Integration'.

case in point is West Germany's ultimate success in taming the political influence of pressure groups that claim to be the collective representatives of specific minority populations. As we have seen, Willy Brandt's government switched to a new Ostpolitik line in defiance of the expellee lobby at the end of the 1960s. In other words, within two decades of their state's founding, West German leaders felt strong enough to override the objections of a well-organized minority to a foreign-policy goal that they perceived to be in the wider national interest. Although this transition may not seem particularly speedy or smooth in absolute terms, it appears in a somewhat different light when contrasted with another well-known case of a minority pressure group wielding negative influence over a specific foreign-policy issue in a major liberal democracy: that of the Florida-based Cuban-American lobby in United States policy towards Cuba.

Unlike West German Ostpolitik, American policy towards Cuba has undergone no fundamental change in more than four decades. The policy of isolating the island economically and politically, originally conceived in the cold war conditions of the early 1960s, has continued, and during the 1990s this hard-line approach became even more extreme. New measures such as the Cuban Democracy Act of 1992 or the Helms-Burton law of 1996 further tightened the US embargo of Cuba and made the overthrow of the socialist system a formal precondition of any fundamental improvement in relations.

None of this made sense in terms of traditional assumptions about foreign policy being formulated in accordance with a rational reading of external power conditions. By the 1990s the cold war was over, as was the Soviet Union's extensive assistance to Cuba, and as a result the Pentagon itself admitted that the island no longer posed a military threat to the US. American public opinion moved increasingly in favour of normalized relations with the island state. Business groups at home and abroad pushed steadily in the same direction, as did most of the United States' key foreign allies, which objected to the tightened economic measures of the 1990s. And yet Washington refused to modify its stance towards Cuba, even as it proceeded to build at least some level of normalized relations with every other remaining Communist regime in the world.[25]

Washington's peculiar behaviour towards Havana becomes intelligible only when the role of the Cuban-American lobby in American domestic politics is taken into consideration. The somewhat more than one million Cuban-Americans have grown into an increasingly powerful political force over the past two decades, particularly in southern Florida, where most of them reside. Their political rise was facilitated by the emergence in the early 1980s of the Cuban-American National Foundation (CANF), a well-oiled pressure group that claims to speak for the entire Cuban-American community with its calls for hard-line

[25] For useful overviews, see Louis A. Perez, jun., *Cuba and the United States: Ties of Singular Intimacy* (Athens, Ga.: University of Georgia Press, 1990); H. Michael Erisman, *Cuba's Foreign Relations in a Post-Soviet World* (Gainesville, Fla.: University Press of Florida, 2000); Walt Vanderbush and Patrick J. Haney, 'Policy toward Cuba in the Clinton Administration', *Political Science Quarterly*, 114 (1999): 387–408.

anti-Castro policies. Because Florida, one of the most populous states in the union, is of crucial importance in both presidential and congressional elections, top politicians eager for Latino votes have repeatedly paid close attention to these calls. These domestic dynamics have been largely responsible for the political elite's willingness to stick to an inflexible Cuba policy even in recent years, despite rising pressure for a different approach and growing evidence that Cuban-Americans themselves are by no means united behind the CANF's hard-line stances.[26]

To be sure, the Cuban-American case is not fully comparable to that of the German expellees. Cuba is not as central a policy concern for the United States as Eastern Europe is for the Federal Republic, and the role and character of the two lobbies also contrasts in many ways. But the recent American record in balancing broader national interests with the demands of the Cuban-American lobby is hardly inspiring, and in comparative terms the West German success in taming the territorial revisionism of the expellee organizations certainly seems the more impressive achievement.

The Federal Republic's triumphs do not merit uncritical celebration, however. The successes in the expellee sector came with considerable ancillary costs on both the societal and high-political levels. Many of the problems derived from the Ostpolitik-related rhetoric employed by expellee activists, politicians, and other public figures. Although the talk of a possible reacquisition of the old *Heimat* did contribute to expellee integration, on balance such rhetorical practices did more harm than good, at least in the longer term. The revisionist language sustained illusionary hopes among a minority of expellees, composed largely of older and less economically integrated elements, even in the late 1960s and afterwards, at a time when most of their compatriots had accepted the existing realities. As a result, the shrinking community of true believers grew increasingly isolated, even within the expellee camp. The consequences of this siege mentality became evident in the excessively acrimonious Ostpolitik debates of the 1960s and 1970s. Although some level of conflict was probably inevitable and the hard-line stances of an embittered minority arguably promoted societal integration by alienating the moderate majority of expellees, the embattled radicals suffered serious personal and psychological strain, and the polarized public debate opened up unnecessarily sharp divisions within West German society.[27]

The distortion and dishonesty that long characterized West German public discussions about Ostpolitik in general and its expellee angle in particular also had much broader societal consequences. As recent key studies by Norbert Frei

---

[26] Along with the works in n. 25, see Jorge I. Dominguez, 'US–Cuban Relations: From the Cold War to the Colder War', *Journal of Interamerican Studies and World Affairs*, 39 (1997): 49–75; Jonathan C. Smith, 'Foreign Policy for Sale? Interest Group Influence on President Clinton's Cuba Policy, Aug. 1994', *Political Science Quarterly*, 28 (1998): 207–20; Adolfo Leyva De Varona, 'The Political Impact of Cuban-Americans in Florida', in Antonio Jorge, Jaime Suchlicki, and Adolfo Leyva De Varona (eds.), *Cuban Exiles in Florida: Their Presence and Contributions* (Coral Gables, Fla.: University of Miami North–South Centre Publications, 1991), 53–99.

[27] Hahn, 'Sudetendeutsche'; Böke, 'Flüchtlinge', esp. 202–3; Niethammer, 'Traditionen', esp. 80–1.

and others have shown, the downside of the early Federal Republic's preoccupation with a rapid reconstruction was a widespread reluctance to face the dark legacies of the Nazi era. The country's first decade in particular witnessed a good deal of evasion and avoidance vis-à-vis the recent past. Public discussions of the Nazi period did take place, but they often remained abstract and marginalized or became embedded in broader narratives that elided or relativized German transgressions and accentuated the suffering endured by the Germans themselves. In this atmosphere, the cause of justice suffered severely, as West German courts took little legal action against perpetrators of crimes against humanity until the 1960s, and Adenauer's government, at least initially, invested much more effort in freeing convicted German war criminals from foreign jails than in tracking down unpunished mass murderers at home.[28] The bill for these practices fell due later, particularly in the 1960s, as embarrassing revelations about neglected de-nazification shook the Federal Republic's domestic stability and damaged its international prestige.[29]

The prevalent public portrayal of the expellees' past experiences and present demands facilitated these broader processes of evasion and relativization. Selective narratives of the expulsions, combined with reaffirmations of desired territorial revisions, had several deleterious effects. They perpetuated old stereotypes about the Germans and their eastern neighbours; systematically downplayed the complicity of the German people in the crimes of the Nazi era; and used exaggerated accounts of German suffering to justify dubious historical comparisons on the one hand and raw post-war revisionism on the other. The selective public memory thereby created helped to foster an atmosphere in which difficult questions about individual responsibility and state–society relations during the Third Reich could long be evaded. In the words of Michael L. Hughes, this process was 'tailor-made for masking moral agency' and for suppressing investigations of German guilt for Nazi transgressions.[30]

The costs of manipulative tactics vis-à-vis the expellees were also very clear in West Germany's top-level politics in general and Ostpolitik in particular. By the mid-1950s, Bonn's political elites had become captives of the revisionist rhetoric they had cultivated primarily for the purpose of courting the expellees and other presumed nationalists at home. As a result, difficult decisions about policies towards Eastern Europe were repeatedly postponed, while fully unrealistic discussions about revisionist policy options were allowed to rage on long past the point at which they might still have served useful domestic purposes. The costs of these practices became increasingly clear during the late 1950s and the 1960s when they delayed a reconciliation between West Germany and Eastern Europe, fuelled negative stereotypes of Germans that foreign leaders, particularly in the Eastern bloc, could use for their own purposes, and perpetuated an unhealthy political

---

[28] See esp., Frei, *Vergangenheitspolitik* but also Moeller, *War Stories*; Hughes, 'No Fault'; Brochhagen, *Nürnberg*. For a less critical perspective, see Herf, *Divided*.

[29] See e.g. Schildt *et al.*, *Dynamische Zeiten*, 77–165.

[30] Hughes, 'No Fault', 209; Moeller, *War Stories*.

atmosphere of dishonesty and deceit at home. Nor did such troubles end with the onset of the new Ostpolitik of the 1970s. The extreme bitterness of the West German debates accompanying these policy changes was a direct result of earlier political practices, and although revisionist rhetoric largely faded from the head-lines during the rest of the Social–Liberal era, its revival under Helmut Kohl's lead brought back many of the old problems. The Chancellor's tactical manœuvring with the eastern border problem, particularly during the German reunification process, refuelled old fears of German aggression and at least temporarily strengthened the opponents of the changes that the peaceful revolutions of 1989/90 ultimately brought about, including reunification itself.

The formal sealing of the Polish-German border in 1990/1 officially removed the main revisionist issue from the international agenda, but the long shadow of the expellee lobby's actions has occasionally continued to darken the prospects for German–East European relations even thereafter. Various interventions by the Sudeten-German Homeland Society, channelled primarily through the CSU and the Bavarian state government, repeatedly delayed progress in the negotiations that ultimately led to the important Declaration on Reconciliation signed by the German and Czech governments in January 1997.[31] Similarly, Polish fears of possi-ble expellee attempts to reacquire land in the former German territories have continued to burden relations between Warsaw and Berlin even in the context of Poland's impending entry to the European Union.[32] To be sure, the issues pushed by the expellee groups have remained secondary at best in the greater scheme of interactions between reunified Germany and the key East European states. But the fact that they continue to make some difference even now, more than half a century after the expulsions, highlights the extent to which the instrumentalized expellee politics practised in the Federal Republic had lasting—and partly unfore-seen—consequences.

The overall success of the West German approach to the expellee problem therefore has to be judged with caution. The relatively smooth integration of the uprooted millions was in many ways a striking success story. But the West German practices also caused major problems, particularly in the political sphere. For far too long the country's political elites indulged in tactical opportunism, telling expellees and other nationalistic audiences what they wanted to hear, with scant regard for existing realities or possible long-term consequences. To be sure, the politicians had to secure a domestic support base for themselves and their policies, and in that endeavour the millions of expellees and other presumably nationalistic voters were a factor to be considered. In addition, it could be argued

---

[31] Vladimir Handl, 'Czech–German Declaration on Reconciliation', *German Politics*, 6 (1997): 150–67; Andreas Götze, 'Der schwierige Weg zur Verständigung', *Osteuropa*, 45 (1995): 1034–47; Emil Nagengast, 'Coming to Terms with a "European Identity": The Sudeten Germans between Bonn and Prague', *German Politics*, 5 (1996): 81–100.

[32] Klaus Bachmann, 'Von der Euphorie zum Misstrauen: Deutsch-polnische Beziehungen nach der Wende', *Osteuropa*, 50 (2000): 853–71. Salzborn, *Heimatrecht*, offers a wildly exaggerated portrayal of the expellee lobby's contemporary influence.

that, at least during the immediate post-war years, a more honest portrayal of the harsh political realities might have overburdened not only the expellees but also the fragile democracy then taking root in West Germany.[33] But on such an important and emotional issue as Ostpolitik there was a need for firmer leadership from the country's political elites. By the late 1950s and early 1960s at the very latest, Bonn's top politicians could have done much more to correct the worst distortions of the entirely unrealistic revisionism that still dominated public discussions of their country's Eastern policy options. Many subsequent problems at home and abroad could have been avoided, had the Federal Republic's elites invested less time in nourishing illusionary hopes and shown more courage in preparing the ground for what they knew would be painful but necessary decisions.

[33] For interesting—although exaggerated—general arguments along these lines, see Heinrich Lübbe, 'Nationalsozialismus im politischen Bewusstsein der Gegenwart', in Martin Broszat *et al.* (eds.), *Deutschlands Weg in die Diktatur: Internationale Konferenz zur nationalsozialistischen Machtübernahme* (Berlin: Siedler, 1983), esp. 333–6.

Bibliography

ARCHIVAL SOURCES: EXPELLEE MATERIALS

Sudetendeutsches Archiv, Munich (SDA)

Arbeitsgemeinschaft zur Wahrung sudetendeutscher Interessen
Sudetendeutscher Rat
Sudetendeutsche Landsmannschaft, Kanzlei des Sprechers (B 4)
Verband der Landsmannschaften (VdL) (B VIII)
Nachlass Dr. Walter Becher
Nachlass Wenzel Jaksch
Nachlass Rudolf Lodman von Auen
Nachlass Hans-Christoph Seebohm (B IX)

Archiv des Bundes der Vertriebenen, Bonn (ABdV)

ZvD/BvD: Jahresberichte, 1957–1958
ZvD/BvD: Protocols of the Präsidium, Bundesvorstand, and Bundesversammlung, 1949–1959
BdV: Jahresberichte, 1959–1969
BdV: Protocols of the Präsidium, Bundesvorstand, and Bundesversammlung, 1959–1969

Archiv der Landsmannschaft der Oberschlesier, Ratingen (ALdO)

Bundestreffen, 1951–1968
1956, Bochum (Bundestreffen)
Bundesministerien, sonstige Behörden, AA, Bundesregierung, 17.11.1949–31.12.1956
Presse, Rundfunk, Fernsehen, 1961–30.11.1964
Presse, Rundfunk, Fernsehen, Filme, 1.12.1964–31.8.1967
Korrespondenz mit Parteien und Abgeordneten, 1951–31.5.1966
Korrespondenz mit Parteien und Abgeordneten, 1.6.1966–31.10.1968
Korrespondenz mit Parteien und Abgeordneten, 1.11.1968–31.8.1969
Korrespondenz mit Parteien und Abgeordneten, 1.12.1969–28.2.1970

Archiv des Instituts für Zeitgeschichte, Munich (IfZ)

ED 720 (collection of internal CSU materials from the 1950s, donated by Professor Alf Mintzel)
ED 706 (materials of the Bavarian GB/BHE from the 1950s, copies from the NL Walter Becher in *Bayerisches Staatsarchiv*)

ARCHIVAL SOURCES: GOVERNMENTAL DOCUMENTS

Bundesarchiv, Koblenz (BA)

Bundesministerium für Vertriebene, Flüchtlinge und Kriegsgeschädigte (B 150)
Bundeskanzleramt (B 136)
Gesamtdeutsches Ministerium (B 137)
Bund der Vertriebenen (B 234)
Nachlass Herbert Blankenhorn (N 351)
Nachlass Franz Blücher (NL 80)
Nachlass Max Hildebert Boehm (NL 77)
Nachlass Heinrich von Brentano (NL 239)
Nachlass Karl Carstens (NL 1337)
Nachlass Axel de Vries (NL 1412)
Nachlass Hans Furler (N 255)
Nachlass Karl Theodor Freiherr von und zu Guttenberg (NL 1397)
Nachlass Walter Hallstein (NL 266)
Nachlass Jakob Kaiser (NL 18)
Nachlass Waldemar Kraft (NL 267)
Nachlass Georg Baron Manteuffel-Szoege (NL 1157)
Nachlass Karl Georg Pfleiderer (NL 1286)
Nachlass Hans Schlange-Schöningen (NL 71)
Nachlass Hans-Christoph Seebohm (NL 178)
Nachlass Franz Thedieck (NL 174)

Politisches Archiv des Auswärtigen Amtes, Bonn (PA/AA)

Büro Staatssekretär
Ministerbüro (MB)
Politische Abteilung 2 (B 10), 1949/1951–1958; Abteilung 3, 1950–1964; Abteilung 7, 1953–1964
B 150 (Aktenkopien)
Nachlass Ferdinand von Duckwitz
Nachlass Albrecht von Kessel

Parlamentsarchiv, Deutscher Bundestag, Bonn (BT/PA)

Ausschuss für Heimatvertriebene/für Angelegenheiten der Heimatvertriebenen und Flüchtlinge
Ausschuss für Gesamtdeutsche und Berliner Fragen
Ausschuss für auswärtige Angelegenheiten

Kommission für die Geschichte des Parlamentarismus und der politischen Parteien, Bonn (KGParl)

Arbeitsgruppe zur Frage der Beziehungen zu den Ostblockstaaten im Ausschuss für auswärtige Angelegenheiten ('Jaksch Ausschuss') (1960–1)

OTHER ARCHIVES

Archiv der sozialen Demokratie der Friedrich-Ebert-Stiftung, Bonn (AdsD)

SPD-Parteivorstand (PV, Neuer Bestand and Alter Bestand)
Bestand Kurt Schumacher (Abt. II)
Bestand Erich Ollenhauer (Abt. II)
SPD-Präsidium
SPD-Bundestagsfraktion
Seliger Archiv im Archiv der sozialen Demokratie, including: Nachlass Wenzel Jaksch;
   Nachlass Ernst Paul; Nachlass Richard Reitzner; Seliger-Gemeinde, Organisationsakten.
Nachlass Heinrich Albertz
Nachlass Fritz Erler
Nachlass Fritz Sänger
Nachlass Carlo Schmid

Archiv des Deutschen Liberalismus, Friedrich-Naumann-Stiftung, Gummersbach (ADL)

FDP Bundesvorstand
FDP Bundestagsfraktion (A 040)
Arbeitskreis Aussenpolitik (AK I)
FDP Bundesparteitage (A I)
Ausschuss für Aussen-, Deutschland-, Europa-, und Sicherheitspolitik
Gesamtdeutscher Ausschuss (A 27)
Bundeshauptausschuss (A 12)
Bundesvertriebenenausschuss (A 13)
Materials of Erich Mende (A 26, A 31)
Nachlass Franz Blücher (A 3)
Nachlass Thomas Dehler (N 1)
Nachlass Karl-Hermann Flach (N 47)
Nachlass Reinhold Maier (A 34)

Archiv für Christlich-Demokratische Politik der Konrad-Adenauer-Stiftung, Sankt Augustin (ACDP)

CDU Bundesvorstand (VII-001)
CDU Bundesvorsitzende (VII-002)
CDU/CSU Bundestagsfraktion (VIII-001)
Arbeitskreis V der CDU/CSU Bundestagsfraktion (Aussen-, Verteidigungs-, Deutschland-,
   und Ostpolitik) (VIII-006)
CDU Bundesgeschäftsstelle (VII-004), including Bundesvertriebenenausschuss; Landes-
   verband Oder-Neisse
Exil-CDU (VII-004-C/I)
Nachlass Eugen Gerstenmeier (I-210)
Nachlass Hans Globke (I-070)
Nachlass Johann Baptist Gradl (I-294)
Nachlass Walter Hallstein (I-341)

Nachlass Linus Kather (I-377)
Nachlass Kurt Georg Kiesinger (I-226)
Nachlass Hermann Kopf (I-027)
Nachlass Heinrich Krone (I-028)
Nachlass Ernst Kuntscher (I-202)
Nachlass Ernst Lemmer (I-280)
Nachlass Otto Lenz (I-172)
Nachlass Erich Mende (I-269)
Nachlass Hans-Joachim von Merkatz (I-148)
Nachlass Clemens Riedel (I-094)
Nachlass Edelhard Rock (I-401)
Nachlass Erich Schellhaus (I-378)
Nachlass Josef Stingl (I-168)
Nachlass Franz Thedieck (I-051)

Archiv für Christlich-Soziale Politik der Hanns-Seidel-Stiftung, Munich (ACSP)

Landesversammlungen (LV)/Parteitage (PT)
Bundestagswahlen (BTW)
Nachlass Josef Müller
Nachlass Gerhard Schuchart
Nachlass Hans Schütz

Pressearchiv, Deutscher Bundestag, Bonn

Article collection on *Vertriebenenverbände* (microfilm reels 4612–14)

Stiftung Bundeskanzler Adenauer Haus, Rhöndorf (StBkAH)

Reden, Interviews, Aufsätze
Bestand B 10, 11, 12 (microfilmed correspondence, party materials) III/21, 22, 23, 24, 38
   (copies of correspondence and other materials)

Willy-Brandt Archiv (in Archiv der sozialen Demokratie), Bonn (WBA)

Personal papers of Willy Brandt

CITED PUBLISHED SOURCES

Ackermann, Volker, *Der 'echte' Flüchtling: Deutsche Vertriebene und Flüchtlinge aus der DDR 1945–1961* (Osnabrück: Rasch, 1995).
Adenauer, Konrad, *Erinnerungen*, 4 vols. (Stuttgart: DVA), i. *1945–53* (1965); ii. *1953–55* (1966); iii. *1955–59* (1967); iv. *1959–63* (1968).
—— *Briefe*, ed. Hans-Peter Küsters, 4 vols. (Berlin: Siedler), i. *1945–47* (1983); ii. *1947–49* (1984); iii. *1949–51* (1985); iv. *1951–53* (1987).

Adenauer, Konrad, *Teegespräche*, 4 vols. (Berlin: Siedler), i. *1950–54*, ed. Hans-Jürgen Küsters (1984); ii. *1955–58*, ed. Hans-Jürgen Küsters (1986); iii. *1959–61*, ed. Hans-Jürgen Küsters (1988); iv. *1961–63*, ed. Hans Peter Mensing (1992).

—— *Konrad Adenauer im Briefwechsel mit Flüchtlingen und Vertriebenen*, ed. Hans Peter Mensing (Bonn: Kulturstiftung der deutschen Vertriebenen, 1999).

Adomeit, Hannes, *Imperial Overstretch: Germany in Soviet Policy from Stalin to Gorbachev* (Baden-Baden: Nomos, 1998).

Ahonen, Pertti, 'Domestic Constraints on West German Ostpolitik: The Role of the Expellee Organizations in the Adenauer Era', *Central European History*, 31 (1998): 31–64.

—— 'The Expellee Organizations and West German Ostpolitik, 1949–1969', Ph.D. dissertation (Yale University, 1999).

—— 'The Impact of Distorted Memory: Historical Narratives and Expellee Integration in West Germany', in Rainer Ohliger, Karen Schönwälder, and Triadafilos Triadafilopoulos (eds.), *European Encounters: Migrants, Migration and European Societies since 1945* (London: Ashgate, 2003).

Akten zur auswärtigen Politik der Bundesrepublik Deutschland, 8 vols. ed. Hans-Peter Schwarz (Munich: Oldenbourg, 1989–2001), i. *Adenauer und die Hohen Kommissare 1949–1951* (1989); ii. *Adenauer und die Hohen Kommissare 1952* (1990); iii. *1963* (1994); iv. *1964* (1995); v. *1965* (1996); vi. *1966* (1997); vii. *1967* (1998); viii. *1968* (1999); ix. *1969* (2000), x. *1970* (2001); xi. *1971* (2002).

Akten zur Vorgeschichte der Bundesrepublik Deutschland, ed. Institut für Zeitgeschichte and Bundesarchiv, 5 vols. (Munich: Oldenbourg, 1976–89).

Albrecht, Willy, *Kurt Schumacher: Ein Leben für den demokratischen Sozialismus* (Bonn: Neue Gesellschaft, 1985).

—— (ed.), *Kurt Schumacher: Reden, Schriften, Korrespondenzen* (Berlin: Dietz, 1985).

Aly, Götz, *'Endlösung': Völkerverschiebung und der Mord an den europäischen Juden* (Frankfurt: Fischer, 1995).

Anic de Orsona, Marija, *Die erste Anerkennung der DDR: Der Bruch der deutsch-jugoslawischen Beziehungen 1957* (Baden-Baden: Nomos, 1990).

Applegate, Celia, *A Nation of Provincials: The German Idea of Heimat* (Berkeley, Calif.: University of California Press, 1990).

Archiv der Gegenwart: Deutschland 1949 bis 1999, 10 vols. (Sankt Augustin: Siegler, 2000).

Ashkenasi, Abraham, *Reformpartei und Aussenpolitik: Die Aussenpolitik der SPD Berlin-Bonn* (Cologne: Westdeutscher Verlag, 1968).

Auswärtiges Amt (ed.), *Die Auswärtige Politik der Bundesrepublik Deutschland* (Cologne: Wissenschaft und Politik, 1972).

—— *Die Auswärtige Politik der Bundesrepublik Deutschland* (Cologne: Wissenschaft und Politik, 1995).

Bachmann, Klaus, 'Von der Euphorie zum Misstrauen: Deutsch-polnische Beziehungen nach der Wende', *Osteuropa*, 50 (2000): 853–71.

Bachstein, Martin K., *Wenzel Jaksch und die sudetendeutsche Sozialdemokratie* (Munich: Oldenbourg, 1974).

Bade, Klaus J. (ed.), *Neue Heimat im Westen: Vertriebene, Flüchtlinge, Aussiedler* (Münster: Westfälischer Heimatbund, 1990).

—— Hans-Bernd Meier, and Bernhard Parisius (eds.), *Zeitzeugen im Interview* (Osnabrück: Rasch, 1997).

Baring, Arnulf, *Aussenpolitik in Adenauers Kanzlerdemokratie* (Munich: DTV, 1969).

—— *Sehr verehrter Herr Bundeskanzler! Heinrich von Brentano im Briefwechsel mit Konrad Adenauer, 1949–1964* (Hamburg: Hoffmann & Campe, 1974).

—— *Machtwechsel: Die Ära Brandt-Scheel* (Stuttgart: DVA, 1982).

Bauer, Franz J., *Flüchtlinge und Flüchtlingspolitik in Bayern 1945 bis 1950* (Stuttgart: Klett-Cotta, 1982).

Baumgartner, Frank R., and Beth L. Leech, *Basic Interests: The Importance of Groups in Politics and Political Science* (Princeton: Princeton University Press, 1998).

Beasley, Ryan K., Juliet Kaarbo, Jeffrey S. Lantis, and Michael T. Snarr (eds.), *Foreign Policy in Comparative Perspective: Domestic and International Influences on State Behavior* (Washington, DC: CQ Press, 2001).

Becher, Walter, *Zeitzeuge: Ein Lebensbericht* (Munich: Langen-Müller, 1990).

Beer, Matthias (ed.), *Zur Integration der Flüchtlinge und Vertriebenen im deutschen Südwesten nach 1945: Bestandsaufnahme und Perspektiven der Forschung* (Sigmaringen: Thorbecke, 1994).

—— 'Flüchtlinge—Ausgewiesene—Neubürger—Heimatvertriebene: Flüchtlingspolitik und Flüchtlingsintegration in Deutschland nach 1945, begriffsgeschichtlich betrachtet', pp. 145–67, in Matthias Beer, Martin Kintzinger, and Marita Krauss (eds.), *Migration und Integration: Aufnahme und Eingliederung im historischen Wandel* (Stuttgart: Franz Steiner, 1997).

—— 'Im Spannungsfeld von Politik und Zeitgeschichte: Das Grossforschungsprojekt "Dokumentation der Vertreibung der Deutschen aus Ostmitteleuropa"', *Vierteljahrshefte für Zeitgeschichte*, 49 (1998): 345–89.

—— 'Die Dokumentation der Vertreibung der Deutschen aus Ost-Mitteleuropa: Hintergründe—Entstehung—Wirkung', *Geschichte in Wissenschaft und Unterricht*, 50 (1999): 99–117.

Bender, Peter, *Neue Ostpolitik: Vom Mauerbau bis zum Moskauer Vertrag* (Munich: DTV, 1995, 2nd edn.).

—— 'Wandel durch Annäherung: Karriere eines Begriffs', *Deutschland-Archiv*, 33 (2000): 971–8.

Benz, Wolfgang, 'Der Generalplan Ost: Zur Germanisierungspolitik des NS-Regimes in den besetzten Ostgebieten, 1939–1945', pp. 45–57, in Wolfgang Benz (ed.), *Die Vertreibung der Deutschen aus dem Osten: Ursachen, Ereignisse, Folgen* (Frankfurt: Fischer, 1995).

—— (ed.), *Die Vertreibung der Deutschen aus dem Osten: Ursachen, Ereignisse, Folgen*, 2nd edn. (Frankfurt: Fischer, 1995).

—— Günter Plum, and Werner Röder (eds.), *Einheit der Nation: Diskussionen und Konzeptionen zur Deutschlandpolitik der grossen Parteien seit 1945* (Stuttgart: Frommann-Holzboog, 1978).

Biess, Frank, 'The Protracted War: Returning POWs and the Making of East and West German Citizens, 1945–1955', Ph.D. dissertation (Brown University, 2000).

—— 'Survivors of Totalitarianism: Returning POWs and the Reconstruction of Masculine Citizenship in West Germany, 1945–1955', pp. 57–82, in Hanna Schissler (ed.), *The Miracle Years: A Cultural History of West Germany, 1949–1968* (Princeton: Princeton University Press, 2001).

Bingen, Dieter, *Die Polenpolitik der Bonner Republik von Adenauer bis Kohl 1949–1991* (Baden-Baden: Nomos, 1998).

Bischoff, Detlef, *Franz Josef Strauss, die CSU und die Aussenpolitik* (Meisenheim am Glan: Anton Hain, 1973).

Blanke, Richard, 'The German Minority in Interwar Poland and German Foreign Policy: Some Reconsiderations', *Journal of Contemporary History*, 25 (1990): 87–102.

—— *The Orphans of Versailles: The Germans in Western Poland, 1918–1939* (Lexington, Ky.: University of Kentucky Press, 1993).

Blankenhorn, Herbert, *Verständnis und Verständigung: Blätter eines politischen Tagebuchs 1949 bis 1969* (Frankfurt: Propyläen, 1980).

Blasius, Rainer A. (ed.), *Von Adenauer zu Erhard: Studien zur auswärtigen Politik der Bundesrepublik Deutschland 1963* (Munich: Oldenbourg, 1994).

—— 'Erwin Wickert und die Friedensnote der Bundesregierung vom 25. März 1966', *Vierteljahrshefte für Zeitgeschichte* (1996), 539–53.

Blumenthal, Werner, and Bardo Fassbender (eds.), *Erklärungen zur Deutschlandpolitik: Eine Dokumentation von Stellungnahmen, Reden und Entschliessungen des Bundes der Vertriebenen—Vereinigte Landsmannschaften und Landesverbände, i. 1949–1972* (Bonn: Kulturstiftung der deutschen Vertriebenen, 1984).

Blumenwitz, Dieter, Klaus Gotto, Hans Maier, Konrad Repgen, and Hans-Peter Schwarz (eds.), *Konrad Adenauer und seine Zeit: Politik und Persönlichkeit des ersten Bundeskanzlers, ii. Beiträge der Wissenschaft* (Stuttgart: DVA, 1976).

Boehm, Max Hildebert, 'Gruppenbildung und Organisationswesen', pp. 521–605, in Eugen Lomberg and Friedrich Eddings (eds.), *Die Vertriebenen in Westdeutschland: Ihre Eingliederung und ihr Einfluss auf Gesellschaft, Wirtschaft, Politik und Geistesleben, i.* (Kiel: Ferdinand Hirt, 1959).

Böke, Karin, 'Flüchtlinge und Vertriebene zwischen dem Recht auf die alte Heimat und der Eingliederung in die neue Heimat: Leitvokabeln der Flüchtlingspolitik', pp. 131–210, in Karin Böke, Frank Liedtke, and Martin Wengeler (eds.), *Politische Leitvokabeln in der Ära Adenauer* (Berlin: Walter de Gruyter, 1996).

Booz, Rüdiger Marco, *'Hallsteinzeit': Deutsche Aussenpolitik 1955–1972* (Bonn: Bouvier, 1995).

Bösch, Frank, *Die Adenauer-CDU: Gründung, Aufstieg und Krise einer Erfolgspartei, 1945–1969* (Stuttgart: DVA, 2001).

—— 'Die politische Integration der Flüchtlinge und Vertriebenen und ihre Einbindung in die CDU', pp. 107–25, in Rainer Schulze (ed.), *Zwischen Heimat und Zuhause: Deutsche Flüchtlinge und Vertriebene in (West) Deutschland 1945–2000* (Osnabrück: Secolo, 2001).

Bouvier, Beatrix W., *Zwischen Godesberg und Grosser Koalition: Der Weg der SPD in die Regierungsantwortung: Aussen-, sicherheits- und deutschlandpolitische Umorientierung und gesellschaftliche Öffnung der SPD 1960–66* (Bonn: Dietz, 1990).

Bracher, Karl-Dietrich, 'Die Kanzlerdemokratie', in Richard Löwenthal and Hans Peter Schwarz (eds.), *Die zweite Republik: 25 Jahre Bundesrepublik Deutschland* (Stuttgart: Seewald, 1974).

Brandes, Detlef, *Grossbritannien und seine osteuropäischen Alliierten, 1939–1943: Die Regierungen Polens, der Tschechoslowakei und Jugoslawiens im Londoner Exil vom Kriegsausbruch bis zur Konferenz von Teheran* (Munich: Oldenburg, 1988).

—— *Der Weg zur Vertreibung: Pläne und Entscheidungen zum 'Transfer' der Deutschen aus der Tschechoslowakei und aus Polen* (Munich: Oldenbourg, 2001).

—— and Václav Kural (eds.), *Der Weg in die Katastrophe: Deutsch-tschechoslowakische Beziehungen 1938–1947* (Essen: Klartext, 1994).

—— Edita Ivaničková, and Jiří Pešek (eds.), *Erzwungene Trennung: Vertreibungen und Aussiedlungen in und aus der Tschechoslowakei 1938–1947 im Vergleich mit Polen, Ungarn und Jugoslawien* (Essen: Klartext, 1999).

Brandt, Willy, *Friedenspolitik in Europa* (Frankfurt: Fischer, 1968).

—— *Begegnungen und Einsichten: Die Jahre 1960–1975* (Hamburg: Hoffmann & Campe, 1976).

Brauers, Christof, *Liberale Deutschlandpolitik, 1949–1969: Positionen der FDP zwischen nationaler und europäischer Orientierung* (Münster: Lit, 1993).

Bredow, Wilfried von, and Hans-Adolf Jacobssen (eds.), *Misstrauische Nachbarn: Deutsche Ostpolitik 1919/70. Dokumentation und Analyse* (Düsseldorf: Droste, 1970).

Brentano, Heinrich von, *Deutschland, Europa und die Welt: Reden zur deutschen Aussenpolitik*, ed. Franz Böhm (Bonn: Siegler, 1962).

Brochhagen, Ulrich, *Nach Nürnberg: Vergangenheitsbewältigung und Westintegration in der Ära Adenauer* (Berlin: Ullstein, 1999).

Broszat, Martin, *Nationalsozialistische Polenpolitik, 1939–1945* (Stuttgart: Fischer, 1961).

Browning, Christopher, 'Nazi Resettlement Policy and the Search for a Solution to the Jewish Question, 1939–1941', pp. 3–27, in Christopher Browning (ed.), *The Path to Genocide: Essays on the Launching of the Final Solution* (Cambridge: Cambridge University Press, 1992).

Brües, Hans-Josef, *Artikulation und Repräsentation politischer Verbandsinteressen, dargestellt am Beispiel der Vertriebenenorganisationen*, Ph.D. dissertation (University of Cologne, 1972).

Brügel, Johann Wolfgang, *Tschechen und Deutsche*, 2 vols. (Munich: Nymphenburger Verlagshandlung), i. *1918–38* (1967); ii. *1939–46* (1974).

Buchheim, Hans. *Deutschlandpolitik 1949–72: Der politisch-diplomatische Prozess* (Stuttgart: DVA, 1984).

Buchstab, Günter (ed.), *Adenauer: 'Es musste alles neu gemacht werden': Protokolle des CDU-Bundervorstandes 1950-1953* (Dusseldorf: Droste, 1988).

—— (ed.), *Adenauer: 'Wir haben wirklich etwas geschaffen': Protokolle des CDU-Bundesvorstandes, 1953–1957* (Dusseldorf: Droste, 1990).

—— 'Geheimdiplomatie zwischen zwei bequemen Lösungen: Zur Ost- und Deutschlandpolitik Kiesingers', pp. 883–901, in Karl Dietrich Bracher *et al.* (eds.), *Staat und Parteien: Festschrift für Rudolf Morsey zum 65. Geburtstag* (Berlin: Duncker & Humblot, 1992).

—— (ed.), *Adenauer: '... um den Frieden zu gewinnen': Protokolle des CDU-Bundesvorstandes, 1957–1961* (Dusselforf: Droste, 1994).

—— (ed.), *Adenauer: 'Steligkeit in der Politik': Protokolle des CDU-Bundesvorstandes, 1961–1965* (Dusselforf: Droste, 1998).

Buczylowski, Ulrich, *Kurt Schumacher und die deutsche Frage* (Stuttgart: Seewald, 1973).

Byrnes, James F., *Speaking Frankly* (Toronto and London: Heinemann, 1947).

—— *All in one Lifetime* (New York: Harper, 1958).

Carstens, Karl, *Erinnerungen und Erfahrungen* (Boppard: Boldt, 1993).

Clay, Lucius D., *Decision in Germany* (New York: Doubleday, 1950).

Clemens, Clay, *Reluctant Realists: The Christian Democrats and West German Ostpolitik* (Durham, NC: Duke University Press, 1989).

Confino, Alon, *The Nation as a Local Metaphor: Württemberg, Imperial Germany, and National Memory, 1871–1918* (Chapel Hill, NC: University of North Carolina Press, 1997).

Connor, Ian, 'The Bavarian Government and the Refugee Problem, 1945–50', *European History Quarterly*, 16 (1986): 131–53.

—— 'The Refugees and the Currency Reform', pp. 310–24, in Ian Turner (ed.), *Reconstruction in Post-War West Germany: British Occupation Policy and the Western Zones, 1945–1955* (Oxford: Berg, 1989).

Connor, Ian, 'Flüchtlinge und die politischen Parteien in Bayern, 1945–1950', *Jahrbuch für deutsche und osteuropäische Ostkunde*, 38 (1995): 133–67.

Crotty, William, Mildred A. Schwartz, and John C. Green (eds.), *Representing Interests and Interest Group Representation* (Lanham, Md: University Press of America, 1994).

Czaja, Herbert, *Unterwegs zum kleinsten Deutschland?* (Frankfurt: Knecht, 1996).

De Varona, Adolfo Leyva, 'The Political Impact of Cuban-Americans in Florida', pp. 53–99, in Antonio Jorge, Jaime Suchlicki, and Adolfo Leyva De Varona (eds.), *Cuban Exiles in Florida: Their Presence and Contributions* (Coral Gables, Fla.: University of Miami North–South Center Publications, 1991)

De Zayas, Alfred M., *Die Anglo-Amerikaner und die Vertreibung der Deutschen: Vorgeschichte, Verlauf, Folgen* (Munich: Beck, 1979).

Diehl, James M., *The Thanks of the Fatherland: German Veterans after the Second World War* (Chapel Hill, NC: University of North Carolina Press, 1993).

Divo-Institut, *The October 1965 German Election Study: Post-Election Study, Oct. 2, 1965–Oct. 23, 1965* (Ann Arbor, Mich.: ICPR, 1975).

Documents diplomatiques français. 1957/2 (Paris: Impr. Nationale, 1991).

Dokumente zur Deutschlandpolitik, ed. Bundesministerium für Gesamtdeutsche Fragen/Innerdeutsche Beziehungen (Bonn: Bundesdruckerei, 1955–97).

Dokumente zur Deutschlandpolitik: Deutsche Einheit. Sonderedition aus den Akten des Bundeskanzleramtes 1989/1990, ed. Hanns Jürgen Kusters and Daniel Hofmann (Munich: Oldenbourg, 1998).

Dokumente zur Deutschlandpolitik der Sowjetunion, i. (Berlin [East]: Rütten & Loening, 1957).

Dominguez, Jorge I., 'US–Cuban Relations: From the Cold War to the Colder War', *Journal of Interamerican Studies and World Affairs*, 39 (1997): 49–75.

Du Buy, F. H. E. W., *Das Recht auf die Heimat im historisch-politischen Prozess* (Cologne: J. P. Bachem, 1974).

Eberle, Richard, 'The Sudetendeutsche in West German Politics, 1945–1973', Ph.D. dissertation (University of Utah, 1986).

Eberlein, Klaus D., 'Die Wahlentscheidung vom 17. September 1961: Ihre Ursachen und Wirkung', *Zeitschrift für Politik*, 9 (1962): 237–57.

Eckardt, Felix von, *Ein unordentliches Leben* (Düsseldorf: Econ-Verlag, 1967).

Elsing, Ludwig, 'Polenpolitik der SPD 1960 bis 1970', pp. 55–65, in Werner Plum (ed.), *Ungewöhnliche Normalisierung: Beziehungen der Bundesrepublik Deutschland zu Polen* (Bonn: Neue Gesellschaft, 1984).

Elzer, Herbert, 'Adenauer und die Saarfrage nach dem Scheitern der EVG: Die Pariser Gespräche von 19. bis 23. Oktober 1954', *Vierteljahrshefte für Zeitgeschichte*, 46 (1998): 667–708.

Erisman, H. Michael, *Cuba's Foreign Relations in a Post-Soviet World* (Gainesville, Fla.: University Press of Florida, 2000).

Europa-Archiv (Oberursel: Europa-Archiv, 1947, 1948).

Evans, Peter B., Harold K. Jacobson, and Robert D. Putnam (eds.), *Double-Edged Diplomacy: International Bargaining and Domestic Politics* (Berkeley, Calif.: University of California Press, 1993).

Fait, Barbara, and Alf Mintzel (eds.), *Die CSU 1945–1948: Protokolle und Materialien zur Frühgeschichte der Christlich-Sozialen Union*, iii. (Munich: Oldenbourg, 1993).

Falter, Jürgen W., 'Kontinuität und Neubeginn: Die Bundestagswahl 1949 zwischen Weimar und Bonn', *Politisches Vierteljahrsschrift*, 22 (1981): 236–61.

FDP-Bundesvorstand: Sitzungsprotokolle, 3 vols., ed. Udo Wengst *et al.* (Dusseldorf: Droste), i. *Die Liberalen unter dem Vorsitz von Theodor Heuss und Franz Blücher 1949–1954* (1990); ii. *Die Liberalen unter dem Vorsitz von Thomas Dehler und Reinhold Maier 1954–1960* (1991); iii. *Die Liberalen unter dem Vorsitz von Erich Mende 1960–1967* (1993).

Fehrenbach, Heide, *Cinema in Democratizing Germany: Reconstructing National Identity after Hitler* (Chapel Hill, NC: University of North Carolina Press, 1995).

Fink, Carole, 'Defender of Minorities: Germany in the League of Nations, 1926–1933', *Central European History*, 5 (1972): 330–57.

Flechtheim, Ossip K. (ed.), *Dokumente zur parteipolitischen Entwicklung in Deutschland seit 1945*, iii/2. *Programmatik der deutschen Parteien* (Berlin: Wendler, 1963).

Foreign Relations of the United States (Washington, DC: US Government Printing Office, 1969–93): 1946/vi; 1947/ii, iv; 1948/ii, 1950/iv; 1951/iii; 1952–4/v, vii; 1955–7/v, xxvi; 1958–60/ix.

Foschepoth, Josef, 'Grossbritannien, Sowjetunion und die Westverschiebung Polens', *Militärgeschichtliche Mittteilungen*, 34 (1983): 61–90.

—— 'Churchill, Adenauer, und die Neutralisierung Deutschlands', *Deutschland Archiv*, 17 (1984), 1286–301.

—— 'Adenauers Moskaureise 1955', *Aus Politik und Zeitgeschichte*, 22 (1986): 30–46.

—— 'Westintegration statt Wiedervereinigung: Adenauers Deutschlandpolitik', in Foschepoth (ed.), *Adenauer und die deutsche Frage* (Göttingen: Vandenhoeck & Ruprecht, 1990).

—— 'Potsdam und danach: Die Westmächte, Adenauer und die Vertriebenen', pp. 86–113, in Wolfgang Benz (ed.), *Die Vertreibung der Deutschen aus dem Osten*, 2nd edn. (Frankfurt: Fischer, 1995).

Frantzioch, Marion, *Die Vertriebenen: Hemmnisse und Wege ihrer Integration* (Berlin: Dietrich Reimer, 1987).

Franzen, Erik K., and Hans Lemberg, *Die Vertriebenen: Hitlers letzte Opfer* (Berlin: Propyläen, 2001).

Frei, Norbert, *Vergangenheitspolitik: Die Anfänge der Bundesrepublik und die NS-Vergangenheit* (Munich: Beck, 1996).

Frohn, Axel, 'Adenauer und die deutschen Ostgebiete in den fünfziger Jahren', *Vierteljahrshefte für Zeitgeschichte* (1996): 485–525.

Fuchs, Stephan, *'Dreiecksverhältnisse sind immer kompliziert': Kissinger, Bahr und die Ostpolitik* (Hamburg: Eva, 1999).

Gaida, Hans-Jürgen, *Die offiziellen Organe der ostdeutschen Landsmannschaften: Ein Beitrag zur Publizistik der Heimatvertriebenen in Deutschland* (Berlin: Duncker & Humblot, 1973).

Garner, Curt, 'Public Service Personnel in West Germany in the 1950s: Controversial Policy Decisions and their Effects on Social Composition, Gender Structure, and the Role of Former Nazis', *Journal of Social History*, 29 (1995): 25–80.

Garton Ash, Timothy, *In Europe's Name: Germany and the Divided Continent* (New York: Vintage, 1993).

Gaus, Günter (ed.), *Staatserhaltende Opposition oder hat die SPD kapituliert? Gespräche mit Herbert Wehner* (Reinbek: Rowohlt, 1966).

Gebel, Ralf, *Heim ins Reich! Konrad Henlein und der Reichsgau Sudetenland* (Munich: Oldenbourg, 1999).

Genscher, Hans-Dietrich, *Erinnerungen* (Berlin: Siedler, 1995).

Gerhardt, Ute, 'Bilanz der soziologischen Literatur zur Integration der Vertriebenen und Flüchtlinge nach 1945', pp. 44–63, in Dierk Hoffmann, Marita Krauss, and Michael Schwartz (eds.), *Vertriebene in Deutschland: Interdisziplinäre Ergebnisse und Forschungsperspektiven* (Munich: Oldenbourg, 2000).

Gilcher-Holtey, Ingrid (ed.), *1968: Vom Ereignis zum Gegenstand der Geschichtswissenschaft* (Göttingen: Vandenhoeck & Ruprecht, 1998).

Gimbel, John, 'Byrnes Stuttgarter Rede und die amerikanische Nachkriegspolitik in Deutschland', *Vierteljahrshefte für Zeitgeschichte*, 20 (1972): 39–62.

Giordano, Ralph, *Die Zweite Schuld oder von der Last Deutscher zu sein* (Cologne: KiWi, 2000).

Glaab, Manuela, *Deutschlandpolitik in der öffentlichen Meinung* (Opladen: Leske+Budrich, 1999).

Glatzeder, Sebastian, *Die Deutschlandpolitik der FDP in der Ära Adenauer: Konzeptionen in Entstehung und Praxis* (Baden-Baden: Nomos, 1980).

Goetzendorff, Günter, *Das Wort hat der 'Abgeordnete . . .': Erinnerungen eines Parlametariers der ersten Stunde* (Munich: Herbig, 1990).

Gotto, Klaus, 'Adenauers Deutschland- und Ostpolitik, 1954–1963', pp. 3–91 in Rudolf Morsey and Konrad Repgen (eds), *Adenauer-Studien III: Untersuchungen und Dokumente zur Ostpolitik und Bibliographie* (Mainz: Grünewald, 1974).

——— (ed.), *Konrad Adenauer: Seine Deutschland- und Aussenpolitik 1945–63* (Munich: DTV, 1975).

——— (ed.), *Der Staatssekretär Adenauers: Persönlichkeit und politisches Wirken Hans Globkes* (Stuttgart: Klett-Cotta, 1980).

Götze, Andreas, 'Der schwierige Weg zur Verständigung', *Osteuropa*, 45 (1995): 1034–47.

Granieri, Ronald J. *The Ambivalent Alliance: Konrad Adenauer, the CDU/CSU and the West, 1949–1966* (Oxford: Berghahn, 2002).

Gray, William G., *Germany's Cold War: The Global Campaign to Isolate East Germany, 1949–1969* (Chapel Hill, NC: University of North Carolina Press 2003).

Grebing, Helga, *Flüchtlinge und Parteien in Niedersachsen: Eine Untersuchung der politischen Meinungs- und Willensbildungsprozesse während der ersten Nachkriegszeit 1945–1952/3* (Hanover: Hahnsche Buchhandlung, 1990).

Greschat, Martin, ' "Mehr Wahrheit in der Politik!" Das Tübinger Memorandum von 1961', *Vierteljahrshefte für Zeitgeschichte*, 48 (2000): 491–513.

Grewe, Wilhelm, *Rückblenden 1976–1951* (Frankfurt: Propyläen, 1979).

Griffith, William E., *The Ostpolitik of the Federal Republic of Germany* (Cambridge, Mass.: MIT Press, 1978).

Grosser, Christiane, Thomas Grosser, Rita Müller, and Sylvia Schraut, *Flüchtlingsfrage— das Zeitproblem: Amerikanische Besatzungspolitik, deutsche Verwaltung und die Flüchtlinge in Württemberg-Baden, 1945–1949* (Mannheim: Institut für Landeskunde und Regionalforschung, 1993).

Grosser, Thomas, 'Die Integration der Vertriebenen in der Bundesrepublik Deutschland. Annäherungen an die Situation der Sudentedeutschen in der westdeutschen Nachkriegsgesellschaft am Beispiel Bayerns', pp. 41–94, in Hans Lemberg, Jan Křen, and Dusan Kováč (eds.), *Im geteilten Europa: Tschechen, Slowake und Deutsche und ihre Staaten 1949–1989* (Essen: Klartext, 1998).

——— 'Von der freiwilligen Solidar- zur geordneten Konfliktgemeinschaft: Die Integration der Flüchtlinge und Vertriebenen in der deutschen Nachkriegsgesellschaft im Spiegel neuerer zeitgeschichtlicher Untersuchungen', pp. 65–85, in Dierk Hoffmann, Marita

Krauss, and Michael Schwatz (eds.), *Vertriebene in Deutschland: Interdisziplinäre Ergebnisse und Forschungsperspektiven* (Munich: Oldenbourg, 2000).

Grossman, Atina, 'A Question of Silence: The Rape of German Women by Occupation Soldiers', *October* (1995): 43–63.

Gutscher, Jörg, *Die Entwicklung der FDP von ihren Anfängen bis 1961* (Königstein/Ts.: Anton Hain, 1984).

Haberl, O. N., and H. Hecker (eds.), *Unfertige Nachbarschaften: Die Staaten Osteuropas und die Bundesrepublik Deutschland* (Essen: Reimar Hobbing, 1989).

Hacke, Christian, *Die Ost- und Deutschlandpolitik der CDU/CSU: Wege und Irrwege der Opposition seit 1969* (Cologne: Wissenschaft und Politik, 1975).

Hacker, Jens, *Der Ostblock: Entstehung, Entwicklung und Struktur 1939–1980* (Baden-Baden: Nomos, 1983).

Haerendel, Ulrike, 'Die Politik der "Eingliederung" in den Westzonen und der Bundesrepublik Deutschland: Das Flüchtlingsproblem zwischen Grundsatzentscheidungen und Verwaltungspraxis', pp. 109–34, in Dierk Hoffmann, Marita Krauss, and Michael Schwartz (eds.), *Vertriebene in Deutschland. Interdisziplinäre Ergebnisse und Forschungsperspektiven* (Munich: Oldenbourg, 2000).

Hahn, Eva, 'Die Sudetendeutschen in der deutschen Gesellschaft: Ein halbes Jahrhundert politischer Geschichte zwischen "Heimat" und "Zuhause"', pp. 111–34, in Hans Lemberg, Jan Křen, and Dusan Kováč (eds.), *Im geteilten Europa: Tschechen, Slowaken und Deutsche und ihre Staaten 1948–1989* (Essen: Klartext, 1998).

—— and Hans Henning Hahn, 'Flucht und Vertreibung', pp. 335–51, in Etienne Francois and Hagen Schulz (eds.), *Deutsche Erinnerungsorte*, i. (Munich: Beck, 2001).

Handl, Vladimir, 'Czech–German Declaration on Reconciliation', *German Politics*, 6 (1997): 150–67.

Hapke, Hans A., 'Aussenpolitische Einstellungen der Vertriebenen als Funktion von Diskriminierung', pp. 416–53, in Carl Christoph Schweitzer and Hubert Feger (eds.), *Das Deutsch-polnische Konfliktverhältnis seit dem Zweiten Weltkrieg* (Boppard: Boldt, 1975).

Harasko, Alois, and Heinrich Kuhn (eds.), *Rudolf Lodgman von Auen: Ein Leben für Recht und Freiheit und die Selbstbestimmung der Sudetendeutschen* (Nuremberg: Helmut Preussler, 1984).

Hartenstein, Michael A., *Die Oder-Neisse Linie: Geschichte der Aufrichtung und Anerkennung einer problematischen Grenze* (Egelsbach: Hänsel-Hohenhausen, 1997).

Hecker, Hellmuth, *Die Umsiedlungsverträge des Deutschen Reiches während des Zweiten Weltkrieges* (Frankfurt: Metzner, 1971).

Hehn, Jürgen von, *Die Umsiedlung der baltischen Deutschen: Das letzte Kapitel baltischdeutscher Geschichte* (Marburg: Herder-Institut, 1982).

Heidemeyer, Helge, *Flucht und Zuwanderung aus der SBZ/DDR 1945/1949–1961: Die Flüchtlingspolitik der BRD bis zum Bau der Berliner Mauer* (Düsseldorf: Droste, 1994).

—— 'Vertriebene als Sowjetzonenflüchtlinge', pp. 237–49, in Dierk Hoffmann, Marita Krauss, and Michael Schwartz (eds.), *Vertriebene in Deutschland: Interdisziplinäre Ergebnisse und Forschungsperspektiven* (Munich: Oldenbourg, 2000).

Heinemann, Isabel, 'Towards an "Ethnic Reconstruction" of Occupied Europe: SS Plans and Racial Policies,' *Annali dell'Istituto storico italo-germanico in Trento*, 27 (2001): 493–517.

Heinlein, Stefan A., *Gemeinsame Sicherheit: Egon Bahrs sicherheitspolitische Konzeption und die Kontinuität sozialdemokratischer Entspannungsvorstellungen* (Münster: Waxmann, 1993).

Heitmann, Clemens, *FDP und neue Ostpolitik: Zur Bedeutung der deutschlandpolitischen Vorstellungen der FDP von 1966 bis 1972* (Sankt Augustin: COMDOK, 1989).

Henke, Klaus-Dietmar, 'Die Alliierten und die Vertreibung', pp. 58–85, in Wolfgang Benz (ed.), *Die Vertreibung der Deutschen aus dem Osten: Ursachen, Ereignisse, Folgen*, 2nd edn. (Frankfurt: Fischer, 1995).

Henkys, Reinhard (ed.), *Deutschland und die östlichen Nachbarn: Beiträge zu einer evangelischen Denkschrift* (Berlin: Kreuz, 1966).

Hentschel, Volker, *Ludwig Erhard: Ein Politikerleben* (Munich: Olzog, 1996).

Herde, Georg, and Alexa Stolze, *Die Sudetendeutsche Landsmannschaft: Geschichte, Personen, Hintergründe. Eine kritische Bestandsaufnahme* (Cologne: Pahl-Rugenstein, 1987).

Herf, Jeffrey, *War by Other Means: Soviet Power, German Resistance and the Battle of the Euromissiles* (New York: Free Press, 1991).

—— *Divided Memory: The Nazi Past in the Two Germanys* (Cambridge, Mass.: Harvard University Press, 1997).

Hiden, John, 'The Weimar Republic and the Problem of the *Auslandsdeutsche*', *Journal of Contemporary History*, 12 (1977): 273–89.

Hildebrand, Klaus, *Von Erhard zur Grossen Koalition 1963–1969* (Stuttgart: DVA, 1984).

Hintze, Peter (ed.), *Die CDU-Parteiprogramme: Eine Dokumentation der Ziele und Aufgaben* (Bonn: Bouvier, 1991).

Hirsch-Weber, Wolfgang, and Klaus Schütz, *Wähler und Gewählte: Eine Untersuchung der Bundestagswahlen 1953* (Berlin: Franz Vahlen, 1957).

Hoensch, Jörg K, 'Initiativen gesellschaftlicher Gruppierungen in der Bundesrepublik Deutschland bei der Ausgestaltung der deutsch-polnischen Beziehungen', in Wolfgang Jacobmeyer (ed.), *Die Beziehungen zwischen der Bundesrepublik Deutschland und der Volksrepublik Polen bis zur Konferenz über Sicherheit und Zusammenarbeit in Europa* (Brunswick: Georg-Eckert-Institut für internationale Schulbuchforschung, 1987).

Hoffman, Dierk, and Michael Schwartz (eds.), *Geglückte Integration? Spezifika und Vergleichbarkeit der Vertriebenen-Eingliederung in der SBZ/DDR* (Munich: Oldenbourg, 1999).

—— Marita Krauss, and Michael Schwartz (eds.), *Vertriebene in Deutschland: Interdisziplinäre Ergebnisse und Forschungsperspektiven* (Munich: Oldenbourg, 2000).

Hofmann, Daniel, ' "Verdächtige Eile": Der Weg zur Koalition aus SPD und FDP nach der Bundestagswahl vom 28. September 1969', *Vierteljahrshefte für Zeitgeschichte*, 48 (2000): 515–66.

Holtmann, Everhard, 'Flüchtlinge in den 50er Jahren: Aspekte ihrer gesellschaftlichen und politischen Integration', pp. 349–61, in Axel Schildt and Arnold Sywottek (eds.), *Modernisierung im Wiederaufbau: Die westdeutsche Gesellschaft in den 50er Jahren* (Bonn: Dietz, 1993).

—— 'Politische Interessenvertretung von Vertriebenen: Handlungsmuster, Organisationsvarianten und Folgen für das politische System der Bundesrepublik', pp. 187–202, in Dierk Hoffmann, Marita Krauss, and Michael Schwartz (eds.), *Vertriebene in Deutschland: Interdisziplinäre Ergebnisse und Forschungsperspektiven* (Munich: Oldenbourg, 2000).

Hrabovec, Emilia, *Vertreibung und Abschub: Deutsche in Mähren 1945–1947* (Frankfurt: Lang, 1995).

Hrbek, Rudolf, *Die SPD, Deutschland und Europa: Die Haltung der Sozialdemokratie zum Verhältnis von Deutschlandpolitik und West-Integration (1945–57)* (Bonn: Europa-Union Verlag, 1972).

Huber, Wolfgang. 'Die Vertriebenendenkschrift von 1965 und das Verhältnis von Kirche und Öffentlichkeit', pp. 380–420, in Wolfgang Huber (ed.) *Kirche und Öffentlichkeit* (Stuttgart: Klett, 1973).

Hughes, Michael L., 'Restitution and Democracy in Germany after the Two World Wars', *Contemporary European History*, 4 (1994): 1–18.

—— *Shouldering the Burdens of Defeat: West Germany and the Reconstruction of Social Justice* (Chapel Hill, NC: UNC Press, 1999).

—— ' "Through No Fault of our own": West Germans Remember their War Losses', *German History*, 18 (2000): 193–213.

Hupka, Herbert, *Unruhiges Gewissen* (Munich: Langen-Müller, 1994).

Imhof, Michael, *Die Vertriebenenverbände in der Bundesrepublik Deutschland: Geschichte, Organisation und gesellschaftliche Bedeutung*, Ph.D. dissertation (Philipps-Universität Marburg, 1975).

Irving, Ronald, *Adenauer* (London: Longman, 2002).

Jacobsen, Hans-Adolf (ed.), *Misstrauische Nachbarn: Deutsche Ostpolitik 1919/1970. Dokumentation und Analyse* (Düsseldorf: Droste, 1970).

—— and Mieczyslaw Tomalka (eds.), *Bonn–Warschau 1945–1991: Die deutsch-polnischen Beziehungen. Analyse und Dokumentation* (Cologne: Wissenschaft und Politik, 1992).

Jakobsmeier, Werner, 'Das Münchener Abkommen—unüberbrückbarer Graben zwischen Bonn und Prag?', pp. 177–203, in O. N. Haberl and H. Hecker (eds.), *Unfertige Nachbarschaften: Die Staaten Osteuropas und die Bundesrepublik Deutschland* (Essen: Reimar Hobbing, 1989).

Jansen, Hans-Heinrich, 'Karl Georg Pfleiderer: Gegenentwürfe zur Deutschlandpolitik Adenauers', *Historisch-politische Mitteilungen*, 4 (1997): 35–72.

Jansen, Silke, *Meinungsbilder zur deutschen Frage* (Frankfurt: Lang, 1990).

Jarausch, Konrad H., *The Rush to German Unity* (Oxford: Oxford University Press, 1994).

Jaworski, Rudolf, *Vorposten oder Minderheit? Der sudetendeutsche Volkstumskampf in den Beziehungen zwischen der Weimarer Republik und der ČSR* (Stuttgart: DVA, 1977).

Jolles, Hiddo M., *Zur Soziologie der Heimatvertriebenen und Flüchtlinge* (Berlin: Kiepenhauer & Witsch, 1965).

Juchler, Ingo, *Die Studentenbewegungen in den Vereinigten Staaten und der Bundesrepublik Deutschland der sechziger Jahre* (Berlin: Duncker & Humblot, 1996).

Juling, Peter (ed.), *Programmatische Entwicklung der FDP von 1949 bis 1969: Einführung und Dokumente* (Meisenheim am Glan: Anton Hain, 1977).

Kabinettsprotokolle der Bundesregierung 1949–1958, 11 vols., ed. Hans Booms *et al.* (Boppard am Rhein: Harald Boldt, 1982–2000).

Kather, Linus, *Die Entmachtung der Vertriebenen*, 2 vols. (Munich: Olzog), i. *Die entscheid-enden Jahre* (1964), ii. *Die Jahre des Verfalls* (1965).

Killian, Werner, *Die Hallstein Doktrin: Der diplomatische Krieg zwischen der BRD und der DDR 1953–1973* (Berlin: Duncker & Humblot, 2001).

Kitzinger, U. W., *German Electoral Politics: A Study of the 1957 Campaign* (Oxford: Clarendon Press, 1960).

Klotzbach, Kurt, *Der Weg zur Staatspartei: Programmatik, praktische Politik und Organisation der deutschen Sozialdemokratie 1945 bis 1965* (Berlin: Dietz, 1982).

Koehl, Robert L., *RKFDV. German Resettlement and Population Policy, 1939–1945: A History of the Reich Commission for the Strengthening of Germandom* (Cambridge, Mass.: Harvard University Press, 1957).

Koenen, Gerd, *Das rote Jahrzehnt: Unsere kleine deutsche Kulturrevolution 1967–1977* (Cologne: Kiepenheuer & Witsch, 2001).

Koerfer, Daniel, *Die FDP in der Identitätskrise: Die Jahre 1966–69 im Spiegel der Zeitschrift 'liberal'* (Stuttgart: Klett-Cotta, 1981).

—— *Kampf ums Kanzleramt: Erhard und Adenauer* (Stuttgart: DVA, 1987).

Köhler, Henning, *Adenauer: Eine politische Biographie* (Berlin: Propyläen, 1994).

Korte, Karl-Rudolf, *Deutschlandpolitik in Helmut Kohls Kanzlerschaft: Regierungsstil und Entscheidungen 1982–1989* (Stuttgart: DVA, 1998).

Kosthorst, Daniel, *Brentano und die deutsche Einheit: Die Deutschland- und Ostpolitik des Aussenministers im Kabinett Adenauer 1955–1961* (Düsseldorf: Droste, 1993).

—— 'Sowjetische Geheimpolitik in Deutschland? Chruschtschow und die Adschubej-Mission 1964', *Vierteljahrshefte für Zeitgeschichte*, 44 (1996): 229–56.

Kosthorst, Erich, *Jakob Kaiser: Bunderminister für gesamtdeutsche Fragen 1949–1957* (Stuttgart: Kohlhammer, 1972).

Kramer, Mark, 'The Early Post-Stalin Succession Struggle and Upheavals in East–Central Europe: Internal–External Linkages in Soviet Policy Making', *Journal of Cold War Studies*, 1/1 (1999): 3–55 (part 1); 1/2 (1999): 3–38 (part 2); 1/ 3 (1999): 3–66 (part 3).

Krause, Michael, *Flucht vor dem Bombenkrieg: 'Umquartierungen' im Zweiten Weltkrieg und die Wiedereingliederung der Evakuierten in Deutschland, 1943–1963* (Düsseldorf: Droste, 1997).

Kraushaar, Wolfgang, *1968 als Mythos, Chiffre und Zäsur* (Hamburg: Hamburger Edition, 2000).

Kreile, Michael, *Osthandel und Ostpolitik* (Baden-Baden: Nomos, 1978).

Krekeler, Norbert, *Revisionsanspruch und geheime Ostpolitik der Weimarer Republik: Die Subventionierung der deutschen Minderheit in Polen 1919–1933* (Stuttgart: DVA, 1973).

Kroegel, Dirk, *'Einen Anfang finden!' Kurt Georg Kiesinger in der Aussen- und Deutschlandpolitik der Grossen Koalition* (Munich: Oldenbourg, 1997).

Krohn, Maren, *Die gesellschaftlichen Auseinandersetzungen um die Notstandsgesetze* (Cologne: Pahl-Rugenstein, 1981).

Krone, Heinrich, 'Aufzeichnungen zur Deutschland- und Ostpolitik, 1954–69', in Rudolf Morsey and Konrad Repgen (eds.), *Adenauer-Studien III: Untersuchungen und Dokumente zur Ostpolitik und Biographie* (Mainz: Matthias-Grünewald, 1974).

—— *Tagebücher,* i. *1945–61,* ed. Hans-Otto Kleinmann (Düsseldorf: Droste, 1995).

Krzoska, Markus, 'Wladyslaw Gomulka und Deutschland', *Zeitschrift für Ostforschung*, 43 (1994): 174–213.

Kühnl, Reinhard, *Die NPD: Struktur, Ideologie und Funktion einer neofaschistischen Partei* (Frankfurt: Suhrkamp, 1969).

Küsters, Hanns-Jürgen, 'Konrad Adenauer und Willy Brandt in der Berlin-Krise 1958–1963', *Vierteljahrshefte für Zeitgeschichte*, 40 (1992): 483–542.

—— *Der Integrationsfriede: Viermächte-Verhandlungen über die Friedensregelung mit Deutschland 1945–1990* (Munich: Oldenbourg, 2000).

—— 'The Kohl–Gorbachev Meetings in Moscow and in the Caucasus, 1990', *Cold War History*, 2 (2002): 195–235.

LaFeber, Walter (ed.), *The Origins of the Cold War, 1941–1947: A Historical Problem with Interpretations and Documents* (New York: Wiley, 1971).

Landsberg, Ludwig, 'Verbände der Vertriebenen und Geschädigten', pp. 515–62, in *Verbände und Herrschaft: Pluralismus in der Gesellschaft* (Bonn: Eichholz, 1970).

Lee, Sabine, 'CDU Refugee Policies and the Landesverband Oder/Neisse: Electoral Tool or Instrument of Integration?', *German Politics*, 18 (1999): 131–49.

—— *An Uncertain Partnership: British–German Relations between 1955 and 1961* (Bochum: Brockmeyer, 1996).

Lehmann, Albrecht, *Im Fremden ungewollt zuhaus: Flüchtlinge und Vertriebene in Westdeutschland 1945–1990* (Munich: Beck, 1991).

Lehmann, Hans-Georg, *Der Oder-Neisse Konflikt* (Munich: Beck, 1979).

—— 'Die deutsch-polnische Grenzfrage: Eine Einführung in den Oder-Neisse Kon-flikt', pp. 37–54, in Werner Plum (ed.), *Ungewöhnliche Normalisierung: Beziehungen der Bundesrepublik Deutschland zu Polen* (Bonn: Neue Gesellschaft, 1984).

—— *Öffnung nach Osten: Die Ostreisen Helmut Schmidts und die Entstehung der Ost- und Entspannungspolitik* (Bonn: Neue Gesellschaft, 1984).

—— 'Oder-Neisse Linie und Heimatverlust: Interdependenzen zwischen Flucht/Vertreibung und Revisionismus', pp. 107–16, in Raimer Schulze, Doris von der Brelie-Lewien, and Helga Grebing (eds.), *Flüchtlinge und Vertriebene in der westdeutschen Nachkriegsgeschichte: Bilanzierung der Forschung und Perspektive für die künftige Forschungsarbeit* (Hildesheim: August Lax, 1987).

—— (ed.), *Deutschland Chronik 1945–2000* (Bonn: Bouvier, 2000).

Lemberg, Eugen, Friedrich Edding, and Max Hildebert Boehm (eds.), *Die Vertriebenen in Westdeutschland: Ihre Eingliederung und ihr Einfluss auf Gesellschaft, Wirtschaft, Politik und Geistesleben*, 3 vols. (Kiel: Hirt, 1959).

Lemberg Hans, Jan Křen, and Dusan Kováč (eds.), *Im geteilten Europa: Tschechen, Slowake und Deutsche und ihre Staaten 1949–1989* (Essen: Klartext, 1998).

Lemberg, Hans, and Wlodzimierz Borodziej (eds.), *'Unsere Heimat ist uns ein fremdes Land geworden . . .': Die Deutschen östlich von Oder und Neisse, 1945–1950. Dokumente aus polnischen Archiven*, i. (Marburg: Herder-Institut, 2000).

Lemke, Michael, *CDU/CSU und Vertragspolitik der Bundesrepublik Deutschland in den Jahren 1969–1975* (Saarbrücken: Dadder, 1992).

Lemmer, Ernst, *Manches war doch anders: Erinnerungen eines deutschen Demokraten* (Frankfurt: Scheffler, 1968).

Lenz, Otto, *Im Zentrum der Macht: Das Tagebuch von Staatssekretär Lenz 1951–1953*, ed. Klaus Gotto *et al.* (Düsseldorf: Droste, 1988).

Leugers-Scherzberg, August H., *Die Wandlungen des Herbert Wehner: Von der Volksfront zur Grossen Koalition* (Berlin: Propyläen, 2002).

Lilge, Carsten, *Die Entstehung der Oder-Neisse Linie als Nebenprodukt alliierter Gross-macht-politik während des Zweiten Weltkrieges* (Frankfurt: Lang, 1995).

Lindemann, Mechthild, 'Anfänge einer neuen Ostpolitik? Handelsvertragsverhandlungen und die Errichtung von Handelsvertretungen in den Ostblock-Staaten', pp. 45–96, in Rainer A. Blasius (ed.), *Von Adenauer zu Erhard* (Munich: Oldenbourg, 1994).

Lübbe, Heinrich, 'Nationalsozialismus im politischen Bewusstsein der Gegenwart', pp. 329–49, in Martin Broszat *et al.* (eds.), *Deutschlands Weg in die Diktatur: Internationale Konferenz zur nationalsozialistischen Machtübernahme* (Berlin: Siedler, 1983).

Ludwig, Michael, *Polen und die deutsche Frage* (Bonn: Deutsche Gesellschaft für auswärtige Politik, 1990).

Lumans, Valdis, *Himmler's Auxiliaries: The Volksdeutsche Mittelstelle and the German National Minorities of Europe, 1933–1945* (Chapel Hill, NC: University of North Carolina Press, 1993).

Lüttinger, Paul, *Integration der Vertriebenen: Eine empirische Analyse* (Frankfurt: Campus, 1989).

Luza, Radomir, *The Transfer of the Sudeten Germans: A Study of Czech–German Relations 1933–1962* (New York: NYU Press, 1964).

Maas, Johannes (ed.), *Dokumentation der deutsch-polnischen Beziehungen nach dem zweiten Weltkrieg* (Bonn: Siegler, 1960).

Maier, Charles S., *Dissolution: The Crisis of Communism and the End of East Germany* (Princeton: Princeton University Press, 1997).

Marcowitz, Rainer, *Option für Paris? Unionsparteien, SPD und Charles de Gaulle 1958–1969* (Munich: Oldenbourg, 1996).

Marrus, Michael R., *The Unwanted: European Refugees in the Twentieth Century* (New York: Oxford University Press, 1985).

Martin, Hans-Werner, '*. . . nicht spurlos aus der Geschichte verschwinden': Wenzel Jaksch und die Integration der sudetendeutschen Sozialdemokraten nach dem Zweiten Weltkrieg, 1945–1949* (Frankfurt: Lang, 1996).

Marzian, Herbert (ed.), *Zeittafel und Dokumente zur Oder-Neisse-Linie, 1945–April 1968*, 6 vols. (Würzburg: Holzner, 1956–69).

Mastny, Vojtech, 'Soviet War Aims at the Moscow and Teheran Conferences of 1943', *Journal of Modern History*, 47 (1975): 481–504.

Meiklejohn Terry, Sarah, *Poland's Place in Europe: General Sikorski and the Origin of the Oder-Neisse Line, 1939–1943* (Princeton: Princeton University Press, 1983).

Meinicke, Wolfgang, 'Probleme der Integration der Vertriebenen in der sowjetischen Besatzungszone', *Jahrbuch für ostdeutsche Volkskunde*, 35 (1992): 1–31.

Meissner, Boris (ed.), *Die deutsche Ostpolitik 1961–1970: Kontinuität und Wandel. Dokumentation* (Cologne: Wissenschaft und Politik, 1970).

Mende, Erich, *Die neue Freiheit* (Munich: Herbig, 1981).

—— *Von Wende zu Wende 1962–1982* (Munich: Herbig, 1986).

Mensing, Hans Peter (ed.), *Adenauer: Briefe 1945–1947* (Berlin: Siedler, 1983).

—— (ed.), *Adenauer: Briefe 1949–1951* (Berlin: Siedler, 1985).

—— (ed.), *Konrad Adenauer: Briefe 1951–1953* (Berlin: Siedler, 1987).

Merkatz, Hans-Joachim von (ed.), *Aus Trümmern wurden Fundamente: Vertriebene/ Flüchtlinge/Aussiedler: Drei Jahrzehnte Integration* (Düsseldorf: Walter Rau, 1979).

Merritt, Anna J., and Richard L. Merritt (eds.), *Public Opinion in Occupied Germany: The OMGUS Surveys, 1949–1949* (Urbana, Ill.: University of Illinois Press, 1970).

—— *Public Opinion in Semisovereign Germany: The HICOG Surveys, 1949–1955* (Urbana, Ill.: University of Illinois Press, 1980).

Messerschmidt, Rolf, *Aufnahme und Integration der Vertriebenen und Flüchtlinge in Hessen, 1945–1950: Zur Geschichte der hessischen Flüchtlingsverwaltung* (Wiesbaden: Historische Kommission für Nassau, 1994).

Meyn, Hermann, *Die Deutsche Partei: Entwicklung und Problematik einer national-konservativen Rechtspartei nach 1945* (Düsseldorf: Droste, 1965).

Mintzel, Alf, *Die CSU: Anatomie einer konservativen Partei 1945–72* (Opladen: Westdeutscher Verlag, 1975).

—— *Geschichte der CSU: Ein Uberblick* (Opladen: Westdeutscher Verlag, 1977).

Miszczak, Krzysztof, *Deklarationen und Realitäten: Die Beziehungen zwischen der Bundesrepublik Deutschland und der (Volks-)Republik Polen von der Unterzeichung des Warschauer Vertrages bis zum Abkommen über gute Nachbarschaft und freundschaftliche Zusammenarbeit 1970–91* (Munich: tuduv, 1993).

Moeller, Robert G., 'War Stories: The Search for a Usable Past in the Federal Republic of Germany', *American Historical Review*, 101 (1996): 1008–48.

—— ' "The Last Soldiers of the Great War" and Tales of Family Reunion in the Federal Republic of Germany', *Signs*, 24 (1998): 129–45.

—— *War Stories: The Search for a Usable Past in the Federal Republic of Germany* (Berkeley, Calif.: University of California Press, 2001).

Moersch, Karl, *Kursrevision: Deutsche Aussenpolitik nach Adenauer* (Frankfurt: Societäts, 1978).

Möller, Horst, 'Die Relativität historischer Epochen: Das Jahr 1945 in der Perspektive des Jahres 1989', *Aus Politik und Zeitgeschichte*, B18–19 (1995), 3–9.

Moravcsik, Andrew, 'De Gaulle between Grain and Grandeur: The Political Economy of French EC Policy, 1958–1970', *Journal of Cold War Studies*, 2/2 (2000): 3–43 (part 1); 2/3 (2000): 4–68 (Part 2).

Morsey, Rudolf, *Die Deutschlandpolitik Adenauers: Alte Thesen und neue Fakten* (Opladen: Westdeutscher Verlag, 1991).

—— 'Die Deutschlandpolitik Konrad Adenauers', *Historisch-politische Mitteilungen*, 1 (1994): 1–14.

—— and Konrad Repgen (eds.), *Adenauer-Studien III: Untersuchungen und Dokumente zur Ostpolitik und Biographie* (Mainz: Grünewald, 1974).

Muller, Jerry Z., *The Other God that Failed: Hans Freyer and the Deradicalization of German Conservatism* (Princeton: Princeton University Press, 1987).

Müller, Rolf-Dieter, *Hitlers Ostkrieg und die deutsche Siedlungspolitik* (Frankfurt: Fischer, 1991).

Münch, Ingo von (ed.), *Dokumente des geteilten Deutschlands* (Stuttgart: Kröner, 1968).

Münz, Rainer, and Ohliger, Rainer, 'Vergessene Deutsche—Erinnerte Deutsche: Flüchtlinge, Vertriebene, Aussiedler', *Transit: Europäische Revue*, 15 (1998), 141–57.

Naimark, Norman M., *The Russians in Germany: A History of the Soviet Zone of Occupation, 1945–1949* (Cambridge, Mass.: Harvard University Press, 1995).

—— *Fires of Hatred: Ethnic Cleansing in Twentieth-Century Europe* (Cambridge, Mass.: Harvard University Press, 2001).

Neumann, Franz, *Der Block der Heimatvertriebenen und Entrechteten: Ein Beitrag zur Geschichte und Struktur einer politischen Interessenpartei* (Meisenheim: Anton Hain, 1968).

Niclauss, Karlheinz, *Kontroverse Deutschlandpolitik: Die politische Auseinandersetzung in der Bundesrepublik Deutschland über den Grundlagenvertrag mit der DDR* (Frankfurt: Metzner, 1977).

Niedhart, Gottfried, and Norman Altmann, 'Zwischen Beurteilung und Verurteilung: Die Sowjetunion im Urteil Konrad Adenauers', pp. 99–117, in Josef Foschepoth (ed.), *Adenauer und die deutsche Frage* (Göttingen: Vandenhoeck & Ruprecht, 1990).

Niethammer, Lutz, 'Traditionen und Perspektiven der Nationalstaatlichkeit für die BRD', pp. 57–102, in *Aussenpolitische Perspektiven des westdeutschen Staates*, ii. *Das Vordrigen neuer Kräfte* (Munich: Oldenbourg, 1972).

Nittner, Ernst (ed.), *Dokumente zur sudetendeutschen Frage 1916–1967* (Munich: Ackermann-Gemeinde, 1967).

Noelle, Elisabeth, and Erich Peter Neumann (eds.), *Jahrbuch der öffentlichen Meinung 1947–1955* (Allensbach: Verlag für Demoskopie, 1956).

—— *Jahrbuch der öffentlichen Meinung 1957* (Allensbach: Verlag für Demoskopie, 1958).

—— *Jahrbuch der öffentlichen Meinung 1958–1964* (Allensbach: Verlag für Demoskopie, 1965).

—— *The Germans: Public Opinion Polls 1947–1966* (Allensbach: Verlag für Demoskopie, 1967).

Noelle, Elisabeth, and Erich Peter Neumann (eds.), *Jahrbuch der öffentlichen Meinung 1965–1967* (Allensbach: Verlag für Demoskopie, 1968).

—— *Jahrbuch der öffentlichen Meinung 1968–1973* (Allensbach: Verlag für Demoskopie, 1974).

Noelle-Neumann, Elisabeth, 'Die Verklärung: Adenauer und die öffentliche Meinung 1949 bis 1976', in Dieter Blumenwitz *et al.* (eds.), *Konrad Adenauer und seine Zeit*, ii (Stuttgart: DVA, 1976).

Olson, Mancur, *The Logic of Collective Action: Public Goods and the Theory of Groups* (Cambridge, Mass.: Harvard University Press, 1965).

Oppelland, Torsten, 'Der "Ostpolitiker" Gerhard Schröder: Ein Vorläufer der sozialliberalen Ost- und Deutschlandpolitik?', *Historisch-politische Mitteilungen*, 8 (2001): 73–94.

Osterheld, Horst, '*Ich gehe nicht leichten Herzens . . .': Adenauers letzte Kanzlerjahre: Ein dokumentarischer Bericht* (Mainz: Grünewald, 1986).

—— *Aussenpolitik unter Bundeskanzler Ludwig Erhard 1963–66: Ein dokumentarischer Bericht aus dem Kanzleramt* (Düsseldorf: Droste, 1992).

Otto, Karl A., *Vom Ostermarsch zur APO: Geschichte der ausserparlamentarischen Opposition in der Bundesrepublik, 1960–70* (Frankfurt: Campus, 1982).

Overmans, Rüdiger, 'Personelle Verluste der deutschen Bevölkerung durch Flucht und Vertreibung', *Dzieje Najnowsze*, 26 (1994): 51–65.

—— ' "Amtlich und wissenschaftlich erarbeitet":. Zur Diskussion über die Verluste während Flucht und Vertreibung der Deutschen aus der ČSR', pp. 149–78, in Detlef Brandes, Edita Ivaničkova, and Jiří Pešek (eds.), *Erzwungene Trennung: Vertreibungen und Aussiedlungen in und aus der Tschechoslowakei 1938–1947 im Vergleich mit Polen, Ungarn und Jugoslawien* (Essen: Klartext, 1999).

—— *Deutsche militärische Verluste im Zweiten Weltkrieg* (Munich: Oldenbourg, 1999).

Pape, Matthias, 'Die Deutschlandinitiative des österreichischen Bundeskanzlers Julius Raab im Frühjahr 1958', *Vierteljahrshefte für Zeitgeschichte*, 48 (2000): 281–318.

Patton, David F., *Cold War Politics in Postwar Germany* (London: Macmillan, 1999).

Paul-Calm, Hanna, *Ostpolitik und Wirtschaftsinteressen in der Ära Adenauer* (Frankfurt: Campus, 1981).

Perez, Louis A., jun., *Cuba and the United States: Ties of Singular Intimacy* (Athens, Ga.: University of Georgia Press, 1990).

Persson, Hans Åke, *Rhetorik und Realpolitik: Grossbritannien, die Oder-Neisse Grenze und die Vertreibung der Deutschen nach dem Zweiten Weltkrieg* (Berlin: Berlin-Verlag, 2001).

Plato, Alexander von, 'Fremde Heimat: Zur Integration von Flüchtlingen und Einheimischen in die neue Zeit', pp. 172–219, in Alexander von Plato and Lutz Niethammer (eds.), '*Wir kriegen jetzt andere Zeiten': Auf der Suche nach der Erfahrung des Volkes in nachfaschistischen Ländern. Lebensgeschichte und Sozialkultur im Ruhrgebiet* (Berlin: Dietz, 1985).

—— and Wolfgang Meinicke (eds.), *Alte Heimat—Neue Zeit: Flüchtlinge, Umgesiedelte, Vertriebene in der sowjetischen Besatzungszone und in der DDR* (Berlin: Verlags-Anstalt Union, 1991).

Pond, Elizabeth, *Beyond the Wall: Germany's Road to Unification* (Washington, DC: Brookings Institution, 1993).

Protokolle des CDU-Bundesvorstandes, 4 vols. ed. Günter Buchstab (Düsseldorf: Droste), i. *Adenauer: 'Es musste alles neu gemacht werden'. 1950–53* (1988). ii. *Adenauer: 'Wir haben wirklich etwas geschaffen' 1953–57* (1990); iii. *Adenauer: '. . . um den Frieden zu gewinnen'. 1957–1961* (1994); iv. *Adenauer: 'Stetigkeit in der Politik'. 1961–1965* (1998).

Prowe, Diethelm, 'Die Anfänge der Brandtschen Ostpolitik 1961–63: Eine Untersuchung zur Endphase des Kalten Krieges', pp. 249–86, in Wolfgang Benz and Hermann Graml (eds.), *Aspekte deutscher Aussenpolitik im 20. Jahrhundert* (Stuttgart: DVA, 1976).

—— 'Der Brief Kennedys an Brandt vom 18. August 1961: Eine zentrale Quelle zur Berliner Mauer und zur Entstehung der Brandtschen Ostpolitik', *Vierteljahrshefte für Zeitgeschichte*, 33 (1985): 373–83.

—— 'The Making of "ein Berliner": Kennedy, Brandt and the Origins of Detente Policy in Germany', in David Wetzel (ed.), *From the Berlin Museum to the Berlin Wall: Essays on the Cultural and Political History of Modern Germany* (Westport, Conn.: Praeger, 1996).

Putnam, Robert D., 'Diplomacy and Domestic Politics: The Logic of Two-Level Games', *International Organization*, 42 (1988): 427–60.

Pütz, Helmuth (ed.), *Konrad Adenauer und die CDU der britischen Besatzungszone 1946–1949* (Bonn: Eichholz, 1975).

Rabe, Karl-Klaus (ed.), *Von Oggersheim bis Oberschlesien: Union und Vertriebenenverbände im politischen Einklang* (Bornheim: Lamuv, 1985).

Rathkolb, Oliver, and Barbara Coudenhove (eds.), *Die Beneš-Dekrete* (Vienna: Czernin, 2002).

Reichel, Peter, 'Die Vertriebenenverbände als aussenpolitische "pressure group"', pp. 233–8, in Hans-Peter Schwarz (ed.), *Handbuch der deutschen Aussenpolitik* (Munich: Piper, 1975).

Reichling, Gerhard, *Die deutschen Vertriebenen in Zahlen*, 2 vols. (Bonn: Kulturstiftung der deutschen Vertriebenen), i. *Umsiedler, Verschleppte, Vertriebene, Aussiedler 1940–85* (1986); ii. *40 Jahre Eingliederung in der Bundesrepublik Deutschland* (1989).

Repgen, Konrad, 'Finis Germaniae: Untergang Deutschlands durch einen SPD-Wahlsieg 1957?', pp. 294–315, in Dieter Blumenwitz et al. (eds.), *Konrad Adenauer und seine Zeit*, ii (Stuttgart: DVA, 1976).

Richter, Werner (ed.), *Die Mauer oder der 13. August* (Reinbek: Rowohlt, 1961).

Ritter, Gerhard A., and Merith Niehuss, *Wahlen in Deutschland 1946–1991: Ein Handbuch* (Munich: Beck, 1991).

Rock, David, and Stefan Wolff (eds.), *Coming Home to Germany? The Integration of Ethnic Germans from Central and Eastern Europe in the Federal Republic* (Oxford: Berghahn, 2002).

Rogers, Daniel E., *Politics after Hitler: The Western Allies and the German Party System* (London: Macmillan, 1995).

Rossler, Mechtild, and Sabine Schleiermacher (eds.), *Der Generalplan Ost* (Berlin: Akademie, 1993).

Rudolph Hartmut, 'Fragen der Ostpolitik im Raum der Evangelischen Kirche in Deutschland', pp. 460–539, in Wolfgang Huber and Johannes Schwerdtfeger (eds.), *Kirche zwischen Krieg und Frieden: Studien zur Geschichte des deutschen Protestantismus* (Stuttgart: Klett, 1976).

—— *Evangelische Kirche und Vertriebene 1945 bis 1972*, 2 vols. (Göttingen: Vandenhoeck & Ruprecht, 1984 and 1985).

Rupieper, Hermann-Josef, *Der besetzte Verbündete: Die amerikanische Deutschlandpolitik 1949–1955* (Opladen: Westdeutscher Verlag, 1991).

Rütten, Theo, *Deutschland- und Gesellschaftspolitik der ost- und westdeutschen Liberalen in der Entstehungsphase der beiden deutschen Staaten*, Ph.D. dissertation (University of Bonn, 1984).

Salzborn, Samuel, *Grenzenlose Heimat: Geschichte, Gegenwart und Zukunft der Ver-triebe-nenverbände* (Berlin: Elefanten Press, 2000).

—— *Heimatrecht und Volkstumskampf: Aussenpolitische Konzepte der Vertriebenenverbände und ihre politische Umsetzung* (Hanover: Offizin, 2001).

Salzmann, Rainer (ed.), *Die CDU/CSU im Parlamentarischen Rat: Sitzungsprotokolle der Unionsfraktion* (Stuttgart: Klett-Cotta, 1981).

Sarotte, M. E., *Dealing with the Devil: East Germany, Detente, and Ostpolitik, 1969–1973* (Chapel Hill, NC: University of North Carolina Press, 2001).

Schertz, Adrian W., *Die Deutschlandpolitik Kennedys und Johnsons: Unterschiedliche Ansätze innerhalb der amerikanischen Regierung* (Cologne: Böhlau, 1992).

Schieder, Theodor, *et al.* (eds.), *Dokumentation der Vertreibung der Deutschen aus Ost- und Mitteleuropa,* 5 vols. (Bonn: Bundesministerium für Vertriebene, Flüchtlinge und Kriegsgeschädigte, 1953–61), i. *Die Vertreibung der deutschen Bevölkerung aus den Gebieten östlich der Oder-Neisse* (1954); ii. *Das Schicksal der Deutschen in Ungarn* (1956); iii. *Das Schicksal der Deutschen in Rumänien* (1957); iv. *Die Vertreibung der deutschen Bevölkerung aus der Tschechoslowakei* (1957); v. *Das Schicksal der Deutschen in Jugoslawien* (1961).

Schildt, Axel, and Arnold Sywottek (eds.), *Modernisierung im Wiederaufbau: die westdeutsche Gesellschaft der 50er Jahre* (Bonn: Dietz, 1993).

—— Detlef Siegfried, and Karl Christian Lammers (eds.), *Dynamische Zeiten: Die 60er Jahre in den beiden deutschen Gesellschaften* (Hamburg: Christians, 2000).

Schillinger, Reinhold, *Der Entscheidungsprozess beim Lastenausgleich 1945–52* (St. Katharinen: Scripta Mercaturae, 1985).

Schissler, Hanna (ed.), *The Miracle Years: A Cultural History of West Germany, 1949–1968* (Princeton: Princeton University Press, 2001).

Schlarp, Karl-Heinz, 'Alternativen zur deutschen Aussenpolitik 1952–1955: Karl Georg Pfleiderer und die "Deutsche Frage" ', pp. 211–48, in Wolfgang Benz and Hermann Graml (eds.), *Aspekte deutscher Aussenpolitik im 20. Jahrhundert* (Stuttgart: DVA, 1976).

Schmid, Carlo, *Erinnerungen* (Berne: Scherz, 1979).

—— 'Besuch der Universitäten in Warschau und Krakau: Tagebuch einer Polenreise im Jahre 1958', pp. 191–203, in Werner Plum (ed.), *Ungewöhnliche Normalisierung: Beziehungen der Bundesrepublik Deutschland zu Polen* (Bonn: Neue Gesellschaft, 1984).

Schmid, Günter, *Entscheidung in Bonn: Die Entstehung der Ost- und Deutschlandpolitik 1969/70* (Cologne: Verlag Wissenschaft und Politik, 1979).

Schmidt, Michael, *Die FDP und die deutsche Frage, 1949–1990* (Hamburg: Lit, 1995).

Schmidt, Robert H., *Saarpolitik 1945–1957,* 3 vols. (Berlin: Duncker & Humblot, 1959–62).

Schmidt, Wolfgang, *Kalter Krieg, Koexistenz und kleine Schritte: Willy Brandt und die Deutschlandpolitik, 1948–63* (Wiesbaden: Westdeutscher Verlag, 2001).

Schmoeckel, Reinhard, and Bruno Kaiser, *Die vergessene Regierung: Die grosse Koalition 1966 bis 1969 und ihre langfristigen Wirkungen* (Bonn: Bouvier, 1991).

Schmollinger, Horst W., 'Die Deutsche Partei', pp. 1025–111, in Richard Stöss (ed.), *Parteien-Handbuch: Die Parteien der Bundesrepublik Deutschland 1945–80,* i (Opladen: Westdeutscher Verlag, 1983).

—— 'Die Nationaldemokratische Partei Deutschlands', pp. 1922–94, in Richard Stöss (ed.), *Parteien-Handbuch: Die Parteien der Bundesrepublik Deutschland 1945–80,* ii (Opladen: Westdeutscher Verlag, 1984).

Schneider, Andrea H., *Die Kunst des Kompromisses: Helmut Schmidt und die Grosse Koalition* (Faderborn: Schöningh, 1999).

Schoenbaum, David, and Elizabeth Pond, *The German Question and Other German Questions* (Basingstoke: Macmillan, 1996).

Schoenberg, Hans W., *Germans from the East: A Study of their Migration, Resettlement and Subsequent Group History since 1945* (The Hague: Nijhoff, 1970).

Schöllgen, Gregor, *Willy Brandt: Die Biographie* (Berlin: Propyläen, 2001).

Schollwer, Wolfgang, *Liberale Opposition gegen Adenauer: Aufzeichnungen 1957–61* (Munich: Oldenbourg, 1990).

—— *FDP im Wandel: Aufzeichnungen 1961–1966* (Munich: Oldenbourg, 1994).

Schönhoven, Klaus, 'Aufbruch in die sozial-liberale Ära: Zur Bedeutung der 60er Jahre in der Geschichte der Bundesrepublik', *Geschichte und Gesellschaft*, 25 (1999): 123–45.

Schraut, Sylvia, *Die Flüchtlingsaufnahme in Württemberg-Baden, 1945–1949: Amerikanische Besatzungsziele und demokratischer Wiederaufbau im Konflikt* (Munich: Oldenbourg, 1995).

—— ' "Make the Germans Do it": Die Flüchtlingsaufnahme in der amerikanischen Besatzungszone', pp. 119–40, in Sylvia Schraut and Thomas Grosser (eds.), *Die Flücthlingsfrage in der deutschen Nachkriegsgesellschaft* (Mannheim: Palatium, 1996).

—— 'Die westlichen Besatzungsmächte und die deutschen Flüchtlinge', pp. 33–46, in Dierk Hoffmann and Michael Schwartz (eds.), *Geglückte Integration? Spezifika und Vergleichbarkeit der Vertriebenen-Eingliederung in der SBZ/DDR* (Munich: Oldenbourg, 1999).

—— and Thomas Grosser (eds.), *Die Flüchtlingsfrage in der deutschen Nach-kriegsgesellschaft* (Mannheim: Palatium, 1996).

Schulze, Rainer, 'Growing Discontent: Relations between Native and Refugee Populations in a Rural District in Western Germany after the Second World War', *German History*, 7 (1989): 332–49.

—— (ed.), *Unruhige Zeiten: Erlebnisberichte aus dem Landkreis Celle 1945–1949* (Munich: Oldenbourg, 1990).

—— 'Forgotten Victims or Beneficiaries of Plunder and Genocide? The Mass Resettlement of Ethnic Germans "Heim ins Reich" ', *Annali dell'Istituto storico italo-germanico in Trento*, 26 (2001): 493–517.

—— 'The German Refugees and Expellees from the East and the Creation of a Western German Identity after World War II', pp. 307–25, in Philipp Ther and Ana Siljak (eds.), *Redrawing Nations: Ethnic Cleansing in East–Central Europe, 1944–1948* (Oxford: Rowman & Little, 2001)

—— (ed.), *Zwischen Heimat und Zuhause: Deutsche Flüchtlinge und Vertriebene in (West) Deutschland 1945–2000* (Osnabrück: Secolo, 2001).

Schwartz, Michael, 'Vertreibung und Vergangenheitspolitik: Ein Versuch über geteilte deutsche Nachkriegsidentitäten', *Deutschland-Archiv*, 30 (1997): 177–95.

—— ' "Zwangsheimat Deutschland": Vertriebene und Kernbevölkerung zwischen Gesellschaftskonflikt und Integrationspolitik', pp. 114–48, in Klaus Naumann (ed.), *Nachkrieg in Deutschland* (Hamburg: Hamburger Edition, 2001).

Schwarz, Hans-Peter, 'Das aussenpolitische Konzept Konrad Adenauers', pp. 97–155, in Klaus Gotto (ed.), *Konrad Adenauer: Seine Deutschland- und Ostpolitik* (Munich: DTV, 1975).

—— 'Adenauers Ostpolitik', pp. 207–32, in Wolfram F. Hanrieder and Hans Rühle (eds.), *Im Spannungsfeld der Weltpolitik. 30 Jahre deutsche Aussenpolitik* (Stuttgart: Bonn Aktuell, 1975).

—— (ed.), *Konrad Adenauer: Reden 1917–1967: Eine Auswahl* (Stuttgart: Klett-Cotta, 1975).

Schwarz, Hans-Peter, 'Adenauer und Europa', *Vierteljahrshefte für Zeitgeschichte*, 27 (1979): 471–523.

—— (ed.), *Entspanung und Wiedervereinigung: Deutschlandpolitische Vorstellungen Konrad Adenauers* (Stuttgart: Belser, 1979).

—— 'Adenauer und Russland', pp. 365–89, in Friedrich J. Kroneck and Thomas Oppermann (eds.), *Im Dienste Deutschlands und des Rechtes: Festschrift für Wilhelm G. Grewe zum 70. Geburtstag am 16. Oktober 1981* (Baden-Baden: Nomos, 1981).

—— *Die Ära Adenauer, 1949–1957* (Stuttgart: DVA, 1981).

—— *Die Ära Adenauer, 1957–1963* (Stuttgart: DVA, 1983).

—— *Adenauer: Der Aufstieg 1876–1952* (Stuttgart: DVA, 1986).

—— *Konrad Adenauer: Der Staatsmann 1952–1967* (Stuttgart: DVA, 1991).

—— 'Vortasten nach Warschau', *Die Politische Meinung*, 42/326 (Jan. 1997), 87–95.

—— 'Die Regierung Kiesinger und die Krise in der CSSR 1968', *Vierteljahrshefte für Zeitgeschichte*, 47 (1999): 159–86.

Schweigler, Gebhard, *Nationalbewusstsein in der BRD und der DDR* (Düsseldorf: Bertelsmann, 1973).

Schweitzer, Carl Christoph, and Hubert Feger (eds.), *Das deutsch-polnische Konflikt-verhältnis seit dem Zweiten Weltkrieg* (Boppard: Boldt, 1975).

Selvage, Douglas E., 'Poland, the German Democratic Republic and the German Question, 1955–1967', Ph.D. dissertation (Yale University, 1998).

Siebenmorgen, Peter, *Gezeitenwechsel: Aufbruch zur Entspannungspolitik* (Bonn: Bouvier, 1990).

Siekmeier, Mathias, *Restauration oder Reform: Die FDP in den sechziger Jahren: Deutschland- und Ostpolitik zwischen Wiedervereinigung und Entspannung* (Cologne: Janus, 1998).

Simon, A. K. (ed.), *Rudolf Lodgman von Auen: Reden und Aufsätze* (Munich: St. Jörg, 1954).

Slapnicka, Helmut, 'Die rechtlichen Grundlagen für die Behandlung der Deutschen und Magyaren in der Tschechoslowakei 1945–1948', pp. 155–92, in Richard G. Plaschka, Horst Haselsteiner, Arnold Suppan, and Anna M. Drabek (eds.), *Nationale Frage und Vertreibung in der Tschechoslowakei und Ungarn 1938–1948* (Vienna: Verlag der öster-reichischen Akademie der Wissenschaften, 1997).

Smelser, Ronald M., *The Sudeten Problem 1933–1938: Volkstumspolitik and the Formulation of Nazi Foreign Policy* (Middletown, Conn.: Wesleyan University Press, 1975).

Smith, Jonathan C., 'Foreign Policy for Sale? Interest Group Influence on President Clinton's Cuba Policy, August 1994', *Political Science Quarterly*, 28 (1998): 207–20.

Soell, Hartmut, 'Deutsche Sozialdemokratie und die Sudetendeutsche Frage vor und seit dem Münchener Abkommen', pp. 91–132 in Wolfgang Götz (ed.), *Die Sudetendeutsche Frage: Entstehung, Entwicklung und Lösungsversuche 1918–1973* (Mainz: Hase & Koehler, 1974).

—— *Fritz Erler: Eine politische Biographie*, 2 vols. (Berlin: Dietz, 1976).

Sommer, Michael, *Flüchtlinge und Vertriebene in Rheinland-Pfalz: Aufnahme, Unter-bringung und Eingliederung* (Mainz: Von Hase & Köhler, 1990).

Sonnewald, Bernd, *Die Entstehung und Entwicklung der ostdeutschen Landsmannschaften von 1947 bis 1952*, Ph.D. dissertation (Freie Universität Berlin, 1975).

Spaulding, Robert Mark, *Osthandel and Ostpolitik: German Foreign Trade Policies in Eastern Europe from Bismarck to Adenauer* (Providence, RI: Berghahn, 1997).

SPD-Fraktion im deutschen Bundestag: Sitzungsprotokolle, 3 vols. (Düsseldorf: Droste), i. *1949–1957* (ed. Petra Weber, 1993); ii. *1957–1961* (ed. Wolfgang Holscher, 1993); iii. *1961–1966* (ed. Heinrich Potthoff, 1993).

Statistisches Bundesamt (ed.), *Die deutschen Vertreibungsverluste: Bevölkerungsbilanzen für die deutschen Vertreibungsgebiete 1939/50* (Stuttgart: Kohlhammer, 1958).

—— *Die Wahl zum dritten Deutschen Bundestag am 15. September 1957*, ii. *Wahlbeteiligung und Stimmabgabe nach Geschlecht und Alter der Wähler: Ergebnisse einer Repräsentativsstatistik*; iii. *Textheft* (Stuttgart: Kohlhammer, 1958).

—— *Die Wahl zum 5. Deutschen Bundestag am 19. September 1965*, ii. *Strukturdaten für die neuen Bundestagswahlkreise*; vi. *Allgemeine Wahlergebnisse* (Stuttgart: Kohlhammer, 1965).

Stehle, Hansjakob, *Nachbar Polen* (Frankfurt: Fischer, 1963).

—— *Deutschlands Osten—Polens Westen? Eine Dokumentation* (Frankfurt: Fischer, 1965).

—— 'Seit 1960: Der mühsame katholische Dialog über die Grenze', pp. 155–78 in Werner Plum (ed.), *Ungewöhnliche Normalisierung: Beziehungen der Bundesrepublik Deutschland zu Polen* (Bonn: Neue Gesellschaft, 1984).

—— 'Adenauer, Polen und die deutsche Frage', pp. 80–98, in Josef Forschepoth (ed.), *Adenauer und die deutsche Frage* (Göttingen: Vandenhoeck & Ruprecht, 1990).

—— 'Zufälle auf dem Weg zur neuen Ostpolitik: Aufzeichnungen über ein geheimes Treffen Egon Bahrs mit einem polnischen Diplomaten 1968', *Vierteljahrshefte für Zeitgeschichte*, 43 (1995): 159–71.

Stein, George H., *The Waffen SS: Hitler's Elite Guard at War, 1939–1945* (Ithaca, NY: Cornell University Press, 1966).

Steinert, Johannes-Dieter, *Vertriebenenverbände in Nordrhein-Westfalen 1945–54* (Düsseldorf: Schwann, 1986).

—— 'Flüchtlingsvereinigungen—Eingliederungsstationen: Zur Rolle organisierter Interessen bei der Flüchtlingsintegration in der frühen Nachkriegszeit', *Jahrbuch für ostdeutsche Volkskunde*, 33 (1990): 55–68.

—— 'Organisierte Flüchtlingsinteressen und parlamentarische Demokratie: Westdeutschland 1945–49', pp. 61–80 in Klaus J. Bade (ed.), *Neue Heimat im Westen: Vertriebene, Flüchtlinge, Aussiedler* (Münster: Westfälische Heimatbund, 1990).

Steininger, Rolf, *Eine Chance zur Wiedervereinigung? Die Stalin-Note vom 10. März 1952* (Bonn: Neue Gesellschaft, 1986).

—— (ed.), *Die Ruhrfrage 1945/46 und die Entstehung des Landes Nordrhein-Westfalen: Britische, französische und amerikanische Akten* (Düsseldorf: Droste, 1988).

Stent, Angela, *From Embargo to Ostpolitik: The Political Economy of West German–Soviet Relations 1955–80* (Cambridge: Cambridge University Press, 1981).

Stöss, Richard, *Parteien-Handbuch: Die Parteien der Bundesrepublik Deutschland 1945–80*, 2 vols. (Opladen: Westdeutscher Verlag, 1983 and 1984).

Strauss, Franz Josef, *Die Erinnerungen* (Berlin: Siedler, 1989).

Sundhausen, Holm, 'Jugoslawisch-deutsche Beziehungen zwischen Normalisierung, Bruch und erneuter Normalisierung', pp. 133–51, in O. N. Haberl and H. Hecker (eds.), *Unfertige Nachbarschaften: Die Staaten Osteuropas und die Bundesrepublik Deutschland* (Essen: Reimar Hobbing, 1989).

Szabo, Stephen F., *The Diplomacy of German Reunification* (New York: St Martin's, 1992).

Taborsky, Edward, *President Eduard Beneš: Between East and West 1938–1948* (Stanford, Calif.: Hoover Institution, 1981).

Taschler, Daniela, *Vor neuen Herausforderungen: Die aussen- und deutschlandpolitische Debatte in der CDU/CSU Bundestagsfraktion während der Grossen Koalition, 1966–1969* (Düsseldorf: Droste, 2001).

Teltschik, Horst, *329 Tage: Innenansichten der Einigung* (Berlin: Siedler, 1991).

Teschke, John P., *Hitler's Legacy: West Germany Confronts the Aftermath of the Third Reich* (New York: Lang, 1999).

Texte zur Deutschlandpolitik, 12 vols., ed. Bundesministerium für Innerdeutsche Beziehungen (Bonn: Bundesdruckerei, 1966–73).

Ther, Philipp, 'The Integration of Expellees in Germany and Poland after World War II: A Historical Reassessment', *Slavic Review*, 55 (1996): 779–805.

—— *Deutsche und polnische Vertriebene: Gesellschaft und Vertriebenenpolitik in der SBZ/DDR und in Polen 1945–1956* (Göttingen: Vandenhoeck & Ruprecht, 1998).

—— 'Expellee Policy in the Soviet-Occupied Zone and the GDR', pp. 56–76, in David Rock and Stefan Wolff (eds.), *Coming Home to Germany? The Integration of Ethnic Germans from Central and Eastern Europe in the Federal Republic* (Oxford: Berghahn, 2002).

—— and Ana Siljak (eds.), *Redrawing Nations: Ethnic Cleansing in East–Central Europe, 1944–1948* (Oxford: Rowman & Little, 2001).

Tiggemann, Anselm, *Die CDU/CSU und die Ost- und Deutschlandpolitik 1969–72: Zur 'Innenpolitik der Aussenpolitik' der ersten Regierung Brandt/Scheel* (Frankfurt: Lang, 1998).

Timmermann, Heinz, 'Im Vorfeld der neuen Ostpolitik: Der Dialog zwischen italienischen Kommunisten und deutschen Sozialdemokraten 1967/8', *Osteuropa*, 21 (1971): 388–99.

Trachtenberg, Marc, *A Constructed Peace: The Making of the European Settlement, 1945–1963* (Princeton: Princeton University Press, 1999).

Unger, Ilse, *Die Bayernpartei: Geschichte und Struktur, 1945–1957* (Stuttgart: DVA, 1979).

Unionsparteien 1946–50: Protokolle der Arbeitsgemeinschaft der CDU/CSU Deutschlands und der Konferenzen der Landesvorsitzenden, ed. Brigitte Kaff (Düsseldorf: Droste, 1991).

Vanderbush, Walt, and Patrick J. Haney, 'Policy toward Cuba in the Clinton Administration', *Political Science Quarterly*, 114 (1999): 387–408.

Verhandlungen des deutschen Bundestages: Stenographische Berichte (Bonn: Bundesdruckerei, 1949–91).

Vierheller, Viktoria, *Polen und die Deutschland-Frage, 1939–1949* (Cologne: Wissenschaft und Politik, 1970).

Vogtmeier, Andreas, *Egon Bahr und die deutsche Frage: zur Entwicklung der sozialdemokratischen Ost- und Deutschlandpolitik vom Kriegsende bis zur Vereinigung* (Bonn: Dietz, 1996).

Volkmann, Hans-Erich, 'Adenauer und die deutschlandpolitischen Opponenten in CDU und CSU', pp. 183–205, in Josef Foschepoth (ed.), *Adenauer und die deutsche Frage* (Göttingen: Vandenhoeck & Ruprecht, 1990).

Wachs, Philipp-Christian, *Der Fall Theodor Oberländer: Ein Lehrstück deutscher Geschichte* (Frankfurt: Campus, 2000).

Wagner, Wolfgang, *Die Entstehung der Oder-Neisse-Linie in den diplomatischen Verhandlungen während des Zweiten Weltkrieges*, 3rd edn. (Marburg: Herde-Gesellschaft, 1968).

Wambach, Manfred Max, *Verbändestaat und Parteioligopol: Macht und Ohnmacht der Vertriebenenverbände* (Stuttgart: Ferdinand Enke, 1971).

Weber, Petra, *Carlo Schmid: Eine politische Biographie* (Munich: Beck, 1996).

Wehler, Hans-Ulrich, *Nationalitätenpolitik in Jugoslawien: Die deutsche Minderheit 1918–1978* (Göttingen: Vandenhoeck & Ruprecht, 1980).

Weidenfeld, Werner, *Aussenpolitik für die deutsche Einheit: Die Entscheidungsjahre 1989/90* (Stuttgart: DVA, 1998).

Weitz, Eric D, 'The Ever-Present Other: Communism in the Making of West Germany', pp. 219–32, in Hanna Schissler (ed.), *The Miracle Years: A Cultural History of West Germany, 1949–1968* (Princeton: Princeton University Press, 2001).

Wenger, Andreas, 'Der lange Weg zur Stabilität: Kennedy, Chruschtchow und das gemeinsame Interesse der Supermächte am Status quo in Europa', *Vierteljahrshefte für Zeitgeschichte*, 46 (1998): 69–99.

Wengst, Udo (ed.), *Auftakt zur Ära Adenauer: Koalitionsverhandlungen und Regierungsbildung 1949* (Düsseldorf: Droste, 1984).

—— 'Die CDU/CSU im Bundestagswahlkampf 1949', *Vierteljahrshefte für Zeitgeschichte*, 34 (1986): 1–52.

Wille, Manfred, Johannes Hoffmann, and Wolfgang Meinicke (eds.), *Sie hatten alles verloren: Flüchtlinge und Vertriebene in der sowjetischen Besatzungszone Deutschlands* (Wiesbaden: Harrassowitz, 1993).

Winkler, York R., *Flüchtlingsorganisationen in Hessen, 1945–1954: BHE, Flüchtlingsverbände, Landsmannschaften* (Wiesbaden: Historische Kommission für Nassau, 1998).

Wirz, Ulrich, *Karl Theodor von und zu Guttenberg und das Zustandekommen der Grossen Koalition* (Grub am Forst: Menzner, 1997).

Wolfrum, Edgar, 'Zwischen Geschichtsschreibung und Geschichtspolitik: Forschungen zur Flucht und Vertreibung nach dem Zweiten Weltkrieg', *Archiv für Sozialgeschichte*, 36 (1996): 500–22.

—— *Geschichstpolitik in der Bundesrepublik Deutschland: Der Weg zur bundesrepublikanischen Erinnerung 1948–1990* (Darmstadt: Wissenschaftliche Buchgesellschaft, 1999).

Woller, Hans, *Die Loritz-Partei: Geschichte, Struktur und Politik der Wissenschaftlichen Aufbau-Vereinigung, 1945–1955* (Stuttgart: Klett-Cotta, 1985).

Zarusky, Jürgen (ed.), *Die Stalin-Note vom 10. März 1952: Neue Quellen und Analysen* (Munich: Oldenbourg, 2002).

Zeidler, Manfred, *Kriegsende im Osten: Die Rote Armee und die Besetzung Deutschlands östlich von Oder und Neisse 1944/1945* (Munich: Oldenbourg, 1996).

Zeiträg, Ingeborg, *Die Selbstdarstellung der deutschen Vertriebenen als Reflex ihrer gesellschaftlichen Situation*, Ph.D. dissertation (University of Hamburg, 1970).

Zelikow, Philip, and Condoleezza Rice, *Germany Unified and Europe Transformed: A Study in Statecraft* (Cambridge, Mass.: Harvard University Press, 1997).

Zimmer, Matthias, *Nationales Interesse und Staatsräson: Zur Deutschlandpolitik der Regierung Kohl 1982–1989* (Paderborn: Schöningh, 1992).

Zimmermann, Volker, *Die Sudetendeutschen im NS-Staat* (Essen: Klartext, 1999).

Zündorf, Benno, *Die Ostverträge: Die Verträge von Moskau, Prag, das Berlin-Abkommen und die Verträge mit der DDR* (Munich: Beck, 1979).

Zur Mühlen, Patrik von, Bernhard Müller, and Kurt Thomas Schmitz, 'Vertriebenenverbände und deutsch-polnische Beziehungen nach 1945', pp. 96–161, in Carl Christoph Schweitzer and Hubert Feger (eds.), *Das deutsch-polnische Konfliktverhältnis seit dem Zweiten Weltkrieg* (Boppard am Rhein: Boldt, 1975).

Index

Note: Entries categorize West Germany's policies on expellee issues. Terms are given in abbreviated form.